THE
DIVINE IMPERATIVE

A STUDY IN CHRISTIAN ETHICS

THE

DIVINE IMPERATIVE

EMIL BRUNNER

Professor of Theology in Zürich

TRANSLATED BY OLIVE WYON

THE WESTMINSTER PRESS

PHILADELPHIA

PRINTED IN THE UNITED STATES OF AMERICA

CONTENTS

5

CONTENTS

7

PREFACE TO THE GERMAN EDITION

THE question, "What ought we to do?" the great question of humanity, is the entrance to the Christian Faith; none can evade it who wish to enter the sanctuary. But it is also the gate through which one passes out of the sanctuary again, back into life; but in spite of the fact that the question—so far as the actual language is concerned—is unaltered, it has gained new meaning. No magic transformation has taken place within the sanctuary of faith; the human being who passes through those portals, both on his way in and on his way out, is the same human being: erring, imperfect, weak. But something has happened to him within the sanctuary, which, although it has taken place in secret and is only partially visible to the eyes of the world, has made him a different person, something which has opened his eyes and his heart to a reality which he never knew before: the reality of the living God. There he stands—as one who has been touched by God, whose heart has been pierced by Him, as one who has come under the stern judgment of God and has tasted the Divine mercy, as one who can never seek the meaning of his life and the answer to that great human question anywhere else save "there"—there he stands, this weak human being, in the midst of life, among other people; but because he comes "from thence," he now has another "position" in this world, and it is *this* which makes him a Christian. What this means for the answering of that question constitutes the subject-matter of Christian Ethics.

We have heard much of a "demand for Ethics." If by this is meant that it is necessary for Christendom to be continually considering this question, and a sign of poverty and bewilderment if it can give no clear answer to it, then that "demand" is only too plainly justified; for no clear answer has been given for a long time. But this "demand" *may* be—like the cry for a "strong man"—merely an expression of shrinking from responsibility, which desires an authoritative promulgation of a law which·will settle all difficulties once for all, which will lay down beforehand what everyone has to do or to leave undone in every situation—in a word: the demand for the doctrinal authority—binding on the conscience—of the Roman Catholic Church. I have called my book a "Protestant Ethic" in order that those who desire to hear *that* answer to the "demand for Ethics," may be saved the trouble of reading it. The infallible criterion of a Protestant ethic is this: does it claim to give *that* answer? or does it refuse to do so?

Neither the moralist, nor the theologian, nor any teacher of any kind can give the decisive answer to the decisive question of life; that is the province of another, and the reading of a book is not likely to disclose the secret. It is not the task of ethics to give the actual answer to this question; its task is simply that of careful reflection about what it might mean to receive this reply, in view of the manifold problems of practical life; thus its pronouncements are not ultimate and decisive but penultimate and preparatory. It is possible to "go on one's way blameless" and to lead a healthy Christian life without having read this or any other work on ethics. The task of ethics, like that of theology as a whole, is rather negative than positive: to clear away the difficulties raised by our own minds which prevent us from understanding the message. However modest may be our view of our work in the light of that primary and decisive element—yet in view of this second consideration we have no right to belittle the significance of such reflection.

There are already more than enough works on *ethics*—even those bearing the name of "Evangelical" or "Protestant"— why then should we add to their number? We would reply with a counter-question: Is there really such a work on *ethics*? It may seem an audacious statement, though it would not be very difficult to prove its veracity, that since the time of the Reformation no single work on *ethics* has been produced which makes the Evangelical faith its centre. It was only in the course of my work, as I began to seek for help and counsel from others, that this amazing fact became clear to me. This discovery only intensified my sense of obligation at least to make an attempt to fill this gap. I believe that I am fully conscious of the dangers and difficulties which beset such an undertaking; hence, although my book represents the work of many years, I only venture to call it a "sketch," of whose imperfection I am painfully aware. But I believe that in my consideration of the subject I have advanced so far at least that the work of others who are striving in the same direction, and upon whose co-operation I count, may be furthered by it.

At the present time two tasks confront a Protestant theological ethic. The first and the most important is a fresh consideration of the bases and fundamental conceptions of an evangelical doctrine of right conduct. To-day the struggle is being waged round these fundamental questions, which have been ignored both by the Church and by theology for centuries; to-day we are concerned with the whole, not with matters of detail. This process of reflection has begun with vigour and I am glad to admit that in it I have learned much that is important from many people, especially from my friends Karl Barth and Friedrich Gogarten. The fact, however, that I believe that my work can carry the process a step further in this direction is connected with my own view of the second task confronting the Church: that clarity concerning the bases of ethics is itself dependent upon thinking through the concrete problems of particular spheres of life. On this side, however, those who really know something about the bases of ethics have hitherto not done very much, so that the obstinate prejudice has persisted, that nothing at all has been done in the realm of ethics. The knowledge of the bases must be proved by the fact that it will shed some clear light upon the definite problems of practical life. It is only to be expected that my attempt, in which both tasks have been kept in view at the same time, will be regarded as insufficient from both points of view; some will think it premature to go beyond questions of principle, others will think it superfluous to spend so much time on such questions and will regard the treatment of particular questions as superficial. The former hesitation troubles me far more than the latter: indeed, from the outset I accept the reproach as justified: the fundamental work is far from complete. At the same time, I am convinced that even in this realm we shall not make progress if we fail to attempt the second task. So far as the second misgiving is concerned the study of the history of ethics has taught me that every ethic deals with a selection; I would be glad if the reader would regard all my discussion of questions of detail merely as "illustrative."

Owing to the subject-matter of ethics, the moralist is necessarily constantly touching on subjects in which the theologian—like the philosopher—is not a specialist, and thus everywhere there lurks the peril of dilettantism. To try to avoid this pitfall, however, would lead to such unnatural isolation, that from the very outset the moralist's work would be unfruitful. Whether I have succeeded in escaping this danger without renouncing contact with "the other faculties" the reader must decide. I do not cherish the ambition of being at home in all these sciences, but I have felt the responsibility of trying to survey those spheres which contain ethical problems as fully as possible. It is of course self-evident that here in particular I am especially conscious of the imperfection of my attempt.

The considerable addition of notes and supplementary material to the text of this work arose out of a similar need. Its purpose is not scholarly—my relation to real scholarship will probably remain all my life that of an unfortunate lover—but its aim is this: to maintain converse with men—past and present—who have thought about these questions already, and to permit the reader to take part in this interchange of thought. Therefore the choice of that which is said or left unsaid is more or less accidental, depending on the direction of my interest at any particular time. In spite of this, I venture to hope that the reader will also find this part of my work of service to him.

In conclusion it is my pleasant duty to offer my cordial thanks for their unselfish co-operation to all the many people who, directly or indirectly, have helped in the making of this book: to my colleagues both within and outside of the Theological Faculty; men and women in practical life; especially to the Rev. G. Spörri in Aarau, who gave me much valuable counsel while I was engaged in correcting the proofs of this work; for the index and for much patience, to my dear wife.

E. B.

ZÜRICH

March 1932

TRANSLATOR'S NOTE

THE present translation is a complete version of the book published by Professor Emil Brunner in 1932, under the title: *Das Gebot und die Ordnungen: Entwurf einer protestantisch-theologischen Ethik* (2nd edition) (lit.: The Command and the Orders: an Outline of a Protestant Theological Ethic). The new English title was given to this version with Dr. Brunner's consent and approval.

This book aroused very great interest when it first appeared in German, and it has won a high place for itself in the realm of theological literature. Four eventful years have elapsed since the German original was published. In reading the English version this fact should be borne in mind. Dr. Brunner wishes me to say that although he has no desire to alter the *substance* of the book, had he written it this year he would certainly have placed the *emphasis* rather differently, particularly in the chapters dealing with the problem of the State.

The section at the end of the book, under the heading: "Notes and Appendices," will be found to be of peculiar interest. Some of the most valuable matter in the book is in this section. Some of the longer Notes merit special attention; for instance, the note which deals with the "Catholic and the Protestant Conception of the State" (pp. 679 ff.), and the one on "Socialism" (pp. 668–72). Owing to the length of the book, in a few cases some of the quotations from Luther, Calvin and Heidegger have been left out, and occasionally a note has been abbreviated, but in no instance have any references been omitted.

In conclusion, the translator wishes to express her very cordial thanks to the many friends who have assisted her in this task. In particular she wishes to thank the Rev. A. E. Garvie, M.A., D.D., D.Th., for his kindness in reading the text of this translation and for much valuable advice. For help in points of detail the translator is also indebted to the following friends: Rev. Denzil Patrick, M.A.; Dr. Karl Polanyi; Dr. Else Sander; Professor William E. Wilson, B.D. Finally, the translator would also express her thanks to Dr. Brunner himself for the prompt and courteous way in which he has dealt with her inquiries.

OLIVE WYON

LONDON

October 1936

BOOK ONE

THE PROBLEM

CHAPTER I

THE PROBLEM OF THE GOOD: AN IMPERATIVE
CHALLENGE

1. In any discussion of the problem of the Good at the present day, however free from prejudice, the following response will be inevitable: on the one hand, there will be an extraordinary variety of definitions of the actual nature of the Good, and, on the other, many people will declare that it is useless to ask the question: "What is the Good?" since it is impossible to answer it. The spirit of the typical "modern" man is relativistic and sceptical (1); he is weary of all systems, averse to all doctrines, and contemptuous of all creeds; that is, he has a habit of mind which meets every ethic—and not the Christian ethic alone—with the "superior" attitude of one who is too "advanced" to care about "this kind of thing." Such men feel that they have known too many ethical systems, all of which claimed to be absolute, to be able still to believe in any one of them; above all, they have seen too much of the miserable discrepancy between high-sounding ethical creeds and the human reality behind them, to be any longer impressed by them. They do not attempt to refute them; indeed, they will admit that these systems may all be based on excellent arguments. But, after all, this only shows that good reasons prove nothing. For what do arguments prove, if an opposite theory can be based equally logically upon an impregnable principle? As a genuine sceptic, the modern man knows that he is only invincible when he thus "suspends judgment," when he adopts the ancient tactics of the ἐποχή. Is it possible to attack this position? (2)

In any case this position cannot be attacked directly. Genuine scepticism can successfully resist all direct attacks in virtue of its elasticity. Supposing we change our tactics and wait and watch? Do we not then perceive that even the sceptic has his own quite definite ethical way of life? No man who acts at all can escape from the necessity of ordering his life in a certain way. A man who acts, makes decisions, ranks things above or below, sets a high or a low value on

17

things, is acting according to definite principles—even though theoretically he may deny these principles—and he is acting with the consciousness—although in theory he would certainly deny it—that it is right to act in such a way. No sceptic allows himself to be dubbed a "gas-bag," an irresponsible human being. But this means that actually, every person, whether he is conscious of it or not, has his own "ethic," a fragmentary and disavowed tendency towards permanence and order in his own conduct and in his practical relations with his fellow-men.

Even a person who lets himself "drift," in order to escape from the necessity for decision, is still constrained by the same necessity, by the very fact that he decides to drift. We may indeed imagine theoretically a purely detached consciousness in which man is a mere spectator, in which we regard our own conduct simply as a natural fact; practically this could only occur as a highly pathological and exceptional case. To be a man, a person, means the impossibility of evading this necessity for practical decision.

2. Therefore, the moment that human consciousness exists the problem of ethics is raised, the question of right conduct must be faced. Further, it is also impossible to avoid setting up a principle of order, a definite scale of values to express preference, whatever theoretical position may be afterwards adopted towards this principle. For we cannot make the smallest decision save in the light of a superior purpose, a norm, a commandment; indeed, we cannot avoid having one *supreme* idea of purpose and order—although this may be still very indistinct, and we may be only dimly aware of it (3). Experience confirms the thought of Christian anthropology, namely, that man must always have "either God or an idol" ("*entweder Gott oder Abgott*"),[1] even when the idol is only distinguished from God in a purely formal manner by the fact that it will always be a more or less changeable deity.

Thus it is true that man—although he does so reluctantly, and does not admit it—actually always gives a reply to the question: "What is the Good?" In the last resort, therefore, moral scepticism, like all scepticism, is a flight from one's own reality and a form of self-deception. Every one who acts, every one who lives as man with a human consciousness, acts

[1] This idea is brilliantly worked out, with a wealth of illustrations from modern literature, in the work of the literary philosopher SPOERRI: *Die Götter des Abendlandes.*

"ethically"; that is, he acts within the dimension determined by the ethical question.

3. At this point two misunderstandings need to be removed. Firstly, we cannot set repose as one half of life over against the active life as the other half, and, so to speak, seek a refuge from the ethical question in a Nirvana of "in-action." For this flight itself is an act, and even repose, as *human* repose, is an act, which is at least initiated by a decision, and is generally accompanied by more or less continuous decision. Even man's sleep is not simply ethically neutral. Secondly, it is impossible to compare the technical or the artistic element with the ethical element and then complain of the arrogant supremacy of the ethical element as unwarrantably one-sided. For the ethical element is not a special material of life, but it is a particular way of ordering all the functions and relations of our life, whether they be technical, artistic, or anything else. Indeed, strictly speaking, there is no such thing as ethical *conduct*, but only an ethical ordering of technical, artistic, and scientific action. If, for instance, I prepare some soup and carry it to a hungry man, my action is technical, and ultimately physiological, it is a muscular movement; the ethical element enters only into the order to which this act belongs. Hence ethics can never compete with the technical, artistic, scientific part of life, with the material of life itself.

Thus the problem of right conduct, and its principle, belongs to human existence as such: if we deny this we distort the picture of human life. We can only meet the moral sceptic by proving to him that in order to be able to preserve his scepticism, he must have a distorted picture of life, to which no real life corresponds, not even his own.

In so doing, however, we have admitted the necessity for distinguishing between the *theory* of ethics and the moral actuality itself. Theoretically we may evade the ethical question, practically we *cannot*. Thus there are two kinds of "ethics": that which is actually lived and recognized in life, the actual ordering of relationships according to a principle of *super*- and *sub*ordination; and the ethic which is theoretically formulated, and perhaps theoretically rejected.

The original ethic—both in the genetic and positive sense— is undoubtedly the former. We have to do therefore first of all not with ethical theories, but with the various practical possibilities of ordinary life in an ethical manner, beside which it is a secondary question to what extent these "ordering-principles" are also accepted in theory, or are indeed even clearly perceived. These possibilities are as manifold as mankind; but they can all be grouped round a few particular main tendencies, which (certainly, in a process of abstraction) *can* be presented, and this is absolutely necessary for the right understanding of the problem of ethics.

CHAPTER II

THE PHASES OF THE IMMANENT MORAL UNDERSTANDING OF THE SELF

1. In the following pages we shall be examining some especially important "principles," which give to human life a definite "tendency" or permanent order; if in so doing we range these one above the other and describe them as "stages," this is not intended, in any way, as a description, however condensed, of a *development*, but the "stages" are merely introduced as phenomena, purely for purposes of comparison (1). Further, it will be obvious that in this description we are dealing with *abstractions*, which never actually occur in this kind of isolation from one another, since these different principles, in some way or another, are always present in the same person both alongside of and yet after one another, so that it is impossible to speak of a present, actual unity, but only of a tendency towards such a unity, of a preponderating principle of order. It is however only possible to know reality by means of such abstractions, human reality no less than that of Nature.

2. *Immediacy.*—When we enquire into the reason for permanence in the sphere of human practical life, what first presents itself is Nature as it exists in its immediate, instinctive, but organically uniform and "unbroken" course of the life-functions. In human life this only occurs in extreme instances, as, for example, in the case of the small child, or—to a lesser extent—in the case of the so-called "primitive" human being. For the distinctive element in human nature is the fact that man is not directly united with his nature, as it is, but that through his capacity for reflection, for asking questions, and for making decisions, he can view it, as it were, from a distance. All we can say, therefore, about the extreme instance to which we have just referred, is this : it has no relation to the problem of Ethics. For here the moral "agent," the human being who makes decisions, is absent. In such cases we can only surmise that the human element in humanity has either not yet come to birth, or that it has already been extinguished. But when we find this non-reflective, instinctive union with his nature—as for instance in the vitalistic philosophy of life of a thinker like Klages—either explicitly proclaimed by reflecting human beings as an ideal, or implicitly willed in a

vague, half-conscious manner, apart from any articulate theory, we are then confronted by a quite different phenomenon (2).

3. *Custom.*—The breach with immediacy takes place through reflection; in it the current of the natural life is arrested; reflection, and on the basis of this, decision, takes place. Self-determination has begun. But this breach with immediacy may vary in intensity. There is a middle stage between immediacy and self-determination, namely, where "others" are present, who drag "me" out of immediacy, without obliging "me" to complete this breach by full self-determination. Where this happens, the individual human being remains in contact with society in a certain dim obscure way. But this does not help us to know *why* he allows himself to be bound—and in this instance the fact that he allows it to take place is the sign-manual of humanity. It may be due merely to imitation or habit, but it *may* be due to religious awe, or fear, or to considerations of utility or to aesthetic feeling, or to various other causes. This stage therefore has no characteristic content; its distinguishing characteristic is formal, namely, the fact that the individual does not take the whole responsibility for his conduct on his own shoulders, but that at least in part he transfers some of it to "others," to "people" in general, to the community, the clan, etc. (3).

4. *Intelligent Purpose.*—The first way in which man uses his capacity of being independent of the actual through the faculty of reflection is by using his intelligence to control the purely natural function of life: self-preservation, and the preservation of the species. Man here demonstrates his intellectual independence not so much by the formulation of "ends"—which indeed remain purely natural—as in the artificial construction of means, through which the natural "ends" can be more surely and fully attained. These "means," viewed as a whole, we call *civilization.*[1] The intellect is here only the *means* to an end. The end is the mastery of nature for practical uses through the intelligence which makes tools and organizes. Here too, the relation between one man and another is on the natural plane, although it is realized through the intelligence; it is this: mutual security and mutual utility through co-operation and exchange. Since here the intellect is only a means to an end, there is no experience of any mental

[1] We are not here concerned with civilization as a task to be achieved but as the highest meaning of life. On the former point see below, Chapter XXXIII.

expansion which is not directed towards a definite end, the characteristic mark of this kind of life is the rigid ordering of this means to an end, or a peddling kind of economy. A man who lives in this limited way, as a "self-contained, finite being" (Tillich), is the kind of person we call a "Philistine."

This existence, however, necessarily suffers from an internal contradiction which must somehow make itself evident; the conflict between the natural "end" and the means which itself becomes an indirect end, that is the mind, between self-preservation—for instance, in the selfish use of other men— and the community, which is becoming a purpose to itself. On the one hand intellect and community are not desired as ends in themselves, but only as means, therefore only "what is absolutely necessary"; but once the intellect has been awakened it does not allow itself to be treated thus. It disturbs the Philistine's complacency by shaking his confidence in his security; he becomes apprehensive, anxious, and this drives him to seek for new ways of preserving his sense of security: Philistine existence is full of this tension caused by the conflict between fear and the effort to create security. On the other hand, the intelligence may finally get the upper hand, and may triumphantly assert its own independent right to exist— in which case this stage is then abandoned.

It is worth while paying some attention to this stage, because it is the predominating principle in the life of the average man. To look at life from the point of view of the rational end is regarded as a reasonable way of living. It is that view of life which was erected into a system in the Utilitarian and Positivist ethic of the nineteenth century; it is that which mainly predominates among the masses of our contemporaries—and indeed in the social upper stratum no less than in the lower— although no man has ever lived nor ever will live who was merely a "Philistine." Such a person would resemble the "ultimate man" in Nietzsche's horribly amusing eschatology.

5. *Sensible Infinity, the "daemonic element."*—While it is characteristic of the *bourgeois* that he desires everything in safe and sufficient measure, but no more, the same desire, without being materially altered, may assume a very different form. The object of desire remains the same, but it is desired to an infinite extent. While in the former case the natural sense element is connected with the limiting, controlling element of the mind, with the intelligence, in the latter it is connected with the element which longs for vastness, for the infinite,

23

that is: with the element of boundless phantasy. Phantasy weaves a romantic halo of infinity around the goods of sense, and the will grasps this boundless wealth of the finite with both hands. The real object of desire is not so much the finite object itself, as the self which asserts itself in this desire. Man desires to become conscious of his limitless existence, and to enjoy his liberation from all restrictions, his freedom. He desires to play, it matters not with what, to enjoy himself, it matters not in what medium. Therefore he does not seek security but danger, adventure, daring experiments. He intoxicates himself with the infinite possibility which his imagination brings before his mind's eye in glamorous colours and of which he is conscious in the unrestricted independence of his own will. This kind of person is the dominating man, the masterful man, the adventurer, who as a robber-baron or as a general, as a captain of industry or a politician, as a speculator on the Stock Exchange, or a Don Juan, exults in his empty freedom, which, just because it *is* empty, must be filled with sense-content if it is to be real at all. Such a man may exploit his fellow-men, or he may be philanthropic in a condescending way, in order to enjoy his solitary greatness in this condescension, and to find in the dependence of others the necessary foil to his own freedom.

But even *his* Self is greater than he knows, and it revenges itself on him in the unrest with which it drives him from one adventure to another; he can never really enjoy his power and his greatness because actually it is not infinite but only comparatively greater than that of others. This is the man who "rushes from desire to satiety and in satiety pines for desire."

6. *The Aesthetic Element as a Form of Life* (4).—The intellect, at first only used as a means to an end, now becomes conscious of itself as a self-end.

Man no longer investigates merely because it is useful to do so, but for the sake of truth; he works, not in order to gain his own security but for the sheer delight of "working." Culture is superimposed upon mere civilization. Culture as a principle of life is the aesthetic aspect of life. Here the intellect wishes to gaze at itself in the forms it assumes, in its inner accordance with law, which cannot be explained as a purely "natural end." The means by which this is accomplished is by the construction of mental images, in science—to the extent in which it is purely theoretical, and not practical and technical —and above all, in art. For here the question of mechanical utility does not arise. But if science and art are really to be more than pleasant recreations, if they are to be the controlling force in life, they must unite in one supreme comprehensive act of contemplation, of world-vision, by which the world, precisely through this act, becomes a cosmos, a work of art, a theorem, or a drama (5).

The intellect here regards itself as the force which creates culture, and in it man believes he has found the meaning of himself. Human existence gains its human quality from participation in this culture-process, and the genius represents the maximum of humanity. Human greatness and human worth are measured by this standard.

There are two varieties of this existence connected with culture: the more objective kind which is mainly concerned with the creative process, and the subjective kind which is more interested in the *man* who creates beautiful forms, that is, in the creative force, the genius. The genius, rather than culture, is then regarded as the place where the meaning of the cosmos becomes real and manifest. The former, more objective variety, appeals most to the man who cares about civilization, leading indeed to a merging of the two; the latter kind of culture appeals more strongly to the dominating, forceful type of man. "Energy or force is the quality of mind which distinguishes those who excel other men" (Beethoven)(6). Hence this second type is the purely aesthetic type. It represents the intellect in the enjoyment of itself, and also the expansion of the self to a world-self, regarded from a cosmic point of view. I assume that it is unnecessary to produce evidence in support of this statement; this view of human life could be illustrated a hundred times over from literature and philosophy, from the Renaissance down to the time of Nietzsche. To-day this view of man's nature dominates the intelligentsia as much as the "Philistine's" view dominates the mass of mankind.

But this aesthetic intoxication is speedily followed by disillusionment; even this "enthusiasm" has its dark background. "Your resemblance to the Divine causes deep misgiving." It is no accident that behind German speculative Idealism, in which this aesthetic view of life has found its most magnificent expression, lies the pessimism of Schopenhauer. This feverish attempt to make the creative faculties in man absolute is necessarily accompanied by despair of finding any absolute meaning in life at all. This intensification of the problem leads either to one still higher (7), to mysticism, or it ends in a scepticism which only plays with the problems raised by the mind.

7. *The Moral Idea.*—Hitherto we have been dealing with ethical decisions and indeed with those which define life as a whole, with "totality-views of life." This is the element common to them all. The distinctive element, however, that which makes it possible to range them as stages in an ascending series, consists in an increasing inwardness, that is, in making the spirit independent and distinct from the actuality of nature. The path which we have been describing is the spiral of immanental self-consciousness.

And yet we might also say: hitherto we have not been dealing with spiritual existence at all. For even genius is natural immediacy, the mind as nature, actuality, not as self-determination. Genius is a quantitative, not a qualitative conception; for every one has a little genius and no one is an absolute genius. Genius, as the word implies, is the spirit as a natural endowment. What genius produces therefore is culture—a thing of the spirit (*Geist-Sache*). Thus here also there exists, as in the earlier "stages," the opposition between the *form* and the *content* of decision. Man decides in favour of this life determined by the aesthetic element; only as such is life human and only as such is life real; but the "What" of this decision does not correspond with the "That"; the material personality (*persona-quid*), that is, self-knowledge and self-determination to freedom and responsibility for one's determination, does not correspond with the formal personality (*persona-quod*). Here too, in a spiritless way the necessity for decision in human existence has been ignored. Here therefore one has not yet become a person.

The emergence of the moral element in human life means that man has realized himself as a *person*; it means that the whole of life is now regarded from the point of view of decision, self-determination, freedom, responsibility.

The *quod*—the inevitably personal character of human existence—becomes *quid*, in the act of recognizing that the Ego, in the act of decision, is aware of itself, and determines itself in the light of this fact. The content of life is now sought no longer *out*side but *in*side the self; further, it is no longer sought in the self as it exists by nature but in its quality of *self-determination*.[1] The idea of freedom and autonomy has

---

[1] No one has grasped what is here intended, and presented it so clearly and fully, as FICHTE, in his *Ethik* of 1798; cf. especially the beginning of the first and the close of the second main section.

been born. No longer are we concerned with that empty freedom of infinite possibility which dissolves life into phantasy and endows Nature with a daemonic character, but with definite freedom. The αὐτός which has thus been recognized implies the νόμος. Such freedom is an inner necessity. Even in the building up of civilization and in the creation of culture, a spiritual principle of law is at work. Civilization is controlled by the logic of the understanding; in culture reason imposes law on sense. But this law affects the object, not the subject; it is accordingly a merely hypothetical law—*if* you wish to count correctly or to create something concrete, then do so and so—it is not categorical. "It shall be"—but not "*Thou shalt.*" Until the imperative—"Thou shalt"—has been perceived and accepted the contradiction is not removed which arises out of the fact that although I am always involved in decision I do not know that this fact of decision constitutes the basis of my existence. The "Thou shalt" of the Categorical Imperative means the emergence of the idea of personality.

This emergence is prepared by *custom* (8). Before man is aware of his own moral responsibility, he knows the moral demand of the community upon him, which he obeys not merely from the fear of social consequences, but in a dim, obscure but reverent awe of the *Nefas*, of that "which one may not do." There are νόμοι ἄγραφοι which *must* be obeyed.

The moment at which the νόμοι, which, here and there, in a casual and disconnected way, have fenced off a section of life, coalesce and become the *one* law, and the instant at which the dim "*one* ought" becomes the clear "*I* ought" is one and the same. The process by which the many commandments have become one law corresponds to the process by which the law becomes more and more interior, until at last it becomes "mine," that is, a law which I do not receive externally, because it speaks "within me."

Only now is the Ego no longer bound up with culture, but is an end in itself; only now is life faced with the stern demand for decision, whereas formerly it was a game. No longer can man regard time as something at his own disposal, for at every turn time comes to him burdened with this serious quality of decision, and it is called: the present moment. Here alone does the Ego count unconditionally as an entity which cannot be reckoned up in arithmetical terms, which cannot be measured by any quantitative standard, that is, as a *person*. The "other man," accordingly, the "fellow-man," is no longer merely the subject of culture or of civilization, which has value only in so far as and because it co-operates in the work and is the bearer of those object-values, but he also now comes under consideration as a person, since he also stands under the same law of freedom. The *one* moral idea demands from me recognition of his freedom as much as of my own, it limits my caprice in relation to him through the demand for unconditional respect and justice.

Then has the spiral movement of increasing inwardness here found its inmost point? Scarcely; for behind this moral idea there stand problems which no process of introspection can solve.

As the individual human being reflects upon himself, upon the "right life," he stumbles upon the mysterious fact of a law which speaks within himself, saying to him, "Thou shalt." The natural tendency of man to say positively: "I will," which even in spiritual creation, even in the work of genius, would like to pursue its course unhindered, is confronted by a higher authority; but the source of this authority, and its relation to me as an existent and volitional being, and, also to the world in which I live, is obscure and indeed incomprehensible. Can this be "my better self"? And if so, what does this mean? What is the origin of this sense of disharmony which becomes most acute when I refuse to do what the law "within me" commands? How is it that I do not act in accordance with this law "within me"? Can it be that this challenging authority, which has the right to judge my actions, should more properly be called "Thou" than "I"? But if this authority is a "Thou," then is this issuing of commands the only way in which it manifests itself to me? If it possesses its own mode of being, should not its relation—as being—to my being and the being of the world also be that of a higher, controlling personal authority? Thus, instead of making its presence felt in this ambiguous manner, ought it not rather to give an unambiguous proof of its own existence? Does such a clear evidence of itself exist? Is there such a revelation of Divine Being? Here introspection ceases and leads to the question of religion, of Divine revelation.

Without leaving the sphere of phenomenological reflection, we will now examine the relation between ethics and the religions of the world, reserving the Christian religion for treatment at a later stage.

CHAPTER III

MORALITY AND THE RELIGIONS OF THE WORLD

1. The line of thought we have been pursuing up to this point is abstract in character; for these "stages" do not exist in the detached way in which they have been described; further, this line of reasoning is abstract in that it isolates man and severs him from a reality which exists independently of all civilization, culture and all that posits itself: the reality of religion (1). Not only are civilization and culture historically often decisively dependent on religious ideas and emotions, but, above all, as a fact of history, morality—coupled with the closely related phenomenon of law, and the custom which unites both—never appears apart from religion. From the empirical and historical point of view religion is the source of all "good breeding" and of all morality (2). The consciousness of "right and wrong," of that which is permitted and that which is not permitted, commanded and forbidden, is very closely connected with the consciousness of "the Holy" (3).

The common element both in morality and in religion is this; the caprice of the human being swayed by his desires and by his passions is checked by the erection of a barrier, surrounded by the numinous awe of "the Holy." In all religions, in the "most primitive" as well as in the "higher" religions, there exists this "Law," which proceeds from a divine will, these "prohibitions" which protect some object or some sphere of life from human aggression, these frontiers which man is forbidden to cross, and which subjectively, from feelings of religious awe, man does not dare to cross. *Nefas!* "Thou shalt not!"

The content of these "prohibited" actions may not be "ethical" according to our present way of thinking—"you may not kill a particular animal—you may not enter a certain place"; still, the fact remains that only through such prohibitions does man learn that his positive desires must be controlled by duty, and his negative reactions by the knowledge of prohibitions. However the relation between religion and ethics may be defined, this, in any case, is common to both: that this limitation of human self-will takes place, not through the arbitrary imposition of man, but through the mysterious self-authentication of an invisible court, proceeding "from that which is hidden," which man obeys from a sense of reverent awe. Although it is clear that the rationalistic theory which derives belief in the gods from fear is false—"*timor primus in orbe fecit deos*"—and also that no real religion has ever existed apart from a sacred "awe" (reverence: *Ehr-furcht*) which is absolutely different from "fear," it is also evident that this sense of reverent awe is a matter of fundamental importance for the moral consciousness.

2. But just as it would be wrong to explain religion in a rationalistic way from the moral consciousness, it would also be wrong to take the opposite course. It is possible to maintain that the conception of an autonomous, purely immanent morality only appears on the very verge of historical reality, within the restricted area of a rationalistically emancipated culture; but, on the other hand, it is also certain that the moral consciousness provides documentary evidence for its independent existence apart from the religious consciousness; or perhaps it would be more correct to say, it acquires it. For in the beginnings of human historical life which we can still observe or infer with comparative certainty, not only are religion and morality indissolubly united, but so also are religion and law, culture, social order, and art. But where this (relatively) primitive state of affairs has been left behind, we see that the relation between religion and morality is not that of one-sided dependence, but rather of mutual influence. This mutual influence is, however, so complicated and so varied that it is impossible to disentangle the threads which compose it; this intricate web of mutual influences varies with the type of religion concerned as well as with the general intellectual level of a people.

The relation between the various conceptions of the Good Life—the right way of ordering all the circumstances of life— and religious conceptions, varies greatly (4). In a Pantheon we may see, for instance, a god who is regarded as the author and preserver of morality as a whole, or, on the other hand, we may see a number of gods, each one of whom governs a particular sphere of life. The independence of morality is also expressed in the fact that the gods themselves are regarded as subject to the moral law, that to some extent they disobey it, and are indeed extremely immoral in their behaviour, and thus that they can only expect to receive their just punishment from some impersonal world-law which is not further defined or known. Almost everywhere the sanctity of the oath, the law of hospitality, and the right of sanctuary, are conceived as directly connected with the will of the gods; other spheres of morality, however, are either very loosely connected with the divine, or they have no connexion with it at all. At one point we may detect an increasing influence of morality upon religious ideas; at another point we perceive how morality itself acquires greater depth through the influence of religious ideas and feelings; or again, we may see how the two drift apart, and religion and morality are severed from each other. The most amazing phenomenon of all is the fact that certain gods who are represented as the guardians of a particular province of morality, offend most crudely against this law themselves, and give man an extremely bad example (5).

3. In spite of the great variety this picture contains it is possible to formulate the following "law." The more closely morality is connected with religion the more the content of morality is mingled with the ritual-irrational element, the more, for instance, does the conception of moral purity tend to merge into that of the magically sacred. Judged from the moral standpoint, this means that the more deeply the sense of the Holy penetrates a people, the more morality is burdened with a priestcraft which has no ethical influence or significance. Or, to put it the other way round: the more that morality severs its connexion with this system of taboos the more it becomes "humane" and rational, the more also it becomes secular and tends to approach the borderline of mere utilitarianism or of mere *bourgeois* decency. Thus morality seems to possess its deepest meaning in the religious sphere, and its greatest clarity in the rational consciousness, and both stand in a relation of unavoidable tension to each other. The rational purification of morality always seems to be connected with a loss of moral sentiment and of reverence for the law as such (6).

The reason for this is manifest; for where morality drifts away from its moorings and loses touch with religion, it comes inevitably into closer contact with the spirit of culture (civilization); increasingly, therefore, its very basis becomes secular, and in the process it loses its independence, so far as the purpose of civilization and the value of culture are concerned.

But where religion itself becomes "spiritualized," that is,

31

where it disengages itself from its numinous, irrational, ritual element, this takes place in one of two directions: either in the direction of mystical speculative pantheism, or in the moralistic, deistic and rationalistic direction. In the latter case the religious sense is almost equated with the sense of culture; religion becomes an arid commonplace affair, the idea of God tends to be equated with the idea of an immanent moral law of nature or the world law, and the religious man tends more or less to be identified either with the "honest citizen," or with the "intellectual," to whom culture is everything. Here morality and religion can merge into each other, without fearing any irrational taint through the magical element. For religion itself has lost all sense of awe and has almost entirely lost its independence, so far as the world and culture are concerned. In the "ethical religion" of the spirit of the Enlightenment ethics and religion have become fused into a unity (7).

Where *mysticism* is concerned it is a different matter. Here the religious element maintains its full independence, its "Other-worldliness" over against all culture and secular existence. But this kind of religion, to the extent in which it becomes mystical, becomes ascetic, that is, remote from the world, indifferent to the life of the world, and thus remote from humanity and indifferent to humanity. Therefore the more fully mysticism develops along its own lines the more it absorbs all morality into religious asceticism; and isolates the human individual both from his environment and from his fellow-men.

4. Confronted by these facts it is impossible to answer the question concerning the presence of a "universal moral sense," a *consensus gentium moralis*, a "unity of the moral consciousness" with a plain "yes" or with a plain "no" (8). An affirmative answer can be given so far as the fact of the "sense of ought" is concerned, for the difference between good and evil, right and wrong, is present wherever there are human beings. Further, we must also grant to those who defend the view of the *consensus* that among all peoples and at all times it can be proved that there does exist and has existed a certain agreement in reference to the content of the idea of good and evil, right and wrong. But we must also immediately add, this agreement is very limited in character. A negative answer must be given in view of the fact that there is scarcely one moral commandment which is everywhere accepted as final,

that, on the contrary, the moral codes of the various peoples and civilizations completely contradict one another, not merely in points of detail but in principle. Could it indeed be otherwise, when we know how the various religious conceptions conflict with one another? Could we possibly conceive that the ethic of Buddhism or of Brahmanism, with its world-denying tendency, should *not* be wholly different from the system of morality which has grown up in China, with its emphasis upon ancestor-worship? How can the morality of the mystic who renounces the life of the world be the same as that of the Parsee or the Muslim who seeks to conquer the world? How can the morality of the deeply serious religion of Egypt be the same as that of Greece with its delight in culture?

To try to discover an "original moral common sense" behind these influences of the various religions is simply a wild-goose chase. It is as futile as it would be to try to discover the common element in religion, the religion of reason, behind all the individual faiths. The "religion of reason" of the Enlightenment, or the "essence of religion" of speculative Idealism and Liberal theology, is essentially a particular phenomenon, standing alongside of the various 'historical religions; in the same way, the "autonomous morality" of the enlightened reason of a person to whom this abstraction has become a principle of life, is essentially a particular phenomenon, taking its place alongside of morality, and is closely connected with religion, that is, with a living religion. Neither the rational "religion of reason" nor rational morality are either religion or morality "in itself" or "in its purity." The impossibility of this conception will come out still more clearly in the following chapters.

CHAPTER IV

THE RATIONALIZATION OF THE MORAL IN PHILOSOPHICAL ETHICS

1. The Moral precedes every kind of ethic. It is, of course, true that the moral does not precede all reflection; for reflection, the break with immediacy, is the presupposition of the moral consciousness. But this kind of reflection is not scientific; it can even to some extent take place "directly" and indeed "instinctively." There is a moral "common sense," a faculty which cannot be interpreted in one sense only, and one which it is very difficult to define, which, nevertheless, is an important reality; but this moral "instinct" is concealed and veiled partly by religious and partly by secular non-moral motives and "principles," which we have already examined at an earlier stage in this enquiry. It is of the very essence of the moral, as a reflective and systematic form of consciousness— that is, a consciousness which presupposes reflection and regards life as a whole—that it can easily be combined with a process of rational consideration, and is then further determined by it.

On the other hand, it cannot be taken for granted that all thinking individuals or races will have an ethic. Many civilized groups possess moral systems; but it seems to have been reserved to the sphere of civilization determined by Hellenism and Christianity to possess an ethic.

It would, however, be wrong to conceive ethics merely as the "science of morality," in the sense, for instance, in which aesthetics are the science of Beauty. Ethics, as the philosophy of the good, penetrates far more deeply into man's understanding of himself than any other kind of science. The origin of ethics in Socrates and Plato already betrays its wholly practical purpose, which is also absolutely accepted by Aristotle, although he is so much more theoretical.[1] Philosophical ethics has never wholly renounced the idea of being a doctrine for life. Thus it has also become a vital factor, an historical force of the highest order. When we remember what the Stoic ethic has meant for Roman law, and what the Stoic

---

[1] A glance at the first chapter of the *Nicomachean Ethics*, where ARISTOTLE subordinates ethics to politics, makes this quite plain. Cf. also PLATO: *Phaedrus*, pp. 229 ff.

and the Aristotelian ethic has meant for the Christian Church, and for the social, political, and cultural outlook of Europe, we cannot rate the importance of ethics too highly, that is, purely from the point of view of life, without reference to science as such. Western morality is just as much determined by ethics as ethics by morality. Ethics does not merely express the self-interpretation of a period; it is also one of the outstanding forces which have shaped it.

Philosophical ethics, as a science, is not essentially theoretical but practical. In all its important forms it arose not out of the need for the theoretical knowledge of morality but out of the need for moral clarity. It aims to complete the process of natural moral clarification. In ancient Greece, in particular, it arose out of the desire to give clarity and stability to the moral will at a time when the traditional basis of the Ethos in religion and tradition was no longer sufficient for the awakening spirit. From Socrates onwards it is the attempt to base morality upon the human reason itself, without the additional aid of irrational-religious and irrational-conventional sanctions. Philosophical ethics, therefore, since its beginning with Socrates, is at the same time a rational ethic, the erection of a standard for the will and for conduct which can be established in accordance with reason. It partakes of this character even where in some form or another it makes use of the idea of God. For even this Idea of God is an entity which arises within rational thought, since in the context of the argument on which it is based it is regarded as "necessary." A philosophical ethic is not necessarily an irreligious ethic; but its distinguishing feature is the fact that it always categorically rejects the basis of a transcendent revelation; in this sense it is always "an immanental idea"(1).

In the following pages, in which we give a rapid survey of the main possibilities of this ethic, our attention cannot be directed towards the content of these ethical systems—for this the presuppositions are at present lacking—but solely towards the strictness of its connexion with the argument. We have to examine these systems in order to see whether they fulfil what they promise, namely, a rational argument for morality.

In the philosophical ethic as usual there are actually only two great systems which confront one another, which are related to the fundamental contradiction in philosophy as a whole: the Naturalistic view of ethics, which starts from the fact of existence, and the Idealistic view, with its sense of obligation or the Moral Idea. Pantheism, which bridges the contrast between existence and obligation in a speculative manner, has never been in a position to develop an independent ethic; indeed to it ethics is more of an embarrassment than anything else. Logically Pantheism should place a doctrine of contemplation or of aesthetic symbolism in the place of ethics. In point of fact, however, the pantheistic moralists have usually helped themselves out with an ethical theory which was half Idealistic and half Naturalistic; Spinoza, for instance, does this in his ethic, which is a mixture of this kind (in so far as it is possible to call it an "ethic" at all).

2. The Naturalistic system of ethics in all its forms consists of the more or less logical attempt to explain the moral life from natural facts, or to base "morality"—that is, the "right" life—upon such facts. So that which ought to be, the principle of "right," must be simply a condensed form of such rules of experience, which make it possible for the individual to determine the most complete realization of his purely natural interest or desire. Ethics then means—according to its theoretical content—the natural causal explanation of the supposedly mysterious supernatural "morality," and in its practical content it is simply Utilitarianism. The sense of obligation and the "moral laws" are abbreviated forms of the experience of humanity in respect of that which I find useful and pleasant. Whoever observes these laws is not "good" but clever. After its most well-known representative we call this the ethic of Epicureanism (2). This ethic is individualistic, for it starts from the standpoint of the isolated individual; it is egoistic, for it aims solely at the interest of this individual, of the Self; it is eudaemonistic, for it makes the principle of conduct "happiness," the well-being of this isolated individual. From this point of view the community exists merely as the sum of all such individuals, and it has significance for it only in so far as the individual, if he wishes to attain his end, in a "prudent" way, must equate his claims with those of society; since if he does not do so he will fall under its chariot wheels and be crushed to death. Ethics is the theory of individual adaptation on the basis of individual striving after personal happiness. The main features of this Epicurean ethic have also been reproduced in modern times by various important and influential thinkers, as also in actual practice they play a great part(3).

The Naturalistic ethic, however, has rarely appeared in this crudely logical guise. Rather the Naturalistic moralists, especially in more recent times, while holding firmly in principle to the bases of their theory, have always felt the need to come rather nearer to that which in our sphere of culture is held to be "morally good." On the one hand they thought they could do this by means of a more refined psychology; on the other hand, by taking into consideration the idea of evolution. Human nature indeed, like that of every other living creature, is aware not only of egoistic feelings and instincts but also of "altruistic" or "social" instincts; thus the satisfaction of these needs also forms part of natural happiness(4). It was believed that it would be possible to construct a whole new system of naturalistic ethics upon this new discovery, whose picture of the "moral" element in human nature would be in greater harmony with the traditional picture. But when we examine this theory more closely it is easy to discover a confusion of thought. Either such things are done as though the satisfaction of the altruistic instinct were the same as that which other ethical theories would call "ethically good," which is not the case at all, since there it is not instinct with which we are concerned but duty; or two distinct motives are at work if a person does something "altruistic," because it is congenial or pleasant to him, or because he feels himself under an obligation to do it. Sometimes, however, the sense of obligation is really intended, but it is believed that it can be traced back to the altruistic instinct, and this can be explained as the source of the sense of obligation. Morality—as generally understood—only begins where the natural instinct breaks down, that is, where one "ought" to do what one does not want to do(5). The choice before the naturalistic moralist is either to deny the existence of such a "sense of ought" or to give up his Naturalism.

In this embarrassing state of affairs it was thought that the idea of evolution would help(6). The sense of obligation, it was argued, is simply a reflection in feeling of that which human experience has found useful. But here, too, the same confusion exists. If I am concerned with the question of the utility of certain conduct to humanity as a whole, then I am faced with the question: Shall I obey this feeling of obligation or not? The fact that the "feeling of obligation" suggests to me what will be useful for the community still does not mean that I will to obey this feeling against my own self-interest.

37

On a naturalistic basis this is only possible if that which is useful for the community is also useful for myself—which brings us back to the Epicurean doctrine of expediency. Granted that the idea of evolution may explain the conscience, the sense of obligation, yet in so doing it deprives it of its power. At the very moment that I perceive that this is all that conscience means, namely, that it represents the experience of utility for the community, it ceases to impose any obligation upon me.

Alongside of this "altruistic" ethical theory which oscillates between duty and impulse, which belongs in the main to the ethical thought of the nineteenth century, there appears to-day another theory, more or less opposed to it, which emphasizes the unrestricted right of the Self, of the individuality. The "pleasure" principle is here replaced by the idea of power or of individuality. This is the ethic of "self-expression." If this ethic were logically carried out it would utterly destroy all systems of ethics(7). The whole of ethics would be summed up in one sentence: "Always do what you like best! For you there are no rules, save one: to obey no rule." In reality, however, behind this programme of self-expression there lie, as a rule, deeper ideas and forces to such an extent, indeed, that they destroy the logic of Naturalism. In this theory, the "Self" which is to be expressed is not simply the natural individuality, but "the law of its nature," its idea, its deeper content, in contradistinction to the "Self" as it actually exists at the moment. In any case, however this "deeper" element may be defined, it is evidently something which does not yet exist, something which ought to be, and this means that the Naturalistic basis has been abandoned. Wherever the Idealistic ethic of duty makes itself felt, there, as its counterpart, arises the romantic ethic of individuality, which in the interest of the genuineness of the will and therefore also of the genuineness of morality, denies every general law; and thus, just because it does stand for the idea of duty, it contradicts itself(8).

3. The most obvious contrast to the Naturalistic ethic of the desire for happiness is the Idealistic ethic of duty for duty's sake. An act is not good if I do it because I like doing it, but only if I do it because I ought to do it, because I "may" not do otherwise. Thus the principle of the Good can never·be sought in my own impulses but only in the law which confronts me.

That will is good which wills what it ought, that is, the

will which is *obedient* to the law. It is not the content of the will which makes it good or bad—the same action can at one time be good and at another time bad—but the "form" of the will, that is, its harmony with the law. The "content" of the will may be desired; it cannot be prescribed. In order that it may be "good" it must first of all be described as commanded by the law; thus it is not the end set before the will which makes it good, but the fact that it aims at obeying the law. Henceforward let us describe this ethical theory by the name of its greatest representative, Kant. I call this theory "Idealistic" because this law, which qualifies the will for the Good, is exactly the same as the Idea of the Good.

But in order to make this ethic possible as a rational philosophical ethic two other conceptions are necessary, that of immanence and that of universal validity. If an ethic is to be possible as a rational ethic, if it is to be conceived apart from any kind of transcendental revelation, then this law must exist in my reason. And if it is really to command me, then it must exist in my reason as something which is binding on every one without exception; but this means that it must be the same for every one. Its power as law is based on this very fact of its universal validity. The Idealistic ethic of duty —if it is carried out in the strictly rational sense—is a universal ethic of duty; in the strictest sense of the word it is legalistic. Finally, there is a third point: it must be possible to maintain that this legalism as such will extend to the possibility of telling every one what he has to do in particular cases. Out of the form of legalism the content of the Good must be evolved. This relation of obligation to existence, however— without the Christian idea of Creation, or the idea of a divine Law of Nature (as understood in the philosophy of religion)(9) —can only be created by the assertion that the Good—so far as its content is concerned—is what should be, conceived as acting as a natural law. The universality of the law, trans- ferred from the sphere of obligation to that of existence, supplies the content of the obligation(10). It is at this point, obviously, that the Achilles' heel of this system becomes evident, and criticism has always concentrated all its force on this particular point. Behind this demand for a way of acting which can be conceived possible as a natural law, a principle has actually been introduced which contradicts the fundamental idea of the system, the idea, namely, of well- being. The formal rational conception of law, however,

39

provides no foundation for the idea that the Good ought to be that which furthers the welfare of all. Kant has transformed a limiting conception into a constitutive idea. It is true, of course, that the Good, ethically conceived, is something which can be conceived as a universal—but with the claim to universality it ceases to be an ethic of duty. But the Buddhist ethic of renunciation conceives itself to be just as universal, in this sense, as the ethical theory which aims at the welfare of all, or as any kind of Perfectionist theory. It is impossible to deduce any material definition of ethics from the mere principle of the possibility of its being made universal. In spite of the powerful impression which the Kantian ethic made in its own day, and continues to make, it can never really satisfy anyone, since it does not fulfil what it promises. It describes the "form" of the "good will," but it cannot say what should be done.

4. Therefore alongside of this ethic—or between it and its exact opposite, Epicureanism—there have constantly arisen other forms of ethical theory, which we recognize as attempts to solve this problem. The individualistic ethic of self-realization, which, after its first and greatest exponent, we call the Aristotelian ethic, starts, like Epicureanism, from the principle of happiness—like the latter it is individualistic and eudaemonistic; but it combines with the idea of happiness that of the specifically human possibility. Put in an abstract way this means: the concept of man is at the same time posited as an Idea. All men are rational beings—that is the *concept* of man. Upon this is based the second statement: all men ought to live in a rational manner: this is the *Idea* of man. The word "reason" is, however, used each time in a different sense: in the first instance it is used as a formal entity, and therefore also as an ethically neutral entity—the power of formulating an "end" and of thought; in the second instance it is determined materially and ethically—the fact that reason defines its own end, and the recognition of this fact—*right* thought. The contradiction is glaring. No sense of obligation can be evolved from the actual constitution of humanity without some logical sharp practice. It is impossible to define what man ought to be from that which he actually is. The secret of the Orphic saying: "Become what thou art!"— which, rightly understood, is the secret not only of ethics but also of religion—cannot be solved along the rational line which is here indicated, although it is quite certain that the

relative power of conviction of such an ethic is based upon this very secret(11).

From the point of view of content, however, both Individualism and Eudaemonism have always come to grief over this ethical theory, which aims solely at self-realization. Hence—mainly in more recent times—attempts have been made to find another way of reconciling that which is with that which ought to be. Is not Spirit an historically objective fact, and therefore a super-individual fact? Can we not, therefore, gain fresh light on the problem of ethics by regarding it from the point of view of this super-individual process of the development of Spirit?—for this process actually exists, it is actually taking place, and can therefore even be regarded as a process of nature. So the Good is then conceived as that form of action by means of which we share in the cultural development of the history of the race. Ethics is based upon the philosophy of history; indeed it is regarded as merely the individual aspect of that universal process. It is, of course, obvious that this theory has no room for the "sense of ought"; it deals simply with existence as it is—even though it may be conceived as a spiritual form of existence; hence this ethic is presented in the indicative and not in the imperative mood, and as far as possible the problem of Evil is ignored; for if it were not ignored, the question would inevitably be raised: "What would happen if this 'spiritual' action were not to take place after all? Supposing man decides *against* instead of *for* this universal process?—What then?" If it is the concern of ethics to tell man which path he should choose, when two possibilities lie before him, then this ethic based on the philosophy of history certainly does not solve the problem of ethics, rather it evades it—this comes out very plainly in the fact that in this theory the individual human being, the person, is lost in the maze of an abstract spiritual process(12).

5. A final possibility of avoiding Kantian formalism without giving up Idealism or *a priori* principles seems to be the "material value ethic"(13). That which makes the will good— so it is here argued—is not an abstract formal "accordance with law" but substantial yet spiritual values. These values are not empirical objects of desire—otherwise indeed the Kantian criticism which characterizes all volition which is determined by material ends as merely natural desire, would be justified; all that could be established would be a desire,

but no obligation; rather these values, though objective, are spiritual entities, and the will can be described as "good" or "bad" according to its choice or rejection of these values. These values, as "entities," which alone confer "value" on the empirical object, are of an *a priori* nature, they are real ideas. It seems as though the problem of Ethics has been solved; the material *a priori* has been found.

In reality, however, we are merely in danger of falling a prey to an illusion. First of all we must make it quite clear that "value" is not an *a priori* intellectual conception—but—according to the ordinary use of terms—it is a psychological and emotional conception. In the language of the present day by a "value" we mean something which corresponds to a definite need, or, to put it more exactly, the quality by means of which something corresponds to a need. Hence values fluctuate according to needs. It is not the desire which makes the value—in this the criticism of the common psychology of pleasure is right; we desire the values because they are valuable, they do not become valuable because they are desired. But they are not valuable "in themselves," but "for me," for instance, for my body, in particular circumstances.

Now it is true that there are spiritual elements which we call valuable; but the very fact that we gather up that which is spiritually valuable under the same concept as the physically valuable indicates that it is not this conception, the "value," which is distinctive of the spiritual. There are values of civilization and of culture, but this simply means that culture, which is something spiritual, also has reference to our desires; beyond the fact that it is of a spiritual nature, it is also of such a kind that it can be desired. It is the same with the so-called ethical values. That they are "values" does not establish their ethical and normative character, but their capacity not only to be classed as obligatory but also as desirable. The enquiry into the question of the scale of values leads to the same goal. Where there is a scale there is a law of order; where values are arranged in a scale, they are ordered according to a law of degrees. This law is, however, not itself a value; but it is indeed this law which prescribes to the moral will the scale of that which is to be desired. Thus the ethically decisive element lies in this law of the scale of values, not in the values themselves. It is not the values but the ordering of the values and the willing of the values in accordance with this order which decides whether a thing is good or evil. The conception of value does not help to solve the problem of ethics(14).

Thus this survey of philosophical ethics brings us to the unsatisfactory conclusion that none of these systems achieves a real synthesis; each ethical system approaches the phenomenon of morality in very different ways; each is right, up to a point, compared with the rest; the excellence of one shows up the weakness in another; thus—in varying degrees —each has its own particular value, and each has its special weakness; thus this unsatisfactory situation cannot be overcome by any kind of "synthetic ethics."

CHAPTER V

THE DEEPENING OF THE PROBLEM BY THE DEEPENING OF THE CONTRADICTION

1. The philosophical ethic of reason, which has arisen out of the need to give greater security to ethical thought than it possesses in its popular form, and to get rid of the contradictions which cling to it, is not only unable to do this since it has itself been split up into a number of systems based on reason, but the opposing views have now reached a state where it is impossible to reconcile them. Even the relative uniformity of moral "common sense" has been completely destroyed by philosophical reflection. Rational philosophical reflection from Aristippus and Epicurus down to Mandeville, Stirner, and Nietzsche has succeeded in justifying all that had hitherto been regarded as abominable, and in casting suspicion on all that had previously been regarded as good. In comparison with the contradictions which appear in the sphere of philosophical ethics the pre-philosophical *consensus gentium moralis* appears a compact unity; it has been reserved to philosophical ethics to call the obviously evil good and the manifestly good evil. It is no longer possible to bridge over these contradictions. For who can reconcile the herd morality of Utilitarianism and the Super-man of Nietzsche, the Hedonism of Aristippus or modern Vitalism with the rigorist Kantian ethic? Who can reconcile the personalism of a man like Scheler with the impersonalism of thinkers like Spinoza or Schleiermacher? Through philosophical reflection the situation has become, in the full sense of the word, hopelessly contradictory.

2. Ought it not to be possible, however, to overcome these contradictions by carrying to its logical conclusion the particular system which approximates most nearly to the heart of the problem of ethics? This would mean, of course, the abandonment of the eclectic method. A moralist with a serious, scientific outlook will always choose this line of thought rather than the eclectic process of the combination of various elements into a system. There can be no doubt that of all the ethical theories which deal with this question, by far the most hopeful is the ethic of Kant; this ethic is the most serious attempt there is to understand existence philosophically

from the simple experience of moral responsibility. It was in Kant's conception of duty that the man who was most keenly aware of the distinction between good and evil found himself best understood, in this theory, that is, which is in opposition to all eudaemonistic and culturally aesthetic modifications of the sense of obligation; Kant's ethic will continue to attract pre-eminently those who are concerned about the peculiar nature of morality, in distinction from considerations of utility, the instinct to create, and the experience of beauty. Then are the contradictions which we thought we perceived on a first superficial acquaintance only apparent? Or at least are they such that on a more thorough examination it will prove possible to overcome them?

Before we enter upon the examination of this question I must make a preliminary observation. We are not now dealing with the possibility of a formal critical ethic, which, as such, does not claim to define the Good in any way, but simply to demonstrate the force of the good will—whatever it may be materially—in a way which could be applied universally. Such a proceeding is indeed necessary, but its importance is purely scientific; it does not set out to deal with the question with which we are here concerned, that is, to develop the Good systematically in a rational form, or at least to provide the basis for such a deduction of particular requirements from a general principle. Kant placed his ethic deliberately alongside the Christian ethic, and made no secret of the fact that the formal principles he had discovered produced exactly the same ethic as that of the Gospels—although the basis is different. Thus we are here only concerned with the Kantian ethic to the extent in which it attempts to define the Good, and to demonstrate the possibility of discovering, by the use of reason, what we should do, or abstain from doing, in any given situation. Let us then enquire whether this theory can overcome those contradictions which complicate the question of ethics.

3. If we start from the most fundamental antithesis of all, from that between an ethic based on immanence and one based on transcendence, then certainly the intention of Kant at this point is not clear. Can it be that a theonomy lies behind his principle of autonomy? Is it then possible that he had found the point where both become one, and thus the point at which the contradiction is overcome? Above all, the recent publication of Kant's *opus postumum* has shown us, most impressively, the

way in which Kant wrestled with this very problem. It has shown us equally clearly that a solution of this problem along the lines suggested by Kant is impossible. His essentially Idealistic point of view can never be combined with the recognition of a "divine substance"—as Kant expresses it— that is, with the recognition of a personality which confronts *me* as *Thou*.

The rationalism of the philosophical ethic can never be combined with the recognition of a divine self-revelation. The principle of autonomy, as Kant conceives it (and is forced to conceive it), the immanence of the logical consistency, presupposes a point of identity between divine and human knowledge in reason, without which transcendentalism breaks down, and with which faith in God and in Revelation cannot be combined. Ultimately, the philosopher would have to give up the attempt to base ethics on reason, if he desired to see it based on God, that is, on the self-revelation of the Divine will. But in this case a philosophical ethic would have been transformed into a theological ethic.[1] This possibility does not exist within philosophy. Autonomy and theonomy cannot be combined. And yet Kant in particular never gets free from theonomy. That which as a philosopher he cannot acknowledge, just because he philosophizes thoroughly, holds him in its spell. For who could the Legislator be save God? What does a "Thou shalt" mean, if it does not come from God?(1)

This fundamental antithesis, however, manifests itself at all the decisive points of the Kantian ethic. If we try to remove the antithesis between that which is and that which ought to be (which is, indeed, the presupposition of all ethics), into man himself, we are obliged to split the Self of man into an intelligible Self and an empirical Self. The intelligible Self is then the Legislator of the Good, and at the same time the pure will. The results of this division are well known: the empirical Self becomes a sense-bound creature, without freedom, the intelligible Self becomes a God.[2] But the Self which is conscious of responsibility and can have a "sense of guilt" does not exist. The metaphysical

---

[1] Here we are not alluding to a "conflict of faculties," but simply to integrity of thought. An ethical system, of which revelation forms a constituent element, is a theological ethic.

[2] Cf. the last phrase of Kant which has just been quoted. It is at this point that Fichte's mysticism takes its rise.

dualism of idea and appearance has obliterated the ethical dualism of good and evil. The Greek Platonist conception of man, which is inseparable from Idealism, that is, the sense of detachment, of the opposition which exists between the realm of "spirit" and the realm of "sense," combined with the view which holds the "sense-life" responsible for the evil in the world, re-appears in this theory, although Kant did not intend it.

The fundamental contradiction of the transcendental ethic comes out particularly clearly, therefore, in the problem of evil. Two irreconcilable points of view confront one another. The one arises from the analysis of the "good will." If the Good is harmony with the law of the Good, then every deviation from the law is not bondage to sense, but disobedience to the law, and the conception of radical evil is unavoidable. We are on the verge of the profound mystery of the Christian doctrine of Original Sin. On the other hand: if we take the principle of autonomy, and the identity of the Law-giver and the Self seriously, then the inmost part of the will is indeed not only in harmony with, but is identical with the Divine Will, thus evil can only be due to the non-intelligible, empirical, and causally-determined Self; thus it is not really an evil will but merely a hindrance. If the supreme court of appeal is really "I," and not "Thou," then the presupposition of autonomy holds good, there is a point of identity between the Divine and the human will, and evil is merely a secondary phenomenon.

4. The antithesis becomes most evident, however, at the point at which criticism has always been most insistent: in the question of the content of the "Thou shalt." The whole Kantian ethic is based upon the contrast between what is and what ought to be, idea and appearance, action based on duty and action based on material desire. We have already[1] pointed out how embarrassed the Kantian ethic is by the simple question: What ought man to do? From a different point of view this ethical theory commands our utmost admiration just because it does *not* answer this question, because it avoids laying down any rules and regulations for specific conduct beforehand, and because it simply looks at the will as it is formally determined by law. Here, at any rate, there is no trace of the much decried "legalism" of the Kantian ethic. For this formalism, if literally carried out,

[1] See above, pp. 39 ff.

would mean that the "good" element in conduct could never be perceived beforehand; obedience to the moral law at any given time is alone good. But this truth could only be maintained if we could go further, and say: the only good is obedience to God's command as it is manifested to us in changing circumstances. There is no trace of this in Kant, however. On the contrary, the same formalism which points in this direction requires also the possibility of determining beforehand all the possible ethical content. For, as we know, it is only the transcendental conception of law and not the theological conception of command which is legitimate in the Kantian ethic(2). Law, however, in contrast to command, is that which is not intended for any particular time, it is non-individual, it is timeless and universal. As a rational moralist, that is, as one who thinks of the good will not in view of an actual Divine command but in view of the law, Kant also believes absolutely in the possibility of an ethical system, that is, in the possibility of constructing timeless valid norms of duty for actual conduct. Were he not to do so, he would no longer be a philosophical moralist in the sense' named, but only a philosophical critic on the threshold of a theological or a religious ethic(3).

Now, however, it becomes evident that neither the formal conception of the good will, and of personality, nor even the conception of maxims which can be unconditionally universalized, provides an adequate definition of conduct. The difficulty is due to the fact that the Kantian philosophy offers no link between the world of existence—and, indeed, the concrete world, as it *now* is—and that which ought to be. The imperative "Thou shalt" is a stranger in this world, it has nothing to do with things as they actually are. On the contrary, the bridge between action in the sphere of the world as it is and as it ought to be, has been broken by the opposition—for Kant necessary—between duty and sense-desire. The metaphysical dualism of idea and appearance, which lies behind all Idealistic philosophy here manifests itself as a negative ethical principle(4). Actually Kant should have moved forward to an ascetic ethic of absolute renunciation of the world. For him neither the idea that God is the Creator of the world, nor the ambiguous pantheistic idea of the *lex naturae* (which made the Stoic ethic so fruitful in the practical sphere), come within the range of possibilities. As a metaphysician Kant knows that the only possible union between the world of being and that of what ought to be is either the symbolism of art or faith in the Creator, that is, religion. Kant, however, is unable to allow the latter to influence his ethical theory, because it would destroy his principle of autonomy. It is well known that Kant ultimately came to terms with Eudaemonism, in order to reach a material ethic at all, and this, in itself, shows very clearly the fundamental difficulty in his theory. He is forced to recognize the presence of natural and cultural goods without being able, from the standpoint of his rigoristic principle, to value them ethically as such. From the point of view of his abstract Idealism it is impossible to see the value of life, and of all that serves life. Kant's actual alliance with Eudaemonism can only be understood when we remember that Kant was not merely an Idealist, but that he was an Idealist with a Christian foundation, and that in the conception of God the Creator, Christianity provided him with a link between that which is and that which ought to be, which, although it had no logical right within his system, was, nevertheless, firmly established in his real thought.

5. Thus the very element within the ethic of reason which makes it possible to take the whole question of morality seriously—the antithesis between that which is and that which ought to be—is also the very element which makes it impossible to give content to this "sense of ought." Every attempt, however, to escape from this unfortunate situation on the ground of a rational ethic, as represented either by the ethic of values or the ethic of culture, weakens this antithesis, and leads to a corruption of the sense of duty in a Eudaemonistic sense; that is, the idea of duty has been so weakened or polluted by other influences that it has become a conception of duty which is partly vitalistic and hedonistic, and partly aesthethic and cultural. Moral duty is no longer regarded as duty—in the real sense of the word—it is simply desire or inclination somewhat glorified. The Categorical Imperative has lost its force, and has become merely a desire for culture or for life. Reverence for the command: "Thou shalt" is replaced by enthusiasm and the ethos of beauty(5), whereby the Good is good because it is beautiful. The Good is no longer the Command, it is "value"; thus conduct is no longer controlled by duty but by inclination. Only at a later stage in this book can we deal with the fact that even behind this corruption of ethical principle there is a certain

amount of truth, the truth, namely, that happiness, and not only duty—love and not merely obedience, the individual as well as the universal element—has a right to a place within any real ethical system; finally, we ought to realize that even the law (Nomos) has not the last word in ethics. But within a sphere of thought controlled by an immanental ethic dominated by the idea of autonomy, such ideas could not fail to have a debilitating influence.

6. If then it is impossible to solve the problem of ethics within the sphere of immanental ethics based on reason, because irreconcilable antitheses are continually and inevitably re-appearing, we may put the final question: Can *religion* solve the ethical problem? In attempting to answer this question, however, we must take care not to fall into the error of the Enlightenment, by examining "religion" in general for this possibility. For "religion" in general does not exist; what does exist are definite "religions," which, as we have seen, adopt very different attitudes to the problem of ethics, sometimes opposed to one another. Thus we do not mean that rationalized form of "religion" of which the thinkers of the Enlightenment type speak, that "religion" of Immanence which has its own place within a philosophical speculative system, but which within the sphere of revealed religion is only another name for the depths of the human spirit; no, what we mean here is a real religion of revelation(6), in which God confronts the human "I" as "Thou," in which man does not dispose of the divine truth, but receives it in an act of self-communication on the part of God, and in which this act of communication is not the same as the deepest act of self-reflection but an event, in which from beyond human possibilities God Himself discloses Himself to man.

Revelation is only known in faith; where and what revelation is, is a statement which can only be ventured upon as a confession. It is here that the Christian Church comes forward with her confession that God has spoken to her in His Word. Science may examine the content of this confession of faith, she may compare the distinctive character of "Christian conceptions" compared with other conceptions, but in the last resort science has no right to pass judgment on the claim of faith or on the claim of revelation. This claim remains the act and the venture of faith, which is willing to witness boldly to the grounds on which its venture is based.

One who has wandered hither and thither in search of the Good without receiving a satisfactory reply to any of his questions, will find that revelation is prepared to give an answer to his question, which we put to the believing Church in his name—and in our own name too, since we never approach this subject from the standpoint of wholly convinced believers but are ourselves also striving to increase our own faith.

Can it be that *here* we have found the answer to the question of the Good?—an answer which removes those antitheses which entangle "natural" morality and ethics, an answer in which the question of morality is seen in its purity—that is, free from "sacred" and ritual irrationality—and is yet grounded in something which is higher than human reason; an answer in which the Good is both in the highest sense human, and yet in the highest sense Divine; an answer in which the conflict between the empty but pure form of the command and its concrete but impure ethical content is ended; an answer in which good and evil are clearly distinguished from one another, without merging again into one at an innermost point; in which the opposition between good and evil comes out as clearly as possible, yet without rending humanity into two separate metaphysical halves; in which the individual is taken seriously, yet not at the cost of the community, and the community is taken seriously, yet not at the cost of the individual; in which physical well-being is not denied in order to exalt spirituality, and the spiritual is not depreciated as a merely accompanying phenomenon of the physical; an answer which absorbs all knowledge which is possible from the side of man, and yet which unveils and removes all the error which manifests itself in the contradiction of opposing views; in a word: Does the Christian faith give *the* answer, the *only* answer, and the *whole* answer to the ethical problem?

The Christian faith ought to give an answer to this question. If it is certain that in the revelation given to it it does possess *the* truth, not *a* truth, the truth which is given by God, and not merely a truth which has been discovered by man, through the processes of knowledge, that it possesses absolute and not relative truth, then surely this certainty includes an affirmative answer to that particular question. Christianity is convinced, not merely that it *sees* these antitheses and sees them far more clearly than others, but that they are not so many different antitheses but one single antithesis, and that this antithesis, once it has been truly perceived for what it is, is at the same time removed. Thus in faith there lies an "understanding" of these antitheses which also sums them up in one, with an intensity which human powers could never attain; and faith possesses a solution of that one single contradiction, which, because it is seen and felt in all its painful urgency, is no longer a matter of theory, but a matter of life and death; it is perceived "existentially," that is, it is seen to be an act of humanity as a whole, and, as such, it can only be removed by an act of God as a whole, which affects humanity as a whole.

This means that the purely phenomenological line of enquiry which we have followed up to this point is over. If we want to know the meaning of faith, we can never find it as neutrals, as mere spectators. This "explanation" and this "removal" of the contradiction—and it is in this that the intensification and concentration on one point consists, and also the transcendental character of this process—is no mere general theory of the universe, offering to the speculative thinker the attractive possibility of a synthesis; but the answer of faith, in so far as it proceeds from faith, is a "witness" which can only be perceived in its real meaning by faith. Yes, indeed, there *is* an answer to the human question concerning the Good; but this answer is of such a character that first of all it alters the question of the questioner in such a way that he is no longer the one who asks the question but one who is questioned, that he no longer sees himself beset by contradictions, but he perceives that the contradiction permeates his own nature. The answer of Faith to the ethical problem is the Word of Sin and of Grace.

CHAPTER VI

THE CHRISTIAN MESSAGE AS THE REVELATION
OF THE GOOD

1. The Christian message is first and foremost the message of
the Bible, the message of the Old and of the New Testaments.
The "Church," as the community of those who have heard
and understood this message, proclaims it in this sense. It is the
message by which the members of the Church "have been
taken captive," for which they are bound to witness, and to
try to win others, since in it they have found the truth for
their own lives, the Word of God, through which He lays
His claim upon the world, in order to "save" it. Hence it is
the message which, although it proceeds from the Church, is
addressed to the world, to the world which does not believe,
in order that it may believe.

It is the message of the Old Testament: the Word concerning the Creation, which is "very good," because it is the
work of the good God. But Evil has crept into this good
creation because, and in so far as, man has faithlessly forgotten
and denied the existence of his Creator and Lord. Here there
is no "intrinsic" Good. What God does and wills is good; all
that opposes the will of God is bad. The Good has its basis
and its existence solely in the will of God. An idea like that
in the religion of Zarathustra: that God became Lord because
He chose the Good, the idea of a law which is even higher
than God Himself(1) is unthinkable in the Old Testament.
God is not merely the guardian of the Moral Law and of the
moral ordinances, but their Creator(2).

The Good is based on the Holy. "Ye shall therefore be
holy, for I am holy."[1] The Holy means God, as the unconditionally sovereign Lord of the world; a thing is holy because,
and in so far as, it is His property and is recognized as such.
The holiness of man consists in knowing that he belongs to
God. In so far as he acknowledges in his life, and in his
existence, this property-right of God, and thus obeys the

[1] Lev. xi. 45; xix. 2.

53

will of God, he is good. No one has a claim on a man, or on a people, save God alone, and this claim permeates all the relationships of life. It is the only valid norm. Hence the "religious" element is also the "ethical" element, and the "ethical" is "religious."

Man's relation to God is based on God's "covenant" with man; it is therefore a bond of loyalty. God does not make His sovereign rights over man felt as a blind natural force. He makes His claim felt on the basis of the fact that He has first of all graciously addressed him. Man's goodness can be no other than a response to the prevenient kindness of God. His obedience is not blind and forced, but free; it is based upon the grateful knowledge of what God is to us, what He wills for us, and what He does for us. It is only on this basis that God makes His claim. The phrase which expresses the ethical content of the New Testament is true also of the Old Testament: "We love, because He first loved us."[1] Man owes his God nothing but love, based on holy fear, and his relation to God and his intimacy with Him may and can be realized in no other way.

The same truth applies to the sphere of human relationships. The thought of the Old Testament, which is so entirely theonomous and theocentric, is also entirely human and social. God wills to reign, He wills to be King in His "Kingdom." *His* will alone is to be realized; but God *wills* community. God the Creator loves His human children. Therefore loving Him means to love mankind; to be united to Him means to be united to man. His will is wholly a social will, a will for a people, for a community; therefore God recognizes no service of God which is not at the same time a service of man. Unlike the God of the mystics or of the pagan thinkers God does not desire a service addressed to Himself alone; He does not wish to draw men out of the world to Himself. Religion is no more autonomous than morality is autonomous. Here, above all, that element which is so characteristic of other forms of religion is lacking, namely, the sphere of the "sacred," the "Saint," the religious man, who stands out in his sacred dignity, the hermit, who leads a private "life of communion with God." It is of course true that this idea of a "sacred sphere" does occur in the Old Testament now and again—but only as that which is being contested or overcome(3). He who wills to serve God must

[1] I John iv. 19.

exercise love and mercy, must know himself one with the need of his people. This is the service which is well-pleasing to God, and this is the Good.[1]

2. In this respect also the New Testament is only the fulfilment of the Old. The covenant with God in the Old Testament was a promise; in the "New Covenant," whose symbols are bread and wine in remembrance of its Founder,[2] it has become a reality. Only now does the meaning of the Old Testament become fully clear. The Good is that which God does; the goodness of man can be no other than letting himself be placed within the activity of God. This is what "believing" means in the New Testament. And this *faith* is the principle of "ethics." "Whatsoever is not of faith is sin";[3] for it does not proceed from a heart which is united to God. Hence it may appear outwardly good, it may agree with an external law—but inwardly it is useless. "For the Lord looketh on the heart."[4] To let God have His way within me means to base my life, in its depths, on Jesus Christ; it means believing in the gracious Divine Word uttered in Jesus Christ; it means to be "crucified" and "raised" with Him(4).

Here alone does it become completely clear that while God draws man to Himself He does not draw him out of the world. For God Himself comes *to man*. Here, in man, He wills to meet him. The riddle of the twenty-fifth chapter of Matthew is solved only by the Incarnation: because God Himself, as man, came to man, it is possible to recognize in each man the God who comes to us. The Incarnation of God is the fact in which theocracy and humanity are inseparably united. Henceforth there is no love of God which can ignore man, and no love of man which can ignore God. But the Incarnation of the Son of God also means the Cross of Christ. Here alone is the meaning of the word "love" disclosed; for here alone is it possible to distinguish between *Eros* and *Agape, Amor* and *Caritas*. For one who has not died to himself "in Christ," and through that Divine surrender is not consecrated to self-surrender and "sealed," *Eros* and *Agape* always merge into one another, love is still limited. Love which has no limits and makes no conditions is love "in Christ."

This love is the "new commandment" which yet, as John

---

[1] On this point see my article: *Die Bedeutung des Alten Testamentes für unseren Glauben—Zwischen den Zeiten,* 1930, pp. 30–48.
[2] I Cor. xi. 25.   [3] Rom. xiv. 23.   [4] I Sam. xvi. 7.

mysteriously suggests, is also the "old commandment."[1] It is, of course, true that, in some way or another men knew that love was the real Good. But before Christ love was one commandment among others, and unconditioned love was not understood. It could not be understood until God Himself had defined its meaning *realiter*: in the Cross of Christ(5).

The Good is simply and solely the will of God. But the will of God is the will of God for the Kingdom. Only in the New Testament conception of the Kingdom of God does the theocratic idea of the Old Testament receive its full meaning; nothing is good save union with the sovereignty of God through this will; but this sovereignty of God also means complete fellowship with man, the communion of God with men—"the household of God" as it is called in the Epistle to the Ephesians[2]—and the fellowship of men with each other. God the Father, men His children, bound to Him by His own love, who through this love of *His* are also united to each other. It is this absolute will of God for community which was revealed in the Cross of Christ as the final and real meaning of all life. And this revelation, as the way in which and the place at which God meets man, makes it possible for man to love "in return." Here there is far more than the revelation of a new idea of the Good. This "idea" is also a fact; this "word" possesses meaning only as the "word made flesh." If love is severed from this *fact*, immediately the meaning of the word "love" becomes quite different. The meaning of this Ethos is inseparably connected, in faith, with this *fact*.

3. Therefore the "dogma" of the Church—the doctrine of the Person and Work of Christ—rightly understood simply means the effort to secure the Ethos of the New Testament against a pagan or rationalistic misinterpretation. The doctrine of the divine Humanity of Christ—or, to put it briefly, the Incarnation[3]—is, rightly understood, simply the securing of the knowledge that God's will is wholly a will for humanity, that theocracy absolutely implies humanity; but this does not mean a mere "idea" of humanity—for there was no need to re-discover the idea of humanity after Socrates; this

---

[1] 1 John ii. 7, 8.

[2] "Now therefore ye are no more strangers and foreigners, but fellow-citizens with the saints, and of the household of God" (Eph. ii. 19).

[3] The connexion between the new Ethos and the Incarnation was first expressed by Paul, in Phil. ii. 4; the exhortation to "look not every man on his own things, but . . . also on the things of others," is based on the coming of the Son of God to man.

revelation of God's will for humanity is more than this: it is a gift, and therefore a reality. For the Divine Humanity is indeed God's gift to humanity. In this fact lies the possibility of our becoming human; this Christ is the real ground of a life in love. To understand Him means to understand that we belong to our brethren.

The second main dogma, likewise, that of "satisfaction," is, rightly understood, simply the basis of the right Christian Ethos. Only he who sees at the Cross of Christ, *quanti ponderis sit peccatum*—and this can only be done by one who sees what the Atonement has "cost"—knows evil in its vast extent. Only he who there sees his own guilt condemned, takes it really upon himself; and he alone knows that in his *guilt* he is united with the whole of humanity. He alone ceases to judge others; he alone becomes even in guilt a brother. Here alone the worst enemy of true community, the Pharisaism of "wishing to be better," is rooted out. And at the same time the despair engendered by the sense of guilt, which always means impotence to achieve the Good, is removed. For the word of the Cross is the word of reconciliation and forgiveness, and as such is the foundation for, and the source of, a new active existence.

This was the real meaning of the dogma. But it was defaced and obscured by the hierarchical-sacramentarian and the hierarchical-juridical Church. The Reformation was needed in order to re-discover the meaning of the dogma—and its *ethical* meaning in particular. It betrays a terrible lack of vision to maintain that Luther treated the ethical problem far too superficially. Since the days of the Apostles no one has taken the ethical problem so seriously as Martin Luther. This alone made him a Reformer. The Reformation as a whole is simply one long protest against moral levity, one long struggle for the reality of the Good. That was the whole point of the struggle for the *sola fide* in the fight against a "righteousness of works." For moralism, with its legalism and self-righteousness, is at all times the worst enemy of true morality. It was for this reason that the two ethical questions which are usually relegated to the background were placed in the foreground of our enquiry, namely, the question of the basis of the Good, and the question of the possibility of achieving the Good, that is, the question of the agent. The first question led us out of a eudaemonistic and anthropocentric definition of the Good—away from the Aristotelian and Thomist conception (that the

Good is that which is adapted to human nature)—back to the truth of the Bible, namely, that only that which God wills is good; and thus that we are to will what God wills, because He wills it. The second question led us back to faith as the source of all Good in union with God. Both, however, mean the same thing; nothing is good, nothing in the whole world, save union with God. From this new interpretation of the Biblical Ethos there arose a third: the new relation to the world. God does not will the "cloister," but His rule in the world. Thus He wills that man should serve Him not apart from the world and the community of mankind, but in the world and in community. The obvious sinfulness of the world is no reason for turning one's back on it, but a reason for "hallowing" it.

Therefore this "secularity" of the Reformed Faith differs entirely from that of the Enlightenment and of Free Thought. Here, indeed, there is no idea of the emancipation of man, but of his union with God; there is here no question of "freedom of conscience" for every individual, in the sense of the autonomy of reason, but, on the contrary, of the union of the individual to the Word of God, to Christ as "King." Erasmus had to learn from Luther, and the opponents of Predestination from Calvin, how deep is the gulf which separates the view of the Reformers from that of "modern" thinkers. The *sola gratia* and Predestination(6) mean the same thing, namely, that the true Good lies only in the power of God and not in that of man; that no other human goodness and good conduct exists save that which is based on the free gift of God.

4. Thus we see that in the Christian message "the Good" is explained in such a way that the difficulties which surround this question in the natural ethos are finally overcome. In the first place, the Good is based solely on God's transcendent revelation, on His covenant and His word; thus its basis is wholly "religious." For this very reason, however, it is truly "human" and "ethical," for its meaning is love, union with other men. This theonomy dispenses with the irrational and "magical" element; and this clear humanity has the depth of the Holy. The service of God can only be realized as the service of man; and the true service of man is only possible as the service of God. Secondly: here the antithesis between freedom and necessity(7) is removed. The Gospel is wholly a doctrine of freedom. It is concerned with the release of man from bondage. But this freedom is at the same time

complete captivity, indeed more than that: it is absolute dependence on God's action. "If the Son shall make you free you shall be free indeed."[1] The ancient error, which consists in thinking (in view of the formal freedom of man) that freedom consists in emancipation from all ties, in an empty sterility, in the *liberum arbitrium indifferentiae*, is here revealed in its true colours. Man—who is a creature, not a Creator—finds his true freedom only in complete union with his Creator.[2] Thirdly: the opposition between the moral content and Formalism has been overcome. To the Good, understood in the Christian sense, the Kantian formula can be applied perfectly well: "Nothing can possibly be conceived in the world, or even out of it, which can be called good without qualification, except a Good Will."[3] Nothing is good save obedience to the command of God, just because it is obedience. No reasons of determination from content here come under consideration. The "form" of the will, obedience, is all. But to be obedient to the will of God means: "love your neighbour!" Hence the content of the commandment is not an abstract law, not a programme that can be known beforehand and codified, but it means a swift responsiveness to the needs of others, and action in accordance with their needs in their particular circumstances. Love is determined by "content" to such an extent that it is wholly impossible to conceive of love in terms of rules and regulations.

Fourthly: the opposition between the individual and the universal is also overcome. This Ethos is universal through the unconditional character of the commandment of love, which applies absolutely to all, in all circumstances, and in every kind of situation; it is universal also through the world-wide breadth of the divine will, which wills nothing less than this: His Kingdom. To serve this purpose means to love. And at the same time it is quite individual, at least in so far as it is the individual who obeys, because in solitude and silence and secrecy, in the depths of his being, he hears the Call of God (8); it is also individual because love does not work according to schedule, but simply according to his

---

[1] John viii. 36, 2 Cor. iii. 17 means the same: "Where the Spirit of the Lord is, there is liberty."

[2] "Being then made free from sin, ye became the servants of righteousness . . . for when ye were the servants of sin, ye were free from righteousness" (Rom. vi. 18, 22).

[3] First sentence of the *Grundlegung zur Metaphysik der Sitten*.

neighbour's need, in any given set of circumstances. Finally, the conflict between Eudaemonism and Rigorism is overcome. The Christian Ethos is wholly "eudaemonistic" in the sense that sharing in the will of God means "salvation," "rescue," "blessing," "blessedness," and even eternal blessedness, and love to one's neighbour means that in doing good both to body and soul it helps to make him happy. It is this which constitutes the humanity of love, which differs entirely from rigorism, from the rigidity and coldness of mere devotion to duty. When love impels us to act in a certain way, we are not moved by a sense of duty, but—to use Schiller's ironical phrase—"unfortunately by inclination." At the same time, it is this spirit which is the greatest contrast to everything which comes under the heading of Eudaemonism, in so far as the Good is only achieved when it is done solely in the spirit of love to God and in obedience to His command. This "inclination," this "impulse" is the impulse of a divine constraint, the imperative of faith; it means being guided by the "new law of the Spirit." Therefore in love to God, based upon faith, the antithesis between happiness and duty is removed, because the God who claims me for Himself is the One who gives life to me and to the whole world.

CHAPTER VII

THE CHRISTIAN INTERPRETATION OF THE CONTRADICTION AS SIN

1. The Christian knows that his knowledge of God is based simply and solely upon the divine self-revelation, upon the Divine Word which is a Fact,[1] Jesus Christ. This knowledge of God also contains and forms the basis of man's understanding of his own nature, and of the Good. But this knowledge of God, and this view of the Good, does not merely constitute a positive answer to man's question; it is also a polemical, radically critical denial of man's natural view of his own nature. The message of Christ is a declaration of war on his present, supposed "knowledge"; indeed, its very existence depends on the fact that it triumphs over the previous view. Faith always also exists as conflict with the earlier view, and indeed it only becomes real faith when it clearly perceives its previous error. The "old man," whom faith overcomes, is—ultimately—always a view of God and of the Self; the "new man" can only be established when the error of the previous view of the Self has been clearly perceived. In the New Testament this conflict is described quite clearly as a fight between life and death. The "old man," and with him the old view of God and of the Self, must be "put to death"; he must literally "die" in order that the "new man" may come into existence. Faith, therefore, like the Christian message itself, exists in a polemically critical atmosphere; the believer lives in the midst of this conflict, in so far as he is a real believer, to the end of his life on earth. This conflict, still more than the fight "without," is the sign-manual of the *militia Christi*.

This conflict must also have its counterpart in theological reflection, in theological "eristics"(1),[2] in explicit "discussion" between the Christian and non-Christian knowledge of God and of the Good. In looking at the latter the task which is here laid upon us can be summed up in these two questions: from the point of view of faith how are we to understand natural morality? And, how is this to be over-

---

[1] Literally "Deed-Word" (*Tat-Wort*).—Tr.
[2] The author uses this term to describe a *combination* of apologetics and polemics.—Tr.

come by faith? The former question will be answered in the present chapter, the latter in the next chapter.

The "natural" existence of man—that is, his existence outside the realm of faith—must be understood (like his natural understanding of God and of himself) from the two points of view of *creation* and of *sin*. The discussion with natural morality therefore forms part of Christian anthropology, namely, that part in which the natural view of the Good as part of the natural being of man in general is understood from the point of view of faith. In faith man knows that he has been created by God "in His image," designed for self-determination according to the will of God, to a free self-giving to the generous goodness of God.[1] The distinctive character of man, in contrast to the rest of creation, is based upon the fact that he is designed for freedom-in-God, for a personal existence which is distinct from God, and yet dependent upon Him. But man is also (this is his view of himself in the light of faith) one who has fallen away from God, one who is separated from God, a sinner, whose divinely created nature and connexion with God has been perverted by this sin. Sin has caused a cleavage in human life which runs right through all that is human. Out of this cleavage there arise also those contradictions of natural morality which we have just mentioned. From this standpoint and from this alone can they be understood and overcome.

2. This fundamental cleavage is reflected first of all in the conflict between the independence of reason which is opposed to God, and the relation with God, or religion, which is hostile to reason; in a falsely autonomous and a falsely theonomous heteronomous morality. The false heteronomy and the false autonomy mutually determine each other. Because man does not know that his life depends on God's gracious giving, but makes himself independent over against God, instead of over against the world, because he emancipates himself from God, therefore to him God is only an alien Power, which forces him from the outside, as it presses upon him from the outside. Because he does not know God, the world becomes his "God," and the picture of God itself resembles that of the world. Or, to put it the other way round: because man is separated from God, and has erected an idol in His place, he cannot avoid seeking release from this half-daemonic power in a rational, autonomous culture and

[1] Cf. on this point, in Book II, Chapter XV, p. 161.

morality. Over against the morality which is determined by a false "sacredness," as we see it in all religions in the blending of the ethical and the accidental and irrational elements in the conception of the "holy," the autonomous morality of reason represents the justifiable concern of humanity; over against the emancipated autonomous morality of reason every form of religion, even the most superstitious, represents the right of the holy and divine basis and sanction of the moral.

That kind of religion which stands *alongside* of the secular sphere as something holy, fenced off from the common life, which sets apart a "sacred" sphere of life, and is obliged to express the service of God in a special form of cultus, belongs to the realm of idolatry, which constitutes a perversion of the truth of God.

It is true, of course, that this distorted relation to God is not influenced merely by the fear of the *Numen*; it has some sense of real reverence; but the mingling of divine elements with those which are not divine prevents the development of pure reverence. Hence although even this distorted form of religion is actually the source of the knowledge of a sacred bond, this sacred bond is itself also unholy, accidental in character, and cannot be recognized in a spirit of inward freedom. It becomes a heteronomy, a slavish and legal bond, slavery. The distortion of the image of God is shown in this, that the deity itself possesses the characteristics of the Unholy as well as of the Holy(2), and for that very reason it is not possible to base morality wholly upon the will of God. Thus in all religions morality comes to be regarded as something higher than the gods; accordingly, it is conceived in terms of an impersonal universal Law.[1]

Thus, once this stage had been reached, the time was ripe for the rise of an independent morality and culture, severed from religion altogether. The greater the distance between this kind of morality and the sphere of the Divine and the Holy, the nearer it came to the purely secular sphere; this meant the final transference of all interest to the cultural and vitalistic aspects of civilization. The more emancipated this "culture" became, the less emphasis did it lay on reverence; and with the gradual loss of reverence existence became increasingly secular and naturalistic.[2] Yet, on the

[1] The classic example of this is the Greek idea of *Themis, Dike and Moira*. Cf. R. HIRZEL: *Themis, Dike und Verwandtes*, 1907.

[2] Cf. my work entitled: *Das Grundproblem der Ethik*, Zürich, 1930.

other hand, this "emancipation" from religion was itself due to a dim, semi-articulate sense of the actual presence of a purer Good than that which was represented by the will of the gods and the existence of the gods; it was, above all, a feeling after freedom, a desire for the independent, willed affirmation of the Good, free from all fear of the gods. The dualism, or even the variety, of all autonomous morality is based upon this fact.

3. Now that we have reached this point, as we look back, for the first time that series of stages[1] from which we started becomes intelligible. We might just as well regard these stages as degrees of degeneration as stages in an ascending process of development. In reality both schemata are ruled out, since they are falsely projected into the time-process, whereas here we are everywhere dealing with simultaneity. The more profound the forgetfulness of God, the more deeply does human existence sink down to the level of animal immediacy or natural life. On the other hand, the highest stage, even when only within the sphere of separation from God, means a very close approach to the truth of God. It is characterized by the command "Thou Shalt," by the view of the Good as Law. This does not mean that in this legal view of the Good man is somewhat nearer to the truth, but that he is nearer to the place where the breach occurred, that is, that here man is both very near to truth, and yet very remote from it. Moralistic legalism—Pharisaism of every kind, constitutes on the one hand the place of greatest nearness of God; and on the other the place of greatest distance from God.[2]

It is true, of course, that here man knows that he is faced with something deeply serious, but he has not seen that true seriousness consists in knowing that God alone is good, and that to "take God seriously" means to give oneself wholly and entirely to *His* action, and thus to believe. Therefore the question of the meaning of the Law is the storm-centre in the struggle of the Gospel against the error of the "natural" man. Therefore also the innermost point of this conflict is the conflict against "righteousness of works" or legalism, and the triumph of the Gospel means justification by faith alone.

Thus when we look back at these "stages" we see that they do not denote merely stages of forgetfulness of God, but at

[1] See above, pp. 19 ff.
[2] On this point see KIERKEGAARD's *Furcht und Zittern*.

the same time stages of a gradual loss of meaning and interest in life. From this standpoint the statement of Kierkegaard becomes intelligible, namely, that the pagan is too spiritless to be able in the strict sense of the word, to sin.[1] On the other hand, the series of ascending stages means that the nearer we come to the truth the more acute does our consciousness of evil become. Only the man who knows the law can really *sin*—in the actual explicit sense of the word. Law and sinfulness belong together. It is peculiarly important that the idea of universal sinfulness should not destroy this series of stages from the "better" to the "worse." In another connexion we shall have to lay special stress upon its powerful moral significance. But, on the other hand, this series of stages must not be understood in the sense of a *gradus ad Parnassum*, as a direct way to perfection—as is the custom in the autonomous morality—but only in the dialectical sense, so that each step towards the higher life means at the same time a step deeper into sin. The most sinful stage of all, Pharisaism, stands upon the topmost rung of the ladder.

4. But the fact that the knowledge of God has become obscured also leads to the fatal dilemma—either the formalism of the legalistic ethic on the one hand, or eudaemonistic materialism on the other. In connexion with the Idea of the Good—once the view which holds that the Good is the life given by God has vanished—all that remains is the bare choice between two alternatives: either the abstract law, which demands obedience and disregards life itself, or life which is regarded as good in itself, without any reference to the Divine Will. The formalism of the legalistic ethic has retained from the original knowledge of God the fragmentary idea that one thing alone is good, namely, obedience to the law (of God) as the expression of His will which is always the same, purely for the sake of its "form," that is, simply because it is so commanded (by God). Since, however, the demand has become autonomous, that is, since it has broken away from the thought of God as the Lord and Giver of life, this law has no relation to life; the gulf between that which is and that which ought to be becomes so wide that it cannot be bridged. Secondly, since this law is not the living will of God, it becomes an abstraction, hovering above life in its concreteness as a schematic timeless entity. Therefore it becomes a force which destroys life; it becomes a rigid legalism, so

[1] *Die Krankheit zum Tode.*

65

distorted in its view of righteousness that it can say: *fiat justitia, pereat mundus*—that kind of legalism for which, in spite of its harshness, we have more respect than for the opportunism which has no principles.

On the other hand, the will that desires *life* fights, very naturally, against this deadening legalism. The proposition that the law is for the sake of man, and not man for the sake of the law, leads to the eudaemonistic ethic of culture, utility, and welfare, finally degenerating into hedonism and vitalism, which justifies life as such in its immediacy and instinctiveness. When this takes place man has ceased to respond to any moral claims, and the bare level of human existence has been reached, which, if it could be realized, would erase utterly every trace of humanity. For man is only man in virtue of the claim made on him by God. Life on the bare level of instinctive existence coupled with the entire loss of all sense of responsibility means the end of humanity.

5. Finally, from this point of view we can understand the difficulties of the natural ethic in its definition of evil. When the knowledge that evil is sin has been lost, that is, when man no longer knows that evil means the severance of freedom from union with God, then the conception of evil is confronted with a choice between two irreconcilable alternatives: evil is either the resistance of self-will to the law—and then the principle of autonomy is in danger; for how can the self be both the law-giver and the will which rebels against the law? Or, the autonomy is maintained by the idea of the "intelligible self"—and then evil becomes simply a surface matter, something which hinders the spiritual self by the mere fact of sensuousness; thus, once evil has ceased to be a serious matter, the command "Thou Shalt" has also ceased to be serious. The ethic of the legalistic "ought" reveals its nearness to the "breach" by the fact that in it the riddle of evil is seen in all its gruesome character; and it reveals its distance from it in the fact that finally, in order not to be obliged to renounce the principle of autonomy, it is obliged once again to give up this knowledge. The Platonic ethic, on the other hand, weakens the law in an aesthetic manner by its emphasis on καλοκαγαθία, and at the same time "explains" evil as the result of the metaphysical dualism of human nature, and thus transforms its meaning into that of a tragic phenomenon.

But Naturalism also in its protest against the forcible

66

subjection of life and individuality to the abstract law, has preserved an element of truth. At the same time it has profoundly distorted this truth by eliminating the idea of guilt. Wherever what is and what ought to be are fused into one on the natural level, the idea of guilt naturally disappears.

Thus the picture presented by natural ethics is that of a heap of ruins. The original truth of God has been split up into a thousand fragments, and each of these fragments, by its isolation from the whole, is itself "twisted," distorted into a caricature of the original. Therefore, all who see this situation clearly will realize that it is hopeless to attempt to construct a synthetic ethic, however obvious it may seem. Even the Christian knowledge of God, for instance, does not constitute a synthesis of this kind; for it lacks the main element in a synthesis: the capacity to be applied as a principle. The Christian Faith is what it is, as the answer to the divine Word, as faith in the fact of revelation; it means a real inclusion within the reality of the divine act of redemption. Hence it sets up no principle which could be adapted to a timeless reconstruction of the truth; rather, if it is not to pervert itself, it can never be present in a theoretical manner but only in the act of decision and of being apprehended by God. The restoration of the original whole is not an Idea, but the Divine action, recognized in faith: therefore even the Christian ethic is not based upon a principle, but upon this process of Divine restoration whose meaning is disclosed in "justification by grace alone."

CHAPTER VIII

JUSTIFICATION BY GRACE ALONE AS THE REMOVAL OF THE CONTRADICTION AND THE FOUNDATION OF THE GOOD[1]

1. All natural morality and ethics—whether based on religious or rational grounds—is either eudaemonistic or legalistic. This double possibility is already latent in the twofold meaning of the Idea of the Good itself. We speak of "well-being" and "of being good." In the one instance the dominant idea is that of happiness, the *summum bonum*, in the other it is that of duty and the good will which is determined by duty. In the first instance "to live the right life" means to live in such a way that ultimately things will go well, or that one receives good things, or has a share in the *summum bonum*; the Good is the goal, the moral will is the way to this goal, which for that very reason lies beyond itself. In the second instance the Good is inseparable from the will—as Kant puts it: there is, in fact, nothing which can be called good save "a good will." But this will is severed from life and from "well-being" and therefore remains empty of content. The ethic of eudaemonism remains close to life, but it simply becomes worldly prudence. The ethic of duty, on the other hand, is able to draw a clear distinction between the moral will as obedience and the desires of mere worldly prudence, but the will becomes encased in the lifeless rigidity of legalism.

And yet, although these two ethical tendencies are poles apart from each other, at the decisive point—in spite of everything—they are one. In both instances *man* is the sole point of reference, whether he is concerned with "well-being" or with "being good." Every form of natural ethics is anthropocentric—man desires the *summum bonum* because it is "good" for him. And because in action controlled by the principle of duty man realizes *himself*, his dignity, the dignity of his nature, he lives the good life. Everything revolves round his personal happiness and moral perfection, that is, round *himself*(1). Even where the *summum bonum* is regarded as

[1] Cf. with this chapter my essay: *Justification by Faith, and the Problem of Ethics* in *Gott und Mensch (God and Man)*, pp. 24 ff., and the closing chapter in my book *The Mediator*.

Divine favour and Divine life, and even where duty is regarded as the Divine command, it is man's *self-interest* which moves his will. Whether he be the Stoic who does the Good because only thus can he respect himself, because in so doing, and only so, does he realize his Divine dignity, or whether he be the Pharisee who fulfils the Law of God because in so doing he earns heaven—in either case the whole emphasis is placed upon what *he* does and is, and upon that which *he* desires, and regards as of *value* to himself(2).

Even the ethic which takes duty very seriously is an ethic of self-righteousness, and thus—ultimately—(that is, in spite of its previous opposition to eudaemonism)—it is dominated by a refined species of eudaemonism. The moralist who lives by duty also seeks himself, his moral satisfaction, his own moral dignity. This is the reward which he desires to gain as a compensation for his severity towards himself: that men will not deny him the reputation of being a just and upright man(3). But even the hedonist, even the utilitarian moralist, in so far as he formulates an ethic at all, is *legalistic*. His maxims of utility are universal, he, too, knows a way which man must follow, if he is to be happy. He, too, knows that he is justified by his actions and rendered secure by his general principle.

But the two tendencies converge also at another point. The hedonist and the rigid moralist both believe in the *realization of the good* by man. The goal (of "well-being" or "being good") may be far ahead in the dim distance, but no doubt exists that with every step along the prescribed path we are approaching a little nearer to the goal. *Ut desint virtes tamen est laudanda voluntas.* The good man forges his own happiness for himself, for he himself is the creator of his moral perfection, even when the happiness or the perfection is still imperfect, or will only become perfect on the other side, beyond this mortal existence(4).

Thus natural ethics is dominated by the principle of self-seeking and self-reference. Perhaps we may put it thus: natural *morality* can be distinguished from *rational ethics* by the fact that it is more naïve and therefore less self-conscious. To the same extent, however, it is also more casual and uncertain. A man may indeed achieve many a "selfless" action, almost unconsciously, so that his left hand does not know what his right hand is doing. Then suddenly he will act—just as naïvely and self-interestedly—without the left hand knowing what the right hand is doing. And when, as everyone does in some way or another, the sum-total of the whole life is reckoned up, it will become evident that—and indeed what else *can* he do?—he will still try to tip the balance in the positive direction. Even he—who is so "naïve"—feels in the last resort secure in himself. Natural ethics in every form means achieving self-security.

2. The meaning of these observations only becomes intelligible when we contrast them with that which the Christian message proclaims about the final balance of every human life. "*All* have *sinned.*"[1] The final result of every life is this: a terrifying adverse balance, a "debt" which cannot be paid. And this result, which is so different from that of all other estimates of life, is reached because here the standard is different. "...and they have fallen short of the glory of God."[2] Because the Divine Will is treated seriously, man has no longer anything positive left to offer, with which he might enter God's presence. In the presence of the Holy God all he has falls away from him: "If Thou, Lord, shouldest mark iniquities, O Lord, who shall stand?" (Ps. cxxx. 3). The basis of this judgment, however, is no other than that which is the result of the examination of natural morality and ethics, namely, that in it man seeks himself, that he expects the Good as the result of his own efforts, that he is sure that his life is secure and justified. This is the root of that which the Bible calls "sin."

The difference between the natural and the Scriptural estimate of man comes out most clearly not in view of human *action* but in view of human *existence*, that is, in view of the inward disposition. The natural ethic says: though I may sometimes fail in my external behaviour, my inmost will is good. The Gospel says: though outwardly you may even do some good, yet your inmost heart is sinful(5). It is not merely that man sins, he is not even merely "sinful," but he is a *sinner*. It is not merely the acts which are sinful but the person, the doer. It is characteristic of natural morality and ethics that it seeks exclusively to answer the question "What ought I to do?" It deals only with conduct, not with the *person* who acts. Hence the illusion arises that the individual is able to move step by step towards perfection. But this illusion vanishes when it is realized that the moral failure resides not so much in the sphere of conduct as in the sphere of personality; here the conviction dawns on the mind that

[1] Rom. iii. 23.　　　　　　　　　　　　　　[2] Rom. iii. 23.

whatever one does is tainted by evil, because evil is entrenched in the very heart of the personality. No moral effort can extricate one from this situation(6).

Further, it is this very moral effort itself, or rather the assumption which is bound up with it, that the Good can be attained along this path, which is evil(7). For this is the evidence of self-confidence, self-security, self-reference, belief in the power to redress the situation for and by oneself. Therefore evil does not come out most clearly, in its most obvious form, where natural morality looks for it, namely, in vice, in moral reprobation which everyone can recognize as such, but it appears in the *self-righteousness* of the legalist, whether the latter be a Pharisee, who regards himself as justified in the sight of God, or a Stoic, who suns himself in his own Divine goodness, or the mystical saint, who thinks that he has traversed all the stages of sanctification to the end(8). These all walk in the way of the just, thinking that this path will lead them to the goal. They are all living under the illusion that the Good is that which they are able to realize. None of them know that *God* alone is good.

This self-confident march along a self-chosen path of righteousness is what Paul describes as the "righteousness of works" or the "righteousness of the Law." It is impossible from the "ethical" point of view to discover that it is this which constitutes sin. Indeed, we may go further and say that in the last resort it is precisely morality which *is* evil; as I have already said:[1] legalism is always the worst kind of corruption; or, in other words, *the worst state of man is that in which he has complete confidence in himself.* For this state of mind constitutes the source of all falsity, for it is the denial of the fact that the Good is always the Gift of God, the denial of the fact that man possesses his true self not in himself, but in God, that he cannot live on his own resources, but only on those which God inspires. This fact of evil, therefore, can only be perceived where this "Good" is known, that is, in faith. From the ethical point of view therefore it is impossible to understand the Scriptural judgment on self-righteousness, the severity of the fight against Pharisaism. In this fact the blindness of the moral consciousness, the evil which resides in "being good" on ethical lines, becomes evident.

3. Therefore the chief emphasis of the Scriptural ethic must lie not in victory over lawlessness, but in the fight

[1] See above, p. 57.

against legalism(9). This is why the Law has such a remarkable twofold position in the New Testament. The charge brought by Paul against righteousness by works is not—as an interpretation of Paul's teaching which is manifestly blind to the real state of affairs asserts—a by-product of his thought, applicable only to his own day and circumstances; no, it is concerned with the centre, indeed with the sole content of the message of the Bible, namely this: that God alone is good, that that alone is good which God does. Or, to put it the other way round: that man lives and moves and has his being in God alone, that his life is anchored in God and not in himself, that only by the action of God is he "justified." It is either this—or legalism.

The Law, therefore, in so far as it is understood from the ethical point of view, is "the sting of death"[1] and this means, not merely what sin reveals but also what it "awakens."[2] From the ethical point of view it is the energy, the principle of sin. For this it is which corresponds to the false autonomy of man. Wherever man thinks in a legalistic manner, he *must* see the Good in himself and expect it from himself; God commands, certainly, but it is the part of man to obey. God and man confront each other on the same footing.

The life between God and man is a life with shared parts; man is the equal partner of God, who can treat with Him on a footing of equality. The original source of all sin is the false independence of man over against God, the arrogance of his so-called "equality," the falsity, the ingratitude and the pride of one who has forgotten that his life and all good depends absolutely on God, and can indeed only thus depend. Only now do we fully understand that which has already been said, namely: that the legalistic view of the Good, in its very seriousness, constitutes the point at which man is furthest away from God(10). Whatever else we call "evil" is simply the "manifestation" of this central fact of evil: the evil of alienation from God here appears in an external form. The results of this inmost corruption, of legalism, may be summed up under the conception of the "curse of the Law."

4. The first direct result of his primal sin, of the emancipation from God in legalism, is the alteration of the attitude towards God in man's actual position. The man who has thus severed his connexion with God is henceforth not

---

[1] 1 Cor. xv. 56.   [2] Rom. vii. 8.

merely remote from God, he is *separated* from Him. This is now his relation to God: he is guilty, and therefore in a state of condemnation. It is, of course, true that man is able to some extent to deceive himself about this state of affairs. He feels so sure of himself in his self-righteousness, but this sense of security is only possible by weakening the Law. The Law is toned down(11) mainly by being broken up into so many various "laws," it is adapted in such a way that man can fulfil it. It becomes a matter of commonplace or conventional morality and now decent people can face the Law with equanimity. Others try to find a still easier path by setting aside altogether the opposition between what is and what ought to be. But all these attempts are only partially successful. There is a court of judgment within man which does not consent to this self-deception, just because it is aloof from human self-activity, because it is not involved (entangled in) its active sin:[1] the evil conscience, this so entirely alien power in man, over which all his ideology has no power.

The curse of the Law further manifests itself in the tragedy of the Wandering Jew, which is the tragedy of every human being: in the restlessness of his existence. God challenges him in his "independence": "Now then, if you think you can do the good by your own efforts, well, do it!" And so man starts out on the path towards the goal; but behold! the goal seems infinitely distant. All those attempts to silence the voice of conscience by which man tries to excuse himself for being so far from the goal, are not capable of calming the soul. Resignation itself weighs on the soul like a ton, and dissatisfaction drives it to ever new attempts, whips it up to new efforts, drives man forward feverishly into new tasks, and finally causes the heart to petrify in that rigidity which is so characteristic of all legal existence, and at the same time makes man outwardly so hard.

The legalistic type of person finds it impossible to come into real human, personal contact with his fellow-man. Between him and his neighbour there stands something impersonal, the "idea," the "Law," a programme, something abstract which hinders him from seeing the other person as he really is, which prevents him from hearing the real claim which his neighbour makes on him. To the legalistic person, the person who acts according to principle only, the other man is only a "case," just as for the judge

[1] See below, pp. 155.

73

(in a court of law) the accused is simply a particular "criminal case." He deals with him according to some abstract ruling, not according to himself, not according to his unique being which can never be repeated, not as a person to be met "here and now." Even in his service to others the legalistic man remains shut up within himself; enclosed within his own ideas, he does not go out to meet other people half-way(12).

The other man only occupies a certain "place" in his system; hence, even where he is dealing with others, in the last resort, he is only dealing with himself. Correspondingly also the motive of his action, in spite of all its apparent selflessness, is self-regarding, namely, self-respect. "I owe it to myself, I could not forgive myself if I were to act otherwise." And if such a person acts wrongly from the ethical point of view, he is not so much conscious of having injured his neighbour— that he himself remains in his neighbour's debt—as of having sinned against himself. This is the curse of "Law" under which above all the other stands.

5. But even now we have not reached the ultimate thing which has to be said about the "curse of the Law." *Legalism is un-freedom*, and this, not merely in the sense in which everyone is conscious of this in the representatives of a typically legalistic rightèousness—as inflexibility, feverish intensity, devotion to abstract principles, but in a far deeper sense. The Good that one does simply from a sense of duty is never *the* Good. Duty and genuine goodness are mutually exclusive. Obedience due to a sense of unwilling constraint is bondage, and indeed the bondage of sin. If I feel I *ought* to do right, it is a sign that I cannot do it. If I could really do it, there would be no question of "ought" about it at all. The sense of "ought" shows me the Good àt an infinite, impassable distance from my will. Willing obedience is never the fruit of a sense of "ought" but only of love. This is the paradox: that the sense of "ought," through which alone I learn at all what freedom is in this sense of "ought," unveils to me my formal freedom—announces to me that I am in bondage to sin(13). To feel one "ought" and one's capacity to do what one "ought," is just as much *materialiter* the same thing as the sense of "ought" and freedom are *formaliter* the same thing. The Law makes known to me that my original union with God—which should be the presupposition of the Good—has been destroyed. Hence antinomian Vitalism, the theory of self-expression, the romantic doctrine of immediacy

is true, at least in so far as it expresses the longing for the Origin, however false it may be as an ethic.

The basis of legalism therefore lies in the fact that man has fallen away from union with God. The law is due to sin, although it is true, on the other hand, that it is the Law of God(14). The law is the will of God, in the only form in which sinful man is able to perceive it. The fact that man has asserted his independence of God means that no other relation to God than a legal one is left open to him. On the other hand, legalism is truly evil because it is the denial of the primal truth, that the Good is that which God gives and nothing else at all(15). Autonomy, the self's sense of absolute independence, and legalism are, ultimately, the same thing. Hence the Good can only be restored by the removal of the "curse of law."

6. This takes place, first of all, in the fact that evil is seen in its true colours. It is part of human sin that it hinders man from seeing sin. If man could *see* evil as it is, he would not be *really* evil. It is true, of course, that every one knows something of evil, and the deeper and more serious a person is, the more he knows about it. But he always sees less than the whole truth. His perception is limited to the moral sphere— and is thus not serious. We only see the curse of the Law and legalism as actual sin at the point beyond the Law where the new possibility of life, where χωρὶς τοῦ νόμου God's righteousness becomes manifest. Sin is only seen for what it is, in its true colours, where God gives Himself *personally*, not in terms of thought or of law, when God *comes* near, because man cannot approach Him, for all his efforts, where life, the Good, righteousness, are granted as a Divine gift. It is the Cross of Jesus Christ alone which awakens us from the dream that we can achieve our own goodness by ourselves, since there it becomes evident to us what we "can" do by means of our own "righteousness." For the execution of the Son of God is the work of the highest form of religious and ethical righteousness, that of the Jews, and it was ordered expressly for "blasphemy." In this event man stands revealed. The Cross of Jesus Christ unveils the curse of legalism.

The Cross, however, unveils the curse of the Law in such a way that at the same time it removes it. It shows up the distortion of life(16), by the restoration of the true relationship with God, in the fact that God there reveals Himself as the One who gives life, and the Good, "apart from the works

75

of the Law," without human merit and human effort, "through grace alone." When the origin once more becomes visible, it is also possible to see the Fall. In the incomprehensible fact of God's coming to us—in the fact that this had to happen if God were to come near to us once more, by the "cost" (Luther) of the Divine Forgiveness, by the "expense" which is necessary to re-unite God and man, the depth of human guilt and error may be measured. At the Cross alone can we understand *quanti ponderis sit peccatum*. In this event God is present as the transcendent Giver.

God addresses the unrighteous as though they were righteous—not because they will be righteous one day, but because they are "right" in His sight, because He wills it so. The Law is "taken out of the way."[1] Without any complementary human effort man receives, purely as a gift, that justification which he seeks in vain to attain for himself. The meaning of the whole doctrine of justification by faith— indeed, the meaning of the whole message of the Bible—is this: that it is not man's efforts by way of the Law—and the human way is always the way of the Law—but that God by the way of grace gives the true relation to God and therefore the true existence. For in its actual specific message the Bible does not deal with the God who demands and the man who acts, like every other sacred book; but it speaks of the God who acts and man who receives the Divine gift(17).

7. This is the great inversion of existence. Previously, life, even at its best, is always a life directed *towards* God; now, henceforth life is lived *from* God as its centre. In this new possibility of life the old life is seen to be perverted, and it becomes manifest that the attempt to attain God by our own efforts rather than to base all our life on God, legalism, is the root of sin. Here, therefore, the contradiction of human existence becomes evident: that man is indeed, in actual fact, as a creature, absolutely dependent on God as his origin, while in his morality and his religion his desire is to reach God by his own efforts. All the contradictions of natural morality and ethics which have already been mentioned arise out of this contradiction; and the message of reconciliation is the Divinely saving contradiction which is directed against the former contradiction, and removes it.

This Divine "contradiction," however, is an event, not an idea, just as surely as sin is a reality and not merely an idea.

[1] Col. ii. 14.

Here everything depends upon the fact that we are concerned with an actual event in time and space and not merely with an idea in the human mind. As a human idea forgiveness is no more valid than the remission of a debt merely signed by the debtor. Everything depends on the fact that the creditor signs the paper, and this is an act which must be achieved independently of the debtor. At the Cross the Divine forgiveness was not only pronounced (as it were verbally) but —as a real re-uniting of God with Him from whom He was separated—actually achieved. Without this actual basis both the word "guilt" and also the word "forgiveness" mean something quite different, and in fact, *not* the meaning with which we are here concerned: that henceforth life is a life lived by the grace of God. Reconciliation—the new life(18) means that God has really come to man.

8. But this new life is not bestowed in any merely magical way. Even in this real historical event God is present as Spirit; even the word made flesh is *word*, that is, something that must be heard, known, and recognized. Actually the atonement only takes place for us through *faith*. God thus takes hold of man by winning his heart—indeed, in no other way could He have gained a foothold in man. But the heart is the place where man understands himself(19). Faith consists in the fact that henceforth man knows that his life, his very self, is a gift from God, not a life which is straining after God. This complete reversal of the direction of man's life, the fact that this re-direction or con-version takes place, constitutes the New Birth, the Divine establishment of the "new man"(20). But the fact that this new birth takes place as conversion, as self-knowledge and redirection of the Self, is the Divine hall-mark of this event, which distinguishes it from a magical process. This is what faith means: to *know* that one is thus "born again," to accept life as a gift and righteousness as something outside oneself. The new life is life in the Divine indicative (mood), instead of in the imperative, in dependence upon God, not in search for God. Only now does it become true that the Good is that which God does, not that which man does.

9. So far as ethics are concerned, when we say this we really say two things: Firstly, that at last man is no longer "in-dependent" but that he is "dependent" on God alone; even his righteousness is something outside himself. "Christ is my Righteousness," my new self. No longer does man

77

believe that he can achieve the Good by his own efforts; his confidence is now wholly in God. No longer—as it was previously—is he himself the centre of the picture, but God. This means that, at last, he has become what he sought in vain to become along the legalistic path—in vain, because it is incompatible with legalism, namely, free from himself, free from self-seeking.[1] Before he does anything, he is already in God. In all that he does—without being obliged to search for God—he starts from the fact of his life in God. God is— as it were—always behind him, not in front of him as the legalist believes. This it is which constitutes the· joy and the peace of the new state of life. Secondly: he no longer has to do with a law, but with God Himself, with God *personally*, and this means, with the loving God.

He is now "free from the works of the law." The loving God is One who "apprehends" us, not One whom we "apprehend." His love is not conditional: "I will love you *if* you do so and so . . ."—no, it is unconditional, *gratia gratis data*. Only in this free giving is God seen as He is. The true God is One who *gives* life, not one who *demands* it.

This, however, also means that at last *freedom* has been realized. Freedom means release from the sense of "ought," from bondage to the Law. Freedom is the life founded on grace, on the gift of God. Freedom means being "rooted and grounded" in God(21). Above all, freedom means being free from the obligation to seek one's own good. Freedom is utter dependence upon God, and this means the absolute renunciation of all claim to independence, of all illusory independence over against God. To be free means to be that for which God created us. For us—who are not God— there *is* no freedom in ourselves, no freedom in a self-derived existence; for the creature the only possible freedom is a *deo esse*.

10. Freedom is redemption from "the curse of the law," thus not only from guilt but also from unrest, from dis-peace. He alone can have *peace* with God who no longer strains after God, but who lives in and on God. Peace springs out of a relation with God which is secured by God Himself, that is, the relation of Divine sonship through the gift of God; it is life in the word of God, which He speaks to us and in us, by which He contradicts the bad reality: "Peace and joy in

[1] This freedom from self-seeking has been emphasized especially powerfully in the Reformed doctrine in the idea of Election.

78

the Holy Ghost."[1] The Spirit of God, however, proclaims and gives to us the *love* of God.[2] To have our standing in the love of God through the Holy Spirit indeed simply means living by the gift of God, by the grace of God, that is, having a share in God's own life, which is love.

Henceforward our whole attitude towards the world and towards humanity is completely altered. Faith which is "living on God" means "living in harmony with the purposes of God." Faith means being absorbed into God's own purpose. This must become evident in the fact that we no longer are concerned with self-regarding aims, but with God's interests, with that which God wills. Through faith man becomes a volunteer in the Divine army, one who, because and in so far as he believes, can do nothing else than will what God wills, precisely because his life is based in and on God. Therefore, because he no longer seeks himself, he now seeks that which God seeks, that is, the world, the other man. The will of God for the world now becomes the will of the believer. The ethical impulse is now no longer that of self-respect, but of love(22). The isolation of the self has been broken down; wherever a man has been set free from himself, he has been set free for others. He who lives by the generosity of God himself becomes generous. All that he now possesses of his own he possesses in God; in faith alone is self-love conquered by the love of God. No heart can be conquered by the law. The law can only reveal our own emptiness; the transformation is only achieved by love(23).

Now, however, since man is turned towards others in love the law no longer stands between him and others as a programme or an idea. Love impels him to come into touch with others in the personal way in which God meets us. Only thus do we learn to see others in any real way. Previously there was always "something"—something abstract—in between. Now the "other man" is no longer a "case," he is present himself, as he is. Now you act towards him, your "neighbour," in the way *he* needs, and as you alone can know, since you see and hear him as he is, since you no longer deal with, educate, reform, provide for him on any abstract principle whatever. Hence here something takes place which can never be formulated in any law, something which cannot be foreknown(24). Love is not only the fulfilment of the law, but also its end, and thus the end of all ethics. That which

[1] Rom. xiv. 7.   [2] Rom. viii. 14–16.

ought to be done in love, in the freedom of the Spirit of God, that alone can love, or the Spirit, teach—thus here all general instruction ceases. For those who believe "are led by the Spirit of God."[1] "For who hath known the mind of the Lord, that he may instruct Him?"[2] And after this, who wants to revert to merely "ethical conduct"?

11. Now, however, the question cannot be evaded: does this Christian person, who owes no one anything save love, and who still owes this love, really *exist*?[3] Or is this itself an ideal? If it were simply an ideal, all that I have written would be sheer nonsense. For an ideal implies law, and a life controlled by ideals means a life of ethical effort, not one of spiritual power. When we talk of the New Birth and of Conversion we must speak of something real—or all our speech is vain. So we may answer the question by saying: "yes, this free Christian person does exist wherever faith exists." But faith does not exist impersonally, but personally (Karl Barth); that means, faith is not a possession, but something which happens through the action of God.

As Luther says continually, faith does not exist as *a quality* of the soul, or as "virtue"—as one of the three theological virtues—but faith exists wherever God as the Holy Spirit speaks within the soul, and Himself, within man's self, responds to the call of God. Faith exists only in the actuality of decision, thus as something which must be continually wrestled for and won out of unbelief. Thus faith only exists alongside of unbelief: "Lord, I believe! help Thou mine unbelief!"[4] What I said above about the new life in faith applies unreservedly to faith, but it is not equally applicable to the believer. For the believer is always also the unbeliever, the sinner. *Simul justus, simul peccator.* For faith, in faith, the law has been abrogated; for man, however, "round whose neck there still hangs the old Adam," there exists at the same time the *demand* of God. In the acquittal and encouragement of justification, therefore, the word of God becomes to us who are constantly standing alongside of faith the claim of sanctification. The indicative of the Divine promise becomes the imperative of the Divine command.

The same word, "I am the Lord Thy God, thou art *Mine*," which is the Divine promise to faith, the assurance of His love, to the believer, because and in so far as he is also a sinner,

[1] Rom. viii. 15.   [2] 1 Cor. ii. 16.
[3] Rom. xiii. 8.   [4] Mark ix. 24.

is the demand of God: "Obey Me, believe"(25). Faith itself must continually issue from repentance, as, on the other hand, repentance is only completed in faith. Therefore through faith—for us who are still sinners—the law is not abolished, but is indeed only now rightly set up. But this does not take place in the old sense. It is law without legalism, law interpreted by faith, which knows the grace of God. Therefore it is no longer the law which condemns, but which "instructs." And it is no longer the law which stands between me and my neighbour, but one which drives me in his direction, towards his concrete existence. It is the law behind which stands the loving God. The believer looks beyond law to grace, and from grace back to law. The first commandment is a promise, and grace consists in this, that we are commanded to believe in this promise. Hence faith is obedience, just as obedience is only genuine when it is faith.

It is impossible for us to merge these two words into one. This mutual relation, the dualism of indicative and imperative, must remain. It is good, and willed by God, that Zwingli and Calvin stand alongside of Luther, in order that Luther's doctrine of the liberty of the children of God should not be degraded into the "freedom of the flesh." And it is also good that Luther stands alongside Calvin and Zwingli, in order that the obedience of faith and the emphasis on the instruction of the law should not once more slip into legalism. This does not mean that there are two kinds of Gospel. But these two points of view are like sentries who are commanded to stand and keep watch—at two opposite points—over the one sanctuary. God *demands* the obedience of faith. God *gives* the earnest determination to do something. Faith does not consist simply in passive acceptance; it always means, at the same time, an act of "pulling oneself together," just as believing confidence is only genuine when it is accompanied by the horror of the possibility of being lost. This is law without legalism, freedom without self-will and illusion. It is the love of God, seized and held in the terrible judgment of the Cross, and the holiness of God, made known in His act of reconciliation. The Epistle to the Romans interpreted by Matthew, and Matthew understood in the light of the Epistle to the Romans: this would provide the basis for an evangelical ethic.

CHAPTER IX

THE DEFINITION OF THE CHRISTIAN ETHIC

1. There is no general conception of ethics which would also include the Christian ethic. Such a general definition of ethics does not even exist for rational thought. Were we to define it thus : Ethics is the science of behaviour in accordance with a standard, this idea of harmony with a standard would indeed fit an ethic concerned with moral obligation, but it would not be applicable to a eudaemonistic ethic, and still less to a radically hedonistic ethic or to the individualistic ethic of self-expression. If, on the other hand—as Schleiermacher has done—we sum up all human conduct under the conception of ethics, then this conception is far too broad, since it would include, on the one hand, the technically artistic side of conduct, and, on the other, bad and foolish conduct. If we except ethical scepticism, which is an extreme case, from our enquiry, it is, of course, true to say that all "natural ethics" may be summed up in this (certainly very indefinite) general formal definition: ethics is the doctrine or the science of conduct, which is distinguished from all that is accidental and not based on principle by ultimate principles which characterize it as "right." This definition of ethics would cover the theory of Epicurus as well as that of Kant. But even this conception—broadly conceived as it is—does *not* apply to the Christian ethic.

It is of course true that even the Christian ethic is concerned with the definition of conduct, which as "right" conduct has to be distinguished from conduct which is accidental or wrong; but this distinction or definition does not take place by means of an ultimate principle, which, as such, would be intelligible and valid. It is indeed the result of the enquiry of the previous chapter, that the Christian conception of the Good differs from every other conception of the Good at this very point: that it cannot be defined in terms of principle at all.

Whatever can be defined in accordance with a principle —whether it be the principle of pleasure or the principle of duty—is legalistic. This means that it is possible—by the use of this principle—to pre-determine "the right" down to the smallest detail of conduct. We have already seen how this legalistic spirit corrupts the true conception of the Good from its very roots. The Christian moralist and the extreme individualist are at one in their emphatic rejection of legalistic conduct; they join hands, as it were, in face of the whole host of legalistic moralists; they are convinced that conduct which is regulated by abstract principles can never be good. But equally sternly the Christian moralist rejects the individualistic doctrine of freedom, according to which there is no longer any difference between "right" and "wrong." Rather, in the Christian view, that alone is "good" which is free from all caprice, which takes place in unconditional obedience. There is no Good save obedient behaviour, save the obedient will. But this obedience is rendered not to a law or a principle which can be known beforehand, but only to the free, sovereign will of God. The Good consists in always doing what God wills at any particular moment.

This statement makes it clear that for us the will of God cannot be summed up under any principle, that it is not at our disposal, but that so far as we are concerned the will of God is absolutely free. The Christian is therefore "a free lord over all things,"[1] because he stands directly under the personal orders of the free Sovereign God. This is why genuine "Christian conduct"—if we may use this idea as an illustration—is so unaccountable, so unwelcome to the moral rigorist and to the hedonist alike. The moral rigorist regards the Christian as a hedonist, and the hedonist regards him as a rigorist. In reality, the Christian is neither, yet he is also something of both, since he is indeed absolutely *bound* and obedient, but, since he is bound to the *free* loving will of God, he is himself free from all transparent bondage to principles or to legalism. Above all it is important to recognize that even love is not a principle of this kind(1), neither the love which God Himself *has*, nor the love which He *requires*. Only God Himself defines love in His action. We, for our part, do not know what God is, nor do we know what *love* is, unless we learn to know God in His action, in faith. To be in this His Love, is the Commandment. Every attempt to conceive love as a principle leads to this result: it becomes distorted, either in the rigoristic, legalistic sense, or in the hedonistic sense. Man only knows what the love of God is when he sees the way in which God acts, and he only knows

[1] LUTHER: *Of the Freedom of a Christian Man* (*Von der Freiheit eines Christenmenschen*).

how he himself ought to love by allowing himself to be drawn by faith into this activity of God.

2. "To know God in His action" is only possible in faith. The action of God, in which He manifests Himself—and this means His love—is His revelation. God reveals Himself in His Word—which is at the same time a deed—in an actual event—in Jesus Christ; and He reveals Himself operatively in His living Word, which is now taking place—in the Holy Spirit. Because only conduct which takes place on the basis of this faith (and indeed in this faith in God's Word) can be "good conduct," in the sense of the Christian ethic, therefore, the science of good conduct, of ethics, is only possible within that other science which speaks of the Divine act of revelation, that is, within dogmatics. Reflection on the good conduct of man is only one part of more comprehensive reflection on the action of God in general. For human conduct can only be considered "good" when, and in so far as, God Himself acts in it, through the Holy Spirit. Hence just as this action is connected with the Divine action, so the Christian ethic is connected with dogmatics.

The attempt to make a clear-cut distinction between dogmatics and ethics from the point of view that the one is concerned with Divine and the other with human action spoils both dogmatics and ethics(2). The New Testament proclamation of the Word of God is characterized by the fact that it makes no distinction between the "dogmatic" and the "ethical" elements. The great Christological passages occur in the midst of practical exhortations(3), and moral instructions are always most closely connected with "dogmatic" ideas. As the indicative and the imperative suddenly alternate, as speech about the redeeming love of God flows directly into the claim for human love, so the whole New Testament is an indissoluble blend of "ethics" and "dogmatics." This is true also, more or less, of the great confessional works of the Reformation;[1] this is also true of the greatest—and, indeed, the only genuinely reformatory—dogmatic work of the Reformation: Calvin's *Institutes*(4). Every theme of dogmatics is also inevitably a theme of ethics. Dogmatics does not exist independently, nor does ethics, but dogmatic knowledge as such always aims at existential, that is, ethical, thought, and ethical knowledge is rooted in knowledge of dogmatics.

[1] See especially ALTHAUS: *Der Geist der lutherischen Ethik im Augsburgischen Bekenntnis*, 1930.

We can only rightly represent the whole of ethics as a part of dogmatics, because it is concerned with God's action in and through man. Not only the commandments of God, not only the New Birth and conversion, but also man's sanctification—if it really *is* what it is called—is wholly the work of God, certainly with this distinction: it is that one of His works which is expressed in our own external conduct.

On the other hand, once we have recognized legalism as *the* evil, once we have seen that the Good, in the moral sense, is that which God does in us and through us, how could we possibly seriously consider severing ethics from dogmatics? The specific element in the Christian ethic—as will become abundantly clear in all that follows—is precisely this: that the Good in human conduct only arises out of the fact that it is set within the action of God. All other forms of conduct are legalistic. This is what the authors of the Heidelberg Catechism meant when they summed up all ethics under the heading—which is certainly easy to misunderstand—of "gratitude." Good can only take place in grateful acknowledgment of the action of God. The separation of dogmatics from ethics would lay dogmatics open to the danger of speculative aberrations and ethics to the danger of moralistic distortions.

Really good Christian conduct—speaking from the point of view of principle—ought to have the whole of the Christian knowledge of God "behind" it. Luther, in his Shorter Catechism, has expressed this very well, since he begins the explanation of every commandment with the words: "we ought thus to fear and love God, in order that we . . ."

The God who is thus to be feared and loved, however, is the One who is manifested in His revelation, "the whole God." Every ethical consideration is thus connected with the whole Idea of God. The fact that we gather up this whole knowledge of God in the two main conceptions "God the Creator and the Redeemer" will, in its own place, be justified.

3. If ethics are thus to be placed within the sphere of dogmatics, this does not mean that the error of a "descriptive, in contrast to an imperative," ethic should be repeated(5). It is true, of course, that behind this error there lies the profound idea that the Good is God's gift and God's work, that it is a fruit of the New Birth. At the same time, this idea contains the wrong and dangerous implication, that the New Birth is

a given entity of a natural kind, out of which the Good is "organically" developed. Whoever has once understood what justification means, as contrasted with the (Catholic) idea of "infused grace," can only regard every kind of descriptive ethic as a reactionary interpretation of grace which had been overcome by the Reformation. Not "sanctification" only, but also faith itself, is never real save as obedience to the command of God.

The decisive point of view for ethics—even for Christian ethics—is conduct, not being, although even for the Christian ethic it is the being of man, "the person," which is the decisive point of view for conduct. The new being (*Sein*) of man, in so far as it is regarded only as the work of God, is the "new man" who is based on faith in justification. In so far as in the being of this new man the emphasis is laid on its manifesting itself in a "work," in actions towards others, it forms part of ethics. Yet this ethical element is not a second, independent element alongside of the dogmatic element, but it is simply the emphasis on a special "moment" within it. For just as the Christian Ethic is distinguished from natural ethics by the fact that in it God's action is always regarded as the basis of human action, so it is also characteristic of it that in all action, the *being* of the agent, as that which alone can be really good or evil, is kept in view.

Therefore, in spite of the fact that a uniform division of Christian doctrine into dogmatics and ethics can only take place with the greatest injury to both, there is always an external technical separation, which is forced upon us by necessity, and is indeed justifiable; that is, if this external separation does not denote an inner separation. These considerations may now be summed up in a sentence, in which the special subject of Christian ethics is defined: *Christian ethics is the science of human conduct as it is determined by Divine conduct.*

4. The question now remains to be discussed: In this connexion what meaning can be attached to the word *science*? This question can here be touched only in passing, since it could only be thoroughly explained in the context of systematic theology. From two points of view the possibility of a science of theology is questioned: from the standpoint of a general conception of science, and from the point of view of faith itself.

When we require any branch of study to be scientific,

inevitably this seems to imply an absolute impartiality;[1] but such an attitude is incompatible with a Christian ethic. Such an attitude is only intelligent and practicable as a postulate when it is so determined and limited by the sphere of its subject. Absolute impartiality[2] would be absolute nonsense. The natural scientist is "disinterested" if he is disinterested within the categorically defined limits of the concept of the subject of Nature. A scientist who does not realize this limitation becomes doctrinaire and does violence to facts or to the truth. For instance, the natural scientist who heedlessly applies those categories which are necessary for the study of his own subject to some other sphere of learning, say, for instance, to the spheres of law or of history, and who regards any argument proceeding from any other than the presuppositions of natural science as a violation of the scientific spirit, only shows that he himself is narrow-minded and truly unscientific. Both for the natural scientist and for the humanist there exist different presuppositions, apart from which the subject under consideration—Nature or History—cannot even be visualized. Only within these fundamental presuppositions can there be any disinterested science. A "scientific ethic" constructed on the lines of natural science would never become an ethic at all, but it would remain embedded in a morass of biology or psychology and certainly in sociology.

Hence an ethic which is free from presuppositions has never existed; rather the question is always *what* presuppositions the moral philosopher brings with him. That man is a product of nature and is to be considered in terms of the categories of natural science is just as much a presupposition as the view which regards man as a spiritual being who should be regarded from the point of view of thought. The scientific character of the ethic in question will differ entirely according to the presuppositions. It is not scientific, for instance, to describe Spencer's ethic as scientific and the Kantian ethic as unscientific. Rather in both instances a totally different kind of science is presupposed; in the one case causal science is presupposed; in the other normative science.

But what distinguishes both these varieties of philosophical ethics from Christian ethics is something which seems to make it impossible for a Christian ethic to be scientific;

1 Literally "absence of presuppositions."—TR.
2 Or "absence of presuppositions."—TR.

namely, the universal validity and universal intelligibility or rationality of its principle, which, as has been already made plain, must be absolutely rejected by the Christian ethic. Once, however, it has been granted that the problem of morality assumes a wholly different aspect according as it is regarded from the "causal" or the "normative" point of view, we might reasonably expect the further admission, that it is actually possible to view the problem of morality from a totally different standpoint—a standpoint which excludes both the causal and the idealistic rational views—namely, the point of view of the free action of God. If the natural scientist is obliged to accept the fact that his presuppositions are not sufficient for a genuinely scientific ethic, then surely a wise philosopher should be at least prepared to admit that there *may* be a standpoint which exists outside Reason, a standpoint whence the problem of morality could be treated quite differently from that which the rational view would require. The wise philosopher ought to be all the more ready to admit this possibility since he—of all men—is well acquainted with the insoluble contradictions which are involved in every attempt to construct a philosophical ethic.

Perhaps the philosopher will admit that he has no right to exclude such a "higher" possibility of defining morality before he has examined other possibilities; at the same time he will make it quite clear that he doubts whether such a view of morality is even capable of scientific presentation at all, since science is a concern of reason and not of faith. This brings us to the second question respecting the Christian ethic as science, which starts not from the point of view of science, but from that of faith. This question, however, can only be discussed on the presuppositions of faith, and thus only "within the Church," since here alone do we know what faith means. Is it possible to present the Christian Faith in general, and the Good which is grounded in the Christian Faith in particular, in a scientific manner?

If the relation between reason and faith were simply one of opposition this possibility would be excluded. But this presupposition is not conclusive. Faith in the Word of God does not exclude reason by thrusting it out of the way; on the contrary, faith penetrates through reason, by realizing itself within it. The believer does not deny the validity of the laws of reason, nor the significance of the acts of reason, but only the validity of the "closed reason," of the reason which is based upon itself and is therefore sufficient unto itself. God is also the Creator of the reason, and it is His highest and most glorious creation. Indeed, there are relations between God and reason which do not exist elsewhere between God and the creature. It is not the existence of the reason which is in opposition to God, but only the perversion of reason from a reason which is founded on God to one which is based on itself.[1]

Hence it is not impossible to combine science with faith. Every believer lives at the same time in a world of reason and of science. This world of reason is newly-defined for him in faith by the Word of God, just as he, as a rational being, knows himself to be re-defined by the Word of God. The Word of God makes the human reason the instrument of God. The proclamation of the Word of God by men takes place by means of reason, just as its reception by faith also takes place by means of reason. St. Antony's sermon to the fishes is a touching story; at the same time it is also sentimental(6). It is not possible here to explain any further the more exact relations which exist between the word of man and the Word of God, between revelation and reason, between faith and knowledge.[2]

The scientific presentation or the Christian ethic can certainly never represent the Good as a general truth, easy to be perceived, and based on a universal principle. Were it to do this, it would be an act of treason towards the Christian Faith. The meaning of the Christian ethic is the exact opposite; its task is to work out scientifically the characteristic element in the Christian knowledge of the Good, namely, that the Good, as faith knows it, can never be legalistic, or a matter of abstract principle; thus that the Christian ethic can never count on general recognition in the sense of a truth of reason, but, explicitly, only on the recognition of those who believe. For one who does not believe cannot understand the Christian conception of the Good.[3]

But this does not mean that the Christian ethic makes no claim to universal validity. Whatever God demands *can* only

---

[1] Cf. especially the section in this book which deals with the community of culture, particularly pp. 486 ff.

[2] Here all I can do is to refer to my *Religionsphilosophie* and also to the first chapter in my book of English lectures entitled *The Word and the World*.

[3] On this point cf. my discussion with Rudolf Bultmann in the *Zeitschrift f. Th. u. K.*, 1931, pp. iii ff.

be universal, that is, valid for all men, even if those who do not hear this demand do not admit this validity, and indeed do not even understand the claim to universal validity. The believer alone clearly perceives that the Good, as it is recognized in faith, is the sole Good, and that all that is otherwise called good cannot lay claim to this title, at least not in the ultimate sense of the word. It is precisely faith and faith alone which knows this: that alone is good which God does; and, indeed, faith really consists in the fact that man knows this—and that he knows it in such a way as it alone can be known, namely, in the recognition of faith. But once man does know this he also knows the unlimited unconditional validity of this conception and of the divine demand.

The Christian ethic, therefore, since it cannot be scientific in terms of a general principle, can be scientific solely and simply if it represents its own subject in a strictly objective orderly process of reflection, and in a method which is suitable to its subject[1] and precisely not after the pattern of a causal or normative science. The "organ" of reason is placed at the disposal of faith for its clarification. It aids the process of reflection on that which is not reason, but is always related to reason, precisely because it is related to man as man. It would be easier to demonstrate the form such a "science" would assume by a particular example than by abstract methodological explanations.

It might be asked whether such an ethic ought not rather to be called a theological ethic than a Christian ethic, since the possibility of a philosophical ethic, based on revelation, would have to be admitted. I must confess that I simply cannot imagine a philosophical ethic which would deal with revelation not as a reality but as a possibility, save under the form of the modest but highly significant process of a critical conceptual purification of ethics of every kind, thus, as a purely formal science. Since, however, such an ethic—save for a few beginnings in Kant—has never yet been written(7), and since it is generally understood that ethics deals with the Good as its content, and not with a merely formal conceptual purification, our description of ethics as "Christian" ought not to be regarded as presumptuous.

5. But what is the function of a system of ethics in regard to the central ethical question: What ought we to do? Can ethics tell us what we are to do? If it could, it would mean

[1] Cf. THURNEYSEN: *Das Wort Gottes und die Kirche*, pp. 196 ff.

that the Christian ethic also is an ethical system based on law and on abstract principles. For where ethics is regarded purely as a science, there general, and to some extent timeless, propositions are stated. If these were to define what we ought to do, then the Good would be defined in legalistic terms. Therefore no such claim can be made either by or for ethics. The service it renders cannot be that of relieving us of the necessity for making moral decisions, but that it prepares the way for such decisions. How this takes place can only be made clear in the explication of the part which is played by law within a morality which is not legalistic. The significance of the law is the same as the significance of ethics, namely: that it prepares the way for a voluntary decision, or for the hearing of the divine command.[1]

In this explicit rejection of the legalistic definition of the Good the truly Christian ethic is also distinguished from the Roman Catholic ethic. In accordance with its juridically defined conception of faith and of the Church its conception of the Good is also rigidly legalistic, and therefore its ethical system is fundamentally a system of casuistry. The lesser stipulations are logically derived from the universal law, and by means of a closely woven network of further minor regulations the whole realm of human life is legally defined, so that for every case, in actual practice, it is possible to look up the ethical code and find out what is commanded and what is forbidden. The relation of knowledge in general and application to the particular case is determined by the purely logical relation of subsumption of the particular under the universal. We shall see elsewhere in this book what is the result of this view of the Good. Here it must suffice to say as strongly as possible (reminding the reader of the line of thought followed in the previous chapters) that this conception cannot be combined with the knowledge of justification by faith alone. Ethical "orthodoxy"—the legalistic view of the Good—is just as bad as dogmatic orthodoxy, that is, as a legalistic view of faith and of the Word of God.

It is, however, equally necessary to protect the Christian ethic from the dangers which menace it from the "Left," that is, from the danger of fanaticism. It is, of course, true that God's claim, on the basis of the divine action, can only be perceived by the individual through faith by means of the Holy Spirit; so that "no man can teach his brother"[2] what

---

[1] See Chapter XV. [2] Jer. xxxi. 34.

in the decisive sense of the word the Good really is. But this does not mean that no instruction is necessary, that the decision can only be expected through hearing the Word of the Spirit. It is not thus that the Holy Spirit speaks to us. As for faith in general, so also for the Good, it is true that God's Word is twofold: the Scripture and the Spirit, the unity between the Word that has taken place and the Word that is taking place now. The love of God revealed in Christ, in the Scriptures, is the same love of God which is shed abroad in our hearts by the life-giving Spirit. As the Scripture without the Spirit produces false legalism, orthodoxy, so the Spirit without the Scriptures produces false Antinomianism, and fanaticism. But what the true mean is, what is the true meaning of the law and of instruction for the decision according to the actual command of God, can only be stated in connexion with the explanation of the relevant theological conceptions.

6. The arrangement of ethics arises from the consideration of the distinctive points of view, in their variety, and in their relations to each other. The main formal conception is this: human conduct; for this announces the specific ethical theme. Every system of ethics, even the Christian ethic, is concerned with human conduct. Its main aspects will therefore supply the formal articulated framework of the ethic. We enquire *why* we act, *who* acts, to *whom* we ought to do so and so, and *what* we are to do? Each of these questions is the subject of one of the four sections of the second fundamental part of this work. The material points of view, that is, those which distinguish the conduct of the Christian from all other kinds of conduct, result from the consideration of the relation between divine and human conduct. The will of God, as it is made known to faith through revelation, is both a gift and a task; it is the will of the Creator and the Redeemer; it is always the same and yet it is different every time; as the Will which demands, as the Command of God it can only be known by us through the law in its threefold sense. And indeed these material points of view are valid within each one of the previously named formal statements of the question, and must therefore recur in each section. At the same time nothing will be explained save the Will of God, as it, as the basis of our conduct, qualifies it as "good," that is, the Command of the gracious generous God. This forms the subject of the second fundamental book.

The Divine Command, however, places us in the midst of reality, which, although it is not good in itself, is not severed from the action of God, which takes place apart from anything we do. In so far as the human reality within which we have to act witnesses to faith in the divine action, and in so doing to His will, we have to do with the divine "orders" within which alone our action can take place, and in accordance with which it ought to take place. Thus the subject of the third book will be the way in which the Command of God comes to us, related to these orders of reality—the way in which this Divine Command can be perceived in and through them. But before we enter upon both these questions we must first of all give a brief account of that which can be learned—negatively as well as positively—from the work of other Christian moral philosophers.

CHAPTER X

THE CHRISTIAN ETHIC: PAST AND PRESENT

THE Christian Church has always been conscious, at every period in her history, that within her, that is, from the point of view of faith in Christ, the ethical problem is formulated and solved differently from any other point of view; at no period in her history has she ever wholly forgotten that faith and morality are indissolubly connected. But she has not perceived this *clearly* at every period of her history, and her theology has therefore produced "schools" and systems of "Christian" ethics which were often nearer to the thought of ancient paganism than to that of Scripture, or at least they expressed the truth of the Christian ethic in a very distorted form. There would be no need for me to speak of these systems were it not that these "schools" of thought and these systems are just as alive and influential to-day as at any other period. Here, however, we are only concerned with the theological scientific presentation of the ethical understanding of the Self, and not with the latter itself, thus only with ethics, and not with the morality of historical Christianity.

The Early Church[1] did not produce a system of "dogmatics"; still less did she produce a system of ethics. She was still far too deeply involved in the problems of her own growth and of her own struggle for existence to express her moral convictions otherwise than in the form of instructive and polemical occasional papers, and her own internal struggles were more concerned with the (dogmatic) content of the Faith than with the (ethical) meaning of the Divine Command. But when Augustine took up the cudgels against Pelagianism it became evident that destructive and confusing forces had long been at work under the surface. It is then at this point that fundamental ethical reflection begins. Regarded as a whole Augustine's ethical achievement was of the highest importance; it meant the re-discovery of the distinctively Christian Idea of the Good contrasted with the ethical rationalism and eudaemonism of the ancient world. The influence of Neo-Platonic mysticism, however, and of the

---

[1] Cf. the excellent *Geschichte der Ethik* by O. DITTRICH, Vols. I and II. *Die Geschichte der christlichen Ethik*, by LUTHARDT, is still useful, in spite of the sharp criticism to which it has been subjected by Troeltsch.

popular ecclesiastical ascetic dualism which originated in Hellenism, can be traced as clearly in Augustine's view of the Good as in his view of faith and of salvation. In spite of this, however, the revolutionizing power of his thought was too great for the Church to endure it. "Semi-Pelagianism" ignored Augustine and pursued its own course, and to this day it has set its seal upon the ethic of Catholicism. The clearest and the most powerful expression of this school of thought, with its spirit of compromise, is the ethic of that authoritative Doctor of the Church, St. Thomas Aquinas. At first sight the system of St. Thomas seems most impressive; this is due to its closely-knit, comprehensive character. On a more careful examination, however, it proves to be an inwardly impossible compromise between the eudaemonistic rationalism of the Ancient world and the Augustinian and Pauline view of the Good.

The fact that right down to the present day Catholic moral philosophers are divided into two schools—those who interpret Aquinas mainly from the Augustinian point of view, and those who interpret him chiefly from the Aristotelian point of view—is due to this element of compromise which is characteristic of the system as a whole. Common to both, however, is the recognition of an ethical structure consisting of two "storeys"; the lower floor represents the rational view of ethics, as a system of natural moral philosophy, which explains the law of the Good as something which can not only be known by every one, but can also be fulfilled by every one. The upper floor represents ecclesiastical moral theology, which discloses a higher "Good" to be known and attained by man, in closest union with the supernatural sacramental form. Catholicism creates for itself the theological dogmatic basis of this twofold structure in the doctrine of the Fall, according to which man, on account of the Fall, has not lost the power to do the Good, but only the supernatural gifts of grace of the supernatural state. In the interpretation of the system of Thomism, which by means of dogma has been elevated to the position of an authoritative standard of doctrine, the two currents of thought diverge so widely from each other that the result is that an absolutely opposite conception of the Good dominates in each. The one main school, as, for instance, it is represented theoretically by Cathrein,[1] and practically by the ecclesiastical practice of

[1] CATHREIN: *Moralphilosophie*, 2 vols, 1924.

confession, regards the rational lower storey as the real content of morals; the upper storey, to which "works of supererogation" belong, is removed from the moral sphere to the sphere of the Church's administration of salvation. The interpretation of the Good is here, essentially, exactly the same as that of Aristotle; here therefore ethics is treated as "moral philosophy." The other tendency, of which Mausbach may be taken as the representative, leads in the other direction; it emphasizes the specifically Christian element in the conception of the Good, in harmony with the thought of Paul and of Augustine, to such an extent that the natural Good is distinguished from the real Good as a merely preparatory stage; this line of thought closely resembles the Protestant doctrine of the *justitia civilis*. But this tendency is constantly checked in its development by consideration for the dogmas of the Church; hence it manifests a certain fluctuation, and an inward disharmony and disunion within the system, which, in comparison with the previous school of thought, with its closely-knit, comprehensive system, appears at a disadvantage, so far as its *form* is concerned. On the other hand, so far as its *content* is concerned, this view cannot fail to be congenial to those who are aware of the true nature of the Christian ethic.

According to the definition of the Aristotelian-Thomistic school of thought, for instance, the principle of the Good, objectively, is not the will of God, and subjectively, obedience to this will, but it is "adaptation to the nature of man." The Good is "all that brings man's nature to perfection."[1] "The idea of the Good thus precedes the knowledge of God and is presupposed by it." It is, of course, true that it is one of the duties of man to love God and to give Him His due, just as it is man's duty to act rightly towards himself and his neighbour; man ought even "to produce an act of perfect love, and he ought to repeat this act often during life," but "it is in no way necessary that in every action man should think of this reference to the final end, and will it from this point of view. Otherwise we would have to maintain that a sinner or an atheist who ignores God completely is utterly unable to achieve any morally good action, which is manifestly absurd."[2] The statement that the "goodness or badness of an action depends upon the objects towards which our volition is directed"[3] is also in harmony with this point of

[1] CATHREIN, loc. cit., p. 221.   [2] Ibid., p. 200.   [3] Ibid., p. 205.

view. This statement is expanded and defined more exactly by saying that "a thing is 'good' for a creature in so far as it agrees with its inclinations and capacities or is able to perfect them."[1] "Those ways of acting are good which are in harmony with the peculiar disposition of the person in question."[2] "That the final End of Man is the real norm of ethics, and that this should be in the mind of the doer in every action when he is called upon to act . . . must lead inevitably to an intolerable rigorism."[3] Therefore "the Good means far more than obedience to the commandments," for "it contains not only the actual commandments but also the Counsels, as we say that the Christian Moral Law contains Counsels as well as Commandments."[4] "There are two kinds of good actions: one kind is necessary to maintain the moral order . . . the other kind is necessary merely in order to achieve greater moral perfection. We are under the obligation to perform the former actions by the Law of Nature, but we are under no obligation to perform the latter, they are simply the subject of a Counsel."[5] I would add that these quotations are taken from the work of a leading Jesuit, that this book has a very great influence, that these extracts are from the sixth edition, and that this book has been published with the *Imprimatur* of the Roman Church. It will be obvious to every one who knows the works of St. Thomas that the author rightly appeals to Aquinas as his authority; this is proved still further by copious extracts from both the *Summas* of this prince of theologians.

But the other school of thought can also rightly appeal to St. Thomas. "Human actions are good or bad in so far as they are, or are not, in accordance with the highest divine purpose, to the extent in which they are in agreement with, or in opposition to, God's inward holiness or outward Glory."[6] It is stated explicitly of the principle of "adaptation": "that the sense of obligation to which this gives rise, is not, in itself, actually of an ethical character, that is, unless it is made to serve the highest purpose."[7] Further, in reference to the views of the author whose works we have previously quoted, this writer makes the highly controversial statement that to describe "the essence of morality" as the Aristotelian principle of "adaptation to the rational nature of man" is "wrong."[8]

---

[1] CATHREIN, loc. cit., p. 209. [2] Ibid., p. 205.
[3] Ibid., p. 219. [4] Ibid., p. 219. [5] Ibid., p. 389.
[6] MAUSBACH: *Katholische Moraltheologie*, 6, 1927, p. 26.
[7] Ibid., p. 31. [8] Ibid., p. 32.

The objective points of view of value and of order are subordinated to the ultimate End, and only receive their moral content from it.[1] "The theological virtues, and above all, love, then appear as the fundamental sources whence the rest of the infused virtues proceed."[2] Love is the *nova lex*, "and contains the germ of the fulfilment of the whole Law."[3] Hence the reproach of the Reformers is unjust, "that medieval theology conceives the law of the Gospel as a mass of external prescriptions" like the legislation of the secular or the Mosaic Law.[4] At the same time it is also admitted that "later Catholic moralists have laid too little emphasis on this primary element of the *lex nova* in their anxiety to lay stress on the *lex secundaria Evangelii*."[5] Accordingly, the inadequacy of natural morality is admitted, and is dealt with in the way in which we are accustomed to see it handled by Reformed theologians.[6]

But although this moral theology is evidently based upon the teaching of St. Thomas, and has also received the approval of the Church, the fact remains that its real tendency can never be developed, for ecclesiastical dogma retains precisely those elements which this school of thought—to the extent in which it follows St. Augustine—is forced to reject. Its inner disharmony comes out clearly in the terms in which the following statement is expressed: "Speaking from the Christian point of view, the inner surrender of the will to the Moral Law and to Good, the reverent love to God on the part of the creature, a love which is eager to serve, is essentially, and under all circumstances, morally good, the opposite is morally bad."[7] What the author really wishes to say is this: that everything is *only* good in virtue of this love, and that without this love it is *not* good. But this he *dare* not say. In opposition to Augustine he is obliged to designate as "false" the "denial of the capacity of fallen man to perform naturally good actions";[8] in opposition to Augustine he must deny that "Original Sin has essentially degraded and mutilated the nature of man," since it consists only in the "loss of the dignity of supernature" in its "free over-flowing gracious character."[9] The Catholic cannot really be Augustinian since Augustinianism has been condemned by the Church by the

---

[1] MAUSBACH: *Katholische Moraltheologie*, 6, 1927, p. 31.
[2] Ibid., p. 207. [3] Ibid., p. 67. [4] Ibid., p. 67.
[5] Ibid., p. 57. [6] Ibid., p. 6. [7] Ibid., p. 28.
[8] Ibid., p. 189. [9] Ibid., p. 189.

Bulle ex omnibus afflictionibus(1). The weakening of the New Testament-Augustinian conception of the commandment leads to the further deduction—which is in opposition to the ethical principle of the Augustinians—that here also, as with the Aristotelians, the effect of sin is simply held to be "that in the state of sin man is unable *permanently* to fulfil *all* the commandments, or to avoid all the greater sins,"[1] that here also a way of action is recognized which is beyond the sphere of binding obligation, and the *consilia* are differentiated from the commandments. But the content of the Counsels, of that which lies beyond the realm of natural obligation, is not clearly conceived, since it is held to mean partly love in general, and partly to refer only to the love of one's enemies and to the three monastic vows. Even the "Augustinian" Mausbach says—like the Aristotelians—"the laws of obligation which concern creaturely goods all move within a certain circle, in order to make their fulfilment possible to the *average* man."[2] In saying this the writer both accepts the two-fold system of morality—that is, for priests and for lay people, for monks and for those who live in the world—and he also reveals the legalistic view of the Commandments and the casuistical method of the practice of confession when he admits that it is possible to keep most but not *all* the Commandments. In actual practice the matter-of-fact Aristotelian ethic always predominates; in the sphere of theory it is in continual conflict with an Augustinianism which perpetually re-appears, although it is confined within narrow limits.

It is not necessary to elaborate the main ideas of the ethic of the Reformers(2) at this point, for the whole of this book is simply an attempt to lay fresh emphasis upon these ideas. In this connexion it is important to note the unity of view which exists between the three chief Reformers in fundamental ethical questions. The Lutherans have a bad habit of reproaching the Swiss Reformers with "legalism," while the Reformed Church levels at Luther the reproach of "quietism." If we look at the historical influence of the Reformation in both these spheres it is evident that these strictures are not without some justification; but here we are not concerned with this point at all. In ethical *doctrine* we can discover no more "quietism" in Luther than we can discover "legalism" in Calvin or Zwingli. The emphasis on the supposed contrast

[1] Underlined by Mausbach himself, p. 195.
[2] MAUSBACH: *Katholische Moraltheologie*, 6, 1927, p. 222.

between the two types is usually due to a wholly inadequate knowledge of the actual views held by one's "opponents." Anyone who really knows the four chapters on the Christian Life in the third book of the *Institutio*, or the exposition of the Ten Commandments in the second book, can no longer speak of the "legalism" of Calvin(3); nor can one who has really grasped Luther's doctrine of "the Calling" speak of his "quietism." The great gulf does not lie between Luther and Calvin but between their orthodox followers. Holl has shown in a convincing manner(4) how even Melanchthon misunderstood Luther's doctrine of Justification by Faith, and interpreted it in a eudaemonistic, individualistic, and legalistic manner. Very much the same may be said of the transformation which the doctrine of predestination has suffered at the hands of Beza. In the understanding of the Good we can perceive the same process at work in the Lutheran sphere as in that of the Reformed. First of all, as early as Melanchthon, we see the renewed emphasis on the philosophical (Aristotelian) ethic and its intrusion into the Christian ethic. Likewise in the first Reformed ethical thinker, Danäus, Aristotelianism is at war with Paulinism; in this conflict it is almost impossible to say which gains the upper hand. On the surface, in both instances, the Aristotelian contribution seems to be restricted to formal categories, which are to be filled with a Christian content. In reality, however, these categories contain (or at least imply) a whole system of anthropology—as, for instance, in the idea of "virtue" —namely the individualistic-naturalistic anthropology of Aristotle.

Secondly, the Idea of the Good becomes increasingly legalistic. The doctrine of justification is indeed always presupposed; but there is no longer any understanding of the fact that it brings with it a new interpretation of the Good; it is regarded solely from the point of view of moral power. Here grace is only valued as the *power* which makes it possible to achieve the Good which is commanded by the Law; Luther and Calvin, on the contrary, know that in the doctrine of Justification by Faith it is precisely this Law which is understood from a wholly new angle. The exposition which a man like J. Gerhard gives of the Ten Commandments can scarcely be distinguished from that of any Reformed scholastic thinker; when he goes on to expound the relation between the Law and the Gospel, and the necessity for good works, the similarity of view becomes still more evident. And indeed how could it be otherwise? For in both instances the emphasis laid on the Scriptural authority for the doctrine is tending towards the view of the literal "infallibility" of the Bible and the doctrine of Verbal Inspiration; in both instances, too, the paradoxical statements of the Reformers—which seemed to achieve a unity between conflicting aspects of truth—were broken up, and arranged in orderly and intelligible logical series, and an *ordo salutis* was constructed which was certainly very rational, but was utterly alien to the spirit both of the Reformation and of the Bible. We might perhaps describe the difference between the two points of view in the following way: from the time of Melanchthon onwards the Lutheran doctrine of justification—and the ethic as well—became strongly coloured by eudaemonistic as well as by individualistic and quietistic features, while from Beza onwards the doctrine of Predestination became strongly speculative and arbitrary in character; this led to a rationalistic, activistic, and legalistic tendency in ethics. On the one hand was the "soft flesh of Wittenberg,"[1] and on the other the narrowness and scrupulosity of Puritanism —so alien to the real spirit of Calvin(5).

The Enlightenment, together with Pietism, developed the logical conclusions implicit in orthodoxy. The Enlightenment led to the revival of naturalistic ethics in almost every possible form, from the crudest kind of hedonism to the idea of the Law of Nature as expounded from the Christian point of view. Pietism, conscious of the "forensic" development of the doctrine of Justification, tried to lead men back to a "living" and morally effective central point; but in the process it became entangled in a net of wholly psychological categories, and the Christian ethic was thus at the mercy of an inwardly untrue ideology of "New Birth" and "Conversion." In contrast to the individualism of all these three tendencies, Idealism represents a world-wide universalism; the effect of this, however, was to merge the individual in the abstract world-process and to subordinate ethical to cultural interests. This Idealism also penetrated into theology and its ethic and

---

[1] This expression was aimed at the theologians of Wittenberg, who were inclined to expound Luther's doctrine of grace somewhat in the spirit of the question in Rom. vi. 1: "Shall we continue in sin, that grace may abound?" These theologians were more insistent on "pure doctrine" than on the practical and ethical aspect of Christianity.—TR.

there created the compromise—so difficult to understand—of Neo-Protestantism(6). However different all the ethical structures which have been erected upon this foundation may appear, in this they are all at one: they are all essentially constructed on the basis of the *lex naturae*, or, as one says nowadays, on the basis of "conscience," "the moral sense," on the "ideal," or, still more recently, on the idea of "value." They all reject the idea of Original Sin, the doctrine of the incapacity of man to achieve the Good by his own natural efforts, or else they modify the idea until it can no longer be perceived, and in accordance with this view they give a central place to the good disposition; accordingly, Jesus Christ only plays the part of an ideal, as the concrete example of the moral Idea, that is, only in the pedagogic relative sense. Still, we must admit that even here the ideas of the Bible and of the Reformers still continued to influence human thought; indeed, they constituted a "disturbing" element within an otherwise rational system; to such an extent is this true that it is actually possible to speak of a "mediating theology"[1] in connexion, for instance, with Schleiermacher's theological ethic. Schleiermacher, however—and this is also true of Rothe(7)—combined with the speculative fundamental conception of Idealism a Pietistic doctrine of the New Birth, or (which actually amounts to the same thing) a renewal of the Catholic doctrine of "infused" grace—not the idea of "grace" characteristic of the teaching of the Bible and of the Reformers.

Ideas of this kind, which are totally opposed to the Reformers' Idea of the Good, appear not only in the Neo-Protestant ethic, but also in the "Lutheran" ethic. Even Harless(8), who was the first Lutheran to write a book on ethics under the influence of the revival of Lutheranism, makes it evident that he had not been able to come into contact with the real spirit of Luther. In the first place, like all the other "Lutherans" of this type, Harless sees Luther always through the unfortunate medium of Melanchthon's interpretation. Hence his idea of ethics remains absolutely anthropocentric, and he does not attempt to eliminate the eudaemonistic elements; indeed, he strengthens this tendency by regarding everything from the point of view of "the possession of salvation." Secondly, in his thought (as in that

[1] German: *Vermittlungstheologie*: the name given to the thought of mid-nineteenth-century German theologians who sought to "reconcile" a "Scriptural and pure" religion with the intellectual heritage of German Idealism.—TR.

of later Lutherans) it becomes evident that in the religious awakening at the beginning of the nineteenth century it was Pietism, and not the thought of the Reformation, which was the main factor; the starting-point was not justification, or the word of Divine grace, but the New Birth, regarded as a magical process, which precedes faith. "Whoever has become a sharer in the Holy Spirit has already received life from God, and does not receive it first of all through faith."[1] Harless turns the Reformation paradox: *fides affert, accipit spiritum sanctum,* and: *Spiritus sanctus operatur fidem, fides est opus spiritus sancti,* into a causal series: "From this it follows that . . . I must *first of all* have the Holy Spirit, in order that I may believe." Of course, what this reception of the Spirit which precedes faith actually means is simply Infant Baptism regarded as a magical process, which plays a suspiciously predominant part in this system, as indeed it does in all these Lutheran systems of ethics. The later Lutheran idea that the *Word* is only the *means* of grace, as well as the "orthodox" view of an *ordo salutis*(9) conceived in a temporal-causal manner, had a very prejudicial effect upon the thought of the Lutherans of this type.

These misinterpretations appear in Vilmar(10) in a still more crass form. The New Birth is described without faith being mentioned at all, and accordingly the doctrine of Justification also differs entirely from that of the Reformation. "This act of the acceptance of that which has been offered is followed by the act of God, which we, in our Church, call 'justification.' "[2] That the same misunderstanding of the New Birth appears in the two Erlangen scholars, Hofmann and Frank, is less surprising, when one knows of their close connexion with Schleiermacher(11). The New Birth takes place "in the mysterious depths of the unconscious ground of life"[3] and "now the man in whom this has thus been in-wrought becomes aware of it, and with conscious self-determination he grasps the grace through which he has come into being."[4] Thus the doctrine of Justification is subordinated to that of the New Birth—as in the thought of Schleiermacher—since the one who is born again by "those supernatural influences" "becomes aware" of his state and of the divine grace.[5] Everywhere, as in Schleiermacher, vital images

[1] HARLESS: *Christliche Ethik,* 6, p. 230.   [2] *Theologische Moral,* II, p. 54.
[3] FRANK: *System der christlichen Sittlichkeit,* p. 225.
[4] Ibid., p. 225.   [5] Ibid., p. 221.

predominate, the Word is only "the *vehicle*" of the energy of salvation," the means of grace are only the "*arteries*, through which the blood is conducted from the heart into all the vessels and limbs of the organism"; its task is "to transmit the life which has been received."[1] Here, too, faith is only "inserted" into and "included" in the whole process of faith and conversion[2] whereas Infant Baptism mediates the regenerating influence of the Spirit—without any preceding faith.[3] Here the Holy Spirit works upon the "spiritual nature"(12), and this effect is only *afterwards* appropriated in a free act of self-determination by faith.[4]

So far as I can see it is A. v. Oettingen alone (the Dorpat colleague of Theodosius Harnack) [whose work on ethics surpasses all the other achievements of this group, both in the depth and range of his thought and in his understanding of the challenge of the hour], who has not fallen a victim to this general misunderstanding of the doctrine of the New Birth. With clear insight he recognized and courageously censured the secret eudaemonism, the obvious individualism and the lack of the sense of "ought" in the systems of contemporary thinkers. In all of them the eudáemonism comes out in the one-sided view of salvation—in v. Oettingen this thought is replaced by that of the Kingdom of God; their individualism is connected with the subjectivistic distortion of the idea of the New Birth. For the interest of these Lutherans is not directed towards the gracious Word of God requiring obedience, but towards the subjective psychological process of the New Birth. Similarly, the purely descriptive and therefore illusory and non-realistic character of these ethical systems is due—as in the case of Schleiermacher—to the same cause. Certainly it is the central truth of the Reformation that the Good has its ground and its lasting significance in the divine "indicative," in justification; but this does not mean that it can be turned into an empirical "indicative," into an indicative of psychological statements. Rather to the Reformers, as to Paul in the sixth chapter of the Epistle to the Romans, it remains a "paradoxical indicative," an indicative which does not describe an empirical effect, but which may only be ventured in the act of faith itself, and is therefore always at the same time an imperative. This meaning of justification v. Oettingen alone has perceived—although

[1] FRANK: *System der christlichen Sittlichkeit*, pp. 181 and 180.
[2] Ibid., pp. 224–5.   [3] Ibid., p. 179.   [4] Ibid., p. 179.

even he has not seen this quite clearly—and therefore his ethic has not fallen into the error of eudaemonism on the one hand nor into that of individualism on the other. This, too, is why it has received a realistic character (which makes it stand out so favourably from the ideology and remoteness from life of the others), and which was worked out in his epoch-making work: "Moral Statistics." His "ethical teaching," however, was not understood at that time; the best ethical achievement of the nineteenth century was unnoticed until the present day(13). Frequently we shall have occasion to return to his work. The fatal individualism of that ethic of "Lutheranism" which in many respects is otherwise so valuable, which is only the theoretical reflection of the actual attitude of the Lutheran Church of that day towards reality, cannot be made more clearly evident than in the titles which Harless gives to those chapters in which he deals with the problems of society. After dealing for four hundred and fifty pages with the problems of the individual Christian—with the Christian doctrine of sin and virtue—the last one hundred and fifty pages are devoted to the treatment of the social ethic under titles such as "The Preservation of the Soul within the Secular Calling," "The Preservation of Earthly Goods in the Service of the Soul" and the retrospective effects of such "preservations" upon the community. Once more, the central point of the final section, which deals at least with the concrete forms of community, is the individual, in his independence: the fundamental forms of earthly community ordained by God and their relation to the realization of Christian virtue. It is not surprising that all this ethical labour, even though its merits shine out brightly against the background of the ethical rationalism of the period, was able to exercise very little influence upon the people as a whole, or even upon the Lutheran Church itself.

Finally we must turn our attention to a school of thought which perhaps expresses most fully the main ethical ideas of the Bible—in spite of the fact that even there the fullness of the ethic of the Reformation has not been obtained; in accordance with tradition I will call this school of thought the "Biblicistic" type. It is true, of course, that the ethic of Beck, whom we may regard as the father of this school, suffers from the same fundamental errors as those of his orthodox contemporaries: in his teaching also the New Birth is a process which can be psychologically described and empirically conceived; here, too, the connexion or rather the paradoxical unity between the New Birth, justification, and conversion is not perceived; accordingly his ethic also remains in the air, in the descriptive and subjective sphere(14). Beck's school of thought, however, has produced an ethic in which the Divine Command is emphasized with great force, at the expense of the subjective emphasis upon "salvation"; this line of thought therefore really opens up the subject afresh; from this new standpoint it is possible to perceive the relation between ethics and community—I refer to Schlatter's *Christian Ethic*. In this book we find the "living waters" of the thought of the Bible welling up as from a clear spring. Here we find that liberty of mind which is characteristic of a person whose whole way of thinking is controlled by Scripture; here, from every possible point of view, are sane, excellent sayings, springing out of a devout and courageous heart. And yet even this ethic pays the penalty of the fact that the message of the Reformers has not been rightly grasped in its central significance; and therefore, being constantly distorted, it is criticized and rejected(15). This work does not possess the characteristics which ought to distinguish a theological ethic from a simple popular series of exhortations; its arrangement is confused, and the thought lacks unity. The arrangement of material under psychological headings—will, thought, feeling, power—is arbitrary, and throws no real light upon the whole ethical question; and although the personality of the author certainly guarantees a unified point of view on the many—indeed too many—problems which are stated from the *scientific* point of view, this is far from plain. In the last resort this work is simply a collection of "cases," of good Christian pronouncements on all kinds of circumstances; it is not a work based on a unified conception, which, through a creative and unifying process of thought, has become really scientific; it is a work of "edification"—in the good sense of the word—which serves for the practical guidance of the members of the Christian community. What we need to-day, more urgently than ever, is to take up afresh and carry further that work of reflection on the ultimate foundations of ethical existence, to think out afresh the connexion between faith and works, faith and the Christian community, which was effected by the Reformers, in a fashion which has never been attained to the same extent. If to-day—actually through no merit of our own—we stand once more somewhat nearer to the point where they once stood, than did the theology of the previous century, we may then hope, even with our modest powers, to achieve something which will take us a little further(16). We ought not to look down on the work of our predecessors of last century, but it is our duty to try to learn from them. We neither can nor ought to raise the cry "Back to the Reformation!" although certainly we have to go back there to pick up the thread of thought at the place where it was broken off. The "world" and those who are most remote from us theologically have set us questions which were not only unknown in the century immediately preceding our own, but also to the Reformers themselves. But we do believe most certainly that in Luther, Zwingli, and Calvin the knowledge of God, not only in the "dogmatic" but also in the "ethical" sense did break in as at no other time since the days of the Apostles, and we hope to be able to show by examples how brightly this light shines even to-day upon our problems. To know this we regard as the distinctive calling of the ethical thinker of to-day, and fidelity to this vocation our highest duty.

BOOK TWO

THE DIVINE COMMAND

SECTION I: THE WILL OF GOD AS THE BASIS AND NORM OF THE GOOD

THE Word of God, so far as our will is concerned, is the Command of God. In faith God claims us for His will. He gives us no other faith than that through which we are laid hold of by Him in the "obedience of faith."[1] And the gift of God is not known to us save in the fact that in the word of His grace He calls us at the same time to Himself, and thus into His service. We *may* believe, we *can* believe—this is God's word of grace; we *ought* to believe—this is His Command. *This* is His real, primary, all-inclusive commandment. The *Law*, the laws of the Bible and of "conscience" can be perceived by everyone; the Divine *Command*, however, can only be perceived by him to whom God Himself speaks His Word, in faith. The Law, so far as its content is concerned, is severed from the grace of God; the Command, however, can only be understood as the address of the gracious and generous God, who claims me for Himself the gracious Giver, that I may *belong* to Him. Hence I cannot know beforehand the content of the Command as I can know that of the Law; I can only receive it afresh each time through the voice of the Spirit(1).

There is such a close connexion between faith and the hearing of the Command that we might almost regard both as one. We never gain faith save by hearing the invitation to "Come!" The Command: "Believe!" precedes every act of faith. And yet "believing" simply means the receptive attitude of one who trusts God implicitly, not the strenuous activity of one who is "ordered" to do this or that. Faith and obedience, the word of grace and the Command, are indissolubly connected, so that the one can only be understood in relation to the other. And yet we must and can distinguish between them. The promise of grace and faith refer to my being as it is determined apart from myself; the Divine Command and obedience refer to my being, *not* apart from myself, but as it ought to be determined by means of my will—that is, my being as it ought to express itself in action on the basis of that which has been given to it by God. *Faith* has to do with that which has *come into being* through the act of God—

[1] Rom. i. 5.

or that which is regarded as about to be brought into being in the future—*obedience*, with that which has not yet come into being. Upon the boundary which separates the past from the future, at the present moment, faith looks backward to that which has been realized by God, obedience looks forward to that which has not yet been realized, but in such a way that even faith only gains that realization through obedience, and in such a way that even obedience, from the vantage ground of faith, only sees before it the first step it has to take.

For the *obedience of faith* is quite different from that of the Law; the Command is not the Law. What the Bible calls "the Commandments" do not primarily constitute *the* Command, although, certainly, the "Commandments" do help us to hear the Command. For us the Commandments are primarily the *Law*, and they only become the Divine Command through faith, through the perception of the God who here and now calls us to Himself. Only then do we become aware of its meaning, which we could not really know beforehand, although certainly the Law which is known beforehand ought to lead us to this perception. The Divine Command gathers up into itself the meaning of all laws; likewise it implies this twofold demand: "Come to Me, in faith, and now take the next step, the first one you can see before you!" All the "Commandments" point towards the one "Command": "Love God—and your neighbour." But that also is law, the supreme law, and I can only learn what it means at the moment at which God calls me; I can never know it beforehand. In the following chapters we shall be dealing with this Command as the basis of the Good as a whole.

In what has just been said the real meaning of this Command has been merely suggested, and the direction in which we are to look has been indicated. But we have not said what takes place at that point. Ultimately—it is impossible to say this, but—penultimately—it is possible to say a great deal about it; and without this "penultimate" truth we shall never understand the "ultimate" truth in this matter. In the sixteen chapters of this book nothing will be discussed save this Command; and yet each of these chapters is intended finally to come to a head indicating a point, which the head itself does not touch. Sixteen spokes in a wheel—but in the centre is the hole, and the usefulness of the wheel depends upon the hole—to use once again Thurneysen's profound simile of the Chinese sage.[1] Sixteen times I shall begin "to say it," and yet I shall never be able to say "it," any more than anyone will be able to hear "it," who has not also first of all heard the penultimate truth. What *we* are able to say is related to that which God alone can say—even where we are dealing with the "content of faith"—as the law and the word of grace, that which can be known beforehand and the language of the Spirit. To make this clear is the actual aim and purpose of this work on ethics.

[1] *Komm Schöpfer Geist*, p. 148.

CHAPTER XI

THE DIVINE COMMAND AS GIFT AND DEMAND

PROPOSITION: *We know God's will only through His revelation, in His own Word. Therefore His Command is also primarily a gift, and as such a demand.*

1. There is no such thing as an "intrinsic Good"(2). The hypostatization of a human conception of the Good as the "Idea of the Good" is not only an abstraction in the logical sense; it is due to the fact that man has been severed from his Origin, to that original perversion of the meaning of existence, which consists in the fact that man attributes to himself and his ideas an independent existence—that is, that man makes himself God. This personal estrangement from God transforms personal union with Him into an impersonal abstract idea; thus "the Good," the "Idea of the Good," "the Law," becomes the principle of life, an abstract idea, which has no vital connexion with life and therefore does violence to life. For the *Idea* of the Good did not create life(3), it has no interest in life. It is an alien force which has invaded life; yet it is not a living force, it is merely the shadow of the real force, namely, the will of God. It is He who unites what is with what ought to be, He, the Creator of Nature and of the spirit, of all that exists and of ideas; His will is the source of that which is and the basis of that which ought to be. The fact that (as we all know only too well) a terrible gulf yawns between that which is and that which ought to be, that the relation between them is not merely that of the imperfect to the perfect, but that they are actually in opposition to one another, was not always so—it is the result of that original perversion of truth—of which we become aware in the sense of Fate and Guilt.

Therefore of ourselves we cannot know the Good or the Will of God. It is, of course, true that God manifests Himself as the incomprehensible One, mighty and wise in the works of His creation, with an impressiveness which, even in the most unseeing, awakens awe in the presence of the mystery of the universe, and fills with wonder everyone who has not entirely lost the child-spirit. But being what we are, with our limited vision, this manifestation is not enough to reveal to us the will of the mysterious power which rules in Nature(4).

Nature speaks with two voices—and the heathen know this better than we do, for they are more defenceless in the presence of nature than we are—kindly and terrible, maintaining and destroying life. But even human nature, the human spirit, and its innermost sanctuary, the *conscience*(5), does not know God's will. It is of course true that every one knows "something of the divine"; I suppose everyone makes the distinction between good and evil—with that amazing precision which shows itself especially in criticism of others. But this knowledge always includes an element of ignorance, of misunderstanding, which is the counterpart of man's original sinful misunderstanding of his own nature: that is, that the Good is that which God demands from us, which we have to achieve in our own strength. Man of himself knows God's Law, it is true, but not His Command, and because he does not know the Law as His Command, he does not rightly know the meaning of the Law, which is love.

2. God reveals His own Nature where He manifests Himself as the Giver of life, as the Creator of the Good, where at one and the same time He gives salvation and goodness, life and love. He reveals Himself in a world which misunderstands both God and man, by making a new beginning, in order that He may deliver man from this twofold misunderstanding. God reveals His will, the Good, His self-giving, love itself, not only where He gives us "something"—as He does every day in the ordinary processes of nature—but where He gives Himself. In this event the meaning of the word "love" is defined afresh, and indeed in such a way that only those who understand this event as the real self-giving of God understand the meaning of love. That which *we* call "love" is always a conditional self-giving, whether it be the love of a mother, or the love of country, or the love of an idea. It is always a love which is limited by some secret demand for compensation, or by some relic of exclusiveness. It is never unconditional. The message of Jesus Christ is the message of an historical fact; "the Word was made flesh"—this means that God loves us without any conditions at all. The very fact that this has happened, that in this happening God is the One who acts, makes the love there manifested unconditional. The word "Love" acquires its new meaning through the fact that in Jesus, the "Suffering Servant of the Lord," *God* comes to us. It is thus that God reveals to us His Nature and His Will.

It is His will to *give*. Therefore He can only be revealed in the reality of His giving. It is His will to give Himself, to give His life to man, and in so doing to give salvation, satisfaction, and blessedness. To the extent in which this act of self-giving is achieved, His will is accomplished, and this act of fulfilment also carries with it the restoration of the perverted order of existence. In this event the life of man is once again placed within the orbit of the Divine giving, and in this it becomes good. *The Good consists simply and solely in the fact* that man receives and deliberately accepts his life as a gift from God, as life dependent on "grace," as the state of "being justified" because it has been granted as a gift, as "justification by faith." Only thus can we know the Will of God, that is, in this revelation of Himself in which He manifests Himself as disinterested, generous Love.

3. But this Divine giving is not accomplished in any magical way; it simply takes place in the fact that *God "apprehends" man*; God *claims* us for His love, for His generous giving. But this means that He claims our whole existence for Himself, for this love of His; He gives us His love. He gives us His love in such a way that He captures us completely by the power of His love. *To belong* to Him, to this love, and through His love, means that we are the *bondslaves*[1] of this will. To believe means to become a captive, to become His property, or rather, to know that we are His property. The revelation which makes it plain that the will of God is lavish in giving *to* man, makes it equally clear that His will makes a demand *on* man. His will *for* us also means that He wants something *from* us. He claims us for His love. This is His Command. It is the *"new* commandment," because only now can man perceive that it is the command of One who gives before He demands, and who only demands something from us in the act of giving Himself to us.

He claims us for His love, for the love with which He loves the world and man, for His sovereign love, His purpose of absolute love. That God claims us for *Himself* means that He claims us for the *Kingdom of God*, for a love which is absolutely universal and unlimited. His "glory" means that we recognize Him as the Sole Giver, and as the Giver of all life. His "holiness" means that He alone is supreme, so that

---

[1] The play on the words *gehören* (to belong) and *hörig* (to be bound to another, even to the point of serfdom) cannot be reproduced in English.—Tr.

resistance to His will can only spell misery. But it is also His will to assert Himself and exercise His will as the Supreme Giver, and this is His "love." Apart from holiness the love of God would not be unlimited, it would not be the only ground of life, it would not be the love of *God*. But God possesses no other holiness than this: that He wills to be known absolutely in His real nature, namely, as the absolute Supreme Lord over His Kingdom, as the One who alone possesses life, and the Good, and gives it to man. Therefore the demands of love can never be separated from the claims of God Himself(6).

4. He claims us for *His* love, not for an *idea* of love—and not for a conception of the divine love which can be gained from merely reading the Bible. He claims us for His present, living activity of love, which can only be, and must always remain, His work. Therefore we can never know beforehand what God will require. God's command can only be perceived at the actual moment of hearing it. It would denote a breaking away from obedience if we were to think of the Divine Command as one which had been enacted once for all, to be interpreted by us in particular instances. To take this line would mean reverting to the legalistic distortion of His love. Love would then have become a "principle." The *free* love of God requires us to remain *free*, that we may be freely at His disposal. *You* cannot say what it means to love here and now; *He* alone can tell you what this means for you at this moment.

The Good is simply what *God* wills that we should do, not that which we would do on the basis of a principle of love. God wills to do something quite definite and particular through us, here and now, something which no other person could do at any other time. Just as the commandment of love is absolutely universal so also it is absolutely individual. But just as it is absolutely individual so also it is absolutely devoid of all caprice. "I will guide thee with Mine eye."[1] No one can experience this "moment" save I myself. The Divine Command is made known to us "in the secret place." Therefore it is impossible for us to know it beforehand; to wish to know it beforehand—legalism—is an infringement of the divine honour. The fact that the holiness of God must be remembered when we dwell on His love[2] means that we

---

[1] Psalm xxxii. 8.
[2] Cf. *The Mediator*, pp. 281 ff. and 467 ff. (Eng. trans.).

cannot have His love at our disposal, that it cannot ever be perceived as a universal principle, but only in the act in which He speaks to us Himself; even in His love He remains our *Master* and Lord. But He is our "Lord" in the sense that He tells us Himself what it means to "love," here and now.

It is, of course, true that we know God's love in His Word which is also a *deed*, in the Holy Scriptures. But this Word which has actually occurred as an event can only be perceived as *His* word which is now living and active—Jesus can only be known as the Christ and as "my Lord"—through the Holy Spirit.[1] This applies not only to the knowledge of that which God wills *for* us, but also to that which He desires to have *from* us. There is no faith, as such, apart from conduct. Real faith always means obedience to God; it means a living obedience, offered here and now, at this actual moment of time, to His loving will, which has an absolute and special significance at this particular moment. If faith does not issue in such obedience it loses its meaning, and is perverted—it becomes a mere theory; obedience, too, becomes mere ethical legalism if it is not based on faith of this kind.

5. The fact that God claims us for Himself, is His love, His grace, but even so His claim is still His Command. In a Christian ethic we are not dealing with "counsels"(7) nor with exhortations, nor with "values"(8), with something which we "prefer"—no, here we are confronted by a Command which must be taken in dead earnest. The fact that the Apostles exhort rather than command—which, rightly, is regarded as a distinction between the Old Testament and the New—does not mean that the imperative character of the Divine claim has been in any way modified. The form of the exhortation is simply intended to remind us of the ground on which the Divine claim is based; that is, that every believer can indeed know the will of God for himself, through his faith in Christ. The apostolic exhortation implies that the believer is no longer a minor, and it sweeps away all legalistic heteronomy. Not even an Apostle can tell you what you ought to do; God Himself is the only One who can tell you this. There is to be no intermediary between ourselves and the Divine Will. God wishes to deal with us "personally," not through any medium.

Similarly, the difference between a command and a pro-

[1] 1 Cor. xii. 3.

hibition is not a matter of great importance. Every command is a prohibition and *vice versa*. Indeed, we may say that the distinction is only important to the extent in which the positive form of the Command—which predominates in the New Testament—points to the fact that God's relation to the world, as its Creator, is primarily positive and creative, not negative; hence we too, in the obedience of faith, are absorbed into this positive action of God. As the will of the Creator God's will is essentially positive; He does not will nothingness, the All-One, or Nirvana, but the world. Even in the New Testament there are plenty of prohibitions, and it is precisely the "hymn of Love" (i Cor. xiii) which conceives the commandment of love in a remarkably negative way, because truly Divinely ordered action in love can only take place as it breaks the natural tendency of our will.

6. God's will controls absolutely *everything*. He claims us and our whole existence. Hence both these statements are true: there are *no* "Adiaphora"(9), and—everything is "adiaphoron"—save love. *Dilige et fac quod vis*. Everything is mechanical and therefore neutral—save the ordering of this mechanical sphere by love. And nothing is merely mechanical, since everything, even the very smallest thing, is connected with the whole, and is impregnated with a certain spirit. The Divine Command is imposed on every moment; there are no moral holidays. All life, the "natural" or material, as well as the spiritual, comes under the sovereign sway of God; indeed even the suffering caused by something which we cannot alter is not excepted from this sovereignty; for God also wishes us to offer Him our endurance and our patience, our grateful acceptance, our reverent longing and our requests for His help.

7. It is *His* will that God wills to accomplish in the world; He is not the servant of some purpose outside Himself. God Himself is His own End. In His love, however, He sets up an End outside Himself—without ceasing to be His own End; this "end" is the communion of the creature with Himself, the Creator. This Divine will for "community" is God's Sovereign Will. Therefore salvation, beatitude, the fulfilment of the purpose of life, both for humanity as a whole, and for the individual, is included in God's royal purpose. The tables of prohibition in the Bible may be compared with the notices on power circuits: Do Not Touch! Because God wills to control our life, He commands and He forbids.

This is the "eudaemonism" of the Gospel, and at the same time its absolutely serious view of duty. God wills our true happiness; but *He* wills it, and He wills it in such a way that no one else knows what His will is. It remains outside our disposal, and indeed we do not know it. We never know what is right for us, nor what is best for the other person. We go astray when we think that we can deduce this from some principle or another, or from some experience, and we distort the thought of the divine love if we think that we know what He ought to do for us in accordance with His love. But of one thing we may be quite sure: His will is love, even when we do not understand it—when He commands. as well as when He gives.

Therefore in His revelation God's will is expressed by His sanctions, by rewards and punishments. God alone gives life; to be with Him is life, to resist Him is ruin. It is impossible to exist apart from God; it is impossible to be neutral towards Him. He who is not for Him is against Him. God's Command means eternal life and God means nothing else than this. He is Love. But His will is utterly serious; it is the will of the Lord of Life and Death. Anyone who—finally—resists Him, will only dash himself to pieces against the rock of His Being. This is the holiness of the love of God. As the divine love cannot be separated from His gift of life, so the Holiness of God cannot be separated from His judicial wrath, the denial and destruction of life. To have a share in the will of God, in the sense of union with His will, means salvation; to resist Him spells utter disaster.

The abstract legalistic system of ethics, because ideas have no connexion with life, can only judge this connexion of the moral element with reward and punishment as heteronomy, as the perversion of the moral endeavour. "We ought to do the Good for the sake of the Good"(10). It does not perceive that behind this phrase, "for the sake of the Good," there lies concealed, "for My sake." And it does not understand that the Good is done for the sake of the Good when it is done for the sake of God, in obedience to the Divine Command. We ought to obey God because He commands it, not because obedience means happiness and disobedience means unhappiness. Faith would not be faith, obedience would not be obedience, if things were otherwise. But obedience would not be obedience towards *God*, did we not know that His Command means life and His prohibition death. The primary concern is not that which refers to my Ego, to my life; no, the primary concern is this: that it is God's will, the will of Him to whom my life belongs. But that which refers to *me*, that which refers to *my* life, is the necessary second element for it concerns the will of Him who Himself is life—even *my* life. Obedience would be impure if this second element were made the first. But it would be unreal, and indeed impossible, if this second element, as the second, were not combined with the first. We cannot do anything good which has no significance for life, and we cannot avoid anything evil, unless at the same time we know it to be harmful. It is not the question whether all morality is not mingled with self-interest—without self-interest nothing would concern us at all—but the question is this: is this self-interest regarded as founded in God or in myself? To do the Good for the sake of the Good is only a pale reflection of the genuine Good; to do the Good for the sake of God means to do the Good not because my moral dignity requires it, but because it is that which is commanded by God.

CHAPTER XII

THE COMMAND OF THE CREATOR AND REDEEMER

PROPOSITION: *Since the Divine Command is absolutely concrete, it cannot be formulated in general terms. But since the will of God which demands obedience is the same as His will which gives, He cannot command anything but the obedient imitation[1] of His activity as Creator and Redeemer.*

1. What does God command? Only those who have a legalistic conception of the Good can imagine that they possess the answer to this question. God's Command is His free and sovereign act of commanding, which cannot be condensed into a regulation. But dangerous as it is to be in bondage to the legalism of orthodoxy, it is just as dangerous to fall into the opposite error of a fanatical antinomianism, which holds that it is impossible to lay down any rules at all, that it is impossible to have any knowledge beforehand of the content of the Divine Command. The will of God, which alone is the Good, is made known to us in His action, in His *revelation*. This Divine process of revelation, however, is not only present, nor is it only past; in fact, it is present, based on the past. We know God through His present speech—in the Holy Scriptures. He is the same yesterday, to-day, and for ever, and this not only in what He gives but also in what He demands. But in His historical revelation He has made Himself known to us as the Creator and Redeemer. Thus in this unity of His revelation He is the God of the Bible, the God who is revealed to us in Jesus Christ. As Creator He is the beginning and the ground of all existence, the source of all life; as Redeemer He is the End, the Goal, towards which all existence tends.

Precisely on the borderline between the past and the future stands the *present moment*, the moment of decision. The will of God which approaches us from the past differs from the will of God which calls to us from the future goal; it is different in its content, but its aim is the same. The work of the Creator differs from that of the Redeemer. The will of God is indeed only one, but we can only understand it in this twofold character. We see likewise how God looks at us both from the beginning and from the end, how He looks at this central

[1] Eph. v. 1.

point—which we call the "present"—which stands midway between the past and the future; it is this "present" moment which is so "pregnant" in ethical significance. We cannot control either the past or the future; all that we *can* control is this point, which we call "now." Owing to the fact that, for us, time is divided into the past and the future on the boundary line of the present, we are obliged to conceive of God and His action in a twofold conception, although in God Himself this action is only *one*. But for the very same reason this conception can *only* be twofold. For by our own act of free decision we divide time—which is nothing in itself—into past and future. Anyone who tries to bring in, as a third element, the idea of the Divine Reconciliation, shows that he has missed the ethical meaning of both conceptions.

Rather it is the Divine Reconciliation which is the centre of time, in Creation and Redemption, in which God reveals Himself to us as Creator and Redeemer; therefore our ethical moment of time is time controlled by the Divine Reconciliation; it is the time which lies "between" the Fall and the Resurrection, and is therefore an "interim" ethic; indeed, all genuine Protestant ethics is "interim ethics"(1). Only in the Reconciliation achieved by Jesus Christ do we understand what Creation and Redemption mean. Where these words are used apart from Jesus Christ they have a wholly different meaning. The Creator and the Redeemer whom we know, we know through Jesus Christ alone(2). And the Reconciliation is accomplished by the fact that in Him God espouses our cause as Creator and Redeemer; in the same fact we learn to understand whence we came and what is our eternal destiny. There, in the centre of history, which through faith in "Christ our Righteousness" becomes "now," we know what God wills in that central point, midway between the past and the future, where we stand and have to act.[1]

2. As Creator God is our absolute Lord and the Lord of all existence. In Him alone the existence of the world, and the manner in which it exists, is based. This world, as it is—in spite of everything—is God's world. It is *this world* which He wills, His creation. This life in its incomprehensible variety, this individual, incalculable, irrational, "accidental" existence, is *not* accidental—however little we can understand the fact that this life is not accidental; it is what it is through the will

[1] Cf. my article: *Das Einmalige und der Existenzcharakter*, in *Blätter für deutsche Philosophie*, 1929.

of God. He did not merely will it once, He wills it still. "What our God has created He will also maintain." This is His kindness as Creator, that He loves us just as we are—in spite of everything—that He "makes His sun to shine upon the evil and upon the good."[1] He fills all that lives with His goodness. He gives us this world as our sphere of activity.

Thus because He gives us this world, because in it His will meets us, He claims from us *reverence* for all that is. For the sake of God, because it is His Creation, we should have reverence for every creature. I do not mean "reverence for life" as an ultimate mystical principle(3). This direct reverence for life as the divine does not perceive the distinction between the Creator and the creature; it is pantheistic and its ethical influence. is disintegrating. Life claims our reverence not in itself but as the Divine Creation; therefore we are not to reverence life in a mechanically uniform manner, but in the various "grades" or "degrees" ordered by the Creator.

It is His will that we should distinguish and retain degrees as well as differences. We ought to deal more freely with lifeless material than with living beings, with the lower forms of existence than with the higher forms; for the real object of His self-imparting will in creation is man, the being which alone perceives the call of God and therefore is "laid hold of" by God, over which therefore we have no right of disposal at all. Hence our attitude towards human life above all should be one of reverent awe, a sense that here we have no right to interfere. We ought to reverence the life of the criminal, the cripple and the idiot—since they also are God's creatures.

3. But we should not only *feel* reverence, we· ought to *meet* this existence with reverence. Practically, this means that we should not deal with it according to our own will, but that we should recognize the will of God which speaks to us in it and obey His command in it. Thus the will of God does not meet us in a sphere of duty which hovers above the plane of our present existence, but it meets us in the very heart of existence itself. The world, that which is not "I," is not something material, needing to be shaped and moulded by us. To think it is betrays an impertinent, arrogant habit of mind springing from the delusion that man is a god. The world is not a shapeless mass of matter, it is not a chaos which we have to reduce to form and order. It was formed long ago;

[1] Matt. v. 45.

it is given to us in a rich variety of form. In its *form* the will of God is stamped upon that which exists. We ought to understand this existing shape or order as the expression of the Divine Will, first of all as a gift, and because it is a gift also as a demand. The demand is this: we are to allow ourselves to be limited by this given form, and to respond to the claim which it lays upon us through the existence which it shares with us, and through that in which it is distinct from us. We are to range ourselves within this order.

This applies not only to our natural existence, but also to our historical existence. For this also has been created by God. Even history has been given to us by the providential will of Him apart from whom "not a sparrow shall fall to the ground." Were we to separate that which has come into being through the direct action of God in creation from that which is due to the indirect action of man, in the course of history, we could never maintain: "I, this particular human being, am created by God!" That condition (which we all know quite well apart from faith altogether) in which we seem to be tossed hither and thither on the ocean of Fate,[1] is seen, in the light of faith, to be under the control of God's will as our Creator. What the world regards as "accident" or "Fate," faith knows to be God's creation and His providence. For this reason alone the place in the world—in the natural and in the historical sense—in which we stand, at which our decision must take place, is not accidental, but it is that which has been appointed to us. Therefore God's command for the actual moment reaches us through the world around us, with all its pressure and its restrictions. Even the historically "given" must be regarded primarily as God's Command, telling us to adjust ourselves to it. Since it is the will of God to "conserve" life,[2] we should do so as well. We, too, are bound to "preserve"—in our own appointed place—"what our God has created" in all the world around us: in the animate or inanimate creation, in human or animal life.

4. But the Creator whom *we* know differs from the One who exists in the pagan conception of the universe. Therefore the command "to preserve," which we have received, is "conservative" in a different sense from that in which the word is usually employed. We simply need to look steadily at a "conservative" ethical system, a conservative ethic,

---

[1] Literally *Schicksalsgeworfenheit*. Heidegger.—TR.
[2] Literally "is fundamentally conservative" (*grundkonservativ*).—TR.

"conservative" in the pagan sense (as, for instance, the ancient Chinese ethic), in order to perceive what we cannot mean by "conservative." In an ethic of this kind, with its naturalistic conception of God and of the world, the Given is altogether one with what God wills. This kind of conservative ethic has no knowledge of sin, nor of the redeeming God and His coming Kingdom. Where God, as Creator, is made known in Jesus Christ, man sees not only that God has created the world, but also that it is sinful. The only world we know is a sinful world; all its forms of existence and all its ordinances are sinful. This means that we only recognize the Divine Creation as it is broken by sin; hence the will of God is never expressed *directly* through it; it only reaches us indirectly. Nothing *real* exists in this world which is not willed by God; but there is also nothing in this world which God does not also not will. He wills it in so far as it is His creation; He does not will it in so far as in it the form of creation has been distorted and spoilt by sin.

But to admit this truth does not cancel the previous statement. Since Creation comes first, and sin comes second, the primary duty of man is to adopt a positive attitude towards life—an attitude of affirmation, acceptance, and adjustment to its claims; the negative attitude of denial takes the second place. And as the action of the Creator is distinctive, apart from which the other element, the action of the Redeemer as a second, distinctive element, cannot be understood, so also the Command of the Creator is distinctive; it demands from us a particular response, and it demands it as a primary duty. We are forbidden to adopt the attitude which has become so usual through Idealism and Rationalism, the attitude which, from the very outset, confronts the world and the concrete circumstances of life with the question: what can we make of it? How can we make it different, or better? First of all we must accept the world, adjust ourselves to it, obey its concrete demands, before we can begin to reform it. The lack of reverence among young people, which is so often bewailed at the present time, ought not to be ascribed to secondary psychological causes—as is often done—but to the disappearance of this fundamental truth; this loss of reverence is indeed due to the rational Idealistic view of man's nature as an independent entity. The modern man no longer knows what it means to be placed within an appointed order, and to adjust himself to it(4).

5. Once this point has been made clear—and only then—must we emphasize our second point, namely: that the God who created the world, created it for an *End*. We cannot simply accept the world as it is, not merely because it has become sinful, but because God wills to perfect His Creation. But when we consider God's will from the point of view of His Final Purpose, it looks quite different from the same will viewed from the standpoint of the original Creation. We do not understand the "end" God has in store unless we understand the "beginning," that is, the Creation. But we also misunderstand the beginning, the Creation, if we know nothing of the End. It is, of course, quite true that it is inaccurate to say that it is the idea of Redemption and not that of Creation(5) which is the standard and the distinctive feature of the Christian Faith. The idea of Redemption exists outside Christianity, in India, for instance; hence an ethical system also exists which is controlled by this point of view. But this idea of redemption, and the ethic which is based upon it, differs just as much from the thought of the Bible as Chinese conservatism differs from it. Since this form of religion contains no belief in the Creator, its idea of redemption is disintegrating in its effects; the ethic which it produces works out in abandonment of "the world," that is, in asceticism(6).

But the Command of the Redeemer, who wills to perfect the world, also means a very critical and challenging attitude towards the world in its present state. To identify the will of God with things as they are would be to turn the Image of God into a devilish caricature, and adaptation to the world would mean the service of the devil. By such "preservation" we would not only preserve that which God does not will, namely sin, but we would be maintaining the Divine Creation in a state which is contrary to the Divine Will. For God has planned His creation for an end which is still unrealized, and it is His will that His purpose for this world shall be accomplished. Therefore *nothing* that exists, as such, and as it now is, is God's order and command; rather in that which now exists we always have to seek first of all for God's order and His Command. To claim any existing order as God's order is a pagan conservatism, which is contrary to the Divine Command.

Indeed, we have as much right to say that the Christian Ethos is *revolutionary* as to say that it is conservative. Just as we have a share in the work of "preservation" through the command of the Creator, so also we have a share in the work of the "new creation" through the command of the Redeemer. "The fashion of this world passeth away."[1] "Behold, I make all things new."[2] Therefore: "Be not fashioned according to this world; but be ye *transformed* by the renewing of your mind."[3] A Christian is a person who not only *hopes* for the Kingdom of God, but one who, because he hopes for it, also does something in this world already, which he who has not this hope does not do. Fanatical Chiliasm, which makes the end of all history itself into an historical event, is neither better nor worse than a lazy conservatism and quietism which regards the world as it now is as unalterable, because it lies under the law of death and of Original Sin. In the world of history the Kingdom of God has made its beginning in Jesus Christ, even though in the paradox of the glory of the Crucified; in the world of history the Risen Lord, even though hidden, wills to build His Kingdom by means of men as His instruments. But in this world the Kingdom of God and the Kingdom of the devil will be in conflict till the Last Day. And this will always be the actual ethical situation, at any given moment of time, so long as history remains. This fact sets a definite limit to the possibilities of man's creative activity in this sphere.

6. How can it be possible for conduct to be *at the same time* both "conservative" and "revolutionary"? To assert that both points of view are justified ought not to lead to the one being neutralized by the other. The command of the Creator and the command of the Redeemer each requires a particular mode of expression, in spite of the fact that the one can only be known at the same time as the other. This does not mean that there are two commandments which we have to obey, as if we had to obey alternately the will of the Creator and the will of the Redeemer. It is, however, true, that according to the point of view of each there is a distinction. As the creator assigns us our existence, and our sphere of life, so also God, as our Creator, summons us to submit to the concrete actuality of this existence in a particular sphere and way of life. He tells us in *what sphere* we have to act. In so doing He gives our activity a basis of solid reality. The will of the Redeemer, on the other hand, gives motive and direction to our conduct. As those who are set by the Creator in this real

[1] I Cor. vii. 31. [2] Rev. xxi. 5. [3] Rom. xii. 2.

world we are not only bound to it, but we are to be consciously united with it. "Brothers, remain true to the earth"—this word of the "Anti-Christ" is quite Scriptural. But we are to be faithful to "the earth" as those who through faith belong to the world to come, to the new aeon, in which all creaturely bondage will be done away. We are to act "on the spot," in accordance with the "situation"; we are committed to "realism." But the reason for this behaviour must be in harmony with the Divine will of redemption, that is, love. For from the point of view of redemption in Jesus Christ we know that love is the basis of the Creation; for "all things were created through Him and unto Him,"[1] in whom we know the will of God. Love, then, is the only possible union of the "conservative" and the "revolutionary" elements, which does not emphasize the one at the expense of the other.

To *love* a human being means to accept his existence, as it is given to me by God, and thus to love him *as he is*. For only if I love him thus, that is, as this particular sinful person, do I love *him*. For this is what he really is. Otherwise I love an idea—and in the last resort this means that I am merely loving myself.[2] I can only love a person by allowing myself to be disturbed by him as he is, and wherever he may come into contact with me, in order that I may make his claim on life my own—and especially in that which does not coincide with my own desires. But if we love like this how can we forget that this our fellow-man is not what he ought to be, how can we forget what a goal has been made known even to him in Christ? And how can this knowledge fail to be painfully critical, and yet hopeful and expectant, and directed towards this end? Therefore to include him within the love of Christ—and this alone is what it means to love truly—also means first of all to accept him, and then to try to lead him towards the goal he has not yet seen.

But even so the concrete situation has not been yet taken into account. Indeed "man," or "I, as man," does not really exist; rather my fellow-man meets me as the member of an order—in his particular "class"(7) and "calling," just as I likewise meet him as the member of an order in my "class" and "calling." It is of course true that I am to meet him as my "Brother Man," just as if there were no "class" or "calling"; but I would not do any real service either to him or to the

---

[1] Col. i. 16.

[2] Cf. GOGARTEN: *Wider die Ächtung der Autorität*, p. 34.

others to whom I am indebted, were I to ignore what the order in which we meet each other requires of us. I must render to him not only that which he requires, but also that which is in accordance with his "situation," which is always (although as it were in a reflection) *my* situation too. So far as motive is concerned the only valid reason for my interest in him is the fact that he is my brother. But *how* this is to be realized is determined by the concrete situation in which I have to deal with him in accordance with this actual situation, even when such action may simply consist in the fact that his situation must be altered. It is legalistic, abstract, Utopian idealism to leave out this concrete situation; it means giving no heed to the command of the Creator. But, on the other hand, it is lazy worldliness to do merely what is required by the claims of our order, without trying to attack all that is contrary to God within this situation with the whole energy of love.

7. As Creator God preserves the world with His long-suffering "Yea"; as Redeemer He grasps it, breaks it, and re-creates it. *How* does God do this? He does this in Jesus Christ, in that act of judgment which is at the same time forgiveness, in that act of acceptance and justification which is at the same time renewal, in the sacrifice of the Cross. The divine love is to be known as that which enters into the world, by sacrifice, in order to tear it out of its present accursèd existence.

Thus God's Command becomes known to us as the demand to give ourselves to the world for the sake of the gift of Christ, for God's sake, that we may give a glimpse of the aim which lies beyond this mortal life. He who sacrifices himself pours himself out on the world as the Divine creation; indeed, he pours himself out for the God to whom we belong. But he who sacrifices himself is also quite free from the world, from the curse of seeking the world. This sacrifice is the right way of adjustment and of protest. As the "salt of the earth" it is our function to preserve; through self-devotion we are to attack.

But this self-giving or self-sacrifice must not be interpreted as a principle. For it is impossible to define in legalistic terms what it means to "sacrifice" in any concrete, given instance, or to define how this aggressive and conserving activity is to be carried on. In any case, here the meaning of "sacrifice" is quite different from the meaning which it contains where "sacrifice" is regarded as a principle, that is, in asceticism, which may be in accordance with mysticism and pantheism, but is not in harmony with belief in God the Creator. True sacrifice consists in serving the world within the various "orders" of Society, and, moreover, of wholly personal service to the individual.

CHAPTER XIII

THE UNITY AND THE VARIETY OF THE DIVINE COMMAND

PROPOSITION: *The basis of the Divine Command is always the same, but its content varies with varying circumstances.*[1] *The "Commandments" of the Bible witness to the concrete Divine Command which has been proclaimed; they are thus authoritative expositions of the One Command. Casuistry in ethics is a legalistic distortion of the Divine Command. Ethics can only prepare the way for decision; it cannot anticipate it.*

1. The will of God is made known to us in His revelation in Jesus Christ as a single will which always and everywhere wills the same. As the One who imparts Himself unconditionally, as Love, He wills to be known and recognized by us. In this self-communication He wills to make Himself known and to rule as "the One He is." His *Holiness* is the intense seriousness with which He wills Himself unconditionally, and accordingly wills to possess us. To live as though He did not exist is disobedience, and spells destruction to man, for He alone is Life, and in his Love He wills to impart His life to us. But this does not mean that God has a "double decree"(1), which we have to recognize and then proclaim. The fact that those who ignore God are shattered by the holiness of God, does not mean that this is a "second" will of God; this "other" will is that in which we do not know God as He wills to be known, it is the will of the *Deus absconditus*, His "hidden will"; the only aspect of this "hidden will" of God which concerns us is the reminder that it *is* possible to remain oblivious to the Call of God, and therefore in ignorance of His Will. God only appears "angry" to one who does not know Him in His love, and refuses to be drawn within the orbit of His forgiving love.

2. Hence the Divine Command is *one* and one alone, namely, to acknowledge this God as the God who *is*, to know that He is *our* God; it is the "first commandment": "I am the Lord thy God, thou shalt have none other Gods but Me." That is: to believe in God as the only Centre, as the Origin and End of our life, upon whose love and grace alone our life is based, and in which it is made complete, to fear Him

---

[1] Literally "The Divine Command is always one in its *Why*, and another in its *What*."—TR.

and to love Him. The love which God commands is the love which He Himself is and which He gives. To love Him truly means to let oneself be loved by Him; this is faith, and it is the fulfilment of the first Commandment.[1]

We are never bidden to do anything else. "Love is the fulfilling of the law."[2] From this point of view this obedience-of-faith-in-love alone is the "moral"; everything else—from the ethical point of view—is technique, that is, the search for, and the use of, means which make this love real. The daring saying of Augustine: *Dilige et fac quod vis*, simply means that love is the fulfilling of the law. But directly this Command becomes law it becomes a judgment on all our action. For which of us loves as God loves? The commandment of love cannot be realized as law, but only in faith in the love into which we are drawn and in which we are forgiven. We can love only "through the Holy Spirit," only when *God Himself* takes possession of us, by His love, and does *His* work through us.

3. "And the other is like unto it: Thou shalt love thy neighbour as thyself."[3] The love of God includes the love of man; therefore to be laid hold of by His will, to be freely obedient to His will, means to love our neighbour. There are no "duties towards God" and "duties towards man"(2). There is only the *one* "duty": to love God. And this one duty of loving God is itself the other duty of loving our neighbour. The love of God, His surrender of Himself to man, comes to meet us in the Man Jesus. To love man means to be united to him in love. This alone is the Good. That mystical love of God which is severed from the love of man is something totally different, since it is not based upon the revelation of God in the man Jesus. God does not will to draw any love exclusively to Himself; He wills that we should love Him "in our neighbour"(3).

Where this takes place, God's will is fulfilled—whatever else may happen. But this love is only possible where we do not take it for granted that we know what we owe our neighbour; this kind of love is only possible when we accept our "neighbour" as he is, in the concrete claims laid upon us by the very fact of his existence, when we accept him, in fact, as given to us by God, when we look at him—in the language of Luther—as the "mask" of God, as one in whom God wills

---

[1] Cf. *Die Stellung des ersten Gebotes in Luther's Theologie* in the work by ALTHAUS: *Gottes Gottheit* (*Lutherjahrbuch*, 1931, pp. I–II).

[2] Rom. xiii. 10.   [3] Matt. xxii. 39.

to come into touch with us. Love means the acceptance of love's "bonds," the state of "thraldom" to another. Just as we are held captive by the free, sovereign will of God through the Command of love, and have no right to transform the Command into a law, an independent principle, so also we are united to our neighbour by the Command of love, which excludes all legalistic general rules and every attempt to stereotype human relationships. Thus where our neighbour is concerned there are no isolated "duties," but only the *one* duty—to do to him what the love of God wills should be done to him here and now; thus to fulfil the claim which our neighbour has on us, as he is, here and now. It is love which does not steal, does not kill, does not lie, does not commit adultery, but does its best for its neighbour(4).

4. This is why God is always bidding us do some particular thing, something which cannot be done at any other time, something quite new. God's Command does not vary in *intention*, but it varies in *content*, according to the conditions with which it deals. The error of casuistry does not lie in the fact that it indicates the infinite variety of forms which the Command of love may assume; its error consists in deducing particular laws from a universal law in ever greater and more scrupulous detail; thus it is wrong because it turns the Divine Command into a Law, and then inevitably into the sum-total of all laws. Casuistry tries to imprison concrete life within a net of "cases" as though all could be arranged beforehand, and thinks it can do this by means of an exposition of the law which is modelled on the lines of a legal code, applied in a similar manner through derivation from a supreme principle(5). Love, however, is free from all this predefinition, for it means being free for God, "relaxed as the arrow in the hunter's bow" (Thurneysen), in the Hand of God, and therefore free for our real neighbour. Love is "occasionalist." She does not know the Good beforehand—and by this very fact she is bound both to God Himself and to her actual neighbour.

The particular decision is not anticipated; it cannot be "looked up" in the ethical law-book. The whole responsibility rests upon the individual himself; this kind of love alone is free from heteronomy, as well as from the self-glorification of autonomy. Therefore in its external appearance it is "opportunistic," "lacking principles," while it too, and it alone, is free from all caprice. Each of its decisions is a "discovery," but each of such "discoveries"—if this love is true and real—is "something given." It is the end of the law, as it is also its fulfilment.

5. What, then, is the meaning and the function of the individual "commandments" in the Bible? whether those of the Decalogue or of the Sermon on the Mount? Why is not the command of love sufficient? Why, instead of this, are we forbidden to kill, to steal, to commit adultery, and why are we told that even the lustful glance is adultery? This question requires a twofold answer. Firstly, the Commandments form part of the revelation of the Divine Will. We can only recognize God's will here and now—as we have already seen[1]—on the basis of the previous historical revelation. "It stands written." The non-legalistic character, the "occasionalism" of love ought never to be understood in the sense of fanaticism. We only know the will of God, here and now, on the basis of His revelation in the Scriptures, in Jesus Christ. The Commandments also belong to this revelation. They are witnesses to His revelation, as is everything in the Scriptures, but as such they are themselves revelation, indirectly, that is, when the Spirit quickens the "letter" into life. In His commandments, as in His promises, God shows us who He is and what He wills.

In the Old Testament in particular (and in this respect Zwingli and Calvin had a keener insight than Luther) the Commandments are witnesses to the Covenant which God concludes with His people; therefore they can only be understood from the point of view of the Promise; again, the gracious Promise can only be understood in the light of the Commandments, seen to be the revealed will of God in His claim on man.[2]

6. Secondly, when we ask about the relation of these Commandments to the one Divine Command, we see that they are authentic "expositions" of the One Command. It is part of the condescension of God towards our weakness that He does not merely tell us to do *one* thing, but a variety of things. "The Commandments" are the God-given examples of what His will and His love mean in the concrete situations of life. The Commandments—both of the Decalogue and of the Sermon on the Mount—are God-given paradigms of love,

[1] See pp. 114 ff.
[2] Cf. my article: *Die Bedeutung des Alten Testamentes für unseren Glauben.* *Zw. d. Z.*, 1929, pp. 31–48.

in which God wills that we should learn to practise what we have learned of the command to love.

7. Each of these commandments does two things: it makes the one Command concrete, and it also abstracts from concrete reality. It stands, so to speak, in the centre between the infinitely varied reality of life and the unity of the divine will of love. It shows us what love would mean in this or that more or less "special" but still general case, and it commands us to do this very thing. Then is this the beginning of casuistry? No. It is of the utmost importance to note how unsystematic, how "casual" are all the commandments which are scattered through the New Testament. Here and there a plunge is made into human life and something is "lifted out" in order to make the meaning of love clearer. But the matter which has been singled out is not held fast as such; it is allowed to slip back again. Care is taken to avoid the possibility of even *apparently* dividing life up into various "cases" or "instances" which, as such, could be pre-judged in a legalistic manner. *None* of the commandments in the Sermon on the Mount are to be understood as laws, so that those who hear them can go away feeling, "Now I know what I have to do!" If it were possible to read the Sermon on the Mount in this legalistic way the absolute and binding character of the Divine Command would be weakened, the sense of responsibility for decision would be broken, the electrical charge of the moral moment would be released, the act of decision would gain a false sense of security by having anticipated decision. Neither the "I" nor the "Thou" would be wholly present. Both would only be represented in a very general way—by the universal law. The Commandments of Scripture are not intended to secure the ethical tension of life by inclusion in something universal, in a law which is always applicable, in an impersonal way, regulating human life down to the smallest detail of conduct; on the contrary, these Commandments are intended to show very plainly that the absolute demand for union with God and with our neighbour cannot possibly be deduced from any such universal law. If we conceive these Commandments in a legalistic way, life—that is, the sum-total of all our relations to our neighbour—becomes something which we can survey as a whole, something which we can foresee; the whole surface which stretches out before us is already parcelled out, as though colonists sailing to the New World were to parcel out the land beforehand upon the map. Every case can be

decided beforehand, if we will only look ahead and consider the matter carefully; the law in its general character logically includes within itself all particular propositions. The commandments of the Bible are not meant in this sense. It is true, of course, that the Decalogue might look as though it were intended to be such a prearranged scheme, as though it were a systematic and comprehensive arrangement of the whole sphere of collective life—and indeed this is what it is in so far as it belongs to the "Sachsenspiegel"[1] of the Jews, and serves as a civil code(6). But, in so far as it represents the Divine Command, it is not intended in this sense, nor is this the case with the exposition of this "code" in the Sermon on the Mount. What is the real meaning of this "exposition"? It is not intended merely to "intensify" or to "spiritualize" the divine law, in order that now we may better know— beforehand—what God wills from us; but the Sermon on the Mount means the very opposite: it is meant to show us that even the individual commandment is not something finite, limited, but something infinite, unlimited, that each commandment contains the whole, one, indivisible will of God, the one indivisible commandment of love. This exposition of the commandments also destroys the atomistic view of morality by demonstrating the inner infinity which resides in each "atom," in each individual commandment. It means this: that each commandment requires us to give ourselves wholly to God and wholly to our neighbour, that it is never enough to "do something" which could be determined beforehand. Even the apparently "positive" statements of the Sermon on the Mount—those which speak of the word of hate, the lustful glance, etc.—are to be understood negatively, not positively. In order that we should not think that we can fulfil the Law by doing "this or that," some unexpected point is isolated from the rest, in a quite incidental, unprepared kind of way: even if something like this were to take place, it would only show that the Law is not fulfilled. These indications are quite casual and unsystematic, in order to prevent the misunderstanding of a legalistic anticipation of knowledge, and the possibility of any casuistically juridical interpretation.

8. Only after this point has been made quite clear is it possible to define the meaning of a Christian ethic in greater

---

[1] The *Sachsenspiegel* is a Saxon Code of Law which arose about A.D. 1230. In it Church and State are both regarded as deriving their authority from God; thus they possess equal rights.—Tr.

detail. If the Divine Command is conceived as law, then its meaning can only be expounded in terms of casuistry, the logical juridical process of subsuming and deducing the "case" from the one general law in the minutest particular, in a way which is quite attainable by human effort—that is, the Catholic conception of ethics, which follows logically from the conception of the Divine Command as law. According to this view, the whole of the moral life can be surveyed beforehand; for every possible case there is laid down in the "law-book" what may and what may not be done (that is, it may be looked up in the law-book, where the moral doctrine is worked out in sufficient detail). It is this which gives to the Catholic ethic, down to the present day—to the Papal Encyclical *Casti connubii*—its impressive inclusiveness and certainty.

But this certainty has been dearly bought. The price which has been paid is that of an equally logical, thoroughgoing distortion of that which is intended in the Gospel to be the relation between me and God, between myself and my neighbour. Between me and God, between me and my neighbour, there stands this "something," the law which it is possible to define; the neighbour becomes a "case"; the meaning of the "freedom of a Christian man," the sense of freedom coupled with direct union with the person of God and the person of my neighbour, has been lost; Christianity has returned to Pharisaic Judaism. Later on we shall see repeatedly to what an extent this legalist interpretation of ethics leads to artificial interpretations, and to endless inward struggles (*casus conscientiae*) and difficulties.

It is, of course, true that the Law, that which can be ascertained beforehand, the prescription, the "division" of the land of the future, also has a place in the Christian ethic; the next chapter will deal with this point. We are not Antinomians because we do not wish to be legalists; on the contrary, it will be our duty to guard the inheritance which we have received from Zwingli and Calvin by the careful consideration of this indispensable function of the law over against a fanatical Antinomianism, a danger which actually threatened Luther himself, and since that time has been a still greater danger to a certain kind of Lutheranism. But certainly we shall have much more to say—and especially within a *Christian* ethic!—about the temporary significance of the Law, a significance which ought to be carefully restricted from many different points of view. With all our might we shall have to resist the immense temptation to say, "Now at last we know what is Right," even though it exposes us to the danger of disappointing all those who expect from us what only a Catholic ethic, in harmony with its own point of view, can legitimately offer—namely, the anticipation of one's own decision, release from direct union with God and our neighbour. It should be the first and the most important concern of a Protestant ethic to maintain within the "Children of God" this sense of direct responsibility to God.

By itself ethics can decide nothing beforehand; *nothing at all*. But, by the consideration of all the points of view which have to be considered by one who knows God's grace and God's demand, the Divine revelation in the Scriptures and in the Spirit, who knows God as Creator and Redeemer, it can prepare the decision of the individual as carefully as a conscientious legal adviser prepares the decision of the judge by the most careful consideration of all possibilities. In this interweaving of a definite demand and of its restriction, of our direct connexion with God Himself and with our actual neighbour, and of our indirect connexion through the Law: in this process—ever renewed before every fresh problem—of steering a clear course between legalism and fanaticism—between the aim at the One Good which alone exists, and the variety of all that can be said about the matter, the task of an evangelical ethic consists; the evangelical ethic does not cut such a fine figure as that of her Catholic step-sister, it is true, but, if she does her task well, she possesses this distinctive quality: she deals more seriously with the reality of man and the reality of God.

CHAPTER XIV

THE THREEFOLD MEANING OF THE LAW

PROPOSITION: *The Divine Command presupposes law in a threefold sense: as the* Lex, *which requires simple legal obedience; as the radical law which leads to repentance, and as* guidance *for faith.*

It is characteristic of our present existence (as an actuality created by God, and yet sinful) that it is embedded in a framework of "orders" of a most varied kind. The individual human being does not enter into the sphere of social and natural relations as a free master of himself but, as a psycho-physical and historical being, he is born into the life which is already present, and—as always—already "ordered," and he grows— at first instinctively, more or less unconsciously, within this "organism" composed of a people and of humanity as a whole, as one of its "members." When conscious self-determination and faith awaken, man has already been moulded both by nature and by history, he has already been absorbed into the intricate web of human life with its manifold claims; duties of all kinds chain him to a certain way of living; he is burdened and tied down by a thousand ties. Although he may choose his own path, and may be a believer, for all that he does not cease to be also a member of this natural historical "organism." To each of us life means constant co-operation with others; it cannot be otherwise. Life on any other terms would be impossible.

These orders, these manifold unconscious forms of life which have grown into the form of legal obligations, are partly a kind of natural law, which is carried into effect automatically by the bodily organism—like the process of breathing—and partly established habits, with which we have become imbued by practice from our earliest infancy—a mechanism apart from which life would be impossible, in spite of the fact that all that has thus become habitual is not necessary to or helpful to life, and is therefore capable of being modified. In part, too, they are "social customs" in which— whether good or bad—the community of the nation, clan, or family is realized, and preserves and inherits the experiences of earlier generations; in part, too, they are customs which have taken the forms of law, codified laws and recognized rules for life and for morality, through which the collective community authoritatively, and more or less by compulsion, forces the individual to become part of this body. We describe the sum-total of all these forms of connexion between human beings, in so far as they are also—on the one hand—subject to the control of the will, and—on the other—primarily simply effective as present forces for the maintenance of order, by an artificial word: *Lex*; we describe the sum-total of the motives which have created these "orders," and by which they are maintained, by the word *legality*. Thus we describe a definite custom or a definitely codified law, which controls the relations of the community or the conduct of life, as *Lex*, and the various motives which lead to the acceptance of this existing order—in so far as the question of faith as a basis for life does not come under consideration—as "legality."

2. Since the believer also finds himself within these orders, the question arises: how is he to behave towards them? and how is he to think of them? Were the isolated sections of the *Lex* to be judged by an abstract law of love, the judgment could only be a negative one. Everything connected with this "organism" is permeated through and through with an irrational, casual character, void of all meaning, and full of loveless harshness. Both the attitude of command and that of (legal) obedience—if measured by an abstract law of love— is "sub-ethical." However varied in character, it is a method of *compulsion*, and of yielding to compulsion, whether this compulsion be inward or outward. It is an extremely crude and ethically extremely inadequate way of co-ordinating the life of the individual with that of the community.[1]

But reflection and experience will show immediately that human life—and this means above all else, life in community —would be impossible without this *Lex*, since human beings and historically natural conditions are what they are. Further: even if we were to try to imagine the removal of all that is particular and historical, and were to think only of human nature as it has been moulded by creation and by sin, we would still have to admit the necessity for some kind of *Lex*, if not this one, then one very similar to it. Apart from customs and law (with the obedience to custom and law which this implies), apart from this provisional order, life is an impossibility for sinful human beings. We need this rude order as a framework for all the more refined and spiritual forms of life which are obedient to God. Even if the individual

[1] Cf. KANT's distinction between legality and morality.

believer did not need it on his own account—which is in itself a very rash statement contradicted at a thousand points by experience—he would still need it for the sake of his life with those who have not been influenced by the Word of God, or who are either indifferent or hostile to it. If we were to wait until all men do right, from the spirit of obedience to God, in the meantime humanity would long ago have been ground to powder in ceaseless conflict of all against all, or rather: long ago either the most powerful, or the majority, would have instituted some kind of *Lex*, just as the actual *Lex* has arisen under such necessities and out of such needs.

3. This *Lex*, however, is not only a necessity for life which *we* can see to be necessary. It is rather itself a possibility of life which is given *by God*; according to its function of creating positive order, of making life possible, it is the gift of God, and therefore—on the basis of that which we have already seen—it is the task given by God. It is true that the *Lex* itself is not what God wills, but it is absolutely controlled by the Divine Command. In spite of the element of compulsion which it contains, the *Lex* forms part of the way in which God, at present, preserves life in the created order tainted by sin, it is His way of giving us life, and especially life with one another. God commands us to obey this rude, coercive, arbitrary, external authority, and, indeed, to accept it thankfully from His Hands, and to obey it willingly. This does not by any means close the discussion of the question; but the first necessary point has been made, apart from which the next point would be meaningless.

Thus the believer finds himself involved in a curious situation: from obedience to God he has to obey the *Lex*, in spite of the fact that the latter does not express what God Himself wills; secondly, the believer has to obey the *Lex* from obedience to God *legaliter*—and in no other way—in spite of the fact that obedience to God in itself excludes mere legality. Both these statements simply mean that since the *Lex* is only indirectly the will of God for us, we only have to obey it conditionally. Otherwise, in opposition to what was said in the previous chapter, a legal relation to the will of God would be here laid down, the Divine Command and the Law would be identified with one another. But the word "conditionally" qualifies this statement by connecting it with reservations. "We must obey God rather than men."[1] This does not mean

[1] Acts v. 29.

142

that the relation of obedience towards men—towards human authority working out through compulsion—is abolished; but it is rigidly and unconditionally limited(1). The right of control is reserved to the command and prohibition of God Himself. Thus we can never hear the Divine Command, we can never obey God, if at the same time—for the sake of this Command—we do not also take into account the *Lex* as the expression, indirectly, of the Will of God, as the "framework" which God has set for our life, for a life in love. For although the *Lex*, in itself—owing to human sin—is coarse and stained with sin, yet the reason why God tells us to pay attention to it is simply His love. The crude *Lex*—and with it legality—is necessary for the sake of love, because it is necessary for the sake of life. We are to "give honour to those to whom honour is due"[1]—for the sake of God; this is the Divine Command, for there is no other obligation for us. But we are to give them that honour which is *their* due, and not divine honour—for the sake of God(2).

4. The Commandments of the Bible also belong to this *Lex*, in so far as they are understood as law. Nor can we do without the law in the moral sense. When we reject legalism, as we are bound to do when—in faith—we perceive the Divine Command, we are not ignoring the laws of human life, but we are breaking through them from within because we have discovered their profound and ultimate meaning. Just as the bud breaks through its sheath, so the believing obedience of love must break through the law from within. The law, both in the sense of "laws which stand written," and in the sense of the law which is written on our conscience, is the husk within which God means the fruit of faith to ripen. But, as we have already seen, when the fruit is ripe, the outer covering must be actually *broken*.

But it is God's will, through this discipline, to lead us into the freedom of faith. The Law is the "schoolmaster to bring us to Christ."[2] Hence the ancient writers used to describe this function of the Law in terms of its two main elements as the *usus politicus* and the *usus paedagogicus*, that is, as the function which makes order "politically," and as the preparatory function of the "pedagogue"(3). It will be shown later how great is the significance of this whole doctrine of the *Lex*.

5. It is quite impossible to sum up "the Law of God" in one single definition; after all that I have just said, this will

[1] Rom. xiii. 7.   [2] Gal. iii. 24.

be quite evident. Even the Reformers, who took endless pains to try to clarify this central conception, only succeeded in formulating a doctrine which, at this point in particular, betrays a certain confusion of thought and remarkable uncertainty.[1] Is the "Law of God" the *lex naturae* "engraved" upon the conscience or is it the Law of Moses? or is it the Sermon on the Mount conceived as law? or is it the twofold commandment of love to God and love to our neighbour? As we have seen, a conceivable *lex naturae* does not exist, although, on the other hand, it is certain that no human being exists without some moral sense, without a "sense of ought." The Law of Moses has ceased to be to us an actual entity which can be explained in a uniform sense—even the Decalogue, from the purely historical point of view, is subethical in character. The "Law of the Sermon on the Mount," however, summed up in the one commandment of love, if it is taken seriously, does away with the idea of law altogether. From our point of view, knowing in what the True Good consists, it is not difficult to understand that there can be no uniform conception of the Law of God because the genuine Good cannot be understood as obedience to a Law. Our reflections on the function of the *Lex* in ordering human life show that this admission does not mean that the Law is meaningless; but when this has been said the significance of the law is in no way exhausted.

Luther once called the Law the "dialectic of the Gospel"[2] —and indeed no one knew better than he what he was talking about. In order to make this plain we will begin from the point at which the command to love is understood as law, the point at which all the ultimate meaning of the law is concentrated. We will put the simple question: What does God will when He commands this one thing? What does the Sermon on the Mount mean—interpreted as a law? Evidently it means that we are to do what it commands. The command to love, interpreted as law, immediately diverts our attention from the One who commands to that which has to be done. In so doing it becomes one with the "Lex" in the sense in which it has just been defined, and obedience to the law becomes legality. The Divine Command understood as law is not really *God's* command. So we must take the opposite line and say: it is not God's Command which is to be under-

[1] Cf. LOMMATZSCH: *Luthers Lehre vom ethisch-religiosen Standpunkte aus.*
[2] *Luther-Briefe*, de Wette, iv. 46.

stood as law, but the law (and this means also the *Lex* in all its variety) as the Divine Command. What does this mean?

6. If some particular action is really known to be *God's* Command, merely external "right conduct" does not come into the picture at all. Then in all law the one thing that matters is that God claims me for Himself: God alone—claims me wholly. He does not merely wish to have my outward acts, but He wants my heart—as one which is obedient to Him; for when He possesses my heart He also possesses my outward actions. It is true, of course, that He wants it first of all in that which is commanded here and now; but the obedient heart is not a matter of a moment. If I give Him my heart only for this actual moment I do not really give it to Him at all. Man is a whole(4).

Disobedience consists in the fact that it is possible for man to be now one thing and then another; it is lack of wholeness, it is the divided heart. God does not wish to have my obedience as something which is valuable in itself. He wants *me*, my whole personality, in the totality of all my actions, both inward and outward. It means the same thing when we look at it from the other side: He wants me *for Himself*, He wants me to obey Him for His own sake, for love. For an obedience rendered for my own sake would be merely sham obedience, mere legality. The law, understood as the Divine Command, can only mean: "Thou shalt love the Lord thy God with all thy heart, with all thy mind, and with all thy strength."[1] If the Law is really understood as the command of God, it *can* only mean this unconditional love which cannot be in any way divided, a demand for which there are no part-payments. The fact that at every moment humanity is disunited, is only another way of saying that man is in a state of disobedience, of division—that man has "other gods besides Me." And further: if the Law is understood as the command of *God* it is unconditionally serious, it is intended in dead earnest. For God is never casual—God is not mocked.

Thus understood—and how can the Law be understood save as the Command of God?—the Law inevitably becomes our judge. For no one of us loves God with an undivided heart. Thus no one is really obedient to God. The appearance of an approximation to obedience to God always arises only from a confusion of obedience to God with legality. Once this confusion has been perceived, once we have understood that

[1] Matt. xxii. 37.

God does not will to have anything done for its own sake, but that He simply wants to have me myself for Himself, then the sentence of death has been passed upon us. The Law "worketh wrath."[1]

This leads to hopeless despair. Despair can indeed assume many different forms. It may express itself in resignation, or as contentment with a very commonplace standard of ordinary decency, which is used as security against God's Command and His Law. The *Lex* becomes a covering to hide the soul from God. However this "righteousness" may be understood: whether as heroic, or ascetic, or religious, it is always the same process: man believes it possible to split up God's claim into partial demands, and this means: to satisfy God with outward good behaviour. Hence all this kind of morality, whether it takes a secular or a religious form, carries with it a bad conscience, as a sign of its deceitful character.

But this despair can also be experienced directly; life may be haunted by a bad conscience, driving the soul to an anguished fear of judgment; this leads to the piling up of "good works"—and still more to the intensification of religious exercises, becoming more and more "interior," till the summit of this inward effort is reached in the mystical practice of "purgation"—in the endeavour to "appease" the wrath of God and to quiet the troubled conscience in its terrible unrest. Since, however, such intense effort cannot, psychologically, go beyond a certain point, practically, the result is that the soul oscillates between one "way" of despair and another, unless the abscess of despair breaks in the confession: "I can do no more!" This is the diacritical point,[2] the turning point, either away from or towards God; but if the soul finally turns to God, he discovers that He is no longer the God who demands, but the God who gives and forgives.

7. In this experience of the grace of God—which is not possible apart from the Law—the legalistic interpretation of the will of God is seen to be *sin, the* sin *par excellence*, the desire of man to live his own life in his own way, apart from God. This is the dialectical element in the Law: it leads directly to the true knowledge of God, in order that then, at the moment when the threshold has been crossed, it may be seen in its true colours, as absolute ignorance of God, as the real enemy to the knowledge of God. It is not the Law which is the schoolmaster to lead us to Christ; that is not the right

[1] Rom. iv. 15.　　　　[2] Cf. KIERKEGAARD: *Die Krankheit zum Tode.*

way to put it. Rather it is God who leads me to Himself through the Law—if He so wills it—since He does not leave me standing on the threshold, since He does not only allow despair to increase and come to a head, but also—and this is not a matter of course at all—He himself lances the abscess of self-righteousness, and thus makes room for humility and faith. It is He alone who causes the chronic, lingering process to become acute, who precipitates the crisis, and thus effects the soul's deliverance from deadly sickness and heals all her diseases.

One thing is certain: this transformation is the work of God alone; it is not the final stage in an immanental process which comes to a climax in consciousness—as might be imagined from reading Kierkegaard's description of "sickness unto death"—despair itself never leads to the change towards recovery; on the contrary, this transformation absolutely contradicts all that might be expected on the natural plane; all this the Christian Faith knows, with utter clearness and certainty, through the Cross of Christ. The Cross is that event (which takes place apart from the subject) in which both the *final* validity of the Law and its *final* defeat are manifested. The despairing soul only finds its "standing-ground" in the Divine forgiveness at a point which lies beyond its own efforts to fulfil the Law, that is, only in the perfect fulfilment of the Law by Christ. As a dialectical process all this would be superficial self-deception; it only becomes reality through the act of God.

Knowledge of grace presupposes the Law; but this per-ception only becomes complete when man realizes, in utter despair, that he can never achieve the Good, in the legalistic sense, and further that it is precisely this legalistic inter-pretation of the will of God which is sin, namely, the "desire to establish one's own righteousness." Hence the Law is the will of God—on account of sin; from the legalistic point of view, however, this is not the "real" will of God but His "mysterious" will, that is, His will as it alone can and should be understood by the sinner, the unbeliever. Without this Law there is no knowledge of grace. Without the Sermon on the Mount there would be no Epistle to the Romans. Thus: without the Law, in this radical and at the same time dialectical sense it is impossible to hear the real command of God. This is that aspect of the Law which used to be described by the ancient writers as the *usus elenchticus legis,* and

147

it is this which Luther chiefly has in mind when he speaks of the office of the Law.

8. But still we have not said the final word about the Divine Command as law. And this is not merely because even the believer is always also an unbeliever, because even for him repentance remains a daily necessity, into which the menacing law drives him, the Law which applies to everyone who is not "in Christ." It is true that this should be taken into very serious consideration. Faith is not faith if it is not the knowledge that it is only the mercy of God which preserves us from falling over the precipice into the gulf into which we would most certainly fall were His Hand not to hold us up; it is not faith if it is not constantly taking flight from this one possibility for man, and fleeing for refuge to the possibility of God. But we need not dwell on this point any longer; this is the meaning of the Law for unbelief in the believer. But there is still a third point which I wish to raise: that the Law, even for faith itself, does not lose its significance; its significance, I mean, as the God-given exposition of what it means for our conduct to be "in Christ." The fact that we have learnt to believe does not mean that we automatically become one with the will of God. Even in the life of faith God remains "over against" us(5), and we only walk along the right path if God guides us into it.

"But," someone might object, "this guidance only takes place through the Holy Spirit, not through the law." Certainly; but the Holy Spirit only speaks to us where the Scripture also speaks to us: the Word and the Spirit, in the "letter" of the Law and the Spirit which makes it live. The Spirit must expound the Law; but He can only do so if the Law exists and continues to exist. It is, of course, true that Luther says:[1] "If we had enough of the Holy Spirit, we could make 'new Decalogues' for ourselves which would be clearer than that of Moses." Yes, indeed, we could, if . . .! It may, indeed, be true that there is a kind of creative ingenuity in genuine love, and it is not advisable, from an exaggerated desire to be "sane," to contest this. We are all aware of that amazing penetrating intuition which characterizes the outstanding

---

[1] LUTHER: "Habito enim Christo facile condemus leges et omnia recte iudicabimus. Imo novos Decalogos faciemus, sicut Paulus facit per omnes Epistolas, et Petrus, maxime Christus in Evangelio. Et hi Decalogi clariores sunt quam Mosi decalogus sicut facies Christi clarior est quam facies Mosi" (W.A. 39, 47, 25 ff.).

examples of Christian love, who, with an insight only to be compared with the genius of the great diagnostician, discover the hidden distress of others, and with amazing spontaneity do what no one would have expected, because this is what love commands. But few of us possess much of this creative faculty, and most of us have very little indeed. Therefore the commandments of the Bible—and for many people the considerations of an ethic as well—are absolutely necessary. The Apostles themselves experienced this; that is why they used to "exhort" their converts; that is why they ordered certain things to be done which seem to us quite obvious— just because—unfortunately—they were not obvious at all. This is why we must teach the *usus tertius legis*, the *usus didacticus*, the instructive function of the Law, more plainly than Luther did(6).

But the Law, as faith knows it, is no longer the same as the *Lex* which existed "before faith." The change is twofold. Firstly, the isolated demand, the command or the prohibition, is no longer detached—as is the case within the sphere of legality—but all instructions, whether commands or prohibitions, are referred to the "first commandment," made explicit in the fundamental law of love. From the law of love the believer can now himself deduce laws, since he "applies" it to particular cases. The claim to know the Good beforehand, to be able to "deduce" it from the principle of love, which primarily and in principle we must condemn as a misunderstanding of the nature of the Good, is not to be totally condemned—but only if it is regarded as a final principle. This "deduction" of the Good which can be known beforehand and defined in terms of casuistry is not, it is true, the Genuine Good, but it has a place in the definition of the true Good. Whatever I can determine beforehand from the principle of love for a definite situation in life must be illuminating for me in the concrete instance of decision, it ought to direct me towards the Divine Command itself. It is possible that—officially—I may be obliged to act quite differently from the way in which I would wish to act on a preconceived principle, that is, otherwise than I should act "according to the Sermon on the Mount," if this is understood as a law. But this preconceived principle, based on the knowledge of the Sermon on the Mount as law, is not without significance; indeed, it is of the highest significance as showing the right path, as demonstrating what the Good is "in and for itself."

The Sermon on the Mount interpreted as law, and the system of ethics which is designed in accordance with this law, is of the very highest significance for the conduct of one who in faith is seeking to do the will of God—but it is not "Christian ethics." It is the law interpreted in a radical manner—and no more than that.

This comes out very clearly when we look at a second alteration of the law effected by faith. It is no longer the command of the Lord to the slave but the instruction of the father to the son.[1] It is no longer the terrible menacing law of Sinai, but it is now the "easy yoke, the light burden," for it is now seen to be the will of the loving Father, who wills nothing so much as to keep us within His love and His work; thus His commands are to be understood as "instructions for work," the directions for the route, regulations—that is, if we are "in Christ," if we really believe. It is therefore that Law of which the "sweet singer of Israel" sings when he says that he has "his delight in the law"; it is the law which guides the volunteer of God. Thus the law no longer contains an ethical sentiment—the ethical sentiment, indeed, resides in faith—but a more technical function: that of giving the right direction. The general direction, all that can be known beforehand, comes to the assistance of him who in faith is united with God and with his neighbour, that he may really act in harmony with love, and may not make a mistake.

In conclusion, however, we must remind ourselves that all this, which we have analysed in such conceptual abstraction, is always bound up with the reality of life. The seventh Commandment: "Thou shalt not commit adultery," in its simple everyday meaning, the command not to do that which we call adultery, applies also to the believer—as an order for his life, as an order of the community. At the same time, however, he knows, since he understands this commandment in a radical way, that he is an adulterer, and that in his honourable civil state of marriage he stands before God as a sinner who can only exist because of the forgiveness of God. And thirdly, this seventh commandment, interpreted by the radical law, now becomes, through the unconditional commandment of love of the Sermon on the Mount, an instruction, in order that now, as a Christian, he may preserve his life in his married state, and not do as "the heathen do." The law is always powerful according to its threefold function: as the

[1] Gal. iv. 6, 7.

word of discipline, repentance, and guidance. And the law which guides is the same as the civil law radically interpreted from the point of view of love, just as the civil law can only exercise its function of maintaining order, and its pedagogical function, because at the same time it is connected with the commandment of love. Thus the law exercises us at the same time in discipline, humility, and joyful childlike obedience.

SECTION II: THE NEW MAN

CHAPTER XV

THE NEW MAN, AS CREATED AND CLAIMED BY GOD[1]

PROPOSITION: *Since God alone is good, and man is a sinner, God alone can be considered the subject of good conduct, i.e. the Holy Spirit, who in faith begets the new will. But this new will is only real in the obedience of faith.*

1. Every ethical system presupposes a doctrine of man, and, accordingly, contains within itself such a doctrine. It is one of the characteristics of a "natural" ethic, however, that its anthropology is more or less latent. That is, that the question of the nature of man, of the subject of the desired good conduct, is either not seriously considered or is even not considered at all. A natural ethic brushes aside the question: "Who is the *doer* of good actions?" and is only interested in the nature and content of the action itself; or, when it does put this question, it is satisfied with an abstract conception, with the Idea of Man, and does not inquire into the nature of the real man at all(1). It is an essential feature of all anthropology presupposed by a natural ethic, that it defines man in an abstract unreal way, in universal terms.

Underlying the two chief types of philosophical ethics— the Naturalistic and the Idealistic(2)—are two corresponding types of anthropology, both of which possess this character of generality. In the Naturalistic view man is simply a part of nature, a particular kind of animal. His spiritual qualities are only transformed impulse and sense perception. Responsibility and guilt are only appearances; man is not an individual but a sample of a species. In the Idealistic view, on the other hand, man is in his deepest nature (and this is all that matters) divine, the bearer of the one and the same reason. Individuality, with its isolation, is something merely negative, like the bodily nature of man. The spiritual core of the

---

[1] This chapter contains, in the briefest possible compass, an outline of the doctrine of man as a sinner, of the New Birth, and of Conversion, as doctrinal statements of dogmatics. Here it becomes particularly clear that ethics is only a section of dogmatics.

personality is the universal reason, identical in all. In this case also, responsibility and guilt are regarded as illusions.

For a Christian anthropology man is neither animal nor divine, but as a finite, corporeal being he has been created by God with an inherent tendency[1] towards Him, and, therefore, with the capacity for knowing Him(3). Thus man is a being who although, like all that is finite, he is a creature, yet has a share in the knowledge of God's will and life, through God's Word, in which and for which he has been created. Like all other created beings, man has been created *by means of* God's Word; but, unlike all other created beings, he has also been created *in* the Word of God, as the being, therefore, whose peculiarity it is that he is responsible to God, whose Voice he hears, whose claim he recognizes. Man alone has an "I," or, rather, is a Self, but this Self is not itself ultimate reality; it is not based upon itself, it does not possess aseity, but I am "I" only because, and in so far as, God addresses me as "thou"; therefore the distinctive quality of my existence, responsibility, only consists in the fact that I am addressed by God. I am not merely causally "derived from God" like all other creatures, but I am also "derived from God" in the sense that I alone *know* that I come from God, and that I can only really become a person when I know that I am destined for God, and can choose to accept this destiny. Thus the essential mark of man is this: freedom in this dependence.

2. Christian anthropology, however, recognizes that man as he is does not correspond with this description. Man is a being who, although he has been created by God, by the fact that he has turned away from God is no longer in the state of free dependence in which he was created. Christian anthropology regards man as not only responsible but also as guilty, that is, as a being who has perverted his nature by misusing his freedom, and thus has *lost* his freedom(4). Hence man's being contains an absolutely fundamental contradiction, or, rather, man's whole existence bears the marks of this contradiction, stamped upon it in indelible characters. It is not the dual nature of body and soul which constitutes this contradiction, that is, it is not something general, con- stitutional, which can be grasped as a metaphysical principle (Nature—Idea); it is something personal and historical, an *act* which, although for us it may be an incomprehensible

[1] Literally, "determination" or "destiny" (*Bestimmung*).—TR.

153

Primal Act, which lies at the basis of all individual action, is no less an act than the Divine act of Creation which precedes all empirical happenings, but is no less an act on that account. In this twofold act, the Primal act of God and of man, this contradiction originated; therefore man is here not conceived in general terms—of Nature or the Idea—but only in this personal reality of action, in that which makes him personally responsible and guilty. Hence—as will be shown later on— in this contradiction the being of man cannot be recognized in a theoretical metaphysical manner, but can only itself be recognized in an act, in faith.

The central point, the heart of the contradiction in man, is man's self-chosen emancipation, his rebellious breaking away from his Creator. In this emancipation man ascribes to himself, falsely, an independence which, in reality, is un-freedom. The very nature of man is changed by this perversion of the attitude of man to God. For the nature of the "I"(5), in contrast to all else that exists, is also determined by that which it knows itself to be and for which it destines itself. As a sinner, man is a being whose nature has been perverted, one who has been severed from God, one who is remote from God. He is—whether he knows it or not—in conflict with the nature in which he was created; he is "sick" with that "sickness unto death" which, when it breaks out, manifests itself in the form of despair.

But man is not only severed from God and from his original nature—which is deeply penetrated with the spirit of separa-tion and contradiction—but his attitude towards the world and to his fellow-man is also perverted. He is now, in a wrong way, an "individual"—his co-existence with others has been destroyed; at the same time he is also in a distorted way "non-individual": that is, he is a dependent member of a species. Both in his Naturalistic and in his Idealistic anthro-pology man projects theoretically both these "possibilities," which reveal the contradiction at the root of his nature. In the world, too, he behaves in a masterful way, snatches greedily at the world for his own purposes, and, in so doing, is the slave of his lust for the world, enslaved by its spell and its glamour. Thus the two direct results of this fundamental perversion of man's nature are self-seeking and love of the world.[1]

[1] Cf. VILMAR's doctrine of Sin (*Theologische Moral*, pp. 119–369) and that of VON OETTINGEN (*Christliche Sittenlehre*, pp. 391–514).

3. Just as it is true that sin in its deepest roots is an act, so also, on the other hand, it is equally true that in its empirical effect it appears in the form of Fate. Not merely the individual personal acts are hostile to God, but hostility to God now forms part of the very nature of man; the "nature," the character of the existence of man as a whole is now dominated by the contradiction. It would be the task of a Christian anthropology to exhibit these contradictions behind the personal acts, in the being of man, in the present "constitution" of man, as, for instance, the contradiction between an abstract intellectualism (reason) and an unintelligent "savage" sensuality; between a view of truth which is that of a spectator, merely theoretical (theoretical reason), and a practical standard of life severed from existence (practical reason); between a godless rationality and an irrational religiosity. The contradictions within the "natural" ethic and morality which I have just discussed are expressions of this contradiction which now determines the constitution of the nature of man.

But likewise, as this contradiction determines the whole constitution of the individual man, so also it is something which concerns the whole nature of mankind, in which each individual has a share. Therefore all historical life is infected with this contradiction. The whole of history bears the imprint of sin. This is the original mystery of solidarity in sin, which corresponds to the fact of our solidarity in being created by God, the primal mystery, that we all, in the Creation and in the Fall, are "Adam," that "Adam" is both the individual and the community. In spite of the fact that the sin of each individual, when he comes to a true knowledge of himself, is known to be guilt in a most personal way, it is at the same time felt as corporate guilt. At the deepest point of the existence of each individual, at the very roots of his being, there, too, every other individual also has his roots; in Creation and in sin we are, in an incomprehensible way, both individual and yet the whole of humanity (Kierkegaard).

4. The "natural man," that is, man outside the realm of faith, does not cease to be man because of the existence of sin. He has become neither an animal nor a devil, but he remains a responsible person, in spite of the fact that through sin the true personality, the state of freedom in dependence, has been destroyed, so that his freedom has become alienation and his connexion bondage. Hence man in his actuality is the

being upon whom the contradiction has devolved;[1] and not merely is this the case, but man knows it, although in such a way that the contradiction is not removed, but, indeed, is only intensified. This knowledge, which is affected by the contradiction, and which makes the contradiction explicit, is—conscience(6).

Conscience is not the "Voice of God," as it used to be described in the theology of the Enlightenment(7), and as it has since then been usually regarded by popular natural theology. Nor is it the consciousness of the Moral Law, of the "Thou Shalt," nor the judgment of the intellect concerning the agreement or non-agreement of an action with the law(8). All these explanations are rationalizations of the original phenomenon of conscience, which conceal from us its true character. Conscience is something far more sinister than all these images employed by rationalizing methods of interpretation. For the sinister thing about conscience is precisely this, that primarily it has nothing to do with God at all, that it attacks man like an alien, dark, hostile power, as it has been represented in ancient myths and by the great poets of ancient and modern times—who in this respect are so much wiser than the philosophers. It is a kind of knowledge, a perception of our existence as a whole, a sense of unrest, a signal of alarm, which announces the disturbance of order; it is rightly called "con-science" (Gewissen)(9), because it is not something conceptually active, but something which denotes a passive state of existence, it is not a rational but an emotional kind of knowledge, like the inarticulate groaning of a prisoner in his dungeon, which only penetrates into clear consciousness in a dim obscure manner. It is, indeed, simply the man himself as he feels himself in the centre of his existence to be disturbed, injured, affected by the contradiction, the consciousness that "things are not right with him," that they "are out of order," a knowledge which comes to him involuntarily. Of course, he can "evade" the pressure of conscience, he can artificially shut down the noise of this' alarm signal, but he cannot get rid of it.

Conscience makes its presence felt on certain occasions of actual wrong-doing or of failure; but as soon as it makes its voice heard it announces more than this particular instance

[1] The Greek perception of the tragic element in life is the aesthetic reflection of this contradiction; man is the sympathetic spectator of his own existence, in his sense of Fate and guilt.

of wrong-doing or failure. It proclaims this fault as an outbreak of the contradiction as a whole, as a manifestation of "general disorder." It is in this primary sense of "conscience" —the so-called "bad" or accusing conscience(10)—that man first experiences his responsibility. We do not experience responsibility in a neutral way, as is represented in the rational ethic, as the two possibilities which lie before us; the conscience which instructs us beforehand is a product of reflection. The original experience of responsibility is always experience after the event; it reaches consciousness as a sense of guilt about something in particular and immediately forms part of the profound sense of guilt as a whole. In the experience of conscience we learn that "we have lost ourselves," we learn our loneliness, we find that we have been "cast out" and "excluded," and we discover that this is not due to the workings of Fate but is the result of our "guilt"; our decision for action (*Entschlossenheit*: Heidegger) is seen to be actually reserve (*Verschlossenheit*),[1] and we see, too, that the possibility we thought existed does not exist at all.

5. But a good deal of the sinister nature of conscience springs from the fact that it does not tell us "to what" we no longer belong nor from what we are "shut out." As conscience it does not speak of God, but it is the flaming sword which drives us away from the presence of God; it is a force which steps in between God and ourselves and hides Him from us, a force which drives us out into loneliness(11). It is true, of course, that conscience speaks to us of law; but the knowledge of the law did not arise out of the law; rather the law is "written in the heart" as the "practical reason." But the conscience subjects us to the law as the right order of *our* life, it holds up to us the law as a possibility which was once ours and has now been lost; it is the way in which the man who is separated from God, the man whose life is no more lived in God, but by his own efforts, becomes conscious of the unreality of this possibility. Conscience and law, indeed, conscience and legalism, are inseparably united. Conscience does not face sin as though it were that part of man which has remained sound, but it is itself deeply involved in sin. Indeed, it is that which most separates man from God, which drives man most of all into his loneliness away from God.

In conscience—as faith is aware—it is the angry God who

[1] I.e. you remain reserved (or shut up within yourself), even if you open your mind for decisive action.—TR.

meets man, the *Deus absconditus*, the God whose "Face is hidden, beneath an impenetrable disguise." This comes out in the fact that conscience, as such, is wholly unable to tell us that in the presence of guilt and responsibility we have to do with God. Conscience is the fear of God—in the sense of the "fear that hath torment"—hence it drives the soul away from God, and yet it is also the longing of the soul for God; but it so distorts the way back to God that the soul can see nothing clearly; the soul does not know that it is *God* of whom it is afraid and for whom it longs. It is precisely this dullness and obscurity, as of something opaque, which constitutes the sinister element in the fact of conscience. The so-called "good" conscience may, indeed, be a reality, but it is a phenomenon which belongs to the surface of life and is therefore quite secondary; it belongs to the sphere of the *justitia civilis*; therefore it has nothing to do with existence as a whole but only with isolated actions as such.

Hence conscience does not lead to true self-knowledge, which only exists where guilt is understood to imply sin, where the Law is seen to be the command of the God of grace, where the sense of "belonging to no one" is seen to imply that the creature is bound to the Creator, and this means: in faith. Faith certainly is concerned with conscience, but it does not originate "in the conscience"(12); faith awakens when man sees himself, not in the light of conscience, but in the new light thrown upon his nature by the gracious Word of God, in Christ. The conscience is neither a "place" nor an "organ" in man, but it is a way of self-knowledge—it is a kind of pain, a feeling of personal anguish, of sorrow of heart, caused by the fact that we have been wrenched away from our true home. Faith alone can heal this wound; faith binds up and reunites the severed elements; it is faith which restores the wounded conscience—conscious of its total need—and replaces the state of anguish and despair by the state of entire justification. Faith does not do this "in the conscience," however, but by calming the fears raised by the conscience.

The sense of responsibility is never neutral; we become aware of responsibility either along the negative path of the voice of conscience or along the positive one of faith. A conscience in itself, within which faith could be born, does not exist; that is a theory which obscures the truth, a speculative idealistic theory which makes a reality out of that lost possibility, without regarding the conditions of that possibility.

But it is certainly right to say that faith does not eliminate conscience any more than it abolishes law. Rather, through faith the conscience is corrected. First—from the standpoint of faith—its voice is now understood as the accusation of God, as the "impression" which the demanding and judging God makes on the heart of man. Secondly, the divine acquittal which is perceived and accepted by faith is understood as the suppression of this accusation by God Himself. Thirdly, the conscience is refurnished in its critical function as the understanding of the Self which is peculiar to man through the joint knowledge of the command of God as the court of appeal which decides what belongs to and what does not belong to God. It remains a human function, but one which through faith has received a new meaning and new possibilities. This event in the centre of existence, in the "heart," in the knowledge of man about himself in which his new attitude towards God becomes conscious, is the New Birth.

6. The New Birth is not a magical process(13); it is the same thing as the act of faith; it is that state in which man no longer strains after God but receives his life and strength from God; it means living on the powers which flow from "justification by grace alone." Through the New Birth the new person, the being whose life is derived from God, the self which has its home in God, in Christ, and not in the Self, is established. From the subjective point of view the centre of this process is the fact that the soul is at peace, is reconciled to God in the conscience. The hounds of hell are chained. The conscience is no longer allowed to accuse us. Our refuge is in God, and there, too, is our new personality, the new man, "in Christ." As soon as this takes place—and in so far as we believe—both our false unity and our false isolation from our fellow-creatures are removed: in faith each of us is wholly and entirely "the individual," in the sense in which Kierkegaard uses this expression; and in faith all isolation ceases; for in faith each one—so far as he really is an individual of this kind—is at the same time a member of the "Body of Christ," a member of the Christian community, of the Church. And finally, in this process the false bondage to ourselves and our false dominion over the world is removed: in faith the desire for the world ceases to exist—"dead to the world" is the forceful expression used to describe this fact—and at the same time, and only now, there begins a life "directed towards

the world," in service; the new man is free *from* the world
for the world.

7. It is both allowable and necessary to inquire also into
the subjective sphere in which this process takes place. Faith,
by the emergence of which the bad conscience is silenced by
the word of justification, is the work and the gift of God. But
just as the Incarnation of the Word of God in Jesus Christ
takes place not alongside of but within historical existence—
although concealed and only visible to faith—so also faith,
in spite of the fact that it is the work of God, is a personal act.
Indeed, it is the only "fully personal act." For in it alone,
in its achievement, does it come to pass that the person who
outside of faith is disintegrated, is again directed towards the
centre and thus "integrated." Faith is not only knowing
God and the Self, it is not only an assent and a resolve—
the resolve to live no longer in self-dependence, but in
dependence on God—but it is also feeling: the certainty and
joyfulness of belonging to God which lifts us above the abyss
of absolute terror.

Indeed, only in the fact that faith is also determined by
feeling does this knowledge and this assent become wholly
"my" faith, or to use the language of the Bible: faith of the
heart.[1] The heart does not *know*, nor does it *will*, but the heart
can *believe*, and such faith alone is genuine. To use the
expression of Kierkegaard faith is *passion*,[2] a passionate interest,
the strongest and most subjective appropriation of the Word
which can possibly be imagined. This integration of all
functions takes place neither in an act of reason, nor in an act
of sensuousness, nor yet in the aesthetic consciousness which
unites them both, but in the personality as a whole. Faith is
in the highest sense objective, it is the redress of all ills by the
Word of truth alone; and it is in the highest degree subjective:
as "existential thinking," as decision, a new self-consciousness,
even feeling of oneself. In faith that deep fear of existence is
overcome—although it is still present as something which has
been overcome—through the joyful certainty of trust; but it
is this subjective element itself which reposes on and consists
in the Word which has been perceived, in Christ. Faith means
leaving oneself behind—"Christ is my righteousness"—and

[1] On this point cf. the excellent remarks on the "heart" in the language
of the Bible by DELITZSCH: *Biblische Psychologie*, pp. 203 ff.

[2] On this see my lecture: *Die Botschaft Sören Kierkegaards* in the *Neue
Schweizer Rundschau*, 1930.

in that very fact it means being wholly oneself, the removal of division within the personality. For the personality is only truly "itself" when it is with God. Indeed, the power of this integration extends not only to feeling but through feeling and the unconscious right down into the organic sphere, even though this may only be experienced in a very imperfect manner. For even in faith we live "in the body of sin," in "this body of death."[1]

8. Thus, since faith is still very partial and imperfect, since we still harbour a great deal of unbelief, we are constantly forced to renew our decision. The process which, in its divine aspect, we know as "the New Birth," becomes "conversion," when viewed from the human standpoint. That faith only has reality *in actu*—and not otherwise—means that it is only able to direct the Self because it is itself controlled from without, it can only achieve self-knowledge because it is known by God. What we "possess" in faith is not a quality or a possession, the mystery of the divine action and the divine giving is fulfilled—beyond our understanding—in the very fact of our acceptance and our passive yielding to God(14). The new man, the new person, is not simply "present" like a newly planted life-germ, as something which is present to be thought of in biological terms; but the new man exists and continues to exist only in the obedience of faith. This is his reality. Therefore immediately behind the indicative: "Thou art the new man," stands the imperative: "*Be* the new man!" "Put on the new man!"[2] Thus the new man, like faith itself, is both God's gift and God's demand.

It is this very "personality"—which is the only true personality—which must not be conceived in any categories of substance;[3] faith, or the "new man," can only be understood in a personal sense *in actu* of God, and thus *in actu* of man. But to be a person means responsible existence. Thus faith, or the new way of life, means a responsible existence, an existence which complies with moral demands, which perceives that it is being addressed from without; it means a self-knowledge, a self-determination which springs from the deliberate acceptance of one's life from the Hand of God. We have no right to attempt to remove this final paradox. To attempt to resolve it into something which we could conceive with our minds would mean turning the personal into the impersonal.

[1] Rom. vii. 24.   [2] Eph. iv. 24.
[3] Cf. BONHÖFFER: *Akt und Sein*, 1931.

The reality of existence, however, can only be experienced in faith in the Word which lies beyond all experience. And this faith, and it alone, is, as actual obedience towards God, required of us. All the commandments are included in the First Commandment. There is nothing in the whole wide world which we are bound to do save this: to glorify God, and this means: to believe. "Whatsoever is not of faith is sin."[1] Thus we have now returned to the point at which we started; only in the realm of faith man does not see himself in the light of theory; here alone does he cease to regard himself in an abstract and general way; here alone does his "understanding" of himself involve an *act*. It is for this reason that the question of the "agent" must be a primary one in all ethical studies; indeed, it is this discussion which will decide all the other problems. For before the Good can be done the agent must be good. But the only Doer of good deeds is God. Man, therefore, can only do good deeds in so far as God does them in him, in so far as our action is obedience to the will of God, wrought in us by God Himself.

[1] Rom. xiv. 23.

CHAPTER XVI

GOODNESS AND THE "VIRTUES"

PROPOSITION: *The Command of God, so far as the subject is concerned, requires one thing only: existence in love, but this implies the existence of every "virtue."*

1. Good, in the radical sense, does not mean "doing good" but "being good." God wants to have me—myself—for His own, and not merely my actions. In the strict sense of the word no action can be "good"; only the agent of the action can be "good." The aristocratic ethic of the "noble," "well-born" man (Scheler), in contradistinction to the democratic ethic of the "good will," is not wholly wrong; it indicates the weak point in the ethic which deals with man's "disposition"; the ethic of the "good will" does not sound the depths of man's being; it remains in the air, concentrated on moral effort, on the isolated act of the will. It does not perceive that the true Good can never flow from this feverish intensity of effort, from all this labour and pain, from all this painstaking endeavour to attain the Good, but simply and solely from the central source of goodness as a state of existence. The "Good" which issues from effort is, for that very reason, not really good; the Good must descend from above, not be striven for from below, otherwise it lacks genuineness and depth.

On the other hand, the ethic of the good will, when compared with the naturalistic ethic of the "well-born" man, is so far right in that it insists that the Good can never be a natural fact. To have a good disposition does not mean being good. To be good is a personal determination, not a natural tendency. The secret of being good therefore lies neither in the act of the will, nor in the fact of natural birth, but in the new birth, which takes place on the further side of this contradiction—the paradox of the new-born—personal will, or rather: of the person who has become good. The subject of a Christian ethic is neither birth nor race, nor a habit which has become a custom ("inherited nobility") nor is it even "the Christian character," but it is the new person, which, as such, is always something given and demanded, a divine and human "central act," an event which affects life as a whole, the whole being of the self in question.

2. But in so far as this new being is, paradoxically, one

which is demanded, what kind of life then is it that is demanded? As a state of obedience? But that is simply tautology. Then, as a life of faith? But that is not the question. For (on the basis of that which was laid down in the last chapter) we are asking a further question about the moral nature of the life lived in faith. What sort of man is the man who in faith is obedient? This very natural question, however, is the point at which so many Christian moralists, and, indeed, whole centuries of ethical thinking, have been led astray into the false path of a doctrine of the virtues which is contrary to Christian thought. The true being of a man can never be indicated by a human quality, but only—as is implied in the expression "to be in faith"—by the actual state of his relation with God. We ought rather to ask: *Where* is man when he is in his right place? and answer: "True being" means being "in Christ"; for "Christ is my righteousness." God's Being in Christ, however—once again not as a quality but as act—is His being in love. The true being of man therefore can mean nothing else than standing in the love of God, being drawn into His love of man. Or, to put it differently: it means living a life which from its source in God is directed towards man, towards the interests of others.

3. Love in the sense in which the New Testament uses the word, is not a human possibility at all, but it is exclusively possible to God. Love is an "ultimate" eschatological possibility; for it will be the last thing when everything else, even faith, has vanished. Hence the state of "living in love" is not something which man can achieve by his own efforts and in his own strength, but it is something which happens to man in faith, from God. The decisive element in this life in love is therefore always to allow ourselves to be loved by God.[1] Once more it becomes clear how it is that the Good can only be understood from the point of view of justification. As we see from the expression that "man is created in the image of God," we are not in any sense fixed stars: God alone shines in His own light, He alone possesses aseity. We are planets which can only shine in a borrowed light, that is, in His light. "Let your light so shine before men that . . . they may glorify your Father in heaven."[2] To be good in the right way is only possible when we desire to be nothing.

4. Love is not merely an isolated act. Even in ourselves natural love, erotic love, for instance, is not genuine if it

[1] See particularly the First Epistle of John.   [2] Matt. v. 16.

does not develop from "being in love" into real love. Only when a person is truly "in love" is it possible to love. Love is a personal form of existence. Love is not an abstract form of loving, but it is the flowing forth of love. The Divine love is the possibility of human loving; it is the river whence the tiny rivulets of human love can pour themselves into life.

Therefore God only demands one thing: that we should live in His love. In His prophetic message Jesus summons men to "Love!" The apostolic exhortation, which points back to the gift of God in Christ, summons us to "Live in love."[1] Or, still more plainly: to *"Remain* in love." For the apostolic exhortation is addressed to believers, that is, to those who are already in the love of God. This commandment transcends the contrast between mysticism and morality. It is the summons to remain within the giving of God, to return to Him again and again as the origin of all power to be good, or to do good. There are no "other virtues" alongside of the life of love.

Even love is not a "virtue," because it is not a quality which can be assigned to man as such—it is not the light of a fixed star—but it is the state in which man stands in the light of God. The ancient conception of virtue can only spoil the Christian statements about being good. To-day we are rightly very suspicious of all talk of "virtues," indeed we are tired of all such language. For the ancient conception of virtue, which also dominates the whole medieval system of morality(1), turns a quality which depends for its very existence upon the reality of the Divine action into a human acquisition. Behind this present-day revulsion from the "virtuous man"—often decorated with all kinds of "orders" for his virtuous conduct— lies the feeling that there is something wrong in this virtue which man has so to speak "created," that all this talk of "possessing virtues" and of "being virtuous," indeed even the striving after such virtues, and even the mere ideal of virtue, is presumptuous. The idea of virtue leads man to justify himself—and this is the very opposite of all genuine goodness.

There is, however, a second point which is connected with this ancient idea of virtue as a quality which belongs to man as he is in himself, namely, that of the plurality of virtues(2). Once the perversion has taken place which conceives "being good" as a human quality, then inevitably the

[1] The *phrases* are distinctly "Johannine," but the subject is equally "Pauline." Cf. Rom. xii. 1; 2 Cor. v. 15; Phil. ii. 5.

second point follows, that there are a number of such virtues. The result is the atomization of the Good. For then man does not possess one quality, but many(3). Thus he has not merely one virtue but—if he is "perfect"—many virtues. The Good, which is one, is divided into little pieces, goodness is severed from the person as a whole, and qualities are turned into independent entities as "virtues." There then exists a whole system of virtues. The conception of the Good has become wholly externalized.

5. Thus if, in spite of this, the New Testament has adopted the conception of virtue, this can only be understood in one sense, namely, that it wishes to exhibit in the individual virtues the various forms of the one life in love. It is an ancient saying that love is "the mother of all the virtues." This saying suggests that there is no other Good at all save that which consists in living in love, but that this one life appears in a great variety of ways in connexion with the life of others. For as goodness is not something which belongs to man inherently, but only to his existence in relation to God, so the practical manifestation of this life with God is a life in relation with others, determined according to each particular relationship. Thus even in respect of others "virtue" is not *my* quality, something which can be thought of as belonging to the individual, but it is always a "*co*-existence," a way of being related to others.

Even where we speak of a plurality of virtues, the ancient conception of virtue has been fundamentally altered, in so far as virtue is never an individual mode of existence, but is always characterized as *co*-existence. There are no "individual" virtues, like those orders and decorations adorned with which the individual struts about among his fellows; but virtues only exist in life lived in relation with others.[1] Thus as the Self only achieves "goodness" in personal relation to God, so also "virtue" can only be attained in our relations with our fellow-men. And further: as life in love is a life which flows from the love of God, so also the individual virtue, as a particular manifestation of the one goodness, is always something which flows from another dimension, namely, from the fact of life as determined by the existence of our neighbour. For to live in love means concretely to allow one's life to be

[1] Or, more literally: "As the 'I' can only 'be good' in relation to the Divine 'Thou,' so the 'I' can only 'be virtuous' in relation to the 'Thou' of another human being."—Tr.

determined by the existence of others, by being "subject" to their needs and demands. Each virtue is a way of "entering into contact" with another person, of knowing that one "belongs" to him. Thus the variety of the virtues comes not from the self but from the other as the definite way in which through his particular situation or peculiarity my existence is determined by his. If it is impossible to conceive of any individual virtue as a quality of the Self, then also there are no virtues which can be individually conceived. Each virtue, one might say, is a particular way in which the person who lives in love takes the other into account, and "realizes" him as "Thou."

6. Only thus is the variety of the virtues to be understood aright. Truthfulness, for instance, is the special way of living in love, or of living in relation with others, which perceives or realizes the claim of the other man on my knowledge of the truth. Peaceableness is a particular way of living in relation with others in which I perceive the claim of the "Thou" for undisturbed fellowship with me. All these virtues are only really conceived in a personally actual, non-substantial manner, when they are conceived in terms of awareness of the claims of others, as a readiness to re-act, to respond to a definite call. Thus they are all *negative*, not positive, in character. They consist in having one's mind and heart open in a certain direction, but this does not imply that they possess positive content. All the virtues consist in "being ready." In this respect, too, the virtues cannot be defined in reply to the question *How?* but in reply to the question *Where?* The very fact that I—because I am living in love—am not self-centred and isolated, but am in touch with others, constitutes virtue in its varying forms.

There is no need here to deduce and describe the individual virtues. Traditional ethics has gone into this subject already in quite sufficient detail. What we need is to regain the right fundamental understanding of the principle which governs the conception of virtue, which has been so badly distorted both by the ancient tradition, and by the medieval scholastic tradition; we need to break away from the individualistic and anthropocentric conception of virtue. It is, indeed, no wonder that Luther hated Aristotle with such a passionate hatred! For the Aristotelian conception of virtue, which governed his own ethic and through this the ethic of Scholasticism, is the purely individualistic conception, which is dominated by the idea of the individual's self-improvement, till he achieves perfection. One of the most important tasks of a Christian ethic is to break away from this idea as completely as possible.

7. But, once this has been said, a second observation must be made as a secondary consideration. Man does not only consist of distinct acts; his life is also characterized by what one may describe as "settled conditions" or a "state of being." Just as we must not forget the fact of the physical existence of man in considering his power to act in a personal way, so also we must not forget the fact that his life falls into a certain "state" of being in a broader sense of the word. We do not live merely in acts of decision, but in our life there is also a region of the habitual, of that which has come to be in the empirical sense of the word. A detailed doctrine of the New Birth would have to take note of the fact that the act of faith has a reflex influence upon the condition of the person in question, with great caution it is true, but still quite clearly. There does exist what we call *character*, which can be described in empirical terms, the permanent element, the element which goes on working yesterday, to-day, and to-morrow. There is a relative constancy, an attitude, a certain stamp, whose external sign is the fact that we are in the body. And faith extends its influence into this region of the factual, habitual state just as much as sin does. There does exist something which can be described as a "Christian character"— different as this character is from faith, and in spite of the fact that faith is not to be understood from this standpoint. Faith may be "materialized" in a certain state of believing, a habitual state of faith. Hence faith exists as something which has grown thus, and therefore also as something which is growing, increasing or decreasing. The *person* can never be conceived in terms of qualities, but the *character* may be.

And just as this element of habit is one aspect of faith, so it is with love. There is therefore an "exercise in love," a process of growth in love, a more or a less, a "treasure," a power at the disposal of the moment of action, which distinguishes the mature soul from the beginner, there is a really present "excellence" and even a virtuosity of loving. In brief: there does exist what Aristotle and the Catholic moralists mean when they speak of virtue.

In this region virtues do exist as qualities in the person. Here, indeed, there really are individual virtues of which one may have more of one and less of another, just as also in technical excellence one may be "stronger" at one point and "weaker" at another. This point of view should and must also have its place in a Christian ethic, even though this place may be a secondary one; this subject will be treated in connexion with the discussion of the *justitia civilis*. The error of the usual doctrine of virtue does not consist in the fact that it points to these virtues—which really are present in individual persons as such—but in the fact that it makes them the fundamental and the main thing, that it interprets man as a being who strives upwards from "below," rather than as a being who depends on something which is granted to him from "above," that it regards continuity as an ascending rather than a descending scale, that it does not perceive that this order of progression is completely reversed by repentance and faith, that *gratia* is not *superponit naturam*, but that it consists in a "dying" and "becoming new"; that even the "virtue" which proceeds from faith only comes into being when the gaze of the soul is directed, not towards the "I," and that which is present, but towards Christ and His word of justification. We can only speak of this virtue as a "state" without doing harm if we are quite clear that it is nothing natural, nothing constructed by man, if we realize that its growth proceeds from the actuality of faith; otherwise we shall fall into a hopeless morass of Naturalism or Substantialism, which knows grace only as Supernature, and in so doing falsifies its nature from the very root.

But to deal with these virtues is not so much the task of ethics as of pedagogy. The place of pedagogy is the habitual, as its essential categories are practice and custom, although certainly a right pedagogy can only be produced when it looks at that which lies beyond its own sphere. Here, therefore, all that concerns us is to give an indication of this connexion between ethics and the empirical considerations and practice of pedagogy.

CHAPTER XVII

SELF-AFFIRMATION AND SELF-DENIAL

PROPOSITION: *The Command of the Creator and the Redeemer requires the thankful acceptance of our given individual existence coupled with the denial of the self-seeking isolated Ego, in view of the Kingdom of God.*

1. It is the nature of the Ego, or of the Self, that it consists not only of its created powers, but also of its view of its own nature, and of the aim of self-realization which it sets before itself.[1] The fact that God has created man as a person, as a self, means that He has created him in such a way that he must himself determine to be that for which he was designed. This constitutes his freedom; this liberty of self-determination forms the very essence of selfhood, or of personal existence, and, indeed, it *is* personal existence itself; it is this element which distinguishes personal existence from every other form of existence. But God has created man in such a way that only when he determines himself in accordance with his destiny does he become that for which he was created. Only then is he really free. But if man chooses to live on another basis, if, for instance, he chooses to run directly counter to the purpose for which he was created—that is, if he plans his life apart from God, basing all on his own independent existence, he loses both his hopes of self-realization and his freedom. He is still formally free, it is true, that is, he is still a being who understands and determines his own course of action, but he no longer possesses material freedom; he is then forced to misunderstand himself and has no longer any real power over himself. He has become the slave of his own emancipation; in it he is "fixed," imprisoned.

Man is only free when his life is shaped according "to the image of God," that is, when he knows that he is living on the power of God, on the gift of God. If he is living on himself—that is, in a lie, for he can only live on that which he has from God—then he is cut off from God, the source of freedom, and is therefore not free. "Whoever commits sin is the servant of sin."

2. Just as I, as a believer, know the Creator, in Jesus Christ, so also I know that God "acknowledges" me—in spite of what I am, and as I am—and that He desires to possess not

[1] Cf. KIERKEGAARD: *Die Krankheit zum Tode* (beginning.)

only my nature, or my existence, but me, myself. This is the incomprehensible fact: that God "justifies" me, just as I am. In spite of everything He affirms me as His creature and calls me good. He sees in me, what none of us can see, His original creation. Because He sees us thus, we also—but only through Him—ought to look at ourselves also in this light, and should thus "accept" ourselves as from Him. God does not require us to throw ourselves away; no, He requires us to respect ourselves, to use our wills, indeed, even—in view of His gift of life—to have a grateful love of ourselves. If this command to love ourselves takes a less obvious place in the New Testament it is only because this self-love is assumed as a matter of course, since, indeed, the vital urge leads in this direction. A glance at the people of India, or at the spirit of despair so prevalent at the present time, will show us immediately that *this* kind of self-respect and self-love can easily become perverted into the exact opposite. This is why it is explicitly commanded.

This certainly does not mean that God commands us to accept life as it is viewed from the standpoint of merely natural instinct; what God bids us to do is to accept our life as a whole, "gratefully," from His Hands. Just because we are here concerned with His creation and with His gift of life, we are absolutely forbidden to dispose of our own existence. The prohibition of suicide stands by itself, alone, outside the dialectic of affirmation and negation; for it alone has to do not with a modification of life but with life itself, with existence as such. We are tempted to say that the prohibition of suicide is an unconditional, absolutely clear law; and yet to say this would be to intrude into the realm of the divine sovereignty, which is not permissible. At this particular point the Christian ethic differs wholly from the Stoic ethic (which, as we all know, left the problem of suicide an open question) (1); clearly as we perceive this, all that we can say is that we can think of no case in which God either commands or does not forbid man to lay hands upon himself. But this does not mean that self-preservation is taught as an unconditional duty. Just as we have no right to dispose of our own lives, so also we have no right to regard life as an absolute end in itself. Self-preservation is always conditioned by the rule that we may only preserve our life if this is possible without breaking the commandments of God. It is always possible to conceive that it may be God's will that we should die; but it is impossible to imagine that God could will us to end our life by our own act.

3. God does not only will our existence but He wants us as we are. We have an individuality which is given by God and is therefore willed by Him. Hence not only are we forbidden to run away from life, but we are also forbidden to renounce our individuality, and are commanded to accept life with gratitude. To renounce our individuality is in harmony with pantheistic-mystical thought, which does not know God as the Creator(2). It is, of course, true that there is also sinful individuality, due to the influence of sin; of that we shall speak later. But behind all its sinfulness there lies the individuality created and willed by God, which we ought to will in harmony with His will. Above all, we ought thankfully to accept the finite character and the limitations of our individuality; for this belongs to our nature as created beings as such. If we are unwilling to accept these limitations it means that we want to be equal with God. It is the infamous idea expressed in the phrase: "If there were gods, who would not wish to be a God" (Nietzsche), the Satanic defiance of God.

Nature and history are inextricably blended in our individuality. Therefore we must also acknowledge our historical existence, that is, our life in the form it has assumed under the influence of previous generations of human beings.

It is the will of God not only that there should be people of different temperaments, but also people of a different historical stamp; indeed, it is the will of God that history itself should exist, and this very history which we know—in spite of everything! Were we to desire to accept as willed by God only that which has happened apart from sin, then we certainly could not accept our own existence. For apart from sin we would not have come into being at all. Sin has a great share in the fact that we exist at all, it is not necessary to be an "unwanted" or illegitimate child to understand this. In our existence, as it is here and now, we cannot separate the wheat from the tares. But—thanks to the fact of justification—we ought to know, and we may know, that we, as we are, are God's creatures.

4. What then does self-affirmation, the thankful acceptance of our God-given existence, mean in detail? To affirm our existence as God-given can mean nothing less than the recognition of our existence as God's property, and thus to

dedicate it to Him. This is the Scriptural meaning of the word "to sanctify." To sanctify life means to regard it and use it as God's possession. We ought to regard ourselves and, indeed, we may do so—in spite of everything—as instruments which God has taken into His service, which He declares to be of use to Him, and to His purpose. This is the honour which we have from God; and no distress over our daily discoveries of our unfitness for this service should make us doubt or even despair. Justification by grace alone means that God has accepted us as recruits in His army; once this has taken place we can go forth bearing on our banner the amazing device: "Fit for the service of God." The value of our life is thus an ultimate value, but it is not a self-value. We may be joyfully and proudly conscious of this dignity, with the pride of humility, which knows that we possess this value only as a gift. Our high standing is due to the fact that God has rated us so highly.[1]

But this also means that we possess this value as those who belong to God, who thus are no longer their own masters, but the servants of God. To sanctify or to dedicate to God means: to sacrifice, in which act we are both "priests" and "victims."[2] "Priests," in so far as God demands from us this action: "victims," in so far as it is our own life which is to be presented to Him as an offering. It is not only our external life which we are to give to Him, but ourselves, the central core of the personality, which we are to offer up in sacrifice, to give over to death. This brings us to the second part of our theme.

5. Looking backwards, it is our duty to affirm our individual existence as a whole, in the very shape and form in which it has come to us, as a gift from God. But this idea must not lead us astray in our thought about the way of life which lies before us, and about our own decision. God does not only give us the existence which we now possess; He sets this life of ours under the searchlight of His judgment, and summons us to alter our lives. Indeed, in faith He tells us that through Christ we have already become different, that we are "a new creation." This "new creation" only becomes real through the death of the "old man." The fact that we have to die— in every sense of the word—both physically and spiritually,

---

[1] Or, more literally: "We may 'regard' ourselves so highly because God thus 'regards' us."—TR.
[2] Rom. xii. 1.

shows how gravely God judges our present existence. It is true, of course, that God by no means destroys our own estimate of ourselves as "not quite so good as we ought to be"; on the contrary, He heightens and intensifies it. He drives home the conviction: "You are so unfit for God's service that there is nothing in you left to save!" This does not mean—as we like to think it does—that the "sinful element within us" must die. No, our personality as a whole must pass through death. Sin and the sinner cannot be separated. We are therefore summoned to yield ourselves up to this death. We are seriously bidden to despair of ourselves. We ought to know how hostile to God is our individual existence, in everything that concerns us, how deeply this whole "organism" is permeated with this spirit of hostility to God; and we ought to know this not as a theoretical, dogmatic statement, but as a matter of daily practical experience. Here we are not concerned with mere "head-knowledge" but with a knowledge which is also an act of feeling and of will. We are bidden to hate this "Ego," this corruption of the Divine creation, which is, indeed, a constantly renewed and living act, a person, a Self, and, as far as possible, we are bidden to annihilate it, in the light of the fact. of death in which God Himself manifests His judgment.

The totalitarian, absolute way in which this is intended only becomes manifest to us in Christ. True negation of self consists in being placed by Him, indeed in Him, in the divine negation, that is, in His death, in His Cross. Paul calls this being "crucified with Christ."[1] This does not mean something "mystical," but it does mean something very real, namely the divine judgment, which begins with repentance, but does not end there. In Jesus Christ, the Crucified, God pronounces to-day this sentence of death upon us. To believe means to acknowledge that that which takes place in the Crucified One really happens to *me*. This act is not an historic psychological transference which at once becomes sentimental; no, what takes place is this: in faith it comes to pass that God's real word of judgment to me, on me, is perceived. His judgment on *me*—not on "my sin"; for sin in itself is nothing. It is evil because it is the act of the sinner. And I am a sinner, "I," not a part of me but I myself, wholly. This does not mean that "ethically speaking" there is nothing good in man, as this idea is so often understood to mean. It does not mean

[1] Rom. vi. 4 and 6.

that "man has not a shred of righteousness left to cover him." We do not deny that differences do exist between the decent and the indecent, between upright, conscientious, honourable men and those who even contend heroically for the Good, and their opposites. All that I say is this: that this whole moral gradation which for us is absolutely necessary, simply does not count ultimately, that is, in the sight of God, because through all this He sees the one thing which is not individual and differentiated but quite universal: that all men are sinners.

6. This becomes ethically manifest in the relation between individual existence and the community. Every individual existence, every human "I," is in the last resort a being who seeks himself. This self-seeking may be refined, but it is indissolubly bound up with our present existence. In this sense the harsh saying of Grisebach, "The Self is the Evil," is absolutely true. Our life—even though we may be very "socially-minded" and friendly towards other people—ultimately circles round ourselves as the central point. We only absorb our neighbour as it were into our circle, but no effort avails to enable us to break through this charmed circle of self-interest. To all of us, without exception, the command to "love one's neighbour as oneself" becomes a sentence of condemnation. Our attempts in this direction are not only finally useless, but from the very outset (and at bottom this is the same thing) they are not quite honest. In faith we see that this barrier is only broken down at one point: in Christ. This is why there alone do we see in reality what otherwise is merely adumbrated in a parabolic way: love, self-sacrifice.

Hence in the life of faith the sacrifice of Christ becomes the Divine Command to deny ourselves. Self-denial is the ethical aspect of repentance, it is the "Imitation of Christ" on the basis of that which His Divine act—which we can never imitate—means. In the self-offering of Christ "ethics"—human action, and "dogmatics"—divine action, are one. This is why we perceive that the Divine Command for our own action is based upon the Divine action. In the language of ethics, to be "in Christ" means the death of the selfish Ego; it means the willed, deliberate mortification of that will whose poison penetrates the whole of our nature—in defiance of our natural self-will; thus it means an attack "upon oneself," upon the natural instincts, and also upon natural self-will in the form of spiritual self-regard, upon the desire to live for self, upon the spiritual tendency to live independently of others, humbly submitting oneself to the claims of others, of the "Thou," becoming "one who serveth."

7. But this *mortificatio*, this self-denial, has nothing to do with ascetic efforts to achieve holiness; for the evil which is to be "mortified" is not a natural or a metaphysical quality, but the severance of the self from union with God and with our neighbour. Just as man is not evil "in himself," but in relation to God and man, that is, in selfish severance from them both, so also this "mortification" of evil is not something which can happen to the Ego, in itself, but it consists in breaking down that false isolation. Evil is lack of fellowship, the desire to love for and in oneself; therefore the new Good means life-in-fellowship, life lived for other people, love.

Self-denial is not self-torture, it is not the destruction of vital powers, it is not the flight of the anchorite or the monk from the reality of life in community, it is not the ideal of holiness in Greek and Catholic thought and practice, the ideal of the holy hermit—on the contrary, it consists in self-giving to the community. The natural egocentric tendency is replaced by the outward movement, towards other people. For this is the movement of the Christ, into which through faith we are drawn: the will for the perfect fellowship of men among themselves through their communion with God, the movement towards the Kingdom of God. All ascetic holiness is itself the final fulfilment of the egocentric movement, it is the highest form of self-fulfilment, of turning away from the "Thou" to the "I." Sanctification through self-denial, however, means turning away from the "I" to the "Thou"—and in this very movement the Self comes to real fulfilment. "For whosoever will save his life shall lose it; and whosoever will lose his life for my sake shall find it."[1] For the Self only fulfils its destiny when it does not live on and in itself, but in and for the other. Love, as the way of life of those who have been born again, is the realization of humanity—in so far as man has been born again. The new life, as gift and as demand, is life in community. And on the other hand: only through life in community does the old self die, as a life centred in self.

8. Faith, since it means being in Christ, also means being a member of His body, life in the Christian community, union with those who belong to Him(3). In the sense of the ascetic

[1] Matt. xvi. 25.

ideal of holiness, and, indeed, in that of the general religious ideal of holiness, it is possible to be a saint by and for oneself alone. For the Christian there is and can be no private holiness. The phrase "Saints" here always means those who are in the community of Jesus Christ, who are in the Church as the Body of Christ, and, indeed, solely on the basis of the fact that they are within this community. To be a member and to be "holy" is the same thing; for both mean to be dedicated to God, to be united with God, and therefore to be united with other men in fellowship. The Greek idea of perfection, the modern idea of personality, the mystical conception of holiness—all define the true being of man as a way of being which is based on, and to be perfected in, the individual man. Christian thought recognizes that this very insistence on a solitary holiness, this self-centred elevation of the spirit— whether of the Self as an entity which plunges deep into thought, or into creative action, or into the mystical "ground of the soul"—*is* evil—not something evil—and that to be free from oneself, to be free for the lives of others, is the Good. This transformation is the new life of man, given to him by God; it also means, on this "given" basis, that man is to "become" a "new creature"; it means that redemption has begun, but is not completed; it means obedience to the Redeemer's Command.

This kind of self-affirmation, which is the same as self-denial, is not only permitted, it is commanded. The "putting on of the new man," this true "revolution of the disposition," means acceptance of myself because God through His forgiveness has already accepted me. This dignity is just as unassailable as it is incomparable. It is the dignity of those who belong to the "household of God,"[1] it is the joy of the restoration of the divine image which proceeds from God Himself. In truth, selfhood, the dignity of the individual(4), has not here been submerged in some collective entity— neither in the Idea, nor in culture, nor in the race, nor in the All; for the member of the community, in this sense of the word, is the same as the utterly solitary individual who has heard and answered God's call, he is the true "individual." Indeed, the Church, the ἐκκλησία, means the sum-total of all those who have been called out by Christ, of the "elect." The new regard for personality is based upon this fact: that man, as an individual, knows that *God* is continually regarding

[1] Eph. ii. 19.

177

him with favour; he knows for a certainty, in the deep and secret places of the soul, where he is alone with God, that God regards him thus. The Christian is commanded to "boast" of this new standing of his, and with this in his heart he can defy the contempt of the whole world. This "God-dependence" constitutes his true "self-dependence."

CHAPTER XVIII

THE BETTER RIGHTEOUSNESS

PROPOSITION: *The Divine Command, so far as the subject is concerned, can only be apprehended through the Law, which requires three things: life on the level of ordinary morality, complete renunciation of all claims to "virtue," and the striving after perfection.*

1. Life in faith—and this means the Christian life or the life of the Christian—is a life which transcends the law; for it is life lived in the strength of the grace of the God who is continually giving. This does not mean, however, that God has ceased to make demands on man—it does not mean that henceforth the life of the Christian is to be described in terms of spontaneous growth:[1] this comes out most clearly, as we have already seen, in the fact that even for the Christian the law has not been abrogated. On the contrary, the law affects what he is bidden to be—as well as what he has to do—in three ways: it acts as a force which creates order, as a court which judges, and as a guide to the "new man."

From the standpoint of justification by grace alone it follows that God commands us to be good decent citizens. The humdrum civic virtues are not only "unfortunately" included in the government of God, like much else which "unfortunately" exists, but they have their appointed place in the life of the Christian. For only too easily does it happen that in overstrained intellectualism or spirituality one may neglect the commonplace moral demands which—more or less—every one knows and accepts. We ought to be able to entrust a cash-box with complete confidence to a Christian—and this cannot be taken for granted. But behind this commonplace fact lies a truth of great significance. We may indeed say that it was the mission of the Enlightenment in the history of the world to lay its finger on this element of truth. It is certain, of course, that this ordinary conception of virtue, if it be the dominating one, seems intolerably meagre and the resistance offered to it by Romanticism and Idealism was well-founded. But to brush aside in a superior manner all the claims of virtue which aim at a finite, attainable and single Good, to despise the exercise of fidelity and honesty in everyday life, as speculative Idealism and Romanticism tended to do in their highest

[1] Literally "the indicatives of growth."—TR.

179

flights of sentiment—this spirit of intellectual dominance, with its attitude of arrogant superiority to the "vulgar herd," is no better, and indeed it is actually a far more daemonic form of self-righteousness than the self-complacency of the *bourgeois* individual.

2. There is a possible kind of virtue, indeed even "perfection," which is required from one who is a believer. Just as it is possible to be a perfect manual craftsman, so it is required of the Christian that in daily life he should be "blameless,"[1] that he should conform wholly to the demands made on him by the ordinary life of a citizen. What matters here is the man himself, and not merely his disposition, first of all indeed legal, actual conformity to a rule. In this conception of virtue the technical and the ethical elements are inseparably united. What is intended and required is an ordering of life, first of all for its own sake, without considering the motive which lies behind it. One must be able to rely on the certainty that in this or that "job" a man will be thoroughly reliable, that with complete certainty we may expect from a man definitely correct conduct. A theological ethic orientated round the thought of the Reformation would be ill advised if at this point it were to insist on the principle that "all our doings are nothing worth" (1). Within this comprehensive saying room must be made for the quite definite finite tasks of an ideal of virtue. By this I mean what the ancients used to call the *justitia civilis* (2). The fact that a closer examination of all that lies behind this ideal of virtue would immediately disclose the infinite nature of the task and the questionable value of all such virtue, ought not to blind our eyes to the fact that this ideal does exist in its own right.

3. The key to the understanding of this conception of virtue, which, at the present day in particular, is so little understood, is the knowledge of its peculiar "principle." It cannot be a principle in the strict sense of the word; for all that is based on principle, as an Idea, immediately leads into infinity, and does not guarantee that with which we are here concerned: its bearing on the enclosed finite. Aristotle, with his genius, was feeling after this idea, and he tried to define it in that idea of the "mean," which is so difficult to understand and has so often been unfairly abused. In my opinion, certainly, Aristotle was prevented by his individualism and rationalism

---

[1] 1 Tim. v. 7. Cf. the similar expressions "unblemished" and "unblamable" in Eph. i. 4 and Phil. i. 10.

from finding what he was seeking; at least he was not wholly successful; for this element cannot be understood as man's existence for himself alone, as something which affects the isolated man as an individual, as something which could as it were be apprehended mathematically. We seem to get a little nearer to the meaning if we define this idea as "righteousness."[1] But in so doing we must think of this term in the older German sense and not in the Latin and juridical sense, which still lives on in many compound words such as *sach-gerecht, mund-gerecht, kunst-gerecht,*[2] etc. In these words the idea of an attitude of mind is combined with that of actual technical efficiency. To be "righteous" in this sense means to "do one's job" in the *right* way. It is here decisive—we are now in the sphere of legality—that the actual achievement and the attitude of mind should not be separated. Here the statement that "nothing matters save a good will" does not apply. No; here what one does matters very much, or rather, the concentration of the worker and the excellence of the workmanship matter greatly. Here the essential point is this: devotion to a concrete purpose within a very limited sphere, that kind of personal action in which interest in the matter in hand and conscientious anxiety to do it as well as possible are merged into one. It does not matter what the particular "excellence" may be, whether that of the good calligrapher with his perfect handwriting, or the certainty with which a farm labourer can drive his horse and cart through a narrow gateway (so much admired by Gotthelf[3]), or the masterly way in which the statesman pilots the ship of state through perilous waters: all these workers "do their job in the right way," and have a right to be proud of their achievements, and to have a good conscience. This pride in good workmanship has nothing at all to do with self-righteousness or arrogance. Indeed it even forms an essential part of this "righteousness."

4. In this connexion, however, it is no accident that the word *"sach"-gerecht* (*really* or *actually* right) forces itself upon our notice. This conception of righteousness is absolutely determined by the *actual* requirements which proceed from

---

[1] Or *Justice*. German: *Gerechtigkeit.*—TR.

[2] *Sach-gerecht*—really *right*, *mund-gerecht*—just *right* to be eaten or drunk (i.e. palatable). Fig. suitable. *Kunst-gerecht*—*right* according to the rules of art, correct, workmanlike.—TR.

[3] JEREMIAS GOTTHELF is the pen-name of ALBERT BITZIUS (1797–1854), a Protestant pastor, poet and popular writer.—TR.

life in nature and in the natural community. There is an objective adaptability (3) of action to the actual duties of life, or "right conduct"—to which there corresponds a certain human quality of trustworthiness (that is, man can be trusted to perform these duties); we call this quality the "virtue" or "righteousness" of the citizen.

Foremost among these tasks of citizenship are those which control the sphere governed by law. The noblest virtue of the citizen is "right conduct," in the sense of right behaviour within the sphere of society. But all attempts to define this principle of "righteousness" in fixed terms are useless. Even the Aristotelian definitions, taken over by the Catholic ethic, of distributive and commutative righteousness (4) are insufficient as an adequate definition, since they are based upon an irrational idea. The standard of righteousness consists in giving to every man "his due," the *suum cuique*. But who is to determine what is the *suum* for each person? The attempt to define and establish this *suum* in absolute terms leads either to the idea of perfect equality—which destroys all life—or to the Christian idea of love, which breaks through and removes the idea of mere righteousness altogether.[1]

How inconceivable—and yet how indispensable—this conception of righteousness is comes out in another idea of the same kind, in that of equity (*aequitas*), which makes it very plain that true justice cannot be conceived in legal terms. Whatever is equitable—and thus truly righteous (right and equitable)—cannot be deduced from principles, it must be inferred by the healthy human moral sense, almost one might say by the moral instinct. It is something which differs in each case, something which has to be discovered ("to find" the right), and such power of discernment, which, for instance, a judge ought to possess, is something creative. All definitions in terms of principle, all legal definitions, violate the spirit of equity, and thus injure the spirit of true justice and also lead to endless complications. There is no "static" equity, but only an equity which can be discovered at the moment of action, and whoever regulates his conduct by this quality is "just" (or "righteous")—it is, as it were, a kind of natural analogy to Christian love.

5. Thus even the Christian ought to have this kind of righteousness; although in a limited sense, he is even bidden to have it. But even when this has been granted the meaning

[1] Cf. on this point: Chapter XXIX, p. 325.

of the conception of the *justitia civilis* has not yet been fully expressed. Just as we can say that the Christian ought to be a good honest citizen, so also we can say that he ought to "be a gentleman." The English ideal of a "gentleman" expresses, in a condensed form, just as many (though different) aspects of natural morality as the German ideal of the "just man" or the "good citizen." The English conception of the virtues which constitute a gentleman suggests an ideal of "right conduct" in social life. The term "gentleman" also suggests respect for law and order; there is no doubt that even in England the devil would appear to be a perfect gentleman, to human eyes quite indistinguishable from a gentleman. Further, the very idea of "a gentleman" does not lend itself to such distinctions. It does not go deep enough, and for this very reason its value is merely relative; at the same time its value as a popular educative idea is great. Its usefulness is based upon the fact that it is an idea, like equity, which cannot be expressed in terms of abstract principle, but only in terms which denote a certain mobility and power of adjustment to life which is not legalistic.

6. Far more comprehensive and profound than all the ideas which have just been mentioned is the idea of *humanity*. In all seriousness we are urged to preserve and to seek for humanity—that which is specifically human—over against the chaos of sense-bound bondage to instinct. Each man is summoned to act as a watcher on the dykes to see that the wild, overwhelming sea of the sub-human, the elements of blind caprice, of casual lawlessness should not sweep over the field of human life. If we accept the idea of a series of stages (which we elaborated in an earlier part of this work) which leads from the merely natural level up to the moral idea, this should mean in actual practice—even if in a conditional and relative way—that every one of us ought to consider it our duty to play our part in this ascending movement, which is the ideal aspect of the historical process. The relative superiority of Idealism to Naturalism, and the demand for surrender to the great spiritual ideas of Truth, Beauty, and Goodness which result from an honest Idealism—even though they may not be regarded as ultimates—are not mere illusions or ideologies. A life spent in the service of the ideal of justice—as for instance that of Zola during the Dreyfus trial—or of humanity—think of a man like Owen, for instance, or Jaurès—is not only to be recognized by the Christian as something so infinitely superior

to all that is superficial and idle, that it contains an element of real greatness, but this devotion to the ultimate ruling and regulative ideas of the practical reason—along with the heroism which springs out of all this—is required by God. Without this idea of humanity human life loses its elasticity which no faith could restore to it. On the contrary, although faith does not actually produce this idea, it does reawaken it, where it has died out. The vitality and genuineness of justifying faith must be proved by the fact that it does not destroy this vital elasticity and this tendency of life created by the Idea.

The practical idealism and humanism of the doctor who wears himself out in the service of suffering human beings, of the judge who cares more for a just verdict than for his own security, of the devoted Labour leader or statesman, of the scholar, or the minor official with his fidelity to duty, of the self-sacrificing mother who gives herself joyfully to her family, all this, which is included under the heading of the *justitia civilis*, is also—if we may dare to put it so—indispensable, highly valued, and commanded by God Himself, within the economy of a Christian people.

7. But the Idea implies infinity. The Idea is always inadequate. The "Knight of the Infinite"[1] if he is no more than this, inevitably loses his balance; or if, in order to avoid this, he resigns himself and adapts himself then he becomes a Philistine. Something far more serious must be behind the moral idea, namely, the law of God, the demand for perfect love to God and man conceived as law. Without this law God is never taken seriously. But—and this is equally true—without despair the law is never taken seriously. Wherever, behind the summons to be a "gentleman," a "good citizen," a "noble man," to "be helpful and good," the divine law of perfect love to God and man appears, there idealistic enthusiasm (which always has a strongly aesthetic aspect) disappears. When the moral idealist is fully and soberly resolved to shoulder the whole of his responsibility, to tread the path of duty whatever it may cost, that is, wherever the Idea is taken seriously, since it is recognized to be the demand of God, thus, where the conception of righteousness is understood in a radical sense, there, inevitably, it will come to pass that man will first of all despair of his own strength, then of the wholeness of his will, and finally of the purity of his heart. Where the brilliant light of the divine law flames into the

[1] KIERKEGAARD: *Furcht und Zittern.*

184

human reality with its light, the deep shadows which lie within every action, every personal life, become visible. Then pride in one's virtues breaks down, then the difference between "above" and "below" loses all significance. How do I know whether in the sight of God that criminal is really worse than I? How do I know that my guilt, if weighed in God's scales, is not a thousand times heavier than his? There is only one thing which I *do* know, and that is: that before the Divine Judgment Seat I shall be found wanting.

It is no accident that here we pass from the third to the first person. We never make that final discovery in the third person, but always only in the first person. In the third person we only know the Idea of the Good, but not the Law of God as *His* Law. On the other hand, so long as we still know the Good as an Idea we only know ourselves in the third person, and this means that we are merely spectators of our own lives. The turning to the existential, that is, to that situation where I myself am summoned by God Himself, takes place only in faith, where the law of God is concentrated at one point in the one demand: "Repent, surrender!" To hear the law of God as His command, and to become nothing before Him, means the same thing. Just as we are bidden to exercise the commonplace virtues of the ordinary decent man, so also we are bidden to exercise this spirit of repentance, this utter humility, in this profound self-knowledge which reveals our utter emptiness—which leads us to cry out: "God be merciful to me a sinner!" At this point all claim to the acquisition of virtue ceases, although the Divine summons to the virtuous life does not cease.

8. This "state" of humility, however, is only possible in a life of faith, and therefore in a very different sense from that of ordinary virtue. Virtue in the ordinary sense, as applied to civic and social life, is really the Aristotelian *Habitus*. Faith, however, is no *Habitus*, but the most complete actuality. It is possible to *possess* "virtue" in this sense all one's life, but faith can only be constantly received as a *gift*. Only in this faith can we endure repentance. Without it repentance must lead either to madness or to passive resignation. Faith is a gift, but it is also commanded. Indeed, in the last resort nothing is commanded save this: "Believe!" In this one commandment, however, there is also commanded as well— not merely social virtue, but the intensification of every single social virtue, that is, of every single way of being righteous.

185

To faith belongs the perception of the command: "Ye shall become perfect!" Perfection, which looked at from above means love, when viewed from below, means the sum-total of all virtues. Even in faith we cannot evade this view from below. The law as an exhortation requires from us the higher righteousness, it requires us to take the demands of social virtue more seriously. This "perfectionism," which is always based upon the foundation of humility, of insight into the lasting nothingness of all human claims to virtue, is thoroughly Biblical, whereas that which is generally so called, since it denies the *simul peccator*, denies justification and is therefore self-deception.

9. The law summons us to become more righteous. "I *follow after* the prize of the high calling . . ."[1] The New Testament is full of the imperatives of growth. The absolute law—that law which is the schoolmaster to bring us to Christ—requires righteousness. But this we cannot achieve. To the believer, however, who knows what his position is, God commands something which he can do, according to the measure of that which he has received. God takes our weakness into account![2] But He does not modify His demand. For He desires from us what we can do here and now. It is this which constitutes the absolute seriousness of His will. In view of this fact the relative distinctions between "better" and "worse" become extremely important. To fail to make this distinction between the law as it appears before and after the soul has received the Divine forgiveness, actually destroys the moral will by its absolute demand. The God who demands the absolute in the Law demands from us in faith, in His Commandments, something finite, something concrete, that is, something adapted to our moral condition at this moment. There would be no practical demand of God to be considered at all if He did not require from us something relative in this sense. Thus, on this basis, the demand of the relative is the only truly serious practical demand. The Law, however, as the sum-total of the requirements of virtue, shows us the way to that which God here and now demands from us, the better righteousness, the comparative. That, however, this is only something relative does not concern us, but the fact that God requires it, means that it is unconditionally required. Indeed,

[1] Phil. iii. 14.
[2] CALVIN: *In gratia constituti sumus liberati a rigida Legis exactione* (on Rom. vi. 14).

it is not the relative as such that He requires—what He always requires is simply this: that in our present moral condition we should "complete the movement of faith" (Kierkegaard).

The ordinary social ethic is not wrong in demanding that we should become better—the New Testament also does this —but it is wrong in the way in which it makes the demand. This ethic has no sense of urgency—there is always plenty of time to alter! It does not know the "to-day" which is so pregnant with eschatological meaning! It has already absorbed the spirit of resignation. It only knows demands which have been toned down and adapted. Indeed it does not know the Divine Command, which for the Christian stands behind every imperative of growth: God Himself commands you here and now to become better. He commands that you, here and now, in this your highly questionable state of virtue shall complete the movement of faith, and that through this you are to be "better," even in view of the ordinary social demands of virtue. He always commands us to strive after perfection.

Thus, in order to perceive the Divine Command, we must always keep the following three elements in mind at the same time: the social demands · of virtue with their legal finite character and possibility of fulfilment; the absolute law, which summons men to repentance; and the concrete imperative of growth. The fact that we are not perfect is never an adequate excuse, but it only adds to our guilt, just as the sinfulness of all we do never dispenses us from doing what we are definitely told to do. The concrete command of the moment can only be understood from the point of view of the absolute law, because only from that standpoint can we understand the gift of God in Christ, and thus faith is possible. But likewise the concrete demand of the moment can also only be understood from the point of view of social righteousness which provides the substructure for this concreteness.

To put it quite simply, it is in God's mercy (as faith perceives) that He wills, here and now, to have from us something which we *can* do; but since we know this mercy of God as that of the God of forgiveness, we know also that at every moment we should have done something which we cannot do, which He alone has done for us, and, in so far as He wills, which He Himself is doing through our sinful deeds.

CHAPTER XIX

SERVICE

PROPOSITION: *The Divine Command requires one thing only: the service of God, that is, to do that which honours God and makes His will effective. But the God who is revealed in the Incarnation does not desire this service for Himself but for humanity. He requires from us a great variety of forms of service.*

1. God does not desire "something" from us—He desires us, ourselves; not our works, but our personality, our will, our heart. This was the subject of the previous section. God does not desire to have us for Himself so that we may lose ourselves in Him in mystical contemplation, but He desires to possess us for His service. The service of God constitutes the sum-total of all good conduct. It is due to the grace of God that He declares us fit for His service, and that He appoints us to His service. And this is the true obedience of faith: that we are at His disposal, that in all that we do we do His will, in order to please Him, and are wholly there for Him, to "lend Him a hand," desiring to glorify Him. "Whatsoever ye do, do all to the glory of God."[1] Only then is our action hallowed; for to "hallow" means to "dedicate to God." Without this dedication an action may be useful creative, heroic; but it is in no way holy or good.

To act in the spirit of dedication to God means to sacrifice. Hallowed action is sacrificial action. Thus the whole of Christian activity is to be regarded from the point of view of "sacrifice." To do everything one does in the world as a sacrifice to God: this is the holy service of the Christian within the world; it is his "reasonable service."[2] The Good in the ethical sense is the same as the Holy: the Cultus. We are bound to serve none save God alone; and we have no other duty save to serve God.

For this very reason we are not here concerned with that which is everywhere else regarded as "cultus." Sacrifice, and with it the whole paraphernalia of sacred or specifically religious action is abolished by the sacrificial death of Christ.

---

[1] 1 Cor. x. 31.　　　　　　　　　　　　[2] Rom. xii. 1.

Ecclesiastical action, or the "cultus" in the usual sense of the word, whose central point is reconciliation with God, by means of the reconciliation achieved by God Himself, has lost its meaning. No longer do we need to propitiate God nor to win His favour. We *are* reconciled, we *are* in His favour. The repetition of the Sacrifice in the Mass—which in the peculiarly ecclesiastical sense of the word is liturgical action, and forms part of the cultus—betrays some doubt about that which God has done once for all. Where the sacrifice of Christ is taken seriously no action is offered directly to God, and thus there is no cultus(1). The delimitation of a sacred zone of life alongside the secular sphere, of a religious form of action alongside the secular, the distinction between "duties towards God" and "duties towards man" or "duties within the world," which is characteristic of all non-Christian religion, has been abolished. All that is secular is holy, and all that is holy has become secular.

This change is due to the fact that the whole direction of life has been altered: henceforth it is man's duty and privilege to live as one whose whole life springs *from* God—the days of his anxious striving *after* God are over; he now knows only the God whose Face is turned towards the world. God does not wish us to offer Him any special sacrifice, intended for Himself alone; when a man turns to Him, desiring to serve Him, God directs his attention to the world and its need. It is His will that our service of Him should be expressed as our service to the world—through Him, and for His sake. For us there are no holy places, times, persons, acts. There are no special "religious" regulations. The cultus, divine service, our turning towards God, is to be found in life itself.

2. God summons us to serve Him and therefore to serve His world. This brings us to the second point, namely, that no action should be directed towards ourselves. There is no Christian service of self. Service means going out of oneself, being free from anxiety about oneself, being free for others. There is no individual Christian ethic(2). If there were, it would be wrong to say that love is the fulfilling of the law, it would be untrue to say that the expressions "love of God," "love of one's Neighbour" express all there is to say about the Good. God's command places us in relation to our neighbour, not to ourselves. Natural desire is self-interested, it is care for oneself. It is this which constitutes the evil and the misery of the unreconciled person. The call to the service of God tears

189

us out of this state of self-regard; through obedience to this call man, as it were, turns his back upon himself.

This does not mean that the rights of the "I" are ignored. Indeed, before action begins the "I" has already come into its own, or rather, not to its "rights" at all, but to its undeserved state of grace. God Himself has taken away from man all anxiety about himself, He Himself has settled the account. Man's life is secure in God. To believe means: "Don't bother about yourself any more!" God has put all your affairs in order. Whoever lives in faith, in justification, is free from all anxiety about the "I." It is true that we are to "hallow the Self," but what does this mean save that we are to turn it towards God—in service? True sanctification consists in a life turned wholly outwards in love and service, a life free from all self-absorption in any shape or form. All attempts to set up an ideal of personal sanctification alongside of the service of humanity finally end in an unhealthy mystical asceticism. In so far as any consideration has to be paid to the self, such action is of a merely secondary and preparatory character.

Certainly the self must be made fit for service and it must get rid of whatever would make it unfit for service. But such action only gains its meaning and its fruitfulness from the fact that it is undertaken for the sake of the service of others. This again is the great transformation of ethics. All natural ethics aim at the upbuilding of the individual personality. Here, however, we are told that "He who loses his life shall find it."[1] In fact one only becomes a "personality" if one is free from self. But I can only become freed from self if and because I have already found myself in God; or rather, because God has already found me, and I may go forth to life in the sure certainty that I have thus been found or elected.

3. God reveals Himself to us in the fact that He became *man*; to try to know Him in any other way is not in harmony with His will. He wills to be known by us as One who takes the part of *man*. That God meets us in the Man Jesus means that in giving Himself to us He also gives us our brother man. The meaning of the Divine Creation of man, the fact that man is "made in the Image of God," is only fully disclosed in this Divine Act of the Incarnation. The God who is revealed in the God-Man wishes to be loved and honoured by us as the God of man. Further, in the fact that God gives Himself

[1] Matt. xvi. 25.

to us in the Son of Man He wishes so to unite us with man that we shall see that our life is bound up with that of humanity.

The natural orders of creation,[1] which all declare to us the fact that we are united to other men, only disclose their real meaning in the Incarnation of Christ. In Christ we are told that life in fellowship is not a duty, nor something added to life, nor a special aspect of life, but that it is the substance of human life. Human life can only be truly human in *Dualis*, in relation to others, and thus only "from the point of view of the other" (Gogarten).

Thus, in a third sense, the will of God is known to us as personal. God does not only will our personality, He does not only desire to have our personality for Himself, in a personal manner; but he also wants us in such a way as to possess our personal life, that is, our life in relation to society. For only the life which is related organically to society, only the life with the "Thou," is personal life. I cannot live personally with "things." The "I" cannot be personal over against an "it," but only when it is confronted by the "Thou." To live personally means: to live in responsibility and in love. This eliminates the abstract, impersonal element from ethics altogether. There are no Ends, Ideas, Goods, Values, no abstract entities, neither Culture, nor the State, nor "sphere of Spirit" to which the human personal life can be subordinated. There is only one self-end in the sphere of possible experience and it is this: personal life, or community between persons. This is the ethical meaning of the Incarnation, as it is the ethical meaning of the fact that man is made in the image of God.

4. We might call this "Christian Humanism": that personal life is its own end. This Humanism differs in various ways from that which usually goes under this name—but in each instance this variety is only a special aspect of the one truth; the first difference is the fact that the individual purpose of the personal life is based not upon itself, but upon God, upon God's personal revelation, in God's personal Word. The second difference lies in the fact that here the *Humanus* and humanity are not defined in terms of the individual person or self, but in terms of community. Rational (Idealistic) Humanism is autonomous and individualistic. It is not aware that love is the basis and the meaning of life. This difference leads to a third one, namely, whereas Idealistic Humanism is based upon an abstraction, because it is based upon an

[1] See below, pp. 210 ff.

idea of humanity, the universal "nature of man," Christian
Humanism, being based upon the personality of God, is also
based upon the personality of the other, upon that of our
"neighbour," and not upon an abstraction. We cannot love
"humanity"—though we can get enthusiastic and sentimental
about humanity—we can only love the individual concrete
person with whom we come into contact.

This conditional self-end (human personal life as community)
is not based upon itself but upon God's unconditional self-end.
The Purpose[1] of God is His dominion, the βασιλεία τοῦ θεοῦ.
We see the *holiness* of God in the fact that *His* purpose alone
is completely free and independent, that nothing can be good
save that *His* will should be done, in His "royal dominion."
But we see the *love* of God in the fact that He does not desire
to have His glory in anything other than in the coming of
His Kingdom, in the perfect fellowship of men with Him, the
Creator, and with one another. By this I mean nothing even
remotely resembling the ideas of practical reason, of a goal
of culture and humanity immanent in history(3). The Kingdom of God lies beyond the bounds of the philosophy of
history, all processes of culture, and all attempts to unite men
with one another; it is the Kingdom which will be set up by
means of Resurrection and Judgment. Therefore the will of
God cannot be deduced from any kind of Moral Idea; it
cannot be equated with any idea of humanity. But it certainly
includes the humane element in history, to such an extent
indeed, that there can be no "service of God" which is not
at the same time also the "service of man." But in spite of,
and indeed on account of, the hope of the Kingdom of God,
the meaning of the service of man remains something which
cannot be known beforehand, something which always has
to be learned from God afresh. For the ways of God are quite
different from the ways which we can construct by means of
our own moral reason. It is never the will of God that we
should serve Him in any other way than in loving our neighbour; but we have to enquire of Him constantly *what* this
"loving" actually means, expressed in concrete terms.

5. God wills men as His creatures. He wills them accordingly in connexion with His whole creation. He wills that
this world should exist, and He wills also that it should arrive
at its destiny and reach its fulfilment. Therefore in some way
or another the non-human creation is also included in the

[1] Literally "Self-End."—TR.

purpose of God. Hence, just as surely as this order of creation has been placed by God at the disposal of man, so also it is never merely a means, never *merely* material for the use of man. Upon it too there rests the blessing of God; it too has its own dignity; therefore man's power of disposal over it is also limited. Man is related to this other part of creation through his body. Therefore man's bodily existence is included in the Divine Will. God has not created us as spirits or as ghosts, but as psycho-physical beings. Therefore our service, since it is the service of a psycho-physical person, is rendered to a psycho-physical "Thou," to his life as a whole.

Thus there is a fourth fundamental distinction between Christian and rational Humanism: it is concrete, in the sense that it does not despise the sense-aspect of existence. It does not conceive man as an abstract rational being, but as one who is embedded in the visible tangible reality. Platonic Idealism with its contrast between the sense life and the Ideas, with its "Soma-Sema," with its ascetic tendency to escape from the world and from the body, is contrary to the Command of the Creator. The Divine Command does not refer to the soul of our neighbour, nor to his body, but to the man as a whole, to himself as he is. The body also belongs to his personality, as indeed the body is the means of communication between one person and another. Through the body we *act*—apart from the body we would remain in the realm of thought alone. And through the body the other makes himself known to me—apart from it each of us would remain shut up and imprisoned within our own individual existence. Our neighbour is *given* to us through the fact that both he and we are in the body. And it is *this* "neighbour"—this particular person —whom we are to love, and whom alone we really can love. The fact that man is in the body is not only the "end of the ways of God" but it is also the centre, for "the Word became flesh."[1]

6. In a further sense the world of history, with which we are so intimately connected, also belongs to the body. Our neighbour meets us not otherwise than as an historical being, embedded not only in the natural creation, but also in a history, in a civilization and culture, in a "social body." Man "in himself," apart from this historical social body, is just as abstract as man without the physical body. Thus to serve him means also to serve him through and with this

[1] John i. 14.

contemporary world. But just as we say: "Man *has* a body," and in so doing express the fact that although the body belongs to him it is not *himself*, that is, that the physical body is the organ, or the instrument of his personal life, so also we say: Man *has* culture (*Kultur*), not, man *is* culture. The whole of the social contemporary world, also, is subordinate to him. God has created body and soul; but He has created the soul to rule the body. For the perception of the Divine Word takes place through the soul, not through the body, although the body shares in this as an instrument. God has made man able to work and to create civilization and culture and forms of social life, but His aim is that man should create them for himself, and not simply for their own sake.

Hence there are no "intrinsic values."[1] "Values" as independent entities, which to so great an extent dominate the ethics of the present day, are a phantasmagoria. All "values" are derived from the human personality in its psycho-physical being, in the totality of its functions. In themselves they have no separate existence. There are "vital values," because man is a corporeal being. We call anything a "vital value" which forms part of the "vital goods" borne by that which transmits the values, by means of which this bodily life of man is made possible, healthy, and strong. "Economic values" exist because man, in virtue of the fact of his creation, is a being who creates civilization. "Economic values" constitute that kind of the goods of civilization whereby the latter serve an economy of civilization. "Cultural values" exist because man, in virtue of his spiritual nature, is a creative and an intelligent being. They are that kind of spiritual objects through which they correspond to the meaning of spiritual creation. It is not through values that spiritual activity exists, but through ideas, in which divine truth and the destiny of man are mirrored for the Reason(4). They have "value" because relation to them forms part of the wholeness of human personal life.

Thus, because all values exist in reference to persons, and for this reason alone, there exists a recognizable hierarchy or scale of values. And thus because there is a scale of values they are not independent, but are based on something deeper still—namely, on persons. Therefore they are to be wholly subordinated to the person—not because the personal value is the highest—how is it possible to estimate which is the highest

[1] Cf. on this point my observations on the concept of "Value" in Ethics, Chapter IV, Note (14).

value?—but because the idea of value only has meaning at all as a relation to a person. "Value" means: for a person who is "there." There are no personal values, but the person is the basis of the values. The value does not depend upon the fact that the person *wills* something—this is a subjectivistic derivation of the values which is rightly rejected, a conception which does not do justice to their objectivity[1]—but upon the fact that objectively, through divine appointment, certain things are due to, necessary or useful for life: such things are values, but nothing else at all. All values, by the will of the Creator, are subject to the person.

To work out the "system of values" in detail, the relations between value and person, in their different spheres of life, does not constitute the subject-matter of an ethic but of a philosophy of value, which, however, should need to be pre-supposed by an ethic. The decisive point is the knowledge that just as there is no art in itself, no State in itself, no science in itself, but only State, Art, and Science, which men create for the sake of humanity, so also there are no "values" in themselves, but only such as have "value" for the sake of humanity.

7. The situation is different, as has already been suggested, where the non-human creature is concerned. It is indeed related to man(5), but it is not simply there for the sake of man. This non-human creature, like humanity, possesses, in a relative way, a certain "end" of its own, even though it lies, as it were, on the very circumference of the Divine purpose. The more that animal life approaches human life, the more significant and purposeful does it become, and the more remote it is ·from human life the less purpose of its own does it seem to possess, at least so far as we can see. Yet we feel that it is displeasing to God deliberately to spoil a tree or a flower. The dumb creatures have a share in the inviolable character of human life. Hence Albert Schweitzer's protest against the current ethic, "in which no animals are allowed to run about," is certainly justified. But, on the other hand, every kind of ethic is sentimental and finally inhuman whose principle is "reverence for life," that is, an undifferentiated conception of life based upon itself. It is indeed no accident that the New Testament, with its phrases the "Love of God" and the "Love of Man," seems to have omitted this sphere from its practical consideration, but that the sighing of the creation for the redemption of the children of God is placed

[1] Cf. what was said above about SCHELER, Chapter IV, Note (14).

within the sphere of the divine power of redemption. In any case the groaning of creation is to us a necessary sign of our own unredeemed condition.

8. From the point of view of "service" the whole sphere of practical reality is divided into ends and means. The dominion of God alone is the End, the Final End, of existence; everything else is means. Through this end every kind of means is hallowed, and in no other way save by this End can it be hallowed. "All that is not of faith is sin."[1] Whatever proceeds from faith, from obedience to God—whatever it may be "in itself"—by that very fact is hallowed. "In itself" everything is neutral, it is neither good nor bad. There is no Good save to obey God, and there is no evil save in disobedience to God. The End, "to serve God," makes everything holy, and the lack of this End makes everything unholy.

But the statement "the end justifies the means" has rightly fallen into disrepute(6) (in particular in its theocratic use in Christianity), owing to the false definition of this sanctifying End. When this Divine End is interpreted in a sacred or a clerical sense, that is, apart from its reference to humanity, then, certainly, the door has been flung open for the entrance of all kinds of abuses. The *Honour* of God ought never to be emphasized apart from the *Love* of God. It is the amazing wonder of the Divine Incarnation which unites, in an indissoluble unity, the Divine Purpose, and the final ends of all human life, both of the individual and of the community as a whole. Nothing can be devout which in its final intention and effect is unhuman. God never commands anything which is contrary to love. The concrete character of the Kingdom of God is always visible in the stress laid on the *human* aspect of any matter. "Pious" inhumanity, *ad majorem gloriam ecclesiae*, is always based upon a sub-Christian clerical conception of piety.

The question which Kierkegaard raises in his profoundly thoughtful exposition of the story of the sacrifice of Isaac[2] is certainly justified: "Does there exist a teleological suspension of ethics?" This question reminds us that true ethics cannot be conceived in a legalistic general manner, by means of a principle. Only the service which God really commands is good, and this service can certainly look very different from that which man would generally imagine to be "loving service." Obedience to the Divine Command—or, what comes

[1] Rom. xiv. 23.   [2] KIERKEGAARD: *Furcht und Zittern*, pp. 48ff.

to the same thing: the love which God commands—in order to be real must often assume remarkable disguises. Service to the community in particular may demand a way of action which falls hardly on the individual, and may appear to be loveless; this subject will be treated in connexion with the doctrine of the "office." But, however hidden it may be, however indirectly the will of love may express itself—nothing can ever be commanded by God, for the service of God, unless it be at the same time and exclusively service to man, to the Kingdom of the God-Man. In this sense there is no teleological suspension of the ethical because the truly divine —we have just called it the theocratic element, the divine End—is identical with the truly human, with humanity. On the other hand, all that is ethical, by which we mean all that we can perceive directly, is permanently suspended by the Divine Command. For the Christian is never called to act on general principles, but always in accordance with the concrete commandment of love.

CHAPTER XX

THE CALLING

PROPOSITION: *God gives us our calling, and requires from us the fulfilment of the duties of our calling.*

1. God's command is wholly personal, therefore it is wholly concrete. God never requires "something in general," He does not issue proclamations, nor does He set up any kind of programme. He never issues commands into the air—with the idea that anyone may hear them who happens to feel like it! He tells me, or us, or you, as definite persons, to do some definite thing. It is true, of course, that the law which expresses the divine requirements in a general way, and also the promise, the assurance of grace in a general way, both have their appointed place in the purpose of God. Only upon the basis of this law is the individual able to hear the Divine Command. But this Divine Command is itself definite and personal.

The difference between legalistic and Christian morality is this: the fact that the Command is personal means that the Creator Himself turns, personally, towards His creature. "I am the Lord, thy God."[1] "I have loved thee with an everlasting love."[2] "I have called thee by thy name, thou art Mine."[3] It is this "thou," this "mine" and "thine" which alone makes faith real; until this takes place it is theory. But this "thou" is the "thou" of election. Faith means the knowledge that I am one of the elect. But the act by which God imparts to me His election, His eternal purpose for my life, is that of the Calling, the κλῆσις. It is the communication of divine grace to me; through this fact of election the universal promise becomes a reality in my own experience. It is therefore the foundation of the new state of life: for whoever has been called, now belongs to Him, is now "with Him," and may henceforth live in absolute dependence upon Him.

But this calling is also the *call* to His service. It is not *man* in general who is called to serve God, but "thou." And all this is not said in a general way, but its whole force lies in the fact that it is addressed to *you* and to no one else. It is only this personal call, not a universal law—and not even a promise understood in a general sense—which has power to move us. For this personal call is the word of the Holy Spirit,

[1] Exod. xx. 2.   [2] Jer. xxxi. 3.   [3] Isa. xliii. 1.

it is no mere word of man. This call—not the universal law— touches us "personally." To hear this call, really and truly, and to obey it actually means the same thing. If I do not obey the call then I have not really heard it aright. Obedience is grace and grace is obedience.

2. Because the Divine Command is wholly personal and concrete it affects me here and now. The call of God touches me, since it is actual and not an idea, in my reality, not in a possibility which can be ideally conceived. God calls into His service this particular person, in a particular set of circumstances, and at a particular time, that is, here and now. This is indeed the grace of God, the justification of the sinner, that God calls him just as he is, into His service; that God does not consider this particular person, just as he is, too bad for His service. This is the gift implicit in the Divine Command: that the Call, which reaches man in his actual sinfulness, places him, sinful as he is, in the service of God. For if man were to try first of all to make himself fit for this service he would never do anything at all. "Come, just as you are!" in your dirty, torn, everyday clothes! There is no need for you to "change." You *are* clothed with new garments—in virtue of this Call.

This expresses one of the most profound truths of ethics, indeed one of the most profound truths which have ever been conceived by the mind of man, namely the idea of "the Calling," which is so characteristic of the thought and teaching both of Paul and of Luther. When Luther drew forth this forgotten truth from beneath the rubbish heap of the ecclesiastical ethic, which had been corrupted by Aristotelian and ascetic ideas, it was an act of significance for the whole of world history, an act of overwhelming importance(1). It was the immediate consequence of the rediscovery of justification by faith. It meant that God wills to allow a sinful man, in all his actual sinfulness, to work for Him. No law, no abstract knowledge of good and evil is to be allowed to step in and depreciate this service rendered by sinful man, in his real sinfulness, because he is "unclean." There is no other service of God save that of sinful man in his real sinfulness. Through obedience to the Call this service, tainted though it is by sin, within actual conditions also tainted by sin, is hallowed. There is no other "hallowed" service anywhere—a service rendered by "pure" agents, within conditions actually "pure" in themselves, simply does not exist.

3. The idea of the Calling and of the Call is unintelligible apart from that of Divine Providence. The God who says to me here and now: "Act, where you are, as you are," is not One who comes on the scene after all that has been done previously has been done without His knowledge. Nothing can happen apart from Him. He is the One who, behind the *confusio hominum*, through His *providentia* governs not only *Helvetiam* but the world. To Him it is no accident that you are what you are here and now, an accident with which He must come to terms. He Himself places you where you are.

The idea of Providence, however, should be introduced into ethics with great caution; for it has already wrought a great deal of harm within this sphere. It threatens to justify the *status quo*, and in so doing to paralyse the moral will. This, however, is not its own fault, but is due to the wrong use which has been made of this idea, owing to the fact that the nature of the ethical moment has been misunderstood. The time which lies ahead of me differs from the time which lies behind me. I can only contemplate the time behind me, I cannot do anything with it. The past has been withdrawn from the sphere in which I can exercise my will. It is already decided. The future, however, the time which lies ahead of me, is not yet decided, and I am called to the act of decision. Hence, from the ethical point of view, the time which lies behind me differs entirely from the time which lies before me. I do not know this theoretically; for from the point of view of theory all I can do is to contemplate, theoretically therefore also the future becomes the past. This is the curse of theoretical thought, that it kills the future by regarding it as already fixed.[1]

Thus from the ethical point of view we are bound to stand "between the times," and to distinguish between them. The time which lies behind me, ethically speaking, I ought to "forget"(2), because it has been withdrawn from the sphere of my responsibility. It is of concern to me not from the ethical point of view, but simply as the Divine time, as the way along which God has led me hither. The "place" of the action, the here and now, the definite character of the reality in which action must now take place, is the place given by God. This does not mean that from that which now exists I can deduce in a rational manner what I have to do as though I were dealing with a law; for the time which lies ahead of me is

[1] Cf. my article: *Das Einmalige und der Existenzcharakter*

different; here I am responsible. Here I can and ought to decide. But it certainly does mean this: that God wills my present action on the basis of this particular past, and also at this particular place, whatever kind of place this may be in itself. Through the concreteness and personal character of the call, God gives me the definite "place," the sphere *within* which I have to act.

Because God wills that I should act here and now, He takes over the responsibility for the quality of this Here and Now, for the sphere in which I act. He *gives* it to the one who is called as though it were a purely divine work. He relieves him of the responsibility for this place in the world which, as such—like all places, like every form of time and place in the historical world—is not holy but sinful. God "covers" this sinfulness. It is with His forgiveness that He "covers" the past. And because God "covers" it, it no longer exists, it has lost all significance. Now the place is "pure"—however bad it may be in itself. It is "pure" through the Call of God. And this paradoxical purity, this making holy of that which in itself is unholy, through God's forgiving call: this is *the Calling*.

The idea of the Calling characterizes the concrete time and place, the sphere and the content of action (in so far as for the moment it cannot be altered), as God-given and therefore —paradoxically, that is, only in faith—"right." It is only because this is so that we can act at all with a good conscience and with cheerfulness. For every definite place, every definite set of circumstances in which we have to act, if it be considered on its merits, would not bear too close an ethical examination. In order to act with a good conscience I would always be obliged first of all to seek another place; or I could never act with a good conscience. But the Divine Call demands action here and now, and for this reason it gives the good conscience as well; and this good conscience, in spite of the bad place in or at which one has to act, is only possible through the idea of the Calling.

4. All this shows clearly the immense importance of this simple yet daring idea. First of all, apart from it, it would be impossible to act with a good conscience. Our action is always within circumstances and conditions tainted by sin, since our whole actual life is tainted by sin. There is no "place," no sphere of action, which is not in the highest degree dubious. In this the monastic estimate of the reality of life in the world

is absolutely right. Therefore apart from justification through faith and the idea of the Calling only two possible courses of action lie open: renunciation of the world, or compromise. Renunciation of the world is indubitably the more serious solution of the difficulty, hence it always deserves our respect. Medieval monasticism—or at least in some of its original forms—is far more serious than the Protestantism which cheerfully conforms to the world, and turns up its nose at such monasticism. But monasticism is not a real solution, since even the cloister or the hermit's cell is a place within the life of the world, tainted by sin, because it is a human dwelling-place. And if the hermit's cell actually meant complete exclusion from human life, then Satan would be casting out Satan, since for the sake of the Good the only thing that is really Good— fellowship, love—would have been cast out. To forsake the world absolutely is the absolute denial of love. The other way out, that of compromise, is easier and more popular(3). Here the sinfulness of the "place," whatever it may be, is accepted as something inevitable, without any basis of right at all, simply because it cannot be helped, and man performs all his actions with an uneasy conscience. In the dualistic ethic the Catholic Church has made room for both possibilities: in the monastic system it has made provision for those who aspire after perfection to "forsake the world," while its "secular" ethic is adapted to the needs of the masses. It is impossible to avoid this alternative if the truths of justification by faith and "the Calling" are not known.

But a second consideration will throw further light upon the meaning of the idea of the Calling. Where a man who is morally in earnest does not know the idea of "the Calling," he regards the reform of life as a *principle*(4); for everywhere he sees—just like the monk at an earlier period—all that is morally dubious, all that is contrary to sense, and to life itself, in existing conditions and circumstances. He feels himself called upon to "clean up" these places within the world before he can decide to live in them himself, and finally this "cleaning up" process becomes to him life itself—this is what I mean by saying that the reform of life becomes a *principle*. No place in the world is good enough for him until he has put something within it to rights. His whole life is spent in this unceasing endeavour to alter conditions, the personal meaning of life is forgotten, a nervous haste takes possession of him, and finally, since he is forced to admit that all these reforms do not alter anything essential, he falls into a state of mind which is either one of cynical resignation or of irritated hostility to everything and everyone. To-day this is often the fate of those who—from the human point of view—are the very "best" people (speaking in ethical terms); the reform of life as a principle—to be distinguished, of course, from the striving after improvements which are always and everywhere necessary but are subordinate to the personal meaning of life—produces a way of living which ignores real life; this is due to ignorance of the real fact of sin; it is the modern form of fanaticism.

The idea of "the Calling" makes short work of this fanaticism and of the spirit of hopeless acquiescence to which it leads. Here what matters most is not the improvement of one particular place in the world, of conditions and circumstances—although such procedure has its own, secondary importance—nor the search "for the right place for me," but the thankful acceptance of the place, at which I am now set, from the hands of Providence, as the sphere of my life, as the place in which, and according to the possibilities of which, I am to meet my neighbour in love. The idea of the Calling makes us free from all feverish haste, from bitterness, and from the—finally inevitable—hopeless resignation of the reformer; at the same time it keeps the door open for me to undertake such reforming work when it is the duty appointed to me in the exercise of my particular "office."[1]

5. The fact that the "place" in life in which I am set—whose apparently accidental character is seen to be necessary, since it is appointed by God—is actual and concrete implies a concrete task. A particular Calling implies particular duties. But this conception of duty is quite different from the usual idea of duty, that is, to put it more exactly, from the rational, legalistic idea of duty. The ordinary idea of duty is intolerable, owing to its abstract and rigid character. The person who makes an idol of duty is unbearable, with his legalistic mind and his scrupulous attention to the fulfilment of a schedule of "duties"; he is also intolerably self-righteous, feeling so sure of himself because he has fulfilled the tasks he has set himself. Only at one point can we get into real human touch with him, and that occurs when he becomes "tragic" about his "conflicting duties."

The idea of a "conflict of duties," if we examine it carefully,

---

[1] See below, pp. 250 ff.

is the chronic disease which afflicts every system of legalistic morality. A person afflicted with this disease constantly feels that it is "his duty" to perform several duties which cannot possibly be combined with one another. What we usually call a "conflict of duties" is only a particularly clear instance of this state of mind, in which the person concerned feels that duty demands the performance of several duties which actually overlap. Therefore the problem of "conflicting duties" is the point at which this mistaken idea of duty which underlies the expression can become manifest to us.

"Duties," as such, do not exist; this abstract conception, which issues from the concrete requirements of a definite task, is only a temporary form of exhortation (as was explained in connexion with the Law) urging us to try to discover the Divine Command for this particular moment. The Law itself never tells me what the will of God is; nor does my "schedule of duties" throw any light on it. In a situation of this kind I must proceed as follows: with the help of my "schedule of duties" and in the light of the various claims which clamour for my attention and constantly overlap—all of them apparently justifiable and necessary—in the spirit of faith (and this means, too, in view of the actual situation) I must listen to the Divine Command in order that I may be able to do what I am really bidden to do, that is, my real duty.

Then, however, I shall find that *one* thing and *one only* is really commanded, is really my duty, and that the "conflict of duties" is only apparent, and does not really exist at all.

But in saying this I do not mean that the Christian is relieved from the pressure of the sense of conflicting duties. To be a Christian, even in this respect, does not mean something *static*, but it means grace and decision. Only through the painful pressure of the apparent conflict of duties—and indeed of a conflict of duties which is unceasing and constantly repeated —do we reach the perception of the Divine Command, and in so doing joyfulness and confidence in action. Indeed, because faith alone teaches us the seriousness of the Law, the Christian is one who is never free from "conflicting duties," as against those to whom this only happens now and again as a "tragic" event, or as a misfortune. But to faith this is a clear proof that the Divine Command has not yet been heard; once the decision of faith has been made this problem ceases to be painful. Whatever we have dared to do, in the spirit of faith, we may, and indeed we should, regard as the duty which was intended. In any case the Christian must never become "tragic" about it; he may appear so to others—as, for instance, a statesman, who out of responsibility for his people must take a step which will expose him to the reproach of disregarding moral obligations—but he himself knows that this neglect is only apparent. How can it be "tragic" to obey God? Even if he himself only arrives at his decision with much difficulty, trembling, and pain, even if his heart almost fails him as he takes this step, he still acts with a good conscience, and his pain is embraced and supported by a greater joyfulness, the παρρησία of faith.

But the Christian is not only forbidden to be unduly oppressed by the sense of "conflicting duties," he is also forbidden to allow his spirit to become rigid and self-righteous. He is not to be rigid, because in the last resort no law can ever dominate him, since he serves "under the instant orders of the living God," and he faces, directly, a concrete duty. Nor may he be self-righteous, because he knows that he always acts as a sinful man, whose action God only accepts or makes good by His grace. In spite of the fact that the Christian too has his "book of duties," or rather his various books of duties and respects them, he is never in the last resort bound by them; and in spite of the fact that he too distinguishes between responsible and irresponsible action, between conduct which meets the test of life in an upright and honourable manner, and that which lets down the tone because a person has "forgotten himself" (as we say), still he is always fully conscious that even when he is most honourable he still stands before God as a sinner who has nothing to boast of save the fact that the gracious Lord acknowledges him as His servant.

6. Thus it is quite obvious that this idea of vocation ("the Calling") has no more than the name in common with that which is called so to-day. The idea of the Calling has been degraded, so disgracefully, into something quite trivial, it has been denuded of its daring and liberating religious meaning to such an extent, and has been made so ordinary and commonplace that we might even ask whether it would not be better to renounce it altogether. On the other hand, it is a conception which in its Scriptural sense is so full of force and so pregnant in meaning, it gathers up so clearly the final meaning of God's acts of grace—the Calling—and the concrete character of the Divine Command in view of the world in which man has to act, that to renounce this expression would mean losing

a central part of the Christian message. We must not throw it away, but we must regain its original meaning.

Nowadays the word "calling" means little more than the share of duty which falls to the lot of the individual in the whole economy of labour, in the business of earning one's living. It has become an economic conception. But even in the theological ethic it has seldom been understood in the deeper sense. How could it be otherwise when the truth of justification by faith was no longer understood? It was realized of course that Luther had achieved something decisive by his renewal of this conception; but men thought that the decisive element lay in the fact that through this new meaning of vocation the secular, civil, and economic forms of labour, in contrast to the ascetic monastic conception, had become hallowed once more. In so doing the very centre of Luther's ideas has been misunderstood. Certainly, this new respect for the economic, civil, and secular sphere is one of the logical results of his work. But that is only the by-product of a greater transformation. Through the idea of "the Calling" existence in the world is revealed in its sinfulness, and at the same time it is "covered" by forgiveness, while the believer regains a good conscience with which he can take part in the action and life of the world, without feeling guilty of "compromise." To express this in a brief formula: the point is that here world-pessimism is overcome, while at the same time the radical corruption of the world and the absolute character of the divine law are recognized. All that Luther cared about was to secure the possession of *a good conscience in one's Calling*, and to do away with the unsatisfactory alternatives: renunciation of the world, or compromise. Therefore this idea of the Calling is full of eschatological tension and a daring which conquers the world; indeed, we might almost call it a "divine audacity"; and the reason is this: God takes over all responsibility for our action in the world which in itself is sinful, if we, on our part, will only do here and now that which the present situation demands from one who loves God and his neighbour.

The narrowing of the meaning of this term to the civil and economic sphere, however, has made this extraordinarily daring idea into a favourite method of rendering Protestantism commonplace. The world was "joyfully affirmed," the tension between the absolute law of God and reality was removed, and the Protestant "delight in the life of the world" was extolled without suspecting what had taken place; economic excellence now became the highest form of virtue, and the worthy citizen who "fulfils his earthly duty" became, as such, the "dear child of God." Finally the nemesis of world history reached even this idol; the same Capitalism(5) which was only possible as the result of this secularization of the idea of the Calling, has also destroyed it in its narrow *bourgeois* form, since it has dissolved the whole order of callings and has led to an economic crisis which has destroyed all joy in labour and all pride in one's calling, a crisis whose disastrous effect is still dominant at the present day. The unspeakable misery of unemployment is the bitter fruit of this process.

7. The idea of the Calling is only secured against this process of secularization when it is not severed from its eschatological basis. God calls man—in the world certainly, but He calls him to His *heavenly* Kingdom. He does not merely call him *into* the world but *out of* it as well; for the κλῆσις is always meant as ἔκ-κλησις, and in the New Testament the "Calling" always means to have a "share in the heavenly inheritance." This supra-mundane character of the Calling, however, works itself out in the world through the service of the brethren. We can only love our brethren if, while sharing in the labour of this world, we do not forget the heavenly kingdom; to serve our brethren within the world means that within this world we meet our brother-man as our real brother, as one who belongs to the Kingdom of Christ; in every child of man we are to see "one for whom Christ died." It is true that the idea of the Calling appoints us our place in the world; but this particular point implies an infinite circumference, the infinitely broad horizon of the Divine Purpose. Here, at this spot, "you are to do your duty"; yes, but "you are to do your duty here as a citizen of the coming Kingdom of God!" In so far as action in this place is carried out in this spirit of obedience it is "labour in the Lord's Vineyard." The Here and Now constitute the necessary narrowness, the vision of the coming Kingdom, the necessary breadth for right action within one's calling. If there were no narrowness, action would be fantastic, unreal, and fanatical. If there were no breadth, action would degenerate into the self-complacency of the Philistine, with an utter absence of tension. To be "on the spot"—working with the Eternal End in view, *that* is Christian action within the Calling.

CHAPTER XXI

THE NATURAL ORDERS[1] AND THE KINGDOM OF GOD

PROPOSITION : *As Creator, God requires us to recognize and adjust ourselves to the orders He has created, as our first duty; as Redeemer, as our second duty, He bids us ignore the existing orders, and inaugurate a new line of action in view of the coming Kingdom of God.*

1. The Calling teaches us to find the place assigned to us—both in Nature and in History—the place where we have been set in order to serve our neighbour. Indeed, it is only through the idea of "the Calling" that the idea of our "neighbour" becomes definite. Your neighbour is the person who meets you. In the "Calling" your neighbour is given to you; you do not need to hunt for him, therefore you do not need to search for your sphere of service. It is not for *us* to choose the tasks which God has thought out and destined for us. Since *we* are called, here and now, our "sphere of labour" and our duties are appointed to us. Our service consists in the fulfilment of "the duties of our state." We are to do "what our hand findeth to do" in relation to those with whom we come into contact. But then the further question arises, *what* are we to do for them? Is there a norm which determines in what way we are to do that which our hand finds to do? To this question we know the two answers which ought always to determine our action. First of all: we cannot tell beforehand what we ought to do; we can only learn it from our neighbour by listening to the Divine Command. And secondly: we are bidden to show love to our neighbour; but this simply means that we are to serve him. But is there some indication or point of view which can be considered in order to find an answer to the question: *what* is to be done? In point of fact, this indication, which defines the content of the Divine Command in greater detail, is given in the knowledge that it is God the Creator and the Redeemer who calls us into His service.

The Divine Command is not a law which hovers above our actual existence without any connexion with it; it is the

---

[1] *Schöpfungsordnung*: rendered variously: "order of creation," "created order," "natural order."—TR.

command of the God who has created our actual existence. We are not called to do something for our neighbour which is remote from and alien to his existence, but so far as we can, in what we do to him, we are to fulfil that which God means for us in this particular created order. God wills *him*, this particular man, in these particular circumstances. Therefore we too are to will the same for him. Since the will of God is the basis of his life, because he is the work of God and the property of God, his *life* should be sacred to us—not merely his *personality*—which might, indeed, be understood in an abstract way as something purely spiritual—his *life*, with all that belongs to it in accordance with his creation. The "biological" ethic(1) is not wrong in connecting the Good with *Life*; it is only wrong in severing this life from its basis in Creation, and therefore in separating the value of life from the Command of the Creator. Nor is the Thomist ethic wrong when it applies the conception of "adaptation" to the definition of the Good,[1] but it is only wrong in making this an independent entity over against the Divine Will, and thus in severing the Good from faith. In reality, we cannot be obedient to the Command of the Creator if we do not pay heed to the laws of life and to the life which is peculiar to man in accordance with his creation. If we are to serve our neighbour "in life"— how can we do this without paying attention to the biological laws which govern life, without listening to what they have to tell us about the preservation and destruction of life? The Will of the Creator approaches us through them; and if we are to serve our neighbour as a fellow-creature—how can we do this unless we know what is due to man as man? Natural biology and anthropology have their definite place within a Christian ethic.

Further, it is our duty to preserve and develop the life of our neighbour, so far as this is possible to us, according to our knowledge of the processes which maintain and enhance life; and it is our duty to serve him "in his existence as a human being," and in his "growth as a human being"— according to our knowledge of the rules which govern this existence and the growth of human life.

This view of our duty to our neighbour also implies the obligation to make him happy. *Eudaemonism*, too, is not wrong in making happiness a subject of ethical consideration; it is only wrong in elevating it to the rank of a supreme principle.

[1] Cf. Note (3), Chapter XVIII.

To serve our neighbour means to make him as happy as we possibly can. While an abstract rigorism is unable to perceive this, because it severs the connexion between the Ideal and the Actual, faith gives us the certainty that He who commands us is the God who created man not only for life but also for happiness. Wherever the moral instruction of the New Testament enters the realm of the concrete, it illustrates the nature of the service of love with special emphasis by simple examples of doing good and "making people happy"; here the emphasis falls chiefly, indeed, one might even say primarily, upon the ills which afflict the life of the senses, the physical life: the first duties of love to our neighbour are to preserve life (in the ordinary physical sense), to alleviate pain, to give food and drink to those who hunger and thirst.

2. But in yet another way the Will of the Creator approaches us through our neighbour's natural life. The general laws of creation, of the preservation and furtherance of life, and of specifically human life, are not the only laws. For our neighbour does not confront us merely as an individual but as a member and supporter of definite communal "orders," which we may choose to call "created orders" in the narrower sense. By this we mean those existing facts of human corporate life which lie at the root of all historical life as unalterable presuppositions, which, although their historical forms may vary, are unalterable in their fundamental structure, and, at the same time, relate and unite men to one another in a definite way.

When we speak of the Creation and of the created existence of man we ought never to forget, not even for a moment—not even in the isolating consideration of the created order in contradistinction to that of the order of redemption—that we only know the Divine Creation as it has been marred by sin, and the created human being as a sinner. But in the light of this very fact the created orders—in the sense in which they have just been defined—are especially significant. We know them as means by which the divine wisdom *compels* men to live in community—men, that is, who through their sin have become separated from one another, and in their inmost will have lost the sense of corporate life; this means that human life, which is only possible as a life in community, is continually being made possible once more. In them, therefore, we ought to honour, in a very special way, the goodness of the Creator, who makes His sun to rise upon the evil and upon the good, the patience of Him who gives life even to the disobedient, and preserves his life because it is human.

3. This is not the place to expound the natural (or created) orders in detail; this task must be reserved for the third book. But one illustration will show what I mean. The most important example of such an order is the co-ordination of man and woman. The sex-differentiation which determines the whole of life is not to be regarded simply from the point of view of individuality; if this were all, then this difference would be essentially nothing more than one individualizing factor alongside of others. On the contrary, the decisive element in the matter is the fact of the relation to each other which this causes, the fact that the sexes are driven to depend upon each other. A man, if he is to be a man, must depend upon the woman, and the woman, if she is to be a woman, must depend upon the man. This reference to life together, to community, according to the created order, is provided by the natural impulse which attracts the sexes to one another,[1] even if now we only know this created order in the sinful imperfection of an unrestrained sexual-erotic impulse.[2] What it means to live in this sex-relation will be explained later on; here we are concerned only to recognize how in this one created order the meaning of the command to serve our neighbour becomes clear.

Even this particular created order, if we understand it aright, must make it clear to us that an individualistic interpretation of life represents an abysmal misunderstanding. The whole of human existence is built upon the fact that man cannot live as a solitary individual. Each of us, indeed, owes his very existence to the fact of such a relation between two human beings, to union between husband and wife: his very existence as an individual is due to the fact that two have become one, and our more exact knowledge of the biological law of growth—of the ovum and the semen—has only given this truth a still greater impressiveness. But even apart from procreation the fact that a man can only become a husband by means of a woman, and a woman can only become a wife through the man, expresses the same truth. We possess our very existence not in ourselves but—to use the language of Gogarten, who was the first to perceive and point out these things clearly—"we always receive it from another."

This means, however, that our action must be reciprocal;

[1] Gen. ii.　　　　　　　　　　　　　　　　[2] Gen. iii.

our giving to the other must be balanced by our acceptance from the other. Action is proud and makes us proud; acceptance is humble and makes us humble. For action by itself strengthens us in the illusion that we are something of ourselves; acceptance expresses the fact that we need others, that we depend upon them. Genuine action in love is action plus acceptance, or acceptance plus action. Genuine love is a "consciousness of our dependence upon another" and an act of "giving in the spirit of dependence"; it is the renunciation of self-sufficiency, the breaking of the pride of the self.

All the natural orders point to the same truth, whether it be the relation between old and young, father and child, leader and followers, the productive and the receptive, or the natural inequalities which determine the living character of economic life. Everywhere life is permeated by a characteristic, natural inequality, which makes one human being stand in need of another. In passing I would allude to the idea which results from this (whose importance will become clear later on): that the egalitarian conception of rationalism, the Stoic "doctrine of the Primitive State," just as it denies these natural inequalities, logically conceives the nature of man in an individualistic manner. The rational man—the one who is proud of his reason—is the very one who does not wish to admit that he has any need of other people; egalitarian philosophy is based upon the self-dependent, self-sufficient individual. The Scriptural idea of Creation, however, contains not only that of unequal individuality—that we have always known—but that of the correlatively individual inequality which renders one dependent upon another, and thus bases life upon "exchange," "co-operation," and—this alone is decisive—upon community, in the sense of the necessity of being together, or of dependence upon one another.

4. There are also orders which, although they belong to the presuppositions of the present life (that is, to the present historical life with which we are all familiar), still cannot be described as belonging to the created or natural order, because they only have any meaning owing to the fact of sin. The most important of these orders is that of the State and the Law(2). These orders must also be distinguished from their changing historical forms. There has never been a human society without something which resembles the State, and without some kind of legal coercion, and in this historical world there never will be a human society without these

orders, since sin makes both necessary. But without doubt there are states which are better or worse than others, there are legal codes which are better or worse than others. The forms assumed by the State and by the systems of legislation may vary, but their fundamental structure is always the same.

And this fundamental structure—in which again our meeting with our neighbour takes place—points to the same thing(3) as the natural orders: that, whether in receiving or accepting, we must give, that in all our action we stand in need of the other. In these orders, too, we find men in some way or other attached to one another in inequality, so that each one has his *vis-à-vis*, and can only become truly himself in this relation with one who confronts him. It is clear that this is the meaning which lies at the root of the old idea of "rank" (*stand*)—in any case the Reformers, even Calvin and not merely Luther, made this conception of "rank" their own in this sense—and we are ill-advised to renounce this idea so easily on account of its patriarchal and feudalistic colouring, that is, on account of one of the forms it has assumed in the course of history. Behind the abandonment of this idea there is certainly not merely the Christian idea of brotherhood, which, as is well known, was very well combined with the idea of rank and position in the New Testament, but, above all, the individualistic idea of equality of the Enlightenment. To be of equal value in the sight of God does not necessarily mean equality in historical life. Rather, equality always means the removal of fellowship. Fellowship can only exist where people are unequal; fellowship is only possible where we are necessary to each other. I do not need to lay stress on the fact that this line of thought is in the closest harmony with the Pauline idea of the body[1] with its many members.[2]

5. The command of the Creator bids us *Accept!* For we possess our life from Him as a gift, as something which we have received before we have begun to act, something which is independent of our own action. The insane illusion of the modern man, who always regards his creative existence as primary, compared with the world and other men—"the world as the material of my freedom" (Fichte)—should be seen through and combated as an error due to arrogance. We are not first summoned to reform something in others and

[1] In addition to the chief passage in I Cor. xii, cf. also: I Cor. x. 17; Rom. xii. 4, 5; Col. i. 18; Col. ii. 19; Col. iii. 15; Eph. iv. 4; Eph. v. 30.
[2] On this point see Chapter XXVII (p. 300).

in our environment; at first we simply have to accept our environment. Anyone who is really called to be a reformer must prove his worth by showing that he has learnt first of all to respect that which now exists, and to adapt himself obediently to it. Our neighbour and his world are not material which we have to mould first of all. It is presented to us already shaped, in the shaping of which we have to honour the Creator's Hand and Work, in spite of all that human sin may have added to this shape. If we are only willing to accept our neighbour minus the sin which forms part of his existence, we shall never be able to accept him at all. For which of us has not been "conceived in sin"?[1] Reverence for the Creator, whose work, in spite of all human perversion, is the one existing reality, demands as our first reaction obedience to the existing order, and grateful acceptance of the goodness of the Creator in the orders, through which alone He makes it possible for us to serve our neighbour, and, indeed, to live at all.

Our service in the existing orders is always the service of our neighbour; this is due to the fact that—in spite of everything—they are orders which proceed from the Creator, and are therefore "orders of service," forces which prepare the way for real community. The fact that in spite of all human disorder and opposition to the order of Creation, these orders of society are still in existence, is not simply a sign and effect of God's patience and kindness, but it also means the possibility of service, and, in a certain sense, a means of compulsion to service for men who are unwilling to serve. This question, however, will be treated in the next chapter, since this coercive element in the orders is indeed no other than the concrete form of the *Lex*.

6. Adaptation to the existing order therefore, because it has been created by God, is the *first* point in the Christian ethic; but it is never the *last* point. The first thing is always what God wills as Creator; but—even apart from our sin—it is not the last. For He wills to lead the Creation out beyond itself, into the perfecting of all things. God does not preserve the world simply in order to preserve it, but in order that He may perfect it. Therefore His affirmation of the existing order is only conditional—namely, it is conditioned by this *aim*, it is the affirmation of a transitional stage. And secondly: the existing order is not the order created by God, but it is the

[1] Ps. li. 7.

order created by God in its broken condition due to sin. Therefore it also requires from us not only the first point, the acceptance of the existing order, but, on this basis it requires, in the second place, obedience to His will, as we know it, as the will of the Perfecter and Redeemer. On the basis of obedience to existing conditions, in view of the new order which He wills to create (while waiting for the world of perfection, of which we form part through faith), He also demands from us something *new*.

The preservation and furtherance of the natural life is not the distinctively Christian command to love our neighbour(4). There certainly is nothing greater than the manifestation of love, the proof in action that we are here to serve others. But this proof of love cannot exhaust itself in satisfying the natural demands of life. As in faith we know our own final destiny, so also we know that of our neighbour. Service to him must develop into service for his eternal destiny. In spite of all misuse the saying of Amalie Sieveking goes to the heart of the question: "The soul of the care of the poor is to care for the poor soul." Of course this does not mean that any doubt is thrown upon the sanity of the simple act of helpfulness. This remains the foundation. But the distinctive thing about genuine Christian manifestations of love is this, that behind this practical act of helpfulness there is a profound interest in the eternal salvation of our neighbour. How can it be otherwise, if we are really concerned about the interests of the other? For our neighbour this decision is a choice between life and death, heaven and hell. We cannot relieve him of this decision; but we can—if it be granted to us—give him that which is given to us: the word of the grace of God.

If every believer is a member of the Church, then every believer is also a priest, and in principle has to exercise his priestly office at all times. The *priesthood of all believers* is realized in the fact that we take our neighbour extremely seriously, because to him also the Call comes, and perhaps just through us, here and now, it will reach its fruition in him. This meeting, where one meets the other as one sent to the other by God, as one who has been appointed to him by God as needing help, is something very "private" and intimate, and yet at the same time it is a process which can only take place in the greatest "concreteness." A messenger of the King has to proclaim to another the gracious message of the King! Where the contact is of this kind, where one whose sins have been forgiven extends the gift of forgiveness to one with whom he comes into touch, there—and there alone—"love" is expressed, in the sense in which this word is used in the New Testament.

How far removed this love is from all sentimentality is shown in the fact that while we absolutely "accept" our neighbour, we are yet acutely aware of all that is actually wrong in him. The command: "Judge not," reminds us that we must always approach a sinner as a fellow-sinner, never as one who is righteous. But the knowledge of our own sin, and the judgment on it, allows us also to see that which is contrary to God in others, just as we see what is contrary to Him in ourselves, and place ourselves under the judgment of God. This service of criticism, too, if it is performed in this spirit, is a service of love, and this aggressive severity necessarily forms part of the manifestation of our infinite interest in the salvation of our neighbour. The same priesthood of all believers which makes it a duty for every believer to seek the salvation of every brother, makes it also his duty to "call him to repentance." What the world requires in the shape of "tact" is, as a rule, if measured by this demand, irresponsibility, softness, and cowardice. But this duty of warning and blaming, and of rejecting inwardly and outwardly that which is not right, is something quite different in principle from the mania for reforming other people, which regards our neighbour simply as an object of our reforming zeal. In principle the critical *No* is embraced by the *Yes*; it is right only when it is a sign of interdependence.

7. Only now, however, do we perceive the meaning of the orders. They must be preserved—so far as their content is concerned—as they are "in themselves." But their meaning, the reason why they exist, is not "in and for themselves." Their meaning is love. This meaning, however, also becomes a test of their reality. Can that which has lost its meaning still express the meaning which it once possessed? and can it serve in the sense in which it ought to serve? Is service, love, the meaning of these orders? then the lovelessness and unwillingness to serve which has been wrought out through its historical forms is placed under the judgment of God. In the light of revelation the non-sense, as well as the sense, of its historical reality is recognized.

All the orders, the created orders no less than the sinful "orders," are, in their historical form also revelations of human sinfulness and godlessness. And even apart from their historical forms they are revelations of the imperfection of the created world. It is, of course, true that they are indications of the will of God for community, but they are at the same time instruments of an evil, violent, collective egoism, instruments of tyranny, by means of which the collective body holds the individual in bondage, and degrades him to be the mere instrument of egoistic collective ends(5). Precisely on account of their obvious necessity and utility they are at all times in danger of becoming idols by being transformed into absolutes. Wherever, and to what extent, they do become idols, they exercise their influence by destroying life, by alienating man from God. They become false means of securing the life of this world against the divine judgment, and entrenchments behind which the man creeps whom God wills to draw out of the existing order(6). Thus the Divine orders become means of resistance to the Kingdom of God, misused in order to provide a theological justification for conditions which are contrary to the Will of God, because they are contrary to love.

8. Therefore, in view of the world as it is—the environment in which our neighbour lives—the will of God does not merely tell us to adapt ourselves, to accept, but also to resist, to protest, not to be "conformed to this world."[1] The kind of apologetic which is characteristic of a certain conservatism(7), by which, with the aid of the idea of Providence, the existing "order" at any given time is justified as that which is willed by God, and every form of criticism and desire to change conditions is suppressed as "godless rebellion," as disobedience to orders willed by God, can only arise out of a condition in which faith has been badly distorted. Without a living, painful consciousness of the appalling contrast between the world which God wills and the world as it now is, genuine faith cannot be imagined. The spirit which sighs for release from the oppression of the present "order" forms a necessary part of obedience to the Divine Command.

A certain kind of Lutheranism holds the disastrous dogma that the various "orders" are not subject to the command of Jesus Christ, but only to the rule of reason(8). This clever distinction is far too easy to be true. It is true, of course, as the next chapter will show, that the "orders," as the *Lex* in an imperfect and sinful world, can only perform their service if they are understood and used in their own legal spirit; it is also true that it is nonsense to apply to them the Sermon on

[1] Rom. xii. 2.

the Mount as an ideal law. It is true that their characteristic legality can only be understood by means of reason. But it is totally false to draw the conclusion that in the sphere of the "orders" Christ "has nothing to say." Just as the Christian can never forget whose subject he is, so also he can never forget that obedience to this King means love, and he has no right to close his eyes or shut his heart to anything by means of which love is injured by the "orders." He ought never to try to modify this glaring contrast between the Ideal and the Actual, even when he sees that at present these "orders" must continue to exist, by shrugging his shoulders and saying: "Well, that's that!" still less ought he to try to justify the present state of affairs by theological arguments.

Thus God's Command requires from us always—but in a very different way—both adaptation and protest, acceptance of the existing order and resistance to it, because our service of our neighbour requires it. In the actual working out of this obedience the believer will be found now in the camp of those who maintain and justify the existing order, now in that of those who protest and demand a new order. In itself obedience is neither conservative, as the world is conservative, nor radical or revolutionary as the world is revolutionary, but, whether conservative or revolutionary, it is based upon the one unchangeable will of the Creator and Redeemer, who, on that account, because He makes His will effective in a world which is always changing, demands us for Himself, and is always bidding us serve Him in varying ways.

The existing orders, behind which stands the Divine order, constitutes the framework within which our service of our neighbour is to be performed; they form the vessel which we are to fill with the content of love. We have just said that the first thing necessary is not to alter this vessel but to fill it with the new content. But there are vessels which are contrary to this content of love, and it is quite possible that such vessels ought to be smashed. Where the existing order is no longer useful but harmful, it is ripe for destruction(9). But where the necessity for this framework and this vessel is denied, and the orders, because as vessels they must differ from the content, are denounced on principle, or said to be unrecognizable,[1] there human life, thrown back entirely upon the "disposition," falls into disorder and chaos, and in the process the precious content is spilled and lost. The legalism of those who uphold

[1] See Note (3) on this Chapter.

the existing order is bad; but the lawlessness of fanatics is worse; for this leads to the most impossible form life can ever assume, which is indeed no form at all: to anarchy. Therefore it is necessary to take into account the function of the orders as *Lex*, and the question of their basis and their limitations within the command: "Serve!"

CHAPTER XXII

SERVICE AS AN "OFFICE" AND AS A PERSONAL RELATION

PROPOSITION: *The Divine Command is only perceived if we take note of its threefold law: the laws of official duty, by which external community is maintained; the absolute law, by which we recognize the lack of community; the law of love, whose function it is to instruct the believer in his right personal relation with his neighbour.*

1. God the Creator is the same as God the Redeemer. But His work as Creator and Preserver of the world differs from His work as Redeemer. As Redeemer He can only work where His Word is heard, that is, in faith. As Creator and Preserver He works even where men do not know Him at all(1). Therefore His created orders can also be effective where He is not known as Creator. These orders are operative in the whole sphere of sub-human life, in the life of the lilies of the field, which God clothes so gloriously, and in that of the birds of the air "who sow not, neither do they reap," and yet our "Heavenly Father feedeth them." They also operate in the life of man, but in a different way. It is true, of course, that in man, to some extent, the general biological laws are fulfilled unconsciously and involuntarily. But at the same time man finds that what is given by Nature becomes a task to be fulfilled. The created (or natural) orders, in the narrower sense, can only become effective in the life of man by means of his own conscious and willed co-operation.

The ultimate, real meaning of these orders can only be perceived where God is recognized as Creator and Redeemer, in faith, through His Word. But the orders themselves are the subject of a purely rational knowledge. Even the most primitive heathen knows something of these orders—and often he is the very person who knows amazingly more about them than the highly cultivated "Christian" European—and he has also some glimmering of an idea that these "orders" must be maintained, indeed that they are in some way or another "commanded" by some higher authority.

The whole of human life is permeated and supported by orders of the most varied kind. Apart from such "orders" it is impossible to imagine life in the wedded state and in the family, in civilization and culture, in the nation and the State, and finally also in the Church. They form the skeleton of the life of civilized historical humanity. These orders are not God's "created orders," but they do not exist apart from them. As *real* orders, the Creator uses them to preserve the world; He uses them in particular as a firm bond which checks the otherwise inevitable tendency of humanity to disintegrate into atoms. Ultimately, therefore, the necessity for these orders is based upon the Divine Will. In them, although in a fragmentary and indirect form, it is God's Will that meets us. Even a man who does not know God perceives in them something of the Will of God.

2. At this point the *theologia naturalis* becomes absolutely practical. Here, therefore, the most careful distinctions are imperative. Only through faith, through the Word of God in Jesus Christ, do we know the meaning of the orders. But precisely there do we know at the same time that God, as the Preserver of the sinful world, preserves it through such orders which are not His pure "orders of creation," and by means of an obedience to the orders which is not obedience to Him, the true God.

Through faith in the God of revelation we recognize that, in some way or another, God is made known even in these orders, in a certain sense—*aliquo modo*—says Calvin—to those who do not know Him in His actual revelation. And in faith we perceive that God makes use of this—however inadequate —knowledge of His orders, and of this—however impure— obedience to these orders, for the preservation of the world. Primarily these orders are only of any practical use when they really do create and maintain order, however primitive or unjust this ordering may be. Human life cannot exist without such orders. Therefore, even though only in an indirect fragmentary way, they are the Will of God, they are His gift. Wherever man submits to these orders, there, in some way or another, he is obeying God, in spite of the fact that this obedience, since it is not directed towards the Will of God, and does not spring from the spirit of faith, is not genuine obedience but mere legality. But, as we have already seen, even the Christian is commanded to practise this kind of legality; only this obedience is enjoined in faith; therefore the Christian knows both the meaning and the limitation of these legal commands. But he also knows that between the Fall and the Resurrection—that is, in the historical world—the external orders and the legality which is connected with them, con-

221

stitute the Divine means for preserving the world, and are therefore the Will of God. He knows that the fact that God enjoins legal obedience to the existing orders, applies even to him as a believer, and that in the maintenance and establishment of such order, he stands shoulder to shoulder with the unbeliever, and must work with him. This truth lies behind the Catholic proposition that it is possible for the Christian to co-operate with the non-Christian on the basis of "Natural Law."[1] If no more is meant by "Natural Law" than this general idea of the Divine order, we could entirely accept it. But the conception of the Law of Nature will be discussed at a later stage in this book.

3. There is one point about which we must be quite clear: the usefulness of the orders depends upon the fact that they are *real*. Even ideas, even general requirements of an ethico-legalistic character, have their own right and their practical use, but their function is entirely different from that of "the orders." The specific value of the orders consists in the fact that they actually and effectively create *order*. And the fact that they do actually create order is based upon the further fact that, in contradistinction to moral laws, these orders claim no more than legality, but to compensate for this, this legality can be more or less *enforced*. That is why, in this sphere of legality, motives like fear of punishment, utility, honour, respect for conventions, etc., play a great part. But this is not really the point at issue; what does matter is that—by whatever motives—these orders should be effectively maintained. The Christian, too, as a member of his nation, must co-operate in this task of preservation, and the special part assigned to him—through "the Calling"—is: the "office." To act in his "office" means to act in accordance with the legal obligations imposed by the "orders."

Every human being has an "office"(2), just as every human being grows out of the community of his or her own people, and can only live within this community. If the Christian's "official duty" causes pain and perplexity to his conscience, it must simply be endured. The Divine Command is terribly distorted when difficulties of conscience created by the "official order" are evaded by setting up a double morality. There certainly *is* an insoluble dualism between the law of the orders and the commandment of love; but since this contradiction is based upon the sin of all men, it must also be borne

[1] In the fourth section this question is discussed in more detail.

by all. As each human being has been produced by the sex-relationship between husband and wife, and has grown up within the community of the family and the nation, so also he must help to bear the responsibility for the orders, without which a peaceful and civilized social life is impossible. The asceticism of monasticism, on the one hand, and the Pietistic fear of "the world" on the other, which leads men to evade this responsibility, is unethical.

4. The preservation and creation of such orders is not due to faith—this will have become clear from what has been said already—but to the natural considerations of reason. All these orders, in contradistinction to the laws of biology, are only real, to the extent in which they are conceived and willed by the reason(3). God makes use of the human reason with its power of conceiving a purpose, in union with the natural instinct, in the service of His preservation of the world. He gives us these orders by means of our reason, and He preserves them by means of our reason. At the same time the word reason should be here understood in a very broad sense, that is, as the power of conceiving and willing an end. In any case, whatever part faith may have to play in the sphere of the orders, its function is not constitutive but regulative. The constitutive element is the natural impulse and reason. It is not faith, but the rational nature of man, which—from the human point of view—has created the orders, and preserves them accordingly. Faith always finds the orders already present as one aspect of reality, as the environment within which his neighbour confronts him.

Therefore these orders do not obey the logic of faith or of love, but the logic of the human and rational (and that always means also sinful) positing of an end.[1] As orders, however, they are always a means by which sinful humanity keeps the final consequences of sin at bay: that is, disorganization and chaos. Further, since we must accept humanity as it is, in the actual situation of the moment, these orders are also the *only* means by which those final consequences of sin can be kept at bay. By this very fact they prove that they are the gift of the Preserver of the world. But this causes the believer an almost tragic conflict, due to the fact that he feels bound to co-operate with an order which does not harmonize with the commandment of love, which is the

[1] Cf. Luther's exposition of Psalm cxxvii, and the paraphrase by STANGE in the *Z. f. syst. Theol.*, 1930.

sole commandment which he can acknowledge as binding upon himself.

But this impression of being involved in a tragic conflict simply arises from that detachment which belongs to any process of abstract thought. Man must, indeed, love in a concrete way. Therefore the first duty of love which is required of him is to co-operate with others in the endeavour to preserve that order apart from which all human life would become chaos—even if this order "in itself" does not in the least harmonize with that which he, as an individual, would do to another individual out of love, if he were acting solely from love. First of all the basis for human life must be created, the framework, the vessel, in which alone, indeed, human life can exist at all, that is, the orders; therefore the *first* (although not the highest) duty of the Christian is his "official duty." Just as in time of drought the inhabitants of a village would leave their ordinary duties and become an emergency team until the "roughest" work had been done, so also the duty which the "order" or "office" requires comes first in order of urgency, in spite of the fact that what it demands is a very "rough" way of acting, that is, it is only very indirectly in accordance with the commandment of love.

5. Since the one thing that matters is that the orders should be *real* forces for the preservation of order, and therefore unceasingly operative(4), man's first duty—even as a Christian —is the obedient acceptance and preservation of the present, existing order—however imperfect, rough and "loveless" it may be. For, at the moment, this order is the only dam which prevents the irruption of the forces of chaos, because it alone is a *real* order. The only kind of order which would be better than the present one would be an order which could replace it immediately, without any break in continuity. It is at this point that the summons to adapt oneself to the existing order (which reaches us through our Calling) becomes concrete; it is also very important, because it is so difficult, that we should be fully aware that the Christian, in the service of love, is summoned to place himself within an order which is inherently loveless! But this is indeed his duty, for if he refuses to obey this summons he will be neglecting the most urgent form of the service of love, that is, the maintenance of the dyke which protects human life from the irruption of chaos. We do not say that he is to perform this service without feeling it, without pain, without the desire to do all that is possible to

create a better and a more righteous order—how can he help feeling this, if he has the faith that desires to work itself out in love!—still, it *must* be done. This might be called "tragic," were it not for the fact that the Christian knows that in so doing he is bearing a share of his own guilt, and is thus co-operating with God in His gracious work of preservation.

In the obedience required by faith, therefore, the Christian believer must, as it were, first of all forget all he ever knew about the meaning of love, in order that he may help to protect and to further the life of these "orders" themselves in accordance with their own logic. For although these orders are necessary *for the sake of love*, most decidedly the behaviour they require is not the kind which we would expect to mete out to our fellow-man in love, if we were dealing simply with two individuals. Our "official duty" is "harsh," objectively technical: the human relation which it requires to men is external: its method is that of the forcible control of the masses, indeed it seems to be wholly opposed to love. To carry it through it needs the use of force, possibly of physical force, even to the point of taking human life(5).

But it is no use groaning over this state of affairs, nor have we any right to refuse to do our "official duty" because things are so. If such action is necessary, in order to preserve the "dyke" which protects our present civilization, we must simply accept the fact, for love's sake. I must behave differently to my neighbour in my capacity as a judge, a policeman, a bank official, a schoolmaster, etc., from the way in which I would behave towards him in a "private" relationship—as man to man. But consideration for the nation as a whole, of which my neighbour also is a member, requires this distinction.

The dykes within which human life ought to take its course must be of different material, and must be built in a different way from that of personal life itself, although they themselves also form part of human life. The one blood produces both the bones and the delicate texture of the skin. Life in the "official" orders, to perform its service of the maintenance of order, must be of coarser stuff than the life which consists in the relations between one person and another. The rind of life must be hard if it is to protect the soft content of the life within. For the sake of the weak it must be hard. It is this which fanaticism does not understand, against which it rages in its sentimentality. It does not understand this, because, on the one hand, it does not see the created natural element, nor, on the other, the sinful element, within life. That is why it has such a close affinity with rationalism, which regards the existing orders from the point of view of its abstract ideal of justice and equality, as something which is sub-ethical. Fanaticism and ethical rationalism reject the existing orders for the sake of an ideal "better righteousness" because neither of them understands that our concern here is not with a *better* order, but with an *actual* order, that is, one which is effective at the present moment. Until the better order is actually present the one which now exists is the best, because at least it *is* order(6).

6. The fulfilment of one's "official duty," exercised by the mother as mother, the father as father, the teacher as teacher, the politician as politician, the citizen as citizen—is the first duty of one who desires to obey God in the spirit of faith. He must help to construct the receptacle for life in accordance with its own rules(7). But this is certainly not the specifically Christian element in life. As one who knows God as Creator and Redeemer the Christian should be distinguished from others who do not know God, by the fact that he understands both the *need* for these orders, and their meaning, better than they. In these orders he sees the discipline of God for us sinful men, and at the same time he sees in them sin itself. He sees, too, how God uses human sin to work against sin; and in the fact that these necessary orders are so very different from life controlled by love he sees his own sin and the sin of humanity. This perception leads him to repentance. Anyone whose life is controlled by faith cannot help feeling acutely the contrast between the requirements of the order and the command of love, and he cannot help being horrified at the necessity for co-operating with this alien element. How miserable these "orders" are, even when measured only by the standard of ordinary justice and equity. In truth, fanaticism, and ethical rationalism, with its emphasis upon the Law of Nature, are perfectly right in so far as they see and feel the wrongness, the inhumanity, the life-destroying harshness, the coercive and mechanical character of every order that may happen to predominate at any particular time. The genuine believer must feel this still more acutely, for he judges this existing situation not merely according to abstract norms of justice, but according to the commandment of love, which gives to every individual exactly what he and he alone needs(8).

Wherever man is conscious of this terrible contrast he can never be a mere upholder of the present order, even though he may have to base his life upon the orders. A man who swears by the present order is one who cannot see beyond the orders but clings to them as though they were the last word, whereas they are only the first word. This kind of person is never penitent. But God's Command requires that even this law should lead to man's repentance, and this in a double sense: through the knowledge of that which these orders are not, and through the knowledge of that which they cannot and ought not to be. The commandment of love, taken as a law—the requirements of the Sermon on the Mount regarded as a law—is and remains the guiding standard even for life within the orders; for it remains the standard for man, wherever he may be. Even a judge or a politician can never have the right "to have done with it." The contrast between that which God wills and what we do ourselves, in our "official" capacity, remains culpable and terrible(9).

But, in the second place, the perception of this fact only leads to real repentance when man perceives that it is *quite impossible* to get rid of this contrast. We never see the real meaning of "original sin," we never perceive the depth and the universality of evil, or what evil really means in the depths common to us all, until we are *obliged* to do something which, in itself, is evil; that is, we do not see this clearly until we are obliged to do something in our official capacity—for the sake of order, and therefore for the sake of love—which, apart from our "office," would be absolutely wrong. The dualistic ethic of monasticism is so disastrous because it spares us the pain of perceiving this truth. For we only perceive the glaring contrast between the 'Αἰὼν οὗτος to which we are in bondage, and the 'Αἰὼν μέλλων, when this truth dawns upon our minds, and we see what we really are, apart from grace. Only then do we learn to pray aright for the coming of the Kingdom of God.

7. But the matter cannot rest there. Even life within the orders, regarded by itself, is an abstraction. We never meet other people merely within the orders, our relations with them are never merely "official." Wherever any personal contact takes place, a "non-official" element always enters into the process as well—this is so even if this element be present in a merely negative form, that is, that apart from our "office" we have nothing to say or to give to the other person. Now it

is at this point, in *personal dealings* between individuals, that faith has its distinctive opportunity. This, too, in and by itself, is also an abstraction; for no one of us lives, even for a moment, apart from his "office." Even where a man desires to meet his neighbour apart from his "office," in an entirely personal way, he is always at the same time also the father of a family, a government servant, a citizen, etc. But the "office" only constitutes one aspect of life; it is the first point, but not the last, it is the shell which contains life, but not the life itself. Actual life consists in meeting another person in love.

It is a judge's duty to condemn the accused strictly in accordance with the law; but by the law he is permitted—and as a believer he is commanded—to allow the accused, in some way or another, to feel that he has not personally broken off all relations with him, but that in the spirit of solidarity he bears his guilt with him, and "believes" in him, that is, that he remembers his divine destiny. The father of the family does not cease to be the father of a family when a man in distress comes to him and asks for assistance on the grounds that he is his "brother man"; had he no family responsibilities he would doubtless be able to help him more fully, but in any case he *must* help him as his brother man, whatever his own family responsibilities may be. The Divine Command requires us to break through the harshness and impersonality of the official order, so far as this is at all possible, without destroying the order itself. The framework exists for the sake of the content, the skeleton for the sake of the living body. The demand for the personal manifestation of love remains, through faith, supreme and sublime, above all collective demands, and the genuineness of faith must prove itself in this, that the personal element really remains supreme above all the claims of the order.

Most decidedly, however, this does *not* mean that the claims of the order are to be in any way either despised or modified; it does not even suggest that the actually necessary strictness of the "order," of the *Lex*, may be relaxed at any point(10). But what it does mean is this: that all this is only the framework for a life of "heartfelt brotherly love" which is filled with an ardent desire to penetrate through all the nooks and crannies in the official order to reach the "Thou" of the other person, "personally." Now certainly the requirements of the Sermon on the Mount are valid, as *law*, for this sphere, which is free from all that is "official"; this "sphere," however, is not really a "sphere" at all, but it is merely one aspect of a life which is controlled in its whole extent by the claims of "official" duty. Indeed, the characteristic element in the Sermon on the Mount is the fact that it expounds the law of love without taking the claims of the "official order" into consideration at all.

In reality, however, neither the claims of the "orders" nor the Divine Command of the Sermon on the Mount are "law" in the sense that they relieve me of the responsibility of making my own decision. Rather it is the very fact that in each situation it is necessary to stand between the official order and the Sermon on the Mount which constitutes the necessary space, which gives free scope for decision.

At all times I must myself decide what are the respective claims upon me of love and of the order, at this particular moment; or rather, it would be better to say, not what "love" and the "order" say I ought to do, but what kind of service the command to love my neighbour requires from me both in my "official" capacity and in my personal and direct relation with my brother. Further; it is not *I* who have to decide this, but the point is that, in faith, in this situation in which I have to decide, I am to hear the concrete Command of *God* Himself.

8. But, even when all this has been said, we have not yet fully indicated the relation between "person" and "office." As we have already said, the orders possess their own logic, their own autonomy. But this does not mean that we are to regard them as immutably established by Fate. The orders are, indeed, according to their form, the product of the rational life of humanity, as it has been moulded by History and by Nature. Fundamentally, therefore, they are variable. So far as the individual is concerned, of course, they do not vary, just as they are not produced by individuals; but they are variable in so far as the "people as a whole" is concerned, and having said this, we must be content to leave this conception without further definition. But each individual is not merely an individual, he is also at the same time a member of his race or nation; to this extent therefore he is partially responsible for the existing order; and he is also justified in sharing the obligation to introduce a better order.

But this does not mean that every Christian is called upon to be a reformer of the world as a whole. Rather, his call to the work of reform is determined by his "class and calling," that is, by his actual position within the nation to which he belongs. Thus, fundamentally, the individual's share of responsibility is always there, but in a great variety of changing historical forms. The responsibility of the subject of a medieval feudal state, or of the Roman Imperial state, and of the corresponding social order, differs entirely from that of the citizen of a modern national state, or of a democratic commonwealth; a member of a craftsman's guild has opportunities and restrictions which are totally different from those of the proletarian workman who belongs to a Trades Union; the responsibilities of the father of a pre-revolution family (with all its ramifications) are quite different from those which fall to the lot of the father and husband who live in the days of the Women's Movement and of the "Era of the Child." Two points, however, should always be borne in mind: the individual is always responsible, but his responsibility is never unlimited and universal. Responsibility is, indeed, always concrete; therefore it can only be discerned at a particular point in history.

The nature of this "better order" cannot be settled theoretically by sitting round a committee table and drawing up programmes. Nothing is easier than to devise a "better order" on paper; but nothing is so difficult as to find the better order which, under actual internal and external conditions, will become a *real* order. To construct ideological programmes is not only useless, it is harmful, because it breeds illusions, deflates moral energy, and makes the person who gives himself to this business an arrogant critic of the world around him. For the criterion by which the "better order" must be tested is that of *practical possibility*, since we are here concerned with *order*, not with ethical ideas. It is true, of course, that the prophetic message, which cares not a jot for what is "possible" or "impossible," is very impressive and important, for it represents the proclamation of the absolute law; but its significance depends upon the fact that it is presented not as a "programme," but as a general challenge, that is, if it does not demand immediate "political" realization. Wherever we are concerned with an immediate practical challenge, however, we must never forget (as we have already said) that a system which does actually maintain order is the best, so long as the "better" order cannot be immediately realized without any break in continuity.

9. From the point of view of Ethics, what does this phrase "can" or "cannot be realized" mean? What do the words

230

"possible" and "impossible" mean? A great deal of confusion is due to the fact that no distinction is drawn between the "impossibility" which arises from the sin of the individual—and simply indicates his weakness and irresolution—and the "impossibility" which describes the collective condition of humanity, or of a nation, or even of the position of the art of culture,[1] at any particular period. In the case of the individual, to allow the idea of "impossibility" to be used as an excuse for lack of moral effort is simply a sign of moral weakness and levity. In the case of collective life, however, the situation is quite different; here we are confronted by a moral duty, challenging us to consider the question of "impossibility" as carefully and exactly as possible, and to will *only what is actually possible*(11). To will the "impossible" in the latter sense is not a sign of seriousness, but merely of an arrogant and irresponsible fanaticism. Since no order is any use unless it is real, everything depends upon the possibility of achieving the "better order" for which one is striving. If this is *not* possible, then it is wrong to want it, because the attempt to realize the "impossible" will only lead to greater disorder, and even to chaos. It is the duty of the conscientious thinker to weigh just as carefully the pros and cons of the "possibility" of realizing the desired "better order" as it is to examine the question whether the proposed "better" order is really "better" or not.

At the same time it must be remembered that this question of "possibility" is not a pre-determined actuality. It is so at a particular moment; but it is not so when we take into account a longer period of time, during which many changes, both inward and outward, may take place. Even then, how-ever, we ought conscientiously to try to discover whether we can reasonably expect a definite change within this period or not, or even whether we ourselves may be in a position to effect this change, by means of which that which was previously impossible becomes possible. But, in so doing, we must remember that to reckon on Divine help to compensate for the absence of human possibilities does not mean that we are trusting God, but that we are tempting Him. A man who sits down to consider building a tower must first of all count the cost, in order to find out whether he "have sufficient to finish it." Only he should remember that men's hearts are not made of iron.

[1] For the meaning of this conception (*Kultur-Kunst*) see below, p. 251.

231

10. Where the orders are concerned the believer works side by side with the unbeliever. This is true also of the demand for a "better order." It is not necessary to be a Christian to see that a certain order is unjust. Even though we may not believe in a *lex naturae* in the old sense of the word, we do know that there is a very far-reaching *sensus communis moralis*(12). To this we can and ought to appeal where we are concerned with the creation of better orders—and also for fuller obedience to the existing orders. The feeling for what is humane and inhumane, for that which furthers and that which destroys life, for that which is fair and that which is unfair, can (and should) always be presupposed in every "fellow-citizen" without enquiring into the question of his religious faith. It is foolish to imagine—as some Christians do—that only within the sphere of the Christian Faith is there—in this definite sense—good will and moral earnestness. To recall the *splendida vitia* of Augustine in this connexion would only obscure the true state of affairs.

The creation, preservation, and reform of the orders is only indirectly a concern of the obedience of faith; directly, it is a concern of human reason, to which also natural morality belongs. Indirectly, it belongs to the sphere of the obedience of faith; to this extent, at least, that the believer will see the injustice of the existing order more plainly than others, and will be more resolute in working for the introduction of the better order. But he can only discover *what* this better order is, not as a believer, but as a member of his nation, along with his fellow-countrymen, by the use of reason. Here faith merely initiates; it does not create a new order, nor does it claim to be a supreme court. Hence, it is not the task of the Church, as the community of believers, to draw up the plans for the "better order" itself; its task is rather that of aiding those who are working for this end, and of setting in motion those forces which are required for this purpose. The work itself, however, must be taken in hand by the "people as a whole"; within this community no distinction can or should be made between believers and unbelievers. Faith can discover tasks of this kind—for love has keen eyes; but it is necessary that "the *bourgeois* reason" should examine its proposals to see whether they can be carried into effect, that is, to see whether their realization would produce more confusion than improvement. "Categorical imperatives" laid down by the Church, or by "believers," in such matters, are no help at all(13).

On the other hand, things are in a bad way with the Church

and with the faith of Christians when this initiative does not proceed from them, and indeed, as so often happens, when, on the contrary, Christians merely allow themselves to be dragged along the path of reform, against their will, by the secular rational spirit of justice.

Just as faith must prove its reality by searching for opportunities in which love can have free play, within the limits imposed by the official order, so also faith must prove its reality by searching for ways of making this official order itself more just, more humane, more full of the spirit of love, without unfitting it for the purpose for which it exists as an order. In certain instances, of course, faith must force itself also to urge that the reins should be held more tightly—for the sake of love(14).

The believer's most important duty, however, always remains that of pouring the vitality of love into the necessarily rigid forms of the order. The orders are the shell within which life is encased, therefore they are a means and not an end. The end, however, is the personal relation itself. Some orders are better than others; none is wholly good or wholly bad. In so far as it is an *order* it is good; but as an order, owing to its necessary harshness, it is incurably loveless, and even—as such—contrary to the law of love. It is true, of course, that to improve it is not a hopeless task, nor is it unnecessary, but it is still only a matter of secondary importance. The one thing that matters is to do what *can* only be done from the standpoint of faith, namely: to love our neighbour "in Christ," and to serve him as our brother, in any way we can, whether within the orders, or outside them, or in spite of them. Service of this kind, rendered with no other motive, has constantly given rise to the most important changes within the orders which have been thrown off as by-products(15) since the new content has broken the old forms and created new ones. At a time when all the emphasis is laid upon quantitative thinking, upon work "on a large scale," on external changes, it is supremely necessary to emphasize the truth that what is decisive always takes place in the realm of personal relations, and not in the "political" sphere, save where we are concerned with preserving the whole order from a general breakdown. Where the dykes are in danger of breaking down every one must help. But it is quite possible that they have fallen into this precarious condition because the *personal* meaning of life has been forgotten.

CHAPTER XXIII

THE ACTIVE LIFE AS A GIFT AND A DEMAND

PROPOSITION: *God gives and demands the right co-ordination of the means necessary for the successful attainment of an end.*

1. The line of thought which we have been pursuing up to this point has been concerned with the following truths: that conduct can only be described as "good": if it is (*a*) based upon the will of God (Section I); (*b*) if it flows from a personal existence which is determined by God (Section II); (*c*) if it consists in personal service to our neighbour (Section III). But although in this way the necessary presuppositions for good conduct have been demonstrated, such conduct has not yet been defined as real *action*. We have to do "something"; it is this "something" alone which defines the reality of the action, that is, it only becomes real when it emerges into the visible sphere and becomes concrete. Even when—rightly—we speak of an "inward action," a relation to this concrete, visible reality is present at least in the imagination as it is moved by the will; a will which has no intention of coming out into the light of day—whether this is possible is another question—is no genuine resolve at all, but merely a figment of the imagination, an unhealthy playing with the faculty of the will. This desire and this resolve to come out into the external, visible sphere is therefore included in the "good will" because our neighbour is excluded from our inward life, because as the "other" he is always the "other outside me," who is given to me, and can only be reached by me by means of the external world, as an "other" in bodily form, within space.

Were it not for the fact that in our neighbour as such this relation to the external concrete world exists, our external activity would not be ethical at all, but merely technical. In itself the relation between "I" and "it" is technical, not ethical; it only becomes ethical in so far as it is at the same time a relation between "I" and "thou." Thus all ethical action, because, and in so far as, it is "doing something,"

234

because it is a visible alteration of a sensible, spatial reality, is always actualized in a technical action. We could, indeed, be quite content to leave the sphere of external action to technology were it not that the impact of the will on external reality can be ethically interpreted in two or more ways. The contrast between Form and Matter does not rightly indicate the relation between "inward" and "outward" action. Rather, all "matter" which we use for the outward realization of the action is always already qualified in an ethical manner; in some way or another it is already "formed," whether in the literal sense—in the shape of matter formed by technical and artistic action—or in a broader sense, as, for instance, in the fact that, owing to the conditions on which property is held, "matter" is always also related to persons. In this world of ours there is no such thing as matter which is ethically neutral(1). But this means that action raises ethical problems not only by the connexion between the influence exerted by the inward upon the outward aspects of conduct, but also by the action of the outward upon the inward. Thus the way in which the inwardness of the will becomes an outward act through "doing something" is not a purely technical affair—although it always *is* technical—but it is also an ethical matter. It is this subject which will engage our attention in this section of this work. It is well known as the twofold idea of *means and end.* By means of this concept all personal action is related to "matter," and, on the other hand, all material action is evidently determined by persons. The "end" describes the aspect of this twofold sphere which is directed towards the person, and the "means" is that which has to do with neutral matter. Wherever matter which has been "formed" by action is utilized, there, in the "means" which are used, a previously realized "end" has also been used and thus affirmed. Or, to put it the other way round: wherever "something" is done, there, because every "something" lies in the external world of things, a *means* is used; there indeed that End—the "something"—is itself only a means to an end.

All this means that the concepts "Means and End" are relative. Every means, to the extent in which it can in any way be regarded as formed, has arisen as an end, and every end, to the extent in which it is the subject of human action, is not yet *the* end, the final end, but a means to an end. All our action moves between the two ideal End-points: that which is an absolute means, that is, ethical neutrality, and that which is an absolute End, that is, ethical immediacy. The theme of this fourth section is how this relative—mediate —technical element determines the relative-personal final end, and is determined by it.

Since all action is "doing something," and thus aims at the realization of something definite, the conception of success is indispensable in ethics. An action which is not aiming at success is not a serious action, but simply a phantasy. For instance, if a person desires to serve his starving neighbour in the spirit of love he intends to feed him on real food—he wills, that is, to *achieve* the end he has set before himself. Moral action is only serious when it contains this element of the will to "succeed." It is only in this way that the inward movement passes from the merely aesthetic sphere (or the sphere of phantasy) into that of ethics. Success, however, in the ethical as well as in the technical sense is the alteration of reality which corresponds to the end through the means. We can thus call an action "successful" in which that which is willed is really done, is actually realized.

Means exist only in view of the successful realization of ends. It is the will to succeed, and nothing else, which drives action into external reality. Therefore success is not—as is so often said—a dubious ethical concept, but one which is indispensable for ethics in particular. On it depends the reality of the moral(2).

Only now do we perceive that action may be of two kinds; since this is a fundamental question, I must anticipate, and at once explain what I mean; these two ways of action may be described as *demonstrative* and *effective*(3); they can only be understood by the consideration of the nature of personal relations. Our relation to our neighbour is personal, but this personal relation is partly indirect and partly direct. An absolutely direct relation would be one in which we could come into loving contact with our neighbour without any "means"; it would be a non-physical, purely spiritual relation between two souls existing wholly for one another; such a relation would mean a love so great that the one would be transparent to the other. A direct relationship of *this* kind, however, does not exist, we can only perceive one another by means of the body. But a *tendency* towards such transparency is peculiar to *demonstrative* action. Since, however, our relations are not only personal, but always include a certain relation to the world—to which in this instance the body also belongs —our action towards our neighbour also means "doing something" to him by means of the world which affects him. I do not merely will to *show* the other person that I am actuated with a loving spirit towards him, I do not only wish to hold communion with him in love, but for love's sake I also want to "do something" for him, "for love"; I want to give him something, or to help him in some way. Here my action does not affect him directly, but it touches "something," a bit of his world, and is therefore indirect. But even this contrast is relative. I can demonstrate my love by "doing something," and I can work in a demonstrative manner. Whole spheres of our human environment which incorporate a mass of effective action, as, for example, the school or the Church, are "means for demonstration," and on the other hand, the demonstration itself becomes a means of effective action, as, for instance, in all kinds of propaganda. Therefore an action may be successful from the standpoint of "demonstration" but not from the standpoint of "effective" action, or *vice versa*. The failure to distinguish carefully between these two modes of action has caused a great deal of ethical confusion, which has even affected world history as a whole—I need only remind the reader at this point of the "imponderables" in politics, an idea which has so often been misunderstood(4).

2. The fact that we *can* act is not a matter of course. This capacity of representing an inner act—in our case an act of will—in an outward action, and of shaping outwardly that which has been inwardly conceived, is based upon an original creative co-ordination of the outward and the inward aspects of life, which starts from the fact that we are "organized" in terms of "body" and "spirit"; this fact also symbolizes this co-ordination. It is not merely that we *have* a body, but that we *are* physical in our make-up. The symbolism of the body, which has been given to us by the Creator, in itself, before we do anything with it, suggests the spirit which it ought to express, and through which it is to play its part creatively in the world. The body's "serviceableness" to the spirit is not only for show; the body itself indicates that it is eager to be used in this way. Before "we" speak, the body, moved by the soul, has already spoken, and before "we" create, it creates. Our body is not only ensouled, but it is penetrated with spirit, indeed the body is the first educator of the awakening spirit(5).

It is true, of course, that we have to learn human speech and action—and the historical character of our existence is determined beforehand by the very fact that we have to learn these things far longer than any animal—but at first this learning is achieved more or less unconsciously and instinctively. Instinctively we learn human things—not animal things; for our instincts are human and not animal. Our humanity therefore is already given in a natural form, before we learn to use this organ and instrument consciously, and with a sense of responsibility.

But it is not only an individual body which we thus receive —a body which is thus ensouled and "spiritual"—as the basis, and also the instrument prepared for our own demonstrative and effective action, but also the original *social forms* of our human existence, those "orders" of which we have already spoken. They, too, although they have been made effective in the external realm, are not the result of a deliberate, responsible, personal act of volition, but, in the main, they are the result of the workings of human instincts and rational impulses. Half unconsciously, without making any special decision, and without any sense of responsibility, we grow into and thus become part of historical existence(6). The beginnings of human civilization, and indeed even of culture, lie in the realm of the unconscious. Even the creation of genius, of culture at its zenith, contains a strong element of this naturally unconscious life. Thus in the natural endowment of our existence, which through faith we know to be the Creator's gift to us, the union between the inward and outward aspects of human life has already been anticipated; indeed, it is already in being as a process which influences our ethical conduct beforehand. It belongs to the very essence of the development of our natural existence that man, as a moral being, should find already to hand a world of means and ends which, although it is not itself ethical, as a technical and cultural mode of action affects the relations between persons. The Creator provides us, as moral beings, with an immensely varied apparatus for demonstrative and effective action.

3. Where the individual is concerned, however, there is still something further to be said. Each of us receives not merely our natural life—by which I mean all that arises apart from our moral responsibility—but also our environment[1]

[1] Literally "joint-world" (*Mit-Welt*).—TR.

(which has been shaped by history as our environment), from the hand of the Creator and Ruler of the Universe. Each of us steps into an immense historical inheritance of intellectual "goods," which vastly expands the sphere of our power of demonstrating and working, and also shows us the way in which to use these powers(7). To look at this historical inheritance from the outset *only* from the negative standpoint—as a burden and a curse (although there is no doubt that this point of view must also be taken into account)—is ingratitude to the Creator who gives us our life in this way, and not in any other. Thus history—whatever our historical environment may be—shows us, in this inheritance, that successful ethical action is possible,[1] and gives us an ethical "working capital" which is indispensable for our action. In technical method and in science, in language, art, and literature, in the community and in the State, in race and custom, the individual does not merely inherit the final results of that process of unification, but as a living being he forms a vital part of this process and is summoned to play an active part within it. What Schiller says of language, which "sings and thinks for thee," is true of all historical life. Regarded from the ethical point of view it presents an infinitely richly articulated—certainly also ethically highly problematical—system of means and ends, whereby each individual "good" is the product of successful action which is partly technically artistic, and partly ethical(8).

We do not now enquire whether *all* action is successful, or whether the arrangement of means and ends, which is given to us, the existing system of means and ends, is right or not, whether the historical inheritance is not quite as much a curse as a blessing. I shall be dealing with this point later on. What I want to make quite clear just now is the fact that this world in which we find ourselves, with all the historical and ethical influences which have combined to shape it into its present form, is that world in, with, and through which the Creator gives us life. Only when we realize this can we speak intelligently[2] and act successfully. Faith bids us accept this world of ours not as an inevitable fate, but, in gratitude and reverence as the gift of our Creator, as the gift of life which He bestows upon us(9).

[1] See below, Chapter XXVI, pp. 281 ff.
[2] And thus "demonstrate" (see p. 236 for the two kinds of action). —Tr.

4. But still the most important thing has not yet been said. In this history, in this sphere of human conduct and human speech, *God Himself* acts, and speaks to us, as He is in Himself, He shows Himself to us as our Creator and Redeemer "by many infallible proofs." Within history, and on historical lines—and this means in external ways—God meets us in His Living Word.[1] It is not "History," as such, which is the divine revelation, as historical pantheism maintains; history as such belongs only to the sphere of "general revelation," which does not show God to us as He really is, and in which He does not redeem us(10). But, on the other hand, it is true that it is *in and through* this history that His particular revelation in Jesus Christ takes place: "The Word became flesh and dwelt among us, and we beheld His glory"[2]; the Incarnation of the Son of God does not mean only that He assumed our humanity; it means also that this actual historical world of means and ends is controlled by the saving will of God. It is only through real speech, by means of Hebrew and Greek and modern languages, and only through real external action, by historical persons, that God utters His Word, and in secret creates His Kingdom.

Thus God Himself has come out of the invisible and has entered into the visible world, in the fact that His Son "emptied Himself, and took upon Him the form of a servant"; in the Man Jesus of Nazareth God manifested Himself, and reconciled the world to Himself. The Word of God, spoken, written down, and printed by man, and, above all, the Sacrament, is the place where the union of the inward and invisible with the outward and visible is achieved by God Himself, and is made known to faith—as a Divine process of "successful demonstrative and effective action"—as revelation and redemption. Thus through God's act and speech within history itself, there has been initiated a process which unites the interior and the exterior aspects of life, a creative revelation and a revealing process of creation, by which, not as in our own ethical action, merely "something," that is, merely relative ends, are accomplished, but the absolute and universal purpose for the world, the Kingdom of God, is successfully—even though not completely—created. It is in the Mediator that this Divine act and speech takes place, which both manifests the final Ultimate End as truly as it effectively—even if not completely—creates it.

[1] Literally "Deed-Word" (*Tat-Wort*).—TR.   [2] John i. 14.

5. This Divine action, although it is achieved as human action, so far as its final End is concerned (that is, in that in which it is distinguished from all other action), is wholly and entirely the act of God. Through faith we are set within the sphere of His action. Through God's Word received in faith, and through His Act received in faith, we are sharers in that union of the inward and the outward, which is in complete accordance with the Will of God, and is therefore both perfectly good and perfectly successful, namely, the Kingdom of God. It is not we who create the Kingdom of God, it is He who creates it for us, as He creates it for Himself and for His glory. It is not that *we* have to show God to the world, and in so doing the real meaning of life and true love, but *He* shows Himself, and in so doing, ultimately, He says all that is worth saying. But we do not stand outside this His Speech and Action—or otherwise what would it all have to do with us? But it is completed in us, and it will be completed through us. It is achieved in us as His gift. We receive the wholly effective action of God, demonstrated successfully to us by external means, as His gift to us, which contains the absolute End, or purpose of the world, the Kingdom of God. We simply *receive* the *realization* of the Divine Will.

Although this Divine action may be fulfilled in a very fragmentary, indirect manner, cutting right across the continuity of history (see the next chapter), yet it is fulfilled within history and by historical means (*media salutis*). God acknowledges the historical world and Himself uses its possibilities (which He Himself has created) for His Purpose.[1] One illustration will suffice to make this clear: He uses human language, Greek characters and Greek syntax, for the establishment of His Kingdom. Human language becomes a means for making His Word known. The God-Man is not only more than man, He is at the same time true man. His life is not only different from that of a character in human history, but it is at the same time truly historical. He fulfils the meaning of Creation in man according to his natural and historical way of life. In Him it not only becomes manifest what human action ought to be and might be, but in Him it is actually realized. In Him God proves (if I may venture to speak like this) that human nature, as created by God, is not unfit for the realization of the Divine Purpose, although in Christ Crucified this human fitness is only revealed in a very indirect

[1] Cf. p. 240, and the last section of this book as a whole.

way. Thus human nature, as created by God, is potentially able to do what God's Will requires; that is, to *love*: both by showing the spirit of love, and by expressing it in effective action.

But this potentiality only "exists" at all because "He gives it to us" (Barth), and we only possess it absolutely as something which we have received. This potentiality, which had merely been adumbrated in the Creation, He now gives as a reality; that is, through faith in Christ we may live in the Divine love. Thus through faith it is possible both to reveal the love of God and to make it "real and effective," to perform the Divine Will, to work with God for the Kingdom of God, by using the historical means which are now available, the existing system of means and ends. Once again, however, in so far as this possibility actually exists, in so far as it is true, it exists "in Christ." This possibility exists in faith and in faith alone, and this means: only in that indirect hidden way which is in harmony with the hidden character of the Divine Victory[1] in the Cross of Christ; in the most literal sense of the word, this possibility is something "given."

6. But although this realization of the Divine Will is a gift, it is also a demand. The gift includes the task.[2] Thus we are not only to do "something" but in this "doing"—and for us there is no other—we are to do that which glorifies God and serves our neighbour. We are to "demonstrate" successfully for God and to "work" for Him successfully. We ought to do this in faith, and we can only do so in faith. For how could it be possible for us to do what God alone can do? How could our human action be divine action? The very fact that this impossible thing is possible, and that this impossible thing actually takes place when we act as those who have received, as those who have been given gifts by God, as those who "walk in the Spirit," is declared to us by faith. Faith contains the demand to believe in the possibility that God can act successfully through our human action, although it is always tainted by sin. This does not mean that God can make everything that happens—even the betrayal of Judas—a means to His end. That is indeed a proposition of faith, but it is not one which has to do with the Divine Command. Rather the demand which is implied in faith can only mean

[1] Literally "success."—TR.
[2] The play on the words *Aufgabe* (task) and *Gabe* (gift) is impossible to reproduce in English.—TR.

this: that we are to place what we do, according to the rules of such action, in a conscientious arrangement of means to ends, at the service of God and of our neighbour. We are to determine our aims in accordance with the Divine End, and we are to choose the means in accordance with these ends for their successful realization.

Since God Himself, in His revealing action, does not disdain to use the historical world with the means and ends which it contains, He requires us also to use it. To have a part in this corporeal world, shaped as it is by civilization and culture, is not only a gift but at the same time a task; indeed, it is only a gift when it is understood as a task, through active participation in it. Renunciation of the world, the world in which speech and action take place, is forbidden us. We have no right to be dumb and inactive. But not only so, we have no right either to give way to any Christian "snobbishness"; there can be no question of that prudish and arrogant contempt of the peculiar apparatus of means and ends which characterizes the ascetic or semi-ascetic attitude to the world, or the monastic or pietistic and fanatical point of view. It is neither right nor possible for us to contract out of the community of labour of historical humanity, but we ought to enter into it just as we have been placed within it. Through the Incarnation of the Son of God evil prejudices and also cowardly excuses have been taken away from us, so that we can no longer behave as though our action in the world had no reference to the Kingdom of God. In itself it has none, it is true, but it does possess this connexion as a gift, granted to it by God, as Creator and Redeemer.

In the sphere of reality no other action is possible save that which is achieved through the existing apparatus of means and ends(11). The view that the Christian can act in a different way from the non-Christian, as though he could freely dispose of his own faculties and devise ends and means himself, in accordance with the Divine Purpose, as though he could undertake "work for the Kingdom of God" on his own account, or construct his own Christian culture and civilization alongside of, and outside of the present one, is the illusion of monasticism. Through justification by faith the *whole* of our conduct, in all its sinful and secular character, is laid bare; at the same time, as a whole, secular as it is, it is fundamentally "sanctified," that is, it is related to the Divine Purpose of God, to the Kingdom of God. To act means to take our place in the work of the world and to co-operate with it, but we are to do this as those who share in the work of God. We can only "achieve something" by taking part in the work of the world, by using and adapting its means and ends. We are to do this with our eyes open, knowing that nothing in this world of action is free from sin; and, therefore, that no action is free from sin; sin cleaves to every farthing that we spend—yes, even if we give it to the Church or to Missions—to every pen with which we write—even though we may be using the pen to write a sermon which is most acceptable unto God. But the first fundamental thing we learn from justification is this: that God graciously "covers" this sin we cannot remove, and so, in spite of everything, we *may* co-operate in the work of the world with a good conscience, and indeed we *must* do so, otherwise we shall incur the wrath of God.

7. At this point what has been said already about the idea of the Calling is further illuminated by the fact that here we no longer speak in an abstract way of the "place" which is appointed to us, but that we now define this "place" more exactly as the existing co-ordination of means and ends which varies according to circumstances. In our "Calling" we must regard the existing means which are ends, and the existing ends which are also only means, as taken up into the Divine self-end, and thus sanctified. If this does not happen all that remains is this: either we must act with a bad conscience and without being justified in the sight of God—and this means a certain kind of sinful action, since it is a way of action which does not proceed from faith; or—we do nothing at all. To think that, in principle, it is possible to do otherwise, is simply fanatical. No human being who acts can act otherwise than as bound to this world, through the present order of means and ends which it contains. But if a person refuses to act—seeking thus to retain his "purity"—he is simply a parasite who lives on the active world around him.

It is of fundamental importance, especially in all problems connected with the ethic of society—or, to use the language of Gogarten, with the political ethic—to see quite clearly that even for the individual it is quite impossible to act apart from the action of all. Christian ethics have constantly been led astray by the idea that the action of Christians could take place, as it were, in an historical vacuum, bound by no laws save those which it evolves out of its own inner consciousness. To this I would reply: To act always means, in every case (just because we must do "something"), taking a share in the action of the world, using the one inclusive, infinitely varied, co-ordinated apparatus of means and ends which extends throughout the whole world, as it is placed at our disposal by nature, civilization, and culture, and indeed—but I will not dwell on this at the moment—within the existing orders of society.

8. Only after this has been made clear can this further truth be rightly understood, namely, that this existing order of means and ends does not exclude but includes the possibility of free choice and the devising of ends. Ends do not spring out of nothing; they appear because they have been posited by a will. Ends only arise where they have been planned, and as an articulated system, the system of means is only real through these ends, that is, through the purposive will. Therefore, fundamentally, all action, and above all, ethical action, implies the devising of ends and the choice of ends. To be set within the work of the world therefore always means that we ourselves are given the responsible task of devising ends, and the means by which they are to be realized.

As soon as we begin to act we can only act in co-operation; this means, we can only act in view of means and ends, in affirming the means and ends which others affirm. As soon as we begin to do anything we are bound to do it in the same way every one else does it. Even if we are building a church our action does not really differ from that of those who build any other kind of building, both in the narrower technical sense as well as in socially technical relations (use of money, conditions of labour, etc.). But this connexion with the ordinary system certainly does not mean that we are wholly determined by it. For instance it is not pre-determined that we should build a church and not a cinema; indeed, this end can only be understood from the point of view of the Purpose of God which we hold fast in faith. But this end has a reflex action also upon the means. One who takes this "end" seriously will not choose means which, from the outset, would render it impossible to carry out this purpose. For in this instance the end is not independent of the means, since the end is to demonstrate something (through preaching) and the means itself ought to further this end. To preach the Divine message in a church which has been erected with obviously unworthy means is, humanly speaking (at least for a long time), futile.

The end determines the choice of means not only in the technical sense, but also in the ethical sense.

9. Here we are not yet dealing with the question of the norm of good and bad means and ends; all I want to do at this point is to make it quite clear that both the use of the existing order of means and ends and the independent planning of ends, and of means for their realization, is an integral part of ethical conduct. This truth, however, contains an important consideration about the content of ethical action as well; namely, the fact that the ends are also conditioned by the present system of means, and the means by the Divine self-end.

This does not mean that we can freely devise ends in accordance with the idea of love. It is, of course, true, that we have to act in love in a concrete world; therefore we cannot construct an abstract idea of love to meet this situation. The end—which is to love our neighbour and to work for God's glory—is also conditioned by the existing "means," each of which already incorporates ends, and indeed, sinful ends. To act in the world means to work with sinful material—since we ourselves are sinners. In spite of this we are to act, not by making compromises—compromise is inevitable where justification by faith and the idea of the Calling are not known—but by making use of existing conditions as though they were holy, since they have been hallowed by the Divine forgiveness. In themselves the means which are thus used, measured by the law of love, are extremely unholy, whatever we do, in every action we use the whole unhallowed apparatus of means and ends. But through faith it is hallowed, not as our action, but as the action of God. This is *one* side of the question.

The other side of the question, although it is secondary, is just as important: we have no right to believe that our action is approved by God unless we do all that lies in our power to make even these means, as far as possible, conform to the Divine End, that is, to Love. The means which have to be used for a definite good end may even be of such bad quality that in this instance we feel it to be our duty to renounce the undertaking altogether.

10. As a rule the notorious proposition, "the end justifies the means," conceals great confusion of thought, whether it is defended or rejected as a principle. To make it absolutely valid and unassailable we might word it like this: the necessary end hallows the necessary means. In this form it simply

expresses the idea of the Calling applied to the relation between means and ends, and corresponds to that which we have said about action within the world. But in this form it is not a law to be applied, but a rule to guide reflection. Stated in this way, casuistry could not be practised, indeed it destroys casuistry. For what is a necessary end, and what are necessary means? This statement expresses the truth that no end may be set up without estimating at the same time the ethical character of the means which it would require, and that no means may be called "necessary" save through a necessary end—and this means, by an end which, in faith, we dare to claim as in line with the Purpose of God.

Almost all previous systems of Christian ethics have been based upon the illusion that means exist which, in themselves, are neutral; they assume that whenever means already possess an ethical quality, and therefore raise ethical problems, they constitute an exception to the general rule. In reality, however, there are *no neutral means*; hence there can be *no* "purely technical" use of means. This is because all means already incorporate ends, and because, on the other hand, even the ends which we propose are always only mediate ends, never the Divine necessary self-end. The whole earth, with its natural treasures, is legal property, and every instrument of manual labour with which we till the soil is a product of the collective workshop of human action. Each square yard of land which I acquire contains the whole history of law, and the whole history of ethics. And every spade with which I cultivate the ground contains the whole of the production of iron, the whole world economy and, again, the whole of history. It is unpardonably thoughtless to speak of the "ethical neutrality of technology." Technology, just as it is, is always a historical phenomenon permeated and determined by legal, social, inter-human relations of all kinds. Technology, in every sense of the word, although not exclusively, is yet to a very large extent determined by law, morality, religion, and personal factors. Later on we shall be dealing with the fact that it is ethically variable, and why this is so. In any case, technology is never neutral, or "innocent," but, whether good or bad, it is a force which is absolutely determined by ethical standards. Hence to make use of it is never a merely technical affair, but it is always an ethical matter as well. Action which uses these means does not only need to be sanctified in the sense of the dedication of a neutral element

247

to God, but it needs the sanctification which springs from forgiveness, and a transforming process of purification.

We could not act at all if we were determined to act *only* in opposition to the accepted code of behaviour; but we could not act as Christians if we were always to conform to the accepted code, that is, if we were unprepared to strike out on a line of our own. Hence the next question with which we have to deal is that of the norm which should decide whether we are to act in conformity with, or in opposition to, the ordinary code.

CHAPTER XXIV

THE HALLOWING OF THE MEANS BY THE END

PROPOSITION: *The Command of the Creator and the Redeemer requires and hallows the use of the means which reality, Divinely created and yet sinful, offers for successful action. At the same time it demands that all means which are contrary to the purpose of God shall not be used, but shall be definitely rejected, at the price of the renunciation of that which the world calls success.*

1. What then are we to do and not to do, in order to glorify God in the service of our neighbour? We dare to believe, or rather, we cannot help believing, that, in spite of everything, this world *is* God's Creation. Faith teaches us that the world in which our lot is cast is the world which God has given us as our world, through which He gives us life. Thus God wills this natural and historical life, by means of which we exist, and apart from which we would not exist at all. God wills that human beings should exist, that they should have children and bring them up, that they should earn their living by the work of their hands, and should make the world subject to themselves. He wills that men should use reason, His most precious gift of creation, His highest work of creation. Thus He wills the whole activity of the natural historical life in the natural forms of community, in civilization and culture. The criticism of culture (*Kultur*) which proceeds from the Gospel, the warning against the idolatry of culture, against a culture which is autonomous, striving after equality with God, a culture which is in the grip of the insane idea of equality with God, does not mean a fundamental hostility to culture as such. Even when the eschatological tension of Primitive Christianity was at its height, the institutions of marriage, labour, and the State were not rejected; on the contrary, they were explicitly recognized.

Now this means that God actually commands us to use the means by which alone this natural life—inclusive of culture—is created and preserved. The Divine self-end, the growth of the Kingdom of God, includes this natural end: the maintenance and preservation of the natural human life in its own required forms. God has not created us as angels, but as human beings of flesh and blood, human beings who can only manage to live their life in a human way by means of marriage and the family, civilization and culture, by means of the State and the system of law. He wills to build His Kingdom in such a way that this life—which gains its definite character through His Creation and our sin—shall be maintained, until He re-creates it in the new age, as the Kingdom of Perfection. This is why we are commanded to use the means by which it is preserved and maintained.

2. Human "action"—as the deliberate transformation of existing reality, by means of creative and demonstrative action —consists in the production of *goods*, and their *distribution* to persons. All human action consists either in the production or the distribution of goods. A "good" is something which has value; but *value* is that quality of a good by means of which it meets a definite physical or spiritual need of man. As we have seen, there are no "intrinsic values" but only the "values of human life"; in stating this truth the emphasis should be laid now on the idea of "life" (vital values), and now on the thought of "man" (human values). A "good" does not come into existence simply by means of human creation; pure raw material is also a "good." But in an historical world there is no pure raw material. All so-called "raw material" is actually a good which has been moulded by historical and social influences, i.e. by conditions of property, by methods of transport which make it accessible, etc. On the other hand, it is also true to say that man can create nothing but goods—for even his artistic and scientific works are "goods."

We must, however, distinguish the creation of goods from the appropriation of goods, the rendering of service. Only through service does the merely potential value of a good become its actual value. A good which has not been appropriated—as, for example, a lost work of art—has only a potential value and no actual value. Every kind of "good" has its own intrinsic use, but it must develop this "intrinsic" use into something of actual service "to us," either by means of distribution, or by some service rendered. If we think of humanity as a whole, there is no difference between appropriation in the wider sense and appropriation for one's own use; in both instances a "good" develops its potential quality of usefulness into actual utility by means of service—sometimes through service in the more restricted sense—as appropriation of a "good" to the needs of another—and sometimes in the sense of appropriation for "my own needs."

3. All human action may be summed up under these two main types. As such, however, human action is still not ethical but it is either technical or creative, a kind of "creative culture"(1). The motive for this action is primarily simply the natural impulse—whether it be the vital impulse, the biological instinct of preservation, or the humanistic rational impulse which creates in the intellectual sphere from sheer joy in creation. Here too the norm for this kind of action is not primarily ethical but technical; for instance, it may be a "rule of the art" which is concerned with the agricultural or technical skill of the manual or factory worker, or with the "rules of the art" in science or art or politics. In the production and appropriation of "goods" the moral is not a constitutive, but merely a regulative principle. Thus it is easy to understand why it is that Greek ethics, which is essentially determined by the conception of creative activity, never arrives at a clear distinction between the ethical and the technical aspects of human action. Creative action is in itself neither ethical nor non-ethical; but it ought to be placed under the jurisdiction of the ethical, it ought to be hallowed.

Natural creative activity implies a natural form of "community," which is not ethical but pre-ethical, namely *co-operation* and *exchange*. Co-operation is the natural form of the work-community which arises out of the natural purpose of production; exchange is the natural form which arises out of the natural purpose of appropriation by the distributing community. Primarily both are based simply on the fact that naturally the one is bound to depend upon the other; we call them the natural forms of community. Just as man—quite apart from any kind of ethical motive, purely from natural necessity, whether mental or physical—must work, so also he must co-operate and exchange. The natural laws of this co-operation and this exchange we may describe as the technique of social life. This again produces the division of labour —the natural order of callings—which carries with it the determination of the goods which are to be produced, and of the means necessary to achieve this end—whether these "means" are "technical" in the industrial or in the social sense. It is true, of course, that this way of regarding the subject is abstract, since it is actually impossible to separate the ethical from the technical sphere; but we have to use these abstract terms in order to clarify the question; we can, and indeed we ought, to study the whole process of co-operation and exchange apart from ethics; only when we have done this can we rightly determine the part to be played by the ethical element.

4. We are *commanded* to take our share in this whole process of creative human action; for through this human action God wills to maintain life in me and through me in others. In concrete terms this means that I am commanded to take part in this process because through this activity of mine God wills to maintain the life of my neighbour; for so far as my own interests are concerned the natural impulse of self-preservation impels me to take my share in this process. And because it is God who, as our Creator, upholds us in that creative activity which is due to the natural impulse of man, one who through faith perceives this Creator will find it possible to co-operate in this activity as the service of God and of his neighbour, or, to put it more exactly, he will be able to regard this work, and to accomplish it, as the concrete form of his service of his neighbour. This statement, of course, provokes a whole host of objections and queries to which we must pay attention in due course. But if we wish to understand something of our duty in life as a whole, all these questions—these "ifs" and "buts"—must, for the time being, be set aside. Our fundamental service to our neighbour consists in taking part in the production and the appropriation of goods within the natural system of the division of labour or the order of callings which arises out of co-operation and exchange.

Only through my relation to this Divine End does the natural division of labour, or, to be more exact, the definite fashion in which I play my part in this work of preserving human life, and the definite place at which I do this, become my "Calling." Through the idea of "the Calling" I come to know not only the place at which I am to co-operate, but also the way in which I am to co-operate: I perceive that the co-ordination of means and ends which my calling involves, is given to me and commanded me by God. This is the abstract conceptual way of explaining the meaning of that epoch-making statement of Luther when he said that a dairymaid in her work on the farm—by the very fact that she does her duty as a dairymaid—can and should serve God and her neighbour, and that this is more important than all special "work for the Kingdom of God," that is, than all work which is dubbed specifically "religious." She does what every one in her position would have to do, but she does it—and this alone is the ethical aspect of the question—in joyful obedience to the Will of God. The shoemaker makes his shoes to the "glory of God," and regards this service as his service to the Kingdom of God. In principle—at least primarily—there is no need to set up special ends, nor any special choice of means, but this relative end and its corresponding means is hallowed by its relation to the Divine Purpose (or Self-End).

This idea will only become completely plain to us when we note the fact that what we have primarily simply described as "Nature" has its ultimate basis in God's Will as Creator. The "natural forms of community" have been so arranged by the Creator that—as we have already seen—He uses the natural life and the necessity which it contains in order to bind men together. It is a divine method of education which forces people, through necessity, to come together, even where in a selfish way they only seek themselves, and indeed He uses their very egoism itself to accustom them to community and to exercise them in it. And it is the Divine Wisdom of the Creator that He has so arranged the natural process of production and appropriation, in co-operation and exchange, that even one whô only works for himself is working in reality for the whole. The believer ought to perceive this, and he should then absorb this secret will of his Creator into his own conscious will. This is what is meant by the expression: to fulfil one's calling to "the glory of God and the good of one's neighbour." The change which this makes in human action is—at first—only inward; in his calling the Christian does what every one else does in these circumstances; but he does it "in a different spirit." Actually he will also perform it differently, but this is a second point, with which we shall be dealing directly.

5. With the Calling are *given*—primarily—the ends and the means which it requires; they are hallowed by their relation to the Divine End. This holds good even when "in themselves," for instance, they are not neutral (and this is of course impossible) but sinful, that is, contrary to love. The judge must deliver his sentence in accordance with the law in its present state—even though "personally" he may be convinced that this present law is unjust. He does not make any "compromise" when he acts in this way—that is, if he is really acting in the spirit of faith. For he knows that at the moment he cannot create a better system of law, but that in this world law is necessary; but he also knows that so long as

the people who frame the laws are unjust—that is, to the end of our life on earth—there will be no truly just system of law. So also our "Christian shoemaker" must—first of all—do the proper work of a shoemaker, although this involves him in direct contact with the unjust world of money, business, competition, the class-war; and indeed this spirit is not new— it is the unpleasant spirit which always has been and always will be characteristic of the business world as a whole. His business is part of the one great economic sphere which is created by God, yet burdened with a curse; only through taking part in this sphere as a whole can he fulfil his calling, and thus render his primary service to his neighbour. It is of the mercy of God that he may still do his work "to the glory of God" in spite of everything, it is of the mercy of God that God takes the responsibility for all that he cannot alter. There may very well be extreme cases where the contrast is too great, where a "calling" can never be regarded as subject to the grace of God; in such instances a man who is in earnest about doing the Will of God can no longer participate in such action; but at the moment we are not dealing with this problem. The first thing we have to do is to recognize that there is *no* calling which does not raise difficult questions in our minds, questions which the individual cannot answer because he cannot alter the said conditions; we must realize that fundamentally exactly the same could be said of every man-made calling.

The only calling which might be regarded as free from entanglement with this sinful world is that of the monk; but to embrace the monastic life in the hope of escaping from the "world" would only mean falling a prey to an illusion. It is due to the Grace of God that, in spite of this state of affairs, we may prosecute the duties of our calling with cheerfulness and with a clear conscience, as those whom God has placed at this particular post; it is of God's grace, therefore, that we may use the necessary apparatus of means and ends which our calling requires, in spite of the fact that, in themselves, these means are always dubious; thus, to live continually under the Grace of God constitutes the Christian's calling.

6. But although this is the first word upon this subject, it certainly is not the last. The second thing which we have to say is this: that God, as Redeemer, has revealed His will to us, in order to make an end in judgment of this sinful world and to create a new world; thus the God who reveals Himself

to us in this way, also demands from us a new way of acting and a new creation. At the same place where we see that God recognizes history—in the Incarnation of the Word—we see His judgment on this world and the beginning of His new creation. Neither in Rome nor in Athens was Christ born, but in the stable at Bethlehem. It is not as One who is always successful that He is our Redeemer, but as the Crucified. In Christ the hostility of this historical world to God is unveiled(2) and this truth, which is perceived by faith, must be carried out in practice. For the Cross is not "placarded" before our eyes in order that we should simply gaze at it as mere spectators; no, faith absorbs us spiritually into this Death, in order that, as renewed souls, we may live henceforth in newness of life. As citizens of the new world we receive the duties as well as the rights of citizenship; no longer have we the right simply to do as others do, as "the heathen do"; along with our necessary co-operation we are also required to do things differently.

In the light of revelation we see the whole curse of historical life: injustice within the system of law, lack of peace in and through the State, lack of truth in science, triviality and idolatry of beauty in art, the deification of culture, slavery in civilization. We see above all—and this is the real point I want to emphasize—how the real purpose of life is being thwarted at every turn in all the "orders" which constitute the framework of human life: the "ends" sought are so futile and empty, and the "means" used to achieve these ends are utterly contemptible. In very truth, to point to Luther's illustration of the "good dairymaid" certainly does *not* settle this question! Co-operation with others for the glory of God and the good of our neighbour must be our first principle, of course, but there is a second principle, which is just as important, namely: there are occasions when—on principle—we must *refuse* to co-operate with others, occasions when it is our *duty* to act in a different manner.

7. What, then, are we to do if we cannot simply deduce the ends and the means from the existing natural order of callings and division of labour? Obviously we must ourselves devise ends and means, by our own free action, in order that we may correct and supplement the existing order of callings. Behind the new question of the choice of a calling—which in Luther's day evidently caused no one very much trouble—stands the far more fundamental question of the hierarchy,

of the system, of means and ends, this question which inevitably comes at the very beginning of a rationalistic ethic but in a Christian ethic is raised at a later stage; its meaning also is very different. There can never be any question of constructing a "Christian programme of culture." We know that such language betrays an idle and dangerous ideology, forbidden to him who knows the truth about the Creator and about sin. The ethical is not a constitutive but a regulative element in the world of the production and appropriation of goods. It is critical—not constructive—thinking which is here required.

The presupposition of all co-operation is the conviction that this co-operation will serve the Divine purpose of preservation, thus, that through the goods which are thus produced and appropriated, "good" will be done, that the goods will be really valuable, that those by whom they are appropriated will really need them, and that all the goods required will be produced. Thus there are three critical questions:

(*a*) Are the goods which are produced real goods?
(*b*) Will they really be distributed to those who need them?
(*c*) Are all the goods produced which are required?

None of these questions can here be answered materially; here all we have to do with is the main points of view. These, however, must certainly be made clear.

8. The standard by which "goods" are tested is whether they are serviceable, what they are "good for." "Good" in this sense is a relative conception, and therefore as variable as historical life itself. Only in the most general definitions can we say anything universally applicable to the idea of "goods." A "good" (in the sense of "goods") is something which serves the earthly end of human life in accordance with the purpose of Creation, and it is something which serves the heavenly end of human life in accordance with the purpose of Redemption. It is nonsense to talk of a "highest Good" as though it were an absolute(3); the idea of *good* is in its essence relative, that is, relative to the person, and therefore subordinated to the person and to the community of persons. But even apart from that we cannot set up a system of "goods." A hierarchy of "goods" ranged, for instance, according to their "higher" or "lower" rank—in which the former would be the "spiritual" values and the latter the "vital" values— may have its place in a Platonist ethic; it can never have

any place in a Christian ethic. To give food to a hungry person is more important than to press a religious tract into his hand. On the other hand, however, we ought not to attempt to construct a realistic order which works from the bottom upwards, a classification of urgency according to the point of view of preference for the vital aspect of life; otherwise we ought never to build a school or a church until every one has enough to eat. Nor ought we to use the twofold point of view of Creation and Redemption as the principle of classification, whether in the former or the latter sense. A system of *goods and services* (i.e. *values*)(4) from a definitely limited and temporary point of view *may* be justified, but it can never serve as the definition of that which has to be done here and now.

It is, however, possible to claim that there are sham goods (sham values) and sham services—I need only remind you of the spheres of extreme luxury and of vicious pleasure—that there are goods and services which are extreme cases, judged by all the points of view which have been mentioned, which, if controversy arises, must give way absolutely to those which have been proved to be necessary as vital or spiritual values. For the rest, wisdom—real wisdom—will come to the final conclusion: "Everything has its day." On such a conclusion it is impossible to erect any system.

9. The second question leads to a similar conclusion. It is impossible to determine legally to whom, for the sake of God, certain goods should, or should not, be distributed. This would only be possible if we could make our basis some rational method of division, for instance—to give the simplest example —the egalitarian method, or one deduced from it. But the egalitarian idea comes to grief immediately on the rock of creaturely historical inequality, and the inequality (which goes with this) of relative value. What does Bach mean to the Indians? or a university to the Bushmen? The rule of equality cannot be applied even to vital goods, since, thanks to human inequality, it would lead to constantly renewed fresh divisions, or, in order to avoid them, to an enslaving of all by a collective system which would make every one unhappy.

In the case of both questions, however, there should be one critical regulative point of view which could be generally applied. Wherever one group of goods is preferred to another, in a one-sided way, the Christian is bidden to redress the balance(5) ; thus, in a materialistic age spiritual goods should be specially stressed and cultivated; in an ascetic period the main emphasis should be placed upon certain vital values. A false individualism needs to be balanced by the function of collectivity, while the deadening influence of rigid collectivism must be countered by insistence on the natural inequality of all life. For each individual this truth should be emphasized: the more easily I can do without something, the less ought I to have it at the expense of the urgent need of someone else. Through such general considerations, which, in the case of the individual—and it is with him we are here concerned— have to function as guiding laws, the flow of goods is diverted from the direction which it would otherwise take, and production is to be either stimulated or checked; here, however, strictly speaking, no laws can or should be laid down.

10. The third question is the easiest to answer; it is obvious that all the goods required are not produced, nor are all necessary services rendered. Indeed, there are goods and services which do not exist "in a natural way," namely, all those which are determined from the point of view of Redemption. It is true, of course, that what we clumsily describe as the "Highest Good" does not lie within the sphere of our action; but the *means* which are given and willed by God do lie within the sphere of our responsibility, as the highest form of demonstrative action, the proclamation of the Kingdom of God. And there is a "more excellent way" of action to which those who have learned to know the love and mercy of the Redeemer are called, and are enabled to accomplish, that is: the free devising of means and ends, in "works of love." Of course, the natural process of production knows nothing of this, nor does it know anything about the proclamation of the coming Kingdom, and these "works" of self-sacrificing, devoted mercy which only seek the good of others (in spite of the fact that even here the "all too human" element is in evidence), still form the most beautiful chapter in world history. It is true, of course, that here the misunderstanding may arise against which Luther felt obliged to protest with his talk about the dairymaid, as though these "special" works, these literally "extraordinary" works, were in a higher category than the simple fulfilment of the duties of one's calling; but in a certain sense it remains true that here, in this action of love which is not laid down by the rules of a calling, freely designed, springing from individual initiative, the meaning of love stands out more clearly than anywhere else.

11. What then is that "something" which from love and in love we are to do to our neighbour in accordance with the will of the Creator and the Redeemer? In co-operation we are to do what every one does, and we are also to act differently from others. A Christian shoemaker—if this illustration of the early Fathers may be used once more—does not differ from another kind of shoemaker simply by the fact that he does the ordinary work of his calling as a service to his neighbour and to the glory of God; rather he will also do "something special" by not always buying in the cheapest and selling in the dearest market, by treating his assistants not only according to the economic point of view, but by drawing them, as his neighbours, within the circle of his personal care; by the fact that in his municipal party he will not always represent the standpoint of the privileged, but that perhaps in some incomprehensible way he will sometimes help the opposite party; since he will not use his savings simply for himself and his family but that he will have a remarkably open hand for his neighbours who are in want. And therefore also, in quietness, and in small things—or if it is granted to him, publicly and in a larger circle—he will remember his priestly duty, and at the right time and place he will say something "amazing," something which does not simply belong to the subject in hand, something unexpected, about God and eternal things, something which, just because it is said at an unusual time and in an unusual way, will have more demonstrative, attractive, and awakening power than the majority of sermons. For—provided that he has already done all that is possible in the way of outward help—he knows that ultimately this is an incomparably greater service of love than all "works" and "services." In his bearing towards those with whom he has to do he will, in some way or another, "show," let it be noted by his inward attitude, that he meets them as brothers and not as strangers, that he counts them as related to himself because he and they alike are related to God. His Christian life will show itself in independence of that which the world calls "good"; he will let others see that he regards earthly things from an end which lies above history, that he judges and orders them practically from this point of view. In all this, in accordance with the Command of the Redeemer, himself a sinful man in a sinful world, he will strive to do the works of love.

Again and again, however, he will see how little he can really do as an individual. And if this individual is not a shoemaker but a workman, a manufacturer, a leader in the business world or an industrial organizer, a statesman or a scientist, in all that is "special," in all that he does differently from that which every one has to do, he will soon run his head against a wall, and will realize how limited is the scope for acting in such a different way, how powerful and terrible the compulsion to do what in itself is contrary to the law of love, and what he must now do for love's sake, because to refuse to act would be still worse. As a Christian should one not be able to break through these iron bands of necessity? Are there *no* means of doing the "something different" on the grand scale? It is to this question that we now have to address ourselves.

CHAPTER XXV

AUTONOMY, NATURAL LAW, AND LOVE

PROPOSITION: *The Divine Command, in view of the work which has to be done, must be understood in the light of the following threefold law: it requires co-operation with secular society in accordance with practical righteousness; secondly, it exercises the critical function of the absolute law, or the prophetic criticism of society; thirdly, it guides the extraordinary action of the Church in preaching and in philanthropy.*

1. We only become fully aware how limited is the scope for free individual ethical action when we want to "do something," when we attempt to make our will effective through technical means. The act of will alone is free, and therefore, in the full sense, responsible. The more the will is directed towards the external world—as indeed it must be, since it intends to be realized—the more do alien influences intrude. The will is prevented from realizing itself in the external world by a double limit: the material it has to use is subject to its own laws, and the society in which the action has to be performed is likewise subject to its own laws. Ethical action is always, at the same time, technical action, and the ethical action of the individual always also involves participation in a collective life. Both these forms of action are impersonal. In the first place in "doing something" I am not dealing directly with my neighbour but with *things*; and yet there is no effective love of my neighbour without "doing something for my neighbour," that is, doing something by means of *things*; I can only realize my personal will by the aid of technical means. And, secondly, in "doing something" I cannot do that which love urges me to do; but since in "doing something" I must take external action, I come out into the open, into visible human life. I can only do something by means of doing it with others. And by the fact that I "do something" the general practice of society controls my personal action.

Thus "Christian inwardness," the obvious tendency of many earnest Christians to shrink from all external action, is based on good reasons. When the individual attempts to realize ethical action in the external world, he finds it dominated by autonomous forces which are calculated to thwart the whole intention of love. Since this takes place with the apparently inevitable necessity of something laid down by law, it is comprehensible that Christian moralists feel inclined to leave this whole sphere to "reason," to the "lawyers," "to the experts"(1). But to do this would simply mean that real action would be entirely withdrawn from the influence of the Christian ethic. It is *here*, in this borderland between technical action and ethics—in economics, in politics, in public life— that the great decisions are made. If the Christian ethic fails at this point it fails all along the line. The indubitable alien autonomous force which here determines action must not lead us to disown all ethical responsibility. On the contrary, the way in which the Christian ethic solves the problem of autonomy(2) will decide its own fate. Since God requires from us not merely volition but action, He requires us to enter into this "alien sphere," into this realm of the impersonal, and it is His will that we, as believers, shall prove ourselves within this sphere.

2. On the other hand, for the very same reason, that is— because we must act—we have no right to blind our eyes to the presence of the laws which control this situation; on the contrary, it is our business to come to terms with them. It is just as dangerous and unreal to close our eyes to the fact that these autonomous forces actually exist, and thus to leave them out of account, as it is to withdraw from this sphere of impersonal reality altogether. It is indeed a dangerous illusion to hold the sentimental view that the law of love, the "application" of the Sermon on the Mount, can here be asserted as the constitutive principle of action. Fanaticism of this kind, which regards itself as Christian earnestness, and arises from inability to perceive the fact of sin, can lead to no result save to an unfruitful hostility to all that happens in this sphere— and thus to an actual withdrawal from all responsible co-operation, combined with the arrogant feeling that "I would do things quite differently if I had *my* way," when actually I am doing nothing at all. Or, if one does try to effect something, this point of view leads to Utopian experiments which further confuse the issue. In both instances, such fanaticism leads to behaviour which is extremely unpractical and therefore superficial.

Since human action in this external sphere of technical public life is determined by laws which do not spring from faith, what was said earlier about the *Lex* and legality is applicable at this point. This, however, means that here the commandment of love is more narrowly defined through the law of relevance. A Christian who is called to be a statesman is not called to "govern as a Christian," but—and just because he is a Christian he ought to know this—as a good statesman. A scientist is not to conduct his research work as a Christian but as a scientist, a Christian engineer does not build "Christian bridges" but solid bridges(3). This means that the Divine Command, discerned by faith, instructs him to act in accordance with facts. Here love is not a constitutive but a regulative principle. It does not act directly—as a law of love—but indirectly; but in any case it does apply, even in this fragmentary, indirect manner.

3. Our first task is to define more exactly the character of these autonomous forces which determine what is practical or relevant. The simplest of them is *technical* "autonomy," in the narrower sense of the word, that is, that autonomy which "actual things" contain, which lies in the determination by natural law of work on and with things.

The things themselves prescribe how we are to treat them, in order that through them we may create things of value, "goods" in the broadest sense. But this technical "autonomy" is not, as is so often asserted, absolute, but is entirely and in many ways relative. The uniformity which springs from the things themselves is a limiting conception; in reality there are always many ways to the same goal. The way in which things—again in the broadest sense—are "manufactured," is a product of history as a whole. Technical work itself, since it can only be accomplished both directly and indirectly in co-operation, is inter-penetrated by social elements of the most varied kind; thus it is not determined predominantly by natural laws, but by human and spiritual laws. For instance, technical processes differ entirely in a social order which permits slavery from that in which it is forbidden; new technical processes are immediately formed, where a previous process is morally and then legally condemned as harmful to health or morally degrading to human beings. It is a matter of common knowledge that the latest system of the rationalization of economic science was evoked by social factors. Above all, however, the technical sphere (and this is so often forgotten) is wholly dependent on the demand for goods, and thus upon the standard of value, the scales of values, of the "system of values"(4) of a people or of a period, and thus ultimately on man's view of his own nature, on religion, and on man's general philosophy of life. In the presence of these facts the "rules" laid down by natural laws which the things themselves contain, disappear. The autonomy of the technical realm is mainly social: it is the autonomy of an historically given social structure.

4. The simplest and clearest instance of social autonomy can be formulated in this statement:

My necessary co-operative action is determined not only by my situation and my will, but also by the situation and will of my necessary co-operators. The more co-operators are concerned the smaller does the share of the single individual factor in co-operation become, that is, *my* co-operative share. With this we must also combine a second law: *the difference between the product to be attained by means of co-operation, and the aim of one's own will, is conditioned by the degree of homogeneity or heterogeneity of the will and situation of the co-operators.* We must also note that in the "situation" we include the historical situation—that is, the place where our lot is cast, the destined course of the life of each individual, and the process by which individuals are formed into a community, which constitutes their social destiny; thus the autonomy of the social sphere is entirely covered by our two formulas. All that remains is to examine their individual factors in somewhat greater detail.

I myself: that is, the one from whose point of view the problem of the autonomy of co-operative action is stated. It will be in accordance with the task we have set ourselves if we assume that this individual is a "believer." A believer, however, is never merely a believer, but he is always a sinner as well. Even if at this definite moment he were to be wholly controlled by the Divine Will of love, his "situation" as a whole would not be controlled by the Divine Will of love. Original sin, the fact that the single moment is interwoven with life as a whole, and that the individual life is interwoven with the life of the whole community, stamps its character upon my situation. Here I am—not only as one who claims: "I who stand here am wholly determined by the Will of God," but as one who is a product of world history as a whole. The will which has been energized by the Divine Command through faith can do much, for faith can "remove mountains"; but faith does not give me a different body, nor a different historical position at this moment. Thus I am not only a *will* but also a *situation*. I act, when I act, in my "calling," which as such determines, and should determine, my moral will in a definite sense.

The Other: At any given moment my will which is energized by faith, has no power over him. I must co-operate with him, just as he is. Possibly his will may be quite different from mine. It is indeed not my faith as such which has led me to him (the question of action through the Church will be taken up later on) but the necessity of calling the other man to help me to realize my will. I do not deal with him "in the Church," but "in the world," that is, I cannot know whether he is a believer, indeed, in action of this kind—regarded solely from this point of view—I have no right even to wish to know whether he is a believer or not, for my business with him is secular. If I want to work in the world outside I cannot enquire into the religion of those who co-operate with me; I can only select them from objective motives, that is, from the point of view of their effectiveness for the accomplishment of a particular end. The presupposition of such co-operation is simply this: a common will to do "this one particular thing." But I know nothing about the motives of those who co-operate with me, and—at first at any rate—the question of motive ought not to be considered at all. The actual fact of such co-operation is determined by the action required, not by the motive from which it is undertaken; this is so because this kind of action takes place "in the world" and not "in the Church." I mean the same thing when I describe this co-operative action as "civil" action. In this instance the co-operation is sought not for the sake of faith but in order that "this one particular thing" may be realized. At the same time we shall make it quite clear that the motives of those who co-operate have much influence on the actual work.

Others. "Civil" co-operative action, however, implies not "the" other, but "others"(5), because here we are not concerned with personal fellowship in faith, but with a particular kind of activity. The plural number is determined by the process of action, by the "good" which is to be established, not by the actual will to achieve community.

Here "the other" is not my "neighbour," but is one of "the others," that is, of those who are obliged to do this work. My relation to him is not determined primarily by the claims of love but by the law of the particular work. This becomes quite plain when we determine "the other" by "the others." The "others" may be perhaps hundreds of thousands or millions; I cannot have any personal relation to them, but only an objective relation, that is, one which is determined by the matter in hand. For instance, we are citizens of a State—I and millions of others; I must co-operate with them in matters which affect the State. What we call autonomy—in this social sense—simply means this: on the one hand the laws which govern the work in which we co-operate, and, on the other, the existence of the co-operators who themselves, just like myself, are factors within an historical situation.

5. The work for the sake of which this co-operation takes place—here we are not thinking of a community of persons but of comradeship in work(6)—dictates to some extent the laws governing this work. But the dictates which proceed from the requirements of the work as such—technical autonomy—are not those which constitute social autonomy; the latter is constituted by the dictates which are determined by the whole complex of those who co-operate in the work. The more co-operators there are the more is this or that work possible in this or that form. It depends upon the fact whether, and at what price, the co-operators are willing to take a hand in the work which I wish to have done. If the work must be done *now*, and if at all costs it must be *done* now, then I have no other choice than to take the co-operators as they are, and to pay them the "price" which they demand. But it is quite possible that this "price" might be so "high" that I would feel obliged to say: "Rather no work at all, than on these terms!" But, granted that this work *must* be done, at any price, then I am bound to accept the will of those who co-operate. I am forced to do the work in the way in which they are willing to do it with me. The larger their number the less does my will come into the reckoning, thus the greater is the autonomy of the existing situation over against my own will. And the more their desires differ from mine, the greater is the difference between that which is determined by the social autonomy and that which is determined by my will alone. The number and the kind of the co-operators determine the autonomy of the work.

This autonomy may be decreased if I am not tied down to the present moment, but have a longer time at my disposal; that is, if within this period of time I can influence the will of those who are to co-operate in the work. In that case, however, the relation between them and me is not one of co-operation but of "instruction," not of effective action but of demonstration; and from the point of view of effective work this is only a preparatory process. It is characteristic of the ideology of fanaticism that, in order to conceal its shrinking from responsibility in action, it always takes refuge in this preparatory or educative action, or that it draws fantastic pictures of the influence of an individual will upon that of others.

It is, however, important to note that while this realistic regard for the actual state of things (the "given" element) must weigh largely with us, on the other hand we must never forget the other side of the question, the aspect of free choice (the "non-given" element), and in our concern to get the work done we ought not to undervalue the significance of the motives of those who co-operate. Even though a statesman who feels compelled to take a particular course of action cannot allow himself to enquire too scrupulously into the motives of those who work with him, yet, on the other hand, he ought not to ignore them entirely. For the motives of to-day are the creative forces of to-morrow. A Christian statesman—to continue using this illustration—has no right to assume that all his fellow-workers—ministers, people, etc., for instance—are Christians; if he were to wait till he could make a State or even construct a law with Christians, then he might wait till the Day of Judgment! But it would be just as wrong for him to declare that religion has nothing to do with his political action. For, were he to do so, he would also have to assert that morality and a high sense of responsibility have nothing to do with political action; were he to do this, he would defeat his own end, for even a State cannot exist without responsibility.

6. This brings us to a fresh question, which although it is often confused with that of autonomy, is in reality wholly different: the question of the inherent morality or non-morality of the purposes of action. All action, as we have already said, consists in the production and the distribution of goods. This process of production is not primarily determined by motives of morality, but by ends which arise naturally out of our physical, mental, and social nature. In order to describe this process of production as a whole, in its moral neutrality, I have invented the term "art of culture."[1] This includes the "technical" sphere in the narrower sense, and also science, art, the State, law, and, indeed, all the forms of life which are connected with the rational nature of man, which in themselves do not need morality. But although, "in them-

---

[1] *Kulturkunst.* Cf. Note (1), Chapter XXIV.

selves," in an abstract manner, they are independent of the moral, in various ways they are still connected with it. It is these potential points of contact which we must now seek to discover.

Firstly, all work—and in particular all co-operation, of whatever kind—presupposes a certain measure of moral discipline and responsibility. An individual may indeed make something for the sheer pleasure of doing it; but he cannot do this *permanently* without the addition of a moral element; he cannot work his whole life long apart from ethical considerations. A certain number of people might combine for some work for sheer delight in the work itself; but they cannot *remain* together without the addition of a moral element.

We call these two factors the discipline of work and solidarity in work. What type of morality do these two factors imply? It is absolutely impossible to give a clear answer to this question. The scale of ethical motives belonging to this type of morality ranges from the first faint stirring of a sense of duty up to the Divine law of love. When we use the terms "natural morality" or "rational morality" in this connexion, we simply mean this wholly indeterminate type of morality.

But there is a second question which is still more fundamental. Why does man will such ends at all? Why does he not simply sink down to the animal level? Certainly, there is the "impulse"—primarily, of course, this "impulse" is ethically neutral—towards civilization and culture, and, connected with this, towards co-operation. But this impulse or "tendency" is a tendency of the whole man, and is only possible as such, and this means that it always occurs along with a definite self-knowledge, with a definite consciousness by man of himself as man, with some sense of human dignity. Above all, the scale of goods, their integration into life as a whole, the "system of values" which lies behind the whole of the process of culture, is also conditioned by the conception of life in general which prevailed at any particular time, that is, by its religion, its theory of the universe, and its Ethos. The historical life of humanity is a whole, from which we can only isolate the individual "spheres" in an artificial way. For example, to take one "sphere" only, *law* is dependent on economics, politics, the State, on natural factors, and again, on the ultimate interpretation of the meaning of existence, on religion and morality. "Pure law" is an abstraction, which is not even "pure" in the brain of a philosophical jurist, and still less in reality. A system of law formed by "purely juridical" motives(7) cannot be even conceived in an abstract way. Further, it is also based upon certain values, and, above all, upon a definite view of man, of his dignity, his "rights," his responsibility, etc But we could say the same about every other sphere of life. The complete autonomy of the individual spheres of life is an illusion. As products of history they have all been formed by the whole man, or, rather, by humanity as a whole.

Thus the *autonomy* which results from a definite end—for instance, the end of economics, law, or the State—is always merely relative; it refers to a definite structure which is set up and willed, which, however, itself forms part of the historical life of humanity as a whole, and in part it is an idea, which arises from a definite way of thinking and willing; it is, therefore, dependent upon our system of values and our view of existence as a whole. A fresh, powerful, religious impulse—for instance—whether good or bad—immediately creates new forms of economics, art, law, the State, and social life, just as the present corresponding structures are themselves the result of religious influences; the religious influences may not predominate, but still they are there, and have left their mark.

7. Therefore the conception of the *lex naturae* (8) which—as a guiding principle and normative idea of this whole complex of ethical questions—casts its shadow over Christian ethics, primarily conceals a great confusion of thought.[1] The *lex naturae* cannot be discovered as either the *cause* or the *norm* of the existing order. It cannot be said to be the *cause*, for the simple reason that the existing order has been composed of a vast majority of causes, just as a river is made up of an infinite number of brooks and streams which flow into it. Nor can it be said to be the *norm*, for there is no economic system, or system of law, or of the State, or even of art or science which is "right" in itself. Such a *lex naturae* is neither generally accepted—it is possible to maintain the idea even if it is not accepted by many but only by a few—nor can such a conception be laid down as proved.

The idea of the *lex naturae* has slipped into the Christian ethic through Roman jurisprudence from the popular philosophy of the Stoics. It can be most easily maintained, with some appearance of justification, in the philosophy of law as the idea of the Law of Nature. It is, however, not difficult to

[1] See the *Excursus* on the Law of Nature, Note (8) on this chapter.

show how artificial is its union with a Christian ethic. The Stoic doctrine of the Law of Nature springs out of the Stoic view of existence, which in its essence is a legal one; therefore its foremost idea is that of justice. The "Law of Nature" here agrees with the conception of absolute right (we shall be dealing with the relative Natural Law immediately), for that which is right φύσει is indeed that which is *divinely* right. But— as is the case in the Christian Faith—as soon as it is recognized that the Ultimate and the Supreme is not a *law* but the generous Divine Love (which cannot be conceived legally at all), and His sovereign Divine Will, justice has become a relative quality. No Christian can conceive of an absolute justice(9) —save as a Stoic conception. To a Christian, to speak of that which is absolutely Right—as law—seems a contradiction in terms.

This does not mean (as we have already seen) that, for instance, the law, and the idea of justice which it implies, is rendered meaningless; but it *has* become relative. For the absolute law is the same as love, which is not a law at all. All that is "less" than love is relative, an indication of love, and an instrument of love, and as such it is certainly significant, but as such it is relative, and cannot be fixed in any absolute "law," in any kind of *lex naturae*.

Further, even the Latin creators of the idea of the Law of Nature were obliged to introduce a second conception of the Law of Nature which takes the historical reality into account; for it was only too evident that their absolute Natural Law, with its abstractly egalitarian content, could not be applied to historical reality, and that, if it were applied, inevitably its effect would be in the highest degree destructive and unjust. Hence they invented the idea of a relative Natural Law which took into account the historical reality, which had somehow become perverted.

To the Stoic the one disturbing element which marred the beauty of his pantheistically harmonious picture of the world was the fact of sin; yet in the Christian Faith sin, or the "fallen world," was the central point around which everything revolved. Only then did the difference between that which is "just" in the historical world of time and space, and an absolute or timeless justice, become so great that practically nothing could be taken into account save the relative Law of Nature, and thus the Christian ethic, by way of the Stoic Natural Law, did what it could and should have done without making this *détour*: it recognized the idea of a "relative Natural Law," or rather, of a relative norm of justice.

8. This norm, however, just because it is relative, cannot be fixed once for all, but at every period in history, and for each succeeding historical group it must be discovered afresh. This is true of every sphere of civilization; in every form of work, in the sense in which we explained this term earlier in this book, there exists a norm of *positive justice*, in every external human relation a norm of *equity*, and for the whole process of production and distribution within human life and society there is a norm of *humanity* which determines what is of service to man. But none of these norms can be conceived from the point of view of their content; not because this would be too difficult, but because in the very nature of the case it is impossible. Let me make this plain by a brief illustration drawn from the sphere of law.

Ethically speaking, there is no "right law"(10). Every attempt to define such a law ends either in the Stoic idea of the abstract equality of all, which, based as it is upon the individualistic principle, can never be acknowledged by the Christian as "the right"; or it ends in merely formal definitions. Right law will only exist in the Kingdom of God, where there will be no longer any law at all. To the Christian, from the very outset it seems futile to raise the question of the absolutely right Law.

But he may, and indeed should, enquire into the best possible system of law that can be constructed at any particular time. Through his faith in the Creator and the Redeemer he is led to turn his attention in this direction. He cannot and should not seek law outside the context of the existing order—his thought of the Calling and the "office" holds him firmly within this order, and therefore it makes his desires and his action real. But he cannot and also ought not to regard the existing law as the best possible; as one who has been placed within a new order he knows that it is also his duty to seek a new and better law. But he discovers the *standards* for this better law in the idea of the Creative and Redeeming Will of God. The purpose of Creation comes first because essentially the chief concern of the Law is the *preservation* of life within the realm of sin; it is not concerned to win it for the realm of Redemption. But the purpose of the Creator can certainly only be perceived where the Redeeming Will of God is also manifest. The creative purpose of God, determined by His

271

redemptive purpose, is—not the norm, but the *point of view* for the discovery of the best possible form of law. The other point of view is that of existing reality. The same is true of the other forms of civilization in so far as they come under the ethical point of view. This, and not a principle, we might describe as the idea of a *Christian Natural Law*.

9. But though we have thus found the norm for the Christian discussion of the autonomy of the spheres of civilization there is still one thing more to be done—we must glance at the type of action required, and the way in which it ought to be done. The action of the Christian in the "civil" sphere is threefold: simple co-operation, in the confidence that by means of this action God wills to preserve our life; critical co-operation as a citizen, striving with others after a better righteousness; and an "apostolic" action in preparation for the future, in the conviction that only a change in the ultimate bases of life can change the mighty structures of social life.

The *simple act of co-operation*—for instance, in the activity of one's ordinary calling—as action, does not differ materially from the action of those who are not believers. Such action is only determined *materially* by the norms of positive justice, equity, and humanity, which are, in some way or another, also accepted—even if in an indefinite way—by non-Christians, in spite of the fact that the Christian does this work—so far as his *motive* is concerned—from obedience to the Will of God and from the desire to serve his neighbour. As action its aim is success, since the whole point of this work is to achieve something definite. Co-operation follows the lines laid down as relevant to this sphere of life. Here the Christian "wants to do his work well," and he works with others on this basis, whether they are Christians or non-Christians. Thus in the various spheres of civilized and cultural life he acts "according to his calling," or—in so far as the public character of his action has to be especially emphasized—"officially."

His critical co-operation is performed, for instance, as a citizen at the voting booth, or through the membership of his political party, or as a workman in a Trades Union, or a member of a guild, or, if he has the opportunity given to him, by public speaking or by his pen. While he remains loyally obedient to the rules which govern this particular sphere of life, he will do his best to improve the legal rules governing this sphere; indeed, he will try to make them "as good as possible" by co-operating with those who are actuated by the same intentions and motives—even if they are not Christians at all. Here too the standard is success. He knows, for instance, that it is useless to strive after an ideal State, an ideal system of law. What he wants is a *real* system of law, and *real* improvements, and he knows that here there is no room for the "ideal." Just because he is a Christian he is wholly and entirely a "realist"; hence he does not think that the higher he pitches his demands for reform the more earnest he is as a Christian. He knows that his duty consists, not in postulating the best possible system of law, but, so far as possible, in the actual introduction of a better system.

In these two modes of action the fact of being a Christian only comes under consideration in a very indirect way; but because even in one's life as an ordinary citizen it is always the whole person who acts, so also the Christian can always bear his "witness" to that which he feels so vital; but this "witness-bearing" should not be ostentatious, nor should it consist in much talk. Even the man who quietly and unobtrusively does his duty as a matter of course "witnesses" to the power which moves him. But this "background" comes out plainly in the third kind of action, in that which we call "apostolic" preparatory action. Here the Christian acts as a member of the Church, but not "in the Church"; he acts as an ambassador of the Church in the "civil sphere." He feels it to be of great importance to demonstrate and restore the connexion between the practical problems of civil life—as for example that of education—and faith(11). Here he makes no secret of the fact that he speaks and acts as a Christian, and that the fact that he is a Christian means something for his life as a citizen. Here, where we are concerned with the creation of the intellectual presuppositions of all social development, the criterion is what we have already said about faith as one element in the social formation of all spheres of life. What we really require here is a statement showing—by means of a lay theology—the real significance of faith or unbelief in all the various spheres of social life; this should be done by experts (in connexion with the spheres of education, law, social conditions, marriage, etc.)—that is, by persons whose knowledge of these particular spheres is thorough and accurate. This initial effort should then be followed by an endeavour to propagate these ideas as widely as possible, and in some instances, if the time seems ripe for it, even to take political action.

Here, however, success, in the sense of actual achievement, is absolutely secondary in comparison with purity of witness. In this sphere witness is more important than achievement —unless by achievement we mean the energy and purity of the act of witness. Here co-operation is only possible between those whose lives are based upon the same foundation of faith. The chief thing here, therefore, is to make certain, as far as possible, of the motives of those who co-operate, for here numbers mean nothing and truth everything. Here we have reached the boundary between civil and ecclesiastical action, and accordingly a different scale of values has come into view. From the point of view of the Church such action ought to be recognized as a form of "service" and also of "apostolate," two ideas which in their intimate connexion have already found substantial, although limited, recognition in "Home Missions." The object of this action is, to use the abstract terminology which we have already employed: the alteration of the system of values and thence of the intellectual bases of the autonomous spheres of life. Whenever any-one wishes to make far-reaching changes in the structure of society—marriage, law, the State, civilized life, etc.— he must aim at altering the system of values which deter-mines the "production" and the "circulation" of goods(12). The system of values is the connexion between the deepest bases of existence, the interpretation of existence, and the social actuality. All direct civil action is short-lived and changes nothing under the surface; the really shattering changes of the social structure take place as changes in the system of values, which, for its part, depends on faith and unbelief.

10. But important as all this action inspired by faith is, yet in faith it is ·still more important to know that "all our doings are nothing worth," even in the best life. This is not intended as an abstract statement. Rather, this conviction grows out of the very effort to take our civil tasks seriously and thoroughly. It may indeed be imagined—and this is no idle fancy—that a jurist, for instance, may learn to understand this statement of Luther, this principle of Scriptural know-ledge, precisely as a jurist, for instance, in struggling with the criminal law. What does punishment mean? What does it mean to reform? Or a statesman whose idealism has been shattered by contact with harsh realities may become open to faith because he has become convinced of the futility of all

274

his efforts for the good of the people through statesmanship. Here the "idea of the Christian Law of Nature" becomes significant once more, not constructively nor critically—in the sense of making things better—but by the fact that it shows how all that we do is nothing when measured by that which ought to be done.

Here, therefore, the prophetic proclamation of the absolute law has its place, that law which, understood in a really radical way, cancels itself as Law. We understand best the real meaning of those men whom we call the great critics of civilization when we regard them as those who proclaim the absolute law. The value of the radical criticism of civilization—even when it does not spring exactly from Christian thought—does not lie in its "practical use," in the practical possibility of carrying it out.[1] The Law must be proclaimed, precisely in order to show us what we are not, and what we cannot do. The unconditional demand contains its own right and its own necessity; its "usefulness" does not depend on whether it effects a change in external reality. The Law wills, and ought to awaken and quicken within us the consciousness that we are not what we ought to be, that our life is the manifestation of a fallen humanity; this applies not only to the law which affects the individual, but also to that which controls society itself.

The very fact of the *godlessness* of our present conditions, of our social life: the harshness and inhumanity of our system of law, of our political and State action, of our economic "order," can and should make plain to us the meaning of the word "sin." The genuine character of the faith of a Christian may be judged by the intensity (or lack of it) with which he is conscious of the contrast between what he has to do as a citizen, officially, and what the God of love "actually" wills. That which the citizen who does not believe accepts as inevitable, and as a matter of course, should act as a spur to the believer to remind him that we need Redemption. Therefore the way in which a Christian speaks about those harsh necessities of social life shows very clearly whether his faith is genuine or not; if he speaks about them in a hard way, like a pagan Roman, or as one who himself groans under them and grieves that he has to do such things: in the one instance or the other he shows "what manner of spirit he is of." The Ethos can be recognized not only by its active expression,

[1] Cf. Note (8), Chapter XXII.

275

but also by its passive expression: "the Christian may be known by his suffering" (Kierkegaard). The law should work repentance. It is evident that the stinging sense of the contrast between actual conditions and the Law acts, in its turn, as a most effective dynamic, spurring the will of the would-be reformer to action.

11. The Law wills, however, to drive men not only to repentance but to faith. It is not merely that faith drives man outwards, to work, but the work also drives him inwards, to faith. The real home of faith is not in the more or less impersonal world of public work, but in the personal centre, in a man's inward attitude to God and to his brother. To assert this is not false Pietistic "inwardness," but a conviction of faith. God wants to have possession of my hands; but above all He desires my heart. But most certainly He does not desire my heart merely as an emotion, but as a will which is resolute for action, as the obedience of faith. Seen from this aspect the life of faith presents itself in a new way. Faith as faith, as obedience to God and love to the brethren, desires to express itself as *purely* as possible. It will work, of course, but it works in order to show something, namely, to show love and to glorify God. There is a form of action whose whole significance consists in "manifesting" something, just because here man can only co-operate with God by bearing witness; in other words, this action consists in proclaiming what, in faith, we have received. This kind of action also is primarily an individual matter, through the universal priesthood which is implied in the "priesthood of all believers." But just as in civil life the individual does not act merely as an individual, but in and with society, so this action is not only individual but social, and in the narrower sense of the word ecclesiastical. It is the concern of the Christian community as such to provide for the proclamation of the Christian message, and to try to preserve its membership by means of "discipline," from becoming swamped by the life of the world; through its practical service (*diakonia*) it seeks to render tasks of helpfulness and kindness which society does not recognize and is unable to perform. This kind of action is also controlled by "law," but it is not the general law of righteousness, but the particular law of faith and love, which therefore can never really act as law, but only as a guiding principle. From this point of view the Creeds of the Church, and its particular regulations regarding Church discipline, Church order, and

the social work of the Church, ought to be regarded as guidance for action.[1]

Though from the standpoint of "work" success comes first and purity of motive second, from the standpoint of "witness" this order is reversed. To care for purity of motive is the same as to hold fast to the Divine self-end. Therefore this leads to great care in the choice of means for particular ends. The will to work says: "he who wills the ends must will the necessary means." The will to witness says: "if an end makes it necessary to use dubious means, then this end ought not to be desired." The necessary end, we said, hallows the necessary means. But whether an end can be said to be "necessary" always depends on the means which it requires for its realization. It is possible that from the point of view of "work" only, something may seem necessary; but the consideration of the means which it will require may lead to the fact that we feel impelled to question that necessity. However useful a "work" may appear, serving the cause of God and the life of our brother: if the means which it requires are faulty its effect as witness spoils more than the work itself can make good. Faith has an eye for the "imponderables" which the actual politician so often loses sight of altogether. Faith knows that in the cause of God we must be scrupulous in the choice of means, and that we must act quite differently from the way in which we act when it is a matter of building the "dykes," of supporting the orders, or of the acquisition of the goods of civilization and culture. It is of course true that in this world we can do nothing without sinful means; all "Christian work" is stained with blood, even if only on account of the money by which it is supported. Therefore the Christian emphasis on purity of motive is not a *law*: for such a law would make all action within the world impossible. But it is a point which must be considered in connexion with each work, just as much as the usefulness of the work itself. Just because the world, whose outlook is bounded by the "seen and temporal," has little understanding of the value of "witness" it is the special duty of the Christian to take it extremely seriously.

But faith will not only make its influence felt directly in this way, but also in the fact that the individual will seek a "private" way of working behind the established institutions of public life. The distinction between an "official" or "vocational" sphere and a "personal" sphere of action cannot, it

[1] See below, p. 557.

277

is true, be absolute; for even the most public form of action has its private aspect—in witness, and even the most private form of activity in so far as it is operative has its public aspect, in the use of effective means. But as a relative distinction, as a *point of view*, and not as a law, this distinction is certainly necessary. There is a "more" or "less" in public action; there are narrower and wider circles around the personal centre. Therefore it is an essential part of the Christian life that we should seek our *real* work in this *personal* sphere, in the personal relation between one human being and another. It is here that love applies as a law—although indirectly, through the public "office" which we cannot and should not reject; this is the intention of the Sermon on the Mount.

12. But there is still a final step to take. The purely personal only takes place where we no longer do or give "something" to each other—for this something is always an impersonal medium and makes the use of worldly means necessary—but where we give ourselves directly to each other in speech and in communion with each other. The most personal thing of all, therefore, is not *doing* something for love, but *showing* love. This direct expression of love must, however, constantly protect itself from the suspicion of cheap sentimentality by seeing to it that wherever it is possible and necessary it will flower into action. But even action is ambiguous: it too is not an infallible criterion of the inner disposition. But everything depends upon this inner disposition. To love another means to desire to hold fellowship with him, and indeed unrestricted fellowship. As the forgiveness of God towards us expresses the actual fact of His absolute will to have intercourse with us, so also forgiveness between human beings—that "seventy times seven" of the Gospels—is the expression of our unconditional willingness for fellowship, or negatively, of our readiness to set aside all that can come between me and my neighbour as a disturbing element. Even in ethics this state of mind is not an *act*, but a way of living with other people. This way of living finds its direct expression in speech, and still more directly in our bearing, our general attitude, our behaviour, our looks, our tone of voice, and our way of "giving ourselves." The way we look at people is the borderline between being and doing, the window through which one person can look into the being of another.

Thus through reflection on the immediate form of communication our line of thought leads us back to the starting point, back from the act to the agent of the action. But the final, the inmost point, out of which the spirit which desires fellowship springs, is the knowledge of communion with God in faith. Because *we* have been forgiven we *can* and ought to forgive. Because we are loved we may and we ought to love.

Thus the central point and the source of all action is faith itself. It also is an act, the act of "accepting a gift," the act of "letting God say something to you." While we are passive, and submit to the Divine influence, where God's *gift* is concerned—in the promise given us by His Word and His Spirit —where His *Command* is concerned, and His demands are made upon us, we become active, we turn in a certain direction. The final act, then, which is required is the act of believing, that of grateful obedience. This inward turning towards God, which, as such, is the origin of all our turning towards our neighbour, is the one essential necessary act, it is the one act which alone is well pleasing to God; this is "the heart" which "God looks at." Ultimately the decisive worth of every act is in exact proportion to this inward action, which is an act of receiving. Here, therefore, there is no longer any difference between means and end. This act in which man allows God to act is the realization of the Divine self-end in the way in which, here, in this historical world, it wills to be and can be realized. Thus in the rhythm of living faith the act which issues from the "heart," where Christ dwells by faith, after it has been impelled outwards by the pressure of the command to act, under the contrary pressure of the impersonal world returns once more to the starting-point, not in order that it may stay there in a spirit of resignation and detachment from the world, but in order that there it may be purified and gain new strength for the new movement of active love.

CHAPTER XXVI

SUCCESS AND PROGRESS

PROPOSITION: *On the one hand, the Divine Command makes a manifold demand: a progressively fruitful realization of good works; on the other hand, God demands one thing only: to turn in faith to the only action that is fruitful: that of God Himself.*

1. External action differs from mere desire in the fact that through the body it uses means, in order to achieve actual changes in some sphere of human life. God wills that we should *will to succeed*, because He Himself wills success. It is part of the idea of the personal God(1) that even in God will and success do not coincide, but that between them both there lies the empty space of possibility.

Were all that God wills inevitable—as the theology infected by Greek thought has often asserted—then nothing but God would exist; there would be no distinction between God and the world. The distinction between the possible and the necessary in God Himself is the distinction between the *personal* and the *pantheistic* Idea of God. And this distinction alone makes it possible for man to have a relation with God, fellowship with God, a personal link with God.

God wills success, because He desires to bring us, as personal beings, into contact with Himself. Therefore the success which God wills is not merely Himself, but our communion with Himself through it, that is, the Kingdom of God. It is this success which God wills unconditionally, and this alone. All else willed by God is determined by this one consideration. Whence do we know this? From God Himself. Indeed, the fact that He wills this one thing, unconditionally, constitutes the Gospel. Our willing, therefore, is included in this His one unconditioned end, in His self-end, because this end is called "community." Our will, however, would not be a genuine will but merely thought, were it not directed towards success. The Creator has given us a body in order that we should not merely think, but that we should make actual changes in the external order of human life. In action the outward and the inward can no longer be separated. The will presses into the external realm until the work is achieved, and the acting organ is inspired through and through by the will, so that no one can say where the inward ceases and where the outward begins. The tense muscle is will made visible. A will that does not put forth all its efforts until success has been achieved is paralysed.

2. Now, however, the statement that the will which is obedient to God wills success, is rendered problematical by two considerations. First of all: are the results which we achieve of such a character that in them God's own will is realized? And secondly: is success within the power of our own will at all?

Doubtless man can achieve many things successfully; the whole sphere of civilization and of culture is a gigantic workshop of successful action: from the well-aimed throw of a stone by a caveman to the successful achievement of an ocean flight by an aeroplane, from the successful whistle of the hunter who entices the wild beast or calls his dog, to the Divine Comedy or the Ninth Symphony. Wherever technical and artistic creative effort is concerned perfection is possible. But this is not our problem; our concern is with the moral, and, so far as the moral is concerned, we are forced to admit that there is no work which does not bear the imprint of sinful man. There is no work which really and truly, without reserve, glorifies God. There is no work which has not been achieved, in part at least, by sinful wills. Even if the pure source of sincere desire were to exist, still, as *Mahomets Gesang* so impressively puts it, the sinful *material*, with which alone we are able to work, would dim its original purity.

Can we claim perhaps that *progress*, that is, the process of successful achievement which is carried on by a succession of generations, leads us beyond this "tragic" element in life—which indeed is guilt? There is no sense in denying that progress does exist. In the economic and technical sphere, in the field of scientific research and discovery, it is an obvious fact that man is piling up treasure, that our descendants will be able to build upon the foundation laid by the achievements of their ancestors, perhaps for centuries, in unbroken continuity, perhaps in some kind of permanence even for thousands of years throughout the whole of the known history of humanity. A more or less continuous line of ascent leads from the rude stone axe of palaeolithic man to the dynamo. This almost inevitable movement of progress also includes the external unity of mankind, and those advances in the sphere of civilization which we can hardly imagine will not develop still further, such as: greater security guaranteed by the law, a greater extension of the social services, particularly in the care of the weak, and a far more general share in the "goods" of civilization for the masses. But the more we turn towards the centre, the more problematical does progress become. In this era, with its "toll of the road," and its World War, which of us can maintain that human life is more highly valued than it was at an earlier stage in world history? Who can assert seriously that by means of popular education, democracy, and the Press, we are to-day "further on" than we were in the Middle Ages? The means for the furtherance of the Good and for the relief of distress are incomparably greater, but then so are the means of causing disaster. There is scarcely a good invention which is not put to a diabolical use as soon as it has been invented. Modern means of communication have brought men closer to one another, but the individual has become more homeless. Christianity has spread more widely through the world, but so also has a mass atheism which was formerly unknown. And even in the sphere of the individual, who will maintain that to-day it is easier to be good than it used to be? Or even that the people of the present day are better than their predecessors?

3. But let us turn away from all this empiricism and enquire: What does faith tell us about the possibility of progress? Progress, the possibility of successful achievement, and of the intensification and purification of good energies from moment to moment, from person to person, thus also from generation to generation, is *given* by the Creation, and strictly *limited* by sin and death. The act of removing these limits would be identical with the fulfilment of history beyond history, in the realm of eternal perfection. But within these limits there is not only the possibility of progress, but the command to progress. It has already been pointed out that the summons to become better is implied in the Divine Command; it also contains the summons to make things better. The serious nature of action is based on this fact. If a man does not believe that through his action things will become better, he cannot act at all. The meaning of all that we do is the achievement of something which has not yet been achieved, the realization of something which is better than the present actuality; action is only significant when it changes the present into something better.

This is what is meant by "doing good." The aim of a "good work"—even of the simplest act of service—is to remove something which ought not to be. But the obedience of faith is directed by the Divine Command to works of this kind. Melanchthon's saying that "good works are a necessary part of faith" does not mean a deviation from the thought of the Reformation; on the contrary, it is a logical development from it. The more faith, the more good works, but this means the more ethically successful action. Progress is commanded. But this does not do away with Luther's terrifying Heidelberg statement: that even the Christian can do nothing save commit mortal sin—although it is evident that in this statement Luther goes beyond the line laid down in Scripture(2). Measured by the Divine standard no action which we perform is good, "even in the best life." Measured by the Divine self-end all our action is nothing, even that which is most successful. The need of the world, the actual obstacles which must be overcome cannot be overcome by our action, and the actual help required cannot be given by us.

4. This suggests that in order to escape the sentence passed upon us by this truth we should take refuge in some inner region of life. There, where pure thought is born, the undefiled spring rises in its purity, which only becomes corrupted when it reaches the world outside, as we heard in *Mahomets Gesang*. But although this view contains a relative element of truth it cannot stand in the light of the Divine Judgment. It is our will itself which is impure in the sight of God; this is true even of the obedient will of the believer. The fact remains: "There is none good but One, that is, God."[1] To withdraw into "inwardness" does not protect us from the Divine Judgment. The withdrawal does not go far enough; to be able to stand before God we would need to withdraw still further to a "rear line" of defence—and this "rear line of defence" is not within us but without, namely, Jesus Christ. There alone are we protected from the wrath of God; there alone does judgment cease to thunder. There alone the work which is perfectly well pleasing to God is performed, and this is ours—through faith. "Christ our Righteousness." [2]His action, because it is God's action, is good and successful in the absolute sense. For this action removes that evil which no human being can remove: death and sin. It is therefore that kind of action in which God's self-end, the Kingdom of God, is realized, in the midst of the historical world: in faith, in the "Church."

[1] Mark x. 18.   [2] 1 Cor. i. 30.

Faith is completely successful because it is the work of God; not as our own act, but as the act of the Holy Spirit. This is what God desires from us: that we should withdraw to this "innermost line of defence," that we should "flee for refuge" to Himself. Once this has been done, the Good has been achieved—whatever else may have been achieved. Thus God wills that we should see the futility of our own action, and expect success from Him alone, that we should despair of our own action, in order that we may put our whole confidence in His act *alone*. We do not need to wait for God to act; He has already acted; to believe means to have a share in this work, through which God realizes His glory and His sovereignty, and establishes His Kingdom.

Thus over all human action there stands the sign of the Cross, as the sign of human failure. The Cross of Christ is God's answer to the assurance of the "successful" man. In Jesus Christ "successful" humanity is crucified; in Him also the success of the Divine Act of Redemption is revealed. This is the first, fundamental transformation of the idea of success by faith.

5. But the Spirit of God, who speaks to us through the Word, is not only the Spirit who speaks but the Spirit who operates. Even though we cannot build the Kingdom of God by our own efforts, yet God can do this through our action. Just as the Word of God transforms *real* human beings, and translates them into the Kingdom of God, so this change is effected by *human* words and human action. God wills to do His work not only *in* human beings but *through* them. This is the meaning of the "Church" and its "means of grace." Thus it is not wrong to say that the final end is achieved, successfully, through human beings, but it *is* wrong for human beings to imagine that *they* can make their action successful in this way, and can know that it is successful. God alone knows whether, and when, human action is successful in this absolute sense, and thus leads to the final goal. All we can do is to make some more or less reasonable guesses at the truth.

We can only suggest the following hypothesis: that which is really from the Holy Spirit, that which is really done in faith, must be successful, even if, judged by the natural standards of success, it looks like the opposite. Thus, truly successful action, like the new man, remains "hidden till the Last Day." Success can never be measured by the natural empirical standards of success, but only by those over which we have no control. Even if instead of "faith" we say "love," and lay down the right principle: that all action which proceeds from love is successful, whether the service rendered be small or great, effective or ineffective, yet here too the final verdict remains with God alone.

But this has effected a second transformation of the idea of success. The *motive* of conduct becomes our standard of success. We do not infer the goodness of the action from the fact of success, but we deduce success from the goodness of the motive (which is ultimately hidden from us). "Success" is changed from an empirical idea to one of faith. This does not mean, however, that the earlier naïve idea of success is ruled out of court. For where action is really inspired by love, there action takes place by means of a will which is set on the successful accomplishment of an actual change. Genuine love is concrete. It desires to give real help, to bind up wounds successfully, to heal actually, really to feed and to comfort. Love does all in her power to achieve this success. But when she has done all she can she says: "We are unprofitable servants";[1] God alone can do good.

For this very reason love is content to do "what comes to hand," and not, primarily, to make great plans. Work on the grand scale is not the primary concern of love; it is secondary. What most people call "great," faith tends to regard with some suspicion, and the assurance with which men prosecute the "strategy of the Kingdom of God"(3), with which they exalt "great actions" as the work of the Kingdom of God, always betrays the fact that their idea of success has not yet been rectified. The believer knows that action on the grand scale, however unavoidable, however urgent it may be, has not only succumbed to the impersonal,[2] but that it also leads people to overestimate the natural quantitative kind of success. The larger the means, the less is it possible to control the motives, the less from the point of view of faith is the prospect of success.

It is true of course that God makes use of the strangest means for the building of His Kingdom, He even uses evil. The hardening of Pharaoh's heart, the treachery of Judas, become means for the accomplishment of His ends. But this only takes place indirectly—in that indirectness of His hidden operation, which is unintelligible to us, like God's providential rule as a whole. He does not establish His Kingdom directly

[1] Luke xvii. 10. [2] See above, p. 281.

285

through the hardening of Pharaoh's heart, but through the faith of Moses, nor through the treachery of Judas, but through the obedience of Jesus. Only where God's Will is known in this direct way, in the way which reveals love, does that which God wills come into being. Thus the believer knows that God also makes use of our "civil," secular action— whether this takes place with or without faith—for His ends, and indeed in such a way that the believer knows that he has been placed in the midst of this secular activity by God; but he does not confuse this activity with real action, nor the success which lies on this plane, and must be sought on this level, with real success. He knows the meaning of the world and the Kingdom of God, and he distinguishes between the ideas of success which belong to these different planes.

6. Connected with these ideas is a third consideration, which further modifies the idea of success: demonstrative action is higher than energetic activity. A person who "reveals" love is more "successful"—in the last resort—than one who does loving actions. Even an awkward attempt to help a sick person does him good if he sees that his attendant puts all his care and love into the effort, and this sense of well-being means more to the patient than service rendered by trained hands. Such action suggests the kindness of God, and it creates and expresses community. In this historical world the Kingdom of God is not created by energetic activity but by "demonstrative" action—although the "energetic activity" may share in this process, in so far as it is either "demonstrative," or prepares the way for "demonstrative" action. For it is created by the knowledge of the Divine love. Revelation, the Word of God, is not "energetic activity" but "demonstrative" action, however much it may use this activity for its own ends.

The objectivity of the work of reconciliation is not objective in the "active" sense, but in the sense of "demonstrative" action, that is, it is objective only for faith, just as the objectivity of the divine operation in the Sacrament is not "effective" (*opus operatum*) but "demonstrative": *verbum visibile*. The *regnum gratiae*, in contradistinction to the *regnum gloriae*, is based upon the *promissio dei*.

This opens up a new ethical possibility. Even action which is "without success" can become successful by its "demonstrative" value. Through the power of the demonstration the hidden power masters the coarse realities which stand in the way. The action of God in the Cross of Christ is not only the ground of our action, it is also our example. It is the sign that love is free from all that is known as "success." Henceforward every action is successful which witnesses with power to the gift we have received. An act, like the death of a martyr, for instance, in spite of the fact that it effects nothing in the sense of success, yet can be in the highest degree successful in the sense of demonstration (or witness). This thought constitutes another warning against the current standard of success, in particular for everything the Church does *as* the Church, that is, for all action which aims at creating faith. Here success counts for nothing; purity of witness counts for everything. This means in practice: let the Church guard herself from political entanglements as from the devil(4).

7. Only now do we venture to say a closing word about progress. We may put it thus: the Christian is very anxious "to progress," but he is very little concerned with "progress." He does not attempt to define progress. In faith we know that what we place upon the credit side may perhaps be placed by God upon the debit side of our account, and *vice versa*. At the same time we know that God's work progresses to the end of time. The divine waters have subterranean currents and come to the light of day at unexpected places. Human successes, on the other hand, even the greatest, when looked at as a whole often have a remarkably short life. That which seems most insignificant may suddenly emerge in its eternal significance, and the "drama of world history" (Kierkegaard) may prove to be merely blind confusion. We are not standing upon a tower whence we can survey all that is happening in the world. But what we can and ought to do is this: to stand faithfully at our post, and to do what is commanded us, whether it be "great" or "small," knowing that God's standards are very different from ours.

If, however, from our own point of view we try at least to look with some dim comprehension at the "course of the Kingdom of God in the history of the world," the picture we see resembles less that of a triumphant campaign than that of a besieged fortress, which is constantly sending out more or less victorious sallies. Every action which really proceeds from faith—whether small or great—is a sally of this kind. But if victorious sallies are to be made then the warriors must constantly withdraw into the fortress, in order that they may gain new strength. The real act is not the sally, but the holding of the fortress, not the world-transforming activity, but the defiance of faith. It must suffice us to know that God Himself undermines the enemy's positions underground, in order that when their time comes they may fall into His Hands. In our visible battlefield we shall see again and again how the efforts of the defenders are followed by increased efforts from without, so that there can be no question of victoriously breaking through the enemy's lines. It is our task to "hold fast and believe"; this faith holds the certainty of final victory, which will not be achieved historically but at the end of the ages. It is good therefore for us that it is so, that all the more surely we may learn what it means to say: *Soli deo gloria.*

BOOK THREE

THE ORDERS

INTRODUCTION

HAVING found the *starting point* for a Christian ethic in the first book, in the second book we developed the chief *points of view* from which conduct must be considered if we are to be able to hear the Divine Command. In every case in which the individual has to act, the one essential is that—through faith—and taking his neighbour into account—he should be able to perceive the will of God in the work which has to be done; and indeed the Will of God is to be known as the Will of the Creator and Redeemer revealed in Christ, who wills one thing alone, and yet is always demanding something in particular, who demands, as one who has previously given, and who indicates His concrete Command by a threefold law. Good action—when it does take place—consists in the union of all these elements, which, indeed, only seem to be separate in the act of intellectual reflection, but which are really one in the act of obedient listening. This explains the meaning of the word "love."

But it was precisely this explanation which pointed to the existing reality as the sphere in which the Good is to be realized; that is, this actual reality defines for us our course of action. Here we see not merely particular spheres of life *within* which we are to act, but orders in accordance with which we have to act, because in them, even if only in a fragmentary and indirect way, God's Will meets us. Hence we call them "Divine orders." Each of these spheres of life, with its "orders," presents itself to us first of all as a definite way of common life, as a form of social organization; it is our task to discover the meaning of this existing reality, and this means, to find the meaning of community. The third book deals with the following questions: What is real "community" within each of these social "orders"? Thus, what is the Creator's intention for these orders? What does it mean to live within them in love, as an individual? And how ought love to express itself within them?

The aim of the first section is, firstly, to show why it is that here we regard life in community, and not the life of the individual, as the concrete realization of the moral ideal; from this also we derive a general doctrine of society. Secondly, in this section we seek to show how the individual social groupings spring out of the nature of man, and we describe their peculiar characteristics. The following five sections will deal with these "orders" in detail.[1]

[1] Cf. H. D. WENDLAND: "Zur Grundlegung der christlichen Sozialethik," *Ztschr. f. syst. Theol.*, 1930, pp. 22–56; LOEW: *Zwischen den Zeiten*, 1926, pp. 60–75. J. WENDLAND's *Handbuch der Sozialethik* (1916) is based upon entirely different presuppositions.

CHAPTER XXVII

THE INDIVIDUAL AND THE COMMUNITY[1]

1. Even in the theology of the present day the subject of the individual and the community is usually treated as a problem of adjustment. The individual is an independent entity; the community makes certain claims on this individual, and *vice versa*, and the task of ethics is supposed to be to balance these claims as fairly as possible, taking into account both the rights of the individual and of the community. Experience seems to force us to accept this view as the natural one, and the distinctive task of Ethics is simply to discover how this necessary adjustment can be achieved in a just manner. The experience of humanity shows us how both these one-sided tendencies, a one-sided individualism and a one-sided collectivism, are perpetually involved in conflict with one another. Now it will be the tendency to break up the historically existing forms of community, to emancipate the individual, which will gain the upper hand, and then the pendulum will swing in the other direction, and the freedom of the individual will be suppressed by collectivism. This conflict already appears in Ancient Greece—for instance, between Socrates and the Athenian *Polis*—we see it again in the struggle for liberty at the close of the Middle Ages, in the Renaissance and the Reformation, and once more, in modern times, between the "individualism of a Nietzsche, a Kierkegaard and an Ibsen," on the one hand, and Socialism and Communism on the other. We do not perceive that this superficial classification violates historical reality, and "lumps together" the most incompatible elements. What has the "individualism" of a Kierkegaard to do with that of the Renaissance, the Enlightenment, and the most recent movements in favour of liberty? He stands far closer to the "collectivism" of the Middle Ages than to the individualism of the author of *The Individual and His Property*! On the other hand, however, if we go deeply enough, we see how closely Marxist Socialism and Communism

[1] This chapter contains the outline of a Christian Sociology.

293

is related to the individualism of the Enlightenment of the eighteenth century; what a great gulf lies between Luther's protest against the authority of the Catholic Church and the philosophy of Jean Jacques Rousseau!(1) The fact that an individual arises to protest against a collective force is an event which may mean all kinds of different things, just as a mass movement also may mean many different things. Evidently, this problem demands some clear thinking, if this confusion is to be removed.

2. It was real individualism when Socrates, in the name of reason, protested against the standards accepted by the Athenian community; it was real individualism when Descartes —in his *cogito ergo sum*—expressed the will of the Renaissance movement for liberty, and laid the foundation of modern philosophy. But the habit of mind which desires to strike a just balance between individualism and Socialism is also dominated by this individualism.

The whole of modern philosophy is a "Robinson Crusoe"[1] affair, expressed in abstract terms; it is an attempt to interpret the individual human being solely in the light of his own personality, and society as the coalescence of such individuals(2). This attempt corresponds absolutely to the attempt made at the same time by science to explain the world of phenomena in terms of isolated atoms, and it is perhaps scarcely accidental that almost at the same time that the eighteenth- and nineteenth-century theories of atomistic physics broke down men began to reflect anew upon the nature of the relation between the individual and the community.

For us the definition of the relation between the individual and the community is not a philosophical but a theological problem(3). To the Christian Faith both these ideas—the "individual" and the "community"—appear to be untrue, and sinful. No adjustment between the two is possible, for it is impossible to make one "Good" out of two kinds of sin. In the Christian Faith the individual is so defined that he cannot be imagined apart from the community, and the community that it cannot be imagined without the individual. By this I do not mean the obvious reflection that Robinson Crusoe on his desert island is an abstraction which would not occur in real life, that actually individuals always live in communities. On the contrary, what I mean is this: that the

[1] Literally *Robinsonade*—a vivid phrase for which we have no equivalent in English.—TR.

individual as such does not and cannot exist at all, that the very *conception* of the individual implies and includes that of the community.

Human existence, as such, is existence in responsibility. This does not mean that man ought to *know* that he is a responsible being, as an ethical truth; no, I mean something which lies behind all ethical consciousness and conduct, namely, that the very being of man owes its *humanitas* to the fact that human life *is*, in its essence, responsible existence. Just as the tension of a suspension bridge is due to the fact that it hangs between two supporting towers and in so doing unites them, so also the peculiar tension which gives its quality to human life—responsibility—is determined by the fact that the "I" is always confronted by the "Thou." This unity through tension *is* the human element; apart from this responsibility human existence simply does not exist. Thus, the fact that man's existence *is* responsibility means that an "I" can only be developed in touch with a "Thou," or, as Gogarten (one of those who have re-discovered this truth) puts it: "The 'I' "comes from the 'Thou'."

But the "Thou" is not a simple fact any more than the "I." The other must be given to me in a definite way, in order that I may recognize him as this "Thou" to whom I owe my being. I must listen to the claim that proceeds from him to me, the claim that makes me a responsible being. I can neither make myself the "I" who listens, nor can the "Thou" make himself into the one who addresses me(4). We must be so made for one another, the "Thou" must be given to me in such a way, that in him I perceive both these facts: firstly, that I am responsible to him, and secondly, that my life consists in this fact. The power which alone can make the "I" responsible to the "Thou" is God. To be responsible to the "Thou" means to be bound up in the bundle of life with the "Thou" by God Himself. Our responsibility can only be based on the Divine claim. When we say that God has so created us that this claim of the "Thou" is our very life, and thus that we have been *created* in His image, we mean that this responsibility is not an extra, alien element in life, but that it constitutes our *human* life itself—(and we have no other life than a *human* life)—we mean that we have not been posited, as things are posited, but that we have been created in such a manner that only as we respond to this claim upon us do we fulfil the purpose for which we have been created.

Human existence, in contradistinction to every other kind of existence known to us, is existence-in-responsibility, a form of existence in which man is not an "object" but a "subject," a being who is addressed and summoned to "reply." This means that this being of man is not self-centred and isolated, but that his being consists in a relatedness; it is being related to the origin and the goal of life.[1] The concrete expression, however, of this existence-in-responsibility is the actual fact of one's responsibility to the "Thou," to the other. In saying this I do not deny, on the contrary, I explicitly affirm the profound truth uttered by Pestalozzi: "God is our nearest relation." But the fact that God is thus related to us means that this intimate relation can only become concrete and real in a relationship with the human "Thou"(5).

The *meaning* of this existence, however, as a responsible reciprocal existence, is *Love*. Every human relationship which does not express love is abnormal. In Jesus Christ we are told that this love is the whole meaning of our life, and is also its foundation. Here the Creator reveals Himself as the One who has created us *in* love, *by* love, *for* love. He *reveals* to us our true nature, and He *gives* it back to us. In Him it becomes clear to us that our "natural" life has not ceased to be a human existence, an existence-in-responsibility, one that responds to a summons; it is obvious, however, that we do not make this response positively, but negatively; we do not respond by accepting our responsibilities, by manifesting love; no, our response takes the form of irresponsibility and lovelessness: we still live as human beings, it is true, but we are misshapen human beings. Thus even our "natural" sinful existence, is a kind of *co*-existence(6), but it is *co*-existence in the negative sense; it means separation from our fellows, and, indeed, hostility towards them. It is not an unrelated existence, but it is an existence which "contracts out," that is, it is an existence which withdraws itself both from God and Man. This explains how it is that in this false definition of co-existence both the "I" and the "Thou" receive a false distorted meaning, but that at the same time the "I" and the "Thou" do not sever their relation with one another(7). The distorted meaning shows itself in this: that henceforth "self-existence" or "self-hood" stands in a permanent relation of opposition to co-existence, to the community, that the false "self-existence"

[1] Literally *Sein-Woher* and *Sein-Wohin* (Being-Whence and Being-Whither). —TR.

and the false "co-existence" are in perpetual conflict with each other. On this basis a right definition and realization of the relation between the individual and the community—which could indeed only be an adjustment—is impossible.

3. Radical individualism only became possible within the sphere of Christianity; for until then man was always regarded as part of the cosmos, as a member of the universal organism. This pantheistic idea, which is the quintessence of paganism, exerted a great influence until the emergence of the Christian idea of Creation and of Sin—this idea which no longer interprets God, man, and the world as a continuum, in which each merges into the other, but as particular, separate entities; it was this development of thought which lay behind that emancipation of the individual rational Self which constitutes the very core of the history of modern thought(8). The Self which is autonomous by means of reason has no need either of a God outside itself, since, fundamentally, it is itself Divine—or of any human "Thou." In its own reason, indeed, it anticipates everything that another Self could offer it. The autonomous rational Self is also the self-sufficient Self; one who sees in Reason the actual substance of human existence—whether he will or no—has inevitably become an individualist. The reason within "me" is self-assured, and its essential content is immanent "within me"—how then can I be bound to another? I am bound to him in virtue of that "bond" which is my "freedom": in him I respect one who bears within him the same Reason which I also bear within myself. In him I respect—myself, according to the depth of my own being.

It is no accident that the figure of Robinson Crusoe and the idea of a "desert island" gripped the imagination of the period of the Enlightenment; for Robinson Crusoe is the symbol which expresses the philosophy of life prevalent at that time. It is the idea of the self-sufficient individual, to whose existence the coming of a second and third individual does not *essentially* bring anything new. It is the idea of the *contrat social*, which derives the State from the contract concluded by individuals; it is the idea of economic Liberalism, which derives the welfare of the community from the egoism of individuals.

From three different angles the attempt has been made to transcend this idea of the self-sufficient personality, but without real success. These three attempts may be thus summarized: the Positivist doctrine of the causal dependence of the individual on his environment(9); the universalism of Idealistic philosophy, and finally, the Romantic theory of the organism.

The Positivist theory of environment, or the sociological view of life as a "continuous adjustment" of "relations," controlled by the biological view of conduct, believes that it can transcend the individualism of the Enlightenment by showing the causal dependence of the individual upon his social environment. Whether this attempt goes so far as to claim that the individual is simply the product of his environment, or whether a high degree of independence is granted to him(10), is, from *one* point of view, a matter of indifference; in this view there is no room for community. Here man is conceived as the centre of a web of effects woven by various causes and thus as an object among other objects. For effects—causal relations—can only exist among objects. Causal determination is not community. Indeed, causal determination is the exact opposite of community. Causal determination and community are mutually exclusive. Collectivism, understood in a causal sense, is not the opposite of individualism; on the contrary, it is its necessary correlate; the atom (*individuum*) has a mutual causal relation with the other atoms. Positivist sociology (Spencer) is just as individualistic and lacking in the sense of community as the Rationalism of the Enlightenment.

Idealistic universalism seeks to transcend individualism by setting the individual within the whole context of the growth of Spirit and of timeless Ideas. The life of the spirit is held to consist only in participation in these supra-individual unities of meaning, in universal Spirit, which, as objective Spirit, creates in historical forms an expression of its superiority to the individual Self. The individual here possesses significance only in so far as he is the "bearer" of these supra-individual values and truths. "The individual human being, as a vessel containing 'values,' becomes an object of love."[1] "Love means being judged equal in value."[2] Here, therefore, just as the individual as a person disappears behind the abstract conception of Spirit, since in himself he becomes a meaningless medium, "in" whom Spirit manifests itself, so also here there is no real community(11). For unity in Spirit, in the Idea, is not community at all. Nor are the objective creations of the human spirit, such as the State, culture, science, art—

[1] SPRANGER: *Lebensformen*, p. 172.   [2] Ibid., p. 61.

community; at their best, they are means to, instruments of, community, but they do not *create* real community; rather they only create great common forces, "something" which binds men together, purposes—even if ideal purposes—for whose sake men will unite, but never real personal community, that is, a direct relation between persons. Here the ideal of community, of the highest form of love, is thus expressed: "There is a Super-Self which finds itself again in the Other."[1]

The Romantic theory of community, that of the organism, manifests itself here as everywhere as a blend—and certainly not an insignificant one—of Idealistic and Naturalistic elements. It oscillates between the Idea of universalistic Idealism and the Positivist idea of the causal product, just as the idea of "organism" stands mid-way between the Idea and the causal product. Just as certainly as the organism is reality— the reality which is present wherever anything vital is present— so also this "blend" is something which corresponds to reality. The Romantic theory of organism—just because it occupies this middle position—possesses a fruitfulness and a close relation to real life which is lacking in both the other theories. It is, however, the most dangerous perversion of truth, just because it oscillates, because it can never be actually "nailed down." If we emphasize its Platonic aspect, then it seems opposed to Naturalism; but if we accept its strong statements about the organism as the principle of community, then it turns away from Idealism. One thing, however, it does say clearly and that is its main contention: the individual is subordinate to the whole, the individual is only a member of the whole community, whose duty it is to serve the community(12). For this very reason it also does not know true community. For community only exists where the individual knows that he is in direct and unique relation with the other person, not where he is conscious of being a subordinate part of a greater "whole." Every kind of "being" or of "the whole" which is regarded as "superior to" the sphere of personal relations destroys both the meaning of "personal" life and the meaning of community. The individual person is never part of a greater whole; there is nothing in the world "greater" or "higher" than the personal. The truly personal is at the same time the truly social, expressing itself as love. All supposedly superior "wholes"—the State, the nation, etc.—into which romantic sociology incorporates the individual, are in

[1] SPRANGER: *Lebensformen*, p. 172.

reality only instruments which serve the ends of persons, and their personal relations to each other in community. They are "orders," which are created for the sake of man, for the sake of love.

4. The Christian conception of the Church makes it quite clear that in the Christian understanding of community the individual and the community are so related that the one cannot be thought of apart from the other. As the Greek word ἐκκλησία shows, this conception of community is inseparably connected with the idea in which the individual is conceived in his most complete personal responsibility—the idea of election (κλῆσις). The Church is the community of those whom God calls, of the elect, *communio electorum, sanctorum*.[1] The Church is not one community among others—and in so far as this is so, in so far as she is a sociological legal structure the subject will be treated in its own place[2]—the "Church" is rather the Divinely created order of community restored by Jesus Christ in His Atonement, and it is the community of the Redeemed, directed towards the perfecting of the Creation. The *communio electorum*, the ἐκκλησία of the κλητοὶ is *the only true community*.

Here the individual is completely united to his fellows. A Christian cannot possibly be an isolated individual; to be a Christian is to be a member of the Body of Christ. But this is only a simile, it is not an organic principle. For this does not mean a relation to life based on vitalistic analogies, but real community, through faith in Christ. A man becomes a Christian through the Word of God, which God gives to the individual through the Christian community. In this Word he receives his life, his new being; "having been . . . begotten again . . . through the Word of God, which liveth . . ."[3] The Church is the witness to the Word which creates faith. Hence there is no faith, and therefore no possibility of being a believer, outside the Christian Church. Only within the Christian community do we receive that which makes us "individuals," believers, namely, the Word and the Sacraments.

He who receives the Word, becomes by this most literally—in the sense in which Kierkegaard used to teach—"this particular individual." The fact of election alone creates real, responsible, self-reliant personality. True freedom only comes

---

[1] Cf. the beautiful exposition of the Reformation Idea of the Church by ALTHAUS: *Communio Sanctorum*.

[2] See below, Chapter XLIV ff.   [3] 1 Peter i. 23 (R.V.).

to those who know that God Himself addresses us—as we are—treats us as worthy of His love, and draws us into His own life. Here there are no longer any intermediary courts of appeal, not only no human courts, but also no "angels, principalities, and powers" and no abstract Ideas, Values, or Laws. All that is secondary, and is simply intended to serve this one end, the *personal* relation between God and Man. Election is the proclamation of the immediacy of the Kingdom under its personal overlord. In the fact of election alone do we begin to perceive, in the light of eternity, the significance of the word "Thou"—"I have called *thee* by *thy* name; *thou* art Mine."[1] Here there is nothing between God and man, between the person who is being created and the One who creates, nor is there anything above them. Here man is face to face with his God, in the most intimate personal relation. Here alone does the "individual" exist.

Thus the same thing that unites me to the Church, unites me directly to the Kingdom of God, makes me an "individual." Indeed, the Church is simply the assembly of the elect, of those who have been "called." Here not only are the individual and the community not mutually exclusive, but they *are* one and the same thing. Here it becomes evident what a distorted view of individual existence is that which is conceived without a "thou," and how false is every kind of "community" which does not consist of this responsibility towards the *Thou.* Here each is both giver and receiver, as one who receives and also as one who gives. This is that "still more excellent way" to which the simile of the "body" (I Cor. xii) refers: the love of God (I Cor. xiii).

Real love only exists as love which is a response to the Divine Love. Therefore real, "absolute" love exists only "in Christ," that is, "in the Church." The Church means that community among men which is based upon fellowship between God and Man. Or, to put it differently, we might say, with equal truth: there is no love save "Christian" love; for a χριστιανός, a "Christian"[2] can only exist "within the Church," as a member of the Body, whose Head is Christ. Thus, whether we say: "true community or true love can only be found within the Church," *or*: "both 'fellowship' and 'love' exist only in the 'Christian' sense," we really mean the same thing(13).

And indeed, how could it be otherwise? If it be true that

[1] Isa. xliii. 1.   [2] Acts xi. 26.

man is created not only *by* but *in* the Word of God—that is, that man can only be himself (become a *person*) by responding to God, and, indeed, by responding to Him in accordance with His Call, then there can be no real existence as a Self apart from fellowship with God. And as true self-existence is fellowship with God, so also, on the basis of this fellowship with God, it is also fellowship with our fellow-man. The attitude of man towards God is not only that which determines his own existence as a self, but also his existence in relation to other people, which is, indeed, indissolubly connected with his existence as a self. Fellowship with God creates fellowship with man, and genuine human fellowship is only possible as it is based upon fellowship with God. Thus human fellowship rests upon the same foundation as fellowship between man and God: the Divine establishment of fellowship, the reconciliation in Jesus Christ, in which—both towards God and man—the perverted solidarity, the "community-in-lovelessness," in isolation, is reversed and brought back into the direction for which it was created, to solidarity in responsibility, into the way of love. *Faith* is the act of sharing in this process of restoration. This faith, however, is only possible through the Word of God, which the Church can only mediate through her message, because, and in so far as, she is able to *witness* to her own faith.

5. Thus in the idea of the Church it becomes evident that a truly personal existence and solidarity in fellowship, or love, are two aspects of the same thing. I can only experience solidarity, I can only be in fellowship, in love, in so far as I am truly a *person*; and only in a real personal existence, as one "personally" called by God, can I be in genuine corporate fellowship with others. To make this quite clear we need to present briefly the converse of this truth, that is, the possibilities which exist outside this divinely-given possibility both of personal existence and of solidarity.

The Self can never cease to be a subject. But if it is no longer a responsible Self, it is an untrammelled Ego, living its life on a basis of complete freedom of "self-expression." It still remains a subject which knows, experiences and creates, which has a world of objects over against itself, it still remains one which transmits human civilization and human culture; it has not lost "personality" in the formal sense of the word. Further, even when it turns away from the "Thou" it is still bound to the "Thou." But its connexion with the other is not based on responsibility, or on love, but on possessiveness. It wants "something" from the other, it makes our fellow-man an object of our will; thus the Self does not respect the personality of the other, although in a certain way he does acknowledge it. Practically, the "I" treats the "Thou" as a *thing*, and his relation to him becomes one not of fellowship but of dominance. The Ego regards the personality of the other as a useful or serviceable object, or as something to be enjoyed, it becomes a *means* to an end, whether this End be a natural end, an end of civilization or a cultural end. The Ego desires "something" from the other, whether this "something" be sense-enjoyment, service, or knowledge, or whether it be his bodily or his mental individuality, his actual existence enjoyed in a physical or intellectual way(14). Even in this latter case, which is so often confused with community, the other exists *for me*. Even the aesthetic pleasure in the other person which gives its special colour to friendship(15) is not really community. In the erotic relationship the enjoyment of the sexually emphasized individuality, in friendship the individuality, apart from sex, is the "something" which is sought. Certainly the other person is intended, is sought, his person, but not as one person forming the mutual complement to the other, but as some one who exists "for my sake"; and even when this commerce of giving and receiving is mutual, as in the genuine erotic and friendship relation, this mutual *enjoyment* remains the decisive element. For that very reason, as such, it is not yet community, it is not yet a real personal relation.

This means, however, that it is undeniable that in this relation "I" also am not personal. For the personal or non-personal character of the Self is determined by this fact: whether the one who confronts him, the "Thou," is recognized as personal or not. Both mean the same thing: to the exact extent in which the "Thou" is recognized by me as "Thou" or not, I myself am a responsible, personal being or not. Of course, over against the "It," the object, the "Thou-as-object," I am indeed a subject, namely, a self which purposes, knows and creates, but I am not a *personal* being. Not only the "Thou" but the "I" is depersonalized. The truly personal self and the community arise and disappear in the same act.

6. Our previous enquiry, however, has been abstract in character, in so far as we have assumed that the Self could completely sever itself from its relation to God. That this is

not the case was fully proved by our treatment of the subject in Book I. The "natural man," the man who is outside the revelation of Christ, is not simply separated from God, but his relation to God and man is perverted. This perversion becomes evident in the fact that the natural man does not *really* know God, and does not *really* love man. He "knows" God in a perverted way, either in a eudaemonistic natural sense, or in a legalistic sense.[1] And his relation with man is either legalistic and self-righteous, or it is a degraded form of love. The natural man is either very rigid, on principle, in his dealings with others—he is, indeed, conscious of responsibility, but he conceives this responsibility from the point of view of an abstract conception of duty—or he is lax and unprincipled; he loves, of course—his friend, his child, his beloved, his fellow-countryman—but this love is partisan and selective, and is therefore limited and selfish. He is, indeed, conscious of his responsibility as father, as husband, and as patriot, but this sense of responsibility is limited and particular. It is not unconditioned, it is not love in the sense of rising above the opposition between law and sympathy, that love which is just as "pure" as the law of duty, and just as "warm" and "personal" as sympathy. Thus, here love and responsibility exist only in this relative and imperfect sense.

Wherever this element of responsibility and of love is treated lightly, the objective character of our relation with the "Thou" is likewise toned down, and the way is opened for "something like" community. Indeed, this "something like" community is what we usually mean by "Community," a form of community which is not absolute, which is permeated through and through with the spirit of impersonal values. The Greek conception of "friendship" provides a classic illustration, both in its abstract description by Aristotle and in its representation in classical literature. This "natural" community we find, of course, among all peoples, and in all lands, in the relations between husband and wife, parents and children, the members of the same tribe or nation, and between friends. Just as there is a natural morality, so also there is natural community. But it is just as limited, and for the same reasons, as natural morality.

A particularly clear criterion of this limitation is the necessity of balancing in some way or another the claims of the "I" and the "Thou," the oscillation between an undigni-

---

[1] Cf. what is said above about "religion" on pp. 28 ff.

fied self-surrender to the forces of collectivism, and a self-assertion supported by "justice"—that is, based upon the rational equality of the claims of the individual and the community. This process of balancing claims is, as I said at the beginning, the hopeless attempt to solve the ethical problem of "The individual *versus* the community." It is hopeless, because here neither the "individual" nor "the community" is rightly understood, in their profound meaning, nor can they be understood. Thus this attempt to strike a balance between the claims of the individual and the community is also determined by that primal act of separation from the Source of Life; it, too, belongs to the natural sphere, to man as a sinful being.

The contradiction which this adjustment seeks to remove, is that which exists between a collectivism which infringes the rights of the community, or, to put it still more strongly, between the predatory and the gregarious types, between the slave and the master. But such an adjustment is like the attempt to square the circle.

This "adjustment," that is, this desire—and a perfectly right desire—to eliminate the false element in both these forms of human relations, can only be either a miserable compromise or no "adjustment" at all, but the discovery of the point above the contradiction in a quite new definition of the relation between the individual and the community which renders this adjustment wholly unnecessary: in love, which is both true freedom and independence of the Self, and the true union between the "I" and the "Thou"—true community.

The adjustment can be effected neither by love in the non-radical sense, nor by responsibility in the legalistic sense. Love which is not absolute is always—in some way or another—particular (i.e. not universal). In the form of mother-love or friendship it is strong, but partisan. In the shape of love of one's country, or rather of one's own nation, it is powerful, but unjust. As the "love of humanity" it is pallid, abstract, unreal, since it deals with *ideas*, not with *persons*. Responsibility, however, conceived in a legalistic way, does not will community as love, but it wills equal freedom for all on a basis of *justice*(16). It absolutely respects the sphere of life of the other, but this clearly defined barrier leads to separation and isolation. Justice may, indeed, be able to remove strife, but it cannot create community. To define our relation to others

305

in terms of justice means renouncing all hopes of community from the very outset. Justice is like an impartial division of a territory, but it is not *communio*.

7. Real *communio* is simply and solely love without conditions, which is only possible in reply to God's way of loving, which is without conditions. The man who loves without conditions, that is, to put it concretely, the man who loves his enemy— he alone is wholly independent and wholly in community. He alone does not allow his attitude to be determined by the attitude of the other, since he loves him "in spite of himself." But since he does this, he no longer loves him "*for* something," but simply because he is his fellow-man, not because he is a man of a certain kind, but simply because he exists. That is what it means to love our neighbour. The love of our neighbour is not a general idealized love of humanity, but the unrestricted recognition of the other man, without considering what he is like, the recognition of the existence of the other in his Divine claim on me(17). This is what it means "to love" "in Christ." For we can only love like this when we know that we are all loved in this free generous way, that is, in the knowledge of the *sola gratia*.

This love does not respect barriers, it transcends them; it means going out towards the other, identifying myself with him; it means "loving one's neighbour as oneself," the renunciation of one's natural and just reserve, it means sacrifice. Sacrifice means rising above the level of justice(18). Sacrifice, therefore, transcends reason. The "living sacrifice"[1] means the way of life of one who knows through faith (so far as this knowledge is genuine) that he is the property of the God who reveals Himself in sacrifice. Sacrifice is the highest form of *self-denial*. But this same sacrifice is also the highest form of self-affirmation. For only in this spirit of sacrifice does the Self live as one who is chosen by God, as one who is gathered up into the life of God Himself, as a "citizen" of the Eternal Divine realm. The life of sacrifice is the Christian's freedom, the "Christian's patent of nobility," alongside of which every other kind of distinction looks forced, like a person who gives himself airs, a cheap imitation of true nobility. The truly *royal* person is the person who sacrifices himself freely for love's sake. Every other kind of distinction secretly seeks something for itself, fame, or worldly honour, self-interest, or pleasure; hence it is not free, it is always bound to "something." One

[1] Rom. xii. 1.

who loves is not bound by anything at all, save by the claims of his fellow-creatures, which make him free even while they bind him.

In this freedom, however—and this is the last difficulty to be removed—the natural *individuality* is set free. The person who loves is the person released from all tension and rigidity, the person without caricature, masquerade, or pose. He is released from bondage. Rigidity and tension are caused by passionate desire. Such passion also stamps an individuality with its own seal, but it marks the person with an artificial stamp, with something unreal, with a caricature. The unloving person is compelled to seek *himself* and to *seek* himself. The loving person, on the other hand, does not need to seek himself at all, for he has been *found*. He is free from anxiety about himself, free for others. Hence his creative powers are set free. Just because, unlike the legally-minded person, he knows no *clichés*, no barriers or regulations—to use Thurneysen's expression once more—he is "perfectly poised like the arrow in the bow of the hunter"; he can also express the natural wealth which every created being possesses, involuntarily, without knowing he is doing so. The individual essence of a human being only prospers where its development is not deliberately sought. People of great love are people with a most distinct individuality—although this individuality is not so striking as to attract the attention of the curious; when it reaches this stage it is already almost a grotesque caricature. Like all that is natural and genuine, the individuality of the loving-hearted person is unobtrusive.

In conclusion, I would point out once more that the love of which I have been speaking is that which is only possible in the act of faith, that is, as a gift. It is not something continuous and permanent, it is an event; but it is certainly of the essence of the life of faith, that this love, like faith itself, should penetrate life more and more—that life which still, however, remains the life of a sinful human being. "Men and women of love," who exhibit this kind of growth, certainly do exist, and their memory is rightly treasured by the Church; it is no part of fundamental Protestant doctrine, if rightly understood, to deny this possibility.

CHAPTER XXVIII

RELIGIOUS AND MORAL PRACTICE AS LIMITING CASES OF THE MORAL[1]

THE fundamental misinterpretation of the Self as a substance or reason based upon itself, the Greek idea of man, has misled Christian ethics into making the disastrous distinction between an individual and a social ethic. In the individual ethic the right nature of selfhood "in itself" (the doctrine of Virtue), and the "duties man owes to himself," were discussed as a separate doctrine; man's relation to his neighbour was relegated to a special second section, in spite of the fact that the New Testament statement that "love is the fulfilling of the law" was constantly reiterated, and that frequent emphasis was laid upon the truth that the command to "love your neighbour as yourself" implies all the other commandments. Instead of taking this truth seriously, and exposing the traditional theory of Greek ethics to a penetrating criticism, in the light of this truth, the Greek view was taken over without any criticism at all, and, for good or ill, the Christian Ethos was stretched to fit into this framework which really crippled it. Even down to the present day the superstitious belief in this twofold division is deeply embedded in the thought of Christian moralists—not only of Catholic moralists (where this confusion of Aristotelianism and Christianity is at least in harmony with their general line of thought), but just as much in that of Protestant moralists.

This process would be inexplicable were it not for the fact that the development of the Christian Ethos itself was already tending in the same direction. This misinterpretation, in the form of an individual ethic, is due to the influence of mystical ideas on the interpretation of faith, and to the influence of ascetical ideas on practice. Henceforward, the "life of the soul with God" became possible as a higher kind of religious duty; pre-occupation with oneself came next, while the question of man's duty to his neighbour took the third place, being depreciated to such an extent that it became a merely "secular" affair. This ethical scale: God—the Self—the world (the neighbour) seemed to be inherent in the "inwardness" and the "depth" of the Christian Ethos. Actually, it was the one

[1] An outline of Christian "asceticism."

great error, which corrupted equally both faith and ethics and made Christianity, fundamentally, a monastic business. A Christian individual ethic is a thoroughly monastic idea and is therefore wholly unscriptural.

Then are there no "duties towards God" and "duties towards oneself," just as there are duties to our neighbour? If the standpoint of duty were the one which determines ethics, then certainly there would be very little to say against this threefold division, and this individual ethic would be justified. But the characteristic element of a genuine Christian ethic is that it does not start from the idea of duty at all, but from that of Divine grace; this point is constantly emphasized, and is, indeed, made quite explicit in the doctrine of justification by faith. This doctrine strikes a fatal blow at mysticism and asceticism; it also shows, however, that the threefold division (of God, the self, and the world) is a fundamental error.

A. *Our Relation to God in the Ethical Sense: Religious Practice*

1. Faith alone is good : for it fulfils the First Commandment, glorifies God, and presses its claims upon us. We have already dealt fully with the question of how far faith is both a gift and a task. Whether it be a gift, or a task which arises out of a gift, this truth holds good : this faith is always the presupposition of "works," it is the fundamental, all-inclusive fact, which can no more be compared with action than cause and effect can be compared with one another. The command to love God is not a moral command; it is not on the same level as the love of man, but it indicates the root of all morality. To place it upon a level with the other Commandment means that we have totally misunderstood the words, "and the other is like unto it." Yes, the two are "like," as the spring and the brook, the tree and its fruits are "like," as the person himself and the works which the person does are "like." It is in faith that personality is constituted—for man's origin and his being consist in his relation to God and this new constitution of the person lays the foundation for his new relation to his neighbour —love.

Therefore our relation to God cannot itself be placed within the sphere of the moral as the presupposition of all that is moral. Our relation to God has been constituted by the act of Christ and does not need to be established by any action of ours. Henceforth, our action does not take the form of striving *after* God, rather it springs from our life *in* God. The cultus as a means of bringing us into touch with God (and this is the real significance of the cultus) is abrogated, in principle, by the sacrifice of Christ. Our relation to God through prayer is rather the "exercise of faith," it continually renews the actual relation which, in principle, has been restored. As soon as we perceive that in this relation to God we are simply and utterly the recipients of a gift, the expression: "our duties towards God," has become unsuitable, or at any rate it has become very misleading.

There are no duties towards God, in the way in which there are duties towards our neighbour. We do not bring anything to God, we simply receive. The meaning of the "cultus," henceforth, is expressed in the receptive attitude of those who offer their thanks, their praise, and their petitions, in the act of prayer.

But as soon as that mistaken view predominates in which man's relation to God is legalistically conceived—that is, as soon as man's relation to God is regarded not as a presupposition but as a state which has yet to be attained (as in mysticism, and in asceticism with its "righteousness of works")—it is evident that a division must be made between God and the world as the object of our action; it is then obvious that the larger half must be given to God and the smaller to man. Therefore renunciation of the world, and of all contact with the ordinary life of man, is always logically connected with mysticism, and with every serious form of religious belief which tries to create a relation between God and the soul of man. If man must fulfil his "duties towards God," then only the *homo religiosus*, the monk who lives far from the life of the world, can be a truly god-fearing man. The more time and strength a man spends on these duties the more "devout" he is. The goal of such piety is necessarily the hermit's cell; life in the world, contact with men, is always felt to be something which really ought not to exist, and the more this "piety" uses up a man's time and strength(1), the deeper is his distaste for the ordinary life of man.

2. We can only clear the way for a genuinely evangelical view of *prayer* if we reject this idea of a special "duty towards God." Prayer does not come under the heading of the "fulfilment of duty," it belongs to a different dimension: to the dimension on which fulfilment of duty is based, where ethics are constituted. From this standpoint it becomes possible to

understand the remarkable fact that in the New Testament so much is said of the urgent need for prayer, and yet so little of prayer as a human activity.[1] The development of religious asceticism belongs to a period where the fundamental misunderstanding had already taken place. It is characteristic of the place of prayer in the Christian life that it is not placed alongside of other forms of action, but that it permeates time and the visible sphere with a certain quiet and almost shy insistence, by reminding us to "pray without ceasing."[2] We are to pray always, all our action is to take place in the presence of God, that is, it is to flow from union with God in prayer. From the point of view of principle prayer ought not to be something alongside of other things, just as God is not something else alongside of the world. Prayer is not the content of ethics, but, like faith, the presupposition of ethics.

Yet if, in spite of this truth, we are bidden to keep the Sabbath, that is, if we are bidden to observe fixed times for prayer, this is a concession to our human frailty, lest the exhortation to "pray without ceasing" come to mean—for us—that we "never" stop to pray at all. In the New Testament in principle the Sabbath is abrogated; but as a means of securing order, as a necessary method of training, as a God-given means of discipline, we, too, have our special "Lord's Day," with its special forms of worship. Still, we are free to determine how, and when, and how often these special observances are to take place, according to our experience. The cultus, as an act which occupies time, as a special act, no longer comes under the heading of the "fulfilment of our duty towards God," but under the heading of "religious exercises"; as such it constitutes the boundary line of the ethical sphere, "looking upwards," just as exercise in self-discipline constitutes the boundary line at the other end of the scale, "looking downwards." The cultus is concerned with the realm which is higher than the ethical sphere; self-discipline is concerned with the region that has not yet become ethical.

3. The presupposition of the true Good—faith, is not created in solitude, in the practice of "being alone with oneself and with God" (which is the illusion of mysticism), but in com-

[1] It is perhaps not accidental that only on the fringe of the New Testament, in the Pastoral Epistles, does a kind of religious asceticism make itself heard.
[2] 1 Thess. v. 17.

311

munity. "How shall they believe in Him whom they have not heard? and how shall they hear without a preacher? . . . So belief cometh of hearing, and hearing by the Word of Christ."[1] At the point where faith is born in a man's heart he is not face to face with God in solitude, but he is in the presence of the man who speaks to him the Word of God. He does not receive faith directly from God, but indirectly, through the word of a human being. Behind the faith of the individual is the Christian *community*, the Church, and, indeed, the local congregation, acting at a definite place, at a definite time(2). We shall be dealing later with the character of this order of community, that is, with the visible Church. We are here concerned with the fact that the faith of the individual arises in and through the Church, although the other, secondary fact is also true, namely, that the Church consists of the faith of individuals. Therefore the first and the most essential "means" of awakening faith and of strengthening faith is not an individual but a social process, the act of placing oneself within the Christian community, and of sharing in the proclamation of the message, and in the life of the Church.

The Word of God, which as an historical Word is by the will of God united with history and with the fellowship of the Church, must therefore always be sought at this "point." In this deliberate practice of listening, constantly renewed, man expresses his rightful attitude towards God, an attitude which is essentially one of receiving, and, indeed, of receiving in union with others. In this self-determined act of turning towards God as the Source of our being we give God the glory, and we do what we can to awaken, maintain, and strengthen faith.

The practice of private *Bible Study*, on the contrary, is secondary and derivative, since the Scriptures are only a substitute for the *viva vox ecclesiae*. The Word of Revelation is not primarily and mainly, but only in the second place, a *written* Word, although we are quite sure that this Scripture is the *Canon*, which guides the living proclamation of the Word. The place of the Bible is primarily in the Christian community, not in the hands of the solitary believer. The public proclamation of the Word is not merely a subsidiary explanation of the Word of Scripture, made necessary by the individual believer's imperfect understanding of the Scriptures, and, therefore, one which the mature Bible student can afford

[1] Rom. x. 14, 17.

to ignore, but, just because it is public, connected with the community, it is the primary form of the Divine Revelation of the Word.

In close connexion, however, with the Protestant idea of Revelation and of the Church, the Reformers declare that each individual member of the community is, in principle, an independent, mature Bible student. For the Church consists of the fellowship of those who themselves have access to the Word of God. Therefore the reading of the Scriptures belongs necessarily to the practice of our right relation with God, since it expresses this immediacy in which God wills to speak to each individual in his daily life. It even precedes prayer, for prayer is the answer to the Word which has been given by God, and the Christian can only pray on the basis of the fact that God has made Himself known to him. Thus the empirical fact that the true Christian life can only grow out of contact with the Bible is based upon the fundamental conditions of revelation and faith.

4. The answer to the Divine Word is the prayer of adoring gratitude and trustful petition. Prayer is faith *in actu*. Like faith itself it is a divine gift, and on the basis of this fact it is a divine demand. We *must* pray; where there is faith it cannot be otherwise. We *may* pray; faith is the highest expression of the communion with God which has been granted to us. We *are* to pray; for God wills to be sought again and again, even in faith. Prayer is the breath of the believing soul. Every true act of faith is at the same time an act of prayer. But for the sake of this kind of prayer the deliberate kind of prayer, the prayer which is practised as a special act, an act which takes time, is necessary. Even this "special" prayer forms part of that prayer which is the highest we know, since it is intimately related with faith itself. But the relation of the one to the other is quite irrational; it cannot be summarized in any definition or in any law, but, at the most, in the rules of spiritual hygiene. Faith, the life of prayer, therefore, although it is a criterion of genuine Christian life, is not an object of scientific investigation, but of practical "ascetic" instruction.

Midway between prayer and Bible-reading is the practice of *meditation*, which has its place, its definite and necessary place, not merely in the mystical life but also in the life of faith. The Word of Scripture must not only be read, but it must be spiritually "eaten," chewed, and digested. The just man is one whose "delight is in the law of the Lord."[1] True prayer must also proceed from profound reflection upon our own lives, as well as from the study of God's Word. For God desires to speak to us not only through the Word of Scripture but also through our experience of life. Meditation is the spiritual act through which the Word which is preached, prayer, and our experience of life are united, in order that they may thus mutually penetrate the soul as a whole. Were "Christian mysticism" nothing more than an emphasis upon the necessity for such meditation there would be nothing against it. Here, however, we must again remind ourselves that to over-emphasize and isolate this element from the rest of life opens the door to grave dangers in the life of faith, and to a serious misunderstanding of the Christian Revelation. Just as Bible-reading apart from prayer and meditation becomes a merely intellectual exercise, so also prayer and meditation become sentimental or fanatical unless they are closely connected with the Bible. Indeed, all religious "exercises" may easily become perverted, in the sense that the "exercise" itself may come to be regarded as a "good work." This danger develops into real injury as soon as the relation to the source has been lost, that is, as soon as the distinction between the works which proceed from faith, and faith as their source (whose comprehension this exercise seeks to further) has been lost.

B. *The Relation to the Self: Moral Practice*

1. Good is fully described by the one word: *Love*, and, indeed, in the New Testament sense, as love of our neighbour. Therefore self-regarding action can only indirectly be called "good." This, as we have already shown, is the great transformation in ethical thought, wrought by the Gospel. By yourself you cannot be good; you can only be good in your relation to the other. The Good is never a unit, it is always twofold. But even the individual life is absorbed into this twofold life. Here we are not concerned to contest the justification for self-directed action (self-cultivation, self-control), but we are concerned to gain the right point of view for its interpretation. Self-directed action can only be understood as action which is on the very outermost fringe of community action(3). Just as our action with regard to *things* has no inherent ethical significance—as such it is rather technical,

[1] Ps. i. 2.

creative, or artistic action, but not ethical action—but only acquires ethical significance through its relation to the community, so is it also with self-regarding action. Self-cultivation and self-control, for instance, are not good in themselves, but, in themselves, they are still ethically neutral, like technical action. There is a kind of self-cultivation and self-control which can be placed at the service of all sorts of rascality. Self-cultivation and self-control is only good when it is exercised for the sake of 'love. Self-directed action, or acts which affect one's own body, only gain ethical significance when they are related to the life of the community, that is, to life ruled by love.

One example, which is often adduced as a "striking" proof of the independence of an individual ethic, may be used to illustrate this point; I mean the practice of masturbation. Why is it morally objectionable? At the present time we see how completely the individualistic conception breaks down at this point, when confronted by the ethical demand to show why this habit is morally objectionable. The fact is that it can only be understood from the point of view of our relation to the "thou." This habit is bad because it misuses for solitary pleasure that which was intended for social use(4). Further, the objectionable character of all irregular eroticism, πορνεία, in the narrower and in the broader sense, can only be rightly understood from the point of view of community, that is, from the point of view of marriage. The sex instinct is intended by the Creator for that form of community in which alone it fulfils its personal meaning, through a responsible common life and through fidelity in love, that is, for marriage.[1]

If the objection is raised that the Creator desires to be glorified in the individual as well, in his physical and spiritual life as an individual entity, we would reply: we know no other will of the Creator than that which has destined me for existence in love, and this means for existence in community. Severed from this connexion with the community all the gifts of Creation are misused; while in this relation, even that which I myself am to *be*, according to God's Will, finds its fulfilment— precisely in so far as love becomes real. In this very fact, that existence for the sake of others, the Cross of Christ, becomes the standard of all ethical judgment, the direction of the natural or rational ethic is transformed. "I" am not a means for the "thou," but I become a Self only in relation to the

[1] Cf. the next section.

315

"thou," and all my natural gifts only find their fulfilment in the service of the "thou." Therefore all self-cultivation and self-control is only indirectly an ethical demand but, as such, it does exist. The development of the Self, of the personality, is the principle of the Greek ethic, not of the Christian ethic. For the Christian ethic maintains that a true "I" can only come into being in relation to a "thou," that is, only in community—and, indeed, not merely in the fact that the individual and the community influence each other mutually, but in the fact that community is absolutely fundamental: thus that without community the "I" is not merely onesided, but is also fundamentally perverted.

2. Once this has been granted then all action which must inevitably take place in solitude and be directed towards the Self, falls into its right place, and may henceforth be estimated at its true worth(5). Such action is justified from the point of view of *discipline* and of *education*—both of which are intended to equip the individual for service. Here the negative point of view of discipline comes first, and not education, as in the Greek ethic, because here it is seen that the Good is not realized in the continuity of natural desire but in breaking it down. The much vaunted "positive" character of the Christian ethic is based upon a confusion of the Christian Ethos with the ancient rational Ethos. As the Cross of Christ is the place where we learn to know God, so also self-denial(6), self-surrender to the death of Christ, is absolutely the first requirement. Certainly, this action presupposes something positive: psycho-physical existence and its positive development. But this does not take place on the ethical plane, but on the naturally creative plane(7). The life-urge does not have to be first created by the good will, but it is already there, like the urge to creative and technical action, which grows out of motives which are certainly not ethical. In a word: there is no sense in commanding men to love themselves, for by nature self-love is already present. The command to love one's neighbour "as oneself" is not to be understood as an imperative but as an indicative. "Ethical self-love" is an expression which can only be used by those who are not yet clear about the meaning of the nature of ethics. The first thing that the awakened spirit of obedience has to do, so far as oneself is concerned, is not to "cultivate" oneself but to take up a discipline, to restrain forcibly, to prune self-love, to break with oneself—*sibi ipsi*—that negative of the New Testa-

ment which has been misinterpreted as the asceticism which renounces the world. At the same time the ascetic idea may well be closer to the meaning of the New Testament than the enthusiastic emphasis on "development" in the cultural ethic of Idealism.

Self-denial, in its original sense, is always intended for our neighbour's good; but in order to make this possible it must be "practised." One who has not learned to deny himself something which is quite lawful will not be able to renounce that which he is called to give up in the way of duty. Hence, self-discipline, as "self-directed" action, is the practice of resistance to the natural urge, it is educative asceticism (ἄσκησις originally meant *exercise*), in order to make oneself supple for the service of love(8). But even the duty of self-control in pleasure originates here. The person who is not self-controlled makes himself unfit for service. On this point, however, in view of the fact that this subject has already received such full treatment elsewhere, there is no need to say more.[1]

3. The duty of *self-cultivation*—in the sense of all kinds of development of our natural powers of body and mind—springs from the fact that although the life-urge is present, frequently, if left to itself, it follows the line of least resistance, that is, to the fact of *laziness* of every kind. Were laziness, as Fichte thinks it is, the original sin, then certainly self-cultivation would head the list of human duties. If this were so, then evil would be quite harmless, it would be merely disturbing, like the action of a brake on the wheel of life. It is not the lack of will but the perverted will which is evil. But the perverted will can certainly assume the form of laziness.

This is why the moral will must come to the assistance of the natural impulse. The sum-total of all these extra aids we call *moral cultivation*(9), since we are here using the word in its original sense. Even this action is only indirectly ethical, in so far as it only renders the powers of a man ready for service, but is not itself service. Therefore self-cultivation, like self-control, can also become a means for all kinds of evil; it is not itself moral, but it is necessary for morality. A person whose powers are not trained can neither take his share in the work of the community, nor can he normally exercise direct service

[1] Cf. the very pregnant observations in ROTHE's *Ethik*, Vol. III, pp. 464–526.

to his neighbour. A man who wishes to make successful "thrusts" must first of all have learned to fence.

4. But self-directed action in solitude is not only necessary in this very indirect way, but it is needed also in a way whose connexion with an existence controlled by love will be obvious to every one. Doubtless we were quite right when we said with reference to action that there was no need to make a distinction between the act of preparation and the act of realization, since both, even if only in thought, are related directly to the Other, and to service. There is, however, another kind of action which lies midway between action and mere practice for the sake of practice, which, therefore, naturally manifests itself as a self-directed action: *self-examination*. The more this practice is related to the concrete and the actual, the more naturally it forms part of real action, as the point of clarification in the circulation of desire and action, disposition and deed; and the more "normal" it will be, even if its accomplishment is directed absolutely to the Self, and if it requires a certain amount of solitude. But where it leads to self-introspection, its value becomes questionable, and where it becomes perverted into self-dissection there already perversion, auto-eroticism, has begun. It may well be, of course, that ocasionally the simple act of self-examination which is closely connected with conduct may prove insufficient, that a deeper kind of self-examination, and one which will occupy a good deal of time, may be necessary—even to the extent of clarification by means of psycho-analysis; but this brings us to the border-line of pathology, which lies outside ethics·in the sphere of medical psychology. Every human being will reach this boundary now and again, and perhaps frequently; but that this is a boundary is shown clearly by the fact that to the extent in which it becomes independent as self-inspection it certainly lies outside the directly ethical sphere. Self-examination, which is such an "individual" business, illustrates and confirms our statement that self-directed action is only ethical to the extent in which it refers to existence in community. The most important and the most correct kind of self-examination is that which has its place in meditation and is limited to that.

Self-examination, when it turns its attention to the community once more, is called watchfulness, that is, it is the attitude of preparation and preparedness for the fight, springing out of self-examination, in view of specially weak points in one's defences. Out of it there arise good resolves, without which a life of love cannot be imagined, and this in spite of the fact that the road to hell is supposed to be "paved with good intentions." Intentions are laws which have been drawn up by the individual, which, like the law in general, can support the will in the act of decision, but which are dangerous as soon as they become independent and make it impossible to listen for the Divine Command at the actual moment.

This whole subject, with all its ramifications, deserves careful thought and fuller treatment. But to enter into these questions in detail would lead us into the sphere of pedagogy and practical exhortation which lie outside the domain of ethics.

CHAPTER XXIX

LIFE IN LOVE

1. To live the life of faith means to be in community. Community, however, means life with the Thou. From the ethical point of view the secret of faith is this: that the individual self loses its loneliness, that the "I" breaks through to the "Thou" —that the "I" which was insanely shut up within itself, and as such made the other an object for its own use, seeking to dominate the other from love of power or for its own enjoyment, is liberated, that this insane egocentricity has been healed, because the "I" has been forced open to admit the "Thou." That fellowship with God which the Word of God creates in faith is at the same time fellowship with man. The divine fellowship of faith must prove its truth and reality in the human fellowship of love. "If a man say, I love God, and hateth his brother, he is a liar."[1] If we do not hate our brother we love him, for we are always either loving or hating people. Neutrality is a form—and a terrible form—of hatred. There is no possibility of not hating save one: to love, and indeed "to love thy neighbour as thyself." This is the miracle, that the water flows upwards: no longer am "I" the central point in my life; there are now always two central points, the Self no longer merely regards life from the point of view of the "I" but also from the point of view of the "Thou." And this is no mere illusion of aesthetic sympathy, but it is a reality. It is with this reality that we must now deal in more detail.

2. In love, the other, the "Thou," is always given to me as a whole, as a personal whole; it is of the essence of love (and in this lies its difference from all other forms of relation) that it always sees the other person as a whole, and not from the point of view of one of his functions only. Indeed, we might simply define love in these terms, for love alone acts in this way. Love means regarding the other "as a whole," seeing and desiring a person as a whole. All other kinds of relation with the other are, in some way or another, partial, and therefore impersonal and neuter in character; they are connected with individual functions or aspects. A relation to an individual function of the other person—for instance, to his function of knowledge—is not love, but it is an impersonal

[1] 1 John iv. 20.

320

form of "community" in knowledge, which we must reckon
among the natural forms of community for definite purposes.[1]
But just because love always deals with the other as a whole
it is really impossible to describe it, or to outline the rules
which should govern its conduct. Law only exists where something can be isolated in an abstract manner. The more abstract,
the more impersonal the relation, the easier it is to formulate
laws. Even love itself can only be described in negative
terms, as is the case, for instance, in the hymn in praise of
love in I Corinthians xiii. Love is life itself, without all the
corruptions which cling to it in the form of sin. Therefore love
is absolutely the "eschatological possibility," the final meaning,
the final realization which, like faith, we can only speak of as
a divine miracle, which is not at our disposal. But if we want
to speak about it, nevertheless, we can only do so by
emphasizing, in an abstract way, certain elements which form
part of the other viewed as a whole. We can lay stress on the
"environment" within which we meet our "neighbour"; this
will form the subject of the following sections. Or we can lay
stress on some individual functions which stand out particularly
clearly when we meet him as a whole. We meet him as an
individual and as a being who feels his individual existence,
as one who knows and wills(1). Just as he himself, in spite of
the unity of his personality, in each of these respects is a
different person, so also love, in spite of the unity of its nature,
must be differentiated in view of each of these functions. We
repeat: love alone is the right personal relation, for it alone is
community. There are no "other virtues" alongside of love,
like justice, truthfulness, or other equally necessary and
justifiable modes of relation with others. As we have seen
already—we are commanded to meet our neighbour *only* in
love(2). Love is the unconditional will to community, and it
only appears in different forms, according as this spirit of
community is active in feeling, knowing, or willing.

3. Firstly, the "Thou" is given to us as an individually
existing person, who is conscious of his individual life. The
individuality of the other is, however, precisely that which
separates us from him, partly in so far as he is "the other,"
and then in so far as he is "different." It is true, of course,
that there does exist a natural analogy to love, namely,
natural sympathy, the divine miracle that we can "feel"
with the life of others, and, indeed, that we are drawn to feel

[1] See below, pp. 330 ff.

321

this so intensely that the life of others seems as real to us as our own. But this natural sympathy is accompanied also by an equally strong power of antipathy, and it is therefore conditional, changeable, and also—because it is determined by self-interest—partisan. Thus it is not able to overcome the feeling of strangeness which comes between me and the other person. To base an ethic upon feelings of sympathy really means to build upon the sand. This sympathy is powerless against dispositions which are "foreign" to its nature—indeed, as such it always feels them to be hostile—and still less can it accomplish anything against the separation between "me" and "thee." The natural feeling is that every one is closest to himself.

And yet sympathy has an important place within ethics, not as natural sympathy, however, but as sympathy which proceeds from love, which suffers and rejoices with the members of one Body, whose presupposition is indeed the fact of this "body."[1] Here, in particular, there appears the profound contrast between every mere rational ethic and the ethic of love. Reason may, indeed, be able in some way or another to do justice to the other in the fulfilment of his objective claims, but it is unable to identify itself with him in feeling. It despises—partly rightly and partly wrongly—mere "attraction," rightly, because of its casual nature, wrongly, in so far as attraction is an indication of real identification, real love. The relation of reason to another person may be "pure" but it is always "cold." Love, however, is both "pure" and "warm."

Love, indeed, sees the life of the other person as "my life." In faith the other person is known and recognized as a fellow-member in the Body. And as union with the uniting Head is not merely a matter of the reason but of the "heart"—the centre of the personality—so, also, is our union with our neighbour. "If one member suffers, all the members suffer with it."[2] God does not merely *respect* us, He *loves* us. Whoever through faith has a share in His will does not merely respect his neighbour, he loves him, and the characteristic sign of love, compared with the rational attitude of respect, is just this: sympathy, the purified form of the experience of feeling the other person as "a bit of myself."[3] Certainly—to recall a familiar truth—the "Christian" does not simply possess this

[1] I Cor. xii and Eph. iv. [2] I Cor. xii. 26.
[3] The allusion is to the folk-song: *Der gute Kamerad* (The Good Comrade).—TR.

love as a passive quality any more than his faith is a passive quality. This love, through faith and with faith, is at the same time always a demand. But when Kant emphasizes—and from his rational premises perfectly rightly—that it is ridiculous to demand a feeling, so also from the premisses of faith it is equally natural to *demand this feeling*; this means, however, that we have to remind ourselves that in faith this feeling, in so far as faith is living, *is* there already.

Thus, the first effect of love is to overcome natural antipathy and natural emotional indifference; for both these states are due to the fact that the "I" has cut itself off from contact with the other. It is this overcoming of natural negative feelings by positive feelings which strikes us most in the outstanding examples of Christian love; they shame us and amaze us by the universality and the intensity of their sympathy, which always carries with it a profound intuitive—one might almost say instinctive—understanding of the other from within, and identification with his individuality. This sympathy, however —like natural love—is not merely something passive, a sharing in joy and sorrow, but it is also a very powerful stimulus to action. This emotion merges into volition; the loving person desires to see the loved one happy, and desires to make him happy, and to banish his unhappiness; here once more the other is viewed as a whole—in body and soul. Genuine sympathy issues in active helpfulness.

4. Secondly, the other meets us as one who knows, and we owe him community in knowledge. Since, however, even from the point of view of the purely natural impulse, knowledge wishes to impart itself, love as community in knowledge manifests itself mainly as a readiness to receive what the other has to impart. Thus love shows itself mainly as the ability to listen. The egoist cannot listen. The rational person aims at independence in knowledge; he wants to be free from being obliged "to let people tell him things." Love willingly listens to what she is told. In saying this we do not mean that in matters which depend on rational knowledge the claim of the reason to be independent is not justified. Love accepts willingly that which *must* be imparted, that which I cannot know by my own efforts: the self-communication of the person himself, and the self-communication of the inevitable fact of the difference of his point of view. Love wishes to "see things from the other's point of view," and in order to be able to do this she needs to receive the communication from the other.

Here, too, it is a sign of lovelessness when a person thinks that he does not need to receive anything of this kind from the other. The right perspective of knowledge—the perspective of love—arises only from seeing things from the standpoint of the other, by allowing his view, which necessarily differs from my own, to have its full validity. This is the genuine tolerance of love. It cannot, however, be related to faith itself, since faith is the presupposition of this tolerance, of this perspective. Faith, in so far as it is the reality of the divine speech with me, does not share in the relativity of all that is secular and human; but *my* faith, *meum credere*, does share in it. The perception of this distinction even makes it possible to exercise tolerance in matters of faith while at the same time holding firmly to one's own convictions(3).

But I also owe the other person my knowledge, in so far as he needs it. The spirit of the miser is as bad in spiritual relationships as it is in material things. Above all I owe him the best that I have, that is, faith itself. The priesthood of all believers is already implicit in the commandment of love. I owe the other man the truth. Truthfulness is the requirement of community in the sphere of knowledge. Truthfulness does not require me to tell the other all I know; nor even all that he would like to know. For all that we know is not at our own disposal; a secret imparted to us in confidence, for instance, does not belong to us. Here, again, love, that is, the desire for the good of the other person, is the standard. A certain reticence is just as necessary for community as great frankness. Truthfulness is injured not by reticence but by lies. Lying is such a fundamental destruction of community because it falsifies speech, which is the means of establishing community, and it makes the value and the function of speech uncertain. Lying shakes the very basis of community, and makes it insecure. To lie is like poisoning the spring from which the whole village draws its water. Lying in the ethical sphere is like false coinage in the economic sphere—"security" has been made insecure—in the realm of logic it would be equivalent to destroying the law of identity. A person who sees for the first time that it is possible deliberately to use words to express something which is not in accordance with facts—that is, that what you say with your lips contradicts what you are saying in your mind—feels as though an abyss had suddenly opened at his very feet.

In spite of this, however, the command to be truthful

remains subordinate to the command to love, and this means that it is always subordinate to the free personal command of God. For the sake of love untruthfulness is lying because it destroys community. Even the law of truthfulness makes no exception to this rule, that there is "in itself" nothing good, but only that which God wills, that which creates community. Even the law of truthfulness, unconditional as its validity seems at first sight, cannot bar the way to the Divine command and cannot destroy the supremacy of love. It is possible to conceive an instance in which we might have to tell an untruth in order to obey God and to love our neighbour as ourselves. But such instances lie outside the sphere of our own control, both negatively and positively. Primarily, what makes the idea of lying in cases of necessity so dubious is the fact that it refers only to the "I" and not to the "Thou." Lying in cases of necessity means the elimination of responsibility in favour of self-preservation. But even when it is understood in its more refined "altruistic" sense—that is, when some one says what is not true in order to help another—its dubious character is not removed. The idea that we can serve others by untruthfulness cannot in itself free the actual untruthfulness from the stain of lying, since when I use speech I am never dealing simply with this one particular individual, but also with society as a whole: for all distortion of truth shakes the "security" of society. The ordinary view of lying in case of necessity, for love's sake—that is, as an imaginary instance postulated by casuistry, as a justification for lying "in such instances"—must be condemned. But in point of fact it is always possible that an exceptional case might occur—although the chances are a thousand to one against this ever taking place in the experience of any particular individual(4).

5. The most important way in which I meet the other is when I meet him as *one who wills*. For, in the main, it is the will of the other—by means of which he ranges himself alongside of me as a kind of independent centre—which menaces the centrality of my own existence. The claims of the other person on life, which conflict with my own, force themselves upon my attention, first and foremost, in the attitude of his will.

The natural will is always a *will to power*—even if this were only power over my body. The will always desires to appropriate something "outside" itself for the Self and through the Self. Therefore in the will of the other person we necessarily experience the limitation of our own endeavours after power. It is our natural sinfulness which makes us treat the other person who meets us as a piece of the external world, and thus desire to draw him into the sphere over which we exercise power. Since, however, he treats us in exactly the same way conflict is inevitable. But it is not only the conflict between the two wills which creates an ethical problem; it is also wrong to subjugate one who does not resist and treat him as an object, that is, it is wrong, for instance, to impose one's will forcibly upon an ignorant child.

From the purely utilitarian ordinary standpoint the settlement of claims to power by contract is "good"; the ethic of reason requires more than this: in accordance with its principle of the unity of reason in me and in the other man it requires the inner recognition of the other as equally entitled to the same treatment. Thus, it produces the fundamental principle of the rational law of nature, the idea of equal rights. This is the principle determining the conditions of community which is the logical result of the supreme principle of the ethic of reason: absolute respect for reason, both in myself and in the other.[1] Here community is regarded from the point of view of justice; indeed, here community is the same as justice. I and the other remain "alongside" of one another, respecting each other mutually in the one Reason. There is no closer relation between us, no fusion of souls; reason can only regard "fusion" of personalities as an intrusion into the sphere of the other person. It does not know love. Love is not the recognition of the other person as an equal, but it is identification with the other person. Love not only recognizes the claim of the other, but makes that claim her own; the truly loving person loves her neighbour as herself.

6. It is important to understand the *irrational* and *unconditional* element in this relation. Love does not only make the justifiable claim of the other person her own, she accepts the person of the other as a whole, including his evil unrighteous will. She does not affirm his evil will, it is true, but she does affirm the person of the other, including this evil will; she transforms the sphere ruled by two—I and Thou—into *one*. Love does not "resist evil"(5), she takes it upon herself, she allows herself to be wronged. Only after this process of identification has taken place—after "I" and "Thou" have become one—does love make any attempt to restrain the other from

[1] See above, pp. 297 ff.

pressing his urgent and harmful claims, or to find some way by which these claims may be adjusted; all this, however, is done in a spirit of entire freedom from a regulative conception of justice, which can only be deduced from the principle of equality. The very fact that such rigid lines of demarcation can*not* be drawn, is due to the *irrational* nature of love, which distinguishes it, fundamentally, from legalism of every kind. Love strides over all man-made barriers, brushes aside the "claims of equity," and presses forward to meet the other. This spirit which laughs at obstacles, which acts in the most uncalculated way, this spirit of amazing freedom, which dares to take all risks, and gives itself into the hands of the other without making any personal demands—what is it but the very "principle" of love?—sacrifice. Sacrifice is something transcendent so far as the rational ethic is concerned,[1] it is the realm which lies above and beyond all visible justice. Therefore—apart from the truth of Christianity—it is not an ethical idea but a religious and ritual conception, and even within Christianity it only becomes ethical through its religious source: the sacrifice of Christ is the foundation of the Christian Ethos, therefore the idea of sacrifice is its "principle."[2]

7. But this is only one aspect of love, the passive side. Love not only renounces her own security in order that she may not set her own will in opposition to the will of the other, but she desires to secure for him the perfect Good. Like the Ethos of reason she honours in the other person his higher destiny; but in this she also includes his psycho-physical needs. She does not separate his rational nature from his bodily nature, since she regards personality as a whole; she is able to unite both because in the Divine Will in Creation both the bodily nature and the eternal goal of man are posited as a unity. This faith alone gives the standard by which I know what I ought to will for the other; apart from this the relation always falls either into an abstract spirituality which is hostile to the bodily nature of man, or into a false, eudaemonistic sensuousness. One who loves does not regard the wish or the desire of the other as this standard of action; nor does he adopt an attitude of superior knowledge, and try to act as guardian to the other; he knows that his only guide is love, that love which feels with the other's need, and is aware of his eternal destiny. Love, therefore, is just as far removed from the frigid "schoolmaster" attitude of the educationalist who lays all the emphasis

[1] See Note (18), Chapter XXVII. [2] Rom. xii. 1. Cf. p. 306 above.

327

on duty, as it is from the enervating indulgence of the eudaemonistic man of the world.

In the very fact of its identification with the other love contains a negative element, something which rejects, an element of judgment; but this element of judgment is embraced by the deeper spirit of unification. In love I will the other person to be as he is, that is, as God *gives* him to me, and yet at the same time I will him to be different, as God wishes him to be. But since, before all else, God wills that *I* should be different, since, before all else, I must remember that by nature I oppose my will to that of the other, the first and also the surest sign of genuine love is my acceptance of the other person—that attitude which does not correct others, or "pull people up," or demand, or resist. For masochists are few and far between in the human race. Therefore the distinctive mark of the Christian Ethos—not merely of the Middle Ages, with its ascetic errors, but also of Primitive Christianity and of all genuine Christianity(6)—is passive love, self-sacrificing surrender—which, from the psychological point of view is the highest activity.

8. But what am I to do if these claims conflict with each other? I cannot do two exactly opposite things at the very same moment! Am I then to solve the problem with the aid of a parallelogram of forces, of an arithmetical method, or by ignoring one of the claims? or in some other way? In point of fact the doubling and multiplication of the "Thou" places us in the midst of a totally new situation; here I am no longer simply in community with my neighbour, I am in society. Real community, love, is never given to a collective body, even if this body were to consist of two people only; real community only exists between the "I" and the single "Thou." As soon as my relation to the "Thou" is disturbed by the thought of another "Thou" which makes its claim upon me, I find I am no longer in the personal sphere, in the strict sense of the word "personal," but I am in the realm of the various "orders" of human life. It should be noted that the commandments of the Sermon on the Mount never reckon with the doubling or multiplication of the "Thou," but simply with the individual. That is its "abstraction," which is necessary just in order to show the non-abstract, purely personal relation of love, in all its purity.

In reality—as we saw at an earlier stage in this book[1]—

---

[1] See above, pp. 210 ff.

we are never concerned merely with the isolated individual, but always with the "orders" as well. Wherever we meet our neighbour, in some way or another, we are also acting "officially." Likewise we never have to deal with an individual only as our "brother-man," but at the same time we also have to deal with him as a member of the historical community. Now it is evident that the way in which the Ethos of love—"community" in the true ultimate sense of the word—is broken by the presence of these forms of community, by the "orders" and their concrete demands, is due to the way in which these orders themselves are constituted with regard to the personal relation of community. The main object of the following chapters will be to examine this structure of the natural forms of community from the point of view of the Christian idea of love, in order to be able to establish both the modus and the coefficient of the refraction which love experiences within these orders.

CHAPTER XXX

THE NATURAL FORMS OF COMMUNITY

1. Hitherto we have always spoken of community in the singular. In the strict sense of the word there is only one form of community: union in love. Not only does the "Thou" here come into its own, side by side with the "I"—for that would be merely justice—but here alone does the "I" really enter into the "Thou"; here the barriers in which the Self was imprisoned are broken down and the gates are thrown open for the entrance of the "Thou." No longer does any alien element come between "I" and "Thou," no impersonal abstract "end," no natural or spiritual "interest," no Idea, no general truth, not even any secondary motive of self-interest, in any form, either on the side of the "I" or of the "Thou." All these relations, however refined and spiritual they may seem, are in the last resort self-regarding. It is always the "I" which seeks enrichment through them; the "I" makes use of the "Thou" for something—however "spiritual" this "something" may be. It is only in love that all claim to this "something" is renounced. This is the meaning of the statement that we do not love our neighbour[1] for any of his qualities but simply because he is.[2] Where this is the relation between the "I" and the "Thou" there is community, there is love. And where this relation does not exist between two persons there is no "community," but only some kind of connexion for a particular purpose.

2. But just as Nature is always full of parables of the Kingdom of God, so also the natural solidarity which exists among men is full of parables of this kind of community. In ordinary parlance, however, and in the view of the average man, the analogy is regarded as the actual reality, and the name "community" is given to its mere shadow. The very fact that the word is used in the plural, that we can speak of "communities" (i.e. forms of community), shows that we are not dealing with "community" in the strict sense of the word. We must now quickly run through the series of their possibilities, stringing them together at the same time on the thread of the idea of real community. Even in this relative sphere the distinction

---

[1] Literally "because he is *such*, but because he is there."—TR.
[2] See above, p. 306.

between personal and impersonal, between community of interest, purpose and ideas on the one hand, and community of love, or between persons, on the other, is significant and also customary.

By community of purpose or of interest I mean that kind of community which comes into being when persons are only brought together, and held together, by some objective purpose, whether it be that of a Joint Stock Company for the exploitation of a lode of potash, or a Male Voice Choir, or a Citizens' Defence Force, or a Literary Club, or an Academy of Science or of the Fine Arts. Nor do ideas create community in the strict sense of the word; ideas are as impersonal as money or as any other commonplace "purpose."

In spite of this, however, we do well to distinguish community in the sphere of ideas from that of some mere impersonal end. Though ideas may themselves be impersonal yet they have this quality: they can remove natural barriers. In the historical process ideas have formed one of the outstanding methods by which the natural barriers between individualities, classes, ranks and nations have been removed; thus although ideas do not create community, they do create an important basis for it. The "universalistic" sociology of the present day makes a great mistake in thinking that ideas create community. Ideas create powerful collective bodies, ideas are high explosive for barriers between nations (symbolized by the Great Wall of China) which separate human beings, nations, and classes. Thus even if they do not create community, since they are impersonal "spiritual things," yet in the fact that they draw men together for a common purpose they do serve as a preparation for true community. At the same time, we ought not to forget that they are also the most dangerous opponents of true community(1). Here, as elsewhere, we see the paradoxical relation between the Idea and Faith: thought is quite close to faith and yet it is far from it.

3. This double aspect becomes clear when we compare it with the "natural community between persons," for example, love between man and woman. It is here that the word "love" has its origin. From this experience, more than from any other, the truth gradually dawns upon us that we, as human beings, were never meant to lead a solitary existence, that our whole existence is framed on the assumption that our fundamental reality consists in the relation between *two* persons, and that *no* human being can ever attain fullness of

being as an isolated individual, but only through surrender to another person. Why, then, do we hesitate to speak here of real community, of real love? We do this because even this experience of love, whose eternal and absolute nature has so often been believed and sung, is, in point of fact, not absolute but limited. "Love" in this sense includes certain natural elements; if these elements disappear the sense of "community" is in danger of disappearing too. *Eros*, pleasure in the sex-emphasis of the individuality of the other, depends upon a "something." Eros exclaims: "I love you, because you are so attractive or so . . " but it cannot say, as real love (love of our neighbour) can: "I love you, simply because you *are*."

It might be more possible to say this of mother-love, the other powerful form of natural love. But gladly as we recognize that this is perhaps the nearest analogy to what is called "love" in the New Testament(2), yet it would be a false idealization of mother-love to deny that it too is limited in character. It is true, of course, that the loving mother really does say to her child: "I love you, not because you are this or that, but simply because you are you"; this is the great thing about mother-love, in which it is higher than the love between man and woman. But the mother says this only to her own child because it is *her* child; she is partisan, unjust, partial. Something more than mother-love is present where a mother treats a strange child with the same love as her own. Even mother-love is only an analogy and a foreshadowing of absolute love. Even the mother loves the child *for* "something," namely, because it is *her* child.

4. In speaking in this way about community based on ideas, and of the natural forms of personal community, we must not forget that this is an abstract way of describing isolated and extreme instances of the formation of real community. When human beings actually unite, they never do this either from an intellectual principle or for "pure love"; in such cases there are always several motives at work, so that it is difficult to define the inward character of the "community" produced by such a connexion. Therefore we must not only examine this inward aspect, but the concrete forms assumed by community themselves, in and through which this inward spirit of community may be realized. These types of community, in which human beings combine, are endless. And yet we can sum them up under a few main headings,

which will throw light on the ethical aspect of human life, in spite of the abstract terms which must be used.

These types of community fall into their natural groupings as we examine the main functions which drive the individual into community.

The fundamental type for all the rest is community between the sexes. It is the "cunning of Nature," says the student of natural science, it is "the wisdom of the Creator," says the believer, that has secured the preservation of humanity by the fact that it has combined this most important end with the strongest instinct and impulse in human nature. The propagation of the race, from the human point of view, does not occur primarily for the sake of the preservation of the race, but because man has such an urgent and clamorous sex-instinct. The fact that marriage and the family exist is based first of all upon this factor, and then also upon other factors, among which erotic love is perhaps not even the decisive one. The constitutive element in marriage and the family is: *the blood*. It is this which draws man and woman together, it is this too which, in a quite different way, binds parents and children together, and further, which makes the clan and the nation into a unity.

The second form of community arises out of the impulse to work for a living. It is, of course, true that it is possible to work alone, and above all to enjoy things alone, and possession of "things" does more than anything else to keep people apart. On the other hand, need demands co-operation and exchange, and the prospect of a fuller livelihood, and above all of a more complete security impels men and women into economic groups, societies, and clubs of all kinds. Economic life to-day is very rarely οἰκονομία in the old sense of the word, that is, a household (or house-community) sufficient to itself, as was still assumed by Luther. The economic community stands independently over against the "house," the family, and the State, and it presents ethics with its very special problems.

The third and greatest form of community, a form which still exercises a controlling influence, is the State, the national and legal community, which has grown up out of the striving to gain security for the economic and family life of a people against disturbance from without, and for stability of conditions or "peace" within. The web of motives which lead to the formation of the State and which condition the maintenance and increase of the power of the State is infinitely complicated. But the one which sets the standard for the rest, the one which is the real basis of the rest, is still the necessity of creating, by coercive means, an adjustment of all the competing spheres of will and power which cannot come to rest either in the economic or in the cultural process, and of delimiting the unity which has thus been formed by the method of power and of securing it against all other similar unities. Might and right are the two forces which set their seal upon the State.

5. While these three forms of community, because, essentially, they are based upon nature, are clearly outlined, and of great historical stability, the case is quite different with those forms of community which originate in purely intellectual impulses. The community of culture is difficult to grasp and to describe; and even the individual structures within this great group are not characteristic as forms of community. It is true, of course, that there is no "education" without a share in the "life of culture," no science without placing oneself within the "scientific process," no art without the realization of a style, which gives unity to a larger group of culture or to a greater epoch. And yet here the problem of community recedes behind the questions of the actual subjects in hand, although this state of affairs has been exaggerated far beyond its rightful proportion by the individualistic habit of mind. Finally, even culture, education, art, science, are still products of the life of the community—not of the State, but of the community of the people as a whole—and can therefore only be rightly understood from that point of view, without the necessity of depreciating the contribution made by the great individual, the genius.

Finally, the *Church*—that is, the "visible" Church, which, just because it *is* visible, must be reckoned among the natural forms of community—is in exactly the same position. Where the social character of the Church—the Church as a visible, organized body—predominates, as a rule this is not due to her own particular impulse of faith, but rather to the need for creating order, and maintaining a clear-cut distinction between herself and the world outside; in this she resembles the State. We can indeed only regard the Churches as communities based on faith. But although it is perfectly true that the real genuine fellowship of love only issues from faith, it is also true that what gives the historical Churches, as social

334

institutions, their compact character, their concrete actuality, is not so much this spiritual unity as their legal constitution. The true Church, however, which is indissolubly connected with the visible Church and yet distinguished from it, the unity which continually produces afresh real love from within herself, just as faith is continually given to her afresh—this Church does not belong to the external forms of community, but she is the presupposition for the right understanding of these forms, and she makes it possible both to criticize and to purify them; indeed this Church is the presupposition for Christian Ethics as a whole.

6. These forms of community exist; with the exception of the Church, they are all independent of faith, and of the love which flows from faith. They exist because of the psycho-physical nature of man. Their nature and their existence are recognized by means of reason, not by faith, by means of the purely natural power of cognition which is given to every man just because, and in so far as, he is a human being. In them the life of a community is achieved, before faith comes upon the scene at all. Faith finds these forms of community already present, or rather the believer finds himself and others placed within this framework. Therefore he has to come to some kind of understanding with them. How he is to do this constitutes the most difficult problem of Christian ethics, precisely because they are so foreign to the nature of faith, and because they are based upon a standard of law which is totally different from that which is known by faith. This, in itself, shows us how stupid it is to declare that this whole sphere lies outside the interest of faith. When faith is confronted with this view of the autonomy of these forms of natural community, she feels—not indifference—but a sense of the difficult and weighty problems which it raises. What should be faith's attitude towards these forms of social life?

These forms of community may indeed exist and be known apart from faith, but this does not mean that their significance and their true nature can be rightly known outside the sphere of faith. They are created by the natural psycho-physical powers of men; but this does not mean that they have been created aright, in accordance with the Divine Will. It is true, of course, that every normal man has some idea of the nature of marriage and is equipped with the natural forces which enable him to enter into the community of sex, to love a woman, to beget children, and in some way or other to educate them and bring them up. Accordingly marriage, family life, and the education of children exist outside the range of the influence of the Christian revelation. But the clear knowledge of "right" marriage, of the *right* estimate of the value of children, the *right* aim of education is not a universal possession of human reason. All who know history are aware of the extent of the revolution which Christianity has effected in this very sphere, and every one who knows the present day knows how with the disappearance of the Christian Faith there goes hand in hand the decay of the institution of marriage and chaos in the sphere of education. Therefore the most important task of a Christian ethic of society is that of throwing light upon the relation between the natural existence and understanding of the existing forms of community, and the Divine Will, perceived by faith.

7. The decisive conception which results from our previous enquiries into the definition of this relation is that of the *Divine Orders*(3). Here we must turn back to the definitions which we formulated in the second part of this work. All these existing forms of community conceal within themselves Divine orders of creation; these "orders"—in spite of the fact that in their present form (constantly changing with the fluctuations of history) they witness quite as much to human sin—and are indeed deeply influenced by sin—as to the Divine Creation—have been given by the Creator in order to make it possible to maintain human life within them as "life in community," or at least, that such "community" may be their aim. The natural forms of community are thus not merely parables, analogies of true community, but they are also the means of a divine training for community. Through them, *nolens volens*, man is placed within society, has its claims laid upon him, and is shown the meaning of true community. Again, to the believer who knows their real meaning in the creative will of God, in Christ, they are *means of service* to the community. Everywhere in the natural state of life in community he discovers an anticipation of that which faith tells him is the meaning of human life; that is, co-existence, dependence on others, and the fact that we owe our very being to others. What the natural human reason recognizes as "vitally necessary regulations," as "necessary presuppositions of our natural and psychical existence," faith regards as the ordering of the Divine Goodness in Creation, by means of which He gives us life, through which He gives us to each

other, requires us to live for one another, and thus educates us for a life in common.

The first, and the most essential point, in the attitude of the Christian towards these orders is that he should recognize these social structures produced by human, natural, and rational impulse as not merely human creations, and accordingly as human tasks, but, above all, as Divine creations and Divine gifts. Just because, and in so far as, they are gifts of God they are not merely existing facts but they are also sacred tasks. They are concrete instructions to work, given by the Creator God to the individual human being. This truth forbids us to "renounce the world"; it forbids an attitude of would-be "spiritual" indifference towards these matters of community. Through this fundamental perception the individual man is claimed by society for all its fundamental functions—not through the bare necessity to live, but through the will of God; not in self-constructed ends and delight in activity for its own sake, but in obedience to the Divine Command which is concealed within these orders. Through these orders man, while in the midst of society with its "secular" tasks, is at the same time "enclosed" in the Will of God; on the other hand, what he is doing here and now he may regard as *God's Work* (4). Only through the perception of this truth is the ascetic conception of life completely eradicated; at the same time this truth eliminates all mere "secularism" of outlook. One who, in faith, dwells within these orders, and renders service through them while he is working in *the world*, is also working *in the Kingdom of God*. This is the meaning of Luther's doctrine of the Calling,[1] which saved the world both from the dual morality of the Catholic Church and from the Utopias of the fanatics who renounced the world, and (this should be carefully noted) was also tacitly adopted by the other Reformers; as indeed this doctrine was, more or less, tacitly accepted as the Old Testament presupposition of the New Testament message.

8. This, however, is only one side of the question. It is true that the unalterable fundamental forms of these orders are the gift of the Creator and Preserver of the world; but the forms in which they appear at any given time, which is constantly changing their historically concrete form, is the

---

[1] Literally "callings and classes (or estates)" (German: *Berufe und Stände*). Cf. *The Protestant Ethic*, by MAX WEBER, Chapter III (and notes). —TR.

effect of human *sin*, and is therefore, like all that is sinful, the object of moral conflict.

Further, even in the permanent forms of these historical data there is expressed, as in all that is historical, the inherited curse of sin. This does not mean that the moral conflict is arrested, but it does mean that it reveals a boundary as final as the boundary of death. All forms of human society, not merely the State, but also marriage and the Church, irrevocably bear within themselves the inherited curse. Every one who participates in them participates in sin. All these orders are not merely under the shadow of the fleeting and the imperfect, a shadow which will only be lifted in the Kingdom of Perfection; no, they are all, also, the stern shadow of the Divine Judgment. There is no human institution which serves society which is not at the same time opposed to the Divine Law. This does not apply merely to the State; there is no pure marriage, because marriage is indissolubly connected with our tainted sex nature. It is quite easy to understand why people with sensitive consciences, aware of the sinful corruption which taints all these forms of community, feel so strongly about it that they would like to run away from them altogether. But this way out is impossible, for were we to do so we would fall into a still worse state, that is, into the radical sin of loss of community, which is also an illusion and an untruth. But in the right Christian "attitude" it is just as essential to recognize this negative element as it is to stress the positive aspect of gratitude for the world as the gift of the Creator. Indeed, where the emphasis is laid exclusively on the world as God's Creation—as, for instance, in trying to combat fanaticism—there, of necessity, the conscience tends to become insensitive to things that are utterly contrary to God's Will; the result is a kind of "quietism" which, if possible, is even worse than fanaticism.

9. What, then, is the right attitude? I would reply—gathering up the threads of my previous argument—a watchful, aggressive, determined attitude of hostility to all that is contrary to the will of God within human life; but this critical and reforming temper must always be based upon a grateful acceptance of human life, coupled with a readiness to serve wherever we may be. This attitude does not mean steering a middle course; it is not a compromise, but a paradoxical way of living which cannot be comprehended rationally; it is not the illuminating Aristotelian doctrine of the μεσότης, but

the Pauline principle of living *in* the world without being *of* it, "as those that use the world, as not abusing it, for the fashion of this world passeth away"(5); only as we learn to live in this way can we discover the Divine Command within the "framework of orders" in which our human life is set. For the Divine Command cannot be discerned by the careless spectator; it is not obvious to every passer-by. No Christian social programme "exists," yet we are called to seek for one, and to seek it constantly. It is a great mistake to declare that some particular existing "order" is "willed by God"; but it is equally pernicious to leave all these questions to "the experts," as though such matters did not concern the Christian Church or the individual Christian. We are summoned at all times to take our place humbly and gratefully in the spirit of service, within the actual social environment in which our life is placed, and in it we are to do the duties it requires as the work God has given us to do; at the same time, we are summoned to protest against the lovelessness which it contains, and to seek to realize a better order. But it is impossible to lay down once for all what it means to combine these two attitudes. All that we can do is to discover this anew in every fresh historical situation, at the particular place where our lot is cast; hence all the general ethical considerations of the Christian moralist—as he views the concrete situation—can never produce any "laws" for conduct; he can merely offer occasional suggestions.

SECTION II: THE COMMUNITY OF LIFE: MARRIAGE AND THE FAMILY

CHAPTER XXXI

THE FUNDAMENTAL PROBLEM OF MARRIAGE

1. *The Crisis of Marriage*

THE critical state of the question of marriage is to some extent a permanent phenomenon within history, in so far as at every period in history monogamy has had to contend with other forms of union between the sexes—legalized or unlegalized.[1] In particular it is a phenomenon peculiar to the history of Christianity, in so far as the strict monogamistic demand only gained universal importance through Christianity, but, if we examine matters thoroughly, we see that at no period in its history did it ever gain a final victory.[2] In the strict sense of the word, however, the crisis in marriage is a wholly new phenomenon, which only in recent decades—we might even say in the last decade—has openly challenged the moral demand of monogamous marriage, both theoretically and practically, to the very widest extent. A mere glance at any of the nineteenth-century text-books on Ethics will suffice to show that at that time this institution was scarcely regarded as a "problem" at all(1). The causes of this crisis are many and varied, internal and external: the destruction of the economic unity of the family by industrial life and the increase in the means of communication, the housing problem of our great cities, the economic, social, legal, political, and intellectual emancipation of women, the numerical surplus of women, the invention of contraceptives, and, above all, profound spiritual changes which can only be suggested by recalling the use of slogans emphasizing the claims of the individual, such as "the rights of personality," or "the freeing of the individual personality from the tutelage of collective groups." Christian society, the Church, and Christian theology would be well advised to take the problem of marriage more seriously than they have done hitherto; it is not sufficient—in a spirit

[1] Cf. WESTERMARCK: *Geschichte der menschlichen Ehe.*
[2] MARIANNE WEBER: *Ehefrau und Mutter in der Rechtsentwicklung.*

of false security(2)—to regard all the problems which are raised as the expression of a libertine spirit, and to say help-lessly: "Well, but what can we do against . . .?" Indeed, without being guilty of exaggeration, we may well maintain that the crisis in marriage presents the Christian ethic with the most serious and the most difficult problem with which a Christian ethic has to deal; indeed, in comparison with this problem even the questions of economic and political justice are of secondary importance. For not only are we here dealing with the very foundations of human existence, but here too all ethical problems are condensed into a complex at one point, so that we are compelled to say: what an ethic has to say on *this* question shows whether it is any use or not. To entrench ourselves behind any kind of tradition—even though it be most venerable—is an escape from respon-sibility. To-day we are not concerned with isolated problems but with the problem as a whole; we are not concerned merely with the question of divorce, nor with that of birth control, but with marriage itself. For it is at this point that our age has gone astray. We are challenged to give a fundamentally new interpretation of marriage, and to give a new meaning to it from the standpoint of faith(3).

Just as it is useless to appeal to tradition on this question, so also it is useless to appeal to isolated passages in the Bible. Devotees of the literalist interpretation of the Bible are par-ticularly prone to this practice, especially on this question, but such procedure reveals a very unevangelical, legalistic idea of the authority of the Bible.[1] It is true, of course, that we can regard the "law" of Scripture to be the Seventh Com-mandment, the commandment of monogamy, and the pro-hibition of adultery. But it is laid upon us as a duty not merely to say what this means, but also to reflect why this is said, and from what point of view, not in order to give a rational argument for the Scriptural commandment (to do which would mean that it had ceased to be a commandment), but indeed a *theological* argument, that is, an indication of the connexion between this commandment and the Biblical view of God and man in general. We may also demand of a theo-logical ethic that it should not make its statements as apodictic doctrines without considering whether they have any relation

[1] We might even maintain that the theological ethic of marriage is the point at which Protestant Ethics has remained either Anabaptist or Catholic, since it here applied the Sermon on the Mount as a "law."

to human reality or not, but that it should develop its doctrines in view of reality, and that means the reality of the present day. Anyone who has sought such assistance for his perplexities from the more recent Protestant ethic knows how little help or light can be gained from this quarter(4).

2. The Argument for Monogamy: The Creation

The principle of monogamy, that is, the assertion that only the marriage between one husband and one wife, an exclusive lifelong relationship, represents in the full sense of the word an ethical solution of the relation between the sexes, cannot be taken for granted. It is of course true that the view of many anthropologists that unrestricted promiscuity, or at last polygamy or polyandry, combined with widespread freedom in the relation between the sexes, was the original state of man, from the historical point of view, has been proved untenable(5), and the fact has been established that already, and even predominantly, in the most primitive stages of human development monogamy was the rule. We may also assume that it is well known that monogamy is the normal state among all civilized peoples, and that polygamy—not to mention polyandry—is exceptional; it is also well known that, apart from Christianity, the claims of monogamy have been stated in all their austerity,[1] thus that even non-Christian thinkers and moralists have tried to meet the demands of monogamy.[2] There is, however, another fact, which cannot be gainsaid, namely, that in classical antiquity the strict monogamous demand is absolutely the exception, and even in the Old Testament polygamy is regarded with complacency;[3] and that the modern man, in particular, does not take it for granted that monogamy is the only right kind of marriage, or is the only kind which can be justified(6). The *consensus gentium* or the *sensus moralis communis* here, as everywhere else, manifests itself as anything but unambiguous. The need to try to discover whether this demand (for monogamy) is based merely on the historically changeable element or upon the eternally valid element in the Christian tradition, is all the more urgent at the present time since the relative character of so many supposedly "eternal" demands has come out

---

[1] Cf. the observations on the claims of monogamy in Stoicism in PREISKER: *Christentum und Ehe in den ersten drei Jahrhunderten*, p. 13.
[2] MARIANNE WEBER: *Ehefrau und Mutter in der Rechtsentwicklung.*
[3] Cf. the article: *Ehe.* AT. by L. KÖHLER in RGG².

clearly in recent years. Another reason for examining this question very carefully lies in the actual fact that the numerical equality between the sexes—one of the strongest external supports of the claim for monogamy—threatens to break down. But where is the argument to begin?

Here, too, it is evident that to begin with the Idea of the love of our neighbour, as representing the Good as a whole, would be very inadequate. For how can we possibly argue that union between the sexes must be limited to union with one person, and that such a union must be lifelong, on the basis of the general idea of the love of our neighbour? The combination of these two heterogeneous elements, *Eros* and *Agape*,[1] sexual relationship, and responsible personal relationship, is not nearly so easy as so many wedding homilies would make it appear. What is the origin of the "monos" in the demand for "mono-gamy"? since the love of our neighbour applies to every one, and in principle the sex impulse, as a natural fact, applies to every other person of the opposite sex, and love—in the sense of *Eros*—is certainly not necessarily always directed towards *one* person?

In shaping an argument of this kind two theories are at our disposal, one is objective and collectivist in tendency, and the other individualistic and subjective; they represent the ancient and modern points of view respectively. The former starts from the natural objective purpose of sex union, the procreation and upbringing of children. From the purely physical point of view, however, possibly the propagation of the race is not achieved more securely by monogamy than by any other kind of sex relation(7). But—when the subject is regarded as a whole—as soon as the irreplaceable value of the family for the breeding and spiritual and moral education of children is perceived, then the advantage of monogamy becomes evident; for not only promiscuity and polyandry, but also polygamy, constitute a hindrance to the unity and permanence of the family, which for its part is the presupposition for the necessary continuity and uniformity of education. From the purely sociological point of view marriage has the advantage over every other kind of order—always, of course, on the presupposition of the numerical equality of the sexes(8). For

---

[1] The Frenchman is more fortunate than we German-speaking peoples at this point, for he uses three words where we only use one: *amour, affection,* and *charité.* In the following pages I use the term *Eros* in the sense of *amour-affection.*

343

instance, if for any reason the female sex were twice as large numerically as the male sex then monogamy—from the sociological point of view—would become sheer nonsense.

At the present time, however, these arguments are not greatly stressed; indeed there even exists a not ungrounded dislike of any argument which bases marriage upon this objective natural end. The feeling is that surely we ought to be able to discover a law which would be just as valid for a childless as for a fruitful marriage? Can it be right to consider that the essence of marriage, that which makes marriage marriage, actually consists only in something "outside" the state of marriage itself, in the physical results of marriage(9)? The modern theory of marriage argues, therefore, from the point of view of the subjective individualistic purpose of marriage: monogamy, and the permanent nature of the marriage bond, is the only possible union of the sexes which does justice to the personal need for full community of life. Since, however, there are other relations in which community of life is experienced, in which the fully personal character of the relation does not require its limitation to two individuals, as for instance in friendship, then the *nervus probandi* for this assertion must be sought in the nature of the sex relation as a subjective experience, or in the nature of the sex love (*Eros*) on which it is based; this, too, is the proof which is usually given by most moralists to-day in support of the claims of monogamy.[1] But it is more than questionable whether this view is really tenable. Is it really the fact that one *cannot* love more than one person at the same time? (For it still has to be proved that one *ought* to love one person only.) Is it really so illuminating and striking to assert that love to one person must inevitably weaken our love for other people? Is the Christian ethic of the present day—at the very moment when *Eros* has become aware of its infinite variety—really going to try to erect the vast structure of monogamous culture upon this frail scaffolding? *Where marriage is based on love all is lost from the very outset.* The lover cannot guarantee that his emotion of love will be either permanent or directed solely to the one person: such a marriage, because it is only possible as a hypothesis, is broken the moment it has been concluded; or rather, it never existed. Even the most honest and ardent

[1] Cf. as examples of the Christian view, the writings of V. ROHDEN: *Sexualethik*; K. ZIMMERMANN: *Not und Hilfe*, which contain much valuable material.

vow of love does not make a marriage. To base marriage on love is to build on the sand. It is this subjective individualism, more than anything else, which has caused the present crisis in marriage.

Neither the naturalistic objective argument nor the idealistic subjective argument can suffice us. The Christian Faith bases the validity of its demand for monogamy on something which lies beyond this antithesis, in a sphere where both subjective and objective are united, and based on something higher; that is, on the *Divine Order of Creation*. Even Jesus Himself, when He speaks authoritatively about marriage, appeals to this order(10). But what does this "order of creation" mean? and how are we to understand it without falling into Biblical literalism? As we have already seen,[1] every natural order (or order of creation) is an order which is given along with what is created; it is an order which, although it has been obscured by the presence of sin, and thus ignored, cannot be eliminated; it is an order of which even the "natural man" is somehow aware, even though it cannot be known as it really is, but only discloses its true meaning to faith.

Thus we have to discover—and this is the meaning of the word "order of creation"—the indication of the will of God the Creator in something which already exists, in something which is already present, apart from, and even against the will of man (in fact, in something *given*), in such a way that in that *givenness*, in that indication, faith may be able to perceive the divine order of creation, and thus discern the reason why *one* man should be united with *one* woman in wedded love. This indication is bound up with two facts; their unity can only be perceived from the point of view of faith in the Creation, so that this indication can be a "proof" to faith alone, while unbelief does not get further than a dim sense of awareness, which it can always shake off if it so desires.

The first fact is this: that every human being is irrevocably the child of one man and one woman, that every father, with this woman, and every mother, with this man, is, irrevocably, the father and the mother of this child. By this I do not mean the mere biological fact that every living creature has arisen out of an ovum fertilized by semen, but I mean something which does not take place outside the human sphere, namely, that a subject, an "existent" (*Dasein*), to use Heidegger's phrase, is united with two other subjects in this unparalleled

[1] See above, p. 210.

345

and unique manner, and not only that this *is* so, but that this "subject" *knows* it. The unique element in this human relation is this: that my existence—not my physical existence, my existence as an object, but my human existence—is thus bound up with two other existences. I, as a child, owe my life (not my physical but my human life) to these two persons. And I, as father or as mother, with this woman or with this man, have given to this person his—human—existence: I, with this woman or with this man, have taken part in the divine miracle of creation. Not a body but a real corporeal person (subject), a human being, now stands there alongside of me as that which has come into being as the result of being united with this woman. Were this being simply an *object*, once the thing was done, we could dissolve partnership and each go our own separate way. But since this being is a subject, just as I am a subject, that is, since this process lies beyond all mere causality and objectivity, since I, the father, as well as the mother and the child, know irrevocably that this fact is irrevocable, then we three persons are bound together in a way in which no other three persons have ever been bound together, in an unparalleled and indissoluble relation. The seeing eyes of all three, our mutual knowledge of one another and of this relation, holds us firmly to one another. This does not mean that we could not drift away from each other, but it does mean that should we separate we would still remain bound to one another because of our knowledge of this indestructible fact which lies at the basis of our existence. This trinity of being we call the human structure of existence. It is clear that this is not a biological fact, for—if, for instance, we think of it from the child's point of view—if the father and the mother separate, the child feels that the bottom has fallen out of his existence. He sees the irrevocable revoked; he feels, or is dimly aware, that his whole existence is clouded by falsity. Nor can the mother or the father really break away from that bond by going away; their knowledge of this fundamental bond still binds them to that trinity of being, although they may deny it over and over again.

This is the one *given* fact, which, as such, every one knows; in some way or another, every one is dimly aware of its profound significance. This fact is not the same as the far more obvious one, namely, that the child needs his father and his mother for the sake of his human development; that human "structure of existence" is independent of the actual presence or absence of children in a marriage. But this secondary empirical fact of the need of the child for maternal care and paternal guidance certainly emphasizes and accentuates this primary truth. It is not for nothing, but it forms part of the essence of human nature, that the human young need their parents so much longer and so much more than all other young in the animal creation; this obvious fact shows most clearly how contrary it is to the whole meaning of life for wedded partners to separate; this, however, is not the basal fact of the argument; it merely points in the same direction.

The second fact, which at first, as it seems, is not connected with any other, is that of human sexual love. It also contains evidence—no more, but also no less—of that "monos" which we seek. For genuine natural love is in its essence monistic. This does not mean—as modern literature shows us *ad nauseam* —that the polygamous instinct does not exist, nor that it is not particularly strong in the male; but it certainly does mean this: that, quite apart from all ethical obligations, those who love each other do feel the intrusion of a third person to be intolerably disturbing, that a strong and genuine love— still quite apart from any idea of ethical obligation—does want the loved one wholly and solely for itself. Where the emotion of love is genuine and strong, those who love each other know that this bond is permanent. It is true, of course, that the impulse towards change and variety does exist, but this does not arise out of the strength but out of the weakness of love—still quite apart from all ethical demands; for indeed we desire to seek the reason for this demand in the realm of *fact*. Even the purely natural emotion of love feels that "more than one" means a division and therefore the weakness of love. Genuine love is single-minded—indeed that is its power. Genuine love—still apart from all ethical demands— always feels: "it is with this particular person that I wish to live alone and for always." This is why love is so serious, so passionate; true lovers feel almost as though they had been thrown together by Fate. This is the theme of the romantic literature of all peoples, at all times, in which all agree, although around this theme of "love" there plays the secondary theme of the vagaries of impulse.

This love-experience itself contains a premonition of that other unique bond due to procreation, even where this connexion does not come to the surface of consciousness. These

347

two "monistic" facts, which are apparently independent of one another, become one in the idea of the divine Creation. It is *one* Creator who created both the structure of existence and also the nature of love, the one for the other. This uniqueness of love has been created by the Creator for the sake of the uniqueness of that "structure of existence"; to Him it is the means for that end; but it is not only a means—for even the Creator never makes use of human relations merely as means. It is His will that in natural love man should experience that structure of existence as a state of being bound together in responsibility, that love should find its own meaning, which is called fidelity, in this fact of being bound together—in that state of being bound together which alone secures that trinity of being as well as the full personal character of the love-relation. So long as love does not become fidelity, sex union simply means—as people rightly say—that the one "makes use" of the other, even though this may be mutual and willed by both sides; it still remains subpersonal, the enjoyment of the other, not identification with the other. It is not the *Eros*, but solely the responsibility of fidelity, which creates that bond which means that one is bound to the other person. In the idea of the Creation all those elements form a unity which outside the idea of Creation fall asunder: the indissoluble trinity of husband, wife, and child, the "monistic" element in the experience of love, and the personal character of the relation between human beings. Only where—in the recognition of the order of creation—husband and wife bind themselves together in love and know themselves bound— marriage means "binding"—has a marriage .(on its subjective as well as on its objective side) been "concluded." *One* creator it is who wills to give life to the human being through two human beings, who to this end uses the means of natural love, and who yet, neither in the one nor in the other, wills any other relation between human beings save one which at the same time is personal: who, indeed, uses this natural element in order to lead to the personal. It is the divine pedagogy of creation which teaches man to understand the meaning of the personal through the experience of love as an existence in community. In order to attain His purpose for humanity the Creator appoints first of all the strongest human impulse as the means to this end; at the same time He also gives to this impulse—as the *human* impulse, which differs from that of the animal—a tendency to strive after the personal, and founds the institution of marriage as a connexion whose meaning can only be recognized and realized through the recognition of mutual responsibility in fidelity. It is not just the desire to *be* together which creates marriage, but only the affirmation of the fact that two people *belong* to each other, and it is only this sense of belonging to one another which fulfils the deepest need of the bond of love, and lifts that sense of having been thrown together by Fate into the sphere of that which is personally free and unconditioned. From the hand of the Creator do I first receive my partner in marriage as "mine," and through this become "his" or "hers." This is the order of creation in marriage; therefore although not a Sacrament—and Protestant moralists ought finally to cease playing with this idea, which belongs to the late Catholic ethic—marriage is a sacred thing(11).

Hence from this point of view alone is it possible to perceive the evil element in sex. It is not the sex element itself which is evil or impure, but it is the severance of the sex element from personal union in fidelity, "sexuality in itself"—in which the sex nature of man is confused with that of the animals, thus in which man forgets that his nature is not only composed of sex functions but that it is also a responsible personal existence(12). The evil in the life of sex is the isolated function, which manifests its hostility to the Divine order by reducing the awful process of procreation and sexual union to a mere trifle, and by refusing to accept responsibility for "the other two." This is why the Creator has implanted shame in our nature as the guardian of the sex impulse. To the extent in which the spirit awakens the sense of shame also awakens(13); through it, however, there vibrates the consciousness that we always experience this awful thing in its distortion by evil. But shame is also evidently related to the "monos": to the fact that virginity can only exist once. Shame guards the threshold of that unique[1] experience in order that it may remain unique. By its very nature the tendency to shrink back, due to shame, can only be removed by the wedded partner's vow of fidelity.

On the other hand, it is only when marriage is understood in this way that we perceive the meaning of individual sex-attraction, namely, that the husband can only become a husband by means of the wife and the wife can only become a wife by means of the husband. This natural attraction to

[1] Literally *Einmalig*—that which can only happen *once.*—Tr.

349

one another is "intended" to show that we are meant for community. The objective meaning of sexuality—procreation —and the subjective significance of the erotic attraction—this twofold tendency to be adapted to each other becomes one, and becomes personal, in the fact that married people live for each other. "Great is the mystery,"[1] the mystery, namely, that the natural foundations of marriage are a symbol and a way of approach to true community. To experience this meaning of marriage is grace—the grace which is in Christ, whose most essential element is the status of forgiveness. And only through the experience of this community does marriage fulfil its meaning. The meaning of the divine order of creation in marriage is this: it is life in community of two persons of different sexes, a community which is complete, based upon the natural foundation of sex love, but only fulfilled in the recognition of the fact that by divine appointment they belong to each other; through whose created distinctiveness the Creator maintains the human race, and through which the sex nature of man, which is disposed for community, can and should realize its personal character. Marriage is in a special sense a proof of the Divine wisdom of the Creator, since in it the natural is so "directed" that at the same time it leads both to the personal character of intimate life in community, and to the universal purpose of the human species; at the same time, however, it only realizes its real meaning in ever-renewed responsible action. Marriage is the "school" of community, created by God, in which man can "learn" that he cannot live as an individual, but only in so far as he is bound up with the other, as also that each one of us has received his or her own life from such a connexion between two persons.

3. Marriage as it is in Reality

When we look at this question from the point of view of the Divine order of creation we see the *idea* of marriage. The reality never corresponds to this idea, any more than any real human being corresponds to the idea of man as the Image of God. Rather, just as there are only sinful human beings, there is also only sinful marriage, that is, marriage which is at the same time adultery. What Jesus has said of the lustful glance,[2] as the absolute law about adultery, makes every one of us an adulterer. "There is none that doeth good, no, not one."[3]

[1] Eph. v. 32.   [2] Matt. v. 28.   [3] Rom. iii. 12.

The *peccatum originale* manifests itself also as that "concupiscence" which has so often been stated by Catholic moralists as the source of all sin—in accordance with their ideal of virginity and the "state of perfection," which however is only one of the many forms of sin, even though one of the most crass and devastating.

People who are full of such concupiscence cannot really "keep" the seventh commandment; here the *non posse non peccare* works itself out as *non posse non moechari*. In the light of this universal sinfulness the various distinctions between "coarser and more refined sins" (in themselves quite justifiable) do not alter the facts; we shall even speak of "coarser" and "more refined" adultery, but in so doing we must bear in mind that the standard for this "coarse" or "refined" does not need in any way to agree with that of the civil legislation, but that it cannot be defined once for all in a general way. We shall be on our guard, especially within this sphere of Catholic casuistry, against following out in detail all its subtle distinctions between the more serious and the less serious sex sins, which as a rule betray a crude naturalism in the treatment of objective criteria(14).

Through this universal sinfulness of all that is called marriage, however, the moral problem of marriage is profoundly modified; all the difficult and fateful decisions connected with this question depend upon whether we recognize or ignore this fact. Here, above all, the ways of an evangelical ethic and of all legalistic systems must for ever diverge; it is at this point that the Protestant ethic is summoned to make a clean sweep of the leaven of legalism, which is still at work within it as its inheritance from Catholicism(15). As a rule it is at this point that the Church loses courage to remain true to her own fundamental convictions; here, therefore, the fact that she has fallen back into the apparently more secure legalistic solution means that she has piled up a burden of guilt on to her own shoulders, which now brings its own punishment in the reaction of lawlessness.

The first modification of the problem caused by reflection upon sin is a new definition of the purpose of marriage, which is added to the conception just mentioned; marriage as *remedium concupiscentiae*. At first sight we might think that attention to the deep corruption of sexual feeling and desire ought to work out in the opposite direction; and this is also the case in so far as the idea of redemption also includes that

351

of the elimination of all the specific sex functions and circumstances of man. "For in the resurrection they neither marry nor are given in marriage, but are as the angels of God in heaven."[1] This saying expresses very clearly the provisional character of the idea of marriage in the order of creation; its practical significance for the believer consists in the fact that it suggests that in isolated instances the duty of marriage may be overridden by some higher obligation. This question of voluntary celibacy will be discussed later on in detail, since here false solutions of immense historical importance are a burden on the ecclesiastical tradition.

But although, on the one hand, from the point of view of redemption, the questionable character of all actual human marriage becomes particularly evident, yet, on the other hand, consideration of the sinful nature of the sex instinct as it now is leads to a new and *positive* (although relative) valuation of marriage. Monogamous marriage—quite apart from what it may be as well—is the *optimum* which, as experience has proved, lies between complete asceticism and a form of sex relation which is more accommodating to the sex desire. The erotic sexual impulse which, in itself, like all that God has made, is pure and good, through sin has become one of the greatest dangers for the life of the individual as well as for that of society(16). To allow it to function freely without any restriction would mean the absolute decline of personal spiritual life and socially moralized life. That erotic Paradise which the sex impulse pictures to the imagination of man as his highest pleasure, is in reality his ruin; at the "Venusberg"[2] man, as man, perishes. Every other form of sex union save monogamy tends to make so much room for the erotic and the sexual elements by allowing so much change, that the impulse instead of being controlled is uncontrolled (or decontrolled)(17). On the other hand, asceticism is not the best way of controlling this impulse—as the superficial psychology of so many peoples and periods in history has believed—in order that it may serve the collective life of the individual and of the community instead of destroying it: for asceticism is too drastic a denial of a fundamental reality of human nature to be more than a fruitful possibility in exceptional cases; as a general and permanent demand it goes too far,

---

[1] Matt. xxii. 30.
[2] Allusion to *Tannhäuser*. Cf. BARING-GOULD's *Popular Myths of the Middle Ages.*—TR.

and completely destroys psychical and physical balance, and through the mechanism of the unconscious and of compensatory processes its effect is almost as sinister as that of unrestricted "self-expression." The order of creation which uniformly points to monogamy proves itself, even in the sinful world, and in its broken condition, the most salutary. Precisely that which erotic people regard as the fundamental fault in marriage—a certain tempering and "domestication" of the wild erotic impulse—is one of the blessings of marriage.

But in saying this we have entered the sphere of relative and comparative considerations. Now this is the second modification which the problem of marriage experiences through the consideration of sin: once it is recognized that we are all adulterers the difference between the different orders of the sex relation become relative. Who would presume to judge whether a man who in the eyes of the civil law is blameless as a married man is really less blameworthy on this account before God than another man who in the eye of the law is living in an "irregular union"? This does not mean that we are to regard these differences as devoid of meaning, and certainly their great importance must not be minimized. All we need to perceive is that these differences lie below the great line which is drawn by God's Law. We are all "below the line," for we are all adulterers, some within legitimate marriage and others outside it. Because a man does not "dissolve his marriage" in the sense in which the term is used in civil law, he cannot, on that account, pride himself on his observance of the Seventh Commandment. The civil law—the law of the State—must never be confused with the Divine Command; it has its own place, certainly, as a particular form of the *Lex* as a whole, and, as such, it is important; we are bound to take it into account, and its requirements are well within the range of human possibility; but we must always distinguish it from the absolute Divine Command. The logical results of this distinction, which has been obscured for the Christian consciousness by a legalistic type of morality, are of great significance for the particular problems connected with the question of marriage. The practical importance of the relation between the Divine Command and the Law (which we examined earlier in this book) comes out very clearly at this point.

The order of creation, the *idea of marriage*, is the Divine *law*, without which no one can perceive the concrete command of God to him in this his particular situation; but it relieves no one of the primary duty of asking: "What is the Command of God?" The Divine Command for the actual moment cannot be discovered by a process of logical casuistical deduction from the law.

It is conceivable that a case might arise in which, in order to obey the Divine Command, one might have to act "against the law." Such a case, for instance, would occur if the dissolution of a marriage had become a duty. This possibility does not exist for a legalistic casuistic ethic; to those who hold such views the question of divorce is regarded as settled in the sense that it can never be right to dissolve a marriage, under any circumstances whatever; it could *never* be commanded by God. For on this view the law is the highest court of appeal. It does not know that the knowledge of the commandment of love—and this means the knowledge of grace—in a concrete case, within the sinful reality, is able to break through what is required in a general way in the law formulated as a universal rule—for instance in the order of creation or the idea of marriage. At this point, as a rule, even the courage of the Protestant Church and its theology fails to take the "liberty of the Christian man" seriously, because it is unable to make a clear and valid distinction between this "liberty" and the "freedom of the flesh."

The Protestant ethic, it is true (in contradistinction to the ethic of Catholicism), has gradually come to recognize the possibility that under some circumstances divorce[1] may be a moral duty; but it has admitted this reluctantly, as a concession, with a conscience which is only partially satisfied, because it has not rightly seen the basis of this conviction; it has therefore isolated this case as something which is wholly unintelligible and exceptional, and it has not taken seriously the knowledge which goes with it for fear "of consequences"; till it is now obvious that this anxiety has caused far greater difficulties. Here, as I have already pointed out, we come upon one of the main reasons for the present crisis in marriage. Even in matters of marriage God is more merciful than the usual theological ethic, and to learn to know this mercy of God aright would be a surer means of defence against libertinism than the legalism which so proudly plumes itself upon its "seriousness" and its "freedom from compromise." Were

[1] Divorce is here only used as an illustration; the subject will be discussed later—p. 359.

it not for the fact that pastoral practice has at all times acted with far more insight than the official doctrine would have permitted, the disaster would have attained greater proportions, and the crisis would have supervened much earlier. It is the curse of "Christian morality" that it always regards the most legalistic view as the "most serious."

The order of creation cannot be revoked, the idea of marriage as the ethical law of God, which shows us how things ought to be, and on which irrevocably and with deep seriousness we come to grief. It is an unalterable fact that the Divine Command can only be discovered *through* this law, and not by ignoring it. The other truth, however, is equally important, namely, that the existence of this universal law relieves no one of the trouble of discovering for himself what God's Command means for *him*, and, finally, that no one can teach another person what God demands from him in this situation, not even in matters connected with marriage. For above all "orders," even above the order of creation, stands the will of God, which here and now requires nothing of me save that I should meet my neighbour in the spirit of responsible love. But no universal law can anticipate what this means in a world confused and corrupted by sin.

CHAPTER XXXII

INDIVIDUAL PROBLEMS CONNECTED
WITH MARRIAGE

1. *Marriage, Love, and Law*

AT an earlier stage in human development, when the prevailing tendency was collectivist, the problem of marriage used to be discussed mainly from the point of view of society, as a problem of law and custom; in the modern era, however, with its individualistic character, the question of marriage has been discussed mainly from the point of view of the individual. This reaction was certainly not unjustified; for the violence done to individual personalities and to the personal character of marriage by the demands of the collective institutions, was so great, that they could not but seem intolerable to a generation which had become more conscious of the individual and personal aspect of life than any previous generation. This is true chiefly, but not wholly, of woman. The polemical description of woman as a "breeding machine" is brutal, it is true, but it describes a no less brutal reality. We may be as horrified as we like by the exaggerated and audacious demands of a writer like Ellen Key and other early champions of the rights of women, and of the rights of love in marriage, and we may see through the illusions which are at the bottom of these demands; nevertheless, I suppose none of us would wish to give up any of the changes introduced by the modern movement. In theological terms, both the significance and the right of the modern movement lie in the fact that it has focused attention on the subjective and individual elements in the institution of marriage over against the objective and social aspects.

Marriage cannot be based upon "love"—it is this which modern people overlook(1); but natural love has been made an essential part of the order of marriage by the Creator Himself. It is not right to marry without this kind of love, and Calvin, who allowed a friend to find a wife for him, is certainly no example in this respect. Calvin was, of course, exceptional, and in his case it is possible to justify such matter-of-fact behaviour in view of his special task in life, but as a general rule such behaviour could only lead to confusion,

356

misery, and disaster in all marriage relations. The history of Puritanism and of Pietism confirms this statement(2). The underestimate of the individual and natural elements over against the spiritual and universal elements revenges itself just as bitterly as the opposite course. In spite of all theories, however "spiritual" they may be, marriage is primarily what most people think it is, namely: the personal concern of two human beings who love one another, who feel drawn to each other by that mysterious force of "love," and who express their feeling for each other by saying: "with you alone do I wish to be united, wholly, and for ever."

But just as there is no true marriage without this element —and to-day in particular it is a very serious matter when Christian parents try to persuade their sons and daughters to marry without this element—indeed, such behaviour is fraught with the gravest danger—so also a life-partnership which is based *only* on this subjective individual element is no marriage. Marriage is not a natural occurrence, but a moral act based upon the foundation of a natural occurrence. Marriage does not consist in the mere fact that two persons feel that they are bound to each other in love, marriage only exists where the divine order of marriage is recognized as binding in itself, and when two people know that they are bound by it. The traditional phrase, to enter into the "state" of matrimony, expresses accurately the meaning of the act. Marriage is an order and an institution, based upon the will of God, whose laws are independent of the will of those who enter into this state. The fact that *these two* particular human beings "enter" together into marriage is based upon the individual subjective fact that they have found each other through love, which in faith is understood as the guidance of God; but the fact that they do enter into matrimony means that this individual and subjective element is connected with something objectively valid, which itself binds them, and whose binding force they affirm in the very act of "entering" into matrimony.

It is true, of course, that marriage springs from love, but its stability is based not on love but on fidelity. Fidelity is the ethical element which enhances natural love, and only by its means does the natural become personal. It is therefore the only quality which can guarantee the permanence of the marriage relation. Through the marriage vows the feeling of love is absorbed into the personal will; this alone provides the

357

guarantee to the other party which justifies the venture of such a life companionship. Marriage which is based only upon love is inevitably accompanied by the fear that love may fade, and thus by fear of the dissolution of the marriage; it may even be accompanied by something still worse (which, owing to the imperfect nature of natural love, is not infrequent) —a secret reckoning on the possibility of freedom to contract another union, should this one prove unsatisfying. "Companionate marriage" or "experimental marriage" is never true marriage, because it lacks the most essential element, that is, the obligation to be faithful. For this very reason marriage is not something merely natural, but, as a divine institution, it is also something holy, whose deepest meaning can only be understood and held fast in faith. It is no accident that strict monogamy (in the sense in which it has been described in these pages) is a product of Christianity, so that with the disappearance of the Christian Faith—or indeed with the disappearance of any kind of religious belief—it is uprooted and fades away; all that is left is the unstable "love-bond" on the one hand and the State-protected institution of "civil marriage" on the other.

The purely individualistic view of marriage involves a complete misunderstanding of the public and legal aspect of marriage. The civil official becomes a ridiculous figure, the "interference" of the State is regarded as a degradation of a union founded on love(3). As a reaction from an excessive emphasis upon the legal and social aspect of the question which formed part of the older tradition, this is quite intelligible; actually, however, the severance of marriage from the system of law and custom is wholly wrong. Marriage, sex relations in general, is a matter which concerns not merely the two interested parties themselves, but the community as a whole; for it is the source of the nation's power, to watch over which is the duty of the guardians of the common weal. This is self-evident not only of the marriage which has already become fruitful,[1] but also of the potentially fruitful marriage. The nation must see to it not only that the well should not be poisoned, but also that it should not be stopped up.

It is therefore necessary that, so far as it lies within its power, the State should protect the meaning of marriage by its *law*, and society by its *customs*, by qualifying all that can

[1] Thus the English philosopher, BERTRAND RUSSELL, in his book: *Marriage and Morals.*

be grasped objectively from the point of view of the idea of marriage as good and evil, right and wrong, and surrounding it with its sanctions. This whole content of the marriage law should also be regarded very seriously by those who from a personal faith know something deeper and better about marriage, and who have laid a deeper foundation for their own marriage. For even the Christian, here as elsewhere, cannot evade the *Lex*, and even if he could he would not do so, for the sake of those who need it urgently. The Christian in particular will not regard the civil official as a superfluous or ridiculous figure, in spite of all apparent Philistinism, but will recognize in him the representative of an extremely important concern of the common weal. In his own action (or in his abstention) he will also acknowledge the laws of the State as binding upon himself, and in principle he will not refuse to accept the unwritten norms of custom; he will do all this, however, in the spirit of obedience to the Divine Command, which is the same as the commandment to love our neighbour.

Law and custom can never create a marriage; again and again the State may give the name of marriage to a union which in its inner quality is not a real marriage: nevertheless, this does not make the marriage any more real. And a true marriage cannot be annulled by the law of the State or by social custom,[1] though what I have just said indicates that the consent of the State forms part of a complete marriage. If, however, marriage is not completed in this way it may be quite as much the fault of the State as of the individual couple. Moreover the blessing of the Church upon a marriage may be, and indeed is, a sensible and significant custom; but in principle marriage, and even Christian marriage, is independent of it(4).

2. *Divorce and Celibacy*

The idea of indissolubility is an inherent element in the idea of marriage; it is based upon that irrevocable nature of the structure of existence, which is the basis of marriage in general, and is implied in the marriage vows, when they are taken seriously. Love, in the sense of *Eros*, is changeful in its very nature, like all that belongs to feeling. But fidelity, as the recognition of an objective divine bond, is essentially

[1] It is not only the recognition of the State which makes marriage valid and obligatory in the moral sense. Hamann's "marriage of conscience" was a real marriage, though incomplete.

unchangeable; or rather, it is related to that which is essentially unchangeable. We cannot "break" love, but we can break faith (or fidelity). We cannot build marriage upon love and be sure that it will stand, but we can do so upon fidelity. The vow of fidelity, which embraces all the fluctuations of love, and all the variable factors in marriage, is the backbone of marriage; in it the unconditional element of the order of creation is taken up into the personal consciousness, into a will conscious of its responsibility. Just as the structure of existence is the *a priori* of all particular experiences, and cannot be affected by their distinctive forms, so the vow of fidelity represents the constancy of the union of these two persons, independent of all fluctuations, both inward and outward. For this very reason, the bond of fidelity is quite different from the bond of love; the relation between the two may be compared with that between spirit and nature. Love and fidelity can only be identical if love is raised above the sphere of nature into the sphere of spirit. Thus it is quite wrong to base the argument for the indissolubility of marriage upon love; it is a mistake to say: "If the love is genuine, it will be permanent!" That is simply bad psychology. Of course love, as a fact of nature, means, "intends," to last for ever, but it cannot guarantee its permanence. It is of course true—and this is one of the mysteries which the Creator has set within the nature of humanity—that love may constantly be re-awakened and nourished by fidelity, in so far as the presuppositions for this are present in any measure. The spiritual, personal sense of being bound causes natural love, which is in itself unstable, to become stable; it is this, and not the rare exception of a naturally permanent inexhaustible energy of love, which is the secret of a "happy" marriage. But this is only possible where the relation between love and fidelity is rightly perceived, where marriage is based on fidelity and not on love, and, especially in a Christian ethic, this must not be overlooked: "where the natural presuppositions for it are present," that is, where marriage is entered from love. The love which is supposed "to come of itself where true Christians marry" belongs to the sphere of Christian legend. Therefore, as I have already said, it is very wrong to contract marriage without love, with the idea that "among Christians this sort of thing does not matter so much after all." Thanks to a false spirituality, in such instances, especially in Christian circles, there is a disastrous confusion between love and feelings of friendship or spiritual sympathy which confuses the whole question. This confusion of thought has caused many marriage tragedies.

For a marriage without love is a misfortune which can only be borne by those who possess great moral force, and it demands such an heroic attitude towards life that most people would feel it to be a task "beyond their strength." A marriage of this kind means such a violation of human nature (which is indeed predisposed for love in its union of bodily and psychic factors), that it is not only a misfortune, but also a constant temptation(5). For centuries "Christian morality," led astray by a false idea of chastity and an ideal of virginity, has so constantly distorted the meaning of this natural fundamental element in marriage, has so firmly tabooed this natural element as "unspiritual," and, by means of the conventions bred by such views, has trained the conscience in such untruthfulness towards oneself and towards others, that the present violent eruption of nature, so long suppressed, was bound to come one day. It is true, of course, that the Reformers—especially Luther and Zwingli—by their general feeling for truth were able to perceive the falsity of the monastic ethic in this particular,[1] and they paved the way for a more realistic and truly Biblical conception of marriage; but at this very point there set in very early a legalistic and pseudo-spiritual Puritanism and Pietism; the realism of the Reformers was lost, and neither the Enlightenment, nor Idealism, nor Romanticism were able to regain the ground which had been lost. This mistaken development, in which, on the part of Christian society, elementary rights were refused to human nature, is the main cause of the present chaos.

A marriage without love, and this means also without sex attraction, should never be contracted. If in spite of this such a marriage is contracted it bears within itself the seeds of its dissolution. It is indeed true that the spirit, especially when it can draw from the well of faith, can fight against nature, and perhaps, against nature, it may maintain the marriage; but even under the most favourable conditions a high price will be paid for this victory, and in many cases this price will be too high. For the sake of the love of our neighbour the only moral thing to do is to dissolve a marriage of this kind.

[1] MACHOLZ, in his book: *Die romantische Ehe und der lutherische Ehestand*, gives an excellent account of Luther's view of marriage contrasted with the Romantic view.

General definitions of principle will never determine when this is the only right line of action. The Christian ethic, supported by the Sermon on the Mount,[1] has always admitted definite reasons for divorce(6). That is precisely the ethically dangerous point. Neither adultery in the crude meaning of the word, nor impotence, nor sterility, nor a serious defect or crime constitutes in itself an ethical "reason for divorce." A human being of strong faith can, under some circumstances, inwardly rise above all this, and can maintain the marriage in spite of all these extraordinary burdens. On the other hand, for people of a certain delicacy of feeling some less crudely disturbing elements constitute a far more intolerable burden. The moral presuppositions of divorce, in contradistinction to the legal presuppositions, can be codified in no law. Between the maintenance of the idea of marriage as an unbreakable relation of fidelity and the command to love one's neighbour as oneself, God's Command must here be perceived in a spirit of free decision, and obedience must be achieved. Here above all the judgment of the Christian believer must shake off all the trammels of civil law: above all it must free itself from the prejudice which is based upon the confusion of thought to which we have already alluded—the view that implies that the maintenance of marriage under all circumstances is what God requires, and that divorce is forbidden by Him, so that divorce can only be considered at all as a concession to weakness. Certainly the fact of a divorce is a sign of weakness, and is a specially clear indication that we are an "adulterous generation." But cases are possible where not to divorce might be a sign of greater weakness, and might be a still greater offence against the Divine order.

In itself it is not natural for a Christian ethic to lay the emphasis on this point; in itself, in this matter its chief emphasis will be on the indissoluble character of marriage. But the legalistic misuse of the idea of marriage by the Christian ethic, custom, and ecclesiastical practice makes it necessary to-day to call attention to the other side of the question, to the moral right of the exceptional case—which indeed is not a rare exception. But it is the height of blindness and inhumanity when the Christian Church urges that the indissolubility of marriage should be made a civil legal statute(7). It cannot even be said that the Church is right when she supports the view which urges that divorce should be made as difficult as

[1] Matt. v. 32. Cf. Note (6) in this chapter.

possible; for in such cases we are not dealing with marriage in the Christian sense of the word at all, but with the question whether it is or is not possible to force people to live a nominal married life. When two people propose divorce, to all intents and purposes, in the ethical sense, the marriage is already dissolved: whether the action of the State in refusing to grant a divorce has any ethical value is a question which cannot be answered directly by "yes" or "no." The value of a "strict" marriage law, however, is all the more questionable the more it leads to untruthfulness or even to the deliberate commission of those acts which are recognized as reasons for divorce. The worth of a law is to be measured not by its "strictness" in the abstract sense, but by the wisdom with which the legislation is adjusted to reality, in order to attain a maximum of social health and decency. From this point of view it is even possible that the State may have to resolve to renounce the exclusive protection of monogamous marriage, and be compelled to extend it to sex relations which are still further removed from monogamous marriage, since, in any case, the present form of marriage can be easily dissolved. Gradually we may have to come to the conclusion that the Lindsey proposals, in so far as they are intended not as a moral, but as a legal reform, must be taken more seriously, although it is quite clear that a "companionate marriage" is no longer a marriage at all. Under certain circumstances this might be the lesser of two evils(8).

Now, however, let us return from this legal circumference of the marriage question to its centre. Once the ethical possibility of divorce within the limits indicated has been admitted —in spite of the fact that indissolubility belongs to the essence of marriage—the question of the re-marriage of divorced persons is raised afresh. It cannot be gainsaid that all second marriages contradict the character of marriage as something which can only take place once. That is true, in itself, of widows and widowers no less than of divorced persons, and every one who has refined feelings will admit (in any case at least for himself) the dubious element in a second marriage. But here also we must recognize how human sinfulness and weakness make the order relative. For in spite of our fundamental scruples, actually in most cases re-marriage is the more decent solution, and the one which corresponds more closely to the ideal, than to remain unmarried, not merely for the widowed, but also for the divorced.

Behind this judgment of the question of divorce lies the view that for the greater number of people "it is better to marry than not to marry." It is of course true that for one who in faith already belongs to the "age to come," where "they neither marry nor are given in marriage," the hope of Redemption makes it impossible to regard the order of creation: "be fruitful and multiply," as an absolutely binding command, while it would be utterly impossible to proclaim marriage as a universal duty, absolutely binding on every healthy human being. In the past, Protestantism, in its reaction against the monastic ideal, both in theory and in practice has gone too near to the other extreme of error, and has from the outset made the unmarried state ethically contemptible; but to-day the very fact of the surplus number of women, the presence of a host of involuntarily unmarried women(9), ought to warn us on no account to allow the idea of virginity to be exposed to contempt.[1] The argument for virginity which forced its way into the Christian Church at a very early stage must be described most decidedly as a serious distortion of the Biblical idea of marriage. Through Platonic Hellenistic mysticism the idea penetrated into the Early Church that the sex element, as such, is something low, and unworthy of intelligent man, an idea which, though it may be quite justifiable within Platonic Idealism, is in absolute opposition to the Biblical idea of Creation. This idea, actualized in monasticism, erected into a standard in the Catholic ideal of virginity, was not wholly overcome by the Reformation; above all it again became powerful in Puritanism and Pietism, and more or less unconsciously and secretly it has determined the thought of Christendom down to the present day. It is the sign of a terrible anti-Christian inheritance, and it has wrought infinite harm and disaster. It is due to this idea that the attitude of the average Christian to the life of sex is so unpractical and so untrue. It is the historical task of our generation resolutely to take up arms against this enemy of marriage and to carry through our campaign to the end;[2] and it is also our duty to understand (from this point of view) the exaggerations on

---

[1] On this point, in the *Symposium* edited by SIEGMUND-SCHULTZE: *Um ein neues Sexualethos*, see the opinion expressed by N. EHLEN, a Roman Catholic, and in SCHLATTER's *Ethik* the fine remarks on pp. 402 ff.

[2] May I remind the reader that this *Ethic* is written first and foremost for the Church, that is, for those who know they belong to Christ, and not for "pagans."

the other side as a comprehensible reaction against the suppression of centuries, and to take this into account, instead of placing ourselves from the very outset (as so often happens) on the side of the conservative opposition.

This idea of virginity cannot rightly be ascribed to the Apostle Paul. His higher estimate of the unmarried state is not due to the contrast between the spirit and the flesh, but wholly and entirely to his eschatology, and—if I may put it so—to his idea of vocation. As a Jew and a Pharisee Paul had from the very outset no understanding of the Hellenistic ascetic view. But the thought of the imminence of the coming Kingdom meant that in his mind the order of creation was altogether subordinate to the hope of redemption. We now see that the form of the Pauline eschatology was due to the limitations of his own day, and with it his emphasis upon the unmarried state; further, even the Reformers always pointed out that Paul desired the capacity for celibacy to be regarded as a special charisma, that is, as a state of life which no one ought to embrace of his own accord; above all, Paul never argued for a "state of perfection" on the basis of this idea of a "charisma."

The fundamental Pauline ideas—the limitation of the order of creation by the ideas of redemption and vocation—are still authoritative and inalienable, even for us. To-day in particular, in view of all this panic about sex problems, we need to summon people to reflect calmly, and to remind them that without sexuality there can be no full humanity. It is of course a false and exaggerated statement to say that only in marriage or at least through sex experience can anyone become fully human; time after time experience has disproved this statement. In particular we owe it to the unmarried women of the present day to offer them this support. On the contrary, it is they who have proved up to the hilt, over and over again, the truth of my assertion. Only the Christian Church ought to draw the logical inference from this statement, and should secure for the women to whom marriage is denied as much scope as possible in life—an attitude which, especially in Christian circles, is still the exception. How idiotic and how cruel it is to repeat constantly: "the woman's sphere is the home," or "the woman's sphere is motherhood," while holding firmly at the same time the principle of monogamy, which, from the point of numbers alone, excludes a third of the women of the present day from the vocation of motherhood. If we

are not prepared to make concessions on the subject of monogamy then there is nothing else to be done but to make it
possible for women to have a worthy substitute for this most
natural vocation of woman.[1]

At the same time, in saying this I have no desire to underestimate the difficulty of the problem raised by the existence of
so many "surplus" women, and the acute distress it causes(10).
The fact that in many countries in Europe one out of every
three women must inevitably remain unmarried (by no will
of her own) is—when we look at the question as a whole, and
not at the individual case—terribly unnatural. In this instance
woman is the victim of our social and political conditions; for
so far as birth statistics are concerned, girls only slightly out-
number boys. The natural order has here been so complicated
by human "civilization" that it makes one wonder whether
these women, to whom society has refused the fulfilment of
their natural destiny, ought not to have a right of self-
defence(11). From the point of view of the individual human
being there is not simply the "right to sex experience," or
even "the right to have a child'; for the child also has a
right to a father and a family, and sex experience is not a
good which can be severed from the responsibility which goes
with it in the natural order. But, on the other hand, where the
sexual nature of human beings is concerned, not only the
subjective impulse, but the objective need for the fulfilment
of those functions for which one is essentially fitted, is so
strong that only in rare cases can it remain unsatisfied without
causing disturbances of a physical, psychic, and even spiritual
nature.

It is most distressing to see how here, too, the law of the
"survival of the fittest" breaks down completely; indeed to-
day it seems rather to be a law that the "fittest" are the special
victims of these unnatural circumstances. But, as soon as we
examine more closely any one of the proposed "solutions"
which are based on the natural law of self-defence, it is obvious
that they are useless. For, to name only one of the most
important—the more that the girls of the present day who
would like to marry but cannot, allow themselves to be drawn
into "free relationships" in order to get sex experience in
some way or another, the less stimulus will there be for the
men to marry; this will inevitably increase the number of

[1] It should be noted that the so-called "specifically feminine callings"
such as nursing and social work, would only meet a fraction of this need.

women who are forced to remain unmarried, and thus the need which has to be remedied will be greater still. On the other hand, it ought to be said that the more decidedly and unmistakably our younger female generation refuses this possibility of a substitute, the smaller will be the number of men to whom this alternative to marriage will be offered, and thus the greater will be the chance of marriage for the individual girl(12). Further, the *main* cause of the surplus number of women must be sought in our social and political conditions, hence the real difficulty will not be removed until there is a definite improvement in the social and political situation.

3. *Marriage and Children*(13)

The sexual nature of humanity can only be understood and rightly estimated from the point of view of the order of creation, that is, in connexion with the question of marriage as a whole. In this sphere every attempt to isolate a particular function is bad, as we have already proved, indeed it is the worst thing that can happen in this respect. Sexual intercourse and procreation are essentially united in the order of creation. Deliberate sterility within the state of marriage is a fundamental contradiction of the meaning of marriage. By this, however, I do not mean, as Christian morality has always been so eager to proclaim, that sexual intercourse is *simply* for the sake of procreation, and must take place *solely* for that purpose. Anyone who thinks at all realistically must immediately perceive to what ridiculous consequences this principle would lead. Necessary connexion and identity are not the same thing. Sexual intercourse is intended by the Creator not only as a means of procreation but also as a means of expressing the love of married people for one another. The very fact that the human need for sex expression is not limited to definitely short periods[1] but is a permanent need, indicates that this, as a characteristic element of human life, is *intended* by the Creator. This again is one of the points at which the conventional Christian ethic, still secretly influenced by the monastic ascetic point of view, has sinned against nature and has inflicted a serious injury upon humanity. To the scandal of all ascetics the New Testament nowhere explicitly bases sexual intercourse upon procreation, but always upon the natural impulse, and therefore it never erects those barriers which are the necessary result of the semi-ascetic point of view. On the contrary—it

[1] Cf. Note (13), Chapter XXXI.

is the Apostle Paul in particular—the supposed representative of ascetic views—who warns Christians expressly against such limitations as a wile of Satan,[1] and is thus in this absolutely in agreement with the views of Judaism(14). The Reformers, too, on the basis of their natural and realistic conception of marriage, held this view. Here too, however, both Puritanism and Pietism broke away from the tradition of the Reformers, and laid renewed emphasis upon Catholic views; indeed, we may even say—at least so far as theory is concerned—that they have brought these views into almost universal acceptance within the Church. If we are ever to master the rebellious uprising of all those natural instincts which have so long been repressed, we must resist this dangerous perversion of truth with all our might; this view is indeed all the more dangerous because it enforces its appeal by the claim to represent all that is most serious and most sacred in the Christian Faith. The Christian ethic must stand for the independent meaning of the erotic and sex element within marriage as an expression of love, not merely as a means of procreation(15). This does not contradict in any way what has been said about the necessary connexion between sexual intercourse and procreation; it only sets it in the right light.

It is an essential part of marriage that it should be fruitful(16). But this does not mean that a true marriage must be *unrestrictedly* fruitful(17). Once more we are here confronted by a prejudice which is widespread in Church circles: namely, that in this matter everything should be left to chance, which will be accepted without question as the Providence of God. Here, in the most important act of which men are capable, reason, reflection, responsible consideration, are to be eliminated; here the supremacy of accident is to be regarded as reverence for Divine Providence, and responsible determination is to be tabooed as an unwarrantable interference with the Divine administration of the Almighty.[2] Theoretically this sort of argument still plays a great part—mainly in theological circles. Practically, however, the passionate defenders of this theory rarely take it quite seriously; for even among them it is a well-known fact that the marriages which are blessed with ten or more children are no longer so frequent as they used to be. Birth control, that is, the use of responsible reflection,

---

[1] 1 Cor. vii. 5.
[2] Cf. the address by the former State-president of Baden, HELLPACH, on *Familie und Volk*.

I regard as a self-evident duty for married people, in spite of the fact that here too, as everywhere else, rational interference with the process of nature brings its special dangers. But those who wish to avoid these dangers must logically renounce any kind of culture.

Thus birth control has been practised from time immemorial, even in Christian families; the fact itself is not new, it is only the name we give to it to-day which is new, and of course certain methods are new. It may indeed be thought—and observations among people on a more primitive scale of culture seem to suggest this—that through the rhythm of the procreation, birth, and suckling of infants the Creator has implanted in man's constitution a purely natural mechanism of control, in order to check excessive fertility. This mechanism seems to be out of order owing to a certain physical degeneration. Whether this be the case or not, at any rate our present civilized life makes it a duty to help ourselves to a large extent, and this must be done by the use of "artificial" or "unnatural" means.

Almost everywhere the noblest method of birth control is held to be that of asceticism within marriage. If an effort which costs people something is the measure of its ethical value then every one will agree with this judgment. For if even monastic asceticism is difficult, it will be quite obvious that asceticism, that is, the living together of married people as monk and nun, must be still more difficult. It is indubitable that even this is not beyond the power of the human will; experience proves it. But this certainly does not mean that this way is the noblest, and actually the best. In any case a person who argues in this way has no right to appeal to the Bible, for the Bible absolutely contradicts him.[1] On our part, however, we must take care we do not suddenly slip into a mistaken literalism in our appeal to the Bible; here, too, we must remain faithful to the line of theological argument. Asceticism within the marriage state *may* be a way; but it means terrible repression, which is dangerous both for body and soul; it contradicts the saying: "What therefore God hath joined together, let not man put asunder." In spite of all this, since every other way is unnatural, in some way or another, let us also recognize this way, and let us prize it highly on account of the individual heroism which it requires. But we cannot see in it the "highest path"(18).

[1] 1 Cor. vii. 5.

"What then?" Earnest Christians have at all times asked themselves this question. No one has so far been able to find a satisfying answer. And yet, conscientiously, and so far as their knowledge extended, people have searched for this way long before contraceptives were known. Their use will be neither better nor worse than the older and more primitive methods, including those recently approved by the highest Catholic authorities(19), an admission which reveals painfully clearly the inward untruthfulness of Catholic legalism.

Under all circumstances we must fight against that hypocrisy in these matters which always acts as though the point at issue were the preservation of sacred principles, whereas, if we examine the ideas of the defenders of the traditional view more narrowly, we find that usually it is simply a question of difference in method. Certainly, all normal people will feel most acutely that in this respect we are living "unnaturally," for the natural order has been disturbed. But, whether as husband or as wife, he or she may twist and turn as they will, both will find that no amount of twisting and turning will release them from participation in this disturbed natural order, both passively and actively, however conscientious they may be. There is no "solution" of the problem along any of the possible lines: neither through leaving all to chance, nor through birth control, nor by control through asceticism, nor in any other way. Here, therefore, there is no general rule; but for that very reason in principle there should be no taboo on certain methods which, although they are new, and—like the other methods—have their own peculiar dangers, are being used.by many people in a spirit of strict responsibility towards God, and when necessary, towards men.

At the present day we can no longer allow natural fertility to take its course, as was the case usually, though not always, at an earlier stage in history;[1] and indeed it is not only negative factors which make this necessary. In addition to lack of space and the costliness of life in cities, there are two other elements about which we can only be glad: the immense decrease in infant mortality(20), and the incomparably higher estimate of the life of women. For the expression "birth control," imported from America, a German woman has found

---

[1] That birth control is no new phenomenon, but that it has always been practised, even in Christian circles, is demonstrated in the article on the *Bevölkerungsfrage* by JULIUS WOLF in the *Handwörterbuch der Soziologie*, pp. 52 ff.

a better substitute in the beautiful phrase "responsible mother-hood." The woman of the present day does not desire to have a child haphazardly, simply because she happens to be married; no, she desires to have a child when she is ready, and because she is ready for it. Any clergyman or social worker who knows the misery connected with the idea of the unwanted child, will be able to appreciate the change of outlook in the individual and in society which is implied in this phrase. The husband also has learnt to respect this right of the wife to have children when she is ready both inwardly and outwardly, instead of whenever the sex impulse of the husband demands. Certainly the indolence and love of pleasure of so many married people, who use the new technical inventions in order to avoid having children at all, without giving up any sex enjoyment, constitutes a serious and increasing danger; but is it really more serious than the unchecked, unplanned fertility of previous centuries? In these days, when people are so often herded together in such appalling numbers, can we really think that depopulation is one of the greatest and most pressing dangers which menace our civilization?(21) I do not venture to express a judgment on this question, but I also dare not refrain from raising it.

4. *Marriage and the Economic Question*

From time immemorial community in marriage also meant an economic community: the family, "the household"—as indeed the Greek word οἰκο-νομία suggests, *economy*—the living cell of the national economy. Indeed, as a rule, this economic factor was absolutely the central point for the contract of marriage and for the stability of marriage, even during the history of the Christian era, down to very recent times. For the wife in particular, marriage—that is, the "household"—also included the whole of her vocational economic activity. This combination of two utterly dissimilar elements is to-day being rapidly dissolved, indeed to a large extent it has already disappeared. In the first place, the industrial development forced the husband to be "out of the house" more than ever, while it also restricted the wife's sphere of activity. It is only the peasant woman who still has a real "domestic sphere," but even she has far less scope than formerly. For all other women the "economy" has become emptier and emptier, till it has often almost faded into nothing. All that used to be made at home can now be bought more cheaply as a factory

371

product, and the work of the house, already thus reduced, has been simplified still further by the use of labour-saving contrivances. To many women, therefore, the watchword: "the sphere of the woman is the home," would mean being condemned to unwilling inactivity, all the more since the children, owing to compulsory education by the State, are away from the house for the greater part of the day. Thus it was not *only* a misfortune that the economic development also drew the woman out of the home into industrial and commercial pursuits. But this process, which was due not to refined methods of educating the people, but to brutal economic laws, has now almost dealt a death-blow to the economic unity of the home; at the same time, however, it has also attacked the very basis of marriage. Although community in marriage does not necessarily require economic unity, it does require, unconditionally, a real living together. And even this life together is to a large extent reduced to a minimum by the merciless demands of industry, and under specially unfavourable conditions it approaches zero. Where the wife is out at work all day and the husband is out at work all night (as a shift-worker), at the most the only time left for community in marriage is the brief week-end.[1]

But there is yet another way in which the economic question intensifies the problem of marriage. The traditional view that the husband must be able to support the family, makes it impossible for many young people to marry when they are at the right age for marriage(22). The increase in "free relationships" is often based purely upon economic reasons. It is, of course, true that one may reply that here it is not economic necessities but the exaggerated demands of the present younger generation which is the cause of the evil; but even when all such cases have been allowed for, there are still sufficient left, where nothing save the absolute impossibility of managing on the income of the young husband alone prevents the founding of a "household" of their own. Here, therefore, the Christian ethic must learn new ways, and the traditional confusion between marriage and economic unity must give way to the elementary requirement, even to the point that possibly at the beginning one must envisage a deliberately childless marriage. In actual practice this has been done for a long time, but wherever religious and ethical

[1] Cf. the excellent article by H. WAGNER: *Gestaltwandel der Ehe*, in the *Zeitwende*, 1931.

ideas have still been operative it has been done with a bad conscience, because the teaching and preaching of the Church usually describes this solution as non-moral. What the Church achieves is this: involuntarily, but compulsorily, it encourages the disorder of "free relationships." But whence does the Church derive its right to lecture a young man who contracts a marriage on this basis because he loves his girl, but loathes a "free relationship," and yet is not in a position to maintain a family on his income? Certainly it is an incomplete marriage, but is it not perhaps the most conscientious solution of this individual problem?

On the other hand, however, modern society should be told very plainly and forcibly, that the only real reason for celibacy and childlessness is often the extravagant tastes and the love of pleasure which characterize so many young people of the present day. Economic greed has destroyed the meaning of marriage, and has also undermined its happiness.

It is probable that we shall have to deal with a still more far-reaching separation between economics and marriage. This will be a hard test for marriage; but it will also free it from a burden, and will allow its real meaning to emerge more clearly. For the combination of marriage and economics, although it is very natural as the realization of complete life unity, has often obscured the meaning of community in marriage, and has turned marriage into a merely business arrangement. In any case, this development will have to prove, and indeed, will be able to prove, that true and complete marriage is possible without the traditional economic community, although on the other hand it would certainly be more natural and more healthy to be able to combine these two elements.

5. *The Emancipation of Woman, and the Relations between the Sexes apart from Marriage*

The question of the relation of the sexes to each other is wider than that of sex community; it is in no sense an accident that we think of this mainly as the "Woman's Question." For until recently woman has rightly felt that her sex individuality has defrauded her of her human rights and possibilities of development, and therefore she strives for release from these fetters which have been laid upon her in the course of her historical development. Whoever knows the story of the lot of woman, and—let no one deceive himself about this— the conditions of serfdom which woman still endures, will be

373

forced to regard the modern movement for the freedom of woman as one of the most significant facts of recent history. Like all movements which aim at liberation this movement has often assumed objectionable and dangerous forms; but this does not alter the fact that, as a whole, it was and is both necessary and beneficial. In any case it obliges us to reformulate the significance of sex-individuality. Here also the twofold standpoint of Creation and Redemption will be authoritative, and will show us the right direction.

God has created two kinds of human beings, male and female. What does this mean for moral existence apart from community between the sexes in marriage? At times the Church has over-estimated the significance of the difference between the sexes to such an extent that at a certain synod it was debated with all seriousness whether woman had an immortal soul as well as man. On the other hand the modern Woman's Movement has under-estimated the significance of this difference to such an extent that it has even denied that it has any influence at all upon ethical existence. The New Testament takes the sex difference seriously in so far as it recognizes it as a definite natural order; at the same time, in its view of the eternal destiny of humanity the New Testament transcends this difference entirely. We find no trace—not the faintest—in the Scriptures of the idea that in our relation to God there is any difference at all between the two sexes—as even Kierkegaard asserts there is;[1] even though there may be no feminine apostles and Church leaders, yet in the community of believers the woman is absolutely equal with the man; experience also confirms the truth that if there is any difference, it consists, at the most, in the fact that woman has a stronger natural affinity to religion than man.

Woman is not only physically different from man, she is also different in soul and spirit; and indeed in such a way that the physical difference—speaking generally—symbolizes the difference in soul and spirit. First of all there is the obvious fact that the feminine nature is receptive rather than productive, that it is directed inwards rather than outwards, that it is quietly retentive rather than enquiring, more inclined to nurture than to generate, more given to tend than to initiate. But whereas *every* woman possesses the physical nature of woman as an absolute distinction, this law of the mental and spiritual peculiarity of woman is not at all absolute.

[1] *Krankheit zum Tode*, p. 250.

374

There are women—and what women they are!—who possess outstanding "masculine" gifts and tendencies. This means that the mental and spiritual differentiation is not so uniform and so penetrating as the physical differentiation. Further, the advocates of the woman's cause lay emphasis on the fact, and rightly, that a certain peculiarity of woman has been either deliberately or artificially bred by their exclusion from certain spheres of the active intellectual life, and by their artificial inclusion in other spheres. How far the mental and spiritual character of woman has really been determined by this it is difficult to say; but it is quite certain that her own understanding of herself, her own estimate of herself, has been most profoundly affected by this fact. What the nature of woman is, and what latent possibilities it contains, no one can say at the present time with any kind of certainty, and it is probable that the thought of our descendants on this matter will be rather different from that which ecclesiastical moralists, in particular, are so sure they know at the present time.

In spite of all this it is certain that the Creator who has created body and soul as a unity, has also created the mental and spiritual nature of woman different from that of the man; this means that woman's sphere of activity is intended to be definitely different from that of man. So long as it is only women and not men who bear children, and nurse them, so long also the domain of woman will be essentially different from that of man.

From the point of view of Creation sex individuality, like all other forms of individuality, is not to be regarded as a mere limitation, but above all as a divinely bestowed treasure. Woman may and should know that the fact of her womanhood offers quite specific possibilities of existence and of service. She should be proud of her distinctive quality, especially in view of the various disadvantages and difficulties which it brings with it. Obviously it is superfluous to impress the corresponding consideration upon the lords of creation, since they are already very full of the sense of the excellence of their own sex. At the same time, for this, as for every kind of individuality, it is true that it is not merely the gift of the Creator but also the product of sin. Woman therefore has to fight against false conceptions of womanhood, just as man has to fight against false conceptions of manhood. It is at this point also that the Emancipation Movement rightly intervenes. Woman has every reason to believe that the present individuali-

375

zation and differentiation of sphere, "hallowed" as it may appear to be by centuries of tradition, has much more to do with masculine violence and with feminine weakness and indolence than with the Divine order of creation.

This is why it is absolutely impossible to put down in black and white, as a universal rule, which spheres of activity "belong" to woman and which do not. This can only become clear through experience, and for this experience first of all the field must be thrown open. This demand applies first of all to the individual. At the same time, however, society also must see to it that the difference between the sexes is not levelled up to such an extent that the greatest and most fruitful tension of human life becomes paralysed, and this simply from temporary utilitarian or rational grounds, which may appear to be practically necessary, but in reality are a shortsighted way of achieving "equality." The criterion of the genuine emancipation movement must always be this, that sex difference—in the broadest sense of the word—is not removed but is fully emphasized. For this is the effect of all spiritual development: that it intensifies the individuality and does not remove it.

The natural sphere of woman is first of all motherhood and the family. It is in the order of creation that motherhood should determine the life of woman in a quite different way from the way in which fatherhood determines the life of man. If the woman feels herself first of all cramped by this fact, it is because—apart from really unnecessary and therefore unjustifiable narrowness—she has a false conception of a "valuable" or "spiritual" existence. A woman who gives herself with her whole soul to the education of her children has a far more real spiritual life than a woman who evades the claims of the family in order to give herself to all kinds of aesthetic and "social" work. Our own generation, with its fatal belief in abstraction, scarcely ever pauses to reflect that intensive labour for the germ-cell of the social organism, the family, means far more than any co-operation in abstract social movements. We ought to be on our guard against the falsely abstract impersonal conception of spiritual life and social life from which even to-day the Woman's Movement is not free.

On the other hand, however, it is a sign of incredible lack of contact with the life of the world at the present time to continue to insist that the solution of the problem is contained in the slogan "The Woman's Sphere is the Home!" For, in

376

the first place, a third of all the women who are available for marriage have no "home" at all in this sense of the word, a home to which they are supposed to belong, in spite of the fact that they would like to possess one very much. And in the second place, even the woman who has a home finds that owing to the effects of modern economic conditions on the domestic sphere she is obliged to seek some way of compensation, even when she is not forced, almost against her will, and to a degree which is not good for the home, to find this compensation in the economic sphere.

Woman in economic life, woman in public life, in any case, whether we like it or detest it, this is a fact with which we have to reckon for a certain space of time, and probably in the near future we shall have to reckon with it far more than at present, without anyone being able to alter things. We cannot reverse the wheel of history; the modern technique of production, of communications and of consumption cannot be ousted or even only reduced in favour of any approximation to patriarchal conditions. In this economic order as a whole, in this economic world which has become completely non-domestic and wholly impersonal, abstract and non-organic, woman has her own place, and probably will have for a long time to come, a place moreover which cannot be given up either from the standpoint of economics, or from the standpoint of the home. We do indeed hope for the time when this artificially abstract, non-organic character of the economic order, which is such a bad soil for the growth of the ethical life, will be, at least in part, overcome. But to make this upheaval the subject of ethical consideration would be sheer phantasy.

Once woman has become a member of the abstract life of the economic order, and once she has become part of the political life which by a process of reflex influence is bound up with it, then the logical consequences must be deduced, and woman must be granted the rights which correspond to her duties. It is a monstrous injustice to expect from economically independent women the fulfilment of exactly the same civil duties as those expected from men, and yet to withhold from them the same civil rights. Every intelligent decent person to-day ought to know that the military service performed by the man is more than balanced by child-bearing on the part of the woman.

The new conditions have also profoundly altered the social

377

relations between man and woman. The old custom, which was based on a widespread segregation of the sexes from each other, which however actually formed an effective protection for marriage, has all but entirely broken down. Men and women form their mutual relationships in the way that they themselves consider right and good; the pressure of public opinion is still present, it is true, but it is obviously declining. Protective custom is only possible in a community where the authorities can keep an eye on all that is happening; in great cities at least, such conditions no longer exist. Ancient custom, which surrounded girls and women with its protection, has lost both its internal and its external force; the double standard of morality which permitted or at least condoned in the man that which exposed the woman to the bitterest humiliation, scarcely exists any longer, and the invention of contraceptives has torn down the last barriers. All this has vastly intensified the problem. All the external supports of monogamy from this point of view have collapsed; almost all that remains is the sense of personal responsibility. At the same time, however, the problem has been reformulated. Even when we glance at the past we see how variable—even among earnest Christians—are the views of what is fitting between men and women. Things about which only yesterday there used to be a loud outcry, against which there was directed all the energy of moral propaganda, are to-day accepted as quite natural and harmless. Morality does not always break down at the point proclaimed by the puritanical, and only too often the Church has made the mistake of simply siding with the defenders of the old order against the growth of newer and perhaps better customs. In this question of freer relations between the sexes it is no trifling matter to extract the kernel of the genuine Christian ethos from the husk of outworn *bourgeois* tradition, and from the shell of a cramping ascetic legalism; on the other hand there is grave danger that here as elsewhere irresponsible individualism may gain the upper hand, and the corresponding responsibility of the Christian Church and the Christian family is serious and weighty. But all these questions are in such a state of flux that the moralist can scarcely do more at the moment than indicate the various points of view in order to warn us against attempting shortsighted solutions in either direction.

The whole situation, which has been wholly transformed by the Woman's Movement, has a reflex influence upon

378

marriage itself. "Christian marriage" has been confused with a patriarchal attitude towards marriage which has no connexion with genuine fundamental Christian principles, but is the product of definite historical conditions and accidental views. The attitude of the man who boasts that "I-am-master-in-my-own-house," which many Christian husbands regard as a mark of genuine Christian piety (and even some Christian wives), can scarcely be deduced from the Divine order in creation; it is quite evident that it springs simply from the egoistical sense of power of the stronger sex, and we may as well admit that certain expressions used by the Apostle Paul are to be regarded as due not to his faith in Christ, but to this peculiar patriarchal view, which was generally accepted in antiquity. We ought not to forget that in the Old Testament the wife is generally regarded as the property of the husband, and that the Jew was taught by his religion not only that woman was different from man but that she was of far less value. To-day we no longer believe that woman is worth less than man, and thus the man's right to act as guardian to the woman has also disappeared. At the present day we cannot even speak about woman as Luther used to do; the present greater respect for the spiritual independence and equality of women is an undoubted gain which has been brought to us by modern cultural development—as for instance in the Romantic movement and the Woman's Movement.

These changes have certainly not made the problem of marriage any simpler, indeed they have made it more difficult; at the same time marriage has gained new possibilities which make the difficulties worth while. On the one hand, the serf position[1] of the wife made married life easier to manage; on the other hand, it certainly made it much more miserable than it is to-day. A true marriage is only possible where the wife is in every way equal to the husband in independence and responsibility. There can be no going back on this development; a woman who drives her own car, and who is empowered by the new legislation to administer her own income independently, can no longer be treated as women used to be treated by their lords and masters; and this is all to the good. Certainly the unity of the management of the family is endangered by this at first, and this introduces into married life an element of danger which should not be taken lightly. But this difficulty is not insuperable.

[1] Still plainly indicated in our abominable German word *das Weib*.

379

Just as it is clear that the wife is a spiritually responsible personality in exactly the same way as her husband, so also it is clear that in the order of creation sex individuality means that the husband's functions in the family differ from those of the wife; and normally the external guidance of family life belongs to the husband. Jeremias Gotthelf, in some of his splendid masculine and feminine peasant characters, succeeded in showing in lifelike, convincing pictures this blend of the impressive independence and responsible authority of the wife, coupled with a self-evident subordination to the "political" guidance of the household as a whole by the husband. The family is the last place in which to make formal democratic experiments. But where there is genuine love, in the double sense of *Eros* and *Agape*, there also will there be a "monarchy" which will arise of itself from the instinct which recognizes the boundaries set by individuality, and all this without any injury to the sense of independence and personal equality. The order of creation of inequality between man and woman is here limited by the knowledge that Redemption has removed this inequality and transcends it; the husband will not insist on his "rights" as leader, and the wife will quietly and willingly concede them to him (that is, so far as the husband does not put himself actually in the wrong), indeed she will even secretly encourage her husband to exercise these rights; even the "emancipated" woman will do this, in so far as she has remained a woman.

* * * * *

Marriage is not only something specially sacred, but it is also a very great gift of the Creator to His human children, and it is one of His most glorious works. According to its original meaning, it blends the natural and the spiritual, the gift and the task, into a harmony not known elsewhere. Especially is it an excellent method of Divine education, in order to bring home to self-seeking man, in his self-seeking, the truth that he can only find his true life not in self-seeking, but in receiving and in giving, in responsible union with the "Thou." Anyone who has ever experienced real marriage can never cease to marvel at the wonders of the Divine wisdom, by means of which the Creator entices man out of the solitude of the "I" into a life of partnership and mutual obligation, through which he gives, in order that he may make demands, and makes demands, in order that he may give. In married life opportunities are given to us which we could have nowhere else, possibilities of service and of experience, of work in common and of growth in independence, of active receptivity and creative sharing, of limitation and of expansion, of repose and of stimulation to work. Indeed it is not an unfortunate accident, but—it is at least also—a deep mystery, that the most beautiful word in our language, *love*, here reveals the ground of its dual meaning: the union of the natural with the spiritual intended by the Creator, the fulfilment of our deepest human longing in that which lies beyond the human sphere. It is of this mystery that the Apostle speaks, of this analogy of the highest, expressed in terms of marriage, in that phrase which, owing to a misunderstanding, has led men to claim marriage as a "sacrament." It is not a sacrament, for it does not belong to the sphere of the "Church," but to that of Creation. But it is a parable which bears witness, and it is able to bear witness because it is the creation of the same God who calls us into the Church by His Word.

In the question of marriage we see particularly clearly why and to what extent there is and there must be a "Christian" ethos and a "Christian" ethic. Marriage is, of course, something "secular" and "natural," which takes place wherever human beings live as human beings, and there is a sense in which every one understands it. And yet deeper reflection and also historical experience show that the true nature of marriage is only disclosed to faith. It is not presumptuous and it is not dogmatic to speak of "Christian marriage" as the truest form of the idea of marriage, not only in the sense that marriage is most perfectly realized within the sphere of Christianity, but also in the sense that here both its significance and its nature have been more clearly perceived. And this connexion with the Christian Faith is more necessary than ever to-day: for the old religions, which, in some way or another, were always the guardians of this sacred institution, have passed away, and purely secular sentiment—arid rationalism—is utterly unable to perceive the meaning of marriage, or, of itself, to solve the problems of marriage.

There is scarcely any other sphere of life in which the connexion between faith and the ordering of life can be seen so clearly as in married life. In countless variety, experience shows that wherever faith is really living, difficulties of married life are overcome, difficulties which are the rocks on which otherwise so many marriages are shipwrecked. How could it be otherwise, since service and mutual forbearance with each other's weaknesses are the meaning and the strength of marriage? How could men reach this idea of the meaning of life apart from the knowledge of Christ? How could one learn the secret of marriage, which consists not in making demands on the other but in finding true happiness in meeting the wishes of the other, without that revelation which reaches its zenith in the saying that "the Son of Man came to serve and to give His life a ransom for many"? Even the meaning of the Law can only be perceived from the point of view of the Gospel, for the meaning of the law is love, which is itself above all law.

But marriage is also an illustration of the fact that truths which are derived from the Christian Faith are operative, and can grow, even outside the Church, outside the circle of those who believe, and thence can even have a reflex influence on the Church itself. The crisis in marriage of the present time is not only the product of godless errors, it is also a product of ideas which sprang out of Primitive Christianity and have grown up outside the Church; these ideas are now ranging themselves against a commonplace and conventionalized "Christian" idea of marriage, and against a "Christian" practice of marriage. All of them, not only Idealism and Romanticism, but even Naturalism and Communism, in their criticism of marriage, and in their claims on behalf of marriage, contain elements of truth which are indeed contained in the Biblical idea of marriage, but which have been neglected or suppressed by Christianity. Hence it is very perverse and irresponsible to estimate the crisis in marriage purely from the negative point of view, instead of hearing in it the Divine Judgment.

Only in the deepest reflection of faith can the truth of marriage be rediscovered; only by the renewal of faith can the energies be released by which the crisis in marriage can be overcome. But this does not mean that the Christian Faith "solves" the problem of marriage. Even the marriage of the best of Christians is not the renewal of Paradise; here, too, there is sorrow, conflict, pitiful sinking of heart, shortsightedness and inadequacy. Indeed, the happy marriage in particular contains special hidden dangers, the danger of being cut off from others, the danger of a wrong kind of self-sufficiency, and of a Pharisaical denial of solidarity with suffering, erring, curse-laden humanity.

Thus while marriage contains a particular grace of Creation it also contains a particular need for Redemption. Even the Christian, and the Christian moralist, stands baffled and helpless before many of the problems of marriage; for knowledge of the order of Creation, like knowledge of the Law, is a long way from being the assistance which is required. We only need to remind ourselves once more of phrases like "marriage and children" or "surplus women" to be aware that so long as marriage exists there will be insoluble problems; so long as man lives "in this flesh" he will never finally settle the problem of his sex nature. Even in the ethic of marriage the final word must be: to live on the Divine forgiveness.

SECTION III: THE COMMUNITY OF LABOUR

CHAPTER XXXIII

LABOUR AND CIVILIZATION

1. It is the destiny of every human being, a destiny which none can escape, to come into the world as the child of a particular father and of a particular mother; so also it is our destiny, which we cannot escape, that we have been placed within a particular civilization. Whatever we do, we do within, by means of, and in co-operatión with, the "civilized world" which surrounds us. By *civilization* (*Zivilisation*)(1) as distinct from culture (*Kultur*),[1] I mean the process by which the forces of nature have been placed at man's disposal for human ends, by the rational activity of man. Civilization is the outcome of labour, or to put it still more exactly, of industrial labour. Labour (or for that matter, civilization) simply presupposes the will to live, the desire to acquire all that is necessary to preserve life, and the intelligence which creates what is necessary by "artificial" methods, as opposed to natural methods, in more adequate measure, and with greater certainty than would be possible to instinct alone. Civilization is a matter of utility, of intelligent purpose,[2] but we must never lose sight of the fact that actually it is always the entire man who labours. This is why civilization always extends beyond the limits of the merely useful and necessary, and in civilization man never seeks solely to secure the necessities of life, but in his dominion over nature he seeks an inward release from bondage to it, an expression of his superiority over nature. But at this point civilization borders on culture.

Primarily man works in order to live. The fact that he *works* in order to live, however, is something by which he

---

[1] The contrast between "civilization" and "culture" (*Kultur*) which is presupposed throughout this chapter is almost impossible to render in English. In the light of the author's own note on p. 627 I here follow, as far as possible, Wilhelm von Humboldt's definition: "Civilization (*Zivilisation*) is the humanizing of the nations in their external organization, and in the spirit and temper to which this is related; to this . . . culture (*Kultur*) adds science and art." (Quoted by ERNST ROBERT CURTIUS in his book: *Frankreich*, p. 3.)—TR.

[2] See above, p. 22.

knows himself to be a human being. Animals do not work; they obey their instincts; they make no resolves, no plans(2); to be able to do these things is the great and dangerous privilege of man; he has no path already traced out for him, he himself must "hack his way" through the jungle; this means that it is also possible for him to follow another course. He may decide not to work, or he may be "submerged" by work. He cannot avoid asking himself whether he intends to work, why he does it, how he will do it, and what he intends to do. All this means that work becomes an ethical question. It is true, of course, that as a rule pure necessity drives him to some form of work. He is so made that only through labour can he rise above nature; but this pure necessity can neither satisfy him, nor deprive him of choice. His intelligence, which freely devises means and ends, offers various possibilities and forces him to decision. But this is not all.

There is no such thing as "man" in the abstract; for man is necessarily a member of some community or another. His intelligence, the natural endowment which makes it possible for him to work, also leads him to this life in community. Intelligent reflection shows him that he attains more in combination with others than each individual could gain by himself, it points him to the two natural possibilities of life in community: co-operation and exchange. Intelligent purpose would lead him into community with others even if he had no other impulse to co-operate with others. But here, too, the specifically human nature necessarily leads to the ethical problem. For now the question arises, how is community to be attained—that community which is sought, in the first place, simply on account of its advantages? For it is indeed evident—as Jeremias Gotthelf shows with classic simplicity in his *Käserei in der Vehfreude*—that even a mere association for work and for exchange is not possible without a background of wider considerations. Just as work presupposes the discipline of work, so also economic co-operation presupposes the need for the "discipline of community" in uprightness, in a reliability which is worthy of trust. Just as surely as intelligent purpose is the substratum of civilization, so also it is impossible to isolate it in the life of humanity as a whole. The co-ordination of labour into life as a whole, and the co-ordination of all who are connected by work, requires ethical decision.

2. This is why work and civilization constitutes an ethical problem, even for theological ethics. Although in itself labour

is non-ethical, and is indeed something quite human and natural, yet, because it is concerned with *human* nature, it becomes an ethical question, for man is man by the fact that he is a responsible being. Labour must be considered from the ethical point of view because it is an act of freedom. Even where our work is concerned we are controlled by the Divine Command.

Although it is evident that man's reflections on work, that is, whether he will work at all, and if so, why? and how? and what kind of work he will undertake? are determined simply by intelligent consideration, yet the fact remains that this process of deliberation, because it *is* an activity of the entire man and because it affects man in community, is encompassed by the Will of God. What does God will?

It is His will *that we should work*. This is not obvious, and the reason why we should work is also far from obvious. History shows us that simple industrial labour, precisely because it is connected with the maintenance of life, was always exposed to the suspicion of being something derogatory, both on the part of a higher intellectual culture as also on that of a higher "spiritual" religion. The Athenian citizen, especially if he was a philosopher, did not work; that was the business of slaves and manual workers(3). Work, compared with the βίος θεωρητικὸς, is a degrading affair, which should be avoided as far as possible. But even the *homo religiosus* of mystical pantheistic religion does not work; for that would attach him to the world which he desires to leave. Fundamentally, the same view was held by medieval Catholic thinkers, although they did recognize work as a means of discipline against sin. The *vita contemplativa* was still the idea of life(4). Work belongs to the fallen world; in Paradise there was no work, and indeed there should be no work there. Work forms part of the curse laid on mankind by God.

It was only the Reformation which removed these influences of an interpretation of life due to factors outside Christianity. Civilization, and thus work, is a Divine order of creation.[1] It is significant that the Divine Command: "make the earth subject unto you," precedes the curse on labour.

3. Man, in virtue of his endowments by Creation, is made capable of using, and by his created destiny is summoned to

[1] Cf. WÜNSCH: *Wirtschaftsethik*, pp. 546 ff., and "Arbeit" in RGG². Unfortunately WÜNSCH follows TROELTSCH in wrongly ascribing the idea of a "Law of Nature" to LUTHER.

use and control the sub-human world—this does not mean, however, that the creature does not possess a relative purpose of its own.[1] For man is to use but not to abuse the creatures; they are to submit to him, but he must not tyrannize over them. Wondering gratitude for this privileged position of man, which forms part of his likeness to God, is impressively expressed in that Psalm[2] which sees the highest reason to praise the Creator in this estimate of man's dominion and superiority over nature: "What is man that thou art mindful of him? and the son of man that thou visitest him? for thou hast made him a little lower than God (R.V. Marg. the angels) and crownest him with glory and honour. . . . Thou hast put all things under his feet; all sheep and oxen. . . . O Lord, our Lord, how excellent is thy Name in all the earth." Thus this distinction between Man and Nature is not Idealistic arrogance but is in line with the injunction to "make the earth subject unto you," and is thus a Divine Command.

The Scriptural idea of Creation draws this sharp distinction between man and the world, which is in contradistinction to all views influenced by a pantheistic cosmology; everywhere else this distinction between man and the world is blurred, and, in the last resort, the necessity for civilization is based essentially upon this idea (I think I may say this, even with the necessary modification which will result from what follows): the distinctive thing about European civilization is not the use of machinery but the will to create a civilization, and this will asserted itself in history by breaking down the barriers which separated the "merely industrial" or "merely useful" kinds of work from the "higher" kinds. It is from the Bible that Europe draws her high ideal of the value of all work which helps to create a civilization.

4. But this is only one side of the question. Work is not based only on the relation of man to the creatures, but above all on his relation to the other man. In the Bible work is conceived as a concern of the community, as service. The Creator wills to give us nothing necessary for our life save through our mutual service to each other. What we conceive as the natural form of community is only the "mask"—to use Luther's expression—the underside of a situation which is turned towards us, which in faith God permits us to see from above as something wholly different. The necessity of co-operation and exchange is the Divine order of service(5). Only through

[1] See above, p. 203.   [2] Psalm viii.

387

this does work gain its peculiar dignity; it is a God-given "calling" for the service of our neighbour. In this service the Creator is honoured, and only in obedience to His will does labour really become service. So long as ordinary manual labour is regarded essentially as an individual concern[1]—as was the case with Aristotle, and also (though from a different point of view) with the medieval monastic theologians—it certainly will be valued less highly than other "intellectual" occupations, whether of a cultural or a religious nature. This scale of value collapses in the light of a higher point of view, that of service. It does not matter a jot what kind of work is used as the instrument of our service; moreover the content of our service is determined by the need of the community, of our neighbour, and the dignity of labour no longer depends on the kind of labour which is performed, but on the reason for which it is performed. The lowest kind of manual labour is of as much value as the "intellectual"(6), if undertaken as the Divine commission to serve, and if it renders a real service to our neighbour. Or rather, this view completely alters the very idea of what is "intellectual" or "spiritual." In the highest, decisive sense the term "spiritual" is no longer applied to cultural or religious work, but to any work which serves the Divine Will and human community. This means a revolution in the concept of the "spiritual" which is as necessary to-day as it was in Luther's days: for we too suffer from that false Greek conception of the "spiritual," which regards the service of the mother in the home, for instance, as less "spiritual" than intellectual or aesthetic activities.

The fact that men must work, and the reasons why they must work, however, also determine how they are to work and what they are to do. That kind of work, and that way of working, is commanded which best serves human life. Through its connexion with the community and with man's control of nature, mere utility is elevated to the plane of service to humanity, and this constitutes its dignity. This ideal of service also constitutes the criterion by which the moral value of any work and its place in life can be defined. Work which is not in harmony with this ideal cannot be performed for the glory of God, nor does it possess the "dignity" of labour. The natural system of callings, arising as it does from the natural purposes

[1] To what an extent labour was regarded only from the point of view of a personal exercise in virtue is shown by v. EICKEN, in his *Geschichte und System der Mittelalterlichen Weltanschauung*, pp. 495 ff.

of life, carried on by means of a community of work, reveals its suitability for service in the fact that it places the individual at the service of the community, even when he only thinks he is working for his own good. In it therefore the Divine order in creation is reflected as the order of service. Hence in faith it is possible to regard the natural calling as God's call to service.

5. There are, however, times and persons on whom it is not necessary to impress the command to *work*; in these instances it is necessary to lay emphasis upon the fact that there is also a commandment about keeping the Sabbath, as a sign that work is not an end in itself, that labour must serve man and life, but that it must not dominate it. It is not that —unfortunately—we *are obliged* to rest, but that—and not at all "unfortunately!"—we *ought* to rest. Only in repose does the human quality in a human being become evident, just as inhuman qualities are revealed in those who cannot rest. In the ability to rest we see whether man is still in control of his work, or whether he is "possessed" by it. On the other hand we not only need rest in order to recover from fatigue, but in order that work shall not get the upper hand and dominate us.

The Sabbath commandment of the Old Testament is no longer a law for us; but it is an indication, which we would do well not to overlook, that our life needs a definite rhythm of rest and labour, if it is not to suffer injury; it needs the rhythm of in-spiration and ex-piration, of expansion and con-centration, of giving out to others and of solitary recollection. Therefore in the Old Testament the Sabbath day of rest has a special connexion with the cultus, and with religious exercises.[1] We are so made that we need special times for prayer, and special days in which we can spend more time on prayer and worship than we can "during the week." But the Sabbath further reminds us of the final end of all human life, which has been attained by Redemption, namely, that God is glorified in that eternal Sabbath, when man "rests from his works" in that Divine worship mentioned by the writer of the Epistle to the Hebrews.[2]

But the Pharisaical and Puritanical idea of the Day of Rest is not in harmony with the meaning of the commandment.

[1] See above, pp. 309 ff.
[2] Heb. iv. 1–11. Cf. the beautiful observations on this point by K. BARTH: *Theologische Blätter*, 1931.

It is essential that the Day of Rest should not be turned into another day filled with duties, the only difference being that these duties are of a religious character. The essence of a Day of Rest should be that it is one day in the week when we "are not obliged to do anything special." Man also needs to use this freedom for play. Play is part of a complete human life; a person who has forgotten how to play has become wooden, rigid. We need play in order to learn once more how to relax. Play is a safety-valve, by means of which the superfluous steam of self-importance, self-conscious dignity, solemnity and over-seriousness can be let off; play is the oil which makes the wheel of life turn less feverishly, and of all play the best is play with children; they are our best teachers in this respect.

6. Rest and play also includes *enjoyment*. The ascetic conception of life would like to exclude enjoyment from the life of the saint; this kind of holiness is contrary to the meaning of the revelation of God in the Scriptures. Enjoyment is an essential part of life, for which God has created us, the joys of the senses as well as of the spirit. The Creator has not given us the capacity for enjoyment for no purpose. It is true, of course, that enjoyment—not merely in the realm of the senses but just as much in the spiritual sphere—is a special danger-zone, because so easily, instead of serving us, it dominates us, and thus becomes a passion; when this happens, instead of making us fit for community it makes us solitary and anti-social, selfish and brutal. The decisive point in this question of enjoyment is not "moderation," this virtue which actually predominates in the Aristotelian-Thomistic ethic(7), but usefulness for service. Whatever assists our life in community is good—whether it be "moderate" or not—whatever harms our life in community is disastrous. The idea of moderation is a very questionable quality, as every one knows who has taken an active part in the fight against alcoholism. This distinction between "higher" and "lower" forms of enjoyment is also false. The sphere of the body and the senses is not "lower" than the intellectual sphere, but it has its definite place in the life of man, since it has been provided for him by God. Only here, too, the principle of what is "serviceable" must be observed. The body must serve the spirit, and the spirit must serve the purpose of God for community. It is from this point of view that all enjoyment should be tested, estimated and defined. There is no occasion to deal more fully with this

subject, since it has already been discussed *ad nauseam* in works of traditional ethics.

7. There are people to whom God has given a special office which requires a heroic renunciation of rest and pleasure; there are times in every life when such renunciation is required. But just as rest and enjoyment may be misused, work can be misused, and control over things—civilization—may become a curse instead of a blessing. "Have dominion over every living thing"[1] is not the only commandment in the first pages in the Bible, for they also contain the command: "Ye shall not eat of the fruit of the tree . . . which is in the midst of the garden, neither shall ye touch it lest ye die," for it is the tree which gives the knowledge of good and evil,[2] and the story of the Fall and of the curse laid upon toil.[3] Man's claim to have dominion over nature is limited by the Divine Will, the purposeful activity of man is limited by the Divine purpose in Creation and in the world. An unrestrained desire to dominate the world and to enjoy the good things of the world destroys the meaning of life, destroys human personality, social relations, and, above all, man's relation with God, for indeed it grows out of a distortion of man's relation with God. Civilization becomes a curse instead of a blessing; instead of elevating human life, it enslaves and degrades it. The story of the building of the Tower of Babel[4]—of the insolent *Hybris* of civilization which tries to storm heaven—is followed by that of the confusion of tongues; this is the double picture of civilization which is shown us in the Bible.

There is always a lurking danger that we may turn our civilizing activity into an absolute. This process is not an offence against an arbitrary command, but it is presumption, for it breaks down the barriers of human nature erected by the order of creation, and therefore destroys it. Civilization, freed from God's control, and throwing off all restraint, gets the upper hand, and man becomes the slave of his own organization and enterprise, the slave of his industrial and of his economic order. Above all, the collective forces which have been created for the sake of civilization, make the individual human being an insignificant cog in its vast wheel of activity. Hence we hear outspoken warnings and protests against this kind of life not merely from the point of view of an aesthetic spirituality and a mystical religiosity, but also from that of the Bible.

[1] Gen. i. 28.   [2] Gen. ii. 17.   [3] Gen. iii. 19.   [4] Gen. xi. 1–11.

8. The degeneration of civilization and of work which is chiefly due to the fact that the meaning of work has been lost, inevitably works out in two directions: in the relation between man and things, and in his relation to the community. When man is no longer bound to God he becomes a slave to the world, for indeed this "bondage" to God is his freedom. The things which are intended to serve man become his masters. To have a mania for "things" is to be "possessed" by them; since man cannot help seeking the infinite, he now seeks the meaning of his life in an infinity of things. His unbounded passion for things hounds him on, from one thing to another, and since he surrounds the "thing" with the magic glamour of that which is worthy of infinite endeavour, of that which is indispensable, he sacrifices his life to it—he sacrifices his manhood to thinghood.

This bondage to things inevitably loosens the ties of community. The mania for things destroys community. Whenever a person is obsessed by this mania, he loses all consideration for others. Conversely, this obsession with things is also a result of lack of community; "things" are all that is left to a human being who, in his egoism, withdraws himself from community. When a person no longer loves human beings he must become infatuated with things: for man is so made that he must love something. Thus it is due to lack of community and the mania for things that labour has lost its dignity and its freedom; it becomes itself a mania, an uncontrollable passion, a form of slavery. From a Divine order civilization has been turned into a curse, and its Divine meaning has become daemonic; for the "daemonic" means being enslaved by something finite which is regarded as infinite and absolute.

9. This question of the daemonic character of civilization is particularly urgent at the present time. Never before in the history of the world has a materialistic and mechanistic civilization so completely dominated life, and in consequence enslaved and destroyed it, as it has to-day. At all previous periods in history civilization was in some way or another anchored to the transcendent and connected with it, and was thereby bound to the unity of the people (*Volksgemeinschaft*). These bonds are to-day decaying. Economic man has become autonomous: this led first of all to an immense outburst of economic energy which issued in a mighty expansion and achieved great things; but this was immediately followed by a desolation of life, a materialism, a disintegration of human

social life, which has no parallel in the earlier history of mankind. This comes out most clearly in our economic order; the abstract concept of value which provides so appropriate an outlet for our boundless mania for "things," i.e. money, not only dominates the world, but it threatens to stifle all that is human, and to drain the last ounce of spiritual life out of humanity. In the economic order, therefore, the problem of civilization, as an ethical problem, becomes most acute. The following chapter will deal with this question. Two other points, however, must be touched on briefly at this point: the question of joy in work, and the problem of unemployment.

It is essential to the Divine purpose of labour that labour can only make people happy in so far as it fulfils its purpose, that is, in so far as it helps man to be truly man, and serves the purpose of life in community. Wherever, whether from subjective or objective reasons, this connexion is absent, all joy in labour vanishes. The disappearance of joy in work, which is so evident at the present time, is not due merely to the fact that the individual no longer regards his work as a Divine Calling, taking it from the Hand of God; on the contrary, the actual conditions of labour often make it practically impossible for the individual to accept his calling from the hands of God. Where the individual worker is simply a minute wheel (which at any moment may be exchanged for another) in a vast piece of machinery, when he does not know what purpose or persons his work will serve, when all he knows is that others will be enriched by his labour, while he himself will remain poor, humanly speaking, he can no longer regard his calling as a Divine vocation. In it he does not experience his superiority over nature, nor his connexion with others in mutual service. At the present time the life of labour has reached such a state of moral disorganization that the "order" of labour has become a dis-order; it is scarcely possible to speak of serving the community in the midst of anarchy(8).

There is no more impressive and appalling expression of this anarchy than the fact that millions of human beings want to work and cannot, in spite of the fact that their work is urgently required by the world. Unemployment reveals the curse which lies upon modern European economic life more plainly than any other fact. Before the nineteenth century scarcely any moralist would have thought of saying that man has a *right* to work: for it seemed unthinkable that anyone

393

could question this right, the *duty* of work was emphasized but not the *right*. To-day the problem with which the greatest economists and politicians are grappling in vain is that of the involuntary unemployment of a great part of the civilized world. What a comment on this "civilization"! The cry of millions: "Give us work!" is a new phenomenon in world history. We have every reason to enquire into the deeper causes of this fact, which means the destruction of all moral value and potentiality(9).

CHAPTER XXXIV

THE NATURE AND THE TASK OF THE
ECONOMIC ORDER

1. *The Economic Order as a Problem of Ethics*

IT is a shameful sign of the way in which the Protestant ethic of the nineteenth century was out of touch with life that it practically ignores the greatest upheaval of social life in the modern world: the rise and the victorious expansion of capitalistic economics. This event transformed all previous conditions of life with unparalleled swiftness and to an unparalleled extent; in so doing it shook the very foundations of the traditional conceptions of social order(1). This is all the more astonishing since the economic order—whatever we may think about it—is that sphere of life in which the strongest natural interest of man—that of the maintenance of life—is felt, and in which the antithesis between the interests of the individual and those of the community appears in its basic form; thus it is the sphere in which we are practically *forced* to consider this problem from the ethical point of view. Further, it is still more difficult to understand why this question was so completely ignored by the Protestant Church, since the Bible —the Old Testament and the New—places the economic problem in the very centre of its thinking; the prophets, as well as Jesus and the Apostles, explain the law of love mainly by using illustrations drawn from the economic order, and their imperatives deal mainly with the ethical aspect of economic life. In any case, an ethic which ignores economic problems has no right to call itself either a Christian or a Scriptural ethic(2).

This fundamental truth must not be overlooked even when we are confronted by the fact that economic questions are extraordinarily complicated and obscure, and that they easily lead the non-specialist into the danger of dilettantism, and the moralist in particular into the By-path Meadow of the construction of visionary Utopian programmes. We shall only escape this danger by holding firmly to that which is our official task: to the task, that is, of considering the fundamental ideas which result from reflection on the Divine Will, and of being on our guard against attempting to draw up anything in the nature of a Christian economic programme. Nothing indeed is easier, but nothing also is more futile, than to outline an ideal economic order from any kind of "ethical standpoint." Since the ideal State of Plato and the Utopia of Sir Thomas More, we know that this is a matter which may possibly find a place in an Idealistic system, but not in a Christian ethic(3). On the other hand, however, to give up all attempts to throw light on the economic question from the point of view of ethics would be tantamount to saying that every system of ethics is bankrupt; this would be the case at a time like the present in particular, when the question of the economic order is so evidently closely interwoven with that of community, and this means, with the problem of ethics. The duty of thinking out what obedience to God within the economic order really means has been laid upon us, and cannot be evaded.

By the "economic order" I mean, without going into subtle definitions(4), the process by which material goods, needed to support life, are produced, distributed, and consumed. The technological side of the economic order—both that of production and of exchange—is not the subject-matter of ethics but of technology and political economy; on the other hand, both as a concern of the entire man and of the community as a whole, both are impregnated with ethical problems, and this leads to the demand for co-operation between political economists and moralists, apart from which, in both instances, a disastrously one-sided view would prevail. A preliminary presentation of the most important economic factors makes it manifest from the outset how closely these problems are interwoven.

The "real a priori" of the whole economic order is the apparently "purely natural"—and therefore ethically "neutral" —factor of the soil. In reality, however, this ethically neutral, "innocent" soil does not exist; the soil has been affected in countless ways—through conditions of property, cultivation, and other ways of "opening it up." It already has its history. It is connected with society by many ties. It is so dominant a social factor that many political economists and moralists prefer to develop the whole social question from the problem of the soil(5). The second concrete factor is *the tools* by which its treasures are taken from the soil and manufactured into concrete goods. But the problem of property (of Capital), coupled with the fact that the chief "tool" of the present day

—the machine, the factory, the large industrial enterprise—
can only be set up and manipulated collectively by co-operation, makes this factor also into an ethical problem. The third,
and most important, factor, is the *working human being* himself,
or in abstract terms, labour, as a combination of physical and
intellectual, technological and social elements, of economic
outlook, of the will to work, of discipline in work, of the
capacity to lead and to be led, of independence and solidarity
—rather, not the human being at all, but man's industrial
community.

The finished "goods," however, the final product of labour,
also constitute a social fact, and therefore an ethically important fact. This final product embodies the claims of all the
different co-operating factors—those contributed by the soil,
by the use of the "tools" (Capital), and by the achievements
of physical and intellectual labour. When we speak of the
"Social Question" we are thinking chiefly of the method of
disposing of the products of labour, of the distribution of
incomes which is closely connected with the actual distribution
of goods. Behind the various methods employed to dispose of
the economic goods—property, interest on capital, wages,
profit, etc.—there lie burning ethical questions, on the answer
to which depends the welfare and the just ordering of Society.
Finally, the question of *consumption*—the use or the enjoyment
of the goods produced—has been, and still must be, a field
for much challenging ethical discussion; it is only right that
this question should receive attention, but it has frequently
received more attention than it deserved.

A clear statement of the purpose of economic life shows still
more plainly the close relation between the spheres of economics
and morality. Although even in the economic sphere the natural
factors will always be of great significance, yet, in the last
resort, the economic sphere can only be understood from the
point of view of its human purpose, and what we regard as an
economic fate is always an *historical* fate. The immediate purpose of all economic activity is to provide the individual and
the community with the material goods which are necessary
for life. But this purpose is not all. Man is not an animal,
incidentally capable of using technological appliances. The
fact that it is *man* who acts in the economic sphere means that
this primary economic purpose cannot be separated from the
general aims of humanity. Man does not act in an "economic"
manner simply "in order to eat," but in order that he may

live, that his *human* life may be preserved. We cannot understand what kind of economic goods man desires and creates, or to what extent, and in what order of urgency, he desires and creates them from the point of view of the actual goods themselves, but only from the point of view of human life as a whole(6); the motive force of every economic system is the "system of values" of the economic community, and its dynamic and its structure finally issue from its "general outlook on life": its faith or its superstition.

Even that "economic man" which classical political economy always presupposes, that caricature of a human being, has only been possible as an abstract conception within a "landscape" quite definitely limited in time and space, in which, for the first time in world history, *laissez-faire* became a reality; there have been not only individuals but even whole epochs (and such will also recur) in which scarcely anyone—if I may put it so—would recognize his own "economic face" in that "picture." The question of ultimate purpose and meaning, however, leads us directly to the question of faith.

2. *Economic Life as an Infringement of the Original Order of Creation*

Wherever there are human beings, there an economic order exists; for man cannot exist without the use of material goods, and man's labour is required to create or restore such goods, and to make them available for distribution. Since God has created man as a corporeal being, He has also created him as a being needing an economic order, and capable of creating an economic order. Thus the economic order forms part of the original Divine order in creation; as such, like all Divine order, it is at the same time a Divine law. Man is commanded to create an economic order. As a rule we do not need to command men to take a passive part, to enjoy economic goods—although this may be necessary when confronted by an ascetic point of view—but we are commanded to undertake active economic *work*. The apostolic injunction: "If any will not work, neither let him eat,"[1] expresses this Divine order in creation in a classically pregnant phrase, since it conceives labour, as well as the enjoyment of the fruits of labour, from the very outset, as a concern of the community; for this apostolic injunction only has meaning on the presupposition of an economic community. It is due to the Divine goodness of the Creator that we have a part in such a community, therefore

[1] 2 Thess. iii. 10.

it is also a Divine Command that we should not be parasites on the community, but active members of it. This applies to every kind of economic order in which a man may be placed.

In itself the economic order is ethically neutral, since on its technical side it has to do with material goods, not with personal relations. But the aim of this neutral activity gives ethical value to the work, and makes ethical demands on the worker. "Neutral action" of this kind must not be neglected; it is wrong to neglect it; we are commanded to perform such action as a definite duty. The end justifies the means, which is itself neutral; thus the economic order, although in itself ethically neutral, becomes ethically significant. Work within the economic order is justified, because, and in so far as, it means sharing in the Divine work of preservation. This idea of the Divine order in Creation wipes out every suggestion that the economic order is "low" or "unspiritual." Economic activity, rightly conducted, is Divine Service. This is its dignity, which was restored by Luther through his idea of "the Calling"(7), after it had been dangerously obscured by the monastic ethic of the Middle Ages.

But this is only one side of the question, and it is the bright side. The other side, the dark side, can never be separated from the real economic order in which we live, that is, from the curse of sin which broods over it. The sinfulness of the economic order—speaking generally—consists in its alienation from its Divine purpose, inherent in the order itself; on the one hand, it has been spoilt by its false tendency to become an end in itself, and on the other by egoistic exploitation by the individual which always works out both as sin and as a curse.[1] This is not merely the character of the economic activity of the individual—for if this were so there might possibly be some activity of a different character—but it is the economic order as such, the order into which each one of us is born. It is not possible for the individual to engage in economic activity without sin. Nowhere does the truth of the doctrine of Original Sin, and the untruth of the individualism of liberty, become so palpably evident as in this sphere. Each of us has an active and a passive share in the universal sinfulness of the economic order(8).

But in spite of this fact the purpose of God for the economic order is not altered. Even within the sinful economic order—and there never has been, and never will be any other—and

[1] Cf. SPANN: *Fluch und Segen der Wirtschaft*, 1931.

399

by its means and by it alone, God gives us life, and what is necessary for life. So far as our life is preserved, it is preserved by this order. Therefore the summons to take an active part in it by our labour is not cancelled by the sinful corruption of the economic order. It is both necessary and possible to serve God and our neighbour even in these orders which, in themselves, are perverted orders of creation. In spite of the fact that all human "callings" are stamped more or less plainly with the curse of evil—for once we see each "calling" in its concrete historical reality, we see that there are really *no* exceptions to this rule—it is both necessary and possible to fulfil a "calling" of this kind in the spirit of faith, and—in the spirit of faith—to perform the "duties of our state" as the work which God has given us to do.

But although the fact of Divine *Creation* hallows and justifies our service within this economic order—a justification which no human sinfulness can alter—the fact of Redemption shakes the foundations of this order, threatening its existence from the point of view of its final purpose. For in the Perfected Kingdom there will be no economic order, and one who already—through faith—has a share in this final purpose can only take part in economic life as one of those who "use the world, as not abusing it," who "buy as though they possessed not," although his calling may force him to play a prominent part in such activity. For the believer, indeed, the unconcern with which the modern man accepts the economic order as a matter of course, the world of finance, for instance, is a thing of the past; he can no more take it for granted than he can take marriage for granted. Thus the New Testament seems to cherish a certain hostility towards the natural state of life; this has often been confused with an ascetic renunciation of economic life, but its intention and its motive are really quite different, since they are determined by the eschatological outlook of the Early Church.[1]

3. *The Norm of the Economic Order*

The economic world in which we live is, to use pagan language, the state "into which we have been thrust by Fate";

---

[1] Paul refers to both—to marriage and to the economic order—in I Cor. vii. 29–31, when he says: "The time is short . . . they that have wives be as though they had none . . . they that buy, as though they possessed not: they that use this world, as not abusing it; for the fashion of this world passeth away."

from the point of view of faith it is our "Calling." The first question the Christian ought to ask in this economic world should not be: "How can I alter it?" but: "How can I serve within it?" None of us knows whether he will ever live to see a different, "better" order, and every one who has eyes in his head can see with what overwhelming force, with the driving power of destiny, economic history in particular drags the individual along with it, how little elasticity is possible within this structure, and, in particular, how closely, even under the most favourable circumstances, natural facts and that historical development which is beyond all human control surround and limit the sphere of free self-determination. We are forbidden to indulge in Utopian dreams and fantastic speculations about the future in order to evade the truth which the Creator wills to hammer into us by the very fact of the overwhelming force of the economic world, namely, that we are living in a "wicked" world, and that we shall live in it to the end of our days on earth. This supposed "organism"[1] of the economic order is a manifestation of that σάρξ (flesh) and of that θάνατος (death) from which only a Divine act of Redemption, that act which is known as the Resurrection of the Dead, can set us free. One who is confronted by this economic world and does not learn this humility will only be able to learn it, at the very utmost, at the hour of his death. Here upon earth we have to bear the curse which forms part of our "expulsion from Paradise," a Divine reaction against our common, primal historical apostasy from our Creator.

At the same time we may know, and indeed we ought to know, that through the kindness of the Creator even this "wicked world" is not wholly unfit to become the sphere in which it is possible to serve our neighbour, and the instrument for such service. It is the wonder of divine grace that even in an "order" which is no order, and in a "community" which does not seem to be a community, it is possible for us, if we take part in this life in the right way, to practise love. Nothing is further from my mind than by means of such ideas either to excuse or to whitewash the present "order" in any way, as will be seen directly. But it is a different matter for an individual to do his work well in this order, whether it is

---

[1] As in the romantic type of political economy, in which the phantasy-picture of an ideal organic economic order is mingled with the actual economic order (cf. SPANN: *Fundament der Volkswirtschaftslehre, Der wahre Staat*).

good or bad, and even in a desperately hopeless situation still to wait for the Command of God; it is a different matter for an individual citizen to join with his fellow-citizens in looking round for ways and means of improving this hopeless situation, knowing very well that even the better order for which they are working, though it may possibly be better, will still not be good. Here as elsewhere let us put first things in the first place, and secondary things second, and at least not distort *this* order.

And yet—even if only to enable the individual to carry on his work in the right spirit in his appointed lot, it is necessary that he should be able to recognize the *Divine* order and the *Divine* law in that which God wills as the "why" and the "wherefore" of this present "order," in order that, in it, here and now, he may be able to perceive the Divine Command. Here, too, the Will of God made known to faith in His order of creation, and in His promise of redemption, must be the guiding principle of our conduct. Although there can be no Christian economic programme—for such a programme could only be an idle Utopia—no economic law of Nature which can be applied as a constructive principle, no system of economic justice which can be deduced, there still are certain guiding lines which here, as well as in the problems connected with marriage and the State, must show us the way. The first of these leading ideas is the purpose of the maintenance of life, which is based on the Divine purpose in creation, that is, the provision of material goods necessary for the preservation of life. The primary purpose of economics willed by God is to minister to human needs, service to life. This implies that the economic order is a means and not an end. To make the economic order into an end in itself, which is so often assumed by theoretical and practical economists, the unrestricted development of the economic process, is inexpedient, and contrary to the Divine order. Man is not to engage in economic activity for its own sake, but in order to live, to live in a *human* way. Thus his economic activity is not intended merely to meet his physical needs but to place at his disposal a surplus of goods which alone makes a human civilized life possible.

But this does not mean—as is so often assumed by Christian theorists—that from the statement that the economic sphere ought to be "humanized" we are to deduce the *a priori* postulate of a specially "humane" economic system.

To attempt to bring economic activity under ethical discipline inevitably ruins it, while the man who blindly accepts the whole economic order and its "autonomy" directly undermines his own life, and indirectly also undermines that of the economic community. For the sake of love, whose will it is to maintain life, we are bidden to observe the *primary* purpose of economic activity, the maintenance of life, first of all; at the same time we must realize that this purpose can never be achieved merely through "humane" means. So long as our economic life is built upon coal and iron, coal mines and blast furnaces will be necessary; so long as men are egoists—not *merely* egoists, but still very largely egoists—special stimuli will be needed in order to secure sufficient economic vitality to guarantee the fulfilment of the primary purpose of economic activity, that of providing the elementary necessities of life. The economic order does not fully recognize the claims of others, implied in the command to love your neighbour, it only recognizes them within certain narrow limits. The autonomy of the industrial order, which causes so much concern to the serious moralist, does not lie only in its technological and natural limitations, but far more in the ineradicable sinfulness of the human beings who engage in economic activity, with whom each one of us has to do, just as we ourselves are also affected by this sinfulness which— here we anticipate—enters, as a permanent factor, into every economic system. The autonomy of the economic order is indeed mainly an historical fact, and as such it is variable, like all that is historical; nevertheless, historical factors, even when they proceed from human action, are forces which are very difficult to control. These truths may be summed up in one sentence: Fundamentally, the sinful autonomy of the economic order can never be overcome, but it is variable, therefore in a relative way it can be overcome. It is impossible to determine beforehand, by rule of thumb, what proportion of humane action can be combined at any given moment with the primary economic purpose of providing sustenance for the race. All that is clear is the general principle, and this is inviolable: the economic order is intended to serve man, therefore both the individual and the community must try to "humanize" it as far as possible; and it is the duty of each individual, in his own place, and of the community as such, to see to it that the economic order is not allowed to make itself absolute, or to lose its purpose of service to humanity.

Where the economic order sets itself up as an absolute, it has become daemonic, and inevitably destroys itself.

The second principle, which springs from the recognition of a Divine order, is this: that the economic system should never be regarded merely as an individual concern, but also as the concern of the community. The Divine order in creation forbids us to conceive the economic life of a nation as the sum total of individual enterprises. God has created man as an individual-in-community. His Divine order in creation is so arranged that it makes the one dependent on the other. The actuality of economic life is based upon co-operation and exchange. The metaphor of the organism—used merely as a metaphor, and not as a structural principle, as in the social and economic theory of Romanticism—is pre-eminently suited to illustrate my meaning. Economic life, like all other living forms of human community, must be based on interdependence, that is, on a mutual relationship deriving from inequality. Thus it is contrary to the purpose of creation either to teach universal equality or to break up society into a number of isolated individuals.

From this it follows that from the point of view of the Divine order of creation, *private property* can neither be affirmed nor denied. Certainly the Biblical idea of personality implies that the individual has possessions of which he may dispose as he wills; for how can a human being become an individual unless he can shape something of his own, of his own free will? Man, who has been created as an individual, needs some space in life in which he can form that which is "peculiar" to himself; the destruction of this sphere (as in slavery, to give an extreme instance) will almost inevitably kill all individual joy in creation, and will also destroy the power to create.[1] At the same time, however, we must admit that in the faith in the Creation we never know the individual otherwise than "as the individual in society." Private property in the sense of Roman Law, the *jus utendi et abutendi*, is opposed to the Biblical idea of Creation. This conception of the meaning of "private" property is really *privatio*, that is, robbing God and our neighbour. The phrase, "that belongs to me," is not only limited by the thing concerned, but also by the fact that with the thing concerned, I am set within society. It is obvious that love never emphasizes "mine" in this way; but

[1] For the way in which Primitive Christianity treated the question of slavery see the *Letter to Philemon*.

justice also, which we seek in the civil sphere, in the light of the Divine order, cannot show a definite boundary. What does "mine" mean, what does "self-acquired" mean, within an economic community which first of all makes it possible for me to acquire anything? We can see the precarious character of the argument for private property, supposed to be based on Natural Law (which modern Catholicism asserts in opposition to the patristic view), from one thing: that, in true Roman fashion, it regards the tax on increment value on landed estate as an actually unjustifiable interference of the community with the property-rights of the individual,[1] where obviously the individual is the privileged beneficiary of values which the community has created—whereas the Fathers regarded private property as a result of the Fall(9). Hence we will not formulate an *a priori* conception of private property or of collective property; all we will do is to assert the idea of "property-in-community" as the critically regulative principle, over against every existing legal economic order, and apply this first on the one side and then on the other.

Individualism is fundamentally perverted and impossible; firstly, because it denies community and makes the individual entirely autonomous; secondly, because it regards community as only useful in cases of emergency, and as a means for furthering the separate life of the individual. The same fundamental conception lies behind *rational Communism*, whose (secular) eschatological aim is anarchy; but it differs from individualism in the fact that it posits an abstract unity as the means to this end. Communism is not community; it is a uniform, non-articulated, mechanical unity. It does not recognize any mutual relationship between human beings, therefore it knows no real exchange; it is like a stream which cannot flow naturally, it has no current, therefore it will become a swamp. It is not the will of the Creator that mankind should be disintegrated into a host of isolated individuals or that we should be forcibly compressed into a kind of collective substance; no, He wills a mutual relation between the individual and the community, as a mutual limitation of the individual and of the community, the moulding of individuality within the intimate life of the community(10).

But in saying this we do not mean either the universalistic system of organic articulation(11), nor the idea of reciprocity contained in the theory of solidarity(12). I would repeat:

[1] Cf. SCHILLING: *Katholische Sozialethik*, p. 92.

just as a point from which we take our bearings differs from a structural principle, so there is no Christian economic system or programme. For we are living in an irrational and sinful economic reality, within which the relative "best" cannot be deduced from any *a priori* system. The economic order is always like the drunken peasant whom Luther describes, who when he is helped on to his horse on one side promptly falls off on the other; it oscillates continually between an individualism which destroys community, and a collectivism which destroys freedom. It is impossible to determine before-hand, by rule of thumb, what is the relatively "right" course to pursue at any given moment; such decisions can only be made as we go along, with that guiding principle in view. The articulate character of economic life, taught by the Romantic school, is just as unreal as the "justice" of a theory of solidarity is Utopian ethics and ineffectual economics. Both for the individual and the community the only general rule is this: to seek to accord each man his due in the midst of community.

The truth that the economic order is a sphere of service ordained by God leads, thirdly, to the statement that every person capable of rendering service is under an obligation to render service, that is, to the rejection of unearned income, economic luxury, or a parasitical existence. But what is a parasitical or luxurious existence? The view which is widely held among Socialists—due to a false theory of value—(value = work) that only manual work counts as work(13), and the deeper view of Tolstoy and Gandhi, that even intellectuals should spend some time on manual labour in order to earn their "daily bread," is not only intelligible but valuable as a reaction against obvious *bourgeois* parasitism, though speaking literally it is incorrect. From the standpoint of one's contribution to the whole the distinction between intellectual and manual labour becomes unimportant—however significant it may be from other points of view. Over-emphasis on manual labour is just as unjustifiable as under-emphasis. Manual work is systematically undervalued by Idealism, which asserts that the different quality of intellectual work and its function of "leadership" make it of "higher value"(14); it is over-emphasized by the "worker," who often does not recognize or admit the importance of the presuppositions of manual labour, or the necessity for such intellectual leadership. From the ethical view of economics every one who does not really serve the community by honest work, according to his actual capacity, is leading a luxury-existence. It is impossible to define exactly, *a priori*, where the line should be drawn. But the general rule, both for the individual and for the community, remains the same; if a man will not work, neither shall he eat.

But this statement also implies a certain *proportion*; for a parasite is not merely one who entirely ignores the obligation to work, but he is also one who partially evades his duty, and lives on the goods procured by the labour of the community. As soon as we try to fix this proportion, in any legal or *a priori* way, we find ourselves confronted by insurmountable difficulties—those difficulties which make it impossible to define the content of the *suum cuique*. What is the standard by which the achievement of work is to be estimated? Or the actual value of the work done? Or the measure of effort it has cost? How can we create a basis of comparison between intellectual and manual work? Does the demand for "equal pay for equal work" conceal the egalitarian idea of equality as a principle of economic justice?

Let me repeat what has been said already: faith in the Divine order of creation controverts all attempts to make the whole of mankind "equal." The egalitarian Law of Nature does not belong to the world of the Bible, but to the context of Stoic rationalism. Now the Creation—quite apart from sin—simply means an incomprehensible inequality, conditions for which we cannot account. The egalitarian idea does not arise out of reverence for the Creator, but out of the desire to dictate to the Creator how things ought to be, on the presupposition that the Creator ought to treat every one alike. Hence, because this idea opposes the Divine order in creation it also works out destructively in life. To try to make everybody equal kills economic vitality(15).

But this does not mean that I have any intention of justifying the inequality which may exist at any particular time by the idea of the Divine order of creation; for this inequality is always—and to a very large extent—also tainted by sin. The actual inequality which may exist at any particular time is always mainly due to some selfish exploitation of advantages, to the brutal determination of masterful, unscrupulous people to exploit to the utmost those who are weaker and more scrupulous. Only those who have fallen a prey to the dreamy illusions of Romanticism, and see everything through rose-coloured spectacles, could venture to maintain that the actual economic order is an "organism" in which "one member helps another." The actual economic world is the scene of a most brutal struggle for power, and it is no accident that it was in the century and in the land of the capitalism of the "Manchester School" that Darwin's theory of the "survival of the fittest" was evolved. Where a whole community leaves the economic order to its own devices, economic life inevitably resolves itself into this intensely ruthless struggle for existence.

Thus, although we are convinced that the theory of equality is contrary to the Biblical idea of Creation, we are also convinced that *this* kind of inequality is still more contrary to it. Because economic life is always a concern of the community, because the aim of the economic order is not only the maintenance of the life of individuals but of the community, the community must be protected against this domination by the individual, above all, the weak must be supported by the power of the community, and by the means of an "artificial" *adjustment* a certain balance must be restored to a people engaged in economic activity. The postulate of a Christian economic ethic is not equality but balance. Thus the idea of equalization is not a constitutive principle but a regulative idea; hence it is not a constructive but a critical principle, which does not permit the formulation of *a priori* laws, but only serves as a term of reference for every particular economic system. In this process of adjustment love goes far beyond all that would be possible as a general rule for a community engaged in economic activity; but even here it is impossible to *establish* justice; it can only be sought. But the criterion which decides whether the adjustment is on the right lines or not is simply this: the *good* of the individual and of the community. An adjustment which would paralyse the vitality of the economic life would be every whit as wrong as the policy of *laissez-faire*, which releases its daemonic energies. In general, however, both for the individual and for the community, it is quite plain that a process of adjustment should be initiated which will go as far as it possibly can; only when it is apparent that to push further would do more harm than good, should it stay its hand. From all that I have already said it is obvious that this adjustment cannot take place merely on voluntary lines; it will need the assistance of the law, with its powers of compulsion; on the other hand, it is also evident that the individual Christian can never be satisfied with the measure of compulsory adjustment effected legally by the community. We shall be returning to this subject later.

4. *The Evil in the Economic Order*

The evil in the economic system is due not to nature—understanding the word in its present-day sense—but to man. But for those to whom the phrase "Original Sin" indicates a reality, this cannot mean that it is due solely to the will of the isolated individual. To-day in particular, when the super-individual elements in the economic sphere stand out more clearly than ever before, evil appears primarily in its *collective form*. We recognize it in two main forms: in that of the super-individual economic spirit—as the "economic spirit of the age"—and in that of the economic system itself.

The *economic spirit*(16) of an age, like the style and general spirit of an age, is a collective phenomenon, a force, which the individual can never entirely evade; its influence is increased by the fact that he is scarcely conscious of it. Thus, for example, the "Spirit of Capitalism"—a sum of economic axioms—is a collective force, like the "Gothic Spirit" (Scheffler) or the "spirit of Roman Law" (Jhering). In itself this force, "the economic spirit," is neutral, but it always provides a happy hunting-ground for evil influences within the economic order, and greatly enhances their effect. It is always a "sinful spirit of the age," and it is peculiarly dangerous because it does not become explicit. This influence has usually completely escaped the notice of moralists. But the ethical significance of the *economic system* itself has also almost entirely escaped their notice; by this I mean the significance of those facts which have a certain common denominator, and, as such, determine the activity of the individual economic subject. Here we find one of the most powerful and manifest expressions of Original Sin. However this system may have come into being, at the present moment it confronts the individual as a force which it is not in his power to evade. So far as his action is concerned the economic system is like a relentless Fate. In any case, every one of us has a share in this collective sin (yes, even when we inwardly resist it), whenever we engage in any economic activity, even if we are merely using economic goods.[1]

[1] The "League of Consumers" is an attempt, on the part of the consumer, to exert some moral pressure on the system.

The evil within the economic order may be summed up, according to its quality, in three main forms: 1. Lack of economic energy: in the language of biology: economic atrophy—in the language of ethics: *indolence*; 2. Excess of (objective or subjective) economic interest; in biological language: economic hypertrophy—in the language of ethics: *the mania for profits and for work*; and 3. Economic *egoism*. To-day it is essentially the two last forms which are important, although with the disappearance of joy in work the first is also not without its significance. The second phenomenon appears, highly intensified, in what has been described as the "daemonic spirit" in the economic sphere(17), that is, the relentless effort to make the economic aim absolute, the madness of "economics for its own sake." In the main, the third form of evil becomes rampant where the economic system tends to a more or less unrestricted individualism, and no effective barriers are therefore set up to protect the weak from ruthless exploitation by the strong. It is the Christian's duty to fight against this evil element in the economic order, in all its forms, for faith has taught him that he is bound to obey God. The Christian should be particularly on his guard against the insidious influence of the "economic spirit"; in spite of the fact that his desire to improve the situation is hampered by almost insuperable obstacles, he must take care that he does not follow the line of least resistance, and end in doing "as the heathen do." He should be aware that the divinely willed meaning of the economic order is not the profit of the individual, but the "common good," the maintenance of the human life of the community, and this knowledge ought to determine his desires and his actions. He must not allow himself to be swept away by the "daemonic spirit" of the economic world, by the "spirit of mammon," the "spirit of Capitalism," or by the tendency to transform economic activity and economic goods into gods; for he knows that he cannot "serve God and Mammon."[1] Indeed, his faith and courage are renewed when he realizes that he is called to serve the life of the community, and that this call means that he is to do his ordinary daily work as a service to his neighbour, and to the Glory of God. The "economic spirit," which is so hostile to God, may indeed be a force which oppresses him in the form of the "spirit of the age," and even tries to capture his soul, but it is not a blind Fate which he

[1] Matt. vi. 24.

is impotent to resist. The power of the economic spirit of an age, hostile to God, resides, in the last resort, in the spirit of the individual, and nowhere else. Here is the point at which the lever can and must be inserted in order to make the economic order better fitted to serve its Divine purpose.

The economic system of a period, or of a people, is, at least in part, the product of this economic spirit, which again has its origin in the "system of values." Faith in the Creator and Redeemer produces a different economic valuation and a different economic scale of values from that of the "heathen." Least of all can the believer resemble the *homo oeconomicus* presupposed by the classic type of political economy, in which self-interest is the only motive which is even considered; nor can he fall a prey to that Utopian philosophy which, like the economic philosophy erected upon the work of Rousseau and Quesnay(18), looks for the welfare of all as the result of unrestricted individual egoism. Although he may have no "Christian economic programme" to suggest, yet he does know something special about the meaning of the economic order, and those guiding principles which control economic labour and the distribution of economic goods. Even if the majority in any nation were to consist of real Christians, it would not mean that we were anywhere near a "Christian economic order"; on the other hand, this might very well lead to something more in harmony with the Divine meaning of the economic order, something more just and humane than that which we now call the economic order(19).

5. The Individual Economic Factors from the Ethical Point of View

Selfish economic exploitation, in contradistinction to political exploitation, consists in the exploitation of advantages in co-operation and exchange in favour of the individual, at the cost of the community. Co-operation and exchange, apart from ethical reasons, come into being because one person needs another. I intend to describe this fact (coupled with the further fact that it is a particular person who is needed here and now) by a coined phrase: "comparative monopoly"(20). The phenomenon of "comparative monopoly" is, by Creation and by History, due to the differences between individuals, and the actual configuration in which they occur. Economic life consists in an adjustment between the different levels of these monopolies. As soon as we desire the economic order as a community, and not as a rigid unity, then we are forced to desire the existence of comparative monopolies. In the rational Communistic economic system this "exchange" is regarded merely as a necessary evil, as the removal of a disturbing element—that is, of inequality—since the ultimate aim is the isolated existence of the individual. The Creator, who has created us for community—for mutual dependence upon one another—has therefore created us with "comparative monopolies"—that is, with reciprocal needs and surpluses. The "comparative monopoly" is part of the Divine order of Creation. But this "monopoly" immediately becomes an economic danger, since the possessor of a monopoly which may happen to be stronger at this point will selfishly exploit it by demanding a higher remuneration than he actually deserves. The more that his comparative monopoly approaches the absolute—that is, when it is urgently required, and he has almost exclusive possession of it—the more the owner of the monopoly is tempted to take a selfish advantage of the other person's need, and to exploit him. From this point of view the different elements in the economic process are manifestly extremely unequal.

The fundamental monopoly, the basis of the whole economic order, is *the land*. Landowners, contrasted with people who own no land, possess what is, in principle, not a relative but an absolute monopoly. The landowner can almost throttle the non-landowner out of existence. Here, therefore, the economic question merges into the political struggle. The fact that the land occupies such an exceptional position raises the pertinent question: Is the actual possession of land or of private property contrary to the meaning of the Divine order in Creation?(21) In any case, from the ethical point of view, this monopoly is far more dubious than others. A monopoly of *tools* seems to do far less harm; for every one can procure tools. But the more complicated and costly the tool—as at the present day, for instance, when "tools" mean machines, factories, and industrial undertakings—the more powerful does it become as a monopoly, the more it tends to develop into an absolute monopoly; here therefore free exchange tends to be transformed into non-moral compulsion.

The third form of monopoly is the *bodily and mental power of work*. Since the power of the monopoly depends on the fact that what is required is rare, and is also urgently needed, capacity for intellectual work is a higher monopoly than strength of body; indeed, so far as the individual is concerned, physical capacity for work, as such, apart from other special qualities, has almost no value at all, because it is so widespread. It is only where a number of human labour units combine to form a union, or where legal regulations restrict freedom of choice, that this capacity for work also gains a considerable monopoly-value. Thus in every economic system human selfishness threatens the position of those who can only offer services depending on bodily strength: in antiquity and in the Middle Ages this was the peasant, who did not own the land; in modern times it is the "worker," who does not own the "tools" (i.e. capital)(22). In the merely economic struggle for existence—quite apart from politics—inevitably he is the one who is most exploited. His only effective means of overcoming his impotence is the formation of strong Labour organizations; in addition, he can use the political method. As an element in the monopoly, the product of labour, the economic product which has been prepared for the consumer, is hardly taken into account at all; it is rather a subject than a means of discussion. In so far as it actually enters into the economic struggle, in the form of capital, it comes under the heading of tools.

Rational *individualism* places no restrictions on the growth of these monopolies, in spite of their dangerous tendencies; rational *collectivism*, on the other hand, seeks to make them ineffective by bringing all kinds of monopoly down to the same level. Individualism produces a "daemonic" vitality in the economic sphere; collectivism produces an equally dangerous paralysis of the necessary economic tension. Individualism breeds the economic beast of prey, and creates the "Might is Right" of the Super-man; collectivism breeds the herdman, and at the same time it produces an "entropy" which means that life is brought to a standstill; this, again, can only be overcome by force. In the light of all that we have just been considering, it is obvious that it is a moral duty to provide the weak monopolies with some "artificial" support, and to restrict the activities of the powerful monopolies. How this is to be done, however, can only be discerned in any given situation where practical action must be taken; it cannot be anticipated in general terms.

This brings us to the question of *economic democracy*(23). Here the attempt is made to balance the powers vested in monopolies by giving equal rights to all, or, at least, by allow-

413

ing every one to have a voice in these matters. The voting paper (whether in politics or industry) certainly does, to some extent, affect production and distribution; of course it does not exert a controlling influence, for that would mean rational Communism; still, it has a certain amount of influence. The value of this corrective idea is indisputable, but from the ethical point of view it is important to remember that its value should not be exaggerated. When the ethical importance of this idea *is* exaggerated it usually means that people have fallen into the error of believing that the majority will always know what is best for the majority. In the last resort, this opinion is based simply on the individualistic optimistic idea of the Enlightenment: that rational self-love will lead to the "greatest happiness of the greatest number." In opposition to this view, we ought to consider very seriously whether economic democracy, if carried to its logical conclusion, would not lead to the ruin of the economic order, in so far as its primary aim of meeting the needs of humanity is concerned? An unconditional, axiomatic belief in democracy might have still more disastrous consequences in the economic sphere than in the political sphere. Behind it there lies the rationalistic desire for "equality," which denies the Divine order in creation, according to which the human community cannot exist apart from energetic and powerful guidance by individuals. In the economic sphere, however, since, on the one hand, its pace is far greater than that of the political sphere, and, on the other hand, it is far more closely bound to technical necessities, the elimination of competent and energetic leadership would be far more disastrous than for the State.

In view of this formulation of the problem, the objection may be raised: while admitting the purely economic disadvantage of an economic democracy, stress is laid on the fact that its intellectual and educational value is great enough to outweigh this disadvantage, since democracy breeds a widespread sense of responsibility. In answer to this objection there are two points I would like to emphasize: first of all, we cannot thus ignore the objective purpose of the economic order, which is, to provide humanity with the necessities of life; this purpose is and must remain the point of view which determines the economic order. Love teaches us that we must stand for an economic order which will really "nourish," whether it be democratic or autocratic. And secondly, in view of our experience of political democracy it is surely rather risky to lay quite so much stress on the intellectual value of the democratic system—and here we mean this particular *form*, not the *spirit*—and to value it so highly and exclusively. "Universal responsibility" may also mean, as experience has shown us, universal irresponsibility, shelving responsibility on the community as a whole, or in point of fact it may mean the transference of responsibility to representative groups or to anonymous cliques. Let us never forget this: as a rule where every one "has his say" the level of output is not particularly high, nor is there any very deep sense of responsibility. This does not mean that the idea of economic democracy, as a corrective, ought to be rejected, but that we certainly ought to question its validity in ethics. Economic democracy is not always a value "in itself," although under some circumstances this may be the case. Only those who cannot distinguish between the orders of ,the "Church" and the "world" will maintain that democracy follows necessarily from the Christian conception of brotherhood.

One aspect of the evil within the economic order is represented by the selfish exploitation of monopolies. The other aspect is the tendency to set up the aim of the economic order, and the economic goods themselves, as an absolute; this leads to the "daemonic spirit" of the economic sphere. Since, however, the latter is intimately connected with the actual structure of the economic order, it will be well to expound this aspect in the light of the economic system of the present day.

CHAPTER XXXV

THE CHRISTIAN IN THE PRESENT ECONOMIC ORDER

1. *The Christian and the Capitalist System*

IT is impossible to define the task of the Christian within the economic sphere if we do not know this economic sphere in its specific historical form. The task of the Christian varies with the kind of economic system within which he himself has to act on economic lines. Failure to perceive this fact is one of the main causes for the almost incredible remoteness of traditional Protestant ethics from actual life; it also explains why the Church, as a whole, in its attitude towards the social question is so completely out of touch with reality. It is true, of course, that there are certain fundamental requirements which are valid in every economic system. But the urgency of this problem *to-day*, for the Christian who "takes his religion seriously," lies in the question: "How am I to come to terms with the realities and demands which are characteristic of the economic order of the *present day?*" We are now aware that the economic system is not ethically neutral; when we look at the question as a whole we see clearly that it is the economic system which decides whether justice or injustice, humanity or inhumanity, service of the community or some private good shall prevail, that is, it decides the ethical character of the economic activity of the individual. An unjust, wicked economic system—whether you will or no—makes your economic activity unjust and wicked. The Church, in particular, needs to realize that at this point the individualistic way of thinking breaks down. Where the economic order has become dis-order, when chaos breaks out, "where the dykes are threatened, then the cry is raised: 'All hands to the pumps.'"[1] I use this illustration because it applies to the present economic system. From the point of view of community the capitalist economy is an unjust and wicked economic system. This statement will be elaborated in the following pages(1). As theological moralists we are under the obligation to enquire into the nature of capitalism, because we must enquire into the basis of the community within which the

[1] See above, p. 233.

Christian has to glorify God and serve his neighbour in his work.

The term *Capitalism* may mean very different things: this variety of idea is due to the way in which first one aspect of its nature and then another is emphasized, and naturally such considerations lead to very different ethical views(2). In my description of Capitalism I shall not use the analytical causal method, but the synthetic method, which tries to understand a phenomenon in its own terms. Thus, following the method of Sombart,[1] I shall try to understand Capitalism as a whole; therefore I shall not study its causes but its nature. Only when this line of approach is followed do we perceive that Capitalism is a wholly *new* phenomenon in history, and that in the main it is not based on material and technological developments— whether in the sphere of production or of finance—but upon phenomena of a moral order, to which these developments are related, partly as causes and partly as effects. Hence I shall not describe Capitalism in general, but that phase of modern Western Capitalism characteristic of the political economy of the present day. Thus, basically, Capitalism appears first of all as an "attitude" of modern man towards the economic sphere as a whole—what Sombart calls the "economic spirit" —and as a pattern of community life; the structure of productive capital ("Capitalism" in the technical sense of the word) is here seen to be a secondary element, which might also be connected with a non-capitalistic economy. We shall perceive at once that the connexion between the economic mentality and the pattern of communal life is very close and intimate; we shall perceive, further, that both are derived from a common source—namely, the view that modern man takes of his own nature; this comes out still more clearly when, following Sombart's treatment of the subject, we illustrate our thesis by indicating the individual elements of this fundamental attitude towards the economic system.

The first element is the principle of profit. "The aim of all economic activity within the framework of capitalism is profit, and, indeed, financial profit. This idea of profit is the counterpart of the idea of 'livelihood' which . . . dominates all the pre-capitalistic economic systems."[2] Money value, an

---

[1] The following sketch of capitalism is based chiefly on the great work of SOMBART (see below, Note (2)). The quotations are taken from the latest description of Capitalism, which Sombart gives in the *Handwörterbuch der Soziologie*.   [2] SOMBART, loc. cit., p. 258.

abstraction which can be expressed in arithmetical terms—
and thus purely quantitative—is the opposite of all the earlier
forms of qualitative valuation. And this idea of value is the
main presupposition for the formation of capital; for only
when one is primarily interested in the abstract money value
can one replace the actual good, without enjoying it, within
the process as capital. "Its unrestricted character is due to the
abstract nature of its purpose,"[1] the unrestrained character
of the acquisitive instinct, and also to its unconditional
character, by means of which "the whole of life becomes one
great business,"[2] and, finally, to the ruthlessness of the
acquisitive temper, since "the intensity of the acquisitive
effort has here reached its zenith, and all scruples based on
ethics or on sentiment have been swept away."[3]

But this new conception of the economic order is necessarily
bound up with a new conception of the relation between the
individual and the community, with *individualism*, that is,
with a "mental attitude, according to which the individual
economic subject feels himself to be exclusively dependent
upon himself."[4] Real capitalism only begins with the transformation of legal conditions in the sense of *laissez-faire*. Therefore, by its very nature, it is necessarily a system which favours
private enterprise and liberty of commerce. The whole
economic order becomes mercantile. The isolated private
enterprise, the "capitalist enterprise,"[5] severed from all
personal interests, and in its fully developed form anonymous,
as a joint stock company, is an absolutely new phenomenon in
history. "No previous century, no other form of culture has
ever developed anything like our Capitalist enterprise, our kind
of business concern." To secure profits, to see to it "that the
debit and credit account in the ledger should close with a
balance in favour of the capitalistic undertaking; all success
lies in achieving this result."[6] Therefore, this economic system
necessarily includes a third element: that of "economic
Rationalization,"[7] that is, the complete spirit of calculation,
the arithmetical reckoning of all economic factors. All concrete
qualities, all personal relations, right up to the direction of
the business, are formalized, standardized, and, finally, reduced
to a common denominator; all values can be expressed
numerically and this numerical value is the only one which

[1] SOMBART, *Handwörterbuch der Soziologie*, p. 259.   [2] Ibid.
[3] Ibid.   [4] Ibid.   [5] Ibid., p. 262.
[6] Ibid., p. 263.   [7] Ibid., p. 259.

is taken into account. It is this which makes the relation between the man who is engaged in economic activity and economic goods, and between himself and other men, such a purely matter-of-fact and "soulless" one.[1] This introduces into the economic sphere a kind of calculating necessity which has nothing to do with the personal motive of the individual, it is the "objectification of the striving for gain";[2] the *entrepreneur*, whether he wants it or not, "must will the successful working of the capitalistic enterprise, and that is, to secure gain."[3] Thus the economic sphere becomes one vast mechanical monster, which runs with a sort of apparently natural necessity, and leaves to the creative and personal element scarcely any other scope than the discovery of the chance of gain.

The effects of this new economic system on the relation between man and his work, man and things, and above all, on the relation between man and society, are incalculable. The following are some of the main results of the severance of labour and property in the means of production; that the outstanding figure in economic life is no longer the person who actually does the work, whether as "worker" or as "technician" or as director, but the one who holds the purse, the "capitalist"; that the system is based, not on the producer but on the merchant;[4] that unearned income is no longer an exception but that the economic system is based upon it. For it is by no means a foregone conclusion that the capitalist himself does any work; his investments yield their dividends even if he does nothing; he may even hand over the management of his concern to paid workers (that is, he can use the brains of other people). The more impersonal the enterprise becomes, the more complete is the severance of the profits of labour (dividends) from the manual and intellectual labour itself. By this very real "abstraction" the relation between the employer of labour (the capitalist), and the one who is employed (as workman, clerk, technician, or manager), becomes completely impersonal, purely numerical; practically, therefore, all "personal considerations" entirely disappear.

---

[1] SOMBART, *Handwörterbuch der Soziologie*, p. 265.
[2] Ibid., p. 266.   [3] Ibid., p. 266.
[4] What this means from the ethical point of view can be seen from the fact that during the whole history of the Christian era, even at the time of the Reformation, the profession of merchant was regarded as one of the last to be adopted by earnest Christians, since it was held to be a calling involving its holder in grave moral danger.

Since, in the so-called "free" contract of labour, owing to the rise in the price of the means of production, the proprietor of this expensive tool (factory, stock) is always the one who has the upper hand, this "freedom" becomes more or less an illusion; thus the capitalist dictates the terms, and it is he who has entire control both of the product of the labour and of the economic system as a whole. This leads inevitably to an increase in the means of production, and, combined with free competition, to the concentration of capital, which for its part again leads to the intensification of the "tools-monopoly" over against the "labour-monopoly"; the main economic power is concentrated in the hands of a few (trust, company, syndicate) and this economic power, again, is transformed into political and social influence(3). More or less, the great owners of capital control the Press, which needs capital, and the State, which also needs capital; they make their influence felt in the Church, which needs money, in the municipalities, and so on.

It is obvious that capital—here we may well use the neutral term, since the individual persons do not appear at all over against the business which they represent—uses this position of power in order to gain still more power and profit. On the other hand, this concentration of economic power—this formation of economic principalities and empires—has the effect of still further de-personalizing economic life; the more powerful the economic groups become, the more must everything be eliminated which cannot be expressed in figures and schedules, the more impersonal, and therefore the more ruthless, must the relation between the employer of labour and the employee become; the more, too, the relation to things is based upon figures. More and more the typical standard representative of the modern economic system is the capitalist who "goes in for" silk or gramophones, as well as for coal and ship-building—who may even turn from the one to the other, as his fancy directs—all he has to do is to buy the necessary shares, together with the directors and works managers who belong to the business. With this spirit of calculation the motive of gain increases automatically and stifles everything else. The concentration of capital leads to the absorption of the middle-class (though this may not yet be a radical process yet it is undeniably increasing) by the two dominant classes: the class of the industrial workers and the—numerically small—class of the capitalists. The *proletariat* comes into being; to the extent in which the capitalist economic system predominates the majority of the population is forced into the class of the dependent workers, who are obliged to depend on the wages or the salary paid by the capitalist, who buys their labour, and controls their work, without their having any say in the matter at all. The only point at which they can express an opinion is the "free" labour contract, whose "free" character diminishes the greater the number of those who can gain their living in this way alone. This proletariat, which includes not merely the "workmen" but likewise the lesser officials (clerks), and the badly paid technicians, forms a special and new *class*, not only in the economic but also in the psychological sense of the term; this class possesses its quite definite psychological characteristics which ought to be noted carefully by the moralist; these characteristics must be explained as due to the following factors: uncertainty of employment; frequent and enforced change of domicile; likewise enforced change of work; complete dependence on the employer of labour, coupled with an increased desire for independence and a consciousness of freedom; the keen knowledge of the economic exploitation of which they are the victims; and· life in the hurry of great cities, surrounded by the artificial conditions of city life (German: *Asphaltkultur*).

Ethically, however, the most serious consequence of Capitalism, so far as the worker is concerned, is that it robs labour of its dignity. It is not modern technique which necessarily renders labour soulless—although a great effort is needed not to let it come to this—but the *position* of the worker in the economic community. Here, too, it is evident that the real ethical problem is not the individual aspect—the relation of the individual to the world of things—but his relation to the community. Capitalism makes labour, and the workman himself, something which can be bought and sold, something which can be exchanged for its numerical value. He (the worker) is merely an "item" in the calculation of profits— and this not because the capitalist as a person is inhuman, but because Capitalism makes this inhumanity necessary. Labour becomes degraded to a mere commodity. "Capitalism treats the man who works as if he were a material object; it disregards his vital quality as a man, and therefore it also disregards his right, as a living human being, to freedom, dignity, and the fulfilment of the meaning of his life. For since the workman is nothing more than a means to a concrete end, the curve of his life is wholly dependent on the material conditions of the labour market; the moment that the concrete purpose of the production of goods is not desired the curve declines; he is then dismissed."[1] In the capitalist economic system the workman is cast out of the economic *community*, since in it he is valued only as an object, not as a subject, and *must* be valued thus. The "objectification of the striving after gain" requires it; it turns this lot into fate. It is *this*, and not in the first place material exploitation, against which the worker rebels; it is this which destroys his joy in work. The real sin of Capitalism against the worker is this: the sin against the sense of personality, and this means against the sense of community in labour.

This picture of the Capitalist system does not entirely tally with the actual economic system of the present day; for, first, Capitalism has not been able wholly to set aside the pre-capitalistic system, and second, for some time past counter-movements have already been set in motion(4). On the one hand, the State, by limiting individual economic freedom in favour of weak "monopolies," by laws for the protection of the workers, by watching over and influencing conditions of labour, by social services, etc., has checked the effects of Capitalism; on the other hand, by means of powerful organization, those who are economically dependent have been able to secure at least a certain influence over the distribution of economic goods; finally, the State, or the community, have themselves become economic entities, and have thus placed themselves as a partly communal-socialist or State-socialist economy over against the capitalist economy. In spite of all this, however, in the main, the economic world of the present day presents the features of Capitalism as we have just drawn them. This is what the economic sphere looks like with which the Christian has to come to terms.

It is, indeed, inevitable that the first effect of this picture should be to awaken a sense of horror, not merely in the soul of a believer, but in every one who still has a soul in this soulless economic world. The expression "monster," which Sombart frequently uses of Capitalism, is no exaggeration. Within this soulless economic "order," which destroys personal relations and reverses the order of nature, is it possible to do any "work" which rises above the world of things, "work"

[1] HEIMANN: *Kapitalismus und Sozialismus*, p. 178.

which is offered as a service to the community, and is done for the glory of God? Is it possible to realize the personal meaning of labour in such an anti-personal economic system? Can, indeed, the proletarian or the capitalist understand at all what we theologians who stand on the mere fringe of this terrible soulless world are saying about the idea of vocation, about the idea of service, and the dignity of labour? Is it not a fact that at this point the collective sin, the opposition to God, in this system, is so powerful, in the negative sense, that the individual cannot prevail against it? So much at any rate is clear: if ever an economic system has a definite ethical character, and if this ethical character of the economic system helps to determine the ethical character of the life of the individual, then this is what we can say about the Capitalist system: it is that system in which all that we can see to be the meaning of the economic order from the point of view of faith is being denied: in which, therefore, it is made almost impossible for the individual to realize, in any way, through his economic activity, the service of God and of his neighbour. This system is contrary to the spirit of service; it is debased and irresponsible; indeed, we may go further and say: it is irresponsibility developed into a system.

And yet we know that no system is wholly the work of Fate. Even in this system the individual to whom God has granted the gift of faith, and from whom He requires a life in faith and love, still has that amount of scope which makes it possible to exercise love, in spite of the fact that he is entangled in the meshes of a system which is opposed to love. Although it is clear that this system arose, historically, out of a definite economic spirit, yet the fact that this system exists does not make it necessary for the individual to become infected with this economic spirit(5). Even as a capitalist it is possible to be an anti-capitalist "at heart," and even to translate something of this spirit—even though it may be a very little—into act. Even as a member of the proletariat—although only with the help of special grace—it is possible to understand the meaning of the words "vocation," "service," "love," and to do one's work in this spirit, as a service to the community within this horrible machinery of the profit system. For—in spite of everything—it is this economic system which supports us all, bad or good; it is this system by means of which God now maintains our lives. As a workman, or a manufacturer or a banker, I may be obliged to do things which run counter to all that can be described as brotherly love; but I need not be infected by the spirit of this economic system; and in the very fact that I do not allow myself to be entangled in this net I can experience the liberty of the children of God, and rise above the world—and in some way or another—I can realize this freedom. To do this remains the first and the chief commandment in a Christian economic ethic, even in the age of modern Capitalism. We cannot let the Christian life wait until a better economic order is here; none of us knows whether he will ever know any better order.

And yet it seems almost an insult to ask those who are the chief victims of this "order" to adapt themselves to it as the place to which God has appointed them; and it *is* an insult if this demand is not accompanied by the clearly expressed will to transform this pseudo-order, which is really anarchy, into a real order, so far as this lies within human power to achieve. But *is* such a change possible? While I seek to approach this subject with all necessary caution, conscious of the danger of "playing with ideas" in a dilettante way, the first point to stress is this: that Capitalism is not only the product of a definite economic disposition, it is also the product of circumstances beyond the range of human control. The most important of these facts are the following: an immense increase in population, coupled with an increased self-consciousness and a higher standard of living; the mechanical technique of production and of transport; further, partly as the result of this, the development of national trade into world trade, and finally, the transition from barter to currency and banking. The economic order of the Middle Ages, with its sense of community supported by a patriarchal personalism, could not do justice to these new facts. The upheaval had to come, and it is idle to ask whether it might have come in another way. So much in any case we see clearly: that several of the features which characterize the capitalist system constitute our destiny for as much as we can see of the immediate future. We cannot go back, behind the Industrial Revolution, behind the world economy—we cannot go back to a system of barter and to the patriarchal order of guilds and handicrafts(6). It would not merely be quixotic to dream oneself back into the Middle Ages, it would also be the greatest offence against love, for the vast masses of the population of the civilized world can only be sustained by means of rational mass production and world trade. To bemoan the impersonality of the present system, its habit of reckoning costs solely in numerical terms, the abstract nature of long-distance communications, has no practical sense, since to-day—even with the best will in the world—we cannot carry on economic life in any other way. In this sense Capitalism is our destiny, which we cannot evade, in which no alterations of the economic system which could be devised as alternatives could alter anything. Capitalism, in the technological sense of the term, will be the permanent factor in every future economic system, whatever it may be called.

We must now translate our abstract observations on Capitalism into concrete terms; that is, we must never forget that the primary aim of the economic system—that of providing mankind with actual sustenance—must always, for love's sake, remain its controlling purpose. This means, that for reasons of humanity we ought to fight against Capitalism only to the extent which can be combined with the realization of this primary aim. The most "humane" economic system is more cruel than an "inhuman" one if it is unable to provide man with that which he needs for his actual existence. It is *this* that constitutes the actual "autonomy of the economic system." Now there is no doubt that since the capitalist system has been established the average standard of life has risen; whether this is due to Capitalism itself is scarcely possible for people like us to decide. But it *is* certain that by means of Capitalism productive energies have been vastly increased. On the other hand, however, experts point out that the lack of method in the individualistic form of the economic system leads to the most disastrous results(7). They point out that, on the other hand, the release of economic energy, which has become an obsession, is accompanied, on the other, by a lack of zest for work on the part of the masses, and that while the standard of living has risen, there is an immense inequality in possessions, and the worker has no rights; the profit system can no longer satisfy real needs, and it creates countless artificial needs; lack of planning in a system based on competition leads to the absurdity of "over-production," and to the still more stupid absurdity of unemployment. The fallacious character of the Utilitarian axiom, "Each person's happiness is a good to that person, and the general happiness, therefore, a good to the aggregate of all persons," was not perceived at first; this was only due to the fact that the ascendancy of this philosophy coincided with the introduction of machinery; this created a prosperity which, due to a misunderstanding, was ascribed to Capitalism(8). Capitalism—that is, the lack of any planned order—can no longer cope with the close interconnexion of all countries and all spheres of life which now exists; in the present world crisis we are experiencing the *débâcle* of this anarchical "order."

However risky it may appear for a non-specialist to give his opinion on a technical problem of such complexity, still it ought not to be forgotten that we are not completely in the dark on this subject. Capitalism is such a perversion of the divine order of creation, that we would feel obliged to assert its economically ruinous character even if—though certainly the contrary is the case—all the experts were to say the opposite. An economic system which contradicts the divine order to such an extent *must* prove the ruin of the people; this is a fact which none can gainsay. Here we are dealing not with technical questions but with the fundamental ethical question: can we as Christians affirm a system which, as such, in its very foundations, is opposed to morality? Or to express it otherwise: have we any right to allow the experts to convince us(9) that *only* this system—whose anti-moral character we know—is in a position to provide humanity with the satisfaction of its daily needs? To this question I answer: No. We are under the obligation to seek for an order which is really order and not anarchy. Capitalism is economic anarchy; therefore the Christian is obliged to fight against it, and to fight for a real order.

2. *The Search for a Better Order*

The fact that no "Christian" or even "just" economic system exists, should not hinder us from seeking for a better and more just system. If, however, as moralists we believed that we could outline a programme for this better order we would in the last resort show ourselves to be simply dilettante visionaries. The better order will not be discovered by people sitting quietly round a committee table, but only in the struggle and effort of those who understand these questions and are deeply involved in them. What we can do, however, is this: we can reflect critically upon those possibilities which have emerged in the course of economic strife as aims of propaganda, for or against which we may have to decide in the very near future.

Rational collectivism or Communism is—or at least appears to be—the very antipodes of liberal Capitalism. It takes over all the essential features of Capitalism with the exception of the two decisive factors: the motive of profit and individualism. The profit motive is replaced by production for use; while private possession of the means of production is replaced by radical collectivization. The transition from the one to the other is effected by means of political force; but there is another point at which force has to be introduced: the economic stimulus, the automatic flow, which is absent from this system has to be replaced by coercion. But this means, partly through the will of the proletariat, partly through the political power which is given to the proletarian authorities, the Communist Party wills to set up an economic system based on a rational "plan," and in so doing to guarantee an equal distribution of goods, and at the same time to provide the community more rationally with a supply of necessities.

In this particular connexion we might disregard as accidental the fact that behind this economic idea there lies a whole philosophy of culture, and that with its propagation there is bound up a whole cultural programme, were it not for the fact that at the same time these ideas are proclaimed as the bases of this economic programme. In this programme, for the first time, the rational idea of equality is taken seriously. It was born out of the abstract rational idea of equality; it is therefore, in the last resort, a radical individualism, as, indeed, comes out clearly also in the "eschatology" of Communism(10). The final point of reference, in spite of all that would appear to the contrary, is the welfare of the individual. For the whole is only conceived in an arithmetical atomistic way, as a conglomeration of individuals; the force exercised by the State is regarded as a temporary provisional measure, as a necessary evil for the moment, which can be allowed to drop out once all "have learned to think in terms of Communism." Here there comes out clearly the self-delusion of rational optimism. Rational Communism is therefore just as much a believer in "progress" as its twin-brother: rational individualism. Actually, however, as the Russian experiment shows, this Communism can only be kept alive by force as it was born out of force. Therefore it is just as much opposed to the Divine order in creation as its counterpart; it is the same system, with the signs reversed.

In so far as Marxist Socialism can still be identified with a programme, the same is true of it as of rational Communism, with the one difference, that it desires to attain its end legitimately by political means and not by violence. It is true, of course, that "socialization" likes to conceal the fact that in practice the term simply means "nationalization." It is obvious that even the Socialist order can only be set up, and maintained, by means of the power of the State—certainly this is conceived as the power of the majority, legally exercised. But there is more in it than this; for here, too, as in rational Communism, the State would be the real economic authority. Only democracy is substituted for the "dictatorship of the proletariat," that is, an economic State-democracy, and this not as a corrective, but as the very essence of the system. As a logical result of all this, therefore, there arises a whole crop of problems, which may be summed up by the words: bureaucracy, demagogy, incompetent leadership, and general irresponsibility. Even this basic idea of a consistent State Socialism has been too deeply influenced by the rationalism of the French Encyclopedists to be able to guarantee, in any way, the realization of an economic national community (*Volksgemeinschaft*).

But this Marxist programme is no longer authoritative for the "Socialist Movement"(11) of the present day—in so far as it does not wholeheartedly accept Communism. The vital element within it—and, indeed, the fact which prejudices its activity in political agitation—is the very fact that it no longer possesses a fixed programme. Its whole aim is being gradually transformed, and is moving in the direction of a principle of co-operation, which issues from an entirely different source, and is connected with the medieval "guild" idea. Broadly speaking, we might say that this kind of Socialism seeks to transfer the bond of unity of the medieval guilds and corporations to the new economic conditions. Whereas French Syndicalism stands closer to the rational anarchist Utopian way of thought, and the German type is only gradually severing itself from the Communistic programme of State Socialism, for some time past the English Socialist Movement has been striving (as in Guild Socialism) with ever-increasing determination towards a goal which derives from a totally different idea of community, or, to put it better, from a real idea of community, not from the point of view of the rational idea of unity at all.

This, again, raises a host of questions. By what power does

this kind of Socialism expect to attain its ends? What guarantee does it offer that the large individual groups will not fight against each other—to the injury of the common weal? How is this co-operative structure to be applied not merely to a national economy but also to a world economy? Or how could a co-operatively constituted national economy overcome the evil of the Capitalist world economy? But in spite of all these misgivings it is impossible to suppress the feeling that the "better" order of the immediate future lies in this direction, all the more since on the *bourgeois* side also we perceive the growth of similar ideas. Even if romantic sociology, with its idea of the articulated structure of the nation as a "body," is far too beautiful to be true, still it contains the idea that the individualism of the present economic system must be overcome, without abstract unity being set up in place of mutual limitation of that which is unequal. The "solution" which seems to be preparing, both on the Right and on the Left, aims at that "mean" between collectivism and individualism which we have shown to be the guiding principle in a general way, which, however, must not be confused with a programme—even with a programme of compromise; it must remain a critical principle, and must therefore never become a principle of construction.

There is, however, one point, which must be emphasized, as the result of all that we have just been considering, namely: that as Capitalism was actually *created* by a definite economic spirit the only force which will really overcome Capitalism will be a *different* economic spirit. Even behind the Communist Revolution there stands a great ethical urge, a powerful idea, a new way of thinking and willing. This new determination has been the driving force behind that upheaval—whatever we may think of the movement in other ways. Thus it was also the idea of community which made Marxist Socialism a power (rather than its scientific programme), and it was the fatalistic idea of historical materialism which paralysed it. In the economic question, if anywhere at all, it is quite evident that mere technological progress, combined with the motive of profit, is unable to produce anything healthy and vital. This confirms what we have already said, namely, that decisive changes in social conditions always issue from a change in the "system of values" of the purposive will. It is at this point therefore that the Church is confronted with her important educational and missionary task. She knows what community is; she knows that community is not something extra added to life, but that it is the very substance of human life itself. She knows that community differs from unity. She knows, too, that community in the world, in the economic sphere, must be different from brotherhood between comrades in the same Faith; but she knows at the same time that real community can be created and nourished by the spirit of brotherhood. It is the duty of the Church to canvass the idea in order that she may help to bring about a better economic community. And, if she is well advised, she knows that in this work she can join forces with all those of good-will, whether Christian or non-Christian. For here we are dealing with that kind of "community" which can be perceived by "reason," although reason is not a timeless entity but has been instructed by the Christian Faith. It is the duty of the Church—not of the Church alone, but still of the Church above all—to revive the idea of the responsibility of all for all, the idea of concrete responsibility in mutual unity; for only out of this thinking and willing can a new order be created, which—while it certainly is not the Kingdom of God—does deserve to be called a "better" economic order.[1]

But this work of preparation does not exhaust the obligation of the Christian to work for the creation of this "better order."· A new order will not come into being simply through a new spirit, but only through direct political action. Even the Christian is placed within the politico-economic struggle for power, and he has no right to withdraw from it. Capitalism, not Marxist Socialism, has turned this struggle into a class struggle(12). In a broader sense class struggle is as old as history itself, in the shape of the struggle of the unprivileged against "exploitation" for an improvement in their position, and of the privileged against the "seditionists" for the existing order, that is, for their own privileges. But modern Capitalism alone has divided the economic world into these two halves: capitalists and proletarians. This struggle is inevitable, for only through it can the better order come into being. Never yet has a class willingly renounced its privileges; it is just as unfair to prohibit a proletarian who wants to be a Christian from taking part in this struggle, as it is to forbid a servant girl from giving notice to a bad mistress. Whether we are

[1] Cf. the fine observations on this subject by the Zürich political economist E. BÖHLER: *Technik und Wirtschaft in den geistigen Entscheidungen der Gegenwart*, 1931.

dealing with the directly economic struggle, that is, with the struggle for power between the economic organizations by economic means of pressure; or with the struggle carried on by the political methods of the formation of parties and the power of Government, the fact remains: no one can or ought to withdraw from this struggle. If a Christian thinks that he ought not to take part in a strike, then he ought also to renounce the advantages which he gains from the struggle waged by others; or rather, if, as a good Christian, he is willing to endure the injustice of his position—so far as *he* is concerned—for the sake of others he ought not to do so.

Where does the Christian stand in this conflict? If all that mattered were the realization of the better order by fighting against the privileged, it would be easy to answer this question. But unfortunately things are not so simple as this, for on the one hand the ranks of the movement which is opposed to Capitalism are divided; on the other hand, not only its methods, but also its ends are such that we cannot expect as a matter of course that even the most conscientious and well-disposed Christian will join one of these opposition groups(13); we cannot take it for granted that anyone ought to expect, quite definitely, that the triumph of one of these opposition groups would mean a victory for the better order; for each of these groups contains a weird blend of right and wrong, of constructive and destructive ideas. Indeed, it is quite possible that a most ardent and self-denying person, one who is willing to go all lengths for the sake of establishing the "new order," might still feel unable to join any of these anti-capitalist groups; his hesitation to do so would be due to his conviction that these groups would do more harm than good, not to themselves, but to the people as a whole.

There are two things, however, which we have a right to expect from every one who does not wish to deny the name of Christ: first, that in his own way, and where his lot is cast, he will support all efforts to achieve the better order; and second, that he will be quite clear in his own mind that every one who does not take part in the opposition movement—of whatever shade of opinion—is simply supporting the existing "order," and this means that he is supporting economic anarchy. Of course, he may feel it right to wait for a time, if he sees signs of the formation of a more effective opposition, with which he wishes to ally himself; but he has *no* right to

431

wait if his delay means that he is virtually bolstering up the existing system.

On the other hand, a Christian ought not to allow himself to be prevented from joining the ranks of a certain opposition group because he sees that even in this opposition, which wishes to fight for the new order, there are injustices and human failings, nor because he perceives that within these ranks there is either indifference, or even open hostility, to Christianity and the Church. For here he is concerned not with the action of the Church, but with the action of the body of citizens as such, where there is no question of anybody's religious creed. Almost without exception the worst that could befall would be the formation of "Christian" parties; for this would bring in a disastrous confusion between the spheres of Church and State. "Christian" political parties are in harmony with the style, and legitimate upon the ground of Roman Catholicism; for here the Church as such has a political and economic programme. The Protestant Church as such has no programme; if she were to have one she would already have become "Roman" at heart. The curse of the betrayal of the Name of Christ broods over the "Christian" social organization for this struggle. We cannot tack this Name on to any of our little political banners(14).

This lack of clarity is also—more or less—peculiar to religious Socialism. Socialism—whatever we may mean by this expression—is an economic-political matter, a civic, not a "religious" matter. It belongs to the world, not to the Kingdom of God. Faith in the Lord Jesus Christ—thank God—stands above the struggle of parties, though it certainly constrains us to enter into this conflict. There is no programme, and therefore also no fighting group, which can be, as such, "religious," any more than it can be a "Christian" group or party; it cannot even exist in the sense that this group, although it does not actually confess the Name of Christ, represents the Cause of Christ. *We* do not know *who* represents the Cause of Christ; on the contrary, from the outset we are forced to admit that many a Christian will find a place allotted to him in the opposite group. The ultimate identification of our own cause with the Lord's cause is forbidden. "Judge not!" Indeed, we ourselves are aware that in this sphere we are dealing with relative concerns, with matters which lie in the undefined region between right and wrong, and with secular matters, in the ordering of which our purely human considerations—

rational and therefore quite misleading—frequently play a predominant part.

But in emphasizing the relative character of economic and political action I do not mean to say that these forms of action are unimportant. I do not mean that we are not to devote ourselves with all our heart to that cause which we have come to feel is the juster side, fighting for it with all our might; above all, making sacrifices and suffering for it. Every one who does this at the post which has been appointed to him will command our respect, whether he is in the camp of our opponents or in our own camp; and his readiness for self-sacrifice should make us ready to guess that that man who is fighting against us, is, in the last resort, a good Christian. If this spirit, if even only something of this spirit, were to enter into the economic struggle for power, indeed even if only those who "seriously desire to be Christians" would carry on the fight in this spirit, this *must* create an atmosphere in which new solutions could be created.

3. The Task of the Christian within the Present Economic System

We must fight for the new and better order, since the present order is such a *dis*-order, that it makes it almost impossible to serve the community. But important as this task is, it is not the first nor the. most important. We ought not to forget that even the new order, when it comes into being, will be sinful; and we ought not to forget that in spite of the fact that the present order is particularly unjust and inhuman, it is not impossible to lead a Christian life within it; in principle we can do this just as well or as badly as in any other order. It is the Christian's duty, in whatever economic order he may be living, to swim against the current; even if he has to fulfil his official duty in accordance with this unjust order, he must always be ready, wherever it is at all possible, to break through, and in spite of its inhumanity to meet his fellow-man, as far as he possibly can, as man, as his brother.

Ultimately, therefore, even within this system of Capitalism the same simple rules of Christian conduct hold good as in any of the earlier more patriarchal economic conditions; i.e. to renounce worry, to refuse to be enslaved in spirit, not to seek our own, but that which profits our neighbour, not to assert our own rights at the expense of others, not to be covetous, or acquisitive, or greedy, not to become inhuman for the sake of things, to be ready to sacrifice our own posessions for the needs of others. The commandments of the Sermon on the Mount hold good to-day just as at all other periods in history; not as a law(15) but as a guide to the Divine Command; they are fixed points which show each one of us just where he is, and in the line of his own possibilities, how he is to order his behaviour towards his neighbour. These commands mean exactly the same as the injunction that every one should exercise his calling as service to his neighbour and to the glory of God, whether he be capitalist or proletarian, manufacturer, workman, or professional man.

It is unfair and absurd to require a Christian business man to conduct his business "according to the laws of the Sermon on the Mount." No one has ever conducted business on these lines or ever will; it is against all the rules of business itself. The "office" of a business man belongs to a specific order which is not that of the relation between one person and another. On this point the business man himself, as well as his critic, ought to be quite clear; he ought to know that, even if he tries to be a just and upright business man, he is still very far from being a "Christian" business man, but that even his business activity is a bit of this wicked world; therefore those who pass judgment upon him ought not to presume to judge him. But, on the other hand, the seriousness of his Christian life must manifest itself in the fact that he fights with all his power against the evil autonomy of his official work, and that he tries again and again to break through it, which means that he treats the people with whom he has to do in business as his neighbours, to whom he owes love, and that he conducts his business as a service to the community.

Nowadays everybody is involved, in some way or another, in the Capitalist system, through some kind of economic action, however small—for instance through buying or saving; but every action, however insignificant, may be made a sign by which we witness to the fact of "Whose we are and whom we serve." The sinful economic order penetrates even into the simplest household, and even in the management of the largest Trusts it is not an absolute Fate.

There are three problems with which every individual to-day in particular has to come to terms: interest, wealth, and luxury. The individual Christian cannot withdraw from the present economic order which is based upon interest on capital(16). Just as he is obliged to give interest, so he cannot

434

avoid receiving interest. The medieval prohibition of interest (usury) was due to a legalistic interpretation of a saying of Jesus,[1] which was uttered under quite different economic presuppositions from those which are present in the capitalist economic system; it is based, secondly, upon the Aristotelian theory of the unfruitfulness of money. The present economic system is absolutely unthinkable without interest; whether it will ever be possible to dispense with it in any future economic system does not concern us here. Interest is the recompense for the loan of an economic good which is to be used for productive ends. Without such a recompense no one will embark on the risk of lending his money and renounce his own enjoyment of the productivity of the economic good. It is impossible to make sacrifice the rule of the economic sphere.

In spite of this fact, from the ethical point of view, interest remains suspect(17); for it presupposes the existence of an income for which we have not worked—even though it may not be true to say that we have done nothing to gain it. Thanks to the institution of interest it is possible to lead a completely luxurious or parasitical existence. Even in the case of a person who is enjoying the interest on capital which he has himself amassed—which cannot be regarded as a general rule nowadays—he is *now* living on the basis of work done in the past; he burdens the community with the obligation of guaranteeing him—at the present time—an unearned income from its present work, on the basis of his own work in the past. This taint clings to interest, even when we are obliged to admit that it is indispensable in the present economic order. From this fact, therefore, we may infer that one who admits the rightness of the saying: "he who will not work neither shall he eat," will accept it as his duty—not, indeed, to withdraw altogether from the economic life based on interest, for that he cannot do—but as far as possible to renounce his own enjoyment of the profit of interest, that is, that what he gains as unearned income, so far as possible he should return willingly to the community. But where the limits of this "possibility" lie, cannot be laid down as a general principle.

This question has already brought us to the second problem, that of *wealth*. To-day wealth is a still greater problem than

[1] Luke vi. 34, 35; cf. also Exod. xxii. 24; Lev. xxv. 36 ff.; Deut. xxiii. 20 ff. In the Middle Ages, the purely legalistic interpretation of this passage made it possible for business based on interest to be carried on between Christians and Jews.

435

it used to be in the past; this is because, as a rule, it is not based upon one's own work or one's own merits, but usually it stands in no reasonable relation to work or achievement. Still less therefore have we any right to ignore the saying of Jesus[1] that it is easier for a camel to go through the eye of a needle than for a rich man to enter into the Kingdom of God. If ever wealth were suspect, from the ethical point of view, it certainly is so to-day. But it is impossible to draw the line between rich and poor; and in the last resort it will not matter *whether* I possess riches but *how* I possess them. Anyone who believes that he has the right to enjoy his wealth as a natural right, simply because it belongs to him according to the law of the land, has no conscience at all. Wealth creates a special calling within which God's will has absolute authority. No one owns his wealth; in every instance he is only the "steward" of his riches. The Roman idea of property is not admissible for the Christian. Wealth for him can never be a means of enjoyment but a means of service. Enjoyment has its place even in the life of the Christian, but only as strictly limited by service. Here above all it must be made clear that he who pays heed to the will of God in his disposal of his "own" riches goes far beyond all that mere uprightness and justice would demand from him, to the very limits of that which is "possible." Where this limit comes every one must decide on his own responsibility before God; here it is our duty to listen to the Command of God Himself. Should this limit be fixed perhaps at "that which is necessary for life"? Whoever lays it down as a rule that no one ought to have more than bare necessities as long as others do not possess what is necessary(18) must be clear in his own mind that in setting up this standard he is erecting a rigorous Puritanism as the norm. For in our world of the present day there are hundreds of millions of people who do not possess the bare necessities of life. This demand practically means coming down to a level which makes all civilized life impossible; unless indeed we conceive "the necessary" not in the sense of a fixed level—the attainment of a minimum of existence by all our fellow-men—but in the sense of the idea of the Calling. In this case, however, the statement is no longer a fixed law with its own content, but a guide to reflection. In this form it should be unconditionally accepted; so long as people round us are in distress it is wrong to claim for ourselves and to enjoy more than we

[1] Matt. xix. 24.

need to fulfil our vocation—in the broadest sense of the word.

We ought not to forget that the demand: first of all procure the necessities of life, and only then (after this has been achieved) the higher goods of civilization and culture, if literally interpreted, would lead to absurdity. Civilization and culture, with its goods—science for instance—is indeed the very presupposition which enables men to procure that which is necessary for life. Only where there is freedom for research, only where people have time and leisure to cultivate art and science and education, will it be possible to create an economic order in which what is actually necessary for life will be provided for every one. As a constructive principle that statement has no sense. But as a regulative critical idea it has a good meaning all the same, and a necessary function. Only with its aid do we learn to distinguish between senseless luxury and the intelligent needs of civilization, extravagance and the use of good things which will make life finer. Being what we are, as human beings, a certain amount of scope is a simple necessity of life; but in admitting this we do not justify for a moment what simple folk call luxury; and every conscientious Christian will make a rule to set the limit to that which is necessary for himself as low and not as high as possible. To desire to fix this limit, however, evinces the spirit of that false Puritanical legalism which ought to be most definitely rejected, not only on general cultural grounds but also on grounds of faith. On this very point it would be advisable to learn what the man who has so often (erroneously) been called the Father of ascetic Puritanism thinks: I mean Calvin. In making this suggestion I do not think I am providing any Christian with a comfortable resting-place(19).

4. The Task of the Church in the Economic Struggle of the Present Day

This question belongs essentially to another connexion; here therefore all I can do is to treat it very briefly in the form of comprehensive theses.

1. The first task of the Church, even in view of actual economic distress and sin, and indeed for this very reason, is the proclamation of the Gospel of the Creation, Reconciliation and Redemption of the world through the God who is revealed in Christ. For it is the Gospel, and not any kind of "social Gospel," which is the salvation of the world, even in view of

the economic situation. What we need is not primarily Christian programmes, but real Christians and real Christian communities, in which the Spirit of God is a living power. Genuine faith, and love which arises from such faith, is the only creative and regenerating force in the sphere of economic ethics.

2. As a community the second task of the Christian Church is that of *service*, that is, the obligation of taking an interest in the victims of the economic struggle by a generous philanthropy. Social politics, however, although it certainly is the duty of a Christian, is not the task of the Church.[1]

3. On the other hand, in her message the Church must not only expound the Divine Command as it affects the individual but she must also expound it for the racial and national community (*Volksgemeinschaft*) and its forms of life. Therefore she must exercise and demand prophetic criticism, just as she has to proclaim the Gospel of the Grace of God in a prophetic manner. From this point of view her task of proclamation is not the development of a programme, or of individual points in a programme, but the awakening of the "social conscience," and the awakening of the conviction that to faith nothing is impossible. Above all she must herself confess the social guilt of Christendom, and must bow to the condemnation of the world as the condemnation of God. Through her proclamation of the growing Kingdom of God she must make strong and living the responsible will of Christian people for the creation of new and more righteous orders. As the one court of appeal, aware both of the order of Creation and of the order of Redemption, she must indicate what is in accordance with the orders of creation and of redemption, and she must claim every man for the demands of love. It is her duty to show the appalling contrast between the actual economic order and an economic order filled with the spirit of Jesus Christ, and it is her duty to proclaim the Will of God as paramount even in the economic sphere. It is her duty to do this, without paying any attention to the opposition of politicians; she must also avoid becoming entangled with actual party politics. It is her duty, precisely because of the economic reality, to make the summons to Repentance: *Repent!* sound forth loudly and fearlessly; it is her duty to show that the evils in the economic sphere come from godlessness, and she must affirm that there is no other real improvement than that which comes through obedience to

[1] See below, p. 555 ff.

the Will of God. To use the phrase of Kierkegaard, she is called to proclaim the "absolute ideal," quite unconcerned as to whether it is "practicable" at the present time. In all this she is not to be concerned about economic and political possibilities; for in acting in this way she is indeed creating the possibility of a better economic order. Then, too, to lend still more weight to her message, she may point out how again and again the spirit of Jesus Christ has been the greatest force behind economic changes and transformations. In all this her message is very far from being an economic ethics. For her business is with the proclamation of the Kingdom of God, not with the ordering of the economic sphere.

4. The Church, as the community of those who believe, must also bear witness to the fact of a different spirit and a different life by her actions. "See how these Christians love one another"—this saying of the pagans points to the strongest missionary force, and at the same time to the strongest force of economic transformation which should and could go forth from the Church. The word of the Church will have little effect if the community of believers does not show a new life even in economic matters, a life by which the world is judged, and at the same time shaken out of its hopelessness. By the actions of her members she must show that the Gospel is not only the power of eternal redemption but also a force for earthly righteousness and humane conduct. Where she is not able to do this her faith too is in a sad plight.

439

CHAPTER XXXVI

THE NATURE OF THE STATE

1. *The Riddle of the State*

ALL enquiry into the nature of the State (as in the case of the problem of marriage) is influenced by the acute practical problems affecting the State to-day. Just as there is a crisis of the institution of marriage, so also there is a crisis of the institution of the State; this is a phenomenon to which earlier times provide no parallel. In this sphere also something is happening which has never happened before, and indeed which could not happen before, since the presuppositions for such happenings did not exist: to-day the very existence of the State, and its nature, is being challenged, not merely by a small group of revolutionary thinkers, but by the masses themselves. The causes of this acute crisis regarding the nature of the State are the same as those which have caused the crisis of marriage: the triumph of the principle of autonomy, the severance of the order of the State from all connexion with the eternal world. Inevitably this has led, on the one hand, to the absolutism of the State, and on the other to the downfall of the authority of the State, as the outcome of unrestrained individualism. Antiquity knew only States with a religious basis; primitive Christianity recognized the State as ordained by God, in spite of the fact that it was actually "without God." The Middle Ages based the State on the Church; the Reformation returned to the standpoint of Primitive Christianity. The "autonomy" of the State was proclaimed by the philosophy of the Enlightenment, prepared by the Renaissance; this view, however, was also, at least in part, derived from a semi-religious conception of reason—from the Stoic doctrine of Natural Law which was permeated with Christian ideas—and was supported by it. It was only after the positivism and materialism of the last century had shaken off even this last remnant of transcendental connexion by its naturalistic explanations of Natural Law, that the State became completely

440

autonomous in the sense of freedom from all transcendental connexions, and this freedom has been its ruin. It is this process of disintegration, and the reactions to this process, which constitute the crisis of the State. Thus this crisis is not due to outward events, but to something which has happened inwardly; at the same time, it certainly becomes manifest in outward events, as, for instance, in the dominance of the power of economic interests over the authority of the State. Reflection on the meaning of the State has therefore ceased to be a merely academic matter, and has become the only means of escaping from the practical crisis. It has also become the duty of the theologian to reflect upon this question, for the Church, the community of believers, cannot understand itself and its task in the world without having its own view of the meaning and the functions of the State.

Whatever form it may assume the State is as ancient as human history itself(1); it was always there, it is now there, and it will be there so long as human history exists. We have no more right to judge whether it should exist or not than we have to judge whether history should exist or not. Thus it is not our business to construct the State, or to seek to justify it from the point of view of its purpose. But since the State never exists apart from human purpose and human action, it is our duty to try to understand its nature, its meaning for our life as human beings—and in particular for our human life as believers—so that we may order our lives with regard to it, and, further, that we may also help to mould it. Even the Christian lives within this order of the State; it is imperative that he should know *how*, by faith, he *ought* to live within the State. Even within the State and in the political sphere the Christian is controlled by the Divine Command.

The State is not the nation, and the nation is not the State, however close the relation between these two entities may be.[1] Rather the State is a definite ordering of the nation, a form of community, and as such it is as independent, and as dependent, as forms can be of their living substratum, as that which has been moulded can be of its creator. Every State not only confronts every individual, but also the collective body of all its "subjects" as an independent entity, and yet it is never anything else than the will and the thought of these very people poured into this mould. It is just as wrong to refuse to recognize this relative independence of the State as it is

---

[1] See below, pp. 455 ff.

to hypostatize it as an entity independent of its living sub-jects(2). The question is, however, what are we to regard as the nature and the shaping power of this form? The answers of the modern theorists of the State to this question, varied as they are, may be summed up under two main heads: posi-tivistic or naturalistic theories, and idealistic theories.

Positivism(3) regards the State as a purely natural fact, the resultant of existing forces within a definite sphere; the State is that condition of balance, at any given time, in which the struggle for power among these forces has, for the moment, ceased. This state of balance then becomes stabilized in a system of law which is "valid" at that time. States are essen-tially forms of domination; even democratic States must be regarded as products of a balance of power. No "idea" is needed for the understanding of the State; he who knows what are the impulses which move men and what are the forces at their disposal for working out these impulses under-stands how it is, and why it is, that States come into being, and why they assume particular forms. Intellectual factors play a very secondary part in the formation of the State—apart, that is, from the intelligence which seeks to discover means corresponding to the ends which have arisen out of impulse; in so far as Positivism recognizes any independent life of the mind, its thought is controlled by the liberal idea of personal freedom, if not by that of anarchy; its slogan is: "Down with the State!"

The Idealistic theory of the State is the exact opposite. It regards the State not from the point of view of its cause but from that of its τέλος, from that of the final meaning at which the State aims—not from the beginning but from the end, not from the point of view of the actual, but from that of the Idea. The State is the idea of humanity, made visible in this form; the State is objective mind, indeed it is the compre-hensive expression (including all intellectual life, all culture) of the Mind which unfolds itself in history. Naturally brutal elements do not belong to its essence but to its contingency, to the incompleteness of its development. Therefore the spiritual[1] life should not and cannot emancipate itself from the State; on the contrary, it should seek its guiding principles in it, as the meaning of the whole, as its fundamental support and its final purpose, and in the State it must know itself as a member of this whole(4).

[1] Taking "spirit" in the widest sense of the word.—TR.

The Romantic theory of the State occupies a middle position between these two theories. In its principle of unconscious vitality and individuation, in its emphasis on the irrational, it inclines to Naturalism, while, on the other hand, in common with Idealism its intention is spiritual and it holds the category of totality and universality. It links Naturalism and Idealism together by the idea of the organism; spiritually interpreted, States are living organisms with an organizing principle, a soul, peculiar to each state; their goal of effort and growth is the realization of this peculiar element in an historically objective form, the permanent structure of which is the system of law and the power of the State(5).

It is perfectly natural that there should be these two or three main fundamental conceptions of the State, which are quite unaffected by the existence of a variety of other less important conceptions. Actually, if one may put it so, the State has two faces—our view of the nature of the State depends on the aspect which we happen to contemplate. It is, indeed, something like a natural growth, irrational, not to be derived from any idea, accidental, and essentially only to be understood from its causes. There is something about the formation of States which forces us to think of the growth of the mountains or of a primeval forest; it carries with it that sense of Fate which we associate with mere *facts*.[1] But it is no less true that the State is a manifestation of spiritual forces and purposes, the bearer of culture, the guardian of justice and of human values against arbitrary violence, and the creator of community in a human society which would otherwise dissolve into atoms. This duality constitutes the riddle of the State(6).

Christian theology is not called to outline a "Christian theory of the State"[2](7) which might, for instance, provide a solution of this dialectical contradiction. In so doing it would only fall a prey to that speculative dialectical Idealism which it wishes to avoid. But it is certainly called to draw attention to the fact that the riddle of the State forces us to consider another riddle, the riddle of man himself. Christian theology does not presume to claim to understand this "riddle," any more than it claims to understand the riddle of the State; but, in spite of all attempts to solve this question—both on

[1] This is the leading idea of the doctrine of the State by KJELLEN: *Der Staat als Lebensform.*

[2] See Note (7) on this chapter, on "The Catholic and the Protestant Conception of the State."

the Right and the Left—it does emphasize the insoluble character of this problem. Most evidently, too, Christian theology *is* called and is under an obligation to point out the connexion between this contradictory element in the conception of the State and that original antithesis of Creation and Sin, by which faith sees the riddle of man, in its very mystery, determined by the Divine revelation. It is for us to show whether it will be a good thing to regard the State as one form of human reality, as part of this antithesis, in order to be able to guide the believer to the right attitude to this question in practical life.[1]

2. *The State as a God-given Order of Sinful Reality*

If man has really been made by the Creator not as a solitary independent individual, but as the "individual-in-community," and indeed in such a way that all human beings are part of this community, then neither marriage and the family nor economic exchange and co-operation can suffice to fulfil the Creator's purpose. In faith we may, and indeed we should, regard the growth of ever larger circles of community to the very limit of a unity which will include all who bear the name of *man*, not as a merely historical fact but as an indication of the Divine Will of the Creator. The Creator has made man not only capable of achieving community and desirous of doing so, but also—in this sense—capable of achieving the order of the State and desirous of doing so; the idea that man is a ζῷον πολιτικὸν is the empirical conception of a situation which faith necessarily connects with the idea of creation(8); this idea (that is, that man is a "political animal") applies equally to the formation of smaller and larger groups of human beings, drawn together by the tendency towards, and capacity for, the creation of "community" by their Divinely created human nature. Just as we dare to say in faith: God wills that human beings should live together in marriage and in the family, so also we may venture to say: God wills that there should be nations with various forms, with one kind of unity which will include them all, and that there should be a humanity which effectively manifests their unity(9).

[1] The most valuable effort to understand and estimate the various modern conceptions of the State, from the strictly theological point of view, is the book by A. DE QUERVAIN: *Die theologischen Voraussetzungen der Politik*, 1931. A less ambitious effort is H. GERBER's *Die Idee des Staates in der neueren evangelisch-theologischen Ethik*, 1930.

But this actual connexion and this symbolical form of unity —I would remind the reader of what was said at an earlier stage in this book about effective and demonstrative action[1]— still does not create the State; still less does it create a system of law. Inevitably, and not merely accidentally, the State contains elements which cannot be understood from this definition of the purpose of community in terms of individual and universal humanity. It belongs to the essence of the State that it should have the power to compel obedience. It is this power of compulsion which gives it this strange double aspect. By force of compulsion the individual State gains respect from other states, and by force of compulsion it maintains its unity over against the opposing will of individuals and of groups. It is by this that the action of the State is a contradiction of the law of love; it is this which makes it a moral problem. In itself compulsion is contrary to love; it is sinful. The compulsive character of the State— and this means what we call the "State"—is not an expression of the will of the Creator(10). For this reason, therefore, the State as community is only community in an imperfect, unreal way, and this order of community is not a created order but it is an order which is also determined by the fact of sin.

The historical picture of the actual life of the State corresponds to this fact. Every State represents human sin on the large scale; in history, in the growth of every State the most brutal, anti-divine forces have taken a share, to an extent unheard of in the individual life, save in that of some prominent criminals. In the State we human beings see our own sin magnified a thousand times. The State is the product of collective sin. The saying of Jakob Burckhardt—referring to Schlosser—that the power of the State is the very incarnation of the Spirit of Evil, although it is not true, does throw one aspect of reality into high relief.

This, however, still does not lead us to the deepest view of the paradoxical nature of the State; without this daemonic, violent power of compulsion we cannot imagine how any unity of a people could have come into existence, and without this power of compulsion the State cannot fulfil its divinely appointed purpose in and for society. It is the State which creates the legal system, without which human civilization would be unthinkable. By means of legal compulsion the State

[1] See above, pp. 235ff.

creates peace within its sphere, and erects a strong dam against the chaos of conflicting forces; thus it preserves intact the settled territory of culture and the humane against the wild inrush of waves of passionate self-assertion—on the part of individuals and of groups—in which all peaceful creative activity would be impossible. In the necessity of the State we recognize the consequences of Original Sin. The fact that we need the State, and a State of this kind, constitutes a very searching call to repentance, and it is this perception which makes us humble. On the other hand, to refuse to recognizè the State is a sign of an arrogant sentimentality which refuses to face reality. Therefore the Christian recognizes the State, which exists whether he will or no, and whose peace and security he "inherits" as a gift of God, as a divinely salutary means of discipline; to adjust oneself to the State and to accept it is both an act of discipline and an act of repentance(11).

Thus in every actual State—and we are not concerned here with the Idea of the State at all—we have to distinguish three elements: the realization of *community*, in accordance with the divine creative purpose; a *disciplinary order*, which creates a kind of community by forcible means, and forms the necessary basis and the harsh framework of civilized life; and an illegitimate, unjust, merely factual selfish, grasping, almost daemonic *exercise of power*. Over every State there broods something of the light of the divine creation and a heavy cloud of anti-divine forces. This should be sufficient to make it clear that it is impossible to define this paradoxical phenomenon in terms of any uniform theory. Now let us turn to the consideration of the individual factors which form the State, in order to understand their ethical bearing in greater detail.

3. *The Power of the State*

The fundamental character of the State is not right but might. Even the despotic State is a State, but it only possesses a "right" as a by-product and in an uncertain sense. "Right," a valid right, may be, but need not be, something different from the sum-total of stable conditions of power, and especially in its relation with the world outside its borders the State does not appear mainly as the creator of law, which appeals to law, but simply as might. But what is might?(12) It is primarily the power which belongs to individuals and to groups to dispose of external things, above all, their own bodies, according to their own will. To this extent power—

let us call it material power—belongs to the created foundation of human existence. Without power there can be no free
shaping of life. In a second, narrower sense, however—and it
is in this sense that political philosophers use the word—power
means the ability of individuals or of groups, by means of
their material power or through psychical and spiritual means,
to move other persons to a definite course of action or refusal
to act, to render, or to refuse to render, service. There is a
purely intellectual power over others, there is also a psychical
power of suggestion, which for its part may have its basis
in the possession of material power, and is then coercive
power in the narrower sense. Now although the power of the
State is based upon the material power of persons—whether
of a few "autocrats," or even of the whole nation—it is blended
with psychical and spiritual power, which is far more important
within the power of the State as a whole than purely material
power. The authority of the State over the individual is not
based first and foremost on its military and police power—
even a stable State is rather embarrassed if a small minority of
its citizens is resolved to hold out in resistance to the bitter
end—but upon the respect which it is able to inspire. Behind
this respect there are concealed the most varied motives, one
of which we must emphasize in particular: a consciousness
of a sacred bond. Whether it be the awe for the *mana* power
possessed by the chief, or the sense of the divinity of the order
of the State, as in ancient Rome, where there is nothing of
this supernatural bond, where the State is entirely secularized,
it has lost its power, though it may possess a large army for
its protection(13).

This undefined numinous background of the authority of
the State becomes clear and conscious in the Christian Faith
as the divine institution of the power of order. Christians of
all ages have known and maintained(14) that "the powers
that be are ordained of God";[1] a right knowledge of faith
knows how to distinguish this from a false theory of Divine
Right on the one hand, and from making the State absolute
on the other(15). Without power the State cannot exercise
either its legal or its social functions. Power is given to it by
God for the sake of order, community, and law. The State is
a secular order; it is not sacred. But it possesses real authority
by divine appointment in spite of all that we have said about
the unholy way in which all States have come into existence.

[1] Rom. xiii. 1.

But just as power, both material and personal, is based on the Divine will, so also it is an almost perfect instrument for that egoism which is opposed to God. The superior material power of the State leads to tyrannical misuse of power and to violent exploitation of the weak; religious power, however, leads to a daemonic misuse of the holy. Material power makes the State terrible; religious power makes it horrible. No sphere on earth provides a better playground for the Satanic element than the power of the State. It appears in its most dangerous form in the idolatry of the power of the State, that is, when the power of the State is confused with the Absolute, with the Holy itself(16). We cannot say only that in the State men express their most savage lust for power, but in the State their will to power receives a wholly different, even a pseudo-religious character. It is therefore no accident that in the New Testament[1] the State is described quite as often under the figure of the Dragon (Satan), as by the title of an authority, ordained by God.

4. The Law

The law is so largely that element in the State upon which its moral necessity is based, that we might almost say: the State exists for the sake of the law. But what is law? As soon as a State exists—in some way or another—law exists. For primarily law is simply the actual, effective, comparatively permanent, and to some extent familiar, order of the conditions which constitute human community, as it springs from the State(17). And there is a theory of law—the positivist—which sees in the law, in principle, nothing but an expression of the actual conditions of power. That the law is "just" is, on this view, first of all a fiction, and secondly, in so far as anything of this kind appears to exist, it is something accidental which is based upon a compromise of power. The Idealistic theory of law takes the very opposite view, holding that the actual law is derived from the idea of law which, for its part, is supposed to be the principle of "just law" or "right right." Unjust law, however, is explained as the imperfect form of the "true" law, which is only in process of development(18). In harmony with this theory is the idea that obedience to the law is not so much a product of fear or a consideration of utility as an "inner bond" due to the idea of law.

Both these theories see one aspect of the reality of law.

[1] Rev. xii. 3.

448

Whoever considers the history of law in an unprejudiced manner—and indeed not its history, but simply the law of the present day—must confess that very often it is far more the expression of might than of right, and that even in the creation of the system of law might has had more influence than right. At the same time we ought to remember that in the creation of a system of law it is never wholly true that might is the only influence at work, but that the sense of justice, the will for a "just law," was present when it arose, and has perhaps been present still more in its administration. Law is nowhere *only* the expression of a balance of power, but it is always also the attempt to restrain and to guide power in the sense of justice. Power is the irrational element in the life of the State; law is its rational factor. And yet behind the law, and indeed, curious as it may seem, behind the rationality of the law itself, there lies that irrational element of religious awe.

Faith recognizes in the law, in so far as it tries to achieve justice, the meaning of that order for which the power of the State exists, that is, the God-given meaning of the State(19). It is true of course that every order which the State creates which prevents anarchy is good, even though it may be wholly unjust. But the intention of the Creator for the State and its power is justice. It possesses a divine sanction for faith even in its imperfect form. For even an imperfect system of law is better than anarchy, than the law of the jungle. But this sanction should never lead us astray into overlooking what is wrong in the system of law: that is, that in the main law arose out of might and the balancing of power. It is of the mercy of the Creator that by means of the mere balancing of power He allows something to arise which resembles "just law."

But what is "just law"? What is justice? From the point of view of the Christian Faith no idea of perfect justice can be conceived(20). For in its very nature justice is imperfect. Only those whose minds are not aware of love can speak of justice as an ultimate. The idea of an absolute justice grew up within the sphere of Stoicism, because here the supreme principle is the *lex naturae*. To the Christian Faith, however, the *lex*, even the *lex creatoris*, is never the final principle(21). It is qualified by two concepts: by the sovereignty of God, which also stands above His Law, and by the Love of God which administers the law, and at the same time overcomes it. Perfect justice is a self-contradictory term; for the perfect can never be merely just(22).

Therefore, in spite of all that appears to contradict this statement it is impossible to define the principle of justice. The *suum cuique*, the principle of the Law of Nature, is possibly an important rule for the discovery of what is just, but all attempts to derive a system of Natural Law from this principle are based, when one looks closer, upon some *petitio principii*. One interpretation of the *suum cuique* alone leads—at least within certain limits—to a logically thought-out legal system: the rational egalitarian Law of Nature(23). When this is examined more carefully, however, it proves to be a purely artificial theory, which has never even come anywhere near to being anything like a real system of law, nor indeed could it do so—a construction of the abstract reason, which is opposed to the idea of Creation as well as to the reality of life. The idea of equality can never be more than a regulative principle; it can never be a constitutive principle of the actual formation of law.

The distinction between justice and love is clear. Love means going out to others, justice means the delimitation of spheres of power, and the protection of these boundaries. Love is concrete and personal, non-deliberate, non-general. Justice, on the other hand, is general, lawful, deliberate, impersonal and objective, abstract and rational. This lawful justice is the presupposition of love. Love which has not passed through this stage would be arbitrary and subjective and sentimental; yet love, while passing through this stage, must rise above it. But even in this subordinate position the idea of justice, precisely in so far as it is an element of law, is of incalculable significance for the historical life.

The idea of justice means that service rendered has a claim to an adequate service, that certain elementary necessities of life belong to every person as "rights," and ought to be recognized as such by the community. Above all, however, the idea of justice contains the idea of constancy, of the objective and effective validity of a rule which has been laid down and which is known to be laid down. Behind this idea of the just law lies nothing less than the idea of the Divine Justice, which likewise does not refer to a concrete content, but to those formal qualities of the adequate correspondence, the reliability and constancy of the Divine action.

Therefore the usefulness of the law is based upon the fact

of its rigidity—a truth which the sentimentalists will never understand. As the usefulness of a watch depends upon its exactness, upon the absolute correctness of its working, or the usefulness of a bridge upon the rigidity of its construction, so does the law depend upon its reliable rigidity, upon the fact that its laws cannot be deflected in any direction. Therefore an offence against the law seems to the simple mind which is aware of justice to be a "deflection" of the law. The just man is one who does not deflect the course of the law. But this rigidity of the law and of its justice includes a principle of elasticity which certainly cannot be conceived from the point of view of its content: that of *equity*, which expresses the demand for consideration of individual conditions and of the common good.

"That which is right and equitable" is the guiding principle for the wise legislator as well as for the just administrator of the law, whereby "right"—in so far as it is conceived in its content—means only the existing and known positive law in its "strict" validity, while the "equitable" means the necessary consideration of the actual historical situation.

The real power of the law, and the strongest cement which holds together the life of the State, does not consist in the power of coercion possessed by the law, but in respect for the law, which also contains that divine element which gives it a binding character(24). Where the sense of this binding character of the law disappears, where the law becomes secularized to a mere compulsory convention, there its solidarity has vanished, however many police truncheons may stand behind it. On the other hand, we must also note that the more sensitive the sense of law becomes among the citizens, the more dangerous it is for the State to administer its unjust law in an arbitrary manner. The fact that to-day the sense of respect for "the sacredness" of the law has very largely been destroyed, is not due primarily to "unscrupulous agitation," but to the class legislation of modern States; both in the creation and in the administration of these laws those rules of adjustment in the sense of equality and that equity in the sense of consideration for the common good which the idea of justice implies, have been grossly disregarded. It is impossible to din into the ears of the people for centuries the idea of universal brotherhood, and at the same time to expect from them respect for an actually unjust state of the law.

451

5. *Law and Force*

By force, or the application of force in the narrower sense, I mean the use of physical means to compel another person to do what we wish.[1] Thus by force we treat the other person —at least at the moment when the force is applied—more or less as an object; we treat him—more or less—as we would treat an inanimate object, a "thing"; "more or less" because even in the application of physical force other elements are always involved, such as psychical and spiritual methods of exercising power. Therefore the use of force, which means the refusal to recognize the other as a subject, which practically confuses the "Thou" with an object, is in itself entirely immoral. To compel another man to do something against his will in itself constitutes the denial of community. It is, of course, true that outside the legal system the use of force may sometimes be imperative—for instance in cases where from love for another our will must act on and for him vicariously, because at this moment, or at this stage of life, he is not capable of acting for himself, as for instance in the case of a child, or a person who is insane, or a sick person in delirium. But such instances do not raise the ethical problem of the use of force; this problem arises where we have to use force in order to coerce another person, an adult who is in full possession of his faculties, because his will disturbs or destroys the purpose of community. Force is then placed at the service of those orders which are necessary for life, and it constitutes the extreme intensification of that which I described at an earlier point in this book as the necessary harshness of these orders. Since, however, the use of force, even with the best of intentions, is such an entire negation of community, society reserves the use of force—with very few exceptions(25)—as a privilege of the legal power of the State. The State possesses the "monopoly of the physical force of coercion" (Max Weber).

Broadly speaking, the usefulness of the legal system (in spite of the fact that every individual enactment of law cannot be imposed by force), depends upon whether it can be carried out by forcible means. Without the possibility of effective coercion the law is not a power of order, but a mere rule in the sense of a public exhortation. Force is based on power; through law the coercive power of the State becomes a moral

[1] Cf. the observations on the use of force in JHERING: *Zweck in Recht*, I, pp. 186 ff.

entity. It is true of course that the justice which is thus forcibly imposed is not itself good, but it is indispensable for the moral existence of the community and even of the individual. Were there no justice which is forcibly imposed there would also be no voluntary justice. This law, too, is a "schoolmaster to lead us to Christ."[1] Indeed, not only the justice which is imposed by force but every kind of order which is forcibly imposed according to some rule possesses this indirect moral dignity and influence. Above all, however, the law which can be imposed by force is the presupposition for the peaceful co-operation of human beings. For where no law of this kind supplies protection against the brutal savagery of general strife, no civilized life is possible.

The possibility of imposing law by force is based upon the superior power of the State. The greater the power of the State, over every individual or group within the State, the more effective is the law. In a weak State law also is weak. The greater the power of the State, and the certainty that every one who breaks the law will be dealt with by the law, the less will the power of coercion be felt. The more that resistance is seen to be hopeless, the more can the use of force remain latent. The usefulness of the law is based upon the unconditional resolution of the State to impose the law by force upon every will that resists it.

In the last resort, owing to the fact that there must never be any doubt about its absolute character, this power is the power to kill.[2] Without the will to enforce the law if necessary by killing the person who resists the authority of the State, every one who came to the point of killing could effectively evade the law. If the State were so squeamish as to renounce in principle the power to kill, it would become the sport of any well-armed gang; for such groups certainly do not reject the power to kill. This produces the remarkable paradox, that the power to kill people, as the last resort of the power of the State, since it belongs to the unconditional superiority of the authority of the Law is—for the sake of the Law—moral; certainly with all the qualifications which result from the foregoing considerations.

[1] Gal. iii. 24.
[2] This power of life and death is the right of the State to self-defence. It has nothing to do with capital punishment. See below, p. 477.

6. *The Nation and the State*

The State is the form, or rather, to put it more accurately, the order of a people; it is only real in and by means of the people. It is not an independent mystical entity, but it possesses reality only in actual human beings; it is only the will of human beings which brings the idea of the State to life, just as the blood of the sacrifices brings the shades of Hades to life. But what is the "people" (*Volk*)? In the last few centuries this word *Volk* has been greatly altered in meaning. Even as far back as the time of the Reformation Luther still uses the word chiefly in the sense of a crowd (*Volk-vulgus*, "much people"). Between him and us there lies the Romantic Movement and modern ethnology. Romanticism laid stress on the historical individuality of a people on the spiritual and intellectual side, while ethnology brought out the significance of the biological conception of the race. Thus the idea of the *Volk* (people), through all these influences, has come to have a remarkable number of meanings. All the isolated elements which together make up the idea of the *Volk* can only be called constituent elements of a *Volk* in a very restricted way, and in very varying proportions.

The basic idea of a people is first of all actual neighbourhood in space—the members of the people who have gone away and settled elsewhere are only like isolated fragments of the parent body—and, secondly, blood relationship. Without a central kernel of families and clans who are akin to each other a people cannot exist, and indeed without this no people has ever arisen, not even the agglomerate peoples made up of colonists. The germ cell of the people is the family. The stability of the family unit is the presupposition for the stability of the unity of the people. But by this very fact the people has been lifted out of the sphere of biology into that of history. The family in its firm unity is not a biological fact, but an historical and ethical fact. By itself, neither blood relationship nor living together makes a people. A people is not a natural but an historico-natural concept.

Thirdly, a people only exists as a community with a common destiny. A common destiny, however, exists for an aggregate of human beings through the State alone. Only the people which has been gathered together into a State experiences history as a common destiny. Thus the State is just as much the condition of the people as the people is the condition of the State. We know no peoples, who know that they are peoples, who are not bound together in a State, or were bound together thus. But we know many peoples in whom we can observe how their consciousness of being a people only arises through their common State. History is stronger than nature; it is so strong that peoples, for the sake of their common destiny, even believe that they have a blood-relationship which can be proved not to exist. Finally we must reckon among the fundamental factors which lay the foundation for the life of a people the actual fact of language. This too is something which is both natural and historical. Above all, the common language permits people to believe in a blood-relationship which does not exist, and it helps to determine in the very strongest manner the will to unity of a people. A bird's-eye view of the peoples, however, would show immediately that no one of these elements is an absolutely necessary condition for the unity of the people, with the exception of living together. The development of a united people, when we look at its fundamental elements, is a very varied process, an irrational fact of history, which cannot be subsumed under any particular formula. Indeed, even living together within a particular territory is an irrational fact of history, inextricably bound up with the sense of destiny.

What we said of the individuality of the single person, namely that it is both a divine creation and a product of sin, is also—and in the same sense—true of the individual people. Peoples are not Platonic Ideas, which have happened to take shape upon the earth, but they are "accidental" groupings in which the riches of individualization, due to the divine creation, and the effects of the most brutal forces of power, are interwoven to form an indistinguishable unity. Of the people too, as of the individual, it can be said: "Behold, I was shapen in iniquity,"[1] and "Thou hast formed me in my mother's womb."[2] Certainly there is *no* reason to glorify the particular individuality of a people—for in what kind of "iniquity" was this our people born! But there is good reason for the thankful acceptance of this collective historical individuality, as well as of the individual historical individuality. Every one ought to know that the fact that he is a member of his own people is his destiny in the sense of a calling which is willed by God(26).

The people (*Volk*), to the extent in which it is consciously

[1] Ps. li. 7.   [2] Ps. cxxxix. 13 (R.V. margin).

summed up in the State, is the *nation*; perhaps we might extend the use of this term to cover peoples which are still struggling to achieve this unity. The common destiny of individuals requires the actual visible expression of their connexion with each other by the State. The national State belongs to the ordinances which God wills that we should maintain. But as a principle the demand: "To each nation its State!" is completely senseless. For what is a "nation"? which of the factors which have been mentioned—blood, language, culture, a common destiny, etc.—is to be the decisive one, since they are never found all together? As soon as one makes a serious attempt with one of these elements it leads to absurdities. Indeed, in order to carry out this principle we would need to wipe history off the slate altogether. For history consists of continual infringements of the principle of nationality, infringements which themselves lead to the formation of "genuine nations"; we need refer only to the nation which is perhaps the most closely knit of all, namely France! The idea of nationality is not a directive principle. The opposite assumption is sheer nonsense. But we must not forget that the national consciousness of the present day, and the national States which correspond to it, are new facts, and therefore that the human process of increasing unity can scarcely stop at this point. The national States of the present day stand midway between individualization and universality. From the point of view of the individualizing of a people they are colossal structures, which, owing to their unyielding nature, actually check the process of individualization, and their formation is based upon necessities which perhaps—in this way—would no longer exist if the still larger form of unity were present. In the nature of man as created by God, there lie energies and needs which are suppressed by these colossal national States, because, on the one hand, they are far too large, and on the other hand they are far too small. The process of history cannot stand still; the tendency to absolutely universal unity on the one hand, and to a return to a more thorough individualization on the other, is inevitably present, and is indicated by historical development. There is actually no reason to present as "the" form of life willed by God the national State in its present greatness and smallness, in this highly imperfect capacity to weld together what is general and give form to that which is individual. Reason as a unity points to the world-State as the goal of historical development, while the variety of natural creaturely life points to the regression to smaller groups. The tasks of civilization and of law require the larger unity; the tasks of a higher culture in a civilized existence, of the intellectual and ethical life, require the further development of the process of breaking up into smaller groups and the greater independence of the latter. From the point of view of this double perspective the formation of the national States of the present day may prove to be a very unpleasant interim stage, dangerous both for peace and for civilization. Actual international life, in which the most vital interests are so closely interwoven, is of such a character that in many respects the frontiers of the national States are felt to be artificial barriers which no longer correspond to reality. Not merely "the nation," but Europe likewise, and in a certain sense humanity as a whole, has become a group united by a common destiny. It is difficult to comprehend why the process of integration should be checked at the present national frontiers, why the actual community of life should not also find expression and an effective order in a more comprehensive community.

At the same time it is absolutely necessary to point out the danger of such centralization; still it is not easy to understand why the opposite process of decentralization should stop at the national frontiers, why it should not go much further still in the opposite direction to a renewal of the variety and colour of life such as that which was seen in the medieval world. Centralism—even the centralism which characterizes the present-day national States—is always a great danger to civilization, and particularism is a necessity of life. The divine order of creation points in both directions—in that of concentration and individualization, to the peculiar and the special as well as to the universal; our attention is drawn in the first direction by the problem of war in particular,[1] in the second, by the relation of the State to autonomous forms of community.

7. The State in its Relation to the other Forms of Community

The function of the State is to create order, in the sense of pacification and justice. It creates the necessary framework of life; but it cannot itself be creative. The modern State has more and more forgotten this limitation, and has tried to

[1] See below, pp. 469 ff.

draw all spheres of life under its control and to dominate them. To the extent in which it has done this it has lost its real authority; it has exceeded its powers, and in so doing it has lost authority. Here too, therefore, we must point out (and not merely where we deal with the other individual spheres of community one by one) that the relative autonomy of these groups is a divine order. The Creator has not created the family, nor the economic order, nor culture as a member of the State(27). All these divine orders of creation precede the State,[1] and have a relative independent aim, which is not primarily bound to the State. It is the delusion of the Idealistic idea of the State to regard the State as the aggregate of all human life; and it is also the lust for power of the State, its greed, which is the reason why it would like to bring everything under its own control. Idealism has become the spokesman of this "totalitarian" view of the State, with its insatiable lust for power.

It is, therefore, the duty of a Christian ethic to point out the injustice and the dangerous character of this tendency. Marriage, the economic order and civilization are prior to the State, and in this "priority"—which is not to be taken in the historical sense—lies the source of their independence. None of these spheres derives from the State; in all these the State can be no more than supplementary. Legitimate—though not complete[2]—marriage exists apart from the State, and the same applies to the economic order and still more to the spiritual factor in culture. A too close connexion with the State, or even a subordination in principle of these spheres of life to the State, must take away their meaning and destroy their vitality; and—this should be noted as very significant—it must also destroy the force and meaning of the State.

It is not the duty of the State itself to engage in economic activity(28), or to establish marriage or to carry on scientific work, or the work of education. All that it ought to do, or may do, is to make a place for the autonomous life of these institutions, in such a way that it can take its place within the life of the people as a whole; thanks to the external means which it possesses it ought to further, support, and co-ordinate the life of these institutions, but it has no right to try to govern them and control them from within. The modern State has

[1] When Aristotle (*Pol.* 1, 2) regards the State as "earlier" than the family, he represents the State absolutism of antiquity.
[2] See above, p. 358.

destroyed almost all the autonomous forms of community which were known both in antiquity and in the Middle Ages. In so doing it has helped to form that stereotyped kind of life and that inner sterility which we lament so much to-day; and the State—like the Church, which has become an institution for everybody, for all kinds of possible and impossible purposes—has lost the sense of its own calling; this is the main reason for the decay of the authority of the State. This intensive centralization is, however, also closely connected with extensive centralization. The national State has required this intensive centralization as the condition of power; it has incorporated those other spheres in order to increase its own power. It is high time for the inauguration of a powerful movement in the opposite direction, with the object of regaining the relative autonomy of the individual spheres. The sphere which is most endangered is that of intellectual and spiritual culture, and the longer this goes on the greater does the danger grow and the more harm is done. In this sense the slogan: "Away from the culture State! Back to the Law State! Back to the independence of autonomous group forms!" is the result of what has just been described. These statements are not made from the point of view of culture and philosophy but from that of theology. They result from reflection upon the meaning of the orders which God has created, upon the mutual limitation which their meaning implies. It will be the task of the next section to give concrete expression to this idea by one single example, that of culture (or education (*Bildung*)).

459

CHAPTER XXXVII

THE ACTING CHRISTIAN IN THE ACTING STATE

1. *The Attitude of the Christian towards the State*

THE paradoxical relation of the Christian to the God-given but sinful world of creation is emphasized particularly strongly in the attitude which he is compelled to take up towards the State. Just as the State has two faces, so the attitude of the Christian who belongs not only to the State but also to the Kingdom of God, is a dual one; where his attitude is not a dual one the Christian faith has either become sentimental or it has been secularized. An unqualified justification of the State, such as is achieved by the Idealistic conception of the State, is impossible from the point of view of the Christian Faith. In its reality the State is always organized selfishness, whether the saying about the *sacro egoismo* is known or not: the thing itself is as old as the State, and it exists wherever the State exists(1). Now the State always tends to make itself absolute, whether this is expressed by the English saying "My country, right or wrong," or the German "Deutschland über Alles," or however the same sentiments may be expressed in any other nationalistic jargon. Thus, because the State possesses unconditional *supreme* power over everything within its sphere, the idea easily arises that it also possesses an absolute right, that it is "sovereign" in the ultimate, religious sense of the word. The Christian Religion meets this claim to sovereignty, this claim to unconditional surrender, with the classic words of the apostle: "We must obey God rather than men."[1] There is an inmost sanctuary where the State has neither might nor right, and that is the place where its relative character is perceived(2).

Every State maintains and increases its power by methods which, in themselves, are ethically wrong. How can it be otherwise if the State is the instrument of sinful, selfish, secular forces? Not only does it tend to make itself absolute within, but it also tends to expand outwards to an indefinite extent, at the cost of others. Imperialism(3) has been characteristic of the history of the State from the time of the great ancient

[1] Acts v. 29.

460

empires of conquest of the East down to the present day. In the Middle Ages a slightly Christian colouring was given to this Imperialism by speaking, for instance, of the "Holy" Roman Empire, of the *Crusades* (with their connexion with the *Cross*); in the period of the Reformation and Counter-Reformation it concealed itself behind confessional interests; in the nineteenth century it became cynically honest and renounced every vestige of transcendent justification. Rather it set itself up as the Transcendent, as the absolute force. Can the Christian ever say "Yes" to this greedy and daemonic monster, by justifying its existence as natural and absolutely binding?

But it is equally impossible for the Christian to say "No" to the State. He must admit the existence of the State as a necessity, and in spite of everything he must thank God for it as a Divine Gift. As I have already said, it is precisely this admission which constitutes a call to repentance, for there is no truth in the saying which Luther, for instance, maintained, that although the State is necessary for the sake of the unbeliever, it is not necessary for the sake of the believer. Luther himself was led astray by this distinction, and Calvin, with his clear knowledge of human nature, rejects it. All of us, even Christians, need the State as a protection against our own unrighteousness. Whenever Christians, in the exuberance of their joy in the Faith, have thought that they could found a commonwealth on family lines, eliminating the element of political coercion altogether, experience has taught them otherwise.

The State exists as a definite condition of our place in the world, as part of our calling. It is therefore an order of service. When we fit in with the State we do not merely experience our sin, but also the kindness of God, who permits us to share in His work of preservation. Through the State we can and should serve our own people. No one has any right to try to evade this service; on the contrary, in faith we recognize it as our God-given task to place ourselves at the disposal of the State, or rather, at the disposal of our people through the State. But this inclusion cannot be unconditional in any sense of the word; we are forbidden to take unhesitating pleasure in the service of the State. Just because the necessity for the State makes itself felt in such an obvious manner—repeatedly, through all kinds of crises—we, as Christians, see our duty to consist not in the cheerful acceptance of the State, but, while doing the duties demanded by the State, to remember our

461

duties to our brethren, which require us to keep a watchful eye upon the extension of the power of the State, since we know how great and imminent is the danger that the State will encroach on these boundaries, constantly reminding the State itself of its duty of service, and meeting its excessive claims with an energetic resistance; we are called—and who else is called if not Christians?—to raise our protest against every form of State absolutism and omnipotence. Times have changed since the Reformation. At that time the great need was to release the State from bondage to the Church; to-day the need is to deliver life from suppression by the State. Our attitude will only be guarded against misinterpretation—at a time like the present, when the authority of the State is actually crumbling away—if we lay all the stress we can upon the authority of the State, opposing both the individualism which seeks to destroy the State and the claims of State omnipotence.

In yet another sense times have changed; to-day we are responsible for the State in a wholly different way from that which was possible for ordinary Christian people in the days of Luther. We no longer live at a time when one could trustfully leave the Elector or the "strict and watchful lords" of Zürich, or the Council of Geneva, to do as they liked in everything that concerned the State; in saying this I do not overlook the fact that there was a great difference between the monarchical system of government in Germany and the republican government of the Swiss cities. For good or for evil: to-day we are all responsible, and even if we do not exercise our political rights we cannot evade our responsibility. The fact that we often feel this burden too heavy for us points to an evil with which I will deal directly, but so long as this evil exists we must indeed stand at our post, in order that we may overcome this evil.

2. *The Christian and "Reasons of State"* (4)

The State cannot be governed and ought not to be governed in accordance with the law of love—for this would do away with its meaning—but in accordance with its own principles which we call "reasons of State."[1] This autonomy is of course only relative and qualified, for it is qualified by the purpose of the State, which is to serve the welfare of the people. But

---

[1] "Reasons of State" or "Statecraft" (*Staatsraison*) mean the maxims which govern the action of the State, the law by which the action of the State is moved. MEINECKE, loc. cit., p. 1.

in order to be able to do this the State needs power. In the process of the acquisition of power, however, empirically and inevitably there are sinister forces at work, forces which cannot be controlled by ethical considerations. To a certain extent we simply have to accept their presence and their influence as a natural fact; for only through them is the State able to maintain order. Here neither love nor justice can be a constitutive principle, but only a regulative one. No State has ever sprung from the "principles of justice." But the existence of law always presupposes the existence of the State.

In saying this we have both formulated the ethical problem of the reasons of State and we have also admitted its insoluble character. The State is primarily not a moral institution but an irrational product of history; the Christian State never has existed and never will exist. Where the State is concerned ethics always lag behind. We can never comprehend the State from studying its purpose; it is "there," given, as a bit of the historical natural world in which we have been placed. In the spirit of faith we can only "understand" it in the light of the thought of the "God who is hidden" within all history; it is never ethically transparent for us, therefore it can never become even approximately "moral." Moralizing has no effect upon it, or can only ruin it(5). And yet: the State is also an ethical body, since it arises through purposeful and responsible action in actual events, and can only be affirmed for the sake of its ethical purpose. State action is therefore always placed under the Divine Command, even though here the Command cannot be anticipated in any kind of law. It forms part of the A B C of all true statecraft that without moral foundations the State must fall to pieces. For the sake of the health of the State, as well as for the sake of the moral energy of its citizens, the State must itself be "just." The "purpose" of the State is the "good" of the people. This Good, however, must not be conceived in the narrow terms of material prosperity; although it is quite clear that the State is not itself the power which creates civilization, education, morality—in the deeper sense—or religion, yet the duty certainly is laid upon it, within the limits of its calling and its possibilities, to support and to further these expressions of life as essential to man as a whole. The doctrine of the moral and religious neutrality of the State is the product of an abstract rationalism, and forgets upon what basis the State itself is founded. By proclaiming this neutrality the State is destroying its own living roots. The bond which most closely unites the people is not the fact that it is convenient to co-operate for certain definite purposes, but the sense of responsibility; but permanently this sense of responsibility can only develop upon a religious foundation. It is of course true that in this sphere of life the State has very little scope for action, since its citizens belong to different religious groups, which must necessarily be left free to remain autonomous; but this does not mean that in principle the State should declare itself to be indifferent in matters of religion. We only need to imagine what would become of the State were it to proclaim its indifference to morals; how could it possibly create a system of law? But in experience we know that morality only grows on the foundation of religion, although it may preserve its life for a time in isolation. The State which is well advised has an interest in the religious life of its citizens; this statement is true, in spite of the doubtful use which has so often been made of it by cunning statesmen.

The autonomy of the State can never mean that it does not come under the Divine Command; this means, practically, that every one who acts in an official capacity, the simple citizen as well as the leader of a political party or a leading statesman, has to try to discover the will of God(6); if he does not do this he does wrong, although in choosing its leaders the people is not required to enquire first of all into the question of their religion. For it is not faith which makes a good statesman, and from the point of view of the whole there may be instances where the "unbelieving" statesman may be the more competent leader. In spite of this, however, for the statesman it is not *also* but *particularly for him* a sin not to enquire concerning the will of God; the rest of us, however, must be on our guard against trying to find out this faith or lack of faith.

But statecraft is limited not only from within but also from without, by consideration for justice between the nations and the good of humanity. A brutal will to power is bad statesmanship. Ruthless politicians, with their abuse of power, are bad statesmen, because they have left out of account the most important factors in the situation. Practical Machiavellianism is a false calculation. Godlessness and trampling on moral scruples, even in intercourse between the nations, is the "ruin of the people." Since, however, by its very nature, the State possesses this tendency, it is the first duty of Christians to put forth all their might to oppose it. The alternative: either the Sermon on the Mount or complete autonomy, is false. The Sermon on the Mount is not a law for the State, but even the State stands under the demands of the will of God, and if it breaks His law it will not go unpunished. The substitution of international law for a condition of anarchy between nations is in the interest of the State, just as it is to substitute the law of the State for the law of the jungle within the single nation. To how great an extent, however, the requirements of moral justice at any given moment can control the decisions of the State depends not only on the good will of the statesman, nor on the good will of all the citizens, but also upon the actual historical situation, which must be understood, and taken into account, in the responsibility of concrete political action.

Political action, in particular, always needs divine forgiveness; it also needs divine guidance; this means that here there are no timeless universal laws which can simply be applied to particular cases; in every instance those who are called to this kind of action ought to try to discover the Divine Command at this particular moment, for these particular circumstances.

3. *The Christian and the Form of the State*

The burning political question of the present day is the question of the form of the State. In a double sense the form of the State has reached a crisis: the older form, which dates from the Middle Ages, has been broken down by events; and in many countries confidence in the modern form of the State, Parliamentary democracy, has been rudely shaken. This matter does concern Christian people, as we can see from the fact that people in America speak of the "God of democracy," while in Germany there are large groups which regard the monarchy alone as "Christian." To both points of view we would reply with a statement which results from reflection on faith: in itself there is no Christian and non-Christian form of the State; no form, in itself, is wholly good or wholly bad(7). It is impossible to decide, here and now, which kind is best, on *a priori* principles; we can only come to a decision on this point in the light of the actual situation. Some years ago it was necessary to emphasize this point over against the unqualified and peremptory claims of a rampant democracy; to-day we need to do the same on the opposite front. But it is not the business of ethics to emphasize one aspect or the other; this is the political task of responsible Christian citizens and statesmen.

The question concerning the best form of the State must be discussed from the point of view of the purpose of the State. That form of the State is best which most effectively realizes the purpose for which the State exists. Here, too, by reflecting on the bases of the State in the Divine order in creation, certain guiding principles are to be discerned, which, while they do not imply the choice of the actual form of the State, do give some guidance in view of the actual historical situation. By the form of the State I mean above all the relation between those who lead and those who are led, or, to put it more generally, the way in which the competences of State action are apportioned. If the State, like the economic order, has a purpose lying beyond itself, then it would be possible to say: political action, in the narrower sense of government, and also legislation, is mainly an "art"; hence so far as possible it should be placed in the hands of experts. But the purpose of the State is not only concrete in this sense, it is also personal; that is, it aims at the formation of the community of the people (*Volksgemeinschaft*) as such. Therefore the people (*Volk*) is not served simply by the appointment of rulers who are specialists in the art of government; for even when this has been done the most important task, that of community, has not been achieved; on the contrary, it has been shelved.

Therefore the question can only be answered if both the very different purposes for which the State exists are taken into account: namely, what kind of State ensures the most competent form of government? and at the same time the closest possible union of the individual members of the people amongst themselves? We will distinguish these two ends for which the State exists by speaking of them as the "technical objective purpose," and the "personal purpose of community," respectively. This twofold purpose of the State makes it clear that as a rule neither complete autocracy nor unqualified government by the people, that is, democracy (which is the ideal of Liberalism), can, as a rule, be the right form of government.

The "concrete purpose": the attainment of the highest possible good of the State, as far as the people is concerned, requires either an autocracy or an oligarchy with extensive powers; for the "concrete purpose" can only be known and realized by experts. On the other hand, the purpose of achieving the fullest possible unity of the people requires that all should take the greatest possible share of responsibility for the State. The comparatively best form for the State—taking circumstances into account—must be sought in creating a compromise between these two points of view.

We reach a similar result if we approach the subject from another angle: from the consideration of the evil element in the State. The presence of evil makes it necessary to have a forceful uniform governing power which can control the sinful will of the individual, and is not distracted by too many conflicting considerations. The presence of evil requires that the authority of the State should resolutely confront the individual. The more people take part in the work of government, the less is the power of State-control. But, on the other hand, as a rule the very fact of the egoism bred by power makes it necessary to set strict limits to the power of the individual ruler, since, if it is not restrained, it almost inevitably degenerates into something daemonic. Anarchy must be prevented by the exercise of authority, tyranny must be checked by democracy. The supporters of modern Fascism forget that the good of the State is too dearly bought at the expense of the deprivation of the members of the State of their rights. The champions of democracy forget that, as a rule, the people as a whole is not a very competent guardian of the common weal, especially if the "common weal" includes the higher kind of leadership, the power which preserves order. Unqualified autocracy nearly always degenerates into tyranny; unqualified democracy nearly always degenerates into mob-rule and latent anarchy. "Democratism," that is, the belief that political salvation depends solely on democracy, arises out of an optimistic view of the goodness of human nature, akin to the spirit of the Enlightenment, and also from an abstract idea of community, which cannot tolerate any inequality, whereas real community is based upon inequality. The modern cry for the "Leader," and for the "ruler with the strong hand," however, springs from a weary longing for repose and for release from responsibility.

There is no doubt that a government is weak in proportion as it is directly dependent upon the consent of the people, and is thus unable to enforce its authority. And it is probable that in unrestricted democracy even those views based on real expert knowledge, or far-reaching aims and energetic enforcement of that which is recognized to be necessary, do not penetrate through the confused mass of irresponsible talk, personal ambition, and that mistrust which always desires to keep to the middle of the road. Here, therefore, leaders can scarcely arise; indeed, the very idea of the need for a leader disappears, and the idea of authority is suspect because at once the fear arises of an abuse of power, whereby it is not noticed that freedom may be equally misused, and that this is just as dangerous. In addition, every democracy suffers from the fact that the universal responsibility of all is rendered to a large extent illusory by the tyranny of cliques and parties. The harm wrought by democratic maladministration of this kind may become so great that there are circumstances in which even an authoritarian form of government would seem to be the lesser of two evils.

On the other hand, those who prefer to bow to authority often fall a prey to illusions, as though the leader were in himself a guarantee of good government(8). Evidently people have still learnt too little from history, which shows plainly enough, in all conscience, that it is precisely the powerful leaders who are rarely able to resist the temptation to misuse their great power in a tyrannical manner. People of this kind usually do not notice that a people which is merely led, must be a nation of children, that is, if it is to be happy in such a situation. People with a strong and resolute sense of responsibility would rather have things less easy, and in return have a share in bearing the responsibility for the welfare of their own country. The cry for a leader is often simply an expression of the spirit that shrinks from responsibility.

The question of the form of the State, therefore, cannot be solved in a general way, that is, apart from particular historical conditions; all that can be done is to hold the "mean" steadily in view: the mutual limitation of both the fundamental elements and of their requirements, as the basic law of the divine orders, where the shaping of the political form of the State is concerned. A new form of the State seems to be the need of the moment; the old form of parliamentary government—that "babbling" of which Carlyle speaks—has come to an end of itself just as medieval feudalism has been finally outlived. The contribution which the Christian can make to this problem is to point out the two main basic requirements: the need to preserve both authority and community; for the State, as well as the nation and the individual, needs both.

4. *The Christian and Force: the Problem of War*

The usefulness of the State, as the means of creating order and peace, is based upon its power to maintain its authority by force against all who resist it. Thus for love's sake, the possession of force by the State is necessary, although, in itself, the use of force is opposed to love. Indeed the relation between love and force is still more paradoxical: for the sake of love the State's reserve of force must be so great that people will feel instinctively: "it is simply not worth while to resist it!" The process of "moralizing" the State can only consist in the fact that the power of the State is kept latent as far as possible. But the difficult ethical problem is not the question of force in the internal administration of a country—the police force—but its use towards the outside world, force in the shape of war. We are here confronted by one of the most controversial ethical problems of the present day; hence at this point we must draw special attention to the difference between the aims of ethics and of preaching and political propaganda. In particular we must make a clear and rigid distinction between war as an abstract and as a topical problem.

War, that is, the readiness of the State at any time to support with all the means of power at its disposal the recognized aims of its policy which are regarded as necessary, belongs to the very nature of the State, so long as it has no better protection of its rights—and this means of its mobile and historically changing law. So long as (more or less) the law of the jungle prevails between States the right of self-defence is an elementary condition of existence which simply cannot be renounced. Every State which is not resolved to maintain and capable of preserving its independence to the utmost, is lost from the very outset. From this point of view a State which is not prepared to defend itself by force of arms might just as well hand itself over to a more virile State, which, as a conqueror, does not hesitate to use these violent methods. To deny, on ethical grounds, this elementary right of the State to defend itself by war simply means to deny the existence of the State itself. This is the justifiable idea (on the condition mentioned) of the "just war," which has always been recognized by all doctors of the Church, Catholic as well as Protestant, but which likewise has also been restricted to the war of defence against the obvious aggressor. Pacifism of the "absolutist" variety is practically anarchy, it is an Anabaptist Utopia(9).

Whoever affirms the State as a necessity must also affirm war as a contingent necessity; the force which each State possesses alone protects it against the force exercised by other States.

But although it is necessary to make this principle quite clear before we enter into any detailed discussion of this problem, on the other hand, it would be futile to speak about war to-day, and of the attitude of the Christian towards it, in terms which were proper to the days of Luther, or even a hundred years ago. The concrete problem of war as it confronts us at the present time is entirely different from the *abstract* view of the problem.

First of all, it is almost tiresome to remark that the same word is used to describe the local incidents which used to be called "wars" and the world-wide conflagrations which constitute the only kind of war we envisage when war is mentioned to-day. Owing to the substitution of a national army for a mercenary army, to the introduction of mechanical and chemical methods of warfare, and to the closely-knit character of all the economic spheres throughout the world, war has now become a method which cannot any longer be reckoned as an item in any political reckoning of gain or loss. The idea of "winning a war" still plays its old disastrous part in the popular mind, but it no longer has any place in reality. In modern warfare all are conquered and none are victors; in modern warfare there is no longer any "non-combatant population." If war were to break out at the present time it is extremely uncertain whether the idea of fighting in "defence of one's country" would have any meaning at all. It is quite possible that in the "next war" the soldiers in the lower ranks would enjoy the largest measure of protection, compared with the rest of the population. Some decades ago war may have been an instrument which, although it was brutal, could be used to resolve intolerable international tension; but to-day, owing to the fact that it cannot be controlled, it has lost even this shred of utility. It seems highly probable that the "next war" would consume the whole of the material and vital energies of the nations of Europe, or of the civilized world, to such an extent that it would be no exaggeration to describe it as a process of "bleeding to death." In view of this fundamental change in what war means, it is unpardonably superficial to try to justify war by means of pictures of the wars of the past with all their glamour of romance. The Christian in particular has no right to live in the past. He in particular

470

ought to know that modern warfare means such a complicated mechanism for the destruction of material, vital, psychical and spiritual goods, such an exhausting process of blood-letting, in which the most valuable blood of all the nations is wasted, such a technical business, which has become entirely divorced from all the ancient "manly virtues," and an international disaster of such vast proportions, whose effects cannot be calculated, of equal horror for the victors and for the vanquished, and, through the fact that it involves the defence-less civil population—women and children—is such a radically unchivalrous method of international strife that all that used to be said in its favour, with some amount of justification, has to-day lost all validity. The development of the technique of warfare, the heightening of war's intensity, and its enormous extension has led to a point where war becomes race suicide. War has outlived itself. It has become so colossal that it can no longer exercise any sensible function. To expect to establish any just order by means of a world conflagration—called war—has become a political madness.

Conflict between the nations will last as long as men are sinners, that is, until the Resurrection from the dead; and to the end of time this conflict will also be waged on brutal lines. But war has ceased to be a method in this conflict; the abolition of this particular method of conflict has become the question upon which the very existence of human civilization depends. New political methods of exercising pressure have already been at work for some considerable time, they too, as things which belong to the sphere of might, are brutal; but at least they are not suicidal for the nations who use them, nor are they murderous for the nations on whom they are exercised. In the next generation to reckon with these means alone will be the criterion of statesmanship. Even the "Machiavelli" of the future will not think in military terms, because he will not be so foolish as to cause his own nation to commit suicide.

When the necessity for war is argued from the point of view of history(10) the supporters of this view entirely over-look the fact that we have reached a point in history at which all analogies drawn from the past break down. The nations have been brought into such close contact with one another, the world has become, to such a large extent, an economic and cultural unity, the idea of an organic connexion between the nations has become such a reality that our traditional political conceptions have become useless. The relation of the nations to one another is already so close—not primarily through ethical developments but through purely natural developments—that it is now far more like that relation which used to exist between the tribes of one people, than like that which till recently existed between the nations, and still forms the basis of our political thought. Objective interest in the abolition of war is to-day greater than all national interests, however justifiable, exactly, as for instance, some time ago the interest in the creation of the unified national State was greater than even the most justifiable interest of the individual tribes. The process of combining in order to form a greater unity is always costly—even the process of forming the present national States cost a great deal; and yet we know that it was inevitable. The hour has now come when a further step towards combination must be taken; for already the one prime necessity of avoiding war—and indeed all that the "next war" would mean—demands it. The concrete situation gives topical significance to that which was said in an earlier part of this book about the necessity for the most universal form of community inherent in the idea of the divine creation, which lifts it far beyond the range of all artificial Utopian theories. To work resolutely towards the formation of this unity is to-day the only "practical politics" worth the name.

To attempt to outline any scheme of the way in which this universal unity is to be attained, however, would be to indulge in purely fanciful speculation. One fact alone can be indicated as moving in the right direction; that is, the development of international law, which is a big step towards this unity. To a great extent—and indeed to a hitherto unparalleled extent—the law of the jungle among the nations has already been overcome, both as the result of purely natural developments and under the influence of Christian thought. In a few decades, to an extent which was wholly unexpected, the administration of international justice has become a fact; the altered temper of the nations has gained an expression, in their estimate of war, which, although it does not yet mean very much in the political sphere, is all the more significant as a sign of the direction in which thought is moving. The nations are beginning to perceive—obviously before their theologians!—that war has begun to outlive its purpose, that war is a way of putting an end to international tension which the world can no longer afford, that the unqualified sovereignty of individual nations no longer corresponds to the actual conditions, that the only alternative to race suicide is the non-military way of settling difficulties between nations. Where war has reached this stage of development it has lost every particle of ethical justification.

To claim that war is the *ultima ratio* of politics is simply a superstition. This is the case only so long as one nation must fear that another will not renounce this *ultima ratio*. Conflict between groups of human beings will last so long as these groups exist; conflict between nations would exist even if war never came into consideration as a method at all, because every one was convinced of its suicidal character; conflict would still exist, even if the idea that it was possible to protect one's nation by force of arms were seen to be an illusion. We have no idea what the substitute for war would be. We cannot play the part of providence, but ethical reflection is called to meet the new facts with new ways of thought. Therefore, if a nation were to disarm, and render itself "defenceless"—in the old sense of the word—in order to prepare the way for the new form of "security," such action would not be a sign of political folly but of political wisdom, since it would demonstrate the possibility of a new way of political action. Again, when conscientious and politically sane citizens refuse to render a service to the State which used to be considered a very real service, but has now, in their opinion, become politically useless, they show political wisdom; this is shown by the fact that they regard this refusal as the Command of God to them, not in the legalistic sense of fanatics, but in the concrete sense of political responsibility, that is, in a quite different sense from those who refuse this service simply on the ground of the command: "Thou shalt not kill," or on the basis of the Sermon on the Mount. They will bear witness to this new point of view by taking without complaint the punishment imposed upon them by the State, knowing well that the State does not yet see what they see, and thus that it regards what they are doing as service to the State as "a refusal to serve."

When a new order is struggling to come into being and to shake off the shackles of the old order, the idea of order itself begins to waver, and this leads to hesitation about the ethical obligation of obedience to the State. An ethical right to revolution which can be expressed in general terms, does not exist; but the necessity does arise of making a choice between the new order which is coming into being and the old order

473

which is falling into decay. Even the Christian cannot evade this necessity, for no one can. Where the old order no longer performs its service of providing for order a new order is necessary, whose "tragedy" consists in the fact that it must first of all do away with the old "order," that it may establish real order in place of a sham order. In itself it is impossible to justify revolution from the ethical point of view even when it takes place for the sake of a better order, for it elevates anarchy to the level of a principle, and in so doing it destroys the basis of all morality. But just as the duty of obedience to the State is always qualified by obedience to God's Command, so also it is qualified by the possibility that God intends to destroy the old order because it has degenerated into a sham. But only unavoidable necessity will avail to protect this dangerous action from the reproach of rebellion against God.

5. *The Christian and the Penal Law*

So long as there are human beings who will not voluntarily leave their neighbours in peace—that is, to the end of history —society will be obliged to use force to protect itself against the violence of the lawbreaker. The right of society to protect itself by means of the criminal law is not questioned, but, on the one hand, there is the problem of the way in which this protective action should be carried out, and, on the other, there is the question whether the law has yet another function, beyond that of protection; for instance, in addition to security we could name the following possible functions: the improvement of the offender, deterrence from crime by fear of punishment, and penalty as expiation. On the second question, however, very great difference of opinion prevails among experts. But there is one point about which no uncertainty should exist, namely, that our present manner of dealing with lawbreakers does very little to "improve" their character; on the contrary it very often has the exactly opposite effect. The question of deterrence by fear of punishment cannot be settled by the argument that experience shows that threats of punishment do not deter the lawbreaker. In point of fact a great deal of wrongdoing does not occur through fear of punishment, and the judge knows nothing about it. But the fourth point—punishment as expiation—is the fundamental problem. On the whole the criminal jurisprudence of the present day is not favourable to this idea. Behind this rejection of this idea, however, there lies mostly either a positivistic utilitarian point of view, or an Idealism which has no understanding at all of the idea of expiation. But the Christian Faith contains the idea of expiation at its heart; it is the task of dogmatics to show the superficiality of the arguments on which its rejection is based. It is right, however, to admit that in the desire for expiation there often lurks a great deal of primitive desire for revenge, a great deal of Pharisaism, as well as (frequently) hidden sadistic tendencies. But even after allowance has been made for all these factors, there still remains a remnant which can only be ignored by ethical thought at its peril. The most convincing proof of this traditional element is the criminal's own sense of the need for expiation. Any man who is not utterly without all moral sense desires in some way to "expiate" the wrong he has done, once he sees that it *is* wrong. Even if only in some vicarious way he wants to expiate his crime. This is not the basis for the theory of expiation in criminal jurisprudence, it does however point towards it. The basis of this theory is not psychological, but, if I may venture to say so, it is of a theological character. It is connected with the correlation of happiness and worthiness with happiness. The true conception appears in the Biblical idea that God Himself "judges," that in the Divine Judgment every one will receive reward or penalty "according to his deeds done in the body,"[1] an idea which is represented in every part of the Scriptures and is never contradicted. It is also the presupposition of the idea that Jesus Christ has borne the punishment for us. If the idea of reward and penalty were not thus connected with good and evil, the Divine demand would lose its moral urgency.[2]

The question is, however, whether the Law is intended to represent this idea, figuratively, in this earthly world of ours? This question should be answered in the affirmative, but within very definite limits, and with many qualifications. It is to be affirmed because God summons men to do His work during their time on this earth. Men are called, so far as possible, to establish justice—in the Divine sense—even upon this earth of ours. Our sense of justice and our understanding of the judgment of God would be dulled—as experience shows us even now—if the Law refused to take over the function of expiation. The Law would lose its sacredness and would become a purely secular affair. Legal theorists injure the idea of law when they consider criminal jurisprudence only from

[1] 2 Cor. v. 10.   [2] See above, p. 120.

the utilitarian point of view of security, deterrence, and the improvement of the criminal. Regarded from this point of view, the Law loses its religious background.

On the other hand, the fact that legal theory has given up the idea of expiation in its traditional form is not only intelligible, but it is a good thing; actually modern positivistic legal reformers have almost always been in the right against their "Christian" opponents. For in practice the old idea of expiation was not only actually controlled by the spirit of primitive revenge, but it was also a fertile soil for the growth of the most hateful, harsh kind of Pharisaism. Certainly the guilty person ought to make expiation. But who is the guilty person? In the whole causal series of crime for reasons of convenience we only hold the last link in the chain guilty, the "agent" of the crime in his obvious act. It is this which constitutes the intolerable falsity of this principle of expiation.

In every crime the first and the chief criminal is—society. For it breeds crime by the brutality of its economic "order," by the paucity of its provision for those who grow up in morally impossible conditions, by the harshness with which it throws upon the street all those who are less talented and successful in life, by the lovelessness with which it meets those who are least adapted to its requirements. A society which invents the most horrible technical devices for war, and by means of compulsory military service teaches every member of a nation the use of these methods, in order to employ them against his brother man, who may happen to belong to the "enemy," and makes it a duty to use these means—such a society has no moral right to wax indignant over the individual criminal, but it should be horrified at his crime as our own. Most people are unable to understand the ethical difference between the "moral duty to kill" in time of war and the prohibition of murder in time of peace. All who take seriously the idea of Original Sin, not merely in a theoretical manner, every time he hears of a crime will feel: "I have only the grace of God to thank that I have not become this criminal." Whoever thinks thus will have lost all desire to have a crime "expiated" in the traditional sense.

But how are both requirements to be combined? By arranging that in the method of punishing the criminal society also helps to expiate the wrong. The idea of expiation must not only be preserved, it must be cultivated afresh and cultivated intensively, but this must be done in such a way that it does

476

not foster an arrogant Pharisaism nor a sadistic enjoyment of cruel punishment, but that in the sacrifice which the punishment imposes upon society, as well as upon the criminal, she will be reminded of her own guilt. This means: in practice we agree with those criminal lawyers who press for the humanizing of the administration of the Law, while in theory we support the conservative representatives of the theory of expiation. The guilty person must expiate his crime; in practice this statement will always mean: all who are guilty must offer expiation. Society must expiate her wrongdoing by trying to compensate, so far as this is still possible, for what has been left undone for the man who has become guilty; at the same time, by the sensitiveness of such educative punishment it must deter the lawbreaker from his crime, and eventually, by its duration it must make the criminal harmless; the criminal must offer expiation by submitting to this forcible education. In many respects this system of punishment will be more costly than the present system; this is only right, for it is this which constitutes the expiation made by society. Capital punishment will have no place within such a conception. It is, of course, true that the State does possess the right to kill, and to contest this means to destroy the power of the State; but it possesses this right for the sake of its necessary function. But this function does not require the killing of the murderer. It is impossible to solve the problem of capital punishment by asking whether "you" could carry out the sentence. Whether "I" could do this or not can only depend upon whether this killing is necessary. To affirm its necessity and then to evade this most difficult duty is sheer sentimentality. What we dispute is the necessity, the *meaning* of capital punishment. The only meaning it *could* have would be that of expiation; but this kind of expiation is one-sided, and therefore Pharisaical. Under certain circumstances the State may have no other means at its disposal, therefore the State ought not to be deprived of this right altogether; but this right should be hedged about with so many restrictions that practically it would not exist. It is not necessary to discuss here the various secondary reasons which can rightly be adduced in favour of the abolition of the death penalty.[1]

The present-day system of criminal administration is a miserable product of compromise, which does not fulfil any of its ends properly. A right system would perhaps be stricter

[1] Cf. the articles on the "Todestrafe" in RGG and RE.

than the present one, since it might keep "incorrigible offen-
ders"—even if they had not committed the most serious crimes
—longer in detention, and possibly they might be kept
permanently away from the rest of society. It would be far
more humane, however, since it would not confine the criminal
under conditions which would destroy his inward life, but
under conditions which would at least contain the possibility
of a moral improvement. Every one who has followed the
course of the latest developments in this sphere will know that
in saying this I am not moving in the realm of fantastic
speculation, but in that of actual experience.

It is a truism that our whole system of law, and especially
of criminal law, is infected with principles which are wholly
opposed to morality. It is far too heavily weighted with the
Roman idea of law, which again is mainly conceived from the
point of view of the protection of private property, and not
from that of the interest of the community; its emphasis is
far too much upon the abstract and universal significance of
the law, and its constancy, and too little upon individual
circumstances affecting particular cases; or, when nowadays
the attempt *is* made to take circumstances into account, as
a rule it only leads to greater leniency, not to greater strictness,
as a result of the general uncertainty in moral sentiment.

Yet in a work of this kind, dealing with Christian ethics as
a whole, it is hardly suitable to probe too deeply into these
questions, with all their countless complications and difficulties.
Indeed, even the "laxity" of the present criminal administration, with which it is often reproached, may be a sign of
something valuable: a person who thinks deeply and finely
is quite unable to punish lightly; he is aware of the doubtful
character of all human standards of punishment; he cannot
judge the man who stands before him in the dock simply as
a "case" in an abstract system of law. From all that has
already been said it will have become quite evident that here,
too, we have no right to rush in with our Christian principles
and poach upon the preserves of the law reformer.

*　　*　　*　　*　　*　　*

In the problem of the State, more clearly than anywhere
else, we see how strangely the divine law of love is violated
by the realities of a sinful world. It is our duty to oppose with
equal firmness the two main errors in this sphere: the quietistic
conservatism which emphasizes the autonomy of the political

sphere of action, to the point of denying that Christian faith either can or should exercise any influence in this sphere at all, and the sentimental radicalism (as for instance the theories of Tolstoy) which believes that it can overcome the autonomy of the political sphere by the power of faith, or, if that is impossible, rejects the State as contrary to the will of God. It is hard to say which of these two errors is the more dangerous —that of false secularization or of false separation from the world. From the purely external point of view the second danger scarcely counts in comparison with the first, since "fanatics" always form a small minority, and their Christian energy and personal earnestness is worthy of all honour. To the majority the necessity for the State is so obvious, and the inertia of the autonomous immoral political action of the State is so great, that the protest of a few fanatics might seem to be not only not dangerous, but, on the contrary, it might even seem very useful. But this line of argument is superficial, and is itself too "secular" to be true. This fantastic "earnestness" which will not admit the necessities which are determined by sin, drove the ancient Church into monasticism, and in Protestantism it has made many of those who "sincerely desired to be true Christians" politically irresponsible and indifferent. Fanaticism, too, where it was "aggressive," led to dangerous anarchist experiments, which because they only apparently began in "the Spirit," ended horribly "in the flesh." At the present time we ought to take very seriously into account the danger that Christian fanaticism, involuntarily but inevitably, may play into the hands of the powers which are endeavouring to break up the orders which are so necessary; we ought to do this, even if these fanatics are of the opinion that all they are aiming at is to substitute a better order for a bad one. Because they cannot decide to work for the order which is the best possible one at the present time, because they are always "winding themselves too high" and are therefore always chasing after an abstract ideal (i.e. the "best order"), because they do not know how to distinguish between the absolute law which appeals to the conscience, and the political programme of the State which can now be realized, they cause a great deal of bewilderment and dangerous confusion, especially in the Christian community. The most dangerous thing about them, however, is not their effect upon the world, but the spirit of Pharisaism which makes such people consider themselves far above all who—in their own terms—"do not take the Gospel seriously." The danger of this attitude is so great because it is so close to the truth, and because it is so difficult to distinguish it from the truly Good, because it is the secret enemy concealed within the Church.

But so far as the outward aspect of this problem is concerned it is obvious that here, as always, the fight must be against a crude secularism. Especially in days of national excitement it becomes painfully clear, with a clarity which almost takes away all heart to preach and teach, how thin is the Christian veneer over the "natural man," especially in political matters. In politics, as soon as the atmosphere becomes heated the Christian forgets that Jesus Christ is his Master; he then talks loudly about "sacred egoism" and the "autonomy" of the political sphere and of the State, in order to provide a "Christian" justification for all he is doing simply from the instinct of mass selfishness, from the purely natural motives of self-preservation and self-assertion. It is not the Christian politicians (*Realpolitiker*) of the *Bismarck* type who are the danger, but the theorists who hang on to their coat-tails and begin to justify what those men did with a sense of deep responsibility in the sight of God as right at that moment, in a general theoretical way; theorists who derive the right of an amoral type of politics from that which these politicians, as a rule, did as a necessity of State, but which weighed heavily upon their souls; likewise, usually it is not the generals who are the betrayers of Christ, but the militaristic scribblers. The worst people of this sort are the theologians who make use of the doctrines of the universal sinfulness of man to conceal national partisanship and unrighteous passion in the cloak of Christian humility and the love of one's neighbour.

The Christian must take an active part in politics because there, if nowhere else, he learns that we are poor sinful human beings, who with the best will in the world cannot do the real Good. He must also take an active part as a citizen of the State, because there he must show whether he really cares about the weal or woe of his brethren, whether he really is in earnest about active love. Only when we know how a man acts in the sphere of the State have we to some extent a reliable criterion by which to judge whether faith has a real penetrating influence on his life or not. Money and power—these are the two *media* which make the depth of one's disposition mercilessly evident. But, here too, and here in particular, we must be on our guard against legalism. A man may be a conservative or a socialist, he may be a democrat or an aristocrat—but these facts tell us nothing about the genuineness of his Christian faith. For political insight and reason, with the same faith and love, lead men along very different political paths. We must be ready to admit that as a Christian it is possible even to be a Fascist or a Bolshevist, not as committed to their ultimate philosophies, which are certainly irreconcilable with Christian faith, but from sympathy with their practical political objectives. The paganism in the ideology of the one and the stark atheism in the ideology of the other, need not necessarily and under all circumstances make it impossible to co-operate with them for purely political purposes, since indeed the ideologies of the less extreme political groups are likewise opposed to Christian principles. The real point is this: in what spirit we take this line of action, the shame and sorrow that we feel in being obliged to follow this line. But just as there are callings which a Christian can scarcely exercise with a good conscience, so also there may be political groups and programmes where the probability is too slight that a man could take part in them as a Christian without betraying his Lord. Woe to a time which could offer only these two alternatives as political possibilities! In this case, there still emerges as the third and extreme possibility that which we first of all declared to be an impossibility: complete abstention from politics. If all that is possible, if one *must* act, is a choice between two obviously godless possibilities, then the only moral course of action is non-co-operation.

In no instance, however, is it possible to frame a policy with a fixed programme or found a definite party which would be empowered to inscribe upon its banner the word "Christian." Politics, state action, is, in every instance, so heavily weighted with the sinful independence of the fallen world, that we can only compromise the name of Christ by taking it as the sign of this or that tendency or group—even if in other ways it may have much to say for itself. Every policy and political tendency stands under the judgment of Jesus Christ, and for each the Christian needs the special forgiveness of God. If this were universally recognized, at least among Christians, the political struggle would lose its most poisonous sting, and political possibilities would be released which apart from this cannot be imagined.

The State is that order, appointed by God, which demonstrates to us most clearly that, in spite of all idealistic glamour, as the New Testament says, we are living in a wicked world. Therefore to live as a Christian in the State means above all to hope for the new world which lies beyond history—beyond history which always was and will be the history of States—for that world where death and killing, force, coercion and even law will cease, where the only "power" which will then be valid is the power of love. It is the *meditatio vitae futurae* which makes it possible for the Christian to do his difficult duty in this political world without becoming hard; and it is this which prevents him from lapsing into irresponsibility out of the fear of becoming hard. Both his joyful readiness for service and his sanity in service spring from this hope. And these two words sum up the whole political ethic of the Christian.

CHAPTER XXXVIII

THE CHRISTIAN IN THE COMMUNITY
OF CULTURE

1. We cannot here examine the relation between the Christian Faith and culture in general; for this theme cannot be the subject of ethics, but only of a universal "Christian philosophy"(1), that is, of a critical philosophy which would be formulated in the light of the Christian Faith, and of revelation as the "judgment" on all culture. This more detailed enquiry into the practical relation of the believer's action to culture as a practical goal ought to be able to refer continually to such a philosophy; we are in the unfortunate situation of being unable to refer to such a foundation; we cannot draw upon the resources of such a fundamental work since it does not exist. What can here be offered is therefore a first tentative attempt, of whose imperfection I am fully aware; at the same time I am equally conscious that such an attempt cannot be postponed.

By culture I do not mean all that has recently been read into this word, namely, the sum-total of all intelligent creative activity in thought and in work. Of course I do not dispute the fact that such an extension of the use of the word, which also includes marriage, the State, and the economic order within the conception of culture, is permissible(2), but our present purpose seems to indicate that a narrower conception of culture should be used. In this connexion, therefore, by "culture" I mean only that activity in which the intellectual element is not a mere means to an end, as in civilization, but is a relative end in itself, that is, in the main, science, art, and education. Problems connected with the voluntary social forms of community will also come within the range of this enquiry, since they touch the circumference of this subject. Our first reflection must be devoted to the universal and fundamental problem of the relation between the believing man and the community of culture, without entering into details connected with the various individual spheres of culture.

483

2. In spite of its various mutual links with morality and with religion, culture should be regarded primarily as an autonomous sphere, which, like the spheres of sex, industry, and law, is ruled by its own laws. The Christian "enters" into this sphere in order that he may impregnate it too with the ethos of the obedience of faith, and also that from the standpoint of faith he may understand it in its (relative) autonomy, and determine its limits. Essentially culture is not produced by morality, but by a spiritual impulse implanted in the nature of man. Close as is the relation between culture and morality—whether this morality be Christian or not—still the fact remains that it *is* merely a *relation*. Not only art and science, but education also, and the social forms of community, are not rooted in moral obligation but in the spiritual impulse, which therefore, from the standpoint of morality, we might describe as a spiritual "natural impulse." The real impulse is not the feeling that man *ought* to create culture, but that he feels he *wants* to do it, and that he *must* do it, because his nature impels him to do so. Thus culture, like marriage and the economic system—and in a certain sense also the State—is based on a spiritual impulse implanted in man's nature, and is thus part of the Divine purpose in creation. We must regard the capacity and the desire for the creation of culture as something which belongs to the primal constituents of the Divine creation of humanity. Animals may have something like a primitive form of civilization, but they never have culture; for they know no creative activity in which the intellectual side of life is freely self-determined(3). The capacity for culture and the desire for culture are characteristic marks of the Divine creation of humanity. Hence culture is both God's gift and man's appointed duty; it is a *gift*, in so far as man cannot help creating culture, and it is a *duty*, in so far as apart from it he has no right to exist, because otherwise he does not realize his God-given purpose in creation. Man's rational nature is given to him in order that he may use it. God is not the enemy of reason, since indeed He has created it; but He is certainly the enemy of all reason which finds its end in itself, which posits itself as an absolute; to this question we will now turn.

3. Man, whom God has created as a rational being, can only fulfil the purpose of his being by the exercise of his reason, and this means by creating culture. Reason has been given to man; but it has not been given to him as his body and his

senses have been given him. Reason can only realize itself in freedom—that is, in the fact that man seizes the opportunity provided by his own powers, in the fact that he transcends the given in reaching out after that which is not given—the "Idea"(4). This freedom is the life-element, indeed, if one may venture to put it so, it is the real substance of reason; without this freedom to raise himself in free self-determination above what is given, man, as man, cannot be imagined. It is precisely this freedom—which previously we called formal freedom— which is characteristic of man. This freedom lives in every rational act, whether in the creation of the artist, in the thought of the scientist, or in the activity of the educationist. This freedom, in the formal sense of the word, is one aspect of the fact that man was made in the image of God, and indeed it is that aspect which, however deeply he may fall into sin, he cannot lose; he could only lose this freedom by ceasing to be a human being at all. In the material sense, however, freedom can be lost and really is lost by sin; this comes out plainly when we say that as a sinner man is no longer true man; in some way or another he is "in-human." It is necessary to hold fast this distinction between formal and material freedom—which has long been familiar to philosophers and theologians—since without it the problem of the relation between reason and revelation, or between faith and culture, becomes hopelessly confused.

It is not only freedom which is an essential characteristic of reason, and thus of culture, but likewise self-purpose and autonomy. The scientist who, so long as he remains within the sphere of science, does not carry on his researches simply and solely for the sake of truth is no true scientist, and the artist who does not work simply in order to create a work of art is no true artist. Science, in spite of the fact that as part of human life it must serve human life as a whole, possesses its law within itself, not outside of itself, and it may only bow to this its immanent law; the same is true of art, and in a certain sense also of education. This is the way reason operates, for its own ends, and independently. Even the theologian who thinks, indeed even the believing Christian who prays, is, in these actions, connected with the laws of reason; apart from them the theologian would not think, he would only indulge in fantastic speculations, and the humble believer would not pray, he would only stammer in a stupid and unintelligible manner. The Creator has not endowed us with reason simply as a present, but as the essential core of life, and this is His Will.

4. But it is the *Creator* who has given us reason; it is He who has created it. Thus at the very point where reason, together with its own individual purpose, is established, there, too, it is limited. It is not itself the Absolute, but it is related to the Absolute, it lives on the Absolute—for this is what God is called, in so far as He is known to the reason. Man has been created by God in such a way that he is never complete in himself; he is only complete through his relation to God. Only when we see this do we reach the material nature of freedom. Its basis and its origin are not in reason as such, but in the fact that God makes Himself known to the reason through His Word, and that man responds to this God who thus addresses him, and in this response becomes responsible, and this means : that he believes. Man could not believe without reason. The animal cannot believe because it does not possess this possibility, that is, reason. From what I have just said, it will be evident that although reason is not the only presupposition of man's capacity for faith, it is certainly an indispensable presupposition, it is, namely, the formal condition of the power to believe. The material condition, however, is the Word of God. Through the Word of God alone—as the Word of the Father, and of the Son, and of the Holy Spirit— can man believe; but by the fact of the freedom of reason he can also refuse to believe. This is sin.

When man refuses to respond through faith, the relative self-end and autonomy of the reason—and thus also of culture— becomes an absolute self-end and an absolute autonomy. This means that man desires to be as God. This is the real origin of evil. Christian faith recognizes this evil as a universal fact which affects the whole field of the rational life of man and consequently that of culture. Culture, which in itself is based on the Divine order of creation, is itself also affected by sin, owing to the fact that man, by his sin, has cut himself off from God. All the culture with which we are familiar owes its origin not only to God but also to sin. The formula which expresses the perversion of culture may be thus expressed : viewed in relation to God it is a false autonomy, and viewed in relation to *man* it is a false abstractness or impersonality, and a lack of community. In order to understand this we must call attention to a truth which has hitherto been neglected.

5. It is of the very essence of Reason that man's understand-

ing of his nature—if based on Reason rather than on God—will always be that of the isolated solitary individual, wholly self-sufficient; but it is of the very essence of faith in the Word of God that man always understands himself as existing in responsibility and in indissoluble relation to a "Thou." Man never learns what "a Thou" really means save where he understands what responsibility means, and this means: nowhere save in faith in the Word of God. It is due to the Divine order in Creation that man is created not merely as an individual, but as an individual-in-community, as a responsible self, related to the "Thou"(5). Thus the perversion of this Creation, sin, is always at the same time the denial of this primal responsibility, towards God Himself, as well as towards "the other" with whom God has placed him. Thus when reason is divorced from faith it always means that the "I" is isolated, that the "I" becomes self-sufficient, that the rational "I" understands itself in the light of its own reason; this produces that "misunderstanding of reason by itself" (Hamann), which consists in the fact that the reason has lost the power of understanding. Therefore the fact that culture is divorced from God, that is, sin within culture, does not mean merely a false autonomy but a false self-sufficiency of the "I," lack of community, or, what comes to the same thing: a false abstractness and impersonality.

Even reason is aware of a kind of supra-individual connexion, but this "supra-individual" element is always an abstraction —an idea, an ideal, a value, a norm, a law. It is not the use of these abstractions which is wrong; such abstractions are necessary; but sin consists in making them into absolutes. Life, and the spiritual life in particular, becomes depersonalized. Reason does not perceive that there is nothing higher than the person save the Person of God, which is indeed the source of personality in man. Where reason, as such, speaks of community, what it really means is that the "I "finds itself again in the "Thou." Reason knows no "Thou" which really confronts the "I"; it cannot see that it is in the very fact of this "over-againstness" that the "Thou" is to be known and loved; finally, even in love to the "Thou" it knows only the self-love of the "I" which finds itself again in the "Thou." The human being who has become abstract through his reason only knows the reason which is identical with itself, which is finally solitary and irresponsible.

Hence reason, which has been divorced from God, may

indeed be aware of supra-individual connexions, forces, and values, etc., and it may realize these in its creation of culture—this is the legitimate nature of reason; but it cannot avoid making these abstract forces absolute, and making the personal element subordinate to them; this is the essential sin of culture. All real creation of culture by men and women is not only the manifestation of the rational nature created by God, it is also the process which transforms abstract-intellectual entities into absolutes, into idols, to which the personal life is sacrificed, which destroy the real life of community. This is the ground of the fundamental opposition between faith and every existing system of culture. In culture man makes himself a God. The symbol of all actual—but not true—creation of culture is the Tower of Babel. It is the repetition in history of that process which precedes all history as a real *a priori*: the event which is known as the Fall. In the Tower of Babel the Fall became historically concrete. The more splendid the system of culture which man erects the more it tends to beget the pride which claims equality with God; the more it produces that defiance which wishes to free itself from dependence on God, that tendency to self-sufficiency which has no sense of responsibility for others, which must inevitably also work itself out in the "confusion of tongues," in lack of community.

6. This is the reason why, in the relation between faith and culture, the critical and negative aspect is so prominent. For faith is not primarily concerned with the existence of culture but with the glory of God, with the desire that God should come into His own. The Tower of Babel of a self-glorifying culture, however, is the greatest, because it is the most imposing and the most dangerous enemy of the glory of God. It is so dangerous because it is itself composed of spirit, and itself possesses the element of "unconditionedness"—the knowledge of an absolute; because it is so easy to confuse this spirit with the Spirit of God;[1] because, above all, sin is here operating in its most original and its most powerful form, as a deliberate act of severance from God, as defiance of God, and arrogance. In itself faith is no more the enemy of culture than God is the enemy of reason. But whereas all the sins of the flesh bear, so to speak, the mark of their shame

---

[1] On this point compare H. BARTH: "Die Geistfrage im deutschen Idealismus" in: *Zur Lehre vom Heiligen Geist*, by KARL BARTH and HEINRICH BARTH.

openly upon their brow, this sin is surrounded by the glamour of spirituality and is therefore so treacherous. This reason dwells side by side with faith, that is why the enmity between the two must be so bitter. It would also be a fatal error to believe that a theoretical perception of this kind would at once sweep away that "misunderstanding of reason by itself," to believe—in short—that once this error had been removed it would be easy to achieve the creation of "genuine," "true" culture. Rather this false autonomy of the reason and of culture belongs to that "Original Sin" which, although we may recognize it in faith, we are a long way from having rooted out, with which therefore we have to fight "existentially," that is, not theoretically, but in the reality of our present existence, in every act of reason and in every contact with powerful rational action. The first reaction of faith therefore will always be this critical attitude towards culture; to it the development of culture will always be secondary; this is primarily due to the fact that culture is also achieved apart from faith, while faith alone recognizes this sinful element in culture, and is therefore able to fight against it. On the other hand, it is easy to see that the representatives of autonomous culture always see first of all, and perhaps only, this element of the negative criticism of culture; this is why, from time immemorial, they have always hurled reproaches against the Christian Faith for its hostility to culture(6).

It is not the business of the believer as such to create culture. That is rather the task of man, apart from faith; or rather, it is not so much a *task* as it is the result of a sense of compulsion. But since the believer, the Christian, must express his faith not outside, but inside the natural orders and in things as they are, to him too it becomes a positive duty to help to create culture in accordance with its own laws. As in all co-operation with the orders, so also in co-operation in the sphere of culture, since the Christian is also a sinner among sinners, this co-operation cannot be achieved save by accepting the conditions which are determined by the order of creation and by the sinful autonomy of this sphere. The Christian cannot produce a Christian culture, any more than he can bring into existence a Christian State or a Christian economic system. Even the culture which he helps to create will be sinful, like all other forms of culture. But, certainly, although his faith cannot be a constitutive principle in this process of cultural development, it will provide new and particular stimuli, due to the

489

spirit of constructive criticism which he brings to bear on the work. Faith will be able to make itself felt as a "regulative principle"; hence in this exact and restricted sense it will still be able to produce something like a "Christian" art, science and education, in the same sense in which—with certain reserves—we may speak of Christian marriage, and—with still greater reserve—of the Christian State. Here, too, the law will hold good, that the further the particular sphere is from the personal centre the less can be the influence of this regulative principle. Still it will be more to the point to explain the meaning of this statement more exactly, not in the abstract but in the concrete material of the individual spheres of culture.

CHAPTER XXXIX

SCIENCE

1. Just as ethics is a scientific problem, so also science is an ethical problem. For science only arises in the form of human conduct, and thus it is connected with all human conduct, both of the individual and of the community, and is, therefore, controlled by ethical standards. But this does not mean that science is in itself moral. Rather—from the ethical standpoint—it is something natural, it is conduct which springs not from moral but from spiritually natural impulses, whose "rightness" cannot be estimated from the point of view of the laws of ethics, but from the point of view of its own laws and its own nature. Science is an autonomous sphere of life. Science does not seek the Good but the True. In faith we know that both the Good and the True have the same origin—God; to recognize this means that we acknowledge Him. But the legitimate object of science is not God (for God cannot be object, therefore man cannot learn to know Him by his own efforts; God alone can make Himself known to man) but the created world, which, as something created, can be object, towards which therefore a theoretical attitude is possible.

The original fact that man was created in the Image of God is the reason why the world is given to him by God as something which he must learn to know, The fact that man is able to do this raises him above the world, as the only being to whom it becomes object. The fact that man is able to regard the world in this objective way, quite apart from its practical use, is a necessity for man, because only as he does this can he gain his spiritual freedom. So long as man remains "immersed" in the world and does not perceive that he can stand back and look at it as from a distance, he is tied to it, he remains a natural being; therefore he cannot live as a human being. Man gains his spiritual freedom and his supremacy over the world not by his technical mastery of the world but by his theoretical knowledge of the world. Even the animal has a certain technical ability, but he never has any science, or knowledge for its own sake. The hour when science was born was an important date in the history of human freedom; at the same time it was also the beginning of a dangerous development.

491

2. Man, even as one who knows the world, never ought to forget that his freedom, so far as the world is concerned, is only a relative and restricted freedom, that although he may be, and indeed is, on a higher level of creation, he is still a *creature*. The fact that man can raise himself above the world by detachment from it, by the process of abstract development of law, which has been characteristic of the development of Western science from the days of its early beginnings in Greece, is not the only possible method of knowing the world. That is the method of knowing by being remote from it; there is, however, also a way of knowing it through being near to it. The method of detachment from things is contrasted with the method of learning to know them by being connected with them, and to-day it is scarcely too much to say that the scientific development of Europe has developed the one at the cost of the other(1). If some one were to mistake the abstract schemata of physics for the reality of the world he would be in a bad way. This abstract way of knowledge, which dissolves all concrete qualitative existence into wholly abstract numerical relations and laws, may be a necessity, and it discloses "truth-above-the-world," truth which proves its value especially in its technical usefulness; but it is only the kind of truth which is perceived by the spectator, from a distance, not the truth with which one is intimately connected, because it is part of oneself. This science, therefore, if it becomes the predominant attitude of the student, becomes very dangerous; it breeds a merely dominating or even tyrannical relation to the world, a one-sided emphasis on the freedom of man *from* the world, without any consideration for the fact that man belongs *to* the world. Thus the world becomes purely a world of *things*, and ceases to be a creature along with man. The immense gain in knowledge and mastery of the external world which characterizes Western development, and especially its modern intellectual development, is dearly bought at the expense of the loss of the knowledge of familiarity with the world which is peculiar to so-called "primitive" people.

In the strict sense of the word only dead matter can be an object; for in everything living there is an element of subjectivity, of that which is "animated." Therefore a science which confuses truth and objectivity must have a deadening effect. It changes the world into a heap of dead elements which are "connected" with each other by abstract laws which can be expressed mathematically—this really means that they are not connected at all. So long as natural things alone are concerned possibly the error to which this gives rise will not be too serious, compared with the gain in knowledge of the law. But where this kind of knowledge which regards everything as an object from a distance, this knowledge through something general, through laws, determines the understanding of man, it must have a destructive influence. It cuts man adrift from his neighbour; knowledge severs the connexion between them and itself becomes supreme. Man as object—this is certainly a reality, but what a horrible lie if it claims to be *the* truth about man! It is beginning to dawn on the medical science of the present day[1] that the purely objective point of view, this kind of knowledge which has no intimacy with its subject, but conceives it only in terms of laws, of general principles, even only in view of the human body, and still more in view of the whole man, is something so artificial that it must end finally in the failure of science to achieve its practical purpose.

3. But the more that science deals with man as a whole, the more dangerous does this confusion between objectivity and truth become. In psychology and sociology, in political economy, and pedagogy, this one-sided objective knowledge has revenged itself harshly. Here science becomes the direct enemy of man, since it dissolves the connexion between the "I" and the "Thou" which is the fundamental human relationship, and places the two over against one another as alien objects. Here, too, the practical result must be to create a master-slave relationship, not a brotherly relationship, full of eagerness to serve. This brings us to an actual situation which is regarded by many with profound concern, but its origin(2) is often misunderstood.

For the origin of this habit of thought, which regards everything solely from a detached objective point of view, lies, as has already been suggested, in the fact that man has forgotten his position as a part of creation, and has set himself up as Creator and master. When man forgets that even he, in spite of his freedom through knowledge, is himself a creature, a created being, and not a creator, then he misunderstands his connexion with the rest of the creation, above all his essential connexion with his fellow-man. He forgets that the world which surrounds him, and especially his fellow-men, cannot

---

[1] Cf. V. v. WEIZSÄCKER: *Medizin und Seelsorge, Zwischen den Zeiten*, 1930, pp. 120 ff., and *Seelenbehandlung und Seelenführung*, 1926.

be known as they really are by an attitude of objective detachment, but only by recognizing the fact that all share in the life of creation(3). The knowledge of this our common "creatureliness" is conditioned by our knowledge of the Creator. Thus our knowledge of the world is not independent of our knowledge of God, and the assertion of this independence, the assertion of a not merely relative, but absolute autonomy of the scientific knowledge of the world, is the cause of a development in knowledge which, fruitful as it may have been for the control of the material world, must inevitably work out as a disintegrating and destructive factor in the collective life of man, and especially in the social life of humanity. Were it not for the fact that alongside of the scientific knowledge and self-interpretation of man there is always another kind of knowledge which in some way or another is aware of that "creatureliness," which takes into account the fact that all creatures are sharers in the same created existence, the influence of this abstract objective way of thinking would be still more devastating than it actually is. Man, made as a creature, cannot wholly forget the fact that he is a creature, and hence he cannot quite forget the Creator. Therefore, there does exist a non-scientific knowledge of things and of men, which, although it is imperfect and restricted in scope, the more it deals with man and with human life in society, is superior to scientific knowledge. Were statesmen, educationists, jurists, economists to deal with their fellowmen simply in terms of scientific anthropology and psychology they would very soon experience or demonstrate the untruthfulness of this picture of reality, just as poets would soon disappear if they tried to keep their creations in harmony with this kind of science.

4. To sum up all knowledge exclusively in terms of the subject-object-antithesis, which in philosophy produces the contrast between Naturalism and Idealism, in the case of the particular sciences leads to the contrast between the method of natural science and that of the humanities. In the one case the criterion is the law of causality, and in the other that of the norm. It was, and still is, a necessity to show these two laws at work within their own spheres. We cannot comprehend either nature or the intellectual life apart from such abstractions. But the view that such abstractions—that the Idea and the law of causality are sufficient to enable us to know the truth—is false, and its effects are devastating. Man—to speak once again of this most important subject—which is

494

both the sphere of conflict between natural science and the humanities—precisely as man, cannot be understood in his humanity in the light of either of these laws, for he is a person(4) and that means: a self-in-community. This abstract habit of thought—whether it be in the natural sciences or in the humanities—does not reveal human reality as it really is; on the contrary, this habit of mind tends rather to conceal both its reality and its truth. Similarly, human community is not to be understood causally, as the resultant of certain forces, nor intellectually, as the concrete expression of an Idea (in spite of the fact that it certainly is both); it can only be understood as the personal. Thus we see that science, if and in so far as it permits man to forget the fact that he is a creature, distorts the picture of reality, and in so doing it also introduces confusion into the life of the individual and of the community.

5. The effects of this deep-seated confusion are more familiar to us and are easier to understand than the confusion itself. The effect of "intellectualism" on the life of the individual and of the community is well known. The intellectualist—that is, the man who believes that the only approach to truth and reality lies in scientific thought—owing to his belief in the laws of Nature, is doctrinaire and out of touch with reality; his emphasis on the "purely objective" approach to truth has a brutal, chilling, and deadening effect. It is impossible to confide in him because he is not personally interested in anyone; it is impossible to have any real human intercourse with him because he keeps every one at a distance by his attitude of cold detachment. No life, no fellowship, no love can flourish in the refrigerator of a purely abstract view of the world. Above all, however, the distorting pictures of truth and reality destroy that higher or deeper knowledge, apart from which life ceases to be serious and worth living. Life has lost its heights and its depths, and the tension of personal decision has been taken away from it(5). The purely scientific outlook on life robs it of all significance, for in the last resort the personal alone has significance.

The distorting effect of abstract knowledge decreases the more this knowledge refers to that which is distant from the personal centre, and it increases the more it refers to that which is near the personal centre. The personal centre itself, personality as such, does not disclose itself to the knowledge of the laws of nature, nor to that of the laws of the human

495

mind, but only to faith. In the Word of the Creator alone can man know that his real state is that of a person who, through his misuse of freedom, has drifted into a false position, and in this false position has lost his true freedom. In faith alone he knows that the responsibility on which his freedom is based also means his connexion with other human beings, which, recognized in obedience, immediately creates a sense of solidarity—community. For this very reason the knowledge of faith is not theoretical knowledge but "existential" knowledge, that is, it is knowledge of such a kind that it is only fully realized as practical decision, and wholly excludes the attitude of a mere spectator.

6. From this point of view we are able to define the character and limits of the autonomy of science. It is not possible to lay down a general rule about the independence or the dependence of science upon faith. It is nonsense to speak of Christian mathematics or of Christian physics; but most emphatically, it is *not* nonsense to speak of a Christian anthropology, or even of a Christian conception of marriage, of law, and of the State, although here, too, the autonomous element of scientific thought is always present. The further the sphere of science is from the personal sphere the more autonomous does the science become, the more legitimate is its abstract conception of scientific law; the nearer it is to the personal sphere, the more the real human being needs to be known, the more faith gains not merely a regulative but a constitutive significance.

But this does not mean that the Christian, in so far as he carries on scientific work, would be in a position to dispense with those "sources of error." Even if he were the greatest genius, and a hero of faith, he could not cut himself off from the limitations imposed upon him by the science of his own day. He cannot "insert" what he knows as a believer into the scientific picture of reality, indeed he cannot even give a different direction to the scientific process. The truth of the Christian view of man comes out very clearly in the very fact that science is always a product of the thought of the community, and not the work of an individual, even in its errors(6). The same human solidarity in guilt appears in the sphere of science as we have discovered to be at work, for example, in economics and in the State. The Christian can certainly stand out against the scientific dogmatism of his own day, and from the standpoint of his faith he can give suggestions of wholly different possibilities of the interpretation of reality, which, especially in connexion with like-minded people, he may perhaps be able to make fruitful even in the scientific sphere. Above all, however, he can warn his contemporaries against the over-estimation of science in our view of man as a whole, and he can attack this exaggerated point of view. For he knows that a supposedly scientific truth which, instead of making man more human, robs him of his humanity, and instead of binding men together in community pulverizes them into atoms, or makes them merely channels for the transmission of an Idea, in the last resort simply cannot be true. The statement, which he knows from his faith, that the True and the Good in their deepest origin are one, will be always before his eyes as the highest principle for the limitation of scientific claims, and will impel him, precisely by means of this limitation, to new scientific enquiry. The certainty that the contrast between science and faith will indeed always become actual, but that it is never based on the actual facts themselves, but only upon our erroneous conception of the matter, must hinder him both from regarding any kind of scientific view of the world as final, and also from the error of confusing the human formulation of the truth of God with the Divine Truth itself.

7. Science is a divine gift of the Creator, and at the same time it is also a divinely appointed task. Therefore in all genuine scientific work there is always—especially when it seeks nothing save truth for truth's sake—an ethos which commands reverence, an attitude which contains something of the spirit of the obedience of the believer, and which, on occasion, inspires men to the greatest sacrifices. The true scientist is obedient to one law of the Creator; that is his nobility. But human science is always also the active expression of that false autonomy which spells alienation from God, and of that arrogance which turns its back on God. Hence science is never an unmixed blessing, it always brings a curse with it, not merely through the practical degradation of scientific knowledge for purposes which are hostile to life, but also in itself, through the artificiality of its abstractions and of existence based upon them. Every one who does scientific work is aware of this, if he also knows what it means to be a human being. To-day we are feeling both in a degree which was previously unknown: the blessings of science, in their power to create freedom, and in their effects for the furtherance of life; and the

497

curse of science, in its intellectualism which destroys life, community and faith(7). The duty of the Christian towards science is this: to show clearly its basis and its limitations, and by means of this critical knowledge to be released from its curse, and freed for its service.

CHAPTER XL

ART

1. From time immemorial the relation between art and religion has been friendly rather than hostile, therefore the problem of faith versus art possesses none of that disjunctive sharpness which has so often characterized the discussion between faith and science. From both sides art and religion seem to be intended to come together; at almost all periods of history religion has sought artistic expression for her own life, above all in the form of poetry—even the Bible, as is well known, is no exception to this rule; art, too, has evinced a particular interest in religion, and especially in its greatest works of art, and in the case of the great masters it has made use of "religious material"(1). We simply cannot imagine Western Art apart from Christianity. It is our duty to reflect on this remarkable relation between art and religion. For even art is a form of conduct: it, too, penetrates deeply into the life of man and determines the form it takes, both outwardly and inwardly; hence it, too, is a problem of ethics.

The living foundation of art is not so much in the existing world as in something which, without losing contact with it, transcends it. It is true, of course, that the power to shape things in an artistic manner is a gift from the Creator, like all other capacities. But its attention is not directed towards the created universe, as such, like science, but to a sphere which lies above and beyond it. The mere "representation" of reality is not art, and the element of representation is entirely absent from that form of art in which the nature of art becomes most evident: music. Thus the origin of art does not lie in the perception of something which is present, but in an impulse to go beyond that which already exists. Art is always the child of the longing for something else. It shapes something which is not present, for and through the imagination, because that which is present does not satisfy man. In this sense it has more to do with Redemption than with Creation. It is an expression of the fact that man is conscious of his need for Redemption—otherwise, how is it that he cannot be content with the world as it is? and it shows that he has a dim premonition and a vision of the possibility of a better world. It is, therefore, an indication, given with the created order, even to fallen man, of man's knowledge of his origin, which he has never lost, of its restoration and its consummation. Art seeks unrealized Perfection. Even where the "material" does not give any suggestion of this Vision of Perfection, the form—which in art is the essential thing(2) —is always born out of the striving after unrestricted freedom and unlimited perfection. It is in the artistic form that man seeks release from the accidental, meaningless, weak, and imperfect aspects of reality; this aspiration becomes particularly clear where apparently all that art reproduces is something already present in the visible world. The process of "ennobling," of intensification, which the existing world undergoes at the hands of the artist, betrays this origin. The influence of art also shows this. It "elevates," it "frees," it "releases," but this process of emancipation, of elevation, and of release, is always accompanied by a shade of melancholy. For this process is not really present, it is only present in the imagination. It is indeed not formative reality, but merely an illusion on the fringe of reality. Its beneficent power may accompany man into life, but it is not able to change it; the power of the real world is too much for it.

2. Therefore, in spite of the fact that art and religion have so much in common, art contains an element of danger which produces a certain hostility towards religion: the danger, namely, of taking the reflection for the reality, or at any rate of resting content with it. Thus art becomes a substitute for faith, which is sought because it does not demand decision, as faith does, but merely the attitude of a spectator, or of one who is swayed hither and thither by the artistic influences around him; that is, it is not a real devotion, it is merely aesthetic. Just as intellectualism accompanies science, so does aestheticism accompany art, and this means that even within this sphere there appears the challenge to decision. For aestheticism—being satisfied with the freedom of illusion—is just as impossible to combine with faith as intellectualism. Both adopt the attitude of a spectator; both mean flight from responsible decision; both therefore destroy that community which is based on responsibility. Aestheticism makes man a creature who enjoys everything and seeks nothing but enjoyment. The man who is entangled in the net of aestheticism feels no responsibility for his fellow-men and *odi profanum vulgus et arceo*. He is an aristocrat, he is self-sufficient; he flees from the world of practical action where

there is so much to disturb his inner repose and upset his balance. True, he desires to have a group of people round him, but he does not wish to serve them, but through their enjoyment he desires to intensify his own, indeed, if they are beautiful or interesting, he wants to enjoy *them*. Therefore, the aesthete may know friendship, or something like it—that is, enjoyment of the individuality of the other person—but not real unity; the union is dissolved as soon as the possibilities of enjoyment have been exhausted(3).

Aestheticism is no more an essential part of art than intellectualism is of science. But in the actual reality of human life, in some way or another they are always connected, though this is certainly more frequent among the members of the art-loving "public" than it is with the creative artist, to whom his work is often a confession of faith, a conflict, and a deed. Even to him, however, it will be a constant danger and temptation, unless he have special grace; hence it is not surprising that faith, where it is not itself subject to an aesthetic misinterpretation, but is fully aware of the demand for decision, does not adopt such an unambiguously positive attitude towards art as, at first sight, might have been expected. It is true, of course, that religion possesses such an attraction for art that it almost amounts to compulsion; but, as a rule, this religion will be pantheism and mysticism, and not the Christian Faith. The prohibition of "images" in the Old Testament, which was necessary as a means of conflict against the pantheism of heathenism, is indeed removed in the New Testament; but the warning which it contains against a solution of contradictions by means of the imagination still remains, and the critical attitude, at a period when art and aestheticism can no longer be separated, may lead to open conflict. Fundamentally, however, in spite of all this, the Christian Faith is aware that, in some way or another, art foreshadows and awakens a longing for that which is to come. A Christian hostility to art can only exist where the Faith is misunderstood; here once for all we ought to correct the widespread and erroneous impression that Protestantism, especially in its Reformed (or Calvinistic) form, has been unfavourable to art, and has proved a barren field for art. When we think of Lutheran (Protestant) music in Germany, and of Calvinistic (Protestant) painting in Holland, and also of the importance of the Protestantism of both confessions in poetry and literature, we feel that it is time this assertion should cease. This does not mean that we dispute the fact that Puritanism manifested as little understanding of art as of nature, but this means very little for those who know how deep, at all points, is the gulf between the Reformed Faith and Puritanism(4).

3. Once the independent value of art has been recognized, however, it may also be valued on account of its influence. In the economy of human affairs it is that function by which the bodily nature of man is united with his psychical and spiritual nature. It corporealizes the spirit and spiritualizes the body. Therefore, especially where, in a false abstractness, the spiritual element is separated from the bodily element, it exercises an incomparably salutary influence, since it re-unites the elements which had been sundered. In this function, too, it gives a hint of the Redemption, which, according to the Christian Faith, will be not release from the body but a spiritualized bodily nature. This spiritualization in art is certainly *only* a suggestion, for it does not take place in reality, but only in a "picture"; but from the "picture" it also has a reflex influence upon the real man, and in so doing it exercises an influence which, though it may not be redeeming, is certainly releasing and preparatory, which the Church at all times has recognized and been able to use for her own purposes. It is true that the opinion often expressed at the present day that art—for instance, music—can become the means of expressing the Word of God as well as, and indeed better than, the human word, is based upon an error. Whoever asserts this does not mean by the Word of God the message of the God who is manifest in Jesus Christ(5). The message of what God has done for our redemption certainly cannot be expressed as music, and what God wills to say to us in Jesus Christ cannot be painted. In this respect the human word is not simply one method among others, for human speech alone can indicate quite unambiguously God's thought, Will, and Work. But music may very well support the word of the proclamation as an expression of the feeling aroused by the Word, and the art of painting may suggest in a pictorial manner what the Word means. This is no small service, and the truly great Christian artists have never wished it otherwise. Wordless art may awaken mysticism but never real faith. Even poetry must give way to simple prose because by the very fact of its beautiful form it only too easily transforms the decision of faith into the enjoyment of art. Where faith speaks directly in the prophetic message and in prayer it will never choose

the actual art form, but often by the energy of its feeling and the earnestness of its reality (which is peculiar to all real faith) it will elevate language likewise to a great power of artistic expression. To the extent, however, in which the artistic intention becomes apparent, the Word will cease to be a message which awakens faith.

CHAPTER XLI

EDUCATION

1. Just as the impulse and the capacity for the knowledge of truth and the creation of beauty have been implanted in the divinely created nature of man, so also is there implanted in man the impulse towards and the capacity for education. Both are the gifts of the Creator, and at the same time also the appointed task of man. Man cannot do justice to the duties imposed upon him by life "spontaneously," but only by the deliberate, purposeful, progressive exercise of his physical and intellectual powers; his human capacities—which distinguish him from the animal creation—can be realized only through "education"; this does not happen "spontaneously" or "naturally," without any effort on the part of man. It is an inherent element in the divinely created nature of man (in contrast to all other created beings) that man must seize the powers with which he has been endowed and make them his own. But the fact that he is a "creature" means that he is unable to seize his powers in *one* act; he can only do this in a continuous and ordered series of acts, which on the one hand, follow the natural process of growth, and yet, on the other, as free acts, break through this process and lead beyond it. In contradistinction to all other beings man can only become himself when he knows his own capacities and strives to realize them. The whole idea of education is based upon this need to realize man's latent powers. What, then, is the content of this idea of education?

From the days of Socrates to the present day philosophy has been trying to answer this question; but this answer is not uniform. Here again it is evident that the two fundamental philosophical tendencies—the naturalistic-positivistic philosophy which starts from the idea of existence, and the Idealistic philosophy which starts from the Idea(1)—follow different paths. Naturalism regards education as *adaptation* to the existing reality, to the "requirements of life," and it regards the process of education as a continuation of the natural process of growth. Education is mainly determined by external factors, and this environment is a conception of objective conditions and biological necessities. Since, however, even the naturalistic educational theorist substitutes something which *ought* to happen for something which would happen "of itself," almost against his own will he places himself within the sphere of the norm, of the Idea; only this Idea, according to its content, is determined by the external reality(2).

In the sphere of education Idealism is, from the outset, superior to Naturalism, in the fact that it acknowledges this normative character of all education. Indeed, we might even venture to maintain that Idealism as a whole has grown out of the question of education, that again and again it nourishes its life on it, and that it reaches its highest point in the sphere of education(3). The idea of education as such—from the days of Socrates and Plato—is the actual theme of Idealism, and the process of education is the principle of its interpretation of the world and of life itself. In its view education does not mean a process of "moulding" by external forces, but the development of potentialities which lie "within me." The great discovery of Plato was the fact that every human being possesses these latent powers, and that it is the specific task of man to allow these latent capacities to be realized in actual life. Plato conceived these "potentialities" as something essentially transcendent, lying beyond and above existing reality, and yet also as immanent, which, even if only partially, can, by means of the Socratic method, be "drawn out" through the process of "reminiscence" from the hidden depths of the human consciousness, and gradually brought into relation with actual life.

All who know that it is impossible to understand humanity without making this distinction between the potential and the actual, without that transcendence of the non-given, and thus without freedom, will perceive that this idea of education is not fantastic, but that it expresses a great truth; to such minds it will also be obvious that this idea of education is far higher than that of Naturalism, as is evident in the very fact that the very use of the word "education" implies the antithesis between what is and what ought to be.[1] And yet the fact that the Idealistic theory of education always has its double and its shadow in the Naturalistic theory reminds us that it must lack some essential elements. Naturalism points out, rightly, that a system of education which is so exclusively

---

[1] Cf. Häberlin: *Ziel der Erziehung*, p. 17: "One must be an Idealist in order to be able to put this question at all (i.e. concerning the aim of education, or the right kind of education)." For Häberlin's view of this aim, see Note (10), Chapter XLI.

orientated "from within," does not place man within reality, but separates him from it, that it places its abstractions (which are remote from life and hostile to life) between man and reality. But Naturalism can only conceive this reality causally and objectively; therefore it again makes it an abstraction.

2. It is at this point that the Christian Faith takes up the tale. Not in the sense that it offers a synthetic ideal of education; such syntheses have been sought very frequently, but they lead us no further, on the contrary they confuse the issue. Rather, our chief concern will be to try to throw light on the Idealistic theory of education by our criticism, showing what is the nature of man in the light of the truths of Creation and Redemption, and, either by limiting or by regulating this theory, we will endeavour to correct it. But in order to do this some previous explanations of a more general character are required.

Every theory of education—however empirical it may appear —is the product of man's definite understanding of his own nature, and to this extent it is either the fruit of a faith or of a view of life,[1] since—whether it admits it or not—it has to do with what man *ought to be*. On the other hand, the effort to sever the question of education from faith, and from one's general view of the world, and to give it an independent standing is so far justified, because in the sphere of education, as in that of science and art, there is a certain autonomy which ought to be considered and should be sought strictly objectively. Even education is primarily an autonomous sphere of life. And yet we see immediately that here, still more than in the sphere of science, this autonomy is only relative. The rules which govern the art of learning may indeed be in a high degree independent of faith and a philosophy of life. But here once again the law of a decrease in autonomy, the nearer one approaches to the personal centre, becomes operative. It is difficult to imagine a system of teaching mathematics which could be described as "Naturalistic" or "Idealistic" or "Christian"; within the sphere of history, however, those epithets cease to be meaningless, and where we are concerned with "genuine human education," with the "disposition," or the Ethos, there the objective autonomy ceases, there the question of education merges into the question of faith(4). If, then, it is true that faith is, or includes, a definite understanding of man, which stands in relation to non-faith as a challenge

[1] Cf. HÄBERLIN: "Die kritische Frage nach dem Erziehungsziel ist eine Weltanschauungsfrage," *Ziel der Erziehung*, p. 14.

to decision—for or against[1]—this implies that the question of education, which has more to do with the personal centre than any other aspect of cultural life, has a particularly close connexion with faith or with its opposite. As soon as we give up the idea that education is the sum-total of "cultivated" potentialities, a sum of dexterities, and maintain that not only does this not exhaust its meaning, but that in this conception it has not yet grasped its meaning at all, that is, that education is not concerned with different particular capacities, but with man as a unity, as a personal whole(5), and therefore that it is mainly determined by the definition of that point of unity, of that personal centre, education ceases to be "neutral." Neutrality exists only on the circumference; the more we gaze steadily at the centre and, further, look at the whole from the centre, which includes the circumference, the more the "neutral" quality of education will diminish, and finally disappear. It is not the technical side of external life, but its integration into the whole, which is determined in this way or that by the very fact of our understanding of this centre. Thus although our understanding of the person is not itself an educational idea, it is the point of view which determines every theory of education. Therefore, just as the Christian understanding of the person differs from any kind of general philosophy of life, although there is not a Christian idea of education, still the Christian idea of personality contains a "principle" which acts as a corrective of every kind of idea of education based on a general philosophy of life(6). Just as the Christian understands the human element in human beings in a different way from that of the Positivist or the Idealist, so also must his view of education differ from theirs; although at the same time he will continue to work with them. Rather, it is only in working with them, as he learns what they think, and as he corrects their ideas by his own, that he is able to learn to express what he himself means by education(7).

3. From the point of view of faith, let me now sum up under three headings what I regard as the errors of the Idealistic view of education; at the same time in this criticism the subordinate right of the Positivist conception will come out clearly. In its conception of education Idealism is *not realistic*, but is remote from reality; it is *not personal*, but abstract; it does not *foster community* but is individualistic.

[1] Literally "in the relation of the Either-Or."—Tr.

It is *not realistic*, for it ignores the power and the significance of the bodily nature of man, and it ignores evil. From Plato onwards Idealism has set the flesh over against the spirit, representing the "flesh" as the enemy of the "spirit"; in this view the "spirit" is regarded as the *real* nature of man, while the "flesh"—as that which is not really human—is identified with evil as that "material existence" which hinders the development of the spirit. This view deprives the "flesh," the natural, of value, and makes evil innocuous. Evil does not issue from the bodily nature of man, but from the spirit; the body, however, belongs necessarily to man as creature. Therefore Idealistic education breeds the illusion—or builds upon it—that "spirituality" as such guarantees genuine humanity(8), and that man in the spiritual core of his being is identical with the Divine Spirit or with Reason.

The second point is very closely connected with the previous one, that is, the *abstract character* of the Idealistic view. For Idealism man's final point of reference is an abstract idea, the Idea—whether it be called divine or not. All "higher life," all that is really human, and this means all that is "spiritual," is adjusted to abstract qualities like culture, value, law, ideas. The meaning of life does not reside in the personal sphere but in devotion to this "higher" realm. The value of man himself only consists in the fact that he is the bearer of this spirit, of these values, that he is the point through which the objective spirit passes on its way to its realization. The impersonal becomes the master of the personal, man exists for the sake of culture, instead of culture for the sake of man(9). Therefore the man who has been educated according to the Idealistic theory cannot find any real relation with the concrete tasks of life; above all he is alienated from those "orders" whose meaning, in the divine order of creation, is that of human community.

This brings us to the third point: Idealism *does not foster community*. Anyone who knows what community means cannot deceive himself by pointing to the "super-individual connexions," the universal purposes, which Spirit contains. That which is common to all does not create community, but merely things which are held in common, and identity. Indeed the Idealist cannot understand community in any other way than as the finding of oneself again in another—as identity(10). But this means: he does not know community. He depreciates the "Thou" just as much as he depreciates the "I"—in the universal Spirit. He does not know the union of the "I" and the "Thou" in the non-identical, in the "over-against-ness" of the real Other. He cannot know this; for his conception of personality is the rational conception, which regards the person as the—in itself indifferent—individual bearer of this universal reason. He regards man as a solitary being, with no relation to others. The theory of identity means this solitary existence in which man is alone with himself even when he ·is with another.

4. In spite of all this, Platonic Idealism has brought to light truth which can never be abandoned, truth which has made it very fruitful, especially in the sphere of education. There is an *a priori*, there is a realm of Ideas, there is something identical, which can only be awakened in the process of "Anamnesis," which can only be brought to light by means of the "Socratic method" of "drawing out." The essence of being human, in its formal aspect, in its formal freedom, in its imperishable *humanitas*, can only be comprehended in reference to the transcendence of the Idea. Without the abstract concepts of thought, without reference to "Eternal Ideas," no human being can become a human being. There is an essential identity of Reason which needs to be grasped in solitary thought, which no individual can impart to another, which, as Socrates says, he can only "bring to birth" as the "midwife" of his knowledge. In all that belongs to the intellectual nature of man, Idealism, and therefore all the education and pedagogy which is based upon it, is right(11).

Idealism is, however, wrong in the fact that it posits this truth as absolute, and makes this penultimate into an ultimate. Idealistic education therefore needs to be supplemented and limited by a realism which knows man mainly as a limited, individual, and natural being, a realism which places the individual in society and in the external world. It needs above all to be limited and supplemented by the knowledge of faith about the nature of personality, which is always a "being-in-community." A human being does not become really personal by his relation to culture, to values, to Ideas, but through the fact that he is related to the human "Thou"; the ground and the norm of this fact lies in its relation to the Divine "Thou." The abstract points of reference of Idealistic education —culture, values, norms, ideals—are necessary; but they are not higher than man himself; they are subordinate to man, to the fact of personal existence, to the fact that the "I" is

always a "being-in-community." Culture exists for the sake
of man, not man for the sake of culture; all that is abstract
and universal must therefore be a servant and not a master.

5. Hence the Idealistic programme of education must
above all be corrected by two principles from the standpoint
of the Christian Faith. The decisive point is not the
"cultivation" or the "development" of the potential capacities
implanted in man—although this is important—but the integration of the individual into the community, not in the sense
of mere adaptation—although this idea has its subordinate
right—but in the sense of concrete obedience and of responsibility in love. Only through obedience and responsible love,
through this double reference to the "Thou" in its difference
from me, can man become truly personal, not through pointing
to ideas and the goods of culture(12). Obedience does not exist
in relation to the Idea—for the relation to the Idea is essentially
always a relation to "me myself," namely, to the depths of
my own being. The Socratic "teacher" who is only a "midwife,"
only the occasion for the free self-activity of the "pupil," must
be supplemented by the concrete authorities whom one is
bound to obey because they are set over one in the divine order
of creation. Idealism has never had any comprehension of the
idea of authority(13); but this idea is deeply rooted in the
idea of the authority of God. And yet the relation of obedience
should not be the ultimate relation between human beings.
The final relation should rather be that sense of obligation
which is responsibility, and that responsibility which is a
sense of obligation, and means: love. But this knowledge,
like this reality, belongs no longer to the sphere of education,
but to that which is higher than education, and also higher
than all the other "autonomous" spheres of life; it is, namely,
the life of faith(14) which must finally control the sphere of
education, as well as all these other spheres.

Faith stands outside the sphere of education both as the judgment on it, and the basis on which it is built. The fact that
a human being is cast upon the act of God alone, through the
word of repentance and reconciliation, does not make him an
educated man. Essentially education is a secular matter,
even where it is ultimately based on and limited by faith
as a regulative principle, and thus becomes "Christian"
education. That which limits cannot itself become that which
is limited. Faith is not an element of the life of education.
All that is secular, even culture and the intellectual life, is

placed by faith under the divine judgment. This boundary must likewise remain as distinct as that between universal and special revelation, as that between the natural man and the regenerating word of God. Man, and his education, comes under the judgment and the promise of God; it is this which absolutely eliminates the difference between the educated and the uneducated, even in the deeper sense of the word. Even the most highly educated person has just as much need of the divine grace and forgiveness as the uneducated, and this forgiveness is not imparted to him through education but through grace. The Church is not an educational institution, but it is the community of the redeemed. It makes no difference whether in this proclamation of the Word of God we are thinking of the "sermon" in the usual sense of the word, or of catechetical instruction to the young; there is no difference in principle. "Religious instruction," as it is wrongly called, has, primarily, nothing to do with education; it is not cultural action, but it is the action of the Church. This holds good even when the Church acts not through any kind of official representatives but through her members in the "priesthood of all believers." Even the father who prays with his children and reads the Bible with them acts not as an educator but as a "priest," not in the "world" but in the "Church."

6. In spite of this *distinction* in principle between these spheres there can never be a *separation* of functions and persons. All ecclesiastical action, even the most central, the acts of preaching and of prayer, are connected with culture by their form. As theology is subject to the rules of science, as prayer is subject to the rules of thought, so also preaching is subject to the rules of all intelligent and effective speech. As the formal element in human existence is the general point of contact for the Gospel as a whole, so also always and everywhere there are individual points of contact which must be taken into account. The pedagogical laws, which circumscribe the conditions of educational activity, hold good also for the preaching of the Gospel, and this activity becomes in a secondary sense also a question of education. "Religious instruction" itself, if it is to be effective, cannot ignore the general rules of the method of imparting instruction. The peculiar content will modify it, as the material always modifies the methods, but it cannot render it useless. But this fact, which cannot be denied, must not be conceived in such a manner that it will permit us to remove a clear distinction.

The fact that the Word of God makes use of human forms, does not mean that it has itself become a human matter. Even where the father of a family, in accordance with his other forms of education and instruction, exercises his office as a priest in his own household, he does not on that account become an educationist; but he remains a "priest" on account of the matter with which he is dealing, although he certainly is an educator, so far as the forms which he is using are concerned. We must take both autonomous spheres into consideration: that of education and that of the preaching of the Word; only then can their positive and negative relations be rightly perceived and understood.

7. This brings us to another important question, which concerns those who carry on the work of education. Who educates whom? The only general answer which can be given to this question is this: every one educates every one else. Educating and being educated lasts as long as life itself lasts. It has been said, and rightly, that the most educative force of all is "life"; this we might call unintentional education. But if by "education" we mean deliberate willed action then education means all that comes under that heading in the purely technical and professional sense of the word. There would be no occasion for us to go into this question at all in any detail were it not for the fact that here prejudices exist which it is very important to expose. Education is not primarily the concern of the school, or even of the State, but of the family. It belongs to the divine order in creation that the child should grow up in the bosom and under the protection of the family, not merely as a physical being—for that is a false abstraction—but as a person. Here the child learns (what is more important than anything else it can learn) to know in an exemplary way the fundamental relation of community, the sense of connexion through the mutual need of one another, the connexion which consists in being "over against" one another, the recognition of the other as one who is unlike myself, whom I am obliged to recognize just because he *is* unlike. What the child learns in this intercourse with his father and his mother, is far more important than anything that he can learn in school—and this is true even if his parents are not ideal but only tolerably satisfactory. The essential thing in the family is not a material or spiritual something but the actual fact of community. In family life the person is always present as a whole and counts as a whole. The family

is not a school—thanks be—but it is far more than a school: it is community, even if it is this only in a relative and imperfect sense. It is this which is the incomparable element in the bond which unites the individual members of the family to each other. The responsibility of the one for the other, the sense of a mutual bond and a mutual obligation, which this responsibility implies, in spite of all imperfection, is still present, in some way or another, even in an only semi-decent family, in a way which exists nowhere else(15).

8. After the influence of the home in education comes—not the State—but the influence of the district in which the child grows up. One of the disastrous results of the modern conception of the State is that the local district is regarded simply as a sub-section, or an administrative district under the State. From the ethical point of view the parish is an independent entity, which, since the disappearance of the tribe, has had to take over the essential function of the tribe as something midway between the family and the people as a whole. Even at the present day the village-community is still an important factor in education. The conscious and deliberate education of the community is achieved mainly by means of the school. It is not the State which is the legitimate supporter of the educational system, but the "school-community"—understanding the word not in the legal but in the social sense— as a combination of families. The functions of culture should only be taken over by the State in cases of emergency, and in a vicarious manner; in themselves they do not belong to its domain. The State is a bad schoolmaster, and it is a great mistake to assume that the whole educational system should be left in the hands of the State. The fact that the school is the concern of the people does not mean that it is the concern of the State. The axiom that the State is the only organization of the people as such is based on no solid ground at all, thus it is not true to hold that all those organizations which the people as a whole creates for cultural ends are for that very reason State organizations. This axiom obscures the truth of the fundamental difference between the building up of cultural and State institutions. The State as a legal organization requires centralization, the building up from above, downwards. Culture, which begins, essentially, with the individual, and as a fellowship, needs the intimacy of the small group, requires to be built up from below. The primary concern of the State is the comprehensive whole; for this reason alone does it extend

513

its organization to the lower spheres, in order that the influence of the whole may affect the individual. Culture, however, has primarily no need at all for a large apparatus and an external unity. It prospers best in the small group, because for it the individual and personal element is the decisive factor. This is true also of education. In itself there is not the least necessity to make education an affair of the State; the private or community school (*Schulgenossenschaft*) is a form of community which is far more in accordance with the nature of the school than is the State school. The reasons which make it necessary for the State to co-operate in school matters are external: compulsory education, the question of finance, and of the external co-ordination of the schools. But this co-operation does not by any means make it necessary for the State to take over the educational system as a whole. There should be State schools only because, and as long as, there are no genuine people's schools. This distinction does not cease to be important even when—at least for the moment —the evil of the State school is seen to be unavoidable. For even within a State school the knowledge that the school must build up from below as a cultural concern, and must not be developed from above, that decentralization in matters of culture is just as necessary as centralization in matters of law, works profound changes in the inner structure of the educational system, and indeed helps to free it from the fundamental evils of uniformity and mechanical bureaucracy.

9. Still more important than this inward separation from the State—and later, too, outward separation—is separation from the spirit of the Enlightenment. Our whole present-day educational system is the product of the Enlightenment. It scarcely matters whether the individual teacher, or the particular educational method, is influenced by the spirit of the Enlightenment, compared with the fact that the whole idea of the "school," as we know it to-day, is only intelligible from the spirit of the Enlightenment. Now I do not wish to deny that the Enlightenment had an important mission to fulfil in its fight against orthodoxy and clericalism, indeed that it actually achieved results of positive value, and that without it the whole rise of modern science could scarcely have been imagined. But the rationalism of the ideology of the Enlightenment, the optimistic belief in "progress" which was bound up with it, as well as its individualism and intellectualism, which infects the whole of our intellectual

life, is now working itself out in our educational system in particular—from the primary school to the university. Radical educational reformers of the present day have indeed grasped something of this fact, and therefore they are rightly directing their efforts mainly against the intellectualism of our educational system, seldom, however, do they see the depths of the evil, because they themselves are still too much under the influence of the ideas of the Enlightenment. It is really tragic that the only great ideas of Pestalozzi which have been realized, or even understood at all, are those which he took over from Rousseau and developed still further, but not those which are peculiarly his own, which he gained from a deeper understanding of man as a personal and social being. The campaign against the ideology of the Enlightenment, looking at the nation as a whole, is hopeless as long as it is not at the same time a campaign against the educational system of the present day which is based upon it.

10. The question of the "Christian school" should be approached from these two points of view: fundamental independence of the State, and emancipation from the ideology of the Enlightenment. Education, especially in so far as it can be school education, is an "autonomous" sphere of life; but this autonomy is limited in scope. The "neutral school" is a fiction of the imagination; the "spirit" of a school, quite apart from all material content, is determined by its general outlook on life and by faith, whether one admits this or not. In this sense it is obvious that the Christian must desire Christian schools. But in principle this has very little to do with the creation of so-called "Christian" schools. First of all, that which to-day is called a school is conceived in a spirit which is essentially remote from the Christian Faith, and is moulded by this spirit, and the "Christianity" of such schools can do little to alter this spirit or this framework. Above all, however, the Christian spirit, which is all that matters, is not in the least guaranteed by the obligation to accept a special Christian Creed or by emphasis upon Christian religious instruction. It is of course true that, under certain circumstances, the formation of such special "Christian" schools may be necessary, but as a necessary evil. On the other hand, this special character would more or less fall away, if the school were not the uniform school of the State but the "community school" formed by the special circumstances of the school community. The only solution of the question will consist in the fact that the popular

515

community which creates the school is itself determined by the Christian spirit; all other attempts are emergency measures of relative and fluctuating value. One thing, however, must be said very plainly in conclusion : the separation of the school from the legal constitution of the Church is an act of the Enlightenment for which even Christians may be grateful. The confessional school, under the control of the Church, is even less desirable than the State school of the present day; this idea is only in place at all within a Roman Catholic conception of the relation between the Church and culture, whereas the guardianship of culture by the Church is an idea which is essentially foreign to the Protestant faith.

CHAPTER XLII

THE FREE FORMS OF COMMUNITY

1. With the preceding discussion of the question of education and the school we have already entered upon the ground covered by our present theme. There are forms of community which are not connected with marriage and the family, nor with industry, nor with the State or the Church, but which develop independently within the sphere of autonomous culture; this is due to the fact that they are based upon the intellectual nature of man, to which the mind is an end in itself. Extreme instances of such social grouping are the community of play, and all free social life. Man feels an urge —based upon his whole "creaturely" tendency—to join with other human beings not for a definite "purpose" but simply for mutual intercourse and "exchange"(1).

This social form of community is not rigidly individualistic or selective. Where it does assume this character it develops into friendship. Friendship is primarily a form of culture, not a moral relationship. Friendship, like love between man and woman, does not spring from ethical impulses but from our natural spiritual impulse. We are not driven to it by a sense of compulsion or duty, but we are drawn to certain people by a certain attraction and inner impulse. Friendship begins with pleasure in the individuality of the other person, its basis is aesthetic. Love of our neighbour is as distinct from it as it is from *Eros*. But in spite of the fact that the basis of friendship is delight in our friend, "delight in being in his company," still it does also contain an ethical motive. Mere delight in the figure, the face, the wit, the peculiarities of the other person is not friendship. Rather friendship only arises where the pleasure we feel is caused by the whole personality of the other, where we are attracted, not merely by "something in him," but "by himself," and where this attraction is mutual. Through this relation to the whole person the ethical element enters into friendship, not primarily as an obligation, but as an object of pleasure. Since, however, pleasure in the moral being of the other is not possible without recognition of the moral demand, the more that friendship is concerned with the whole personality, the more it becomes a bridge leading to the ethical realm. It is the aesthetic aspect of ethics, ethics

517

as a natural fact, as something "given"(2); at the same time this natural fact always develops into a task or a duty owing to its distinguishing feature, that is, because it is delight in something ethical. Friendship is only genuine where it is deliberately regarded not only as a gift but as an obligation.

In spite of this, however, in principle, the relation between friendship and faith is exactly the same as the relation between faith and the erotic, economic and political forms of community. From the point of view of faith friendship is a natural fact which can only become ethical through the love of our neighbour. Real community, *Agape*, is foreshadowed, naturally, in friendship, and in the capacity for friendship; the fact that human beings instinctively form friendships, whether they will or no, is an indication that they are destined for community, in the sense of responsible love. But friendship is not itself such community. For it is not based on the fact that I know that I am under an obligation to serve the other, but upon the fact that I take a delight in him. Friendship does not say: I love you because you are *there*, but it says merely: I love you because you are like this! Thus it is not unconditional but conditional, exclusive and not universal. A person who claims friendship with every one has not begun to understand the meaning of friendship.

This exclusiveness and this limitation seems to be incompatible with the commandment of love. For us created human beings, however, this exclusiveness is no more incompatible with the commandment of love than the exclusiveness of married love. The Creator grants us this special element in friendship, just as He grants us beauty alongside of duty. From the point of view of faith, friendship starts from the standpoint of real human refreshment. What art achieves impersonally, friendship achieves personally. In this special function, which is implanted in our created nature, lies the right to friendship and its exclusiveness. At the same time here too lies the possibility of its corruption and of its disastrous influence. Friendship, like love between the sexes, can degenerate into sheer self-pleasing and possessiveness. Indeed no human friendship is ever without this corrupt element. There is no one who does not secretly regard his friend as his possession, and who does not exploit the necessary exclusiveness of friendship in a greedy selfish manner. Friendship, too, needs to be re-born, and this new birth, even in the highest instance, will only be the beginning of a new life which is never perfect.

Even when "friendship" as a natural phenomenon is placed under the discipline of the obedience of faith it still remains perverted by selfishness. It also constitutes no exception to the statement that all natural community is at the same time the denial of community, thus it is due both to creation and to sin. But there is no need for me to pursue this familiar subject any further.

2. As friendship is the nearest approach of the natural spiritual element to *personal* community, so, on the other hand, custom is the *impersonal* medium between the truly ethical and the natural(3). Within society it means what habit means for the individual; it is "social habit." Habit is not in itself ethical; but it is the only possibility of making the ethical into "second nature"; it is the union between the spiritual act[1] and the natural existence, therefore it is of supreme importance in education. The same is true of custom. All that is spiritual, even faith, becomes a permanent part of the life of society only through custom. That is also why it is not understood or valued by rationalistic individualism, but is regarded as something unworthy of a "free" man, and is accordingly destroyed. This is the reason for the decline of this force in more recent times. Our day is "without customs," not in the sense of bad customs, but in the literal sense that custom in general is largely ignored.

Everything can be precipitated into custom, all that is known, grasped and recognized in the spiritual act, the evil as well as the good, that which is Christian as well as that which is non-Christian. Therefore, the relation of faith to custom is only indirect and ambiguous; "Christian custom" can only exist in that extremely indirect and vague sense in which we can speak of "Christian education," "Christian marriage" or a "Christian State." For the habitual, as such, is something quite different from faith, since faith indeed lives only in act. But seeing that we happen to be psychophysical creatures it is our duty to recognize the dynamic importance even of habit, even of social habit or custom. Where we are concerned with growth, even with the growth of faith, there the soil which nourishes it is supremely important. But the soil from which all spiritual growth springs is custom. It should be an urgent concern of the Church that custom should be moulded into shape as a deposit of faith and not of unbelief, of personal responsibility and not of irresponsibility.

[1] I.e. act of the *spirit*, as opposed to the *body*.—TR.

519

3. For its own ends the cultural life creates a great variety of distinctive forms of community, which we may describe as community forms for intellectual ends. Here the *end* is the intellectual life in the cultural sense—that is, intellect in the abstract, the "values" of "goods" of culture—the community is merely the *means* to the end, as for instance in the "republic of letters" and the Academy, in the circles of poets and literary people and in artistic circles, in scientific societies, and in societies for the furtherance of various cultural ends. Here, too, we find a kind of "border-state" on the frontier of the realm of ethics, that is: societies which pursue a definite ethical purpose simply for the sake of this purpose(4). Here there is a form of contact with the ethical activity of the Church, which can, however, all the more lead such bodies to trespass on her domain and to overlap with her action, since although the ideas which are here operative are very often solely and vitally rooted in the Christian Faith, those whose action is guided by these principles do not need to have any conscious connexion with the Christian Faith at all. Here, then, it is possible to speak not merely of "unconscious Christianity" but of an "unconscious Church." On this presupposition, the element which makes these people a real "community" is simply the message of Jesus Christ, upon which this definite moral will is based. Those who know anything at all about the connexion between the Christian Faith and the development of the modern view of law, the conception of the dignity of women and the value of children, of human dignity as a whole, and who also know how largely these ideas are now separated from all connexion with the Church, and with organized Christianity, cannot help describing this phenomenon as a "secular" or "profane Church." But since in this problem the spiritual content is more important than the *form* of the community let us briefly examine this subject, from the point of view of "public opinion."

Public opinion is a necessary subject of Christian ethics since it is the most important method by which the message of the Church affects the civil community. Public opinion *is* not, it is true, but it *can* be, the "world-conscience." It is primarily an indefinite force, composed of the most heterogeneous elements, and yet, in spite of its indefinite character, it is most influential. It is moulded and formed by the "spirit of the age" and fashionable tendencies, and also by the moral *lex naturae*, various philosophies of life, and religions of all kinds, among them also the Christian tradition and the Christian message. It exercises, however, a critical and productive function—whether for good or for evil, in any case extremely important—in all matters which affect custom, law, politics, and the private life of individuals. It is a kind of secular parallel to the "invisible Church"; it is a collective force, a kind of loosely connected community, that is, a community of "opinion"—in which individuals know they are united, and through which those who cannot do much as individuals are able to influence events on a large scale.

It is not the primary task of the Church to influence public opinion; its duty is rather to educate and inspire the local congregations. But much of that which is known and willed by those who confess the name of Christ is also known and willed by those who do not confess the name of Christ, who indeed do not know that what they affirm and will proceeds from the message of the Gospel; the Church should be ready to acknowledge this as a fact, and she should do nothing to hinder it. Where the Gospel is itself heard and believed, the Church comes into being; but the influence of the Gospel extends where the Gospel itself is not believed. Or, to express this in a simplified formula: the Christian *ethos* is effective even among those who are not Christians. As we have already seen, it is the duty of the Church to influence the formation of the *justitia civilis*, which is a variable force, and this takes place in the form of influence upon public opinion. By its means much is achieved which apart from it would not come into being; by its means much is prevented or abolished which, apart from it, would remain in existence and continue to exert an evil influence on humanity. It is a great power, which can be used for good or evil according to the source from which it is fed. To-day in particular, when the Press and the wireless play such an immense part, that is, when the formation of "opinion" proceeds in a way which cannot be controlled, far beyond any distinctly defined circles, it is an urgent duty of Christendom to perceive the task which awaits her here in particular, and not to leave to the powers of evil these methods which, for good or ill, are always at work on the grand scale. Night and day public opinion is being manufactured; whoever can control it would control the world. It is the duty of Christendom to create public opinion, in the sense that through it and in it Christ should exercise His Sovereignty even over those who do not know Him, so far as this is possible. This

521

outer circle ought not to be despised because it is only an outer circle. For how often already has it happened that from this outer circle, against the will of those who called themselves Christians, things have happened which were more in accordance with the mind of Jesus Christ than that which was done by the official Church. But also we must not over-estimate this influence of Christ on opinion outside the Church, as though here only, in separation from the Church, could the Kingdom of God be found. We have now reached the point where it becomes necessary to enter the last of the circles of community, and to make clear to our minds what is the significance of the Church.

SECTION VI: THE COMMUNITY OF FAITH

CHAPTER XLIII

THE NATURE OF THE CHURCH

1. *The Church of Faith*

THE question of the nature of the Church is the decisive question for theology, and also for every system of theological ethics. The view we hold of the nature of the Church reveals most plainly where we stand in relation to faith; and it is through this belief in the Church that faith is able to influence world history at any particular time. The new view of the Church which Luther gained altered the course of the history of Europe; but Luther's view became obscured, and it has remained more or less concealed until the present day(1). The question of the Church is indeed *the* unsolved problem of Protestant theology. It is all the more necessary to discuss this question in connexion with ethics since in the Church the Divine action (which is the presupposition and point of view of an honest theological ethic) is manifest in its indissoluble connexion with human conduct.

In all that I have said hitherto about Christian conduct the Church was presupposed, although this was not explicitly stated. Whenever we speak of the Christian, of faith, and of conduct inspired by faith, we are speaking of the Church. For faith exists only in the Church; faith and the Church belong to one another as inevitably as the body and the limbs. Whoever acts as a believer, by that very fact acts as a member of the Church, united with the whole body of believers, from which he has gained his faith, which supports and nourishes him in his faith. This is the reason why the Christian ethic is a social ethic.

But this is not the Church of which every one thinks when the Church is mentioned. The Church, in the usual literal meaning of the word, is a definite institution or corporation, something which can be clearly defined within space, a sociological structure which can be clearly perceived; indeed, in our usual way of talking we think of the Church only in the plural: the Catholic, the Lutheran, the Reformed, the Methodist Church. And it is precisely this Church, or rather

523

its relation to that other Church, which is still an unsolved problem(2). The relation between these two kinds of Church is the point at which dangerous short-circuits have been and still are continually being made; misunderstandings at this point create both those forces which cast a heavy shadow over the history of Christianity: a false ecclesiasticism and a false anti-ecclesiasticism. Since we are here concerned with the Church in action, and action in the Church, we cannot dispense with a doctrine of the Church, which ought to be presupposed in an ethic, at least in its main features.

There are three classical definitions of the Church, all of which, each from a different standpoint, say the same thing, and yet only when they are taken together do they express the whole. The Church is the *coetus electorum*, the *communio sanctorum*, and the *corpus Christi*. The first definition contrasts the Church of faith most sharply with the Church conceived as a sociological institution; the third makes it very clear that the Church is not a merely spiritual reality in the sense of a Platonic Idea; the second restores the connexion between the two conceptions.

First; in the New Testament the Church, the ἐκ-κλησία, is the community consisting of those whom God has called. The sole foundation of the Church is the will and the choice of God; God, not man, is the *auctor ecclesiae*. Because, and to the extent in which, God calls men by His word out of the world—where they are "without God and without hope"— to Himself, into fellowship with Him and into His service, there alone, and wherever this takes place, the Church exists. Her ground is the eternal counsel of God; not merely salvation and the service of the individual, but community—the fact that these individuals are bound to each other. The universality of the Church and her social character are not based on the human need for community, but on the Divine will for the Kingdom of God.

Secondly, the Church is called the *communio*—or *coetus*—*fidelium*, or the *communio sanctorum*, since it is a community which, although it is grounded in the eternal, is realized within history. It is not the open proclamation of the Gospel which makes the Church, but man's believing response to this Divine call. The Church is the place where the decision of faith is made. Through this objective-subjective event man becomes a "saint" in the Biblical, not in the Catholic sense of the word; this means that he is a person whom God has apprehended for Himself, and one who willingly submits to this claim;

thus he is one who, by the very fact that God's Hand has seized him, has really become God's "property"; thus he has abandoned the world, with its alienation from God, and has returned to communion with God.

But the Church is not called the *summa fidelium*, but its *communio* or *coetus*. The act of becoming a believer is not a solitary event—although it certainly makes a man an "individual" in the strict sense of the word; but it is the event in which a human being becomes conscious of community, the act by which he abandons for ever all solitary detached existence. Faith means being united not only with God but with our fellow-men. The severed branch is again grafted into the Tree of Life, the individual human being no longer belongs to himself but to the people of God. The *meaning* of this event is community.

Community is both the *cause* and the *effect* of this occurrence. It is the *cause*: for no one becomes a believer save through the influence of others, who, in the very act of confessing their faith, pass on to him the message which made them believers. No one comes to the point at which he begins to believe in Jesus Christ apart from a message communicated to him by others, apart from that impressive chain of witness called "the Christian tradition" which extends from the earliest days of Christianity down to the present day.

The human word is never the ground of faith, but it is always the cause of faith. This connexion may not be very clear: but, in any case, it does exist; certain types of mysticism and natural religion might come into existence without this communication, but no Christian faith ever came into existence in this way. Similarly, faith itself is the effective cause of community, since it is faith which urges one human being towards another; above all it is faith which impels him to join the company of those who have believed before him, and who are now believers. The believer feels it both an inward impulse and an outward duty to communicate the truth he has received. This impulse and this sense of obligation to communicate the message to others are due to the gift of the Word.

Thirdly: the union between this invisible, "other-worldly" cause, and the visible, "this-worldly" effect, is expressed in the simile—both spiritual and natural—of the *Corpus Christi*. Where Christ is, there is the Church, and nowhere else. And the Church is wherever Jesus Christ is; for it is the fact of

His Presence among men which creates community in faith and love. It is only a simile, for believers do not depend upon their "Head," and upon each other, in the same way as the members form part of the body. Christ is present in the call which summons to decision, and it is only through the decision of the response of faith that He takes possession of the individual. Yet this spiritual event is connected with an external word, and this faith again leads to an outward community. For this reason the Church is the only true community.[1] It is real and powerful, like the blood relationship, like the love between mother and child, but it is not, like it, partial and limited. It is spiritual, like the community of ideas, but not, like it, abstract and impersonal. It is the true community, because it is absolutely personal, since it is based upon God's personal call and man's personal answer. It is therefore the only form of community between one person and another—the community of love. At the same time it is completely universal, knowing no barriers of race or class or culture.

The ultimate, absolute End, that is, the Kingdom of God, begins in this community, in the Church. The Church is not based on the fact of Creation, but on that of Redemption, although Creation was designed with this end in view. But it is only the concealed beginning of this ultimate end, hence in itself it is not an end, it is not complete; indeed it is essentially incomplete. As faith is not itself perfection, but is only the certainty of the coming perfection, so also the Church transcends itself, reaches out towards that which is beyond itself. The Church can be only understood in the light of the end. All who belong to the Church are of the company of those "who desire a better country"; they live in the hope of the final fulfilment of "the Promise." Therefore the Church does not stand still, but is ever moving towards the end. She moves towards the ultimate End because she herself is drawn by it. She is, as Barth once said very finely—the "vanguard of God." Therefore she cannot be her own End, but her whole will must be set on that which is "to come," on the Kingdom of God. The Church is the earthly, historical veil which conceals the "Kingdom," or, to change the metaphor, she is already "the Kingdom" in "the form of a servant." The Church and perfection are mutually exclusive ideas; the Church is the community of those who are still sinners; therefore, the Church is always an imperfect community, permeated with

[1] See above, pp. 300 ff.

526

sin. This is not due to the corruption which has entered into it incidentally, in the course of history, but belongs to its very nature; when we see this we have found the key to the understanding of the relation between the Church of faith and the Church as an institution(3).

2. The Church as both Divine and Human

There is no Church, in any sense of the word, apart from human action. This simple sentence contains the whole problem of the Church. We can only understand it in the light of the central paradox of the Gospel—the Incarnation, this paradox which is the inmost heart of the whole of the Christian Faith, the primal mystery. It has pleased God to reveal Himself in a human being, and through this revelation to achieve the salvation of the world; it has pleased Him to be the Revealed One only in this concealment. This is the content of the Gospel: the Eternal Word in an historical, unique event, never to be repeated. It is only through this historical form— only through the "form of a servant"—of this earthly life that the Eternal Son speaks His Word to us, and only in this historical form do we possess this Eternal Word, and therefore we always possess it in historical form(4). The Eternal Word of God which creates faith is therefore always an historical word, that is, a human word. There is no saving Gospel except one that is proclaimed by men(5). The Church exists only where this Word is preached and believed, and wherever this takes place, there is the Church. This is the central affirmation of an evangelical doctrine of the Church. There is therefore no purely divine or purely spiritual Church. It belongs to the essence of the Church that it is at once divine and human, sacred and secular.[1]

For human action is, primarily, secular, and it does not cease to be secular even when it is filled with spiritual power, controlled by the Holy Spirit. Only when this has been perceived —which is the same as the *simul justus simul peccator* of the doctrine of Justification—is Catholic clericalism finally swept away. The recognition of this fact must be the guiding principle of all theological reflection. Even the preaching of the Gospel is a human act, just as the Bible itself, the canon by which all preaching is tested, is a human book. But just as it has pleased God to reveal Himself in a human being, so also it

---

[1] On Luther cf. KATTENBUSCH: *Die Doppelgeschichtigkeit in Luthers Kirchenbegriff*, p. 35.

pleases Him to speak His Word through such human and earthly speech. *We* cannot give this divine qualification to our own word; *we* cannot dispose of the Word of God; if our word becomes the medium of His Word this is due entirely to the Grace of God. But we certainly have received the promise that this is possible, and we have also received the Divine Command to order our action according to the "pattern in the mount," in order that, in some way or another, our action may be "conformed" to the Divine Word. This is true first of all of preaching. Man cannot empower himself to proclaim "the Word of God." Merely to read aloud the word of Scripture is not "to proclaim the word of God." The Bible itself is not simply the Word of God, it is also human testimony, although it does contain the original witness to the Word of God, and must therefore become a testimony in us and through us.[1] This is what the expression "pure doctrine" means: that in this endeavour to "conform" our human word to the Divine Word there are degrees of conformity which can be perceived, even if only in faith, and it is our highest duty to take note of these differing degrees. All that we can do as human beings is to try to express the Word of God in the purest form of doctrine we can find; in so doing, however, we must take the manner of the formulation into account, as well as the matter. The pure doctrine, the proclamation of the Gospel in all simplicity and sincerity, is still not the Word of God. God may speak through doctrine that is less pure, and He may not speak through the purest doctrine.[2] Here, however, it is evident that our action and the divine action are most intimately connected. The statement of the Helvetic Confession: *praedicatio verbi divini est verbum divinum*, is right, if it means this intimate connexion. It is false clericalism, and smacks of priestcraft, if it sweeps away the last reserve and tries to place the Word of God at the disposal of man. Therefore, in faith we may determine where there is "pure doctrine," and accordingly a pure creed; but even in faith we can never determine where God really speaks His word. This is and remains, like true genuine faith, His secret. This is what Calvin means when he speaks of the "invisible Church." But he does not deny the

[1] This is one of the points at which the views of Luther and Calvin differ very widely; for Luther the standard is the *viva vox ecclesiae*, for Calvin it is the written Word, the *illustrior forma* or *doctrina*. (*Institutio*, IV, 8, 6).

[2] Calvin, loc. cit., IV, 1, 12, and 1, 8.

importance of this intimate connexion between pure doctrine, the pure creed and the Divine Word, any more than Luther denies the importance of Calvin's concern for the "invisible Church."[1] Thus the connexion between the human and secular aspect of the Church—human thought, grammar, logic and rhetoric—and the Divine action, may be very close and intimate. But it is only possible through a real relation, that is, in the fact that human action—thought, speech, and teaching—is carried on in believing dependence upon the Divine action. And *vice versa*: thus the earthly nature of the Church penetrates to the very heart of its life.

Where this Word is preached, and is received with faith, there—as we believe, with a faith which is based upon the Divine promise—is the true Church, the Church of faith. Where the Word of God is preached and believed, where two or three meet in the name of Christ, there is the Church. Whatever else may be said about the Church, this is fundamental(6). This statement has *never*—not even at the present day—been understood in all its revolutionary power(7). The meeting of two or three must be recognized to be the Church in however imperfect a form. When a father gathers his household round him to expound the Gospel to them in his humble simple way, or where a layman, out of a full heart, proclaims the word of God to a group of young people, there is the Church. Whoever departs from this rule, whoever thinks that something else has to be added to make this a real Church, has misunderstood the meaning of the very heart of the evangelical Faith(8).

But although it is quite certain that here the Church is present—that is, assuming that here God has really spoken His Word through the simple, sincere human message—this is only the first step. Others must gather round this inmost circle. If the inner reason for this were to be absent then this faith would not be real, the Church would not be there. People who have been touched by faith cannot remain isolated believers. They are impelled to enter into community—the Spirit of God impels them, and the Divine Command bids them do so, and this impulse drives them in two directions: into the community of faith with other believers in their neighbourhood, and into the community of love with those who do not believe, whether by going out to them to communi-

[1] The work entitled: *De servo arbitrio*, will be sufficient to illustrate this point.

cate to them their faith,[1] or by serving them in "works of mercy." Every one who has really and truly received the Word of God cannot and may not remain a private individual; there is no private Christianity save *per defectum*.[2]

In the New Testament the relation between faith and community is emphasized with peculiar impressiveness in the Sacraments, which constitute a special form of the Word. The "word" which is preached is a human message; therefore it is connected with community, and itself creates community. But again and again this particular "word" is misunderstood, and is regarded as independent of community. The mistaken idea, that only through the Bible can we become and remain Christian, constantly reappears. One of the evident reasons for the institution of the Sacraments is the desire to prevent this mistaken idea from taking root. Another reason, closely connected with this one, is the fact that the Sacrament, the *verbum visible*, is the elementary "outward and visible sign" of the "inward and spiritual grace" of the Divine gift of salvation. In any case the Sacrament can only exist as the proclamation of the Word by the Church, and not as a private matter; the *verbum visible* places us inevitably within community. Indeed, the very act of communication, the fact that one member gives to another, and lays his hands upon another, constitutes the real fulfilment of the Sacrament. Thus in a very special way the Sacrament underlines the fact that God wills to give us His Word only through human action, in order that He may force us to abandon our individualism(9). But there is another truth which is equally clearly emphasized in the Sacrament, namely, that God uses earthly elements in order to give us His divine gifts. The earthly element, indeed the sense-element, here occupies a solid position in the very centre of our Church life.

Secondly, the Sacrament implies the existence of the Church in the usual sense, as the worshipping community. The mere proclamation of the Word—apart from the Sacrament—can take place apart from the existence of a worshipping community. Indeed it is the preaching of the missionary which first creates the Christian community. It is therefore definitely not an

---

[1] Cf. KATTENBUSCH, *Die Doppelgeschichtigkeit in Luthers Kirchenbegriff* p. 31, who in his turn indicates the view of K. MÜLLER.

[2] CALVIN, *Institutio*, I, 5: "Whoever does not attend public worship falls into *pestiferos errores*." See especially his discussion with fanatics, ibid., I, 10 ff.

act of worship, and to the extent in which the missionary situation exists this must be so. Worship presupposes the existence of a Christian community, it assumes that the decision of faith has already been made. Therefore the Sacrament does not belong to the missionary situation, and this is why Paul the missionary makes the categorical assertion that it is not his work to administer the Sacraments.[1] But quite apart from the Sacraments the Divine word and faith are of such a nature that inevitably they lead us to "assemble ourselves together" to receive "the Word." The formless Church must issue in the "congregation," the assembly for worship. This sense of impulsion is emphasized by the Sacraments, both by the Sacrament which admits new members to the Church (Baptism), and by the Sacrament which provides the believer with "spiritual food" (the Lord's Supper). It is, however, most important to distinguish clearly between the Church of faith and the worshipping congregation(10). The Church may exist where there is not yet a worshipping congregation, and there may be congregations meeting for worship where there is no true Church. Both statements are fundamental. The third statement, although extremely important, is secondary; the true Church leads of necessity to the worshipping community, wherever faith is living, and external circumstances permit.[2]

Only now, through the *congregatio*, does the definition *coetus fidelium*, coupled with the definition *communio fidelium* (*sanctorum*), receive, so to speak, its normal content. It is, of course, true that *communio* may exist where this *coetus* perhaps does not exist; but the true *communio* will realize itself in the *congregatio*, in the *coetus fidelium*. Not merely because the believer needs the divine Word again and again, but also because he desires to respond to the Divine Word in fellowship with his brethren in the faith, in "prayer and praise." This was the original conception of Christian worship. It is very closely connected with the Sacrament in that very pregnant word "Eucharist." But it is not merely the Sacrament, nor even the cultus, but the desire to hear the Word regularly which creates the necessity for the *congregatio*, and with that the necessity for the definite,

---

[1] 1 Cor. i. 14 ff.
[2] This is true of LUTHER, in spite of RIEKER's assertion to the contrary. Loc. cit., p. 61. Cf. KATTENBUSCH, *Die Doppelgeschichtigkeit in Luthers Kirchenbegriff*, pp. 94 and 101.

sociologically visible entity of the "worshipping community" —the Church.[1]

The new meaning which this gives to the word "Church" is shown by the fact that the secular element now appears in a new and tangible form in the establishment of order. There can be no common worship, nor a worshipping congregation, without order. It is true that the purpose of this order is to serve divine and sacred ends, and that it ought to be established and maintained with direct reference to these ends, that is to say, in the closest possible conformity with the Word of God. But order is order, and what is done in accordance with order is only indirectly connected with faith. Order means that something takes place simply because it has been "ordered." "Now we remain loyal to this order"—until some other order is created. This point is of the first importance for the clarification of the confused problem of Church Law, which will be treated later on.

The Church of faith leads inevitably to the worshipping community, and thus to the definite local congregation. But this means that the Church of faith is primary, even where the local congregation is concerned(11). Indeed the congregation is a congregation only through order, and is real only as an order. It is therefore a fundamental error to find the explanation of the Church in the congregation—just as it is a fundamental error to interpret Luther's "Christian meeting" of this community as a *congregatio*. There is a relation, and indeed a necessary relation, between the Church of faith and the individual local congregation, but the two are not identical. There is a Church even where no local congregations yet exist, but where there is a real Church local congregations must come into being. In a secondary sense, however, when we enquire into the "cause" and not the "ground," the converse is also true: the (missionary) community is the cause of the Church which is only being formed.

This brings us to the question of the connexion between the practice of preaching and the worshipping community, and this means the question of ecclesiastical office. By "office"

[1] Even the Church as a sociologically visible structure cannot be *rightly* understood from the point of view of *general* sociological principles, as TILLICH (*Kirche und Kultur*) or O. DIBELIUS (*Das Jahrhundert der Kirche*) believe; it can only be understood as the Church of faith. There may be worshipping *groups* outside Christianity, but there can be no "Churches" outside Christianity.

I mean the task entrusted by God to every believer, and therefore also to every community of believers, of handing on the message which has been received; indeed, the Church cannot be imagined at all without this "office"—this institution for the proclamation of the Word—apart from all questions concerning the persons who are to do this, or those for whom they are to exercise it, or the methods they are to use. The Church arises out of this "office which preaches reconciliation,"[1] and necessarily leads to it. This "office," however, is the opposite of that which is usually understood by office: it is the universal priesthood of all believers. This "office" has nothing at all to do with order; primarily it is grounded in the nature of the Church of faith itself, apart from all order: hence it must always be regarded not merely from the standpoint of community, but also from that of a divine institution(12). But the "institution"—which produces community—and the "community"—which is produced—are not only necessarily connected, they are actually the same. At any given time those who believe are the "supporters of the institution" who impart faith to those who are ready to receive it. But this means that there is no office outside the Christian community itself, the primary "office" is the priesthood of all believers. This "office," then, is exercised not in virtue of a human commission, but in virtue of the commission which lies in the Word and in faith itself. Therefore it is not an "office" in the usual literal sense of the word.

"Office," in the ordinary sense of the word, has a special double origin: an extraordinary office through a special, direct divine commission, and an ordinary office through a human commission. As a rule the Reformers skate rather lightly over the first type, simply remarking that the extraordinary office of the prophets and apostles was limited to the early days of the Church. This is comprehensible when we remember the fight the Reformers were waging against fanaticism, and in view of reality they were essentially right. And yet it is most important that we should take into account this extraordinary possibility, because only through it does the nature of the ordinary office become intelligible(13). The ordinary office is purely a matter of order, and—as an ordinary office—it originates only in the obligation of the worshipping community to see to it that regularity and order should prevail

[1] So Luther renders 2 Cor. v. 18. Paul's expression is certainly διακονία (*service* or *ministry*).

533

in the matter of public worship. Merely to leave everything to the spontaneous action of faith, merely to leave everything to the "movement of the Spirit," has always proved impossible to combine with the requirements of community life: this has been the case not only in a community which is weak in faith, but always and everywhere, even in the primitive Christian communities.[1] An official order is required in order that the worshipping community may the better perform its divinely appointed task. That in so doing the first consideration should be spiritual gifts, spiritual equipment, does not alter the fact that we are here dealing with an order, one in which, moreover, a rule has to be kept. The spontaneity of faith is necessarily limited by the rationality of order. The two following statements are of fundamental importance: first, that the Church of faith, just as it must organize itself as a worshipping community, must also have the official order which such a community requires; secondly, the mere fact that something is done "officially" does not mean that it has divine authority; an official position in the Church is no guarantee that the "office-bearer" possesses God's Word(14). The relation between the official order and the Divine Word is much less than that between it and "pure doctrine," or the "correct" administration of the Sacraments. In spite of this, however, the fact that the "office" is necessary implies a certain relation with the Divine action. Just as God wills to have ordered communities, so also He wills to speak His word through official preachers—that is, people commissioned by the Christian community; this is true even though He does not tie Himself to the official order, but still more than in the case of pure doctrine, He remains free and sovereign Lord. The other considerations which belong to the question of office are secondary; but the fact that an official order is necessary is based upon the very nature of the human-divine Church in its form as a worshipping community.

The worshipping community cannot remain content with simply meeting for worship. The *Communio sanctorum* means more than just the *coetus*, an assembly for the purposes of worship. Where Christ is present He wills to create; for *Christus non est otiosus*. Faith must be active in love. The community of worship must become a community of life. What we said of the Church of faith, of the "two or three who are gathered together in His Name," is true also of the worshipping

[1] 1 Cor. xiv.

community, in so far as it really contains a living Church of faith. The *communio* must become *communicatio omnium bonorum*. In some form or another, or indeed in a variety of forms, Christian love must manifest itself in works of mercy, and in deeds of service, and this must manifest the reality of the "community life." The brotherhood of worship must develop beyond its purpose of worship, just as surely as love is the necessary sign and fruit of faith.

Through these activities the Church once more enters into new relations with the world; it mingles with the general life of the world and its institutions. The Church of faith makes its influence felt beyond the bounds of the worshipping community in the natural secular relations between human beings, in the natural orders of the family, the economic order, the State and culture. Here again we see how the Church of faith means more than the worshipping community. It is true that the latter can, as such, do much to prepare the way for faith to penetrate the varied activities of the world—this point will be treated later—in principle, however, this is the business of the individual(15). This is not the aim of the worshipping community, which exists in order to awaken and nourish faith, which then "of itself" works out in love in the conditions of the world. For this very reason the Church of faith is invisible, inasmuch as it is present in secular institutions, not as a separate order, nor as a law controlling the development of these institutions, but—as was shown in detail in an earlier part of this book—as a regulative principle, and as a new spirit, revealing and striving to realize the intended meaning of these institutions as created for the service of man. In this sense we may say that it is the duty of the Church, in contrast to all other kinds of non-Christian religious communities, to be secular, indeed to be as secular as possible. This is in accordance with the hidden character of the Kingdom of God in this age, even as it is in accordance with the universality of the Church of faith. Through the members of His Body Christ wills to rule even in the things of this world(16). In principle He uses the secular orders to set up His royal rule in just the same way as He uses the order of the worshipping community. It forms part of the fundamental view of the true character of the Church of faith, that its boundaries do not coincide with the boundaries of the worshipping communities. It is characteristic of the "invisible Church" that she is present within secular institutions as the "soul" is in the body, just

535

as she dwells invisibly within the body of the worshipping community, as its "soul."

Finally, we need to call attention to another necessary tendency of the Church, which goes in the exactly opposite direction. The Church, as we have said, is the community of those who have been "called out," of the "saints," thus of those who are called to be separate from the world. This applies in the first instance not to the worshipping community but to the Church of faith. But just as the worshipping community cannot remain indifferent to that duty of expansion, but, on the contrary, must prepare the way for it, so also it is its duty to be distinct from the world. For the very reason that the worshipping community is the only form in which the Church can become visible at all to the non-believing world, in which the world experiences the Church as a community, it is the duty of this Church, as a worshipping community, to make its distinction from the world plain and clear. So far as the world is concerned it must at least demonstrate its character as a Church, and it is its duty to help its members to make this distinction from the world quite clear. Thus it is the Church's duty to educate her members to emphasize their difference from the world in the right way, in the form of an impressive testimony. This is the idea which underlies "Church discipline."[1] As the social service of the worshipping community indicates its contact with the world, so church discipline is the indication of the distinction between it and the world, the experimental and therefore merely relative representation and realization of the fact of being "called out" from the world, of distinction from it. This duty will indeed vary with the historical character of the environment, as well as with the character of the worshipping community itself at different periods, and under different circumstances, yet, under all circumstances it exists, and in principle it is the same at every period.

This duty, however, can only be performed by means of order, and by this very fact it shows its merely suggestive, relative character. The worshipping community must exercise church discipline through a certain order. The priority of the Church of faith over against the worshipping community proves itself here too in the fact that though the worshipping

[1] HOLL, in his book on *Luther* (pp. 359 and 378) shows clearly that Luther was much concerned about the idea of Church discipline, although at that time he felt it could scarcely be exercised.

community may possibly exclude individuals from the worshipping community, it can never exclude them from the Church. It may indeed "excommunicate" certain persons, but it can never cast anyone out of the Church of Christ(17). That can be done by the Lord of the Church alone. In the very exercise of church discipline the worshipping community will be forced to remain aware of the merely educative and demonstrative meaning of its action. Where the worshipping community believes that it has the power to excommunicate, in the sense of actual expulsion from the Church, it has already become clerical and priest-ridden. Even the worshipping community does not know the boundaries of the true Church(18), even to it they are invisible, and therefore none of its regulations which refer to church discipline have any power to bind the conscience, for no order has such a power, the ecclesiastical order no more than the power of the State. This power is exercised only by the Word and the Spirit of Christ Himself, who may indeed use order in His service, but who delegates His authority to none. In this respect the worshipping community cannot dispense with order if it is to do its service for Christ, but the very fact that it is forced to use it shows most plainly that it is not identical with the Church of faith, however close may be its connexion with it.

Among all that is visibly, tangibly present, next to the Bible the worshipping community is that which stands most directly and most necessarily close to the Church of faith. This is why the one word "Church" is used to describe both. Without the worshipping community the Church of faith cannot exist; for it is the worshipping community alone which is concerned that the Word of God should "have free course and be glorified." Within this Church alone can the Sacraments be administered. She alone is the historical connecting link between the Jesus of History and every period of time, and with every individual. She is, therefore, the "Mother" of all believers. She alone has brought forth the Canon of Holy Scripture, the Bible, which is the standard of the human message of Christ; not only has she brought it forth but she has translated it and made it intelligible by her living preaching(19). Whatever may and indeed must be said, unfortunately with full justification, against this Church and these churches, in spite of everything it is the distinctive indispensable means by which the Church of faith is created, maintained, and—this we ought never to forget—also constantly renewed. She is the mother of our faith[1]. The Church of faith extends far beyond the Church as a worshipping community; there are true members of the Church of faith who belong to no worshipping congregation, just as there are many members of the worshipping community who do not belong to the true Church. Speaking from the point of view of principle, there is no part of the world, no order or arrangement of men where the Church of faith is not also concealed; and there is no worshipping community which is not far too full of secular matters, which do not serve Christ, but on the contrary which hinder and obscure His presence. In spite of this, it is not merely an evil that *one* word only is used to describe these two very different entities: the Church. For the worshipping community, regarded as a whole, and not as an individual, and in principle and not in detail, is the preferred, distinctive necessary order, which in far greater measure than the other orders, because in more direct and necessary connexion with it, serves the Church of faith. Like the other orders she is a divine institution; but in contrast to them all she is that order or institution which serves the Church of faith directly and not merely indirectly. Our next duty, therefore, will be to deal with the subject of this Church, which is the order of the community of faith.

[1] It is CALVIN who frequently stressed the idea that "as God is our Father" in faith, "the Church is our Mother" (*Institutio*, I, 1).

CHAPTER XLIV

THE CHURCH IN ACTION

1. *The Church and the Churches*

THE worshipping community, by its very nature, is primarily a single congregation(1). When we think of the Church as a tangible sociological entity the first thing that strikes us is the single congregation or "local church." In spite of all the limitations which are implied in the preceding observations the Church of faith is, primarily and essentially, represented by single "congregations." But this idea admits far more variety of conception than many people—who talk about a particular "parish" as a definite, clearly defined entity—would lead us to suppose. We need only think of the most modern method of oral communication—by wireless—to realize how fluid is this conception of a single congregation which can be localized. But the conception still has meaning, and the Sacrament in particular will help to preserve this meaning. The local congregation, where people actually meet together in space, where they see each other constantly, and meet in the concrete experience of the "fellowship of giving and receiving" in common worship, will always remain the "germ-cell" of the "visible" Church. As those who are "in the body" we only experience community, in the full sense of the word, through actual contact with each other as physical creatures within space.[1]

It is the primary business of the local congregation to see that its essential purpose is realized, in a way most in harmony with its sacred purpose. All its ordinances must be so arranged that they will further its end; that is, as a worshipping community, as an organic part of the Body of Christ, the local Church will seek to serve the Church of faith, and as far as possible, to frame all its ordinances in harmony with it. This is definitely the concern of the local congregation, not of a superior authority with the name of "Church"—in the sense of a Territorial Church or anything of that kind. The visible Church builds itself up from below and not from above. The decisive element is consideration for its definite purpose, not

[1] Cf. the fine remarks by KATTENBUSCH on this point: *Die Doppelgeschichtigkeit in Luthers Kirchenbegriff*, pp. 99 ff.

539

regard for an organized whole. Therefore it must be able to order its life and worship in accordance with its actual situation. There is a place for considering the question of the uniformity of local congregations, and the creation of a super-congregational bond of unity, but it is secondary. This is the true element in all forms of "Congregationalism"; this, too, is the true idea in Zwingli's *Kilchhöre* principle,[1] the principle of congregational autonomy.

But this does not mean that the connexion between the individual congregations is a matter of indifference. For in any case the single congregation cannot express one of the fundamental elements of the Church of faith, that is, universality. *Credo in unam sanctam catholicam ecclesiam*(2). This *una sancta* cannot be identified with any kind of territorial or national Church, or indeed with that Church which knows least of all what the Church means in the sense of the New Testament, because from the outset it confuses the Church of faith with the Church as an order. But it certainly is essential that the genuine local congregation should always be aware of the unity of the Church Universal, and that, as far as possible, it should try to manifest this truth by achieving a real connexion and a real unity. The local church therefore should always long for unity and fellowship, and should feel shame and distress over the barriers which have been created by the sinful confusion of Christendom. Thus a genuine *Kilchhöre* will unite, as far as possible, with other worshipping communities, and, as far as possible, it will also try to realize the unity of the Church in a unity of outward form, so far as this can be combined with its own peculiar local requirements. In this sense every genuine Church certainly contains an "evangelical Catholicism." Only this secondary element ought never to be achieved at the expense of the primary element; the primary element is that the local congregation should fulfil its particular calling, as fully as it possibly can, a calling which is unique and wholly peculiar to itself.

When we speak of the Church, as a rule we mean some

---

[1] This is a Swiss-German expression. It means a Christian community (as a "parish" or "congregation"), but it also contains the idea of "hearing" (*hören*), and "belonging to one another" (*zusammengehören*). *Kilch* = *Kirche*, *höre* = *the flock* that "hears" the Shepherd's Voice, and by this fact knows that its members "belong to one another."—TR.

larger union of local congregations, such as the National Church of Zürich, or the Methodist Episcopal Church, or the Anglican Church. This is due to historical circumstances, especially to the way in which these churches originated. But behind this way of speaking there lurks the great danger of a false ecclesiasticism, of an imitation of that Church which in the formation of the evangelical churches was still in secret their ideal: the so-called Catholic Church. The idea of unity, and of a strong *esprit de corps*, which is in itself justifiable, usurps the first place, whereas it is only justified if it takes the second, less important place. It is not this great united Church but the local congregation which is most clearly and intimately connected with the Church of faith. The Church of Christ can live without "Territorial Churches" and the like; but it cannot exist without individual communities for worship, without local congregations. The fact that this is so little understood to-day is due not only to the unfortunate example of the Roman Catholic Church, but also to the development of the claims of the State, which likewise deprives the local community of its necessary (relative) autonomy and has degraded it to a mere sphere of administration. The "federalistic" structure of growth from below is still more important in the Church than it is in the State.

In spite of this, however, the necessity for union and uniformity in organization still exists. Isolated individual congregations cannot meet the demands made upon them by their own ideals, not merely on external grounds, but also on the internal decisive grounds which have been mentioned. It is also entirely in order that this tendency to union refers primarily to the country to which the Church belongs. The need to build up from below requires this organic affiliation. It is right and necessary that there should be Territorial Churches (*Landeskirchen*). But the tendency towards union cannot stop there. The idea of the *una sancta catholica* requires some kind of universal unity; indeed, it absolutely requires the greatest possible, the most vigorous and far-reaching union and unity—as far, namely, as the needs of the local congregation and of the national churches permit. The idea which lies behind modern strivings for unity is absolutely necessary; objections cannot be raised to them, but only to the way in which people are trying to realize unity, and this for good Christian reasons.

Above all, however, disunion is a scandal for the Church

of Christ; to see, within the same sphere, different "churches" in conflict with one another, possessing no positive sense of unity, is indeed perfectly scandalous. The word "sectarianism" is ugly, but it describes an ugly thing. Although sects are not based wholly on human arrogance, there is always a good deal of arrogance mingled with the establishment of "sects"(3). As a rule, sectarianism is based on a misunderstanding of the idea of the "holy community"; from the time of Novatian onwards the main factor in the establishment of sects has been a wrong idea of "holiness" (as represented by the Anabaptists, for example). Therefore the "sect" idea is not primarily a sociological conception or an idea of Church order, but it is a dogmatic conception. It is not the kind of order which distinguishes the sect from the National Church—thus it is not the fact that the National Church is a State Church and the sect is a Free Church; there are Free Churches which are not sects in any sense of the word—but it is the view of holiness, and this means the view of justification and of sanctification. But this disagreeable sectarianism is not merely the fault of the sects which happen to flourish at any particular period, but it is equally the fault of the Established Church of that period; this comes out plainly in two facts: first, in its insistence on justification by faith alone the Established (or Territorial) Church has either forgotten or scandalously neglected the truth of sanctification(4); secondly, in its justifiable and necessary caution in the use of church discipline it has allowed this necessary function to drop out altogether. In the ugly guise of sectarianism every "Church" sees her own guilt.[1] But once the separation has been effected, and has become consolidated, then the "sect" becomes a "Church" of a definite type. What the "territorial" or "national" Church ought to oppose is not the actual sect which is now in existence, but the act of forming sects. It is true, of course, that this act is frequently renewed in the maintenance of the group which has thus broken away by a more or less ardent attack on the "secularized" national Church. As a rule, however, in the second or third generation,

---

[1] Is it really so very terrible if a local congregation calls in the aid of the Brothers from Chrischona (a well-known Evangelical Brotherhood near Basle—TR.), if the alternative is to be condemned to years of listening to rationalistic morality, and never a Gospel Message at all? Is it quite certain that loyalty to the National Church should be bought at such a price?

the sect usually approximates more and more nearly to the Church-type; often the difference only becomes intelligible from a study of its historical origins.

The Church of Christ is visibly represented by a painfully large number of larger or smaller groups of churches, all separated from each other, secretly or openly in conflict with each other, from the hierarchy of the Roman Church down to Independency and Quakerism and the smallest ephemeral fellowship-groups which are continually being formed afresh. The Body of Christ is divided into an infinite number of separated opposing sections. It would take a very romantic mind to see in this fact the delightful variety of a spontaneous manifestation of life. Certainly uniformity is not a sign of life, not even of genuine spiritual life. But here we are concerned not with the variety of mere forms but with fundamental antitheses in the understanding of the Gospel, and therefore not with a variety of organs, each of which has its own function, but with a terrible and also inevitable fight against each other. Variety of forms could very well be combined with the *una sancta*(5), indeed it would be a necessary requirement if we regarded the local congregation as the germ-cell. But where differences do not merely distinguish but separate, whether because the form has been confused with the substance, or because the variety actually refers to the central point, to the understanding of the Word of God,[1] then variety necessarily becomes opposition.

But if we test these actually existing "ecclesiastical bodies" by the idea of the Church, then we must confess that no Church exists which has the right to be called the "true" Church. Even the main contrast, that between the Roman Catholic and the Protestant Churches (when one looks at the *actual* preaching of the message and the *actual* church life), does not represent the difference between the false and the true Church. As a rule the "pure Gospel" is proclaimed neither in the one nor in the other, and in the one as in the other, it is rare to find real Christian life, real churchmanship. Were we to ask the Church for her official creed we would know very soon which is the true church; but, unfortunately, how much does this official creed mean? and how much

---

[1] In opposition to the usual view Calvin goes so far as to say that even in the realm of dogma no rigid unity is required; all that is necessary, he says, is to see that the *articuli fundamentales* are taught in a uniform way (*Institutio*, I, 12).

543

better the situation is on the other side—thank God—than the official creed would suggest! The same may be said of the relation between the individual Protestant churches and groups. We willingly leave it to the romantic ecclesiastical controversialists to prove by means of the confessional writings of the sixteenth century, and by *a priori* deductions drawn from them, in defiance of reality, the incontestable superiority of the Lutheran to the Reformed Church;[1] we leave it also to the propaganda speeches of leaders of the Pietist type to boast of the superiority of their Church to any other. We can only mourn: the Church of Christ lies in the dust, whichever way we look, *miserere nobis, Kyrie eleison*! Whether we apply the standard of real doctrine, or of real church life, or of influence on the life of the people as a whole, we have not the courage to assert that this or that church—for instance my own church—if not the "true Church" is at least the Church which contains the largest element of truth. There is only one thing which allows us still to believe in the high advantage even of the Protestant Churches of the present day; in principle they are capable of regeneration, whereas the Catholic Church has elevated error to the rank of a principle, and in this very fact regards itself as infallible. Otherwise we are willing to admit that in it too—comparing its actual condition with the actual state of the Protestant Churches—there are elements of the true Church of Christ which are sadly lacking amongst ourselves(6); I would add, however, that even the Quakers, and even the deliberately non-churchgoing individualists, possess some of the truth of the Gospel which is lacking in every one of the "organized" churches of the present day. The inheritance of Christ is split into sections, and who can undertake to find out who has received the largest piece! There is no other way back to the *una sancta* than the way of truth. This truth of the Reformation is at all times the principle of the regeneration of the Church, over against which all other efforts to achieve unity appear to be either futile or deceptive.[2]

[1] Cf. ELERT: *Morphologie des Luthertums.*
[2] Unfortunately, hitherto even the "Lausanne" movement for Church Unity—as can be seen from the large Report of the first World Conference, and especially from the Report of the Theological Committee (1932)—is guided in its endeavours not so much by the principle of truth as by the spirit of compromise.

2. *Church Order and Church Law*

The Church of faith, as such, possesses no order, save that which is already implied every time the pure Gospel is simply proclaimed. No Church ever came into being as the result of "speaking with tongues"; church life has always come into existence as the result of preaching which is rational, and thus subject to the laws of grammar, logic, and rhetoric. By "order," however, we mean something in a narrower sense, an established rule for church action. The boundary between the two, however, varies a good deal. Even the establishment of the Canon and of an official Creed—however simple and short—as the norm of pure doctrine, is "Church order"; this "order," although it is evidently closely related to the Word of God, is not the Word of God itself. It is extremely important that the distinction between the "order" which is the instrument and the "cause" it serves should be kept quite clear. If this distinction is blurred or ignored a false legalism is immediately introduced, which confuses the "order" with the Divine Command, that is, it confuses an established system, with rules which can be known beforehand, with the living Word of God itself.

The first sign of this false legalism—easy to comprehend and yet most disastrous in its effect—is the view which confuses the letter of Scripture with the Word of God, the legalism of orthodoxy, which misinterprets the Bible, by regarding it as a divine oracle, and wrongly imputes to it an infallibility, a purely divine character, which is contrary to its nature, and indeed to the nature of faith in the God-Man. This legalism is almost as ancient as the Church, and was first overcome in principle by Luther(7). *Christus dominus et rex scripturae*— this principle frees us from all Bibliolatry. The theology of the present day is trying to find its way back to the right understanding of the authority of the Bible, avoiding both the error of Verbal Inspiration on the one hand and the still greater error of the Enlightenment on the other(8).

The second step in the direction of legalism is taken when the distinction between the human confession of faith (dogma) and the Word of God itself is blurred and ignored, that is, "orthodoxy" in the wider sense of the word. The pure doctrine —and it, too, simply and solely as it is understood in its content— the intellectual form in which the understanding of the Word of God is expressed at a certain period, is identified with the

545

Word of God itself, and is declared to be a religious law which is binding on the conscience. From the point of view of evangelical doctrine there is no such dogma with power to bind men's consciences; there is only a creed, or "symbol," which contains the essence of the message of the Christian community; this creed can be revised at any time.

But these phenomena lie beyond that which we have described as "order" in the narrower sense. The Church of faith as such has indeed no order; but since it leads necessarily to the worshipping community it also leads necessarily to order. For no worshipping community exists without order, just as no other kind of permanent community consisting of many human beings can exist without order. The spontaneity of faith alone does not guarantee any regularity or harmony of work in common. It must be supported and limited by the rational element of order, by the rule of action which is made known and observed. This rule may be simple, and elastic, and it may constantly take fresh forms; but it must exist, and where it guides conduct, there, to this extent, conduct is not controlled directly by faith, but only indirectly, and all that is said or done under the direction of this "order" does not possess any directly Divine authority; whatever authority it possesses is only very indirectly derived from God.[1]

The more living the congregation the less will it stand in need of rules, the more elastic and mobile will be its rules(9). Above all, however, the more directly will they be formed by their relation to the holy cause itself, to the work and Word of Christ in the Church and in the world. Just as the "pure doctrine" shares in the Divine authority because it is so directly related to the Word of God, in spite of the fact that this Divine element is in human form, so also the rules of the life of the Church, in so far as they are closely connected with the thing itself, have a share in the Divine authority, in both instances, however, in such a manner that the distinction between the two is preserved. This is the legitimate origin of that idea which is wrongly called the sacred Law of the Church.

To a certain extent even Luther recognized a kind of sacred "Church law,"[2] just as he also recognized certain

---

[1] Paul always makes a distinction between that which he orders as an Apostle and that which has been commanded by "the Lord" and is therefore a rule which is binding on the conscience of the believer.

[2] Cf. KATTENBUSCH, *Die Doppelgeschichtigkeit in Luthers Kirchenbegriff*, pp. 96 ff.

elements of the cultus-Church as absolutely fundamental to the Church of faith: the "orderly" administration of the Sacraments, the regular practice of public preaching, the administration of the office of preaching controlled by definite rules. *How* this was to be done was an indifferent, or at least a secondary matter; but Luther saw clearly that such ordering was essential, that it was a necessity, based on the very nature of the Church as a worshipping community. It is not at this point that Calvin differs from Luther—he too sees plainly that such order is a necessity—no, Calvin's view is different because he regards the sphere which needs to be controlled by this "order" as far larger than the sphere contemplated by Luther. The difference, however, was also due to the fact that indubitably Calvin's view of the authority of Scripture was more legalistic than that of Luther.

But the expression "sacred Church law" does not correspond to the intentions of the Reformers. Both Reformers held that there are certain *institutiones* which are necessary for the Church as an "institution," as a worshipping community; hence, since they are thus willed by God they belong inherently to the Church. But all these ordinances are of such a kind that they are all concerned with the *fact* of order—with rules—but not with its content—that is, they are formal rules. But the content is determined for them by the Word of God. The criterion of this conception is the Sacrament. As a matter of course both emphasize the truth that the Sacrament belongs to the Church of Christ; but they would deny to no one the name of Christian who is not a communicant. It is true that a certain ordered rite is associated with the Sacrament; but the Sacrament does not exercise its influence *ex opere operato*, but only to the extent in which the Word of Christ is appropriated.[1] Thus not even here, at the centre, is a sacred order recognized, in the rigid, that is in the direct, sense of the word. Here also the distance between identity and direct connexion is preserved. This difference is still more clearly preserved in all that refers to the ordering of public worship, and of the various offices in the Church.

In the controversy which has arisen since the appearance of the epoch-making work of Sohm(10), about the relation between the Gospel and Church law, neither side has noticed that the process of transition from mere order and law—in

[1] LUTHER: sacramenta non implentur dum fiunt, sed dum creduntur. WA II, 715, 30.

the sense of Roman ecclesiastical law—varies a great deal. In the strict sense of the word a sacred ecclesiastical system of law does exist in the Roman Catholic Church. For there, firstly, the distance between the human and the divine is absolutely removed in principle in the legalistic conception of the Bible, of dogma, and of ordinances. Closeness of connexion becomes identity. Therefore the Bible becomes a legal code, dogma a religious law which is binding on the conscience, the ordinances of the Church sacred laws, hence too the Sacrament works *ex opere operato*, and the Pope, when he speaks *ex cathedra*, is infallible. And, secondly, the relative distinction between an ordinance and a legal principle is removed. Or rather this second point is the necessary result of the first. We leave it to the lawyers to harmonize the conception of law which is here created with the legal conception of the State; it is obvious that ecclesiastical law, even in its legal aspect, differs from the law of the State. Finally, it is a question of terminology whether it should be called "law" or not.

Protestant ecclesiastical law, as it is called, is a very different matter. In so far as there are legal ordinances in the Protestant Church at all they are of a purely secular kind, even of a politico-legal kind, as Sohm has rightly perceived. In so far, however, as it is legal principles which give legal authority to the ordinances of the Church, they are indirectly of an ecclesiastical nature. The Church calls in the aid of the State in order to confer legal authority on her fluid ordinances, which more or less issue from the nature of the Church as an institution, or a community for worship. Thus materially, in so far as its own peculiar content is concerned, Protestant Church law is ecclesiastical: formally, however, according to its legal character, it is a purely secular affair of the State; in saying this we ought to note that for the Christian even the State is a Divine ordinance(11). Finally, however, there is one misunderstanding which must be cleared away. It is a question of subordinate importance whether the Church calls in the State to her support in such a way that her own ordinances are placed under the protection of its private law (law of association), the law which governs corporations (public institutions), or under the law of the State. The Free Churches, which come under the law of associations, have as little right to appeal to the Primitive Church as their example as the so-called State churches. For they also enjoy the protection of the State for their ecclesiastical ordinances, to which the Early Churches could lay no claim, and even if they could have done so, they would not have done so. If they were clear that even in non-ecclesiastical matters they ought not to use the legal organization of the State,[1] how much more was this the case where the protection of their ecclesiastical ordinances was concerned! In the Primitive Church the relation of the Church to the State was wholly one-sided: the State claimed absolutely, and as a matter of course, legal dominion over the Church; indeed it did not even recognize the existence of the Church at all; the Church, however, demanded no compensation in the form of protection of her ordinances; she could not do so, but also she would not have done so. To-day, however, there is scarcely any kind of Church-group—however closely it may try to imitiate the "Primitive Church"—which would renounce this protection, which, for example, would not hand over an unfaithful church treasurer to the authority of the State. There exist to-day only legally organized Christian communities for worship—whether they come under private or public law.

3. State Church, National Church, Free Church

When we see clearly, from the point of view of principle, the relation between the Church, order, and law, it becomes evident that the differences between the various forms of the legal organization of the Church as an order, although they are not without significance, are still of very secondary importance. It is certainly extremely unnatural when the Church (as a worshipping community), becomes a vital part of the State; for the function of the State is very different from that of the Church(12). Two possible courses of action lie open to the Church, both of which, however, themselves contain great dangers. The Church may try to invest her ordinances, through their close connexion with the Word of God, with the greatest possible authority, and, on the other hand, she may give to these ordinances an authority similar to that exercised by the State. Thus the Church remains an institution with a strong internal organization, which is independent of the State. The danger which here threatens the life of the Church is that this internal organization will develop into an ecclesiastical system of church law similar to that of the Roman Catholic Church. Or, from the very outset, the

[1] 1 Cor. vi. 1 ff.

549

Church may place herself under the protection of the State as an association for worship: then she is threatened with the danger that this "Free Church" will inwardly become a "sect." The emphasis on the Church as a "lawful association" tends to obliterate its distinctive character as a Church; if this takes place, the decisive truth that the Church as a body precedes any of its individual members, and the idea that the Church is a Divine institution and not a human form of community, will be lost. Further, there is a secondary element, which, however, only has reference to the weakness of the Church—but what Church is not inwardly weak? The Church that is free from the State, in spite of her independence in this direction, is equally dependent on society; to put it bluntly, she is dependent on the people who hold the purse. The Free Churches are forced to play for popularity; in their criticism of social conditions and of moral conditions they dare not go to the last ditch; their mouth is stopped by consideration for the members who support them. This need not be so, but as a rule it is so. The State Church is far less hampered than the Free Church in giving her message, although certainly in various other respects—especially in view of her organization as a community and her works of mercy—she is less mobile.

Far more important than this legal difference is the dogmatic difference between the Established and the Free churches.[1] By an "established" Church (*Volkskirche*) I mean a community for worship with a "birthright membership," handed down naturally from generation to generation. Its sign is Infant Baptism. In the "Free" Church (*Bekenntniskirche*), on the contrary, a person can only become a "member" on explicit "profession of faith" or by Adult Baptism, thus proclaiming his or her resolve to join the Church(13). The Free Church appeals to the New Testament, but in so doing she forgets that the New Testament presupposes the early missionary work of the Church, where entrance into the Church on "profession of faith" and by Adult Baptism was a matter of course. But the question of Infant Baptism ought to be explained in a work on dogmatics, not in one on ethics; all that can be said here is this: however many important and weighty arguments the Free Church can adduce in support of her claims she is always menaced by two extremely serious dangers: first, by the danger of the sect, that is, by the failure

[1] Rather a free rendering of the German *Volkskirche* (literally, people's or national Church) and *Bekenntniskirche* (Confessional Church).—TR.

to understand the heart of the Evangelical message—justification by faith. Almost inevitably the Free Church attributes an importance to the human aspect of the "profession of faith," and to a state of sanctification which can be proved, which cannot be reconciled with this fundamental truth (justification by faith), whereas in the "Established" Church it is the very fact of Infant Baptism, and the recognition of all who are baptized as members of the worshipping community, which gives the most explicit indication of the prevenient sovereign grace of God as the only basis of the state of a Christian. Secondly, the fact that the Free Church only recognizes as "members" those who explicitly request to be admitted, means that almost inevitably it tries to separate the wheat from the tares, in this present historical world, and in so doing it becomes a "hole and corner" affair(14). It lacks the breadth of the Established Church; it is wholly unable to influence a people as a whole; above all, it is quite unable to influence youth.

On the other hand, however, it must also be admitted that the established or "national" Church, above all, when it is a "State Church," contains much that is seriously wrong. Here the "tares" are mingled with the "wheat" to such an extent that the distinctive character of the Church is almost obliterated. Once a church has reached the point at which it is possible for her functions to be administered by open atheists and scoffers at religion, when perhaps the majority of her members are merely nominal, and do not care a jot for the Church, when the impression is widespread that it is as natural to belong to the Church as it is to be born, and that membership means *nothing*—then certainly the point has been reached where we may ask: Has not the Church become like salt "which has lost its savour" and is henceforth good for nothing?

And yet the root of the evil does not lie in this organization of the Church at all. What *is* wrong is that no "prophet" has arisen to expose these evils; we need "prophetic" preaching, which will put a stop to this process of taking the Church for granted, which ends in destroying its meaning. Indeed, we might put it thus: we have no preaching which would lead to masses leaving the Church. The trouble is, that the National Church also seeks to curry favour with the people, that it too fears nothing so much as loss of members, whereas this should and might be a sign that it was doing its work properly.

Organization can never be the crucial test for the Church(15). For her the only crucial test is the living Word of God. Where this is absent every form of organization is useless; where this is present every form of organization is endurable. And where the Word of God is present in power the Church will spontaneously arrange her own organization as is most suitable for her purpose, under certain circumstances, and at any particular time. But to expect the deliverance of the Church by means of a new form of organization is exactly like putting the cart before the horse.

4. Church and State

The State and the Church are the two sole forms of community which make a claim to universal loyalty; therefore the relation between Church and State is the greatest subject in the history of the West. This discussion has led to conflict, and will constantly lead to conflict, wherever this claim has been misunderstood. Hence the right understanding of its nature, and of the relation between Church and State, is a matter of great practical importance, for the State as well as for the Church. All that we now have to do is to sum up the conclusions which we have already reached concerning the nature of the State and the nature of the Church.

Our reflections on the nature of the State and of the Church forbid us to place the State, as the natural order, over against the Church, as the supernatural order. The State is also an order which is God-given, and the Church is also—as an organized community 'for worship—a secular order. But whereas for the State the one thing that matters is that order should be secured, for the Church order is not the essential matter. The aim of the State is to be a power which secures and maintains order; but the purpose of the Church is to be a community of believers, through fellowship with God, founded upon the Word of God. The order of the State is the necessary presupposition even of the existence of the Church—as it is for all civilized human life. The God-given authority of the State is based upon this function, and even the Christian is obliged to accept it—within certain limits—by obeying the law. In the Church, however, the order is merely a help and a support for the up-building of the Church as a worshipping community. Therefore our essential relation to the Church is not that of legal or legalistic obedience, but that of a free community of faith.

On the side of the State the danger which threatens to destroy the right relation between Church and State is that of State absolutism, the claim to possess absolute and unlimited sovereignty, which is based, in the last resort, upon a pagan deification of the State. Against this the Church needs to be on her guard, not only in so far as the State actually hinders her in those expressions of life which are vital for her own existence, but also in so far as by its absolutism it poisons the thought of the people, and does violence to the life peculiar to the individual orders. At least the danger is always imminent that the cry: "Christ or Caesar!" will once more become an actual challenge. On the side of the Church, however, there is another danger; this is due to the failure to make a clear distinction between the Church of faith and the Church as an ordered system, as an organized community for worship. The Church only possesses divine, unconditional authority in so far as she possesses the Word of God. But the Word of God is not a law of order, although certainly indirectly it establishes order; but it is the "law of liberty"[1] which can only be obeyed in the freedom of personal decision. The Church, the worshipping community, has very often confused the "law of liberty" with the law of order, with the law of the State, and has claimed direct legal and divine authority for her ordinances—whether for the Canon of Scripture, for her dogma, for her morality, or for her "ecclesiastical" ordinances in the narrower sense—and therefore has also demanded legal obedience. In so doing she herself became a State, and the conflict with the authority of the State was inevitable. The State cannot tolerate this theocratic claim —in the sense of the law of the State—of the Church any more than the Church of faith can tolerate it. This claim equates the order of the Church with the Kingdom of God, and in so doing it confuses the spheres of the State and of the Church.

The true Christian view grants the State its relative autonomy, and deprives the Church as a worshipping community of her claim to absolute obedience. It acknowledges both as equally justified necessary orders, which, in quite different ways, are intended to serve the Kingdom of God(16). This does not destroy the close connexion between the Church as a worshipping community and the Kingdom of God, but it does limit it to that which is essential to the Church:

[1] James i. 25.

to her spiritual functions, the proclamation of her message, and her social service. The close connexion between this Church and the Kingdom of God, however, does not extend to her legal administration, to her resemblance to the State; in so far as the Church is an order she is subordinate to the State, just like any other group of human beings, or any other institution formed for a special purpose(17). The Church is not subordinate to the State in the sense that the State has the right to create her ordinances—for how is the State to know what ordinances are suitable for the Church? She is subordinate to the State rather in the sense that the State has the right to exercise the full power of the law over the Church in all matters which concern the law and order of the State. Church and State must mutually limit each other's activity, since the Church possesses the right to criticize the moral bases of the State, and may make moral demands on the State; the State, on the other hand, possesses the right to include the members of the Church in her legal system of administration, and to repel the false legal claims of the Church. Where the Church exceeds her authority, the State will step in with its power of coercion; but where the State exceeds its authority (so far as the Church is concerned) all the Church can do directly is to offer spiritual resistance, and, indirectly, to bring pressure to bear upon the State through public opinion; finally, she may have to offer the protest of martyrdom.

CHAPTER XLV

THE ACTION OF THE CHURCH

1. *The Functions of the Church and the Offices of the Church*

As we have seen, the nature of the Church of faith is such that it must lead to the formation of a worshipping community, in which the tasks which are in accordance with the nature of the Church, given to her by a divine commission, are performed, through the action of the Christian community as a whole, and this means, through a certain organization. This does not mean that the whole action of the Church is confined to definite ordinances; for if this were the case both the "universal priesthood" of all Church members and the activities of some outstanding individuals with a special Divine Commission would be ruled out. I mean rather that even this direct action of all in the obedience of faith, and this exceptional activity of certain individuals with a special commission, are both *limited* and yet *supported* by the ordinances of the Church. There would soon be no "universal priesthood" if there were no regular and ordered services for worship.[1] But the way in which the individual community for worship, or the individual group of churches (as for instance in a Territorial Church), should arrange these ordinances, is a subordinate question, though it is not unimportant. Two things alone must be kept in mind: that these ordinances should not themselves claim divine authority, and that as far as possible they should be devised in harmony with the divine purpose of the Church, and indeed that this should be their direct intention. This means, too, that they should express, as far as they possibly can, the concern of the Christian community for the best possible and most complete service to the cause of Christ.

So far as essentials are concerned the Church cannot pick and choose. The necessary functions of the Church are implicit in her very nature. A great deal of discussion about the dignity of the ecclesiastical offices might have been avoided if this distinction between the functions and the offices of the Church had been more clearly perceived(1). The basic or primal function of the Church is that of preaching; for it is this which

[1] Cf. 1 Cor. xiv.

establishes a Church, in every sense of the word. We have seen, however, that this basic function is not the only function which is essential and necessary to the Church. There are other functions, closely connected with this basic function, yet different in character, which are necessary for the full organization of a real Christian community for worship; we could, of course, imagine the Church of faith without these functions, but not the Church as an organized worshipping community. Under this heading we would place the administration of the Sacraments, social service, church discipline, and—this has not yet been explicitly mentioned—the ordering of the action of the Christian community or Church government(2).

These four or five functions do not, however, necessarily imply four or five offices. The Church of the New Testament had a larger number of offices; most churches, however, recognize fewer than these. The situation of the Churches of the New Testament was historically unique, one that cannot be repeated, and therefore only through a misunderstanding can it be made into a Divine Law for the whole of the future. Secondly, we must add the fact that all later forms of organization which have also appealed to this New Testament order as their law were actually very far from agreement with their model. For any Church to misinterpret the Church order of the New Testament to the extent of regarding it as a Divine Law finally leads to this: an attempt of this kind to "restore" the Church order of the New Testament actually becomes a fiction(3).

Still more disastrous, however, was the effect of another fiction: the Pauline statement that everything in the Church should be done decently and in order, that God is a God of order and not a God of confusion, was misunderstood by the Churches of the Reformation to mean that all action, above all, all preaching in the Church, and by the Church, was to be connected with an office, and thus with the rule of order. The warning of Paul: "Quench not the Spirit," was either forgotten, or set aside, in this emphasis on the need for order.[1] The consequence was that the Church came to resemble the State. Hand in hand with this went the reduction of the number of offices which has already been mentioned, and this led to the exclusion of the lay element from the activity of

[1] Both LUTHER and CALVIN fell into this error; but, in view of the Anabaptist danger at that time, have we any right to use the term "error"?

the Church. In this connexion I would make the following observations: although the point of view which insists that there should be *rite vocati ministri* in the Church is worthy of consideration, yet this point of view (which concerns order) ought not to be elevated to the rank of a dogma; and important as it is that the Church should have educated and appointed ministers, still there is nothing in the nature of the Church to justify the prevention of the activity of the laity, or the elimination of all unusual elements as impossible. One of the chief reasons for the rise of sects is that the Church has become a legal organization like the State, and a Church ruled by its pastors; this constitutes a malignant growth in the body of the Church.

Our Churches have become poor in offices, and in their ecclesiastical offices either exclusively ministerial or bureaucratic. The paucity of offices, the neglect of all other functions in the concern for preaching, the intellectualistic degeneration of the actual preaching, the resemblance of the ecclesiastical ordinances to the State and the elimination of the lay element —all these factors are mutually related. But when they are all combined they give to our churches their general character—a very unpleasant one—a character which is obviously opposed to the true nature of the Church of faith. This unfortunate situation is due to a variety of causes; I do not mean only that the Pauline exhortation to do things in order has been transformed into the principle of the *rite vocatus minister*, but also the identification (based on wrong exegesis) of the "episcopal" office with the teaching office, the confusion of spiritual equipment with theological study, and many other things as well. Above all, the example of the Catholic Church with its imposing semi-political structure has been secretly at work, with most disastrous results. More or less the whole of the Church history of Protestantism has been blighted by the principle of seeking to imitate as far as possible the secular greatness of the Catholic Church. We cannot here, however, go into this question of structure and the ordering of offices in any further detail.

Among the functions of the Church which have been most badly neglected—due to the intellectualist emphasis of orthodoxy—is that of social service. This kind of action, as we have already said, is mainly a concern of the individual in his life on the secular plane. But the Church as such ought not only to be a community for worship, but it should also represent

557

the Church of Christ as a whole, and therefore it should be a community of life. A Church whose sole social act as a community is to meet for worship must necessarily create the false impression that to be "in the Church" only means listening to preaching and taking part in the prayers. As we have said, the connexion between the Church and the outside world must at least be prepared by the worshipping community. Therefore, even as a community for worship she also has the duty of social service, of social assistance. If a Church produces no living acts of charity for the community as a whole, it is impossible to avoid suspecting that she is sick unto death.

This "social work of the Church" must, however, be limited by two considerations. The duty of the Church is simply to prepare the way for such work; as far as possible, the Church should simply initiate this kind of service and then leave the "secular" bodies to develop it further; this will be still more necessary when the work in question has no direct relation with the faith of the Church. On the other hand, we must also point out that the more the Church resembles the State the less is it fitted to do such service. For this reason the "Innere Mission" (Home Mission) was rightly founded as a service of the Christian Church independent of the organized community for worship. Ecclesiastical bureaucracy — unfortunately this is true — would only have stifled, or at least have severely restricted and hindered, such work. In spite of this the duty remains. Only on one condition, however, can this service be undertaken by the Church without doing serious harm, namely, by a vigorous development of the activity of the laity. Where "the minister" is the Church, the social work of the Church can do nothing but harm, for the preacher is overloaded with tasks for which he is not suited, which push his real work into the background. The overburdened parson is not the result of the fact that the Church is doing too much social work, but that the Church is still too exclusively a Church of pastors.[1] A Church which gives its lay members nothing to do for the Church is in an unhealthy condition.

The function of church discipline has likewise, to a very great extent, fallen into disuse; this is mainly due to the connexion of the Church with the State, and its organization as a national Church. The Church ought to know, however,

---

[1] GOGARTEN does not see this, when he—rightly—warns his readers against the present social activity of the Church in his book: *Die Schuld der Kirche* (*The Guilt of the Church*).

that this absence of any kind of Church discipline inevitably gives the impression that to belong or not to belong to the Church comes to the same thing in the end, and makes no difference in practical life. Here, however, the danger of Pharisaism is great; but we ought to remind ourselves that the one from whom we all learn what Pharisaism means, Paul, addressed himself to this problem with the greatest earnestness. If the Church no longer possesses either the courage or the power to refuse to give Communion to a person who is known openly as one who "sweats" his employees, her power to witness is at a very low ebb. Perhaps the state of the Church is such that she had better not attempt it; but she should be aware that this is a sign of miserable weakness, and she ought to pray that one day she may again be able to do this, knowing that she ought to be able to do it.

Social service and church discipline indicate the connexion between faith and life in the world. This, however, is also the task of preaching. The Church ought to give the world some instruction on the subject of the secular "orders." Of course, the most important thing is that the Church, by her preaching of the Gospel, should create hearts anew, in order that individuals, as new men and women, should create something new in the life of the world and in its orders. But neither preaching nor theological ethics can stop there. As the Church institutes a public confession of her faith, not as a legal statement binding on the conscience, as a dogma, but as an instruction for the faith of the individual and as a manifestation of his faith—so also the Church ought, if she can, to adopt a public attitude towards the great questions of the day in the secular realm[1]. The Papal Encyclicals—in spite of their falsely legal authoritative form—also remind the Evangelical Churches of a neglected duty.

But there is a second point which, in this respect, is still more important. The Church ought to exercise a prophetic office, the office of a "watchman." In her preaching she has not only to expound "the Gospel" but also "the Law," and, under some circumstances, she may even go further than any ethic would ever dare to go: on occasion the individual preacher may and indeed must demand concrete decisions. He may and indeed must do this when he clearly perceives the Divine Command for that particular moment. To-day, too, there

[1] On this point cf. the weighty remarks by KARL BARTH to the Presbyterian World Alliance (at Cardiff) in *Zwischen den Zeiten*, 1925, pp. 311–33.

exists the possibility of a prophetic calling through which an individual has to proclaim the Divine Command, for that moment, to the Church. No one can assume this responsibility for himself, but we ought to be prepared for such an eventuality.

Finally, we have to consider the question whether the Church, as such, ought to enter into politics—whether, since she is an organized social community, she ought to allow her organization, as a powerful factor, to be used in the political conflict. This question must be answered with a very decided "No," for it is utterly opposed to the real spirit of the Evangelical Church; it is only in harmony with the Roman Catholic conception of the Church.[1] If the Church does this she confuses her action with that of the State, and thus for the sake of the "mess of pottage" of a momentary, possibly desirable political advantage, she loses her rights as the firstborn, namely her office of "watchman" above all the political parties; she loses that for which she exists, namely, her spiritual authority.

It is of course impossible for the Church, in so far as she herself is an order, to renounce Church politics entirely. Both without and within she will have such work to do: from time to time she will have to do it without, in order to oppose the false claims of the State, and constantly in order to delimit the boundaries between the order of the Church and the order of the State; she will have to do it within, because, and in so far as, she herself has become an order and a legal structure like the State. Indeed, once the Church has been legally constituted, she has a legislative authority (Synod) and an executive (Church Council), and perhaps also a kind of judicial authority. There are church elections, decrees, edicts, etc. Where the Church·is legally constituted ecclesiastical politics are inevitable. But the Church ought always to be aware that the political element within her is a "foreign body"; as far as possible she ought to try to rise above the machinery of elections and voting, which forces the minority to accept the will of the majority as law, by promoting spiritual unity; she ought never to carry on Church politics as a matter of course[2] as the State is obliged to do. The State is right in using compulsion to enforce order, but

---

[1] Anyone who knows CALVIN's *Letters* will remember how seriously he warns his correspondents against such a mingling of Church and politics.

[2] Cf. the detailed researches of RIEKER into the introduction of the modern democratic idea into the Reformed Church under the cloak of "Church independence" (loc. cit., pp. 144 ff.).

although this *may* be necessary in the Church, it is only "on account of our weakness," that is, because we are unable to establish order by free consent.

Here I will only allude briefly to the function of church government. In the New Testament churches, where the organization had not yet been cast in any kind of legal mould, we see a peculiar mixture of the "democratic," the "aristocratic" and even of a certain "oligarchical" element in the proportionate share in the government of the Church taken by the community as a whole, the higher office-bearers, and the apostolic leaders. But quite apart from the fact that here the spiritual element, the charismatic gifts, drives the element of order into the background, the conditions of the young missionary church in the pagan world cannot be compared with any other situation, which is determined by the interpenetration of Christian views and customs in a general way into the life and thought of the peoples. But although we cannot look at the Primitive Church in the romantic light cast by certain views of the Bible, and thus idealize these communities, we can still see in them (since they are the canonical primitive type of the Christian Church) significant indications of the formation of the Church, even under very different circumstances. Here, in a remarkable way, the fundamental lines of the constitution of the Church coalesce with the general guiding principles which we discovered in our reflection on the subject of the State: mutual limitation by the ideas of democracy and leadership. At the same time we must be on our guard against transferring wholesale the abstract, impersonal schemata which apply in the sphere of the State to the Church with its quite different definition of its aims. The Christian Church is never a democracy; but she must always be a real community. She ought always to have leaders, but the leaders must show that they *are* leaders by the power and the truth of their message. To expect salvation from the creation of authoritative offices means that we have already transformed the Evangelical idea of the Church into the Roman Catholic idea; and this is a grave mistake. The Church must create space for powerful spiritual leadership; and the leaders must make room, as far as possible, for work in common, common care for each other, and for the common responsibility of all the members of the Church. Here too it is extremely important that the principle of order—which can only be subordinate, here, and used to serve higher ends—should not be allowed

561

to get the upper hand, for if this happens the character of the Christian community (or congregation) as the most important organ of the Church of faith will be ruined from the very foundation.

2. *False and True Ecclesiasticism*

The fact that a false and a true ecclesiasticism exists, is due to two aspects of the nature of the Church, namely, that the Church is both human and divine. False ecclesiasticism, ecclesiastical "Monophysitism," clericalism, is based on the fact that the divine element has been confused with the human, and thus that it predicates of both elements that which really only applies to one. Anti-ecclesiasticism, on the other hand, is based upon the fact that the necessary union of the divine and human elements in the Church is denied, and both are separated. True ecclesiasticism, however, consists in the fact that the divine and the human are not separated, but also that they are not regarded as identical with one another. The more serious danger of these two is the first, because it exists within the Church. False ecclesiasticism is the peculiar curse of the Christian Church,

This tendency towards a false ecclesiasticism began in the first century and grew from century to century. The simple and unique conception of the Church as the community of believers, which can have no Head save Christ Himself, whose Divine authority is not based upon some numinous force confronting the individual believer, but simply and solely upon the Word and the Spirit of God, indwelling the Christian community as a whole, gradually disappeared. Its place was taken by the conception of the Church as an institution, something which comes between God and those who believe, itself endowed with Divine authority and the power to impart salvation. This conception of the Church has produced the following ideas: the idea of "salvation" as something substantial which works *ex opere operato* in the Sacrifice of the Mass; the divinely authoritative official hierarchy, reaching its zenith in the Pope, whose word is infallible; and the sacred law of the Church, which binds and looses the consciences of men, which opens heaven to the obedient and casts the disobedient into hell. This is the most complete and most closely knit and therefore the most imposing form of clerical churchmanship, which has transformed the intimate relation between the human

562

and the divine in the Church into an actual identity with the Divine.

The Reformation made a fundamental breach with this kind of ecclesiasticism; in principle the Reformation was a return to the original Christian conception of the Church. But the relics of that theory of the Church which identified the human element with the Divine, which still lingered on in the minds of the Reformers, produced a fresh growth of this malignant error within the Protestant Churches; but since it was also mpossible to forget the objections to this theory Protestantism has wavered uncertainly ever since between a false churchmanship and a lack of churchmanship, and this is still its character at the present day. The thought—or more accurately the feeling—of the average "Protestant" oscillates between a secret or at least half-concealed longing for the imposing splendour of the Roman Catholic Church, and an indifference to all that bears the name of "Church."

Non-churchmanship could not flourish under the dominion of the Catholic Church. The protests of radical monasticism, of mysticism and of the sects were never able to break through this charmed circle, but always led to more sublime, if more hidden forms of the very same kind of ecclesiasticism. The sectarian movements peculiar to Protestantism, while claiming to be a revolt against false ecclesiasticism, only reproduced in another form the evil against which they contended. This was the view of Luther, Zwingli, and Calvin with regard to the Anabaptist movement, and in this their instinct led them aright. The ecclesiasticism of the sects is ecclesiasticism in its extremest and worst form, the will to create the pure Church, the Church of the true saints. The same is true, though certainly with many reservations, and in a very different degree, of Pietism, the offspring of this spirit within the Territorial Church. Its idea of sanctification and of the *ecclesiola in ecclesia* is at least to some extent the product of this conception.

Real "non-churchmanship," or a habit of thought which can see no value in the Church, so far as it still claims to be Christian, is represented by the individualism which is based either on rationalism or on what claims to be a "spiritual" interpretation of religion. If we penetrate to the heart of this point of view, we find that the distinction between the Visible and the Invisible Church is here understood in the sense of the Greek thinkers, as an opposition between form and matter. Christianity, as a purely "spiritual" concern, must not allow

563

itself to be mixed up with externals, like order, organization, or the formation of Churches, or even—if this idea is pressed to its logical conclusion—with sacraments or the "dead letter" of the Scriptures. Hostility to the Church, however, is often not so much the result of theory or principle as of dissatisfaction with the tragic failure of the Church to realize its own ideal. Such people are ashamed of the Church about which they are compelled to wax indignant.

This indignation and this shame are only too well justified, therefore, and to this extent this "non-churchmanship" has good grounds for its attitude. Who would dare to dispute the statement that Jesus Christ and His cause have had no worse enemy down the whole course of Christian history than the Church? What sincere Christian is not seized with horror when he looks at what the Church all down the ages has done or not done, said or not said? If things seem to have been better "since the Middle Ages" this is really an optical illusion: the Church has simply become more insignificant, and the fact that she counts for so little constitutes her greatest guilt. The sharpest criticism of the Church will never come from the outside—for from the outside this guilt is not visible—but from the inside.

Hence the charge we bring against *this* kind of anti-ecclesiastical individualism is not that those who thus stand aloof criticize the Church, but that they stand outside, that they refuse to acknowledge their share in the common guilt, and separate themselves from their fellows in lovelessness and pride. But these faults spring from another fault—ingratitude. For, after all, the Church, which they repudiate for her sins, is their Mother. No man has ever become a Christian without the Church having been his mother in the Faith; for through the Church alone has he received the message, and through the Church alone he understands the message of Christ which makes him a Christian. We do not refuse him the name of Christian; we do not say: the Church did not give *you* the Faith; but we do call his attention to an error which, although comprehensible, is not excusable.

We gratefully accept his criticism of the Church, however, for without it the Church cannot regain her health. It is true of course that every Christian is not called upon to criticize the Church; but every one is called to pray for the Church and her need as the need of his own Church; therefore he should feel this to be his own need, and should mourn over it accordingly. At every period in the history of the Church the greatest sin of the Church, and the one which causes the greatest distress, is that she withholds the Gospel from the world and from herself. Whether the corruption of the message be the orthodox form which does not distinguish between human doctrine and the divine Word of God, and therefore preaches the creed of yesterday instead of the living Word; or the Pietist error which diverts interest from the Word and the Promise of God to the individual and his subjective experiences and feelings; or the Liberal and Rationalistic error which confuses the Word of God with reason, and instead of the message of the Cross offers a religious ethic or a mystical asceticism: in principle it all comes to the same thing in the end, because each error is akin to all the others. The Word of God is only proclaimed where, as the Eternal Word, it speaks as the "present" Word, but always in its own glory, and therefore is proclaimed as the "divine foolishness."

The weakness of the Church lies in the fact that she lacks this "living Word"—that she does not know the reason for her own existence—and consequently has no real message for the present situation. Hence she has no true independence. How can the Church be independent if she is not standing upon her own foundation, and how can she stand upon her own foundation if she is simply concerned with herself? This brings us back to our first point, to the question of false churchmanship, only we are now concerned with the false churchmanship of the present day.

False churchmanship, or clericalism, does not consist in an excessive concern for the visible Church, but it is churchmanship which lacks any real foundation because it seeks that foundation in itself. In other words, it is a churchmanship which, since it does not spring from a concern to proclaim the true Gospel, finds its dynamic—which it certainly possesses—in secular motives and ideas. Once again the Church presents to the world the painful spectacle of an institution which is being carried along by the great forces of the world and of the age, even where its independence is most vigorously proclaimed. The Church allows herself to be carried along by all kinds of "waves" of mighty but quite uncontrollable forces, of varied origin. She has perceived the collective situation and she allies herself with all kinds of elemental forces. Her great desire—and this is the time-honoured scandal of Protestantism—is to keep pace with the times. Yesterday she was Idealist in outlook, to-day she is collectivist; yesterday she was revolutionary, to-day she is conservative; yesterday she was international, to-day she is nationalistic. But this Church is sadly out in her reckoning. When the Church tries to be modern she always arrives too late, and the world—rightly—is only amused by her "modernity." There is only one Church (at least at the moment she can still do so) which can do all this without making herself ridiculous, the Church which really can seek herself only, without becoming involved in a contradiction, because she exists in the removal of this contradiction: the Roman Catholic Church. Protestant clericalism must always break down on the fact that as a Protestant Church it desires to be what is only possible in the Catholic Church(4).

The great danger of the Church, either on a large or on a small scale, is always that of the Grand Inquisitor, that is, its aspiring to be great, its desire to glorify itself. True evangelical insight, however, knows that the Church cannot be great either in doctrine or in love, save in so far as she forgets herself and remembers only the end for which she exists. The saying that "he who would save his life shall lose it" applies to the Church as well as to the individual. Just as faith seeks not herself but the Word of God, so also to the true Church the Church is not the main thing but the divine content which is entrusted to the weak fragile vessel. The watchword of genuine churchmanship is never "the Church," but always and only "Jesus Christ." The more earnestly this message points away from the Church to Christ the more the Church increases in real strength, even in strength to shape life and to serve the people.

*   *   *   *   *

To live in the Church means to live by God's Word. The true Church, the hidden Church of faith, for the sake of which all forms of Church-life exist, consists of those who—to whatever camp they may belong—live in the midst of the world with their faces to the world to come, drawing their life from that future world. They stand with their feet firm on the ground on which the Creator has placed them, but nevertheless as those who, because they know of the fallen state of creation, know also that no act of man and no event of history, but only the final culmination in which all history ceases to be, can restore creation and achieve our redemption.

As those who wait for this consummation they alone truly possess the present; as those who are aware of their weakness they are the strong; as "pessimists" they are those who have true hope.

This hope, by which and for which the Church exists, is the motive power of the Christian life. Hence the first and most important element in life is the possession of faith and hope; action takes the second place. The Christian Ethic can only claim the first place as the result of a misunderstanding. For an action is only "Christian" when the one who performs the action knows that—ultimately—the only thing that counts is *God's* action, not ours. The first and the last word of a Christian Ethic, and its sole meaning, is this: that in all our actions, in all our human social relations, we must never forget this ultimate ground, this final relation, on which all else depends; in every concrete problem with which we are confronted we must never forget the reality of the world beyond, and the action upon us of that eternal world.

NOTES AND APPENDICES

NOTES ON CHAPTER I

PAGE 17, NOTE 1.—In the modern world moral scepticism is represented rather by works of fiction than by a philosophical school; in the former "the modern temper," as the American writer Krutch so aptly calls it, appears as a general outlook on life, or as a certain "spirit" or "temper" which colours everything else. The view of life expressed in terms of theory which was characteristic of ancient philosophers like Pyrrho, Carneades, and Sextus Empiricus, was in any case the logical result of a sceptical theory of knowledge; in the time of Montaigne and La Rochefoucauld, although it was indeed a kind of general outlook on life, it was still only the concern of a small aristocratic upper class, but to-day this spirit has become the general view of life of large masses of people. The sources of this spirit may be found in the main in the natural philosophy of the teaching of Darwin, in Marxist historical materialism, and in the disintegration of all current values by Nietzsche and by psychology; in particular stress must be laid on the influence of Freud's methods of psycho-analysis on the general view of life. In his book entitled *The Modern Temper* Krutch gives an admirable description of the process of decay of the ideal forces which were at the beginning still present within Naturalism. LIPP-MANN's well-known *Preface to Morals* ought also to be regarded as an expression of this spirit. Of course, NIETZSCHE, in his essential intention, is not a moral sceptic but a prophet. But his criticism of all existing morality does not only deliberately carry on the tradition of MONTAIGNE and LA ROCHEFOUCAULD—who for their part are wholly determined in their main line of argument by the ancient moral scepticism of Pyrrho—but in all those who cannot bring themselves to accept his positive faith in the new ethic of the "Superman" it works itself out as scepticism. Once again in the case of Freud it becomes plain that naturalistic psychology inevitably ends in scepticism, if indeed on the other hand it does not arise from it. The nearest approach to a "school" of thought of this kind is perhaps the group represented by the *American Mercury*; among modern novelists who have described this "modern temper" no one has given a better description than ALDOUS HUXLEY, the grandson of the great prophet of the Darwin school.

PAGE 17, NOTE 2.—The process of argument in support of their theories used by both ancient and modern sceptical thinkers is in part the method of antithesis—since they oppose every assertion of their opponents with the argument that the exact opposite is equally probable—and in part the method of psychology, since by showing the origin of the moral conceptions from custom, superstition, and disguised egoism they try to empty them of value. In the language of the present day: moral ideals are wish-fulfilment phantasies, moral laws are social habits, the conscience is a guilt-complex.

PAGE 18, NOTE 3.—Thus for the ancient sceptical moralists *ataraxia* or apathy was the practical guiding principle; behind the sceptical theories of modern thinkers there lie concealed all kinds of positive ideas of value, partly of a vitalistic nature and partly idealistic and humanistic.

NOTES ON CHAPTER II

PAGE 21, NOTE 1.—Thus this "phenomenonology" is not intended in the Hegelian sense, where the stages are always at the same time stages of development in the world process, but rather in the sense in which KIERKEGAARD speaks of "stages" (*Stadien*). It is fitting that even in a Christian theological ethic the comparatively high importance of such stages should be perceived and acknowledged, even though their importance is not absolute. The absence of such an explicit recognition on the part of the Dialectical Theology has given rise to much misunderstanding, as, for instance, has been expressed by TILLICH's criticism of it. (Cf. *Die religiöse Verwirklichung* and *Protestantismus als Kritik und Gestaltung*.) In this respect the controversialist KIERKEGAARD is to us an hitherto unsurpassed example, in that with all his emphasis on the Absolute, and on the absolute contradiction, he yet took the relative, and the relative contradictions, seriously.

PAGE 22, NOTE 2.—To what a great extent "extremes meet" is shown in the fact that the practical attitude of the thoroughgoing sceptical thinker approaches or can approach this boundary line of immediacy. His *ataraxia* may work out as a complete—and deliberately affirmed—act of "letting oneself go," that is, in a return to a human existence which is scarcely distinguishable from the animal level, that is, to practical "Cynicism."

PAGE 22, NOTE 3.—HEIDEGGER expresses the same idea (in the distinction between "Eigentlichkeit" and "man") in an excellent phenomenological description in his book: *Sein und Zeit*, p. 130. Cf. what is said about natural community on p. 304 of this book.

PAGE 24, NOTE 4.—Here, too, the point at issue is not the element of Aestheticism as a content or possibility of life (of which more anon, see below, pp. 499 ff.), but of aestheticism itself, that is, making the aesthetic element absolute, where art, science, culture, self-regarding intellectualism becomes a principle, the "god" of life.

PAGE 25, NOTE 5.—Cf. SCHOPENHAUER: "On the other hand, we might compare the genius, with his unfettered intellect, to a living man playing along with the large puppets of the famous puppet show at Milan, who would be the only one among them who would be aware of all that was happening, and would therefore gladly leave the stage for a while in order to enjoy the play from the boxes: —that is the reflectiveness of genius." (*Of Genius*.)

PAGE 25, NOTE 6.—"One who with talent is born to talent finds in the same his most beautiful existence" (GOETHE). "He who possesses science and art, has religion, he who does not possess them, let him have religion" (GOETHE). SCHOPENHAUER is the philosopher of aestheticism in this form of the deification of genius. It is common knowledge that in Romanticism genius was regarded as the sum-total of the value of human existence. We find a crassly naïve expression of this outlook in the work of the popular philosopher LUCKA (whose works are so widely read) in his book *Grenzen der Seele*, Part II, p. 191 : Genius "is a higher synthesis of nature and freedom, it is a superlative, an ideal of the human, it is the human being we need, released from all bondage to accidental elements. The genius constitutes a living solution of the tragic problem of humanity."

PAGE 25, NOTE 7.—We do not deal with mysticism here because it does not belong to the immanent possibilities of the understanding of the Self, but it belongs essentially to the sphere of religion, although in distinction from all other kinds of religion it is a kind of religion which finds the Transcendent in the "ground" of the Self, and is thus subjective in tendency.

PAGE 27, NOTE 8.—No human being who has ever lived has been without the consciousness of the moral idea, save in the extreme case of the moral idiot, who is indeed scarcely human. For the majority of men and women, however, the moral idea is embedded in custom. Here it is not yet possible to prove that this is not only due to the fact that this denotes the moral self-certainty of the individual Self based upon itself over against something imperfect (as Idealism would claim), but that it is also a sign of superiority. Here I can only say in passing that the language which describes this morally ethical element as *sitt-lich* (moral) is more correct than the individualistic critics of this *Sitt-lichkeit*[1] (morality). The idea of the sociological moralists (of the school of Spencer) who try to explain morality in connexion with the social structure, and the *custom* which has been erected upon it, bring to the individualistic view of morality peculiar to the thought of the Enlightenment an element of truth which ought not to be ignored; but it cannot grasp it itself without, in so doing, giving a naturalistic tinge to morality. How both these elements can be united from the higher Christian point of view of morality and of the community, has been shown particularly finely by A. VON OETTINGEN in his *Sittenlehre* (cf. especially the section on *Custom*, pp. 47 ff.).

[1] There is a play here on the words *Sitte*—custom, and *Sitt-lich*—moral, which cannot be reproduced.

NOTES ON CHAPTER III

PAGE 29, NOTE 1.—This "independence" must not be confused with absence of connexion with anything else, as the following observations will show. Here, however, it is certainly necessary to emphasize the independence of religion, its "autonomy" in relation to culture and morality; this is required in view of the theories of religion which' are naturalistic and positivist in tendency. This truth of the philosophy of religion must here be simply presupposed. (On this point cf. my "Religionsphilosophie protestantischer Theologie," in the *Handbuch der Philosophie*, published by BAEUMLER and SCHRÖTER.)

PAGE 29, NOTE 2.—One of the most impressive modern accounts of the mutual relations between culture and religion, between morality and religion, is contained in MAX WEBER's *Religionssoziologie*. WUNDT's *Völkerpsychologie*, however, has also cleared away a great many positivistic prejudices at this point.

PAGE 29, NOTE 3.—The value of the work of OTTO on the question of *The Holy* in the scientific study of religion is undisputed; he has proved the independence of the religious element in a way which can never be controverted. The only thing that is questionable in his work is the theological use which he himself has made of this truth of the comparative study of religion.

PAGE 30, NOTE 4.—So far as I know we still have no comparative study of religion written from the point of view of the relation between morality and religion—this is indeed urgently needed for many scientific purposes. The great work in three volumes by the Jesuit writer CATHREIN, entitled: *Die Einheit des sittlichen Bewusstseins*, is of course a valuable collection of material, but it is not much more than this; it is also one-sided, being written from the point of view which sets out to prove the Catholic axiom of a *lex naturae* principle of a universal and uniform kind. Among theologians WUTTKE is the one who has paid most attention to this subject. The relevant observations in his *Ethic* (*Das sittliche Bewusstsein und die Sittenlehre der heidnischen Völker*) are still valuable, although in some respects the book is out of date. WESTERMARCK's famous work: *The Origin and Development of Moral Ideas* is a mine of wealth for the study of the religion of primitive peoples, but it provides nothing for the relation between morality and religion in the higher forms of religion. The chapters which refer to this subject in E. W. MAYER's *Christliche Sittenlehre* are therefore of great value.

PAGE 31, NOTE 5.—In this respect the history of Greek religion and morality is typical. In ancient times morality could not be separated from religion. (Cf. LEOPOLD SCHMIDT: *Ethik der Griechen*, and MAX WUNDT: *Geschichte der griechischen Ethik*); here however morality could not be separated from the legal administration and the life of the State, nor from the practices of worship; the one merges into the other. The empirical rules governing the practices of worship are obeyed with as much religious reverence as those which affect human conduct as a whole. But to the extent in which the moral consciousness became emancipated from religion under the influence of philosophy the purely secular principle of happiness, if not even that of undisguised lust, takes the place of a law to which one is bound by reverence. A truly humane ethic was produced only by the religious philosophy of the Stoics and of Neo-Platonism.

PAGE 31, NOTE 6.—The most important and the most well-known example of this historical law is the struggle of Greek philosophical ethics against the morally corrupting influence of the Homeric representations of the gods.

PAGE 32, NOTE 7.—It is to this rationalized kind of religion, the Enlightenment of late antiquity, as it influenced the later history of thought, in particular through Epictetus, Cicero, Seneca and Marcus Aurelius, that we owe the conception of the *lex naturae*, which was destined to play such an important part in Christian theology and in the history of the Christian Church. The discovery of this fact by DILTHEY (*Weltanschauung und Analyse des Menschen seit der Renaissance*) is a landmark in the understanding of our own intellectual history. That which to the theologians and philosophers for 1,500 years was an incontestable *a priori* certainty has now proved to be a contingent fact of history. "Nature," "Natural morality," and "natural religion" is a definite historical phenomenon. But it is evident from the preceding remarks that this does not mean that the problem of natural law and of natural morality, for instance, has been abolished.

PAGE 32, NOTE 8.—If we look more closely into the matter, the controversy between the apparently utterly opposed thinkers, WESTERMARCK and CATHREIN, boils down almost to a matter of verbal difference of opinion. WESTERMARCK does not deny that there is a far-reaching similarity in the development of the moral concepts, and that there is, to a large extent, a wide measure of agreement between these concepts in very different spheres, nor does CATHREIN do more than maintain their "unity" in a very undefined and broadminded way. In view of the obvious fact that much which our present system of morality regards as criminal was or is regarded as a moral obligation by others, he says: "This does not prevent us from maintaining the truth of the universality and unity of the moral consciousness of humanity, if one will only distinguish universal principles from ultimate deductions and applications. . . . The Commandments of the Decalogue are actually known to all peoples practically, even to the most savage, if they are looked at in a quite general way" (*Moralphilosophie*, I, 457). In the carrying out of this principle, however, CATHREIN shows himself so broad-

573

minded that in the end no definite moral Commandment is left in existence. This whole attitude is only possible to one who (like the Jesuit theologians in general, see below, p. 96) regards the moral perception as quite independent of the religious consciousness, and this means: just as long as one regards morality from an entirely external point of view. If, on the other hand, we look at life and society from the point of view of fundamental principles the impossibility of the thesis of CATHREIN becomes manifest. The view of the morally Good, which the Chinese possesses on the basis of his religion of ancestor worship, of his fundamentally conservative and permanent social religion, is just as unintelligible to a genuine Brahman mystic and hermit, and just as repellent, and it must to him seem just as godless as, on the other hand, the Brahman's mystical renunciation of the world, and his lack of all social responsibility, must appear to the filial Chinese. Likewise the old conservative Romans were fully aware what a moral revolution the introduction of the Oriental orgiastic cults would mean for their *civitas*, as well as for that which they called *honestum*. We are making the same experience to-day. The deliberate radical secularization of thought which has been achieved by Bolshevism on the one hand, and by rationalistic Liberalism on the other, empties all ideas of "good" and "evil" not only of their traditional content, but in principle, and nothing is left save the "unfortunately inevitable" adaptation of the individual claims of life to the principle of the least possible friction, or to the principle of the greatest possible exploitation of power. We do not deny that "behind" these religions and views of life and their moral consequences there may lie a moral knowledge which is common to all; but we maintain that this cannot be summed up in any definite formula but only in the law that they all have the possibility of affirming the real Good where it becomes manifest to them as "that which they really knew already."

NOTES ON CHAPTER IV

PAGE 35, NOTE 1.—The reproach, so often levelled at me, that I make the mistake of setting philosophy and theology against each other (e.g. cf. TILLICH: *Religiöse Verwirklichung*, p. 278) would only be justified if there really did exist a truly critical philosophy, which did not think in this sense in "immanent" terms, thus which were either directly related to revelation, or at least left room for it. Up to the present, however, such a philosophy can scarcely be said to exist, and TILLICH's philosophy of religion, with its interpretation of Christianity in particular (see chiefly his *Religionsphilosophie*) simply continues the Western tradition. Revelation is worked into a Neoplatonic system of Immanence, and in so doing its meaning is altered. His understanding of Christianity is absolutely "rational,"

574

in the sense in which he himself uses the conception (cf. *Der Pro-*
testantismus als Kritik und Gestaltung, p. 7, note). Thus Western ethics
is not only philosophical but rational; apart from the fragments in
KANT (see below, note 9), and, at least in intention, in EBERHARD
GRISEBACH's *Gegenwart*, no truly critical system of ethics exists.

PAGE 36, NOTE 2.—Certainly the ethic of EPICURUS is itself not at
all logically "Epicurean," any more than was the life of the philosopher himself. But "all the more sharply it contradicts it in its
argument. To desire virtue for its own sake, means, as he believes,
to chase after vain imaginations; only he who makes pleasure
(well-being) his end has a real end for his activity. . . . It is not
virtue in itself which makes men happy, but only the pleasure
(well-being) which it produces" (ZELLER: *Die Philosophie der Grie-*
chen, IV, p. 447). The inconsistency of Epicurus, from the logical
point of view, arises from the fact that he believed that spiritual
pleasure lasted longer than the pleasure of the senses, and therefore
that, by means of psychological perception, he could give a higher
place to spiritual pleasure. In the pupil of Epicurus, METRODORUS,
the real meaning of the Epicurean principles comes out plainly.
"He does not merely say that all pleasure is *based* upon that which
comes from the pleasures of the table, but that all pleasure refers to
them and is measured by them, and that they alone are the purpose
of all clever and fine inventions. This assertion is only to be distinguished from those of Epicurus by the fact that the latter, more
reflective than his pupil, does not limit his remarks on pleasure
merely to the enjoyment of eating and drinking, but that he says of
all the pleasures of the senses what Metrodorus had just said about
the latter" (ZELLER, loc. cit., p. 444).

The most logical representative of the "Epicurean" ethic is
perhaps the predecessor of Epicurus, ARISTIPPUS OF CYRENE. In
contrast to Epicurus, Aristippus maintains that the pleasure of the
moment is all that counts. It is not our intention to show that this
leads to a life consisting in the mere pleasures of the senses—which
is not true even of ARISTIPPUS—but that all else is only affirmed for the
sake of the pleasures of the senses (cf. ZELLER, loc. cit., II, pp. 305 ff.).

PAGE 36, NOTE 3.—The most important of the later representatives of the Epicurean ethic is HOBBES. His ethical principle is as
follows: the preservation of life with the fewest possible restrictions,
with the least possible danger for the future (*de cive*, 6, 13). Egoism
is the only motive for action. He arrives at a philosophy of society—
his famous doctrine of the State—through the view, that it is this
very egoism which leads to the formation of social groups. "*Omnis*
igitur societas vel commodi causa vel gloriae, hoc est sui, non sociorum amore
contrahitur" (*de cive*, 1, 2). He did not carry out these views con-
sistently however. His doctrine of the State is based upon the statement that every one in the same manner has the same right to
everything. The state of Nature is the *bellum omnium in omnes* (*de cive*,

1, 12). The State is therefore not based upon good-will but upon fear. The State and civilization may be explained as the result of fear of one another.

In the philosophy of MANDEVILLE Epicureanism is developed to the point at which it becomes complete moral scepticism. "The theory that self-love is the source of all human action has never, either before or afterwards, been presented . . . with such brutal frankness" (JODL: *Geschichte der Ethik*, 1, p. 187). STIRNER is just as radical as MANDEVILLE, only his standard of conduct is not so much pleasure as the desire for sterile freedom. "I want to be and to have everything that I can be and have. Whether other people want to be and have similar things—does not concern me. Every one else is only what he is for me, namely my object, and because he is my object he is my property" (JODL, loc. cit., p. 286). Here there is no attempt, by way of the Utilitarian principle, to establish a "virtuous" or altruistic life, but here naked egoism is extolled as the only intelligent method of living.

PAGE 37, NOTE 4.—The pioneer in this sphere of altruistic sensory phenomenalism is HUME, the one who discovered the feelings of "sympathy," and ADAM SMITH, who gave a more refined version of Hume's theory in a very notable way (cf. TH. LITT: *Die Ethik der Neuzeit*, I, pp. 51 ff. in the *Handbuch der Philosophie*, edited by BAEUMLER and SCHRÖTER). Perhaps the most influential of the modern moralists of this school is BENTHAM, who for the first time enunciated as a fundamental ethical principle the view that we ought to aim at gaining "the greatest happiness for the greatest number." In order to establish this fundamental axiom as the ethical standard (the principle of utility), he sets up a whole series of criteria; under the concept of "sanctions" he deals with the motives which should move the individual to will this result, which ultimately can all be traced back to the idea of personal well-being. Closely connected with and dependent upon his thought is MILL's *Utilitarianism*. In his theory, however, still more clearly than in that of Bentham, we perceive a confusion of thought between the effect of well-being and the motive of happiness. Mill distinguishes various qualities of pleasure, higher and lower, but he does not notice that in so doing he has accepted a motive of Idealism, and that through the summons to prefer the higher form of pleasure to the lower kind, he is slipping into the imperative type of ethic. This point has been noticed by a later member of the same school, SIDGWICK, who then frankly breaks away from a one-sided Eudaemonism and tries to erect a system of ethics upon the combination of the motives of pleasure and of duty. Although it is plain that all these systems, from the time of Hume onwards, are based on the confusion between the *feeling* of sympathy and the *duty* of altruism, on the other hand it cannot be denied that they have certain positive merits in their criticism of the formal ethic of duty.

PAGE 37, NOTE 5.—The rational ethic has no means of over-coming the opposition between duty and "inclination"; when it tries to get beyond the bare conception of duty it immediately falls into Eudaemonism. Schiller's attempt to bridge the gulf between the two ends in the idea of "aesthetic education"; thus through connexion with the Beautiful Schiller leads us back to the Greek conception of καλοκαγαθία, and again destroys what he had learnt from Kant: the recognition of unconditional obligation.

PAGE 37, NOTE 6.—The first philosopher to apply the Darwinian idea of evolution on a large scale to the solution of the difficulties of the eudaemonistic ethic was HERBERT SPENCER, in his *Principles of Ethics*; and indeed he not only uses the idea of evolution for the explanation of moral phenomena (for instance, of the conscience) but just as much for the positing of a norm. Conduct "which furthers race-maintenance" is moral conduct (p. 16). The lack of clearness in his conception comes out immediately in the fact that he continues: "which evolves hand in hand with the conduct which furthers self-maintenance. That better organization which makes possible the last, makes possible the first also." "The fore-going exposition shows that the conduct to which we apply the name *good*, is the relatively more evolved conduct; and that *bad* is the name we apply to conduct which is relatively less evolved" (p. 25). In order that this distinction between the "higher" and the "lower," with some apparent right, may be conceived as a natural process, the development of the intellect is everywhere regarded as the real driving force in this optimistically conceived process of evolution. It never entered Spencer's mind that the developed intellect could be far more evil than the undeveloped. He believes quite simply in the equation: a complicated (differentiated) organ-ism = a "higher" organism, even in the ethical sense. Another conception which ought to form the mediation between the process of nature and the higher moral development is that of *adaptation* or adjustment. The moral man is one whose functions "are all dis-charged in degrees duly adjusted to the conditions of existence" (p. 83). Spencer, like a true Nominalist, maintains that the spiritual element—even in the qualitative ethical sense—is due to the capacity for abstraction. The conscience is an abstract sentiment "generated in a manner analogous to that in which abstract ideas are generated" (p. 124). With these attempts to retain the truly ethical element, while explaining it from the standpoint of natural science, there goes hand in hand the older, purely eudaemonistic and Epicurean way of looking at things. Spencer's view of society resembles that of Hobbes, as due to the motive of mutual toleration for mutual advantage (153), and again: "Sympathy is the root of both justice and beneficence" (148). Hence Spencer recognizes ethical prin-ciples (i.e. that which is universally recognized as good), but only "after the same have been rightly explained," namely, according to the causal principles of natural science: "Hence, recognizing in due degrees all the various ethical theories, conduct in its highest form will take as guides innate perceptions of right duly enlightened and made precise by analytic intelligence" (pp. 172-173). But he always considers it necessary to explain that the egoistic motives are just as necessary as the altruistic ones (p. 238). The confused character of this system and its compromises comes out in a kind of lapidary sentence in the beginning of the second volume: "Conduct is good or bad according as its total effects are pleasurable or painful for the agent or for others."

PAGE 38, NOTE 7.—The only representative of this principle of individualism among the more recent moralists is STIRNER. GUYAU's *Morale sans obligation ni sanction* comes from a quite different source: a pantheistic Nature-mysticism; we might even say, if we understand the word in a refined sense: "pan-eroticism." It is not that the Self *ought*, but that it *wills*—in the consciousness of its unity with the All—to give itself to this All, and therefore to all creatures. The concept of "sympathy" of the English Nominalists is here intensified to the point of mystical ecstasy. But to speak of this as an "ethic" is only possible as the fruit of a misunderstanding. Either that surrender takes places or it does not; but there is no question of obligation.

PAGE 38, NOTE 8.—Here we are thinking primarily of NIETZSCHE, although he only claimed to be arguing rationally at the utmost, in his earlier, purely critical period. He is not essentially a philosopher but a prophet, with an incomparable gift of psychological analysis, which is certainly not the portion of prophets as a rule. As a critic of the previous system of ethical thought he carries forward the line which runs through PYRRHO and MONTAIGNE down to LA ROCHE-FOUCAULD, but he also adopts from England the Darwinian idea of selection, which however he applies in exactly the opposite sense from that in which it is used by SPENCER, that is, not in the sense of the welfare of all, but in that of the selection of the aristocratic few. But this positive principle, his real "Gospel," is not to be understood in the purely vitalistic sense—although this feature does stand out very clearly in his thought, in his fight against the negative morality of extreme asceticism or quietism—but in the sense of the Romantic glorification of genius. His "super-man" is a blend of the "man of power" (see above, pp. 23 ff.), and of the genius, in the sense in which SCHOPENHAUER uses the word. If we want to reduce Nietzsche's thought to a system we might call it a "mysticism of Genius," but at the same time we must always remember that his "genius" is never a mere spectator, but that he always wants to act on a grand scale. In the last resort we can only understand NIETZSCHE from the point of view of his sympathetic hostility to the Bible.

PAGE 39, NOTE 9.—When SCHLEIERMACHER, in his *Grundlinien der*

Kritik aller bisherigen Sittenlehre, without further question places KANT with the Stoics he overlooks the fact that the ethic of the Stoics is based upon an Idealistically-Pantheistic view, which as a metaphysic Kant rejects. It is precisely this union of the Ideal and the Actual by means of the ambiguous conception of the *lex naturae* —by means of this theory, both idealistic and naturalistic, of "living in accordance with nature"—which gives possibilities to the Stoic ethic which the Kantian ethic does not possess. The Kantian ethic however also has an Idea of God in the background, but this Idea is not the Stoic idea but the Christian idea—although somewhat weakened by a certain tinge of Deism: but it is now common property from his *opus postumum*, how Kant strove to the very last to eliminate this theological background from his ethical theory, and that he was unable to do so. It is this which gives the Kantian ethic its divided character. We can understand it as a purely critical ethic which describes the form of every kind of morality—even the Christian—under the aspect of the "good will"; with HEINRICH BARTH (*Philosophie der praktischen Vernunft*), we may even regard this line as the really Kantian one, and in so doing forget Kant the moralist, with his views of the Enlightenment type. Only we ought to remember that a critical ethic, in this sense, ought never to deal with the content of an ethic; consciously it should decide nothing as to the "what" of its demands. Or, we may regard Kant chiefly as the rationalistic moralist, who, because he refuses to see the content of the moral anywhere else than in Reason, is obliged to become a legalistic moralist, and to be secretly inconsistent, in order to squeeze the content out of the form of the Law, by its transformation into a law of Nature. The first view seems to me, in view of Kantian criticism as a whole, to be far the most sensible; but then the faithful Kantians of the present day (who thus conceive their relation to their master) are bound to eliminate from his ethical theory those elements of his ethic which are conditioned by Rationalism. This fortunate process of development seems to have begun and to be going on.

PAGE 39, NOTE 10.—This curious idea lies behind the well-known formula: "Act only on that maxim whereby thou canst at the same time will that it should become a universal law" (*Metaphysik der Sitten, Reclam.*, p. 55). Then somewhat further on he says: "Act as if the maxim of thy action were to become by thy will a universal law of nature" (p. 56). By means of this idea, Kant, without borrowing from theology, seems to make up for the lack of that idea of the *lex naturae* in the Stoic ethic. But here there prevails an obvious illusion. It cannot be proved that a society on a purely egoistic basis is *impossible*. And secondly, this principle of the possibility of making the maxims universal does not arise out of the previous definitions, as a criterion of the Good. There are no maxims which could be said to correspond with that Kantian rule. Behind this confusion between the Moral Law and the Law of Nature there lies concealed the principle of Well-being as the *material* principle of ethics: Act in such a way that if every one were to act as you do, a happy human society would result.

PAGE 41, NOTE 11.—The impossibility of the Aristotelian ethic as a method is as evident as its unusual though relative value on the side of content. Once the principle of the superiority of the Spiritual and the Rational over the Empirical and Instinctive has been admitted, certainly a useful ethic can be constructed. Only we ought not to overlook the fact that its individualism, its intellectualism, and the poverty of the purely formal principle of reason render it very limited. In happy inconsequence ARISTOTLE has combined with this idea a whole mass of other motives, which made it possible for him to shape his ethic as the philosophically systematic expression of Greek wisdom in the conduct of life. But its material principle is rather culturally aesthetic than in the real sense of the word moral; it is that of "the cultivated personality." Innumerable are the moralists who have imitated, and more or less successfully continued, the Aristotelian ethic, from the Peripatetic School of antiquity, via THOMAS AQUINAS and MELANCHTHON, down to the ethic of personality of a SHAFTESBURY or a LEIBNIZ, and thence to the latest protagonists of the theory of Self-realization, of whom we may name PAULSEN as a representative. But we must remember that scarcely one of these moralists took over Aristotle wholesale; this was not possible because the whole conception of personality had been changed by Christianity. But from the point of view of formal method PAULSEN's definition of the Moral, as "the normal exercise of the life-functions along the lines of natural capacity and disposition . . . the development of the natural tendencies and powers to their full extent and their full excellence, and their complete use under normal external conditions" (*System der Ethik*, p. 212), is not far from the Aristotelian principle. Here, too, however, that surreptitious change has taken place which managed to evolve the Idea out of the concept and makes a "natural tendency" produce the sense of obligation. In this the principle of "harmony" plays a very questionable part. In order to establish what belongs to the harmonious whole of a personality, and what does not, an idea must be present which appoints to each element its place and its position in the series. But this idea cannot be found within the empirical human being; it is the Moral Law, which transcends empiricism.

PAGE 41, NOTE 12.—We might enquire whether we should describe the ethic of COMTE as Idealistic or Naturalistic. Like SCHLEIERMACHER in his philosophical ethics, COMTE stands midway between the two. Where method is concerned he is certainly naturalistic; he tries to conceive the laws of the human development of society by means of a "physique sociale," and regards "altruism" as the most important factor in this formation of society (the word "altruism" originated with Comte) as an instinct, which, however, can only be rightly known in its true importance by means of the intellect, and, therefore, deliberately cultivated it leads to the truly Moral. But here, far more definitely than in SPENCER, the spiritual life, and above all the will to community, love, is known as the real *ethos*, so that we might almost describe it as a Christian ethic on a naturalistic basis. The endeavour to interpret the spiritual as a fact of nature is Naturalistic; the recognition of an obligation which applies to every one is Idealistic, while the definition of the content of this obligation is Christian.

The philosophical ethic of SCHLEIERMACHER is quite different. It, too, is Naturalistic, in so far as it conceives the spiritual process of cultural development as a natural process; also in the fact that it regards morality only as the continuation of "physics," and therefore sets up no norms, but only—as in the history of philosophy or sociology—describes its laws of growth; on the other hand, it is Idealistic in the fact that the content of this process consists precisely in the supremacy of Spirit over Nature, or as it is called, "in the union of the Spirit with Nature." His Naturalism comes out plainly in his treatment of evil as a purely "abnormal" formation, which stands in the same category as abortion; his Idealism is visible in the unambiguous aim of this development of the complete supremacy of Spirit—and indeed of a wholly abstractly cultural spirituality—over Nature. Even HEGEL's system is not pure Idealism, although it is often described as such. For here too the spirit-process proceeds along inevitably natural lines—although it follows the zig-zag line characteristic of dialectic; here, too, the process rushes on over the individual like a stream, carries him along in its headlong course, and then allows him to disappear. Here, too, the idea of obligation is only permitted to be an auxiliary idea, it is a phenomenon of the stage of "morality," which will be overcome in the course of the process. Above the conscience and its sense of obligation there stands as the goal of the whole development "the State, the reality of the moral Idea" (*Rechtsphilos*, p. 317). WUNDT's great system of ethics is developed by means of a remarkable blending of the ideas of SPENCER, COMTE, and HEGEL. From the first to the last (4–5) edition of this work there is plainly to be perceived a development in the direction of a universalistic culture-Idealism, just as much as the fact that it never arrives at a clear definition of the Moral because the naturalistic fundamental conception is nowhere really overcome. Listen to the following definition of the central problem: "We call . . . immoral every disposition or action which consists in the resistance of the individual will to the collective will"; on the other hand, "the will is moral from the point of view of result, when an action is in conformity with the *collective* will, from the point of view of the disposition, when the motives which determine it, agree with the aims of the *collective* will (Vol. 3, p. 107). The "collective" will is here understood entirely in the empirical sense. So *vox populi vox dei!* All these systems of ethics, which have remained more or less in the realm of theory, are outstripped in historical importance by the system of KARL MARX. In it, MARX, the disciple of HEGEL and FEUERBACH, reveals the latent naturalism of the Hegelian philosophy of history: the dialectic of the historical process is combined with the naturalistic idea of development, and in the place of the spirit which realizes itself there is placed the economic system of Communism which realizes itself. MARX never claims to be a moralist; but his ideas have been understood as an ethical system, and as such have had an immense influence, partly in the negative sense as the ethic of a passivity which almost merges into fatalism and irresponsibility, and partly the opposite, as the ethical justification of resolute class-war and class solidarity. The inner contradiction between the materialistic basis and the—still predominating—Idealistically humane purpose is evident. But Marx should not be understood as a rational moralist —any more than his exact opposite, NIETZSCHE—but as a prophet, and therefore he does not belong to this connexion.

PAGE 41, NOTE 13.—The creator of this new ethical tendency is MAX SCHELER, in his important work entitled *Der Formalismus in der Ethik und die materiale Wertethik*. He has been followed by NICOLAI HARTMANN, whose "Ethik" comes very close to that of his master. The difference between the two will be indicated in the following notes.

PAGE 43, NOTE 14.—SCHELER's ethic—which moreover he himself has abandoned—can only be understood if we read between the lines. Then we see that it is essentially a theological ethic, and indeed to put it more exactly, a Christian and theological ethic of the Augustinian type, thus, according to our definition, it is non-philosophical. But this Augustinianism contains many essentially alien elements, and thus it is impossible to sum up the whole system in a few sentences. The second half of the book is a personal ethic, in which the Moral is absolutely personally conceived, as a personal relation of man to a personal God. The criticism which SCHELER expresses, from this point of view, of every kind of rational ethic, even of the rational ethic of duty, is most apt, and agrees with a great deal of that which is elaborated in the later sections of this book. It is an ethic of love based on grace. With this personalistic ethic, however, there is connected an impersonal ethic of Values, according to which it would seem at first as though the Values were independent entities. Only incidentally do we learn "that all possible values are founded upon the value of an infinite personal Spirit and of the world of values which stands before Him" (p. 94). Whereas at first SCHELER maintains that the scale of values cannot be derived, on p. 97 we learn that the higher values are those which "in feeling and in preference themselves are given as the values which are closest to the absolute Value." Thus they are not absolutely underivable, but only for rational thought. But in spite of this distinction this impersonal ethic of values is in opposition to the personal ethic of the second part. The fundamental law of values: "All that is of positive value ought to be, and all that is of negative value ought not to be" (p. 210)—in itself a quite senseless idea since that which is positively valuable is an ideal total conception, to demand the realization of which is just as foolish as the demand that all thinkable ideas shall be realized, when indeed the reality of the one excludes the reality of the other—and stands in sharpest contrast to the wholly Christian idea of a "sense of obligation" which "goes forth as a call to this person and this person alone, regardless of the fact whether the same call has also been addressed to others or not" (p. 510). Fundamental too is the contrast between the idea that the Moral consists in the choice of the right values, and the idea that there are special ethical values which as such make the choice ethical.

At the same time it becomes evident that these "moral values" are simply what the older ethical theories used to call "virtues," that is, the individual manifestations abstracted from the existence of the ethical personality. If we take the theological personalism of the second part of the book seriously, then all values which are not connected with personality are seen to be relative, so far as the personal is concerned (as indeed they are based upon the personality of God and are to be known as such), but then the value as such is no longer the ethically determinative factor, but the preferring of the "higher" to the "lower" values, the scale of values, or the estimate of their "nearness" to the absolute Value. But this leads us away from a philosophical discussion into a theological one. It is therefore comprehensible that NICOLAI HARTMANN, the protagonist of the proposition of the non-morality of the Idea of God, has felt the need to sever the teaching of his master from this theological background (cf. his polemic against SCHELER, p. 225). But what in SCHELER—even if only from behind the scenes—is intelligible, has become in HARTMANN wholly obscure: the connexion between the values as a whole with the Moral, the relation of the ethical values to the other values, the reason why the ethical values in particular bring with them a sense of obligation. Here too, above all, the question of the scale of values—which is the all-important one—remains unexplained; we are simply told to look to the future for consolation. "Even an individual analysis, if such should exist, is not sufficient for a really thoroughgoing ordering of the values. We should never forget that we stand at the very beginning of our enquiry into the values. . . . We cannot expect certain results at all" (p. 245). With these presuppositions what meaning can an ethic have, since "the Good is the selection of the values

themselves according to the principle of the elevation of the value?"
(p. 351). But if we hold firmly to this statement, then the Good is
not determined by a value, but by the choice of the higher value,
"according to the principle of the elevation of the value." Thus it is
not the value as such which is the decisive point in an ethical
system, but the principle of the elevation of the value. What is said
further about the moral values simply amounts essentially to a
theory of Virtue; thus here too the values are simply the different
forms of the expression of the good will or of being good. But if this
is so it was scarcely necessary to write this enormous book of 750
pages on the theory of Value!

NOTES ON CHAPTER V

PAGE 46, NOTE 1.—"I believe from the bottom of my heart and
after the most mature consideration, that the doctrine of Christ,
when cleansed from all the extraneous nonsense imported by clerics,
is the most complete system which I at least can possibly imagine.
Only I also believe that there is also another system, which grows
out of pure reason and leads thither; but the latter is only for
practised thinkers and not for man in general; and even if it were
to find favour, we would still have to choose the doctrine of Christ
for practical accomplishment" (KANT, op. post., p. 763). Alongside
of the sentence: "the thought of Him (God) is at the same time
faith in Him and His Personality" (p. 776) there stands this one:
"that such a Being exists cannot be denied, but it *cannot* be maintained that it exists beyond the man who thinks rationally" (p. 785).
"God is not a Being outside me, He is merely a thought within me.
God is the Reason which morally and practically posits itself as
Law" (p. 819). "Thus God is not a substance which can be found
outside me but merely a moral relation within me" (p. 826). The
main aim of all these enquiries is to show that the Moral is independent of the question of God. And yet we find a sentence like
this: "There is a Being within me who is differentiated from me in
the causal relationship of influence upon me, which is itself free,
that is, it is not dependent upon the natural law in time and space,
which inwardly judges me (justifying or condemning)," which,
however, goes on to say, "and I, a man, am myself this being, and
this is not a substance outside me" (p. 824).

PAGE 48, NOTE 2.—On this point KANT is quite explicit: "Religion (from the subjective point of view) is the knowledge of all our
duties as divine commands. That type of religion in which I must
know beforehand that something is a Divine Command, in order
to be able to recognize it as my duty, is revealed religion (or one
that stands in need of revelation): on the other hand, that kind of
religion in which I must know first that something is a duty, before

I can admit it to be a Divine Command, is natural religion," that is, "religion within the limits of mere reason," which Kant alone recognizes (*Religion innerhalb . . . Reclam.*, p. 165).

PAGE 48, NOTE 3.—I find the finest expression of this self-estimate of the philosopher which is determined by faith, and yet strictly philosophical and critical in character, in the two latest published works of the specialist in Kantian philosophy in Holland, B. H. J. OVINK: *De zekerheid der menschelijke Kennis*, and *Philosophische Erklärung der platonischen Dialoge Meno und Hippias Minor*. See the sentence in the introduction to the latter work: "Thus I have understood that such a wholly restrained critical enquiry into the fundamental conceptions of all human knowledge is the only philosophy which can fit in with the living spirit of the Christian Faith, because it does not, like all other kinds of Idealism which proceed from the source of the enthusiastic *Eros theoretikos*, lead inevitably to a pantheistic mysticism."

PAGE 48, NOTE 4.—In this sense it is certainly correct to say that behind Kant's anti-metaphysical philosophy there is a metaphysic (TILLICH). Only this metaphysic is not connected with his critical work, but with the relics (which even he possessed) of a non-critical Platonism. But every philosophy which believes it can find the bridge missed by Kant becomes metaphysical and speculative— which ought particularly to be rejected when it makes friendly overtures to Christianity.

PAGE 49, NOTE 5.—This secret or open Eudaemonism is stamped on every type of Greek ethics, even on that of Plato and the Stoics. It is the idea of Beauty and Goodness (καλοκαγαθία), this attractive combination of the aesthetic and the ethical, which stands for the understanding of the True Good, both to the ancient Greek and to the modern thinker. Until the time of Luther no one had been aware of this fundamental defect in ethics; in the theory of KANT likewise only one-half of the Lutheran interpretation of the Good is left. "It is all upside down to describe Luther as the precursor of Kant. The truth is rather that Kant, in his disintegration of the Moral, only repeats—and this not fully—what Luther, who had started from a definite content of the Moral, had first of all discovered" (HOLL: *Gesammelte Aufsätze*, III, p. 547).

PAGE 50, NOTE 6.—Cf. BULTMANN: *Der Begriff der Offenbarung*. BRUNNER: *The Word and the World* (Student Christian Movement Press; London, 1931). What from HEGEL to TILLICH the speculative philosophy of religion has called "revelation" is always meant in the sense of the "religion of Immanence." The fact that the term "revelation" is used in Christianity in a sense which is not found in any other form of religion is treated in my pamphlet: *Die Christusbotschaft im Kampf mit den Religionen* (Verlag der Basler Mission), and my *Religionsphilosophie*.

NOTES ON CHAPTER VI

PAGE 53, NOTE 1.—LOMMEL: *Die Religion Zarathustras*, p. 22.

PAGE 53, NOTE 2.—The rejection of this Biblical principle by Thomism is the logical result of its Aristotelian intellectualism. Cf., for instance, CATHREIN: *Moralphilosophie*: "God's holiness consists in the fact that essentially His will can will only the Good and the Right. Thus it presupposes an eternal standard of all willing which is not subject to the free choice of God, a standard with which the Divine Will agrees not freely but of necessity, so that God's holiness consists precisely in this necessary agreement" (I, p. 186).

PAGE 54, NOTE 3.—There are elements in the Old Testament, it is true, most of which are also found in other religions; but these elements do not constitute the distinctive part of the Old Testament with which we are here concerned. The specific element in the Old Testament is the fact that there is a fight *against* this kind of priestcraft in connexion with worship.

PAGE 55, NOTE 4.—The key to the ethics of the New Testament is contained in the following passages: *Romans vi, vii* and the beginning of *Romans viii*. Here, as nowhere else, we perceive in great clearness and detail the identity of the central points in dogmatics and in ethics. The Sermon on the Mount, on the other hand, although it is the necessary presupposition of Christian ethics, is not its foundation. Its relation to *Romans vi* is that of the Law to the Gospel. For further observations on this topic see below, p. 137.

PAGE 56, NOTE 5.—When H. DIEM, in his informing article on "Die Kirche und Kierkegaard" (*Zwischen den Zeiten*, 1931, p. 305), gives it as his opinion that in the New Testament "there is no kind of new commandment . . . nor ethical norm, but simply the way is shown by which the old law can really be fulfilled," he is, in this respect, following along the lines laid down by MELANCHTHON, but he is not following the accepted Lutheran doctrine (see below, p. 100), and in so doing he overlooks the very thing that is said in the Johannine paradox about the "new commandment." Since, as DIEM himself says, "a new value is given to the object of this love," this implies at the same time also a new understanding of the *meaning* of this love. That it is no new demand to "mortify your members," as DIEM thinks it is, can only be said by someone who forgets what this expression means in *Romans vi*, that this meaning of "mortification" can only be grasped in connexion with the fact of the Cross of Christ. (Cf. BULTMANN: *Aimer son prochain* (*Revue d'histoire et de philosophie religieuse*, 1930, pp. 222 ff.)

PAGE 58, NOTE 6.—If the idea of predestination is thus conceived, then it certainly is "the central dogma of the Reformed Church" (ALEX. SCHWEIZER), and the secret of the moral power of the original Reformed theology. The presentation by MAX WEBER of the doctrine of predestination, and the reasons for its ethical effectiveness, in his famous study: *Die protestantische Ethik und der Geist des Kapitalismus* (*Ges. Aufsätze zur Religionssoziologie*, I, pp. 89 ff.) may be described as at least very one-sided. To Calvin the main point was not the twofold decree but election. The particular form which he gave to this doctrine, however, I regard as unscriptural. (See below, note 8.)

PAGE 58, NOTE 7.—Cf. on this point the excellent observations in A. v. OETTINGEN's *Christliche Sittenlehre*, para. 5. Similarly, MARTENSEN, in his *Christliche Ethik*, I, pp. 185 ff., emphasizes the overcoming of the great ethical contradictions in the Gospel.

PAGE 59, NOTE 8.—When, however, MAX WEBER (loc. cit., p. 93) speaks of the "unprecedented inner loneliness of the single individual," which is the result of the idea of election, this again is most one-sided. For this election is precisely election to true community. The force with which, particularly in Calvinism, the idea of the Church became a reality, the power of forming religious community, is the other side of this very idea of election. The ἐκκλησία corresponds to the κλῆσις. See below, p. 300.

NOTES ON CHAPTER VII

PAGE 61, NOTE 1.—The older kind of apologetic was not wrong in drawing this conclusion; it erred simply by drawing this conclusion from false premises, namely, from that of a theoretical view of life. It was not wrong in making that conflict explicit, but it went wrong when it severed it from the decisive reality of faith, and made it merely the confrontation of two varieties of worldview. On this subject cf. my articles: "Die andere Aufgabe der Theologie" (*Zwischen den Zeiten*, 1929, pp. 255 ff.) and "Theologie und Kirche" (ibid., 1930, p. 397).

PAGE 63, NOTE 2.—In the justifiable endeavour to distinguish the feeling of the Holy from all that is merely rational, OTTO, in his works upon the Holy, has not made a clear distinction between that which is supra-rational and that which is sub-rational, and thus he has drawn a picture of the Deity which often seems more like a picture of a daemon than of the true God. On the other hand— probably under the influence of SCHLEIERMACHER—he has misunderstood the importance of the Holy for the rise and the foundation of morality. WUNDT's *Ethik* (Vol. I, pp. 41–103) gives a careful analysis of the relation between religion and morality, but without a profound understanding of the religious aspect of the question.

NOTES ON CHAPTER VIII

PAGE 68, NOTE 1.—No one has seen this so clearly as Luther, and nowhere has Luther expressed this so clearly as in his *Commentary* on the *Epistle to the Romans*, on the eighth chapter, where he is dealing with the *curvitas naturalis* of the will. See FICKER, II, pp.184, 18; ibid., 185, 14. At the same time Luther does not in any way overlook all those good, spiritual, fine motives of which even the natural man is capable, with which his opponents try to overthrow his doctrine, even down to the present day; he even rises to the greatest heights of the mystical knowledge of God and of the mystical love of God—cf. the catalogue of goods which the natural will desires to possess, on *Romans viii.* 7. (Cf. FICKER, II, 190 and 190, 21.) On this see also HOLL: *Luther*, pp. 155 ff.

PAGE 69, NOTE 2.—In Luther this knowledge is not only present in principle, but it is also fully present, and perfectly clear, from the historico-critical point of view, with reference to all the religions and philosophies known to him. (Cf. VOSSBERG: *Luthers Kritik aller Religion*, 1922.) Similarly PASCAL, above all in his famous *Entretien avec M. de Saci*, has summed up the nature of the non-Christian ethic in a formula; but his Augustinianism, coupled with the refined mystical Eudaemonism peculiar to himself, here prevents final clarity; of the great thinkers after the Reformation KIERKEGAARD alone possessed this clarity. His *Krankheit zum Tode* (Sickness unto Death) stands completely alone, in spite of the flourishing Lutheranism of the nineteenth century. (On this see pp. 100 ff.)

PAGE 69, NOTE 3.—The ethic of the Stoics also recognizes as its highest principle the general Greek principle of Eudaemonism. (ZELLER, loc. cit., IV, pp. 208 ff.) The statement: τέλος δέ φασιν εἶναι τὸ εὐδαιμονεῖν, οὗ ἕνεκα πάντα πράττεται, αὐτὸ δὲ πράττεται μὲν, οὐδενὸς δὲ ἕνεκα (ZELLER, p. 208), applies to all Stoic moral philosophy and practical teaching. But even KANT, owing to the fact that he adheres to the immanental basis of ethics, does not escape from this necessity. The doctrine of the "Interest, attaching to the Ideas of Morality" (*Grundlegung*, p. 88), leads to the result that one does the purely Good because thus "we may expect to enhance the inward value of our own personality." Thus I believe that I have become this "better person" when I have adopted the point of view of a member of the "world of Pure Reason" (p. 95).

PAGE 69, NOTE 4.—"For an individual who throughout a considerable tract of time has seen his forethought principles exerted into act, and is thence enabled to conclude, with tolerable certainty, upon a radical reformation of his character, may reasonably hope that this advancement, provided only its inward principle be good, will so confirm and augment the elastic force wherewith he still presses forward to what is better—as not only to prevent him from quitting while on earth the narrow path of virtue, and urge him with more courageous and unimpeded footstep thitherward. . ." (KANT: *Religion innerhalb, etc.*, p. 70—Reclam. Eng. translation: J. W. SEMPLE, p. 83.) "A good and pure sentiment . . . whereof we are conscious, guides consequently to a conviction of its permanency and steadfastness, although it does so *mediately* only. . . ." (Ibid., p. 73, Eng. translation: SEMPLE, p. 86.)

PAGE 70, NOTE 5.—LUTHER, on *Romans viii. 3* (loc. cit., p. 184, 12.)

PAGE 71, NOTE 6.—Again it was LUTHER—who was in this matter, however, preceded by Augustine—who placed the question of the "Agent," the "captain of good works," in the foreground. . . . (*Leipziger Disputation*, DREWS, pp. 181–184.)

PAGE 71, NOTE 7.—It was STANGE who first of all rediscovered this most profound thought of Luther's, and made it known in his work entitled *Die Heilsbedeutung des Gesetzes* (1904), but even so, he did not make it really fruitful.

PAGE 71, NOTE 8.—It is a well-known fact that even a man like Luther did not perceive for a long time that there was an intimate connexion between mysticism and legalism. His later views of mystical theology were therefore all the more critical—indeed he went so far as to say that it ought to be shunned *tamquam pestilentiam* (*Disputationen*, DREWS, p. 294). Mysticism can never get beyond the idea of the *infusio gratiæ*, and in its connexion with asceticism and the cloister it betrays its secret belief in self-redemption.

PAGE 72, NOTE 9.—There is urgent need for some more detailed presentation of the subject of Luther's attitude to the Law, based on the sources which have recently been discovered. The very inadequate monograph by LOMMATZSCH (*Luthers Lehre vom ethisch religiösen Standpunkte aus, und mit besonderer Berücksichtigung seiner Theorie vom Gesetze*, 1879) is the latest work on this subject. We need equally badly a good presentation of Zwingli's and Calvin's doctrine of the Law.

PAGE 72, NOTE 10.—Romanticism has some dim notion of this; its protest against legalism constitutes its comparatively right element. But it does not see this aright; it asserts an immediacy which ignores the Law, whereas faith only knows immediacy by breaking through legalism. Therefore, as Luther says, the Law "is the Dialectic of the Gospel."

PAGE 73, NOTE 11.—But it is not only this legalistic ethic which is an undue simplification, but the immanental autonomistic conception of the Law as well, since it transfers the Good to the centre of the personality.

PAGE 74, NOTE 12.—The connexion between imprisonment within the Self and the tendency to think in abstractions, and the lack of reality in one's relation to others to which this gives rise, has been made clear by EBERHARD GRISEBACH in a most illuminating and original way, especially in his books: *Die Grenzen des Erziehers* and *Gegenwart*. In this he was preceded by MARTIN BUBER in his prophetic little book: *Ich und Du*; FERDINAND EBNER, again, preceded BUBER with his book: *Das Wort und die geistigen Realitäten*.

PAGE 74, NOTE 13.—Nowhere could it be more evident than at this point that LUTHER and KANT are so close to each other, and yet so remote from each other. Ultimately, with his doctrine of the "moral Revolution" KANT is completely Pelagian: "For, so long as the Moral Law commands 'Thou *shalt* become a better man,' the conclusion is inevitable 'that thou *canst*'." (*Religion innerhalb*, p. 53; Eng. translation, p. 60.) In spite of his theory of "radical evil" KANT completely overlooked—without understanding—Paul's and Luther's theory of the "enslaved will." On the other hand, it must be admitted that LUTHER in his fight for this truth often ended in denying formal freedom and fell into a false determinism.

PAGE 75, NOTE 14.—This is the meaning of the distinction which LUTHER makes between "the law in itself. . ." and the "law according to its office." (Cf. THEODOSIUS HARNACK: *Luthers Theologie*, Vol. I, p. 381.

PAGE 75, NOTE 15.—On this point cf. the important articles by GOGARTEN: "*Das Gesetz und seine Erfüllung durch Jesus Christus*" (*Zwischen den Zeiten* 1928, pp. 368 ff.) and "*Die religiöse Aufgabe der Gegenwart*," in REICHL's paper: *Der Leuchter*, 1931, pp. 56 ff.

PAGE 75, NOTE 16.—This interpretation of Good and Evil as the meaning of the Gospel message we owe to LUTHER. No other teacher, not even AUGUSTINE or CALVIN, approaches LUTHER in this respect. Yet for centuries *this* aspect of Luther's teaching has been concealed, even down to recent days; even those who called themselves "Lutheran" in a most emphatic manner did not know this. The only scholars of the nineteenth century who understood this side of Luther's thought were the two theologians of Dorpat: THEODOSIUS HARNACK (cf. for this section: *Die Theologie Luthers*, Vol. II; *Christus der Träger und Überwinder des Konflikts*, pp. 228 ff.) and—to some extent!—A. VON OETTINGEN. The reader will find the basis for this assertion in Chapter X.

PAGE 76, NOTE 17.—Luther's insistence on making the distinction between the Law and the Gospel quite clear, and his assertion that everything in Christian doctrine depends upon this, can only be understood from this point of view. Cf. my book, *Der Mittler*, especially pp. 253 ff. (Eng. translation, *The Mediator*, pp. 285 ff.).

PAGE 77, NOTE 18.—It has been recently maintained (TROELTSCH, TILLICH) that Luther's doctrine of Justification by Faith is no longer relevant for us at the present day, since our generation does not live under the burden of legalism, and the fear of the wrath of God; this statement entirely overlooks the fact that the language alone has altered; the fact remains. Even at the present day the interpretation of the Good (in Ethics) is absolutely legalistic—the "moral personality" of the modern consciousness simply means that the Good *can* be attained by the Self, independently—and that "sickness unto death" which KIERKEGAARD describes, or despair, is simply a form of fear of the wrath of God. TROELTSCH and TILLICH are right to this extent, however, that we ought to reformulate the old truth in new terms, in view of the new views in psychology. In this chapter I try to do this.

PAGE 77, NOTE 19.—R. BULTMANN has rendered us a distinct service by making plain the existential character of faith by means of his concept of the "understanding of existence" (*Seinverständnis*); only BULTMANN is in danger of neglecting, in a subjective manner, the *fides quae creditur*, for the *fides qua creditur*—the objective character of the Act and the Word of God, as it is explained in dogma, for the existential act of appropriation. When KIERKEGAARD ventures to make the statement: "the subject is the truth" (cf. my article: "*Die Botschaft Sören Kierkegaards,*" in the *Neue Schweizer Rundschau,* 1929) he always implies that the objective correlate of "existential" faith is the "paradox," the "foolishness of the Cross."

PAGE 77, NOTE 20.—For the dubious part played by the idea of "the new birth" in recent "positive" orthodox Lutheran theology, which is conditioned by placing the New Birth before Justification, cf. Chapter X.

PAGE 78, NOTE 21.—"This is namely the formula which describes the condition of the Self when despair has been completely banished: in relation to itself, and since it wishes to be itself, the Self bases its existence transparently upon the power which created it" (KIERKE-GAARD, *Krankheit zum Tode,* p. 11).

PAGE 79, NOTE 22.—With a daring expression LUTHER . . . calls *charitas: "contraria concupiscentia"* . . . (See WA. 7, 504, 8.)

PAGE 79, NOTE 23.—LUTHER, WA. 7, 36, and 37.

PAGE 79, NOTE 24.—This is what Luther means by saying that love does "what lies ready to hand," that the believer does "whatever comes nearest" (cf. WA. 6, 207). It has been too often overlooked that this simple thought is the centre of the Ethic of the Reformation. (See below what is said about *the Calling,* pp. 182 ff.)

PAGE 81, NOTE 25.—On this point cf. the excellent article by ALTHAUS: "*Gottes Gottheit als Sinn der Rechtfertigungslehre Luthers,*" in which, by means of copious extracts from Luther's own words (against HOLL), he proves that Luther's whole intention was to interpret the First Commandment in the light of Christ. Here it is precisely the union of the Divine Command with Divine Grace which is the decisive point.

NOTES ON CHAPTER IX

PAGE 83, NOTE 1.—The distinctive element in Christian Ethics is obscured if we take the view—as does, for instance, B. J. A. DORNER in his *System der Christlichen Sittenlehre*—in which love, as a "moral ideal," is set up as the main ethical principle, and Christ takes a second place as "the realization in principle of the moral ideal."

PAGE 84, NOTE 2.—This separation appeared very early in the development of Protestant ethics (cf. ALEX. SCHWEIZER's report on early Protestant ethics, in *Stud. u. Krit.* 1850), and it dominates the more recent theological ethics which does not start from the fact of the new Birth as an empirical fact, and is therefore not under the anthropocentric and psychologically subjective influence of Schleiermacher. It can also be seen in SCHLATTER's *Ethik*.

PAGE 84, NOTE 3.—The following passages may be given as illustrations of this point: *Phil. ii. 5 ff.*; *1 Cor. viii. 6*; *2 Cor. v. 19 ff.*; and *1 John* as a whole. But in reality the *Epistle to the Romans* does not constitute an exception, as we can see when we remember that in the first chapter, and particularly in the second chapter, the question of the capacity to be "righteous"—that is, the enquiry into the nature of the True Good—is stated as the themes of all the observations which follow, and that from the third chapter to the beginning of the eighth chapter the writer is especially concerned with the "basis of Ethics," as becomes evident in the sixth and seventh chapters. The powerful statements of Pauline "dogmatics" are placed within this context.

PAGE 84, NOTE 4.—In CALVIN's great work the moral reference and the ethical sentiment comes out clearly not only in the glorious, explicitly ethical chapters in the third book, but also in all the "dogmatic" explanations which precede them; whereas in the dogmatic theologians who succeeded Calvin—both among Lutherans and Reformed—this union is replaced by a terrible emphasis on theoretical dogmatics as an independent subject.

PAGE 85, NOTE 5.—The appallingly strong influence which SCHLEIERMACHER has exercised, even on "positive" theology, comes out most clearly in this fact, that almost all the Lutheran moralists of the nineteenth century, from HARLESS and FRANK down to REINHOLD SEEBERG, have succumbed to this psychological interpretation of the Doctrine of the New Birth, and accordingly have followed the descriptive type of ethics. (Cf. the next chapter.)

PAGE 89, NOTE 6.—The question of the possibility of the influence of the Gospel upon imbeciles is a more serious one; but this question belongs to the other question of the psychological limits of human rational capacity; even the imbecile is not simply devoid of reason.

PAGE 90, NOTE 7.—While this book was in the press there appeared an excellent book by the Dutch philosopher, J. C. FRANKEN, entitled: *Kritische Philosophie und dialektische Theologie*, which is by far the most thorough and careful examination of the relation between theology and critical philosophy that we possess. Here, too, there are developed the main features of a purely critical ethic (§ 390–420), which, so far as I can see, are in entire agreement with that which I have postulated as a critical ethic, particularly in making a clear distinction between the formal critical elements, and the rational content, in the system of Kant.

NOTES ON CHAPTER X

PAGE 99, NOTE 1.—Among the good Augustinian statements which were there placed explicitly under the *damnamus et abolemus*, there were such as these: *Non est vera legis obedientia quae fit sine caritate. Liberum arbitrium sine gratiae dei adjutorio non nisi ad peccandum valet.*

PAGE 99, NOTE 2.—Until recently the only available works on Luther's ethics were those of LOMMATZSCH, LUTHARDT, and THIEME; such progress has been made in Luther studies, however, that these works are now out of date. The only book in which this new knowledge is applied to the subject of ethics is O. DITTRICH's *Ethik Luthers*; in spite of the author's profound understanding of Luther, a more comprehensive study of this aspect of Luther's thought is still needed. The only existent monograph on Calvin, the *Ethik Calvins*, by LOBSTEIN, is extremely meagre. And we have practically nothing on the ethic of Zwingli.

PAGE 100, NOTE 3.—Those Lutherans who have not allowed themselves to be "put off" by ELERT (*Morphologie des Luthertums*)—the latest writer to glorify Lutheranism and to despise "the legalism of the Reformed Church"—and have made an independent examination of the current view, would do well to look up what the "legalistic" Calvin says about the Command to observe the Sabbath. (See below, Note 2 on Chapter XXVIII.) It is, of course, quite evident that it is impossible to expect an objective presentation of the ethic of Calvin from an historian of dogma like OTTO RITSCHL, who maintains that Calvin treats the doctrine of Justification by Faith as though it were a "foreign body" (*Dogmengeschichte des Protestantismus*, III) and, in spite of Luther, regards the doctrines of predestination and justification as mutually exclusive. The view that is held by some, that the doctrine of Calvin and Zwingli is "legalistic," proceeds not so much from a real knowledge of the doctrine in question, as from observation of the practice of Church discipline in the Reformed Church. But this is as characteristic of the thought of Calvin as the "Territorial Church" idea, with the "Prince" at the head, is characteristic of Luther. The view of Luther's "quietism," which has become widespread from the time of TROELTSCH, is, of course, equally wide of the mark. To-day, since HOLL's work has become known, it ought to be fairly evident that TROELTSCH understood Luther as little as he understood Calvin. But we can still detect traces of the conclusions which he drew from this distorted view of the Reformers in his *Soziallehren*. It is indubitable that a good deal of this was also due to MAX WEBER's confusion of primitive Calvinism with Puritanism; but it also seems probable that SCHNECKENBURGER's comparison of the different confessions (which suffers from the same complaint) has also contributed to bring about this result. The corrective administered to WEBER by WÜNSCH in his *Wirtschaftsethik* (pp. 331 and 336) is absolutely justified, but it is needed in other spheres as well; we are here dealing with a fundamental misinterpretation.

PAGE 101, NOTE 4.—HOLL, loc. cit., Vol. I, passim, Vol. III, p. 535. Holl, too, has perceived that Calvin is far closer to Luther than Melanchthon; almost all modern "Lutherans" are really followers of Melanchthon.

PAGE 101, NOTE 5.—The opinion which has been current from the time of SCHNECKENBURGER, namely, that Calvin regards "good works" as proofs of election, is only correct in so far as it refers to Reformed thinkers *after* Calvin. This is why there arose so soon that spirit of anxiety and scrupulosity which was so remote from Calvin himself, and also from Zwingli; it was this which—from the days of the *Casus conscientiae* of AMESIUS—made casuistry, founded on the Catholic model, such a favourite exercise. But we ought not to forget that the relation of AMESIUS, the Puritan, to CALVIN may be compared with that of JOHANN ARNDT, the early Pietist, to LUTHER. It is appalling to see how quickly degeneration from the "peak" of the Reformation sets in, even in ethics; even in BEZA and Á LASKO there is a different atmosphere. DANÄUS actually succeeds in writing a work on ethics without once mentioning Justification by Faith. But this disparity is scarcely greater than that between LUTHER and JOHANN GERHARD, quite apart from CALOV on the one side and ALSTED on the other.

PAGE 102, NOTE 6.—Naturally it is impossible to define exactly the boundary line between Neo-Protestantism and "*Vermittlungstheologie*" ("mediating theology"); we may call SCHLEIERMACHER the father of both types of thought. The most important ethical achievement of the more radical type of Neo-Protestantism are TROELTSCH's ethical works, especially his *Soziallehren*. They are actually valuable at the present time, since they raise problems of Christian ethics which have never before been stated so plainly and challengingly; these questions were raised first of all by NAUMANN, but TROELTSCH was the first to formulate them scientifically—I am thinking particularly of the weighty problems of the Law of Nature, and of the autonomy of the spheres of culture. I must confess that I have learned almost more from Ernst Troeltsch—whose theological views differ so widely from my own—than I have from moralists whose theological position was far nearer my own. From the third section of Book II onwards Troeltsch's formulation of the problem will continually occupy our attention. The other important representative of this group is WILHELM HERRMANN; his teaching on

594

ethics—in so far as it can be regarded as ethics at all, and not as a propaedeutic for dogmatics—does not go much beyond Kantian rationalism; the chief thing we can learn from him is the demand for a non-legalistic concreteness in the genuine expression of love, even though Herrmann's rationalism prevented him from fully perceiving the significance of this important truth. On the other hand, Herrmann is a typical representative of the "ethic of the disposition," which is so utterly out of harmony with the ethic of the Reformation and of Scripture.

PAGE 102, NOTE 7.—RICHARD ROTHE, in a certain sense, is the most "all-round" example of a Neo-Protestant, on account of the speculative character of his ethic, which is planned on a large scale, in so far as—at least in his *Ethik*—Christianity is wholly absorbed into his speculative system. From another point of view Rothe is a typical theologian of the *"Vermittlungs"* school, in so far as he has woven into an imposing whole, by means of a formal dialectical art, elements which are positively the most impossible to combine—the Gospel and speculative Idealism. In spite of everything, behind this unscriptural ethic there lies so much profoundly Christian insight, that, even for one who feels bound to take an opposite view, it constitutes an almost inexhaustible mine of ethical wisdom. The same may be said—although at some distance from Rothe—of the ethical teaching of HÄRING, in which good Würrtemberg "Biblicism" fights with Ritschlian-Kantian rationalism. In his charateristic conceptions of the Kingdom of God, of love, and of the revelation of Christ, he does not deny the Ritschlian side of his thought, with its concealed Rationalism hidden by a Scriptural veil; but here too, once more, so much genuine Christian life pervades the theological concepts that we might even class him with the "Biblicists" who are mentioned at the close of this chapter. The central importance of Justification by Faith is recognized by him still less than by SCHLATTER.

PAGE 102, NOTE 8.—We must always give HARLESS the credit for being the first to venture to develop ethics from the doctrine of justification, in the period of Idealism.

PAGE 103, NOTE 9.—It may indeed be correct to say that the phrase *"ordo salutis"* only appears in the eighteenth century (RGG, ·II, 1738), and indeed, as even HASE knew (*Huterus redivivus*, p. 293), under the influence of Pietism through CARPOV; but the *thing itself* has been there from the time of MELANCHTHON, the causal and temporal explanation of that which was still regarded as a paradoxical unity by the Reformers. On this point cf. HEIM: *Das Gewissheitsproblem*, Chapters 13 and 14.

PAGE 103, NOTE 10.—In saying this I do not deny the incontestable merit of VILMAR's moral theology. His doctrine of sin, for instance, in spite of the fact that it is blemished by some Pietistic errors, is an outstanding achievement; indeed, the whole work is not out of date, since it deals in such a powerfully simplified manner with the problems concerned, and with such realism.

PAGE 103, NOTE 11.—"The person who has experienced the New Birth is the subject of theological ethics" (*Theologische Ethik*, p. 84) —this principle of the "ethic" of VON HOFMANN is just as right, if understood in the Reformation sense, as it is wrong if understood in Schleiermacher's sense. VON HOFMANN, however, uses it fundamentally in SCHLEIERMACHER's sense, in the Pietistic sense, that is, that the New Birth is an empirical fact. The descriptive character of this "ethic" is the inevitable result of this point of view.

PAGE 104, NOTE 12.—The causal empiricism of FRANK may be made clearer by the following statements: "The New Birth is the *cause* of conversion (p. 68), faith is the *acceptance* of the working of the Spirit in the realm of the unconscious (p. 69), the becoming aware of the presence of God (in the soul) (p. 70), *the New Birth creates faith*" (p. 72). The descriptive character of the ethical system is based upon the fact that "Christian morality is a reality which has entered upon the supernatural path . . . exists within the Christian community, and in virtue of this reality can become an object of systematic knowledge" (p. 41). VON HOFMANN likewise defines ethics as "a *description* of Christian behaviour" (p. 71). The same conception predominates in the thought of R. SEEBERG, the last outcome of the school of Erlangen—even in his ethical system a strong tendency to Neo-Protestantism is evident. To him also, the New Birth is the *centre* of conversion (p. 68). The advantage of his ethic is his strong emphasis on and development of the ethic of society, a consideration of the formulation of the problem stated by TROELTSCH.

PAGE 105, NOTE 13.—The *Christliche Sittenlehre* of V. OETTINGEN is not even mentioned in the surveys of literature dealing with moral theology in the books of ALTHAUS and WÜNSCH; SEEBERG at least mentions it, although he makes no further use of it. This is all the more amazing because his "moral statistics" which were prepared as an introduction to ethics are, rightly, still greatly valued.

PAGE 106, NOTE 14.—In spite of this, however, I must not omit to acknowledge how much I owe to this work, in particular to BECK's lectures on Christian Ethics (published by LINDENMEYER). I cannot imagine my theological development without it, and I am still grateful to learn from it, in spite of the fact that I cannot accept the "genetic" tendency which colours the whole.

PAGE 106, NOTE 15.—It is more than a mere whim when SCHLATTER (p. 16) speaks, in all seriousness, of people who "do not need repentance"—yet directly afterwards (at the same place) he admits that even the "righteous" need to "turn round," as though "repentance" and "turning round" did not mean exactly the same things in German as in Greek. Rather there is here an inner uncertainty which runs right through Schlatter's ethical teaching. It is expressed in the fact that, on the one hand, he places two fundamental demands alongside of one another, love and justice, in order to get rid of the Reformers' idea of the *justitia civilis* which he abhors (p. 62); on the other hand, however (p. 120), he sets up love as the *one* duty which includes all others. Above all, however, his doctrine of the "righteousness of faith" is anything but Pauline (p. 80), and his continual attacks on the ethic of perfectionism are as little "evangelical" as his doctrine of "higher" and "lower" righteousness (p. 67). Even the distinction he draws between ethics and dogmatics (that "in our knowledge of God we are to note what we have become and perceive it in ourselves, whereas in ethics we are to note what we are becoming and what we want to make of ourselves" (p. 35)) ignores the specific element in Christian ethics just as much as the "indicative" ethic of the Lutherans which he rightly rejects (p. 39). But all this does not prevent me from being very grateful for this work by the Nestor of Biblical Theology.

PAGE 107, NOTE 16.—A welcome document from the new theological situation is the newly revised issue of the *Outline of Ethics* by ALTHAUS (*Grundriss der Ethik*) which in comparison with the earlier view shows clearly the change of direction, and which represents a serious attempt to take the theology of the Reformation seriously, also on its ethical side. But his sketchy manner of presentation, together with his effort to deal with all the burning questions of the present day, make it impossible for him to give that thorough explanation of the fundamental conceptions which are so much needed; this is why, in this form, it can scarcely have that penetrating influence which it deserves, from the point of view of its purpose.

BOOK II

PAGE 111, NOTE 1.—The "Word of God" is not only the principle of a Christian system of Dogmatics but also of a Christian system of Ethics. The ethical thinkers of early Calvinism, as against the Lutherans, were right in making the existence of the person who has experienced the New Birth into an ethical principle. Christian ethics must be just as "theocentric" as Christian dogmatics. This alone is in harmony with the meaning of the Bible, both in the Old and the New Testament. But the Lutherans, on their side, are right when they reject as "unevangelical legalism" the Calvinistic type of doctrine which deals with ethics from the point of view of law, as the exposition of the Decalogue. In point of fact, the ·law is no longer the supreme court of appeal for the Christian life, but the gracious *Word* of God, the gift of Christ, in so far as this also becomes a task, that is, in so far as the gracious Word becomes the Divine

Command. We owe it to KARL BARTH that in this matter also he has said the decisive thing in his lecture: "Das Halten der Gebote" (*Zw. d. Z.*, 1927, pp. 206 ff.). I gratefully admit that only through this conception of the "Divine Command"—which is used in the sense of Luther's exposition of the First Commandment in the "Sermon" on "Good Works"—my previous fundamental idea of Ethics (that is, that the will of God as Creator and Redeemer is the principle of Evangelical ethics) became quite clear to me. On this occasion, however, I believe that I am more faithful to the Reformed tradition, and I believe I see more clearly the specific and differentiated significance of the Law, of the "Commandments" of the Bible, for the perception of the Divine Command, than BARTH seems to do, judging by his previous expressions of opinion. Those who know what a malignant growth subjective anthropocentricism has been within the Lutheran theology of the last century, and how, on the other hand, late Calvinistic legalism (see above, p. 85) has absolutely prevented an evangelical interpretation of the Good, will be in a position to estimate at its true worth the significance of this re-orientation in Ethics—which is indeed not new, but is the real spirit of the Reformation.

NOTES ON CHAPTER XI

PAGE 114, NOTE 2.—This simple statement makes a clear distinction between the Christian ethic and every kind of rational ethic; it also differentiates between the Protestant and the Catholic views of Christian ethics. It is precisely this "intrinsic Good" which is taught by Thomism. The Thomist CATHREIN (op. cit., pp. 191 ff.) explicitly approves of the definition of the Good given by ARISTOTLE and by the modern Aristotelians TRENDELENBURG and ZELLER: "That is ethically good which is desirable and adapted to the rational nature of man according to his peculiar disposition, so that human nature, in so far as it is rational, serves as the primary standard of that which is ethically 'good'." CATHREIN supports this statement with numerous extracts from the writings of AQUINAS, which all come to this in the end: *quod autem conveniens est alicui est ei bonum*, p. 195. Hence knowledge of the Good is independent of knowledge of God, and "is presupposed by the latter" (p. 220). From the time of AQUINAS Thomism has rejected as erroneous the idea that "the essences of things have their ultimate ground in the free will of God" (p. 185).

PAGE 114, NOTE 3.—The Idea of the Good, as is well-known, is represented as the Creator or at least the Cause of the world, by PLATO (*Rep.*, 508 E). But the way in which Plato's thought oscillates between the Idea of the Good and that of divinity shows that here the limits of human thought have been reached, and Plato is obliged to "help himself out" with symbolism. The Idea, as such, does not provide a basis for reality: it merely provides what is necessary for thought. Reality is "contingent," beyond the Idea.

PAGE 114, NOTE 4.—*Rom. i. 18 ff.*: It is just as wrong to deny that Paul recognizes a natural pagan knowledge of God, as it is to equate this knowledge as continuous with the real knowledge of God, possessed by faith. *Rom. i.* 19 never provides an adequate basis (as SCHLATTER maintains it does) for a positive *theologia naturalis*; for the God whom man discovers for himself in nature—apart from Christ—is an idol. Out of the Divine conditional possibility sin makes something unreal. From the point of view of God the Creator, it may indeed be possible to know God in His Creation, but it is not possible to know Him from the point of view of man, who is a sinner. In this view I agree with KUHLMANN, *Theologia naturalis bei Philon und bei Paulus*. His remarks on the problem of natural theology in Paul are worthy of much consideration, although to me they are by no means new; in the terminology of HEIDEGGER they say what I have said already in a somewhat different way; but KUHLMANN makes his controversial statements against my views very easy by implying that I hold views which are not mine at all. For instance, when he argues against my observations on the *Theologia naturalis* (p. 135) he does so on the presupposition that I wish to assert a "continuity" between the natural and the Christian knowledge of God, whereas the case is exactly opposite. Actually, I am wholly in agreement with his statement: "Just as surely as something like God is perceived within human existence, so exclusively is this God always already a product of the εἶναι σοφός, and therefore not the real God, but an idol" (p. 53). But it is the problem of my *theologia naturalis* that man, when he does not know the real God, *necessarily* has idols, and KUHLMANN ignores this problem, since, like GRISE-BACH, he sees in the idea only the human factor, and not the Divine factor. Therefore to him the Law is *solely* the product of the sinful understanding of human nature, whereas for Paul it is precisely the self-manifestation of God—even though of the "wrathful" or "hidden" God. But the God of the Law is not—as KUHLMANN thinks—"an idol" (p. 52), but the real God—the God "whose Face is turned away," to use Luther's expression. The opinions KUHL-MANN advances about the views of GOGARTEN, BARTH, and BULT-MANN are superficial and incorrect; his view that CALVIN, in contradistinction to Luther, possesses a *theologia naturalis* is a pre-conception based upon ignorance which is held by many others. It is well-known that the opposite is the case: LUTHER makes far greater concessions to the *theologia naturalis* than CALVIN.

PAGE 115, NOTE 5.—It is of course true that according to Paul the works of the law are written in the hearts even of the heathen, and therefore the conscience—which is to be distinguished from the practical reason—can raise its voice in accusation. But the "works of the law" are very far from being the Good. Rather it is the view of Paul that the genuine Good can only be perceived through revelation, and indeed only through Christ. These two statements, which only apparently contradict one another, about the natural moral perception, we find also in the teaching of the Reformers. (See, for instance, WA. XXX, 192, 19 ff.) Faith, however, is the sole Good. (WA. 46, 667, 10 ff.) In the fact of idol worship, as well as of a natural moral law, LUTHER recognizes both the *Theologia* and the *Ethica rationalis*. Indeed, in the most decided way he recognizes the "law written in the heart" as the point of contact for the Word of God (WA. 16, 447, 26 ff). LUTHER lays particular emphasis upon the fact that the law written on the heart cannot be lost (*Briefe*, *De Wette*, 5, 150). But this does not mean that the Good is perceived; for the Good consists only in action in faith—whatever the action may be (cf. the classic passage, WA. 10, I, pp. 309 ff.). We find this twofold statement also in CALVIN, only he makes a sharper distinction between the law of God and the law of nature. For him too this implanted law is naturally the point of contact for the word of revelation.

PAGE 117, NOTE 6.—The humanitarian ethic seems possible, owing to the historical fact that the love which is based upon the Christian revelation can exist for a time as an idea even when severed from the ground on which it was reared. Mankind cannot easily forget the Christian idea of the love of one's neighbour, even when it has abandoned the Christian Faith. This idea, once it has been discovered—it was only "discovered" in connexion with revelation—now leads, to a certain extent, an independent existence. But once a generation of materialistic ideology has existed in the world, this idea, severed from its foundation, would become unintelligible, and would cease to be a current idea. The "Christian atheist"—I am thinking of Balzac's Mass of the atheist—may be a possibility, but it is always only a marginal possibility within a civilization in which Christianity is still a living force. Within such a civilization there may even be "unconscious Christianity" (ROTHE) but it cannot exist independently.

PAGE 118, NOTE 7.—These "Counsels" (cf. above, p. 97) define the sphere of spiritual perfection. Thus St. Thomas says: *consilium in optione ponitur ejus cui datur*, and the reason for following them is that thus: *homines melius et expeditius beatitudinem consequerentur* (*S.T.I.*, 2, qu. 108, 4). The doctrine of the Counsels belongs strictly to that of the "State of Perfection," that is, to the monastic life (2, 2 qu. 34 a). The attempt made by modern Catholics to interpret the Counsels as mere methods at the disposal of the one purpose of love (*caritas*), in order thus to preserve the unity of the Catholic idea of life, breaks down when it is realized that in monasticism the Counsels become a Divine Command, that the monastic life is regarded as the state of perfection, and that a particular saving value is attached to obedience to the Counsels. (Cf. the excellent article by SCHEEL, RGG¹, II, pars. 734–40, to which unfortunately there is nothing of equal value in RGG².)

PAGE 118, NOTE 8.—See above, the note on SCHELER's *Wertethik*. The apostle Paul certainly gives "counsels"; but he never connects them with the idea of a higher order of merit; his "counsels" are pedagogical instructions, which are not binding on the conscience, and also do not create a higher spiritual caste.

PAGE 119, NOTE 9.—The problem of adiaphorism is typical of a legalistic habit of thought—of a way of thinking, that is, which does not regard human conduct as a whole, but breaks it up into fragments. At one fell swoop Luther removed this problem (and many others as well) from Christian Ethics altogether, by means of his conception of "The Calling"; "whatever you are obliged to do in the calling given you by God" (he says in effect) "—even if this includes sleeping, resting, playing games, etc.—is right; anything else is wrong." The life of the Christian is a whole, and it is not composed of different isolated sections. With the rise of Pietism, however, the problem of adiaphorism once more entered into ethics, and has never since been dislodged.

PAGE 120, NOTE 10.—The fact that in the New Testament Divine rewards and punishments are clearly promised, and that this doctrine is taught by Jesus as well as by the Apostles, is not something of which the Christian needs to be ashamed, something which we must hide or modify as far as possible. The Gospel would not be the Word of God if things were otherwise. A God who could be mocked would not be a God. It would be quite different if this reward and this punishment were set up as the *motive* of conduct. The Gospel says "no" to this, in no uncertain voice. But this does not mean that we are to do the good "for its own sake." We are to do the good—for the sake of our neighbour, and this, again, for the sake of God. That the love of our neighbour, the total conception of the Good, is not based merely on our inclination or on our natural sympathy, but upon a higher necessity, namely, the Divine Will, is that which makes it "good"; everything else is "evil." "Good for its own sake" is merely an abstract, "watered-down" idea of this obedience to God. Behind this Idea of the Good there lies a dim conception of God, and behind this respect for "the Good" there lies an emasculated "fear of God."

NOTES ON CHAPTER XII

PAGE 123, NOTE 1.—An "interim-ethic" is the slogan adopted by the Eschatological School to describe the conditional and imperfect element—due to the limitations of time and historical development

—of the Ethic of the New Testament; in this expression, better than they knew, they have singled out the characteristic aspect of every genuine system of Christian Ethics. The ethical element is essentially an "interim-ethic," it is essentially provisional, existing "between the Fall and the Resurrection"; it is the way of life of the *homo viator*, who must make resolves, because things have not yet been decided. But the Christian ethic is the only system which—because it is aware of this fact of a decision still in the future (the Judgment)—treats this "interim" period seriously as a period for decision. (Cf. my article: *Das Einmalige und der Existenzcharakter*, in *Blätter fur deutsche Philosophie*, 1929.)

PAGE 123, NOTE 2.—It would be the task of a Christian philosophy of religion to prove that all that is called "Creation" and "Creator" outside the realm of thought influenced by the Bible, is something quite different from that which the Bible describes as "Creation." Not even the religion of the Parsees possesses, strictly speaking, the idea of a World Creator, because it does not possess the Old Testament conception of an unconditionally sovereign and absolutely personal God.

PAGE 124, NOTE 3.—ALBERT SCHWEITZER's *Kulturphilosophie*, and especially his work *Kultur und Ethik*, whose main conception is that of "reverence for life," is a curious and remarkable hybrid, composed of the pantheistic mystical attitude towards life, represented by GUYAU and FOURIER, on the one hand, and of KANTIAN humanistic personalism on the other. Schweitzer's own life-work is the most convincing proof of the inadequacy of this conception for the basis of an ethical system, since he, as a doctor, is obliged to kill a million forms of life in order to preserve *human* life, and knows that in so doing he is acting *ethically*.

PAGE 126, NOTE 4.—There is very little genuine conservative thought amongst us, even in so-called "conservative" circles; for even they have been infected with the ideology of rational Liberalism; the difference between them and the Radicals—apparently based on principle—is mostly a difference of interests; people are conservative because they profit by the existing order. The romantic tendency to glorify the past, an archaic habit of thought, the philosophy which believes in "protecting the home" is not genuinely conservative; it is rather retrospective aesthetic Idealism. Real conservative thought we find among the Reformers, and indeed in Zwingli and Calvin as well as in Luther; only in each one of them their conservatism has a different emphasis, according to their historical situation.

PAGE 127, NOTE 5.—The cause of this misunderstanding lay mainly in the fact that Luther did not make his language clear on this subject. Sometimes he would speak of belief in the Creator as the common good of all men, as the central conception of natural theology; at others he showed quite clearly, and indeed said so with marked emphasis, that he was aware the Christian alone knows what it means to believe in God as Creator.

PAGE 127, NOTE 6.—Cf. MAX WEBER: *Aufsätze zur Religionssoziologie*, II, pp. 146 ff. But the same phenomenon can be perceived within the history of Christianity itself. To the extent in which belief in the Creation recedes—under the influence of Neo-Platonist, pantheistic, mystical ideas—does the abandonment of "the world," asceticism, monasticism, and the hermit life, become usual.

PAGE 129, NOTE 7.—The renewal of the theory of "classes" by GOGARTEN has nothing to do with romantic patriarchalism, even though the actual expressions used may sound rather archaic. This theory is dealing with truths which are independent of definite sociological structures (which, as such, belong to the changing element in history), just as much as the fact that every human being is the child of one man and one woman. Even in the Soviet State that fact remains! This is what GOGARTEN means when he speaks of "classes."

NOTES ON CHAPTER XIII

PAGE 132, NOTE 1.—The idea of a twofold decree, which is incorrectly regarded as the central dogma of Reformed (Calvinistic) doctrine (whereas the only conception which merits this predicate is that of Election) is absolutely unscriptural, and can only be evolved out of *Romans ix* by wrong exegesis. It transforms the conception of divine freedom and of the possibility of being destroyed by God—which is only true existentially—into a metaphysical theory. For the rest the doctrine of Election must here be presupposed. All I can say here is this: that the most recent exposition of the doctrine of Election, which ELERT gives (*Morphologie des Luthertums*, pp. 108 ff.), according to which it is the duty of faith to overcome the idea of predestination, in no case represents LUTHER's views, however much this exposition may be in accordance with "Lutheranism."

PAGE 133, NOTE 2.—Our relation to God and to our neighbour cannot simply be indicated by an "end." The "two Tables" of the Decalogue are not exactly the same in character, as they are conceived in the ethical theory of Catholicism—in which, however, both Calvinistic and Lutheran moralists have often concurred. The First Commandment does not simply "include" the others, but it is the *meaning* and the *basis* of the others. To speak of "duties towards God *and* duties towards my neighbour" means to fall back into a "ritual" interpretation of our relation with God, which has been overcome by the Gospel. Consequently the basis is not found in the "and"-relation.

PAGE 133, NOTE 3.—To say the least, it is misleading, when

GOGARTEN applies this idea in such a way that it seems as though faith only arises "from contact with our neighbour." The God-man—Christ—is not our neighbour, but One through whom alone, strictly speaking, we gain "neighbours," One through whom we are able to perceive our neighbour as such. Therefore in the Two-fold Commandment of Jesus, the love of God remains the First Commandment, while the love of our neighbour springs from it as the Second Commandment. But man's relation to God is not ethical, but it is the basis of Ethics, hence, in principle, it does not occupy time, it does not take up any space alongside of service to mankind; otherwise we would have to retire to the cloister, or to reproach ourselves for not making sufficient space to give the greater part of our time to the special activity of prayer. This kind of "religion" has been overcome by Christ.

PAGE 134, NOTE 4.—The Thomistic, official Catholic ethical theory also reveals its oscillation between Aristotle and Augustine in the fact that it cannot come to a final decision, in its differentiation of the three criteria of the Good (object, circumstances, end), about what it is which constitutes the Good, love, or the objective rightness of the action (in the sense of the principle of adaptation). At first the objective point of view is placed absolutely in the foreground, but afterwards love is then affirmed as the source of all good. (Cf. MAUSBACH, op. cit., pp. 154 ff. with p. 207.) This too is the direct result of the distinction between "natural" and "supernatural" virtues, to which love belongs. The second storey cannot be at the same time the basis of the lower storey!

PAGE 134, NOTE 5.—CATHREIN: God must "make it possible for every human being, in the normal conditions of community, to be able to deduce from these general principles—by means of his own reflection and instruction from without—all necessary or important rules of life (loc. cit., I, p. 456). Thus by the process of simple logical subsumption we proceed to deal with the most particular cases. But it would be an error to think that this is only customary in Catholic morality; as a rule Protestant Ethics is also casuistical, just because it is legalistic; only as a rule its casuistry does not go so far as Catholic casuistry. It is also dilettante in character, whereas in this respect the Catholic system has certainly become masterly. The necessary other side of casuistry is Probabilism, which has therefore been developed by the Jesuits alongside of casuistry.

There is also a justifiable Protestant casuistry, that of the true pastor and "shepherd of souls"; but it has only a preparatory, never a binding value.

PAGE 137, NOTE 6.—From the point of view of the history of religion the Decalogue—and especially in view of its different tradition—cannot be distinguished from the mass of Old Testament laws for the regulation of worship and law, and to this extent Luther is right, when he says that anyone who observes one of the laws of Moses, because it is a law of Moses, is under the obligation to observe them all, and that means, to become a Jew. But it is well known that Luther also had another view of the Decalogue, namely, as the God-given exposition of the One Commandment, and thus not as a system, although applicable to all the essential circumstances of life.

NOTES ON CHAPTER XIV

PAGE 143, NOTE 1.—GOGARTEN: *Wider die Ächtung der Autorität.* Unfortunately, Gogarten does not make it clear where the *limitation* of authority comes in, and he thus develops a conservatism which completely leaves out man's relation to the order of redemption.

PAGE 143, NOTE 2.—See WA. 40, I, pp. 176 ff.

PAGE 143, NOTE 3.—In the dogmatics of orthodoxy a certain confusion of thought prevails with reference to the terms used, since some reckon the *usus pedagogicus* with the *usus politicus*, others with the *elenchticus*.

PAGE 145, NOTE 4.—That is LUTHER's discovery, and after him, of KANT (in his doctrine of Radical Evil) and KIERKEGAARD. This truth destroys the Thomist conception of Ethics—which sums up the Good as a whole, in view of particular virtues, and particular acts—and unhinges the whole system.

PAGE 148, NOTE 5.—Above all, it is CALVIN's concern that this should not be overlooked, as opposed to a visionary enthusiasm of faith which breaks out in Luther now and again, and has become a principle in modern Lutheranism.

PAGE 149, NOTE 6.—SEEBERG is certainly right in saying that "in LUTHER's teaching the threefold use of the law is assumed" (*Dogmengeschichte*, IV, I, pp. 207); but we only need to glance at his *Commentary on Galatians* to perceive how one-sidedly Luther emphasizes the *usus secundus*, and how little use he makes of the *usus tertius*. The educationalist and Church-builder, CALVIN, on this point corrected LUTHER from the outset, although certainly on his part he did not do this without sailing very near the wind in the dangerous matter of legalism.

NOTES ON CHAPTER XV

PAGE 152, NOTE 1.—Most moralists are content to explain the principles of the Good on the one hand, and to outline an ideal picture of the wise or the Good on the other. The human being who is entangled in evil they ignore altogether. KANT's treatment of the problem of evil is an exception; SCHLEIERMACHER, indeed, goes so far as to remove the problem of evil from ethics altogether.

PAGE 152, NOTE 2.—Pantheistic Romanticism has an anthropology of its own, to this extent, at least in that it regards the world-antitheses as reflected in the psycho-physical nature of man; therefore it emphasizes chiefly the organic connexion between body and soul, and the functions in which this connexion is particularly evident: feeling, *Eros*, instinct, and intuition. In its view ethics is replaced by either mystical or aesthetic contemplation as the victory over the contradiction between nature and spirit.

PAGE 153, NOTE 3.—Cf. KUHLMANN: *Die theologia naturalis*, pp. 39 ff., where he uses—very aptly—GOGARTEN's doctrine of Creation for the interpretation of *Romans i. 19 ff.*; without otherwise alluding to Gogarten. The Gnostic idea is to be rejected that the existence of individuality is a result of sin (pp. 40 and 50).

PAGE 153, NOTE 4.—The fresh formulation of the doctrine of Original Sin which KIERKEGAARD has attempted in his work: *Begriff der Angst*, is too individualistic to be satisfactory: KANT's analysis of radical evil undoubtedly comes nearer to the Christian conception of Original Sin. JULIUS MÜLLER's attempt (influenced by the thought of SCHELLING) to explain the Fall by means of a theory of a prehistoric original "Fall of Man," is speculative; on the other hand, SCHLATTER's abandonment of all attempts to construct any doctrine of Original Sin or of the Fall is a far too summary empiricism. HIRSCH's theory (in his *Schöpfung und Sünde in der natürlich geschichtlichen Wirklichkeit des einzelnen Menschen*, 1931): "Creation and sin are one and the same (!), regarded from two points of view, both springing out of man's relation to God, which require each other, and at the same time are opposed to each other" (p. 33). This definition, as it is expressed in this passage, is a Gnostic error. It is not "creation" and "sin" which are the same, but created and sinful existence are indissolubly connected in "personal union"; otherwise God would be the Author of Sin. We cannot go further than the myth of the Fall, since it alone expresses contemporaneously: the priority of the Creation over against sin, the individual element of guilt, and the historical element of the causal and representative unity of the race; only we must recognize and freely admit that the fact that we cannot go beyond this myth suggests the limitations of our knowledge.

PAGE 154, NOTE 5.—Only one who has grasped the actuality of the Self can understand what it means that man does not possess this "Self" in himself, but in the Word of God; the "substance" of man as man is actually not "substance" at all, but: *relationship with God*; therefore it is either Grace or Sin. On this point, cf. the instructive work of DIETRICH BONHOEFFER: *Akt und Sein*, 1931.

PAGE 156, NOTE 6.—On this point, cf. the informing new studies on *Conscience* by STOKER (*Das Gewissen*, 1925) and GÜNTER JACOB (*Der Gewissensbegriff in der Theologie Luthers*, 1929), and also KÄHLER's presentation of the subject, which has never yet been surpassed (*Das*

Gewissen, 1878, and the article on "Gewissen" in HAUCK's *Realencyclo-pädie*, 3).

PAGE 156, NOTE 7.—We are indebted to KÄHLER for the redis-covery of the genuine phenomenon of conscience; for he has dis-entangled it from the rationalistic interpretations of ancient popular philosophy; this process has been carried further by STOKER's work and its main thesis is confirmed (very amply) by the examination of Luther's conception of conscience by JACOB—unfortunately too much influenced by the terminology of HEIDEGGER.

PAGE 156, NOTE 8.—This is the view of conscience in Catholic moral philosophy. It is due to its rationalistic conception of ethics that it holds "that we have to seek for conscience in the intelli-gence." "The conscience draws its conclusions in the same way that the judge comes to his. The judge applies the general laws to a concrete case, or he subsumes actions under a general law. It is thus that the intellect deals with the conscience. For instance, it reasons like this: "What you wish to say, is a lie; but lies are forbidden; then you must not say what you want to say" (CATHREIN, op. cit., I, p. 481).

PAGE 156, NOTE 9.—We have no right to read any mysterious religious meaning into the Greek word συν-είδησις (con-scientia). The συν never refers to God; first of all, it referred to other human beings who shared this knowledge; later it referred to a human subject divided into two parts: one which instructs, and one which is instructed; συν-είδησις ought to be translated as "self-conscious-ness." This has been proved once for all by KÄHLER's researches. Once, certainly, in the New Testament the idea of joint-knowledge with God appears in the remarkable conjunction: συνείδησις θεοῦ, but this qualification of meaning is not due to the συνείδησις itself, but to faith. Otherwise we must grant that KÄHLER is right in maintaining that the conception of conscience is not central to the thought of the New Testament, and that it is not a genuinely Scriptural idea, but that it is a connective idea taken over from Hellenism. This has constantly been confirmed by later research.

PAGE 157, NOTE 10.—The usual distinction between the "judg-ing" and the "anticipatory" conscience takes no account of the depth of the phenomenon, nor of the relation between law and conscience. In modern terminology the one word "conscience" and cognate words are used to cover a great variety of conceptions.

PAGE 157, NOTE 11.—See LUTHER: WA. XIX, 222, 25. (Quoted by JACOB, p. 29.)

PAGE 158, NOTE 12.—This is HIRSCH's point of view in his dis-cussion with GOGARTEN (*Zwischen den Zeiten*, 1923, p. 56), and also HOLL's view in his book on Luther, and in his reply to GOGARTEN (*Christliche Welt*, 1934, pp. 307 ff.). That HOLL has described Luther's conception of conscience wholly in Kantian terms has been fully proved by JACOB's researches, even to those who had not already been enlightened by the work of THEODOSIUS HARNACK. If Luther had really meant what Holl thinks he did by conscience—"the sense of obligation, receptivity for the sense of ought," then Luther's talk about the conscience as the enemy of God would be utter nonsense. Particularly in those ways of thinking which at first horrify us (as THEODOSIUS HARNACK makes clear) does the real Luther come out.

PAGE 159, NOTE 13.—It is incontestable that the Lutherans of last century—here even v. OETTINGEN is no exception—had a magical conception of the New Birth. To presuppose the germ of faith in the baptized infant means emptying the concept of faith of all meaning. On the other hand, it is a mistake to suppose that to deny this magical effect is to deny "baptismal grace" altogether; only the historical interpretation has replaced the magical one: as soon as faith exists we know that we are one with the person who was baptized at a particular time; we know that the covenant word which was then spoken was the prevenient word of Divine Grace, which preceded our present situation.

PAGE 161, NOTE 14.—Naturally, by this I do not mean anything in the nature of "synergism"; synergism doubtless intends to stress the personal character of the act of appropriation, but it does not understand the comprehensive character of grace. It does not understand that it is due to grace that we can thus respond to God. On the other hand, a doctrine of grace which obscures this personal element by the use of naturalistic images of appropriation for the sake of the objectivity of grace is just as incorrect; this has often been done by modern Lutherans, but not by Luther himself. Luther, indeed, also uses naturalistic images, as also does the New Testament, but he uses personal expressions at the same time; above all, in Luther's teaching there is no idea of a New Birth which precedes faith.

NOTES ON CHAPTER XVI

PAGE 165, NOTE 1.—This individualistic and at the same time naturalistic conception of virtue prevails absolutely in the Thomist ethic, so far as natural virtues are concerned; it only partially prevails where the infused supernatural or theological virtues are concerned; it is at this point that St. Thomas's dependence upon ARISTOTLE and his anthropology comes out most clearly. The Aristotelian ethic is the ethic of the active, creative human being, of the man therefore who can be perfect "in himself," in so far as "material" is given to him which he is "capable" of moulding. In accordance with this point of view St. Thomas also defines virtue as *habitus* and *bona qualitas*, and indeed as self-acquired (in contradistinction from the "infused" supernatural virtues), as *acquisita*, gained by activity as the habit of being active (St. Thomas, II, I, *qu.* 55 and 63). The Augustinian conception of virtue as God-given, by being limited to the theological virtues, is explicitly rejected, whereby the theological virtues do not make natural virtue really good, but only fit for the attainment of the supernatural goal (*qu.* 62). This Aristotelian-Thomistic conception of virtue then became that of the Enlightenment.

Page 165, Note 2.—I have already (in Note 7 on Chapter XI and in Note 4 on Chapter XIII) pointed out the contradiction which exists within the Thomist Ethic between the system of the natural virtues and the three "theological" virtues. On the one hand, St. Thomas maintains that, in the last resort, love alone makes an action really good, while on the other hand a system of individual virtues—based on the Aristotelian cardinal virtues—is developed, which do not become real "virtues" through love alone, but which have an independent existence; if this were not so, the whole of this sub-structure would be rendered insecure; or, to put it more exactly, it would become, what it is in the teaching of the Reformers, merely the doctrine of the *justitia civilis.* But the Catholic Church may not teach this. Therefore she is obliged to assert the existence of a number of independent, real virtues, of which it is possible to possess some and not others.

Page 166, Note 3.—The theory of "qualities" plays as disastrous a part in our view of ethics as the theory of "faculty" or "capacity" (German: *Vermögen*) does in psychology; for instance, in pedagogy there is nothing so disastrous as to hold a person responsible for his "qualities." We only have "qualities" in so far as we are not personal. To regard a person in the light of his "qualities" means that we do not take him seriously as a person.

NOTES ON CHAPTER XVII

Page 171, Note 1.—The theory of the ἐξαγωγή (ἐξάγειν ἑαυτὸν τοῦ βίου) is characteristic of Stoicism as a whole, not only theoretically, but in many cases also practically—*Patet exitus.* (Cf. Zeller III, I, pp. 305 ff.)

Page 172, Note 2.—It is also possible to say that Rationalism rejects the idea of individuality, since it does not regard it as an essential element in human nature. Mysticism, however, goes further still. It not only denies individuality as "being different," but also in the sense of "being another."

Page 176, Note 3.—Among all the Christian moralists of last century v. Oettingen alone regarded this idea as regulative for ethics as a whole, and not only, like the rest, "in its own place" within the doctrine of the Church. "In opposition to all 'spiritualistic' personal ethics and all materialistic social physics the object peculiar to moral philosophy makes it necessary to describe and to treat it as a social ethic" (p. 79); "it always leads us back to the idea of community which determines all redeemed life, to Christendom as the redeemed community, united, by faith in Redemption, to the Church as the present form of the Kingdom of God on earth, to the organism of humanity, as one which is to be finally perfected by the laws of the Christian redeemed life" (p. 258).

PAGE 177, NOTE 4.—With this compare my remarks in Chapter XXVII. When HIRSCH (*Schöpfung und Sunde*, p. 9) lays stress on the idea of KIERKEGAARD of the individual over against all collective groups, that is, especially to-day, quite right and just; but when he goes on to speak of the individual as he does, it is evident that, still more than KIERKEGAARD, he fails to perceive that this "individual" can only come into existence "in the Church"; throughout this whole work by HIRSCH the fact that he starts from FICHTE's point of view is only too evident.

NOTES ON CHAPTER XVIII

PAGE 180, NOTE 1.—To some extent SCHLATTER is right in opposing this to a certain way of applying the idea of the Reformation. It must be admitted that this also hits a certain kind of dialectical theology, and I can only accept what HIRSCH—writing critically against both sides—says: "What has previously been brought against the movement of the Dialectical Theology has mostly been at the expense of a weakening or limitation of the Reformation judgment on man—by an approximation to the decided rejection of the Reformation view by ADOLF SCHLATTER, who finds in man some goodness, and some sinfulness, and who bases the necessity of faith in forgiveness on the total rejection of the doer even of individual sins. Now this standpoint of SCHLATTER seems to me to be in opposition to that deeper view of man and of life, and is therefore an impossibility for one who has discovered within himself the unfathomable depths of human life" (p. 98). The only curious thing is that HIRSCH has not noticed that that "movement," that is, that failure to recognize the relative distinctions between good and evil, has not been approved or allowed to pass uncontested either by BARTH or by any other leading theologians of the Dialectical School.

PAGE 180, NOTE 2.—We cannot take too seriously SCHLATTER's unfounded assertion that the theology of the Reformation has "not improved, but rather intensified" the old conflict between Law and the Counsels; for Schlatter has not taken much trouble to understand what he is contesting. Otherwise he would have been obliged to notice that his distinction between justice and love, while holding firmly, at the same time, to the Scriptural statement that love is the fulfilling of *all* law, can only mean exactly what the

Reformers teach. Life in society demands a kind of conduct which, in its character, is on a lower level than love, just as plainly as the merely calculated delimitation of claims is lower than sacrifice. But this kind of behaviour is required by the very fact of consideration for society, that is, by the motive of love. Simply to place justice and love side by side, as Schlatter does, introduces a disastrous dualism into ethics, and makes Schlatter contradict his own statement, a statement which is wholly in line with the New Testament, that love—and love alone—is the fulfilling of the law.

The dualism of the Catholic ethic is quite different. It recognizes that which the moralists of the Reformation call the *justitia civilis*, as something really good, and it has then to add something specific, from outside the realm of ethics for the theological virtues and for the Counsels—works of supererogation and the acquirement of the supernatural good of salvation. As I have already said, this means that among the Aristotelians the tendency prevails to regard this second element as outside the sphere of ethics, while the Augustinians take the opposite view and regard the substructure merely as the *justitia civilis*, as an ethic in itself inadequate—in so doing, however, they come into conflict with the official Church doctrine.

PAGE 182, NOTE 3.—The immanental moral principle of Thomism, the definition of the Good by means of the idea of "adaptation" is not wholly wrong, but only as an ultimate principle. Obedience to God's will includes both the objective, concrete aspect and the subjective and personal aspect of conduct. God wants from us action which is in accordance with actual facts; but there are two mistakes which may here occur: the view that from the standpoint of reason we can absolutely define the right and relevant conduct, and, secondly, that conduct which is in accordance with actual facts makes the action, as such, good.

PAGE 182, NOTE 4.—The Catholic ethic uses the phrase "equalizing justice" for that which is called "arithmetical" by Aristotle: the equal counter-achievement; and it speaks of "distributive justice" where Aristotle uses the term "geometrical," which acts in a proportioned manner in accordance with certain definite claims (cf., for instance, CATHREIN, I, pp. 360 ff.; ARISTOTLE: *Nicomachean Ethics*, 1131 ff.). In both cases, however, the justice is rational, and the mathematical method of calculation is presupposed. But all these moralists skate lightly over this fact, since there is no standard in existence by which we could settle what *is owing* to each one.

NOTES ON CHAPTER XIX

PAGE 189, NOTE 1.—This does not mean that there is no legitimate Christian cultus or "Divine Service," but that this cultus no longer has any sacerdotal significance; to us the Church is no longer *templum*, a τέμενος. "Divine Service" is, as the Reformed Church in Holland puts it so well: "Exercises in Divine Service." On this, see Chapter XXVIII, p. 314.

PAGE 189, NOTE 2.—An individual ethic is only possible within a system controlled by the thought of Aristotle; within the sphere of Protestantism it can only exist as the result of a subjective misunderstanding of the doctrine of the New Birth. To be "born anew" means, from the very outset, to be placed within the community of the Kingdom of God. The New Testament speaks thus of the New Birth (*John iii. 3; 1 Peter i. 3; i. 23*). The new existence of the Christian can only be described as a co-existence (with others). The germ of truth contained in the fatal distinction between an individual and a social ethic is the (certainly necessary) distinction between an ethic concerned with persons and one which is concerned with society as a whole. There is a distinct difference between my behaviour towards "my neighbour," which is direct, and that which comes indirectly through an "order," whether it be that of the family, the State, or the Calling. The exact distinction between the two takes place by means of reflection on "the third." (See Note 5 on Chapter XXV.)

PAGE 192, NOTE 3.—The RITSCHLIAN conception of the Kingdom of God is just as fully influenced by immanental ideas of History as of Reason; it is the Kantian rational idea of humanity, combined with the idea of "progress" contained in the Idealistic philosophy of history. But this is the conception of the Kingdom of God which prevails throughout the greater part of the Protestant West.

PAGE 194, NOTE 4.—The reaction against Idealism visible in GOGARTEN and GRISEBACH, and recently also in HEIM, which sees in ideas *nothing* but self-idolatry, seems to me to have overshot the mark. The Idea should be classed with the Law, and has the same dignity and the same ambiguity as the latter. In spite of ADOLF SCHLATTER, in every system of theological thought—(even in Schlatter's own system)—the Idea is the inevitable form, apart from which all "observation" would simply register a wild chaotic confusion. The Idea is also the formative principle of all civilization —even of a so-called Christian civilization. See below the section on the *Kulturgemeinschaft* (Community of Culture or Civilization), especially p. 509.

PAGE 195, NOTE 5.—The modern view of the world presented by natural science does not in the least alter this Scriptural theological idea; for even the present-day scientist cannot deny that man is the only creature we know who carries on scientific investigation; this means (or to put it more exactly—by means of the existence of the subject determined by *humanitas*—as already Kant has seen in his critique of the power of judgment) inevitably, that we cannot do otherwise than look at all creatures as we look at man.

PAGE 196, NOTE 6.—The *Societas Jesu* has no reason to complain

—as they so often do—that this statement, in its bad sense, is so often ascribed to their moralists; for what else can the following statement of BUSENBAUM's mean if not this? *cum finis est licitus etiam media sunt licita?* (*Medulla theologiae moralis,* in the edition lying before me, 1719, p. 368). And the use which has been made of this statement in the practice of the Jesuits, which dominates their casuistry, is quite well known.

On the other hand, should not Protestant theology do the same, instead of wishing only to approve of the use of means good in themselves? What does this mean in view of the fact that this theology has always justified war? Is killing a method "good in itself"? In the 4th section of this book I try to give a better answer to this question, one which does not leave the door open to clerical and theocratic misuse, nor feign an innocence which no real action in the world ever possessed.

NOTES ON CHAPTER XX

PAGE 199, NOTE 1.—Cf. HOLL: *Die Geschichte des Wortes Beruf* (*Ges. Aufs.,* III, pp. 189 ff.) where the proof is adduced that in the Middle Ages the word *vocatio* was applied first of all, and mainly to monasticism, but was indeed later applied to those living in the world, presupposing always the advantage of the clerical caste. This medieval idea of "classes" was only broken down by Luther's doctrine of the priesthood of all believers, and from 1522 onwards Luther uses the German word "Beruf" (calling) as the most pregnant expression of the new view of life in the world. MAX WEBER has written the history of the secularization of this idea: *Die Berufsethik des asketischen Protestantismus, in Ges. Aufs. z. Rel. Soz.,* I, pp. 84 ff.

PAGE 200, NOTE 2.—Of course this does not mean that we are to forget the past in the psychological sense of pushing it back into the unconscious; we can never come to terms with the present, indeed we can never be *wholly* present, if we have not at the same time absorbed our past.

PAGE 202, NOTE 3.—FRIEDRICH NAUMANN and ERNST TROELTSCH have rendered a great service by laying such emphasis, for the first time, upon the weighty problem of Christian Ethics which lies behind the idea of compromise. The greater part of the third and fourth sections of this book is an attempt to answer the question asked by them. Their own reply could not be adequate, since it lacked the necessary basis of a Christian ethic: insight into the meaning of the doctrine of Justification. But although their conception of compromise is unsatisfactory as a *solution* of the problem, it has been most fruitful as a *question.* Before their time Christian Ethics—Catholic as well as Protestant—had carried on an undignified "ostrich"-policy and a dishonest game of Hide and Seek, and this theoretical situation was exactly matched by practice. The course of affairs in the world was simply neglected; from the ethical point of view it was left to "the experts" as a more or less irrelevant technical matter, and the vast social upheavals which took place—like the rise of Capitalism, for instance—were simply accepted as Destiny. Before NAUMANN and TROELTSCH, A. v. OETTINGEN alone seriously tried to grasp the facts as they were (in his *Moralstatistik*), and to give the principles of a realistic ethic of society (in his *Sitten-lehre*). The utter lack of vision of his contemporaries and predecessors in the study of Ethics is, in this respect, indescribable. In this connection, however, the name of WICHERN ought not to be omitted. The dream which haunted his mind was nothing less than a social policy born out of the Spirit of the Gospel, in the widest sense of the word. But in order to make this idea fruitful a theological basis of principle was required, which he did not himself possess, and was unable to acquire from anyone else. This is more or less true also of STOECKER, whereas the members of the (later) movement of Religious Socialism, although they had such a basis, had one of such a kind that it was unable to combine realism with Scriptural thought; their Ethic was either a sectarian ethic combined with rationalism or—as in the group led by TILLICH—it is only Hegelian-ism with a veneer of Christianity.

PAGE 202, NOTE 4.—This motto may well have been characteristic of the early Baptist movement, in so far as—to use the language of TROELTSCH—it existed as "an aggressive sect." It also describes a certain type of Religious Socialism. At the same time, I must say plainly that the language generally used by Religious Socialism leaves a great deal to be desired in recognition of the profound contradictions within this complex. In the last resort what has a man like TILLICH to do with men like RAGAZ and KUTTER in their earlier years? What has the "Social Gospel" movement in America to do with the European one? It is amazing that even WUNSCH, who might well know better, does the same, as though Religious Socialism were mainly a German affair, whereas obviously that is what it is *not*, and the influence which up to the present it has exerted in Germany is quite insignificant compared with its internal and external influence in other countries. I think it is fitting to speak here of Religious Socialism, because all my work in these sections is dealing just as much with it as with Naumann's problem of Compromise.

PAGE 207, NOTE 5.—Cf. MAX WEBER's well-known study: *Die protestantische Ethik und der Geist des Kapitalismus* (English translation: *The Protestant Ethic and the Spirit of Capitalism*. Translation by TAL-COTT PARSONS—Allen & Unwin, 1930): *Die Protestantischen Sekten und der Geist des Kapitalismus in Ges. Aufs. z. Rel. Soz.*, I, pp. 207-36.

NOTES ON CHAPTER XXI

PAGE 209, NOTE 1.—Even in ethics it is possible to distinguish between a "formal" and a "material" principle. The fact that the "biological" ethic of modern times—mainly since the days of SPENCER—is materially related to life, gives it a vitality and a concreteness which, on the whole, distinguishes it advantageously from the ethic of Idealism. We ought not to forget that MARX as well as NIETZSCHE was influenced by this English ethical theory, and that the later realistic personal psychology, which for its part can mean so much for a truly concrete ethic, likewise has one of its roots in biology (think of BERGSON and SCHELER, for instance).

PAGE 212, NOTE 2.—By this I do not mean that the State has nothing to do with the order of creation (see below, pp. 444 ff.), but that in its definite historical form, as a power of coercion, it can only be understood in view of sin.

PAGE 213, NOTE 3.—By these remarks I intend to show how my own view differs from that of my theological friends, K. BARTH on the one hand, and F. GOGARTEN upon the other. This difference does not only occur at this point, but, as I believe, it runs right through this whole work on ethics. We may define the differences between the two, which are often rather painful in their expression, by saying that in BARTH Creation comes off badly compared with Redemption, and in GOGARTEN Redemption comes off badly compared with Creation. BARTH is certainly right—(as against SCHLATTER, let us say)—in rejecting the identification of the existing order with the Creation, and in protesting against the high-sounding language concerning the Divine order of creation so often used by orthodox Calvinists: he is also right when, in connexion with the doctrine of the *imago Dei*, he warns us against a reaction in the direction of the Catholic modification of the doctrine of Original Sin (cf. especially his work: *Der Heilige Geist und das christliche Leben*, pp. 48–55). But when BARTH remarks, incidentally, "I know, of course . . . of definite orders, which, at this moment, are valid for me, and show me what is the Divinely Created order" (p. 49), in this very confession, even with these justifiable limitations, there lies much more than BARTH will admit, a reality to which he ought to pay far more attention than he does at present. We do not know the Creator through the world, but through revelation; this thesis is right, and it is good Protestant theology. But through Christ we also know the Creator in the world—this statement, which forms the content of the early chapters of CALVIN's *Institutes*, Barth ignores entirely. The fact that the Creation is obscured by sin ought not to make us forget that in spite of this it is GOD's Creation, and that in spite of sin it bears traces of the Glory of the Creator. Those moralists who ignore these "hints" or "suggestions," tend to develop an ethic which leads either to fanaticism or to sterility.

On the other hand, however, it is certainly true that GOGARTEN, in his justifiable emphasis upon the idea of Creation, and the orders of creation, for ethics, takes too little account of the fact that the Creation is hidden, and of the relation of the believer to the coming Kingdom of God, so that his ideas, especially in their crude presentation by FRAU M. V. TILING, issue in a curiously rigid conservatism.

Gogarten is right of course when he says that in the ethical problem we are concerned with practical ("political") decisions:. "for which of the two or three or more possibilities which are open to us at any particular time are we to decide" (*Wider die Ächtung der Autorität*, p. 13), but to argue that this decision must in some way or another be for the existing order and against revolution, if it is to be in accordance with faith, can only be maintained if we overlook the fact that the Christian *Ethos* contains a revolutionary element—that is, the fact that the Christian belongs to a new world—which must also work itself out in practice. These examples may be at the same time an indication that practical moral decisions of far-reaching significance depend on the right relation between the Ethos and Creation and Redemption.

PAGE 215, NOTE 4.—This charge might well be brought against GOGARTEN's over-emphasis upon the doctrine of authority, and of obedience within the secular calling (*Die Schuld der Kirche; Wider die Ächtung der Autorität*). Certainly, to-day in particular, it is the duty of the Church to reiterate with vigour these things which "even the pagan" can know, because so much that the natural man might very well know has been concealed by our ideologies, and has been lost for the thought of our own day; the *sensus communis* needs to be rediscovered, and to this task theology is called as well as philosophy (HEIDEGGER, GRISEBACH). But the Church must not allow even the suspicion of the idea to arise that this is her specific mission, not even in the sphere of ethics.

PAGE 217, NOTE 5.—It is this that GOGARTEN forgets in his—justifiable—fight against individualism. Neither the French nor the Russian Revolution can be charged with a false individualism, but with a false collectivism; they were the Divine Judgment executed upon a corruptly "united world" (to use the apt expression of HIRSCH) of degenerate feudalism. Rebellion against the life-destroying bondage of the individual by collectivism, emancipation, and revolution, has as much relative right as (human) authority. Emancipation from tyrannical authority—whether this authority be that of the father, or the political ruler, or the economic system—is just as necessary in authoritarian days as a closer connexion with authority at a time when men are intoxicated with the wine of liberty.

PAGE 217, NOTE 6.—The modern nationalistic State is a classic example. Nothing tends more to conceal God from man than the State, for it is always able to invest itself with a peculiar glory, almost numinous in character. That is: the State transforms its undoubted relative right—as an order given by God, and as a particular form of human life willed by God—into an absolute.

PAGE 217, NOTE 7.—Cf. the illuminating representation and criticism of Christian conservatism in A. DE QUERVAIN: *Die theologischen Voraussetzungen der Politik*, pp. 116 ff., where an important and very penetrating criticism is combined with a sympathetic estimate of men like STAHL, VON GERLACH, and VILMAR. However, it seems to me that it would be still more illuminating to carry this criticism of the failure to recognize the necessarily revolutionary element in Christian ethics to its logical conclusion. All these conservatives have only seen one thing: the God-given element in history, the necessity of adaptation, of a connexion with authority. They have not perceived that if these ideas are not balanced by the order of redemption they must lead, inevitably, directly to the daemonic use of authority; and it is this very one-sidedness which leads to that historical pantheism which, from the time of RANKE onwards, infects Lutheran theology. DE QUERVAIN has seen, rightly, that it was the lack of the idea of election which led to this departure from the right way, but he does not make the connexion between election and the ethical problem very clear. Through this knowledge of the fact of election faith gains an ultimate freedom over against all the other facts of existence, and the possibility of a critical denial of concrete authority and of historical collective forces. Within "Christian conservatism" the *one* idea of Providence swamps the whole field of ethical decision. Attention to the first article has made the second, where it is not forgotten, at any rate, ethically ineffective.

PAGE 217, NOTE 8.—This tendency was certainly also present in LUTHER himself; but with him it was a deliberately one-sided emphasis, made necessary by his fight against the false union of Church and State in Catholicism, and a falsely legalistic "application" of the Sermon on the Mount as a law for secular ordinances by the Anabaptists. But we need only think of his work: *Von weltlicher Obrigkeit*, or *Von Kaufhandlung und Wucher*, to know that he never left technical questions to the lawyers, in the sense of an abandonment of ethical demands, or in the sense of releasing the "orders" from obedience to the Divine Command. But later Lutheranism, in its cult of Luther, has elevated this historically conditioned one-sidedness of Luther's into a standard, and later still, if not theoretically, at least in practice it has withdrawn these "secular" matters wholly from Christian criticism, and has left them to the "reason" of the "experts."

PAGE 218, NOTE 9.—The fact that in Holland certain ecclesiastical groups are organizing themselves politically as an "anti-revolutionary Party," and that also in certain German Calvinistic circles revolution is regarded as the anti-Christian attitude *par excellence*, leads me to emphasize the truth that *in principle* revolution stands upon exactly the same footing as that of the obedience of the subject to his superior authority. There is, of course, a *relative* difference, which is also an important one, namely, that all political activity must aim at order and peace, and thus that revolution can only be allowed as an exception, as a necessary transition to a new order; but, as such, under certain circumstances, as an unavoidable process of transition, revolution is certainly justified. (See below, p. 473.) But if the motto "anti-revolutionary" were interpreted in a broader sense as anti-Liberalism, there would be no objection to it, if, at the same time, by the use of the word "anti-Conservative," it were also made quite clear that to be "conservative" is in itself no more Christian than to be "revolutionary" or "liberal." Conservatism only becomes "Christian" when it allows itself to be limited by the revolutionary element, and *vice versa*. The fact that in a definite historical situation we are bound to take our stand on the one side or the other is a different question; but this has only a very indirect connexion with our discussion of ethical principle, and should not be confused with it.

NOTES ON CHAPTER XXII

PAGE 220, NOTE 1.—This seems to me to be the important "concern" of GOGARTEN, which BARTH does not understand. Barth says rightly: "We only know the Creator through faith in Jesus Christ; even in the first article there is no "natural" theology on which Christian theology can be based." This must be firmly maintained even against the arguments of HIRSCH's new book. What Hirsch there writes about Creation is speculative philosophy, not the Christian belief in Creation. But Barth does not seem to perceive that the believer, when he thus knows the Creator, in so doing also perceives the working of the Creator in the pagan world, in the sphere of nature, and also the further fact that the Creator does His work by using human instinct and human reason, indeed, even by using a natural or pagan or rational "knowledge" of the Creator and of His ordinances. As Paul (*Romans ii. 14 ff.*) admits that the heathen have a knowledge of the divine law—in spite of the fact that they do not rightly know the Law-giver—so must we, in connexion with *Romans xiii*, also go further and admit that the heathen are, to some extent, aware of the ordinances of God, without rightly knowing Him who creates these orders. This is the element of truth in the doctrine of the *lex naturae*, although it is certainly wrong, on the one hand, because of its rationalism, and on the other, because of its supposed rigidity.

PAGE 222, NOTE 2.—Luther's language, in this connexion, is not quite uniform and clear; the concepts of "Office," "Class," and "Calling" are often used alongside of one another without any distinct demarcation between them. This lies in the nature of the case, since all these words mean things which are very intimately connected with one another. At this point, however, I certainly part company with Luther, and with the general use of these terms, for I use "office," as an artificial word, to describe the objective observance of law, or connexion with an order, in our action within our calling. In so doing I want to make it clear that the same connexion with an objective norm, determined by consideration for the people as a whole, is peculiar to all action within a calling, which we usually only admit of the action of a State or Church functionary. The guardian also acts "officially," and so does the factory manager, the father, the physician. The word "calling" would not be suitable to describe this particular state of affairs, the necessary "strictness" and "rigidity" within action in a calling. The "Calling" is the genus, the "Office" is a *differentia specifica*. In spite of the views of GOGARTEN on the matter I think that the word "Stand" (class or position) would lead to misunderstanding.

PAGE 223, NOTE 3.—Here I use the word "reason" in a very general sense, as the sum-total of all natural human capacity for knowledge, that is, as theology has always used it in its best days.

PAGE 224, NOTE 4.—This expression must not, of course, be pressed in too pedantic a manner. It means the refusal to construct an ideological programme, which does not weigh carefully the pros and cons of the question: Could such a programme be translated into action, here and now? There are some proposals for reform, "good in themselves," which, were they now translated into action, would ruin everything. The demand for ceaseless activity is, however, limited by the circumstances which make a temporary cessation of all order necessary, so that a better order, which is ready to be introduced, may be established. Let me make this clear by means of an analogy. When a railway bridge has to be moved, first of all the new bridge must be built alongside of the old one, until the moment for the new connexion has arrived. Then comes a moment when the line has to be closed: the moment when the connexion is made with the new bridge and broken off from the old one. It is the ambition and the duty of the railway engineer to make this moment of transition as brief as possible: his desire is to make the transition as smoothly as possible. For were he not to do so the harm created by the disturbance to traffic might be greater than the advantages gained by the improved method of communication. A new bridge only has to be built when the old one has become unsafe, whether the pause, the break in the line of communication, is long or short. This analogy would apply to revolution at a period when the old order had become untenable.

PAGE 225, NOTE 5.—A State which would renounce the right of life and death would lose its power to exist. This has nothing at all to do with the justification of Capital Punishment as a method of justice (see below, p. 477).

PAGE 226, NOTE 6.—This is true not only of the order of the State but also of the economic order. I am the very last person to admire the Capitalist system, but the way in which some members of the Religious-Social movement—in their absolutely necessary and justifiable criticism of Capitalism—demand the introduction of Socialism as an alternative, without seriously enquiring whether this hazy Socialism would really be better, sins—to say the least—against the rule of conscientiousness. For with the word "Socialism" they usually connect ideas of an ethical character, in order to recommend it to the Christian conscience; yet they do not stop to reflect how a mere alteration in the economic system would also effect a change of temper and of spirit. The fact that we demand Socialism for some ethical reason or another does not prove that Socialism is the better economic system, nor that within Socialism the spirit of man will be more "social," more closely connected with the community. Here I am not arguing for the one system more than for the other (see below, pp. 426 ff.), but I only wish to draw attention to the short-sightedness of this kind of argument.

PAGE 226, NOTE 7.—This means two things: (a) that there can be no "Christian politics" or "Christian economic policy"; (b) that the Christian is under the obligation to take his task seriously in connexion with politics and economic policy. But as a Christian he must do this politically and not as a Christian, although in so doing he must certainly never forget whose servant he is. The same Lord commands me to meet my neighbour in love, and not to judge, who commands me to take part in politics which have a definite aim in view. One Lord, one motive, but two kinds of Command.

PAGE 226, NOTE 8.—We may indeed go much further and admit that over against the churches of the Reformation, which, in their actual situation, did not proclaim the pure Gospel, fanaticism formed a necessary and useful corrective. In recent times which of us has not been thankful that the Quakers still exist?—almost the only people who, when national sentiment was at fever heat, did not allow themselves to be drawn into hatred and abuse of the enemy, and who were the first to be ready to reunite the bonds which had been broken, and to give help wherever it was required, without taking national enmity into account. How often, throughout the course of Church History, the "fanatics" and "sectarians" have been the only people to represent the truth that "My Kingdom is not of this world"—although they have done so imperfectly or erroneously; how often have they been the force which has made it possible for some necessary new order to emerge. To seek the Right, and to recognize the corrections of the Right which has been spoiled, are two different things.

PAGE 227, NOTE 9.—Although in Calvin's teaching the contrast between the demands of the ethic of society and those of the personal love of our neighbour is not so glaring as in Luther, and accordingly, now and then, Calvin stresses more strongly the unity of the Divine Command, still the light and shade on both sides is equally strong. Luther sees the godless reality more clearly than Calvin, and accordingly he sees more clearly the sinfulness of the means by which we maintain the fabric of the social order. To us it is amazing to see the optimism with which Calvin speaks, for instance, of the State. On the other hand, however, Calvin is not frightened away by that dualism (which naturally he also knows) from asserting God's Command even within society, in the State and in the economic order. TROELTSCH (in his *Soziallehren*) has seen this difference rightly; but he puts everything in a wrong light by his disastrous theory of the Law of Nature (see below, Note 8 on Chapter XXV).

PAGE 228, NOTE 10.—If, for example, a manufacturer—we assume, of course, that he is a man who takes his Christianity seriously—out of a genuine sense of the value of his workmen, pays them higher wages than the business can stand, he serves the community as a whole badly; for the ruin of his business causes economic loss to the community as a whole; certainly a man of this kind will be regarded with far more respect than one who brings his business into a flourishing condition by keeping wages as low as possible in order that at the same time he may make as much profit as he can for himself.

PAGE 231, NOTE 11.—It is the infallible sign of a legalistic habit of mind if in ethics the word "possible" is rejected with horror, in the belief that to take no trouble to do what is actually possible is a sign of seriousness and of trust in God. Even this attitude is certainly to some extent justified as a corrective to a lazy concealment of one's real motive behind the impossible; but here we are seeking for a principle, for the truth, and not for a caricature of the truth, which it is always possible to find. An earnest and sincere Christian, who may happen to be a statesman, has to examine with extreme conscientiousness what is possible and what is impossible; for politics is the art of the possible; one who does not understand this is a bungler and a visionary at this point, and God does not want people of this kind. God wills that a politician also should do his work properly, and this means that he will do what is possible. Certainly in so doing he will try to extend the boundary of the possible in the direction of the commandment of love; but, once this boundary is known, it must be respected.

PAGE 232, NOTE 12.—Here is the place where—as later in the sphere of pedagogy—the theological doctrine of the natural knowledge of God and of natural morality becomes of practical importance. Those who will not acknowledge the *justitia civilis*—and this is the usual attitude of Pietism and the sects—refuse to consider such co-operation. Hence in Germany it was found necessary to form the *"christlichen Volksdienst"* (Christian service of the people), that is, the Christian Party, in order to stimulate the members of the *Gemeinschaftsbewegung* (a Pietist movement within the Lutheran Church in Germany—TR.) to take an interest in politics.

PAGE 232, NOTE 13.—There could be no surer way of completely ruining both economics and politics than to do in these spheres what the pastors and the theologians say. As a rule this is admitted by everyone; only generally people apply this to "others."

PAGE 232, NOTE 14.—The task of ethics is different from that of "Christian" politics and theologico-political instruction. Although an ethic cannot be timeless in character, still it must not confuse its task of teaching all Christians with that of the theological controversial pamphlet, in which the writer has already made up his mind about what must be done in the particular situation in question, and in which he summons his readers to make their own decision in the same way. Thus ethics is able to examine all the possibilities contained in the suggestions put forward by all parties, but it is not its business to decide for one particular policy. Of course, possibly even the theologian will feel that he must come out openly for one particular party, and by his writings and by his speech in public he will defend one point of view against another. But this he does in a personal "private" manner, on his own responsibility, not on that of his position as a teacher of the Church. As such he has no right to range himself either on the side of the defenders of the existing order or on that of a particular opposition group, for he knows that on the one hand, authority, and on the other, liberty, are understood in such a way that the antithesis is a relative one, so that earnest Christians, according to their knowledge, are found on one side or the other. But this is utterly different from the challenging "word" of the prophet which comes to all with unconditional authority, the "word for the times" which is delivered in virtue of a special divine commission.

PAGE 232, NOTE 15.—Someone has once called this the "silent revolution"; it begins with the *Epistle to Philemon*—this classic example of the union of conservative and radical elements in Christian love; its influence works like this: first, a life in "genuine brotherly love" is lived in some place or another; this awakens astonishment, amazement, and admiration; secretly it sets up a standard of living, then it becomes a public demand, a postulate of law, and finally a legal statute. This is the way in which the following rights have been won: the laws of the present day for the protection of women and children, the abolition of serfdom and slavery, and also—as JELLINEK has shown—legal freedom of conscience.

NOTES ON CHAPTER XXIII

PAGE 235, NOTE 1.—The failure to recognize this fact marks the defective realism of traditional theological ethics. It is dominated by the Aristotelian contrast between form and matter, instead of by the Scriptural idea: to be in the world—to be in the Kingdom of God.

PAGE 236, NOTE 2.—Usually all that is said about success is that it lies beyond our own power, and thus that it does not concern us at all; that, on the contrary, to take the idea of success into account makes the ethical will impure. This is only right if the Divine Command has already been heard; after that there is nothing but "blind" obedience; but success must most earnestly be sought in order that the Divine Command of God may be really heard.

PAGE 236, NOTE 3.—This distinction is related to that of SCHLEIER-MACHER's distinction between "symbolizing" and "organizing" action; but this relation is only a formal one, in so far as in SCHLEIER-MACHER the contrast refers to a process which is not ethical at all but "cultural"; the union of the spirit-form with the "material" of nature. Nowhere does Aristotelian aestheticism stand out so clearly and unmistakably as in the philosophical ethic of Schleiermacher, for which reason also the statement—wholly impossible for a real ethic—that "ethics" is only the continuation of "physics" is here quite logical.

PAGE 237, NOTE 4.—Disregard of the imponderable elements (that is, of the effects of a definite political action which show which way the wind is blowing) very often characterizes a so-called *Realpolitik*, and so often makes it unrealistic. However, we ought not to emphasize this point of view to the extent in which FOERSTER does in his *Politische Ethik*; but then FOERSTER does not really know the sinfulness of this world, hence from a Pelagianism of the Enlightenment type he has gone over to a Catholic Semi-Pelagianism and not to Protestantism.

PAGE 237, NOTE 5.—This point of view has been vigorously worked out in the *Sittenlehre* of A. v. OETTINGEN, although certainly often to the very verge of making the personal element a purely natural thing. On the other hand, certain dialectical theologians incline to leave out the natural element altogether (rather in the fashion of WILHELM HERRMANN, which ought to serve as a warning to us)—they disregard the first article of the Creed where God is called "Creator of Heaven and Earth," and they also in this respect show a disregard for the Bible, which, when it speaks of the Creator, has in view mainly Nature and her ordinances. I find the most

extreme form of anti-naturalism in the otherwise excellent book by
A. DE QUERVAIN: *Die Theologischen Voraussetzungen der Politik*. We
have no right, in our anxiety to preserve faith from the dangers of
an over-naturalistic emphasis—(which is certainly our first concern
over against the whole theological tradition)—to fall into the other
extreme, and to place Nature outside the will of the Creator altogether.

PAGE 238, NOTE 6.—In the strict sense of the word, however,
history can only begin with responsibility; but just as that which is
actually ethical is preceded by custom, so all that is human emerges
from a semi-conscious region, and the whole of responsible existence
is based upon a pre-responsible natural spirit-foundation, and this
we must include in the Creation. The fact that we come into this
world as children ought not to be regarded as a result of the Fall!
GOGARTEN rightly warns us against regarding man's relationship to
God as something which has been added later on as though we had
been created first of all as natural creatures, and later as responsible
beings; on the other hand, this truth ought not to be expounded in
such a way that the fact that human life has a natural basis seems
to have no connexion with this fact of the actual creation of man
by God.

PAGE 239, NOTE 7.—The Lutheran ethic—even A. v. OETTINGEN
is no exception in this respect—tends to confuse the fact of an historical inheritance with history itself; this arises out of its erroneous
idea of the Sacraments, and especially from its magical conception
of Infant Baptism. Historical inheritance is always only an "occasion" for a particular historical existence, just as Infant Baptism is
only a symbol—although a God-given sign of grace—which does
not work *ex opere operato*, but only in so far as later on it is *recognized*
as this sign. This is the paradigm for the relation between a particular historical inheritance and history itself. Likewise the extension of the cultural demonstrative instrument (for instance, writing,
printing, wireless) cannot itself be called history in the true sense of
the word, but only the "occasion"; but as such it ought not to be
ignored. Naturalism always makes the occasion into the thing itself;
Idealism, on the other hand, fails to perceive the importance of the
occasion.

PAGE 239, NOTE 8.—This is the important but limited truth of
the doctrine of the "objective spirit," that is, of the ethic of HEGEL
or of SCHLEIERMACHER.

PAGE 239, NOTE 9.—A. v. OETTINGEN is right in combining his
anti-individualism with this idea; for connexion with the historical
inheritance is also at the same time a kind of relation with the
community. But this relation needs to be more clearly distinguished
than it is in his theory from the really personal relationship. The
way in which Naturalism, and historical Romanticism, hands man
over to these historical connexions, and depreciates him as an

individual, can be seen especially clearly to-day in the nationalistic movements. Therefore the above ideas ought not to be forcibly removed from their connexion with the theory of the "individual."

PAGE 240, NOTE 10.—Historical pantheism is just as much the danger which besets Lutheran thinking as an abstract Rationalism is that of the Reformed. In German-speaking countries, in any case, we must continually draw attention to the pantheistic-historical element which has filtered through into German positive theology from the time of RANKE onwards. It is not merely men like ALTHAUS and HIRSCH, but even men like SCHLATTER, who speak of history as though it were more than the field upon which and in which revelation took place, namely, as though it were itself the revelation. But in the New Testament history is called "the world"; the world which "lieth in the evil one" is the world of history.

PAGE 243, NOTE 11.—This is a point of view which is wholly alien to the mind of previous ethical thinkers, because ethics has always been regarded from the point of view of the individual, because it does not take seriously the fact that all conduct is penetrated with the spirit of the world. That too is why ethical thinkers, whether Protestant or Catholic, reject with such indignation the statement that "the end justifies the means," taking it for granted that "pure means" do exist.

NOTES ON CHAPTER XXIV

PAGE 251, NOTE 1.—By the art of culture (*Kulturkunst*) I here mean all that is creative, that is, scientific thought, in so far as it is purely scientific, artistic creation, in so far as it is purely artistic, politics, in so far as it is determined by the actual aim of politics, and economics, in so far as it is determined by the actual aim of economics. Further on in this book I deal with the fact that in all this—and to how great an extent—the whole sphere of culture contains an ethical element.

PAGE 255, NOTE 2.—By this I do not mean that history as such is sinful; in this I agree with ALTHAUS (*Die Gestalt dieser Welt und die Sünde, Ztschr. f. syst. Theol.*, 1931, pp. 319 ff.). It is true that we know no other history than that which is sinful; Original Sin has left its mark on history as a whole. But in spite of this we must hold to the belief that Creation is planned for history, just as the fact of sex refers to the difference between the sexes, and the fact that human beings come into this world through procreation and birth is not in itself due to the Fall—as was asserted by Origen. Such a statement is sheer Platonism, and is opposed to the Biblical idea of Creation.

PAGE 256, NOTE 3.—The "Supreme Good" is a Greek, eudaemonistic conception, not a Biblical conception. From the days of Augustine onwards it has coloured Christian ethics with an unfortunate eudaemonistic element. In its stead the Bible uses the idea of the Kingdom of God, of the Sovereignty of God. This idea includes the highest form of salvation, not as the "Supreme Good," but as the reality of complete fellowship with God and Man, and above all as the realization of the supreme Will of God. By the concept of the "Supreme Good" even the Kingdom of God is subordinated to the desires of man: the idea of "good" as a leading idea in ethics spoils ethics as much as the idea of "value," with which it is closely connected. The patristic ethic took this idea wholesale from the first chapter of the *Nicomachean Ethics*, without noticing how much Eudaemonism and Anthropocentricism it took over at the same time.

PAGE 257, NOTE 4.—It should be stated plainly that the system of values, as it was undertaken first of all by SCHELER and after him by HARTMANN, has broken down; how could such a system be possible, when, as HARTMANN himself admits, it is impossible to find the principle by which the scale of values can be classified? (See above, Note 14, Chapter IV.)

PAGE 257, NOTE 5.—This might also be expressed thus: in the Christian ethic equality is not a constitutive but a regulative principle. It is an ethic which deals with the adjustment of natural differences and sinful inequalities; it is never egalitarian, but it does level things up. Therefore it never aims at levelling all to the same plane, but it does aim at smoothing down inequalities which are dangerous or injurious, while acknowledging frankly that it would be fatal to remove all inequalities. This means that the Creator has created individual life, and that He wills it, and that even eternity must not be regarded as the removal of individuality.

NOTES ON CHAPTER XXV

PAGE 262, NOTE 1.—I cannot understand how it is that HOLL, in opposition to TROELTSCH's views, wishes to deny this fact; he supports this statement by saying that the passage upon which TROELTSCH bases his opinion is not a genuine "Luther" passage (LUTHER, p. 248). This seems quite impossible to believe, since Luther's writings contain so many passages with a similar meaning. But HOLL—in reference to Luther's works on the Princes and Usury—is certainly right at this point: when he contests the view that Luther intended to give up, in principle, all attempts to make the Divine Command valid and effective within the sphere of economics and politics.

PAGE 262, NOTE 2.—In spite of the clear and challenging way in which the problem has been stated both by NAUMANN and by TROELTSCH, even the most recent works on ethics do not exhibit much change in their fundamental attitude. WÜNSCH, in his *Political*

Economy, wrestles earnestly with the problem, and—on the very fringe of theological ethics—TILLICH does the same, but his idea of "autonomy" is more likely to obscure the problem than to illuminate it.

PAGE 263, NOTE 3.—There are no "Christian bridges," any more than there are Christian proofs for the Pythagorean doctrine. But in so far as all human activity is connected with the whole man, and with human society as a whole, the concrete norm is immediately limited by ethical norms; therefore, indirectly, the fact of being a Christian must somehow or another have some influence on the process of building bridges. This point has been fully treated above (see p. 264).

PAGE 263, NOTE 4.—A system of *values* is an artificial expression; it here describes both the principles and system of the values which, in combination with the actual circumstances actually existing at the moment, determine the acquisition and the distribution of goods within a nation, or at a certain period in history. On the other hand, this "value system" is an entity whose effectiveness is in proportion to the way in which it is known. For most people it is regarded as axiomatic, and therefore its influence is unconscious and uncontrolled. It expresses itself for instance as an "economic spirit" (see below, p. 409) or as a political creed, but it is based on ultimate reasons, connected with one's general outlook on life and religion.

PAGE 265, NOTE 5.—With the addition of the third person to the "I" and the "Thou" society comes into being, and with that the problem of the ethic of society; the ethic of society is certainly something particular within an ethic, but it is not the social ethic contrasted with a so-called individual ethic (on this point, see Chapter XXVII, p. 295).

PAGE 266, NOTE 6.—Community between persons only exists, in the strict sense of the word, as a "Church," understanding the word "Church" in its original sense, and not as a legal corporation, but as the *coetus electorum* (κλῆσις—ἐκκλησία), and therefore as a community which necessarily requires the individual as an "individual." For this distinction, see the last section of this work.

PAGE 269, NOTE 7.—KELSEN's *Rechtslehre* attempts to carry through a juridical formalism of this kind; but even this extreme is only possible by means of secret borrowings from the visible sphere of law, in which, for its part, there is always a certain amount of ethical content.

PAGE 269, NOTE 8.—ERNST TROELTSCH has rendered a great service by recognizing the importance of the question of the Law of Nature for the understanding of the Social Teaching of the Christian Churches. At the same time, however, the way in which Troeltsch deals with this question only goes to prove that an "outsider"—and so far as the faith of the Reformation is concerned

627

Troeltsch *is* an outsider—can introduce confusion into a discussion, in spite of all the keenness of his intellect.

Since to-day in particular the problem of the Law of Nature is of extreme importance within Protestant theology, whether it be positive or negative in character, in the following appendix I give a survey of the whole question, which, although at many points it depends upon Troeltsch, does not primarily refer to his views; it is based also upon the well-known work by CARLYLE (the two brothers of that name), upon DILTHEY's *Weltanschauung und Analyse*, as well as upon my own studies in the Catholic doctrine of the Law of Nature.

1. *The Catholic Doctrine of the Lex Naturae and the Law of Nature.*— The Catholic doctrine of the Law of Nature is not so uniform and closely-knit as it might appear to be at first sight. The contrast between Augustinianism and Aristotelianism makes itself felt within it, just as we know to-day that the difference between patristic doctrine, that of the Early Middle Ages, and Thomist doctrine is considerable. In spite of this, there is a far-reaching agreement among the present-day supporters of the Catholic doctrine, in accordance with which the main features may be thus described. The *lex naturae* springs from the *lex aeterna*, the Eternal Divine plan, which, because it is unchangeable, is called *lex*. The *lex naturae* is the *lex aeterna* at work within the created world. It is called the *lex naturae*, in so far as it is implanted by Creation within the creature, in the broader sense: in all created beings it is the unconscious power which is ever at work to produce order in their life; in the narrower sense, it applies to the human rational creature in so far as the will of God is inscribed in the rational nature of man. It is called *lex*, moreover, in the narrower sense, in so far as this will of God is known to man as one which *commands* him, and indeed as a will which is always everywhere the same in its demand for obedience to its commands.

One part of this *lex naturae* is the Law of Nature, namely, that which refers to our relation to other human beings, and indeed more exactly, in so far as this relation ought to be regulated by the principle of the *suum cuique*. This statement, namely, that every one must give every one else his due, is the real content of the *lex naturae* as the Law of Nature. From this all the statements of the *jus gentium* are to be derived, and this *jus gentium*, once more, is the basis of positive law.

It is here, however, that the uncertainty and obscurity begins. The distinction between an *absolute* and a *relative* law of Nature, which plays so large a part in Troeltsch's work, and rightly so, is relegated, most curiously, to the background, in the actual doctrine of Catholic theologians; for instance, in his *Moralphilosophie* CATHREIN does not once mention it; SCHILLING (*Katholische Sozialethik*, 1929), who enters into a vigorous discussion of the views of Troeltsch, and who knows the history of the *lex naturae* very well, mentions it certainly, but almost immediately passes on to something else. Whereas in the teaching of the Early Fathers the contrast between the absolute and the relative Law of Nature is extremely clear and sharp, because in it they saw an expression of the whole contrast between the world as it has been created by God and the fallen world (the relative Law of Nature is that which is adapted to the world which has become sinful, the absolute Natural Law corresponds to the Primitive State), even in the teaching of AQUINAS the relation between the two is no longer regarded as one of contrast or opposition, but as a difference of degree, and is held to be due not so much to sin as to incompleteness or imperfection. Later authors never mention the relative Law of Nature at all. Thus the impression is given that it is possible to derive the regulations governing present conditions from the absolute Law of Nature, "by taking circumstances into account" (CATHREIN); the most striking thing about this statement is its verbal obscurity, i.e. the ambiguity of the expression: "to apply to particular circumstances." Whereas SCHILLING knows exactly and says plainly that this may mean two things: either, the subsumption of the particular under the universal by means of a purely logical process of deduction, or, the alteration of the content of the law itself (of the universal law) in accordance with the actuality which has been thus transformed by sin (God now commands something different because the world has become sinful), but the majority of writers do not mention this contrast between the relative and the absolute Law of Nature at all, and so it looks as though the absolute Law of Nature were the standard even for actual present conditions. The expression "application to special circumstances" permits two things: to argue for the validity of that which is only relatively good, and at the same time to give the impression that it is always only the one absolute Law of Nature which is intended. It is this which gives so much elasticity to this conception.

But where it is honestly admitted that there are two kinds of Natural Law, the absolute and the relative, there is no exact definition of the content of the second, referring to the "transformation formula" which would permit the absolute Natural Law to be applied to existing sinful conditions. This means, that even here, in the last resort, the fiction still exists that it is possible to determine what is valid, here and now, on the basis of the absolute Law of Nature by means of a legalistic process of interpretation. And the whole imposing structure of the uniformity and "freedom from compromise," or the fidelity to law of Catholic social ethics is built upon this fiction! Were the contrast between the absolute and relative Law of Nature openly admitted and carried into practice, at once it would be seen that the relative Law of Nature is *not* a *law* at all, but only a *regulative principle*, from which no definite demands can be deduced, but all that it determines is this: that in the sinful world, so far as possible the absolute Law of Nature must be carried out. Even Troeltsch did not see *this* difference clearly, and yet upon it is based the important fact that allows the Catholic ethic on the one hand to boast of its rigid legalism, and on the other to adapt itself with such elasticity to circumstances. The elastic element is the relative Law of Nature, which has never been reduced to a code, indeed it has never been explicated (so far as its content is concerned), or fixed as a "transformation formula," but it is a secret agent of transformation, where, unseen by the world, the law of high tension is transformed into a tension for actual use, but this transformation is concealed by the ambiguous formula: "application to special circumstances"; and no one ever enquired on what principle this transformation is to be undertaken. Actually, the history of the relative Law of Nature shows how this conception contains the most varied and contradictory elements, and indeed (this lies in the nature of the case) the solution of the most important practical problems is found in this secret region, where no law prevails. No Catholic moralist knows the content of the relative Law of Nature—which sets the practical standard—there is no doctrine about what it contains that is different from the absolute Law of Nature, and there is no principle in existence, according to which it could be derived from the absolute Law of Nature. Therefore it is *not a law at all*, it simply expresses the necessity (which cannot be expressed in legal terms) of adapting the absolute Law of Nature to the sinful reality. It is no accident that the majority of works on Catholic ethics are not aware of this conception at all; for it is extremely unpalatable. But the fact that even in patristic teaching—under the influence of Stoicism—this conception (that is, the application of the concept of law to something which is actually a negation of the law, of that which can be defined in legal terms) could be used at all, is due to the fact (quite apart from the fact that it was possible to borrow it simply from the Stoics) that from the point of view of "relative Natural Law," in the main it was actual legal conditions, actual *laws* (of the State), which were treated. Thus the ambiguity of the idea of law hid from the authors themselves the fact that, whereas the absolute Law of Nature is a law in the sense of systematic unity, of principle, the relative Law of Nature must be described by the expression: absence of principle. This explains a further point: that the relative Natural Law never appears as a constructive principle but only as a principle of interpretation. Ethical demands are never derived from the relative Law of Nature but existing conditions are justified. The relative Law of Nature is an auxiliary idea, by means of which actual facts, in view of the sinful reality, are afterwards connected, in this indirect way, with the absolute Law of Nature.

But even the idea of the *absolute* Law of Nature conceals secret tensions. On the one hand, its applicability depends upon the fact that its content is not only universally valid but that it can be universally perceived, and is to be affirmed by every rational being. History, however, shows that this is not the case at all. Quite "reasonable" people (and nations and periods) have regarded as "good" things which are totally different from each other, and do so still at the present day. This does not, of course, contradict the absolute law, but it does contradict the absolute Law of *Nature*, in so far as by "nature" there is meant the possibility of disposing of knowledge. Here we see the original fiction of Aristotelian anthropology: the doctrine of a universal reason, the confusion of the idea of the *a priori* with an anthropologico-psychological interpretation of this idea. In theological language it means that the failure to recognize the fact that through sin even the "original" rational nature of man has been altered, and has been affected by the contradiction *(Rom. i. 21)*, is suppressed.

Various methods are employed to try to overcome this difficulty. It is said that it is only the most universal propositions which can be perceived by all—but then the fact that these universal propositions produce such very different results must be due either to ignorance of certain facts, or to lack of mental development (cf. CATHREIN, I, pp. 452 ff.), which, however, obviously contradicts the facts of history. Or it is said that these propositions are evident to any "impartial" person (SCHILLING, *Sozialethik*, p. 21); but immediately the question arises: what kind of people *are* impartial? Indeed, in a sinful humanity are there any "impartial" people at all?

It is evident that this is not sophistry, for the doctrine of the Law of Nature is directly connected with natural theology: it is explicitly stated that the right law of Nature "is inseparably connected with the idea of God" (SCHILLING, loc. cit., p. 21), evidently with the *right* idea of God, thus evidently with that which (according to the teaching of Scripture) the natural man does not possess. This leads to the contradictory formula of a "Christian Law of Nature" (SCHILLING, ibid.). But the analysis of the content of the doctrine of the Law of Nature leads to the same point. It is well known that there is an egalitarian-rationalistic Law of Nature, which is clearly distinguished, though not always with the same emphasis, from the doctrine taught by the Church. On what then is the deviation of the Christian Law of Nature from the rational Law of Nature based, since both claim to be based upon reason? In actual fact the so-called Christian Law of Nature is a concept of the Law of Nature which has been modified by the faith of the Bible, therefore it is not really a law of "Nature" but of "Creation," and its difference from the rational Law of Nature points to the fact that faith and revelation must come to the assistance of reason, in order to discover what is truly rational. The absolute Law of Nature, therefore, is based upon the fiction of a natural reason, which in reality is a reason which is instructed by the Christian belief in God, and by the Christian anthropology which arises from this.

To sum up, this line of thought leads to the following results:

The definition of that which is required of us here and now is acquired from a view of "the Good," as it is intrinsically—the absolute (Christian) Law of Nature—determined also by Christian truth, by means of an adjustment (no longer conceived in terms of law) to the concrete historical conditions of the sinful world; in so doing, however, the fact is overlooked that this "natural" knowledge is only present where reason has been illuminated by faith, and that this "adjustment" cannot be conceived in terms of law, or of principle, and is therefore incapable of uniform definition.

2. *The Law of Nature in the Thought of the Reformation.*—Both LUTHER and CALVIN teach a *lex naturae*, but both in such a way that the natural knowledge of the truly rational is very restricted and limited, that only the reason which is illuminated by faith can understand the absolute law of God; Calvin makes this limitation far more evident than Luther does, and indeed Luther uses this conception far more than Calvin.

At the same time both Reformers agree in teaching that the absolute law cannot be carried out within the sinful reality, wherever the conditions of society are concerned; but here it seems as though Luther alone still uses the conception of the *lex naturae* at all. But he does not use it as a law or a principle; on the contrary, he is fully aware that from the point of view of actual history it is irrational in character.

Finally, both the Reformers, in agreement with the Fathers, and in partial agreement with the Scholastic thinkers, teach that the existing forms of society, above all the State and the Family, are divine institutions, but that in their concrete historical form they are products of the natural rational process, thus that the actual laws of this structure have a share both in the sinfulness of the world and in the will of God; in saying this Luther lays more emphasis upon the sinful aspect than Calvin does. The *Lex Naturae* and the Law of Nature is here concerned in so far as—mainly by Luther—emphasis is laid upon the fact, that the knowledge of the immanent legalism within these concrete spheres is predominantly a matter of the reason, and is only indirectly connected with faith. Here, however, every vestige of a system which can be grasped by the mind, of a system of Natural Law disappears; the "doctrine of the Law of Nature" of the Reformers should therefore in essentials be that which is outlined in this book. What God requires for the ordering of the conditions of society cannot be rationally deduced from a rational system, but it can only be discovered on each particular occasion, in obedience to the revealed will of God, by means of the reason.

3. *The Doctrine of the Law of Nature of the Enlightenment and of Modern Times* is not at all uniform. Three main elements can be distinguished within it which were blended together and related to each other in very different ways: (i) The rational doctrine of the Law of Nature of the Stoics and of Aristotle; in which, however, the objective emphasis is transformed into a subjective one (the expression "Law of Nature" is replaced by "Law of *Reason*"). (ii) The Stoic doctrine of the Law of Nature, modified by Christianity. (iii) A naturalistic positivist Law of Nature which elevates the biological laws to norms, and at the same time explains the norms in a biological manner.

4. *The Treatment of this Subject by Troeltsch* suffers from the fact that it takes too little account of the following differences: (*a*) The difference between the subjective (rational) factor and the objective (natural) factor, which was united in the one word *natura* by Stoic Pantheism; (*b*) the difference between the Christian and the Stoic Law of Nature. Sometimes TROELTSCH maintains that both are identical—for only thus could he defend the thesis that this idea has been taken over from Stoicism—and sometimes he points to the difference between them, but on the presupposition of a legalistic conception of true Christianity. TROELTSCH has not perceived the ambiguity of the conception of the relative Law of Nature, and the peculiarity of the Catholic social ethic which is based upon it, and he estimates far too highly the influence of the Stoics in particular upon this fundamental central conception. This conception does not correspond so much to Stoic optimism as to the Christian idea of Original Sin; it is present in Stoicism (as CARLYLE, who is more cautious than Troeltsch, proves), but it only becomes a fundamental conception through the Christian ethic, mainly through AUGUSTINE.

His weakest point is his treatment of the "Law of Nature" in the thought of the Reformers, because here he has no understanding of Luther's dialectic of the Law and the Gospel. On the other hand, I must also say likewise that HOLL has not understood Troeltsch's whole discussion of the question, and its enormous fruitfulness, and therefore he goes much too far in his rejection of it.

PAGE 270, NOTE 9.—On this point cf. the chapter on Law and Justice, pp. 447 ff.

PAGE 271, NOTE 10.—In saying this I only appear to disagree with STAMMLER's theory of "right justice"; for Stammler conceives "right justice" from the very outset as a purely critical idea, and therefore as strictly formal, and in so doing he describes precisely that which, on the side of content, I mean by the best justice attainable at any particular time: the idea of right justice is the presupposition for the finding of the best form of justice, but it is not a principle from which the best form of justice could be *deduced* (natural law), but a formal principle, according to which it is to be *sought*.

PAGE 273, NOTE 11.—The present isolation of the Church and of theology can only be broken down if all lawyers, sociologists, natural scientists, who are Christians will make the importance of the Christian Faith plain in the scientific treatment of their problems. To-day the situation is such, that if a man does not start from the positivist or humanist point of view, scientific objectivity is supposed to be in danger, and difficulties are raised about "theological prejudice."

PAGE 274, NOTE 12.—Since the publication of MAX WEBER's *Religions-soziologie*, positivist prejudice (which implies that causality could only be in one direction, namely from the social forms to religion) even if not overcome, has certainly been modified. There too we find some of the most splendid examples of this opposite tendency of influence, from religion to the social forms themselves, with reference to civilization as a whole. Even SPENGLER's "morphology of civilization," with its description of religion as the soul of every form of civilization, has helped to promote a truer view of this fact. The "economic materialism" of KARL MARX has not in the least lost any significance through this change of view; only the analysis needs to be pushed still further in order to discover the reason for this preponderance of the economic values, and in order to distinguish to what extent this is true of various periods.

NOTES ON CHAPTER XXVI

PAGE 280, NOTE 1.—The speculative idea of *necessitas* in the doctrine of God is always the transition to Pantheism; it is thus conceived by ZWINGLI in the *De providentia*, and occasionally in certain lines of thought by LUTHER in his *De servo arbitrio*. The Scriptural doctrine of Election, rightly understood, is the ultimate defence against this logical conclusion drawn from the idea of Omnipotence. For in the idea of Election the freedom of God is posited as the first point, and the freedom of Man—based upon the divine Freedom—as the second point (cf. GOGARTEN's preface to his edition of Luther's *Vom unfreien Willen*). Against this, on the other hand, Calvin's conclusion from the twofold result of the judgment that there must be a twofold Divine decree also leads to *necessitas*, and therefore destroys responsibility.

PAGE 283, NOTE 2.—None of Luther's expressions are too strong, in view of the strongest tendency in human nature, that of self-assertive freedom; but at a time when determinism in thought and pessimism in feeling predominate we have to take care that we do not yield too much to Luther's one-sided emphasis, for Luther did not shrink from the most rigid determinism when he felt he must at all costs uproot the humanistic conception of freedom. It is incontestable that in the New Testament the emphasis is not upon the fact that the conduct of the believer should not differ from that of the unbeliever, but upon that fact that he is a "new creature." But it is a far cry from this fact to the assertion that (in the present-day sense of the word) Paul was a "Perfectionist."

PAGE 285, NOTE 3.—Naturally the most striking example of this is the Roman Catholic Church; but this quantitative standpoint of success comes out still more plainly, because more naïvely, in certain forms of ecclesiastical "Amerikanismus," which have unfortunately won their way into the life of Europe, and even into Germany.

PAGE 287, NOTE 4.—This is constantly the one great temptation which the Grand Inquisitor proclaims to the Lord as the sole possibility of ecclesiastical success. The Church—with the best intentions—seeks to gain influence for the Gospel by using secular methods of a very doubtful purity, and applies the same methods as her opponents, but in so doing she becomes like "salt which has lost its savour" which is henceforth fit for nothing but to be cast out and trodden under foot of men. For how can a Church which has itself become the world, help the world?

NOTES ON CHAPTER XXVII

PAGE 294, NOTE 1.—When MARITAIN, in his *Trois Réformateurs*, places LUTHER on the same plane with DESCARTES and ROUSSEAU, it is ultimately no worse than when Neo-Protestants appeal to Luther's views on "freedom of conscience," or when MARTENSEN strove against KIERKEGAARD as an individualist who destroyed community. Both LUTHER and KIERKEGAARD were concerned with the struggle for true authority and community against false authority and bondage to collective forces. Where an historical force usurps unconditional authority, true community is impossible. The genuine idea of community must be known by the fact that it recognizes the relative right and mutual limitation of collectivism and individualism, of human authority, and of emancipation from authority.

PAGE 294, NOTE 2.—The history of this "Robinsonade" (a vivid expression for 18th-century individualism—TR.) has been described by DILTHEY in his *Weltanschauung und Analyse des Menschen seit Renaissance und Reformation*. When HIRSCH (in his *Schöpfung und Sünde*, p. 92) gives it as his opinion that "among theologians it is an historical myth which cannot be eradicated, as though such a Self, in its isolation, were essential to the Idealistic point of view," he only shows that he has not yet understood what the theologians mean who say this. The "community of the Spirit" in which the Self (as he understands it) of Idealism knows itself to be "embedded" is precisely, as a community of "Spirit," not real community.

It is precisely the Hegelian idea of the historical process of Spirit, his theory of the objective Spirit, and the whole dialectical conception of history, which lacks the sense of community as much as it lacks the personal element. Whether "the freedom, which we are, does not exist as a single entity" is quite beside the mark, and indeed this question has not been raised; but what has been asked is this: whether this freedom, whether this Self, is from the very outset related to the other (to the "Thou") apart from whom the "Thou" cannot even be imagined, just as we cannot conceive of a suspension bridge which is only suspended from one tower, whether from the very outset freedom is regarded as relation with the "Thou." Certainly HIRSCH is not dealing with this idea of the Self at all. In this theory—in the whole of this speculative doctrine of the Self—the other, in so far as he is present at all, is only mentioned afterwards, as "also a self," just as I am. The fact that Idealism always speaks of the "Thou" as "also a self," and that it can speak so, shows how entirely it lacks the idea of the "Thou." EBNER, BUBER, and GOGARTEN could teach men something really decisive which no Idealist has ever known, and which HIRSCH himself does not yet know.

PAGE 294, NOTE 3.—At the present day, indeed, philosophy is giving increasing attention to this problem. In saying this I do not allude to works like LITT's *Individuum und Gemeinschaft* or SPANN's *Sozialphilosophie*—those are the old solutions; but I mean HEIDEGGER, GRISEBACH, KNITTERMEYER, H. BARTH. F. EBNER—whom I first learned to understand through GOGARTEN, although I had known his work for a long time—ought I suppose to be regarded as the actual pioneer of this movement in thought, coupled with M. BUBER. In a certain sense here, too, the new metaphysic of WHITEHEAD should be mentioned, which also seeks to break away from individualism, from the point of view of the new scientific knowledge. But in the last resort he still remains within the sphere of objectivity, in the *"Es-Welt"* ("it-world" or impersonal sphere) to use BUBER's expression.

PAGE 295, NOTE 4.—I cannot understand how it is that HEIM has so totally misunderstood GOGARTEN. The "claim" of the "Thou" is not the same as "his claims," but it is precisely that which HEIM himself lays down: the fact that alongside of myself as the central point in the perspective of my world there appears another with this very "claim," which in the sense of responsibility I somehow perceive and which in love I ought to affirm. The neutral attitude between the "I" and the "Thou" which HEIM describes (*Glaube und Denken*, p. 429) never exists at all; the Command to love our neighbour—to which indeed GOGARTEN always refers—qualifies our actual situation always as sin, and always requires the acceptance of the "claim" of the other, that is, the abandonment of the attitude in which we ourselves are the centre of everything, and also the abandonment of mere justice (the equal value of both claims), and thus my going forth to the other.

PAGE 296, NOTE 5.—The fact that "God is our nearest relation" we could not know "of ourselves," not even through direct revelation —unless indeed we were prophets in the Old Testament sense— but we know this through the message of the Church and of the Bible. The immediacy of man's relation with God, as even HIRSCH maintains, is not a neutral preparatory stage of the Christian Faith, but is always a kind of paganism. But what Hirsch says about this is a mixture of speculation and Christian knowledge, a kind of Christian Gnosis.

PAGE 296, NOTE 6.—On this point cf. the fundamental observations by GOGARTEN, *Wider die Ächtung der Autorität*, p. 34: "Love is his original being, and in so far it is the presupposition of all his action. He may do what he wills and he may act as he wills, his action will always take place either in love or against love. And according as it takes place in love or not, whether it is done in the spirit of co-operation or of hostility, it is good or evil."

PAGE 296, NOTE 7.—Cf. GOGARTEN, loc. cit., p. 42: "No hostility, however passionate and far-reaching, no opposition, however wild, can burst these bonds, can really sever men from each other, on the contrary, such action only rivets them to one another with iron chains," etc.

PAGE 297, NOTE 8.—Cf. my article on *Secularism as a Problem of the Church* in the *International Review of Missions* (1930). DILTHEY'S work, *Weltanschauung und Analyse des Menschen seit Renaissance und Reformation*, prepared the way for this truth. In the criticism of this individualism I agree to a great extent with that which O. SPANN on the one side, and THEODOR LITT on the other, have alleged against him; but the fact that their criticism is not radical comes out plainly in the text, and in what is said in the following notes.

PAGE 298, NOTE 9.—There is no purely naturalistic sociology; even the sociology of HERBERT SPENCER, and that which is based upon it, never proceeds purely causally—indeed, were it to do so, it would have to cease speaking about man at all; it is rather a mixture of causalism and individualistic rationalism. This applies also to TÖNNIES, whose idea of community is based absolutely upon the rationalistic idea of personality, but who, as a disciple of SPENCER, lays great stress on the causal factors, in the way which is typical of the sociology of the pre-war period. On the other hand, when the starting point is altered, and, as in LÉVY-BRUHL'S work, this is placed in the soul of primitive man, or, as in the writings of HEIDEGGER, in the pre-rational consciousness, which always combines with the consciousness of self-hood the awareness of a relation to the other, there breaks through a wholly new perception of the connexion between "I" and "Thou," which is neither rationalistic nor Idealistic. But this view of community cannot be radical;

it remains a restricted and limited spirit of community, of a kind which will be demonstrated later on in the text. (See above, pp. 303 ff.).

PAGE 298, NOTE 10.—Here I mean that conception of the relation between the individual and the collective whole which until recently assumed the title of "sociology" pure and simple, and which, like Positivism in general, absolutely predominated in this whole sphere. In German sociology, during the last twenty years, a significant change has taken place; universalism and the theory of the organism now contest the field with the previously positivist sociology. Cf. the—to some extent—very pertinent criticism in LITT: *Individuum und Gemeinschaft*, especially pages 205 and 229 (against WEISE and VIERKANDT). It is obvious that Marxist "historical materialism" is only a particular form of this sociology.

PAGE 298, NOTE 11.—The interesting book by LITT, *Individuum und Gemeinschaft*, is an attempt to overcome abstract universalism. LITT perceives that the problem of community is the problem of the "I" and the "Thou." But he evidently has no conception of all the new things that have been said on this fundamental theme since EBNER, BUBER, and GOGARTEN have given us the fruit of their thinking on this subject. He conceives the Self (the Ego) only as a centre of experience and of knowledge, which is "connected" with the other centres by means of exchange of their peculiar aspects. The "impossibility of changing one's position" (p. 224), and the perspective to which this gives rise, is the special element in his theory. This is no small service; but it certainly has very little to do with community. Over against the abstractions of Hegelianism this theory means the assertion of the individual element, but this does not mean that the *personal* element is emphasized. The individual and the "community" (it should be called "the universal") stand in an irreconcilable relation of tension towards each other. The individual is only that which is not universal; the individual, thus conceived, is not wholly absorbed into the universal, he constitutes the incalculable element of resistance in the midst of convenient generalities. But the individual must continually assert himself against the universal and *vice versa*. The more the one has the less has the other. That is also quite correct, where the individual is concerned; but it is the very opposite of the truth where we are dealing with the question of the "individual" and the community. The real individual and the real community are not related to each other by a tension, but by a relation of identity; the truly personal and the truly communal is one and the same thing—it is love. LITT's line of argument lies wholly within the sphere of the intellectual and the aesthetic; the problem of responsibility does not once appear—just as in the writings of LEIBNIZ.

PAGE 299, NOTE 12.—Theories based on the idea of the organism are alive to-day in various forms, in the teaching of BECHER and DRIESCH for instance—with their interest in natural science—as well as in that of SPENGLER and SPANN. Here I refer to SPANN, since he is the thinker who uses his sociological ideas as the basis of his theory of political economy, and of his theory of political science, and is thus enabled to give unusual significance to his ideas. I also need to discuss his views because very often his formulations sound like my own, as, for instance, when he speaks of *Gezweiung* (union of two, a coined word—TR.) as the fundamental fact of human life as a whole (*Der wahre Staat*, p. 39), or when he constantly reiterates as his main argument, that the individual does not enter into the community as a finished article, but can indeed only be thought of within it as a human being (for example *Gesellschaftslehre*, p. 261). But in spite of these apparent analogies there exists between SPANN's idea of the community and my own the vast difference between a romantically interpreted speculative Idealism and the faith of Scripture and of the Reformation. This contrast manifests itself immediately in the definition of the relation between the individual and the community. For SPANN the community is an independent entity, which is higher than the individuals which compose it (*Gesellschaftslehre*, p. 268); it is a whole, which has the same relation to the individual as the organism to its members. Here the analogy of the organism is not a simile, but a constructive principle. "The primary element, the original reality, from which all is derived, is not the individual but the whole, the community" (*Der wahre Staat*, p. 29). "The whole, the community, is the actual reality, and the whole is the primary element, the individual is likewise only really present as a component part of the latter, it is, therefore, that which is derived" (ibid). This Whole is super-individual, it is the true reality; "this (reality) alone awakens, produces, nourishes, and moulds the individual" (p. 43). In the definition of this super-individual whole the thought of SPANN oscillates between a conception which is purely Platonic, spiritual, and based on ideas, and one which is biological, organic, and in harmony with life, characteristic of Romanticism as a whole (cf., for instance, the controversial statements in *Der wahre Staat*, pp. 187 ff., with the remarks on the philosophy of history at the beginning of the book, and in his *Gesellschaftsphilosophie*, in the *Handbuch der Philosophie* by BAEUMLER and SCHRÖTER). But however that may be, SPANN is consciously and deliberately a metaphysician, and the super-existent which in his view is "articulated" in the *Gezweiungen*, is an impersonal Absolute, which he calls "God." But in all the writings of SPANN there is no sign of the "community" as I mean it—of community, that is, which is only real in the relation between persons, which has nothing higher than itself, but is itself the ultimate, which does not subordinate the individual to the whole, but in which the whole is simply the *communio* of the individuals.

639

The peculiarity of his organological conception of community comes out very plainly in his hierarchical structure of society. It is that fundamental idea of a hierarchy which works from above downwards, which we find already in the writings of the Areopagite, and which predominates in medieval Neo-Platonism. At the same time, I would like to make it quite clear, with all possible emphasis, that in spite of all this there is a great deal to learn from this conception of society, and from its application to political economy and to the State, since it is very suitable for breaking down the atomistic individualism which still so largely prevails.

PAGE 301, NOTE 13.—The expression "Christian" is always a little awkward, since it gives the impression of something which is already present and settled; and yet we cannot do without it. Rightly understood, this adjective ought really to indicate that which is not by any means settled and fixed, namely an "existence" in "Christ" and in "the Church" through faith, that is, to something which only exists at all *in actu*.

PAGE 303, NOTE 14.—This "community," which is determined by something, is present in the "forms of community," the social structures of any kind, which will be discussed in the following pages.

PAGE 303, NOTE 15.—Here I mean that which gives to friendship its element of exclusiveness, that which causes me to be the friend of *this* particular person and not of someone else. Natural affinity, a natural pleasure in each other is the presupposition, the "local colour" of friendship. (See below, pp. 517 ff.)

PAGE 305, NOTE 16.—The rational ethic never gets further than Justice. Justice is that part of ethics which can be defined in legal terms. It reflects the anthropology of reason, the conception of the Self as completely independent and isolated. Here, therefore, is the origin of all theories of the Law of Nature; its basic conception —as SCHLATTER confirms in his theory of justice—is the idea of equality, which for its part is based upon the conception of the Self as "also a Self." Since the other is "also a Self," which, measured by the standard of reason, has the same rights, the "right" relationship is necessarily that of equality. To this there corresponds the idea of commutative (arithmetical) justice. Distributive or proportional justice is derived from that through the consideration of an inequality which exists, for some reason or another, but which is not further discussed; from the very outset the "Thou" is inserted as a—so to speak—double-valued or half-valued Self, and on this presupposition equality is then demanded. It should be granted "according to desert." In saying this, it is true, an irrational element has been admitted—that of the original inequality—but this is neither justified for any reason nor, once it has been admitted, is the demand for rational equality abandoned. It might be proved how through this door of distributive justice the "relative Law of Nature" enters into the ecclesiastical doctrine of the Law of Nature. "The dignity in accordance with which" we are to give every man that which is his, is likewise the key to the distribution on the presupposition of which the process can, moreover, go on in a rational and egalitarian manner.

PAGE 306, NOTE 17.—When ALTHAUS (*Communio Sanctorum*, p. 82), following SCHLATTER, thinks that he ought to censure the Reformer's conception of love—which indeed he has described most excellently —by pointing out their one-sided reference to the *need* of the brethren, he overlooks the fact that while certainly CARITAS is only concerned with this kind of need, it does not destroy the natural motives but permeates them. Only the intrinsic nature of love ought to be made plain, and this Schlatter does not do. Love does not shut out a certain knowledge of value and a certain value-judgment, but it is not itself a value-judgment. As an historical judgment, however, what ALTHAUS says remains true: in Lutheranism— and indeed also in Reformed circles—love gained this one-sided character, because it misunderstood its own nature in a legalistic manner, and thus out of the fundamental relationship became a practical rule. This is how it was that CARITAS came to have its narrow and almost technical character of *Liebestätigkeit* (Literally, activity of love, i.e. "works of mercy"—TR.).

PAGE 306, NOTE 18.—On this point see G. SPOERRI: *Das Inkoordinable in der Philosophie, J. J. Gourds*, pp. 32 ff., where this antithesis between rationality and irrationality, between immanence and transcendence, in reference to justice and love is unusually clearly perceived.

NOTES ON CHAPTER XXVIII

PAGE 310, NOTE 1.—The older form of Calvinistic ethics also tends to place alongside of each other "Our duty towards God and towards men," which is taken for granted in the Catholic system of ethics. The "two Tables" of the Decalogue provide the external occasion for this, while Luther simply wished to point out that the second Table is based on the First. It would be worth while to examine this question more fully, in order to find out whether the fact that the two "Tables" are placed side by side—which leads naturally to the fact that the one was immediately ranked higher than the other, was not the cause, or the partial cause, of the early development of an ascetic semi-monastic Pietism of the kind represented by TERSTEEGEN.

PAGE 312, NOTE 2.—CALVIN, the "legalistic" thinker, argues against obedience to the Sabbath Commandment wholly in the spirit of the above remarks (*Institutio*, II, 8, 31). The Sabbath Commandment has been abrogated by Christ; for He Himself is the fulfilment of the Sabbath, cf. pp. 33 and 34.

641

PAGE 314, NOTE 3.—With the introduction of the Aristotelian conception of virtue, whose guiding principle is human self-development, the perfecting of personality in itself, and with the religious correlate of this Ethos, the mystical ideal of life, there also emerges what is utterly alien to the spirit of the Bible: occupation with oneself, "my duty towards myself." No Protestant moralist has ever expounded these "special duties to oneself" with so much loving care as—characteristically!—RICHARD ROTHE, in whose "Ethic" they fill nearly three hundred pages, and indeed, in a logical way, they are related to the question of virtue: the duty of educating oneself in virtuous qualities, virtuous happiness, virtuous energy of personality, etc. Certainly the whole of this treatment of the question is valuable, but all this could only exist in a process of reflection which artificially isolates the self; in reality these virtues do not arise directly out of a process of self-education, but they are the unconscious by-products of the right way of acting and living in community, just as the right and natural kind of gymnastics does not take place before a mirror but on the playing-field. In itself self-introspection is morbid or unethical.

PAGE 315, NOTE 4.—The highest "fruit of the morbid, non-moral individualism of our own day is the glorification of Narcissism by PAUL VALÉRY; it is at least logical and frank, and thus it reveals the *Ethos* of a certain "spirituality" which sets up a standard of its own, and is wholly occupied with the Self in isolation from others. It is not a far cry from VALÉRY to GEORGE.

PAGE 316, NOTE 5.—It is noteworthy how narrow this sphere with which we are dealing has become. The whole "doctrine of Virtue" lies outside it, and within it there are simply the points of contact, where the connexion between the Self and the Community become visible in "I myself," and call attention to themselves.

PAGE 316, NOTE 6.—It is characteristic that in ROTHE's ethic of self-education it is precisely this relevant Christian point of view which disappears; everything is regarded from the point of view of *cultivation*, and that means, the cultural, non-ethical, or only indirectly ethical point of view. Here the Greek basis of this way of thinking comes out quite plainly. Calvin, on the contrary, regards the whole Christian life from the point of view of self-denial; here, of course, there can be no idea of an ethic of individual self-cultivation. The postulate—constantly repeated during the last century—of a "positive" ethic (in Neo-Protestantism, emerging in TROELTSCH, for instance) is at bottom simply a return to the Greek understanding of the Good as "education" or "cultivation."

PAGE 316, NOTE 7.—The failure to recognize this distinction in the thought of SCHLEIERMACHER and ROTHE leads back to the Greek Ethos, or proceeds from it; the cultivation of the self to its perfection of vigour, a kind of athletic ideal of a higher order.

PAGE 317. NOTE 8.—The fundamental Thomistic conception is that of the *Habitus*; that of Scripture is the *actus* in faith and love.

PAGE 317, NOTE 9.—Education is not ethical but cultural. But like all that is cultural it is under the control of the Divine Command. In the sphere of education, as well as in the sphere of economic life, or of the State, the Divine Command must be heard and obeyed. But Idealism, and its successor Neo-Protestantism, makes education itself a moral principle, and indeed even *the* moral principle, because it conceives the moral as self-development; this again is because, in the last resort, it is individualistic, although it lays so much stress upon the historical and the social element in education. The historical and the social element is then a means of education of the Self. Think of the poet's phrase: "When the rose decks herself, she adorns the garden!"

NOTES ON CHAPTER XXIX

PAGE 321, NOTE 1.—Where love has to be described apart from its social setting, the only possible principle of individualization is that of inner variety, that is, the psychological point of view. Here then, in this subordinate position, SCHLATTER's classification of love as will, knowledge, and feeling is justified. But SCHLATTER applies this psychological point of view to the definition of the conditions of community, which is obviously a mistake.

PAGE 321, NOTE 2.—Love should always be the *motive*, even where the *outward* contact has to be determined by justice. The actual character of our "duties" is always determined by our "calling," and therefore by justice; but justice should never be the actual motive. I cannot understand how SCHLATTER can make his ideas of the equal value of love and justice tally with the teaching of the Sermon on the Mount.

PAGE 324, NOTE 3.—Religious tolerance does not mean that the "tolerant" person regards truth as "relative." Precisely because I have a definite Christian faith I am commanded to meet a person whose faith is different from my own not only as a human being, in the spirit of love, renouncing all coercive methods of forcing Christian influence upon him, but also, in view of the imperfection of my own faith, of my knowledge of the Word of God, I ought always to hold myself open to the possibility of receiving correction through other people.

PAGE 325, NOTE 4.—The problem raised by the question: "In cases of emergency should one tell a lie, or not?" is usually discussed in such a legalistic spirit that from the very outset it is sterile; this leads to rigoristic assertions which are in opposition to practical life, and indeed to conscientious conduct. No one condemns lying with more feeling than the Catholic moralists, and in so doing they confirm the above rule. But what certainly does make the problem of lying so particularly difficult is the fact that love, where the individual is concerned, does not permit us to falsify the spiritual means of social exchange. This is the point of view from which KANT proceeds to an unconditional rejection of all lying, in principle. We ought to take this Kantian point of view into consideration (the view, namely, that lying entirely shatters confidence), but we cannot accept his final judgment: that only that is good which, practised by all, would make life in community possible. Love is constantly doing extraordinary things. The principle of always telling the truth is the *Lex*, obedience to which makes decent social life possible; but we must make a distinction between this assertion and that which I am bound to do actually, here and now, out of love for my neighbour. To confuse this suspension of the law of truth with laxity is only possible to one who cannot rid himself of the legalistic habit of mind, and who thinks that the most legalistic point of view is the most earnest.

PAGE 326, NOTE 5.—*Matt. v. 39*. It is pure fanaticism to think that the political method of "passive resistance" has any connexion with the commands of the Sermon on the Mount. Passive resistance is a political coercive method, just as much as the actual use of force; it is even an extremely refined and subtle method of coercion, since, if it is adopted by a private individual against the authority in power, it offers the latter the choice of either renouncing the effort to impose its will, or of making use of the method of force. Thus to the extent in which it virtually consists in holding up all actual authorities to moral contempt, this policy is extremely and subtly immoral, and its glorification by pacifists is a sign of ethical confusion in their thinking. But, on the other hand, the *Ethos* which disapproves of the use of force is based on a powerful moral sentiment, and represents a high ethical standard—that is, so long as it really remains an *Ethos* and does not degenerate into mere "tactics"; if this *Ethos* could be brought to bear on politics, as a regulative and corrective principle of political methods, it would be an event of the greatest importance. The ethical element predominates in Gandhi's personal conduct, the political in the Movement for "Civil Disobedience" initiated by Gandhi.

PAGE 328, NOTE 6.—Nietzsche's criticism of Christianity ought not to be met by laying the main emphasis upon the "positive" element in the Christian Ethos; in so doing we distort it, for indeed Nietzsche saw Christianity far more truly than the majority of his "Christian" opponents. It is, and indeed remains, a fact that the distinctive element in the Christian Ethos is self-denial and surrender, that is, the passive aspect. But what Nietzsche did not understand was the actual greatness and world-transforming power of this passive Ethos; and the point at which he came to grief was this: he confused the pitiful picture of Christianity as it actually is with its essential truth. Nietzsche's realistic analysis of this "average" Christianity, however, has never been surpassed, and it can hardly be contested.

NOTES ON CHAPTER XXX

PAGE 331, NOTE 1.—Ideas create what we call the "doctrinaire spirit," fanaticism, and party passion; ideas create the spirit which can say: *fiat justitia pereat mundus;* every idealist must necessarily— that is, if he is really in earnest and not simply playing with ideas— be "a Knight of the Infinite," in the sense in which KIERKEGAARD uses this expression; he must necessarily be a person who is difficult to understand. IBSEN's "Brand" has no connexion with Christianity; Brand is rather "the legalist," the kind of man who is obsessed by an idea and in bondage to it; by means of this idea he does not become "this individual," in the sense in which Kierkegaard uses the term, but he becomes an isolated individual, who no longer sees human beings as *persons*. See also the anticipatory reply of KIERKEGAARD to this misunderstanding of IBSEN's, in his book *Furcht und Zittern*, with its description of the true Christian in the incognito of the "Philistine."

PAGE 332, NOTE 2.—Our Feminist extremists, who deny that woman is any different from man, ought to insist that the Biblical simile of "God, the Father" should be made equal; God-Father-Mother, as is claimed by Christian Science. The Biblical simile of Fatherhood is not intended to imply that maternal love is something on a lower level, but the idea of Fatherhood is used in order to show that love includes the idea of sovereignty. To the ancient Jew the word "father" meant something quite different from the equation of *Father* with the good-natured "Daddy" which is what it suggests to the man of the twentieth century; the word "Father" in this connexion contains the idea of the *patria potestas*.

PAGE 336, NOTE 3.—The fact that we place the whole of the ethic of society under the conception of the "orders" does not only restore the connexion with the ethic of the Reformation, but it has this further advantage: it shows quite clearly the chief point of view from which faith regards life in society. It is the Will of God that we should participate in this life in community through entrance into these "orders" of community; and in each of these orders in particular He points us to the order of Creation, without the knowledge of which we cannot understand His Command. "The order" is therefore the actual theological category of the ethic of society as such, thus—from the theological point of view—it is that which distinguishes life in society from the personal relation between the "I" and the "Thou," or rather, it is that through which that personal relation receives its particular modification by society. The ethic of society is the manifestation of love as it is determined by the "order." As I have already spoken about this modification in a general way, it is the task of this section to interpret the individual orders, as such, from the point of view of faith, and to show the special way in which they modify love.

PAGE 337, NOTE 4.—When HOLL emphasizes the fact that Luther describes the activity of man within these orders by the image of the "masks" of God, and in so doing makes man the instrument of the Divine activity, this is not, as KARL BARTH seems to think it is, an arbitrary interpretation of HOLL's, but it is a genuine Lutheran idea, and—whether BARTH likes to hear this or not—it is a genuine idea of the Bible: God does *His* work through men. This is how we are to read *Romans xiii*! (Cf. KARL BARTH: *Die Arbeit als Problem der theologischen Ethik, Theol. Bl.*, 1931.)

PAGE 339, NOTE 5.—*1 Cor. vii. 29, 30*. We might very well inscribe this Pauline formula upon the whole of Christian ethics; for it is the formula which describes the way of life in the world of one who is in Christ, and, by this very fact, is in the new world.

NOTES ON CHAPTER XXXI

PAGE 340, NOTE 1.—Even the utilitarian ethical system of JOHN STUART MILL, or the evolutionary system of HERBERT SPENCER, simply takes for granted the permanence of marriage as the final goal of sexual-moral development. Of the theological moralists of the last century I suppose we may say that the one who saw most deeply into the problems of marriage and into the insecurity of the whole question was A. v. OETTINGEN (*Moralstatistik*), while the first to perceive the whole danger of the situation were TROELTSCH and SCHLATTER.

PAGE 341, NOTE 2.—A rather "pointless" discussion of the problem of marriage from the Christian point of view is contained in a book called: *Der Kampf um die Ehe*, a collection of articles published by SCHLIPKÖTER and BÖHME. It is defensive in this false sense, without any attempt to understand more fully the reason for the offensive of its opponents. The paper by ALTHAUS is the only one which suggests the possibility of further developments, a promise which has been fulfilled in his new outline of Ethics.

PAGE 341, NOTE 3.—This is the subject of the book on Marriage by KEYSERLING. In spite of all his efforts KEYSERLING is unable to get beyond his aesthetic and aristocratic conception of the spirit, and the kind of marriage at which he aims would only be possible for elect souls.

PAGE 342, NOTE 4.—SCHLEIERMACHER (*Die christliche Sitte,* pp. 336 ff.) does indeed wrestle seriously with the problem of the Christian argument for monogamy, but he does not get further than the assertion that it is based on the need for uniting procreation and education (*Erziehung*). ROTHE (*Ethik*, II, pp. 265 ff.), like a genuine Gnostic, bases marriage on the fact that each sex is incomplete without the other; he goes so far as to assert: "thus the sexually determined human being is not essentially a complete human person, but it is only the two sexes together which form a complete human person" (p. 225). Then, however, he absolutely contradicts himself by saying in another place—quite in the genuine evangelical spirit—that there is no unconditional law of marriage (V, 10); on the other hand he says that "at the most," he is willing to admit "that it is an unconditional moral demand to love once in a sexual way; but the same cannot be said about the act of entering into the marriage relation" (V, 10). It is impossible to construct an argument for monogamy from such contradictory theses, and this he does not attempt. But the Lutherans also leave us in the lurch. FRANK, for instance, cannot say anything more about the basis of monogamy than this: monogamy expresses the fact that man is a "subject," or the value of the individual, i.e. "that one individual in not only a means to an end where the other is concerned, but that monogamy ensures a life-relationship . . . which can never be achieved with the same truth and intensity in polygamy" (II, 376). VILMAR (II, 188) is content to make a simple appeal to the letter of Scripture ("Monogamy has been instituted and commanded by the Creator as the original natural state. . . . The indissoluble character of marriage has been stated most plainly in *Matthew v. 32*"). HARLESS bases marriage—in a very indefinite way—on the unity between the natural basis and a personal life-relationship (p. 510). All that W. HERRMANN can say about the argument for marriage is this: "The family arises out of the fact that the most powerful natural instinct, by means of which the species makes individuals serve its purposes, is controlled by human beings and used for the purpose of the most intimate personal fellowship" (p. 151). MAYER bases monogamy upon the twofold purpose of reproduction and of psycho-physical complementation (pp. 266 and 271). This statement is only supported by negative arguments, by showing, for instance, that some non-monogamous forms of marriage are unsuitable for the fulfilment of this twofold purpose. SCHLATTER's argument is just as inadequate: "Whoever wishes for love within marriage, will desire unconditional marriage with the one partner, because only by this type of marriage is the whole of one's life and property given to the partner without any division at all" (p. 394). On this point A. v. OETTINGEN (Cf. pp. 647 ff.) comes nearest to the view that I am here trying to suggest.

PAGE 342, NOTE 5.—The MORGAN theory of the development of sex conditions, which to-day plays such a sinister part in the popular literature of the type of the Enlightenment, has been not merely corrected but absolutely reversed by the recent anthropological researches of W. SCHMIDT, MALINOWSKI, and others; at the very beginning of the course of development which we can trace there stands the monogamous family—and indeed this monogamy is often of a very pure and strict type. Only with the progress of civilization do other forms of marriage arise alongside of monogamy. It is well known that Wundt, in his *Völkerpsychologie*, has given his support to this view. Cf. the article *Ehe und Familie* in the *Handwörterbuch der Soziologie*, pp. 112 ff.

PAGE 342, NOTE 6.—This is the turn taken by the problem, which, foreshadowed in Romanticism (but still usually interpreted in a very conservative way), has dominated the situation from the time of Ellen Key onwards. Every one can see that fellowship in love is absolutely justified; but whether marriage too—at the most—is equally justified? But usually the view of Ellen Key is accepted, namely, that compared with the perfection of the love-relationship, marriage is rather a secondary matter of adaptation to conventional requirements. The argument of the modern novel—or rather of the novel which until quite recently was "modern"—defends the "rights of love" over against marriage.

PAGE 343, NOTE 7.—In the post-war period politicians who are concerned about the birth-rate, especially in France, have demanded official recognition for and furtherance of polygamy; and indeed this is not so very surprising when we think of the vast surplus of women. On the other hand, other students of this subject have proved, long ago, that upon the whole, polygamous peoples are less fruitful than those which practise monogamy.

PAGE 343, NOTE 8.—Von Oettingen gives some extremely interesting proofs—of course his statistics are based on material which is now out of date, but his proofs are based on a broad and solid foundation—of an inexplicable natural tendency, after a nation has lost large numbers of men, to restore the balance by an unusual surplus of boy-babies (cf. *Moralstatistik*, pp. 44 ff.). I do not know whether such a movement has begun to appear since the Great War; in any case, even if the movement has begun, it has not yet been able to make up for the great loss of man-power due to the War.

PAGE 344, NOTE 9.—The first people to protest solemnly against the objective theory of marriage in the name of love and of individuality were the Romantics. Schlegel's *Lucinde* is of particular interest for us to-day as the starting-point of the whole modern view of the subject. Cf. also Macholz: *Die romantische Ehe und der lutherische Ehestand.*

PAGE 345, NOTE 10.—*Matthew xix. 4 ff.* Here with all the clarity that we could possibly desire, in a decisive passage Jesus Himself utilizes the conception of the order of creation, and at the same time distinguishes it from the orders, as they are related to sin. Hence I cannot understand how anyone can maintain that the conception of the order of Creation has no Scriptural foundation.

PAGE 349, NOTE 11.—The Reformers themselves pointed out that the New Testament proof for the Sacrament of Marriage is based upon the Latin rendering of the Pauline word μυστήριον

648

(*Ephesians v. 32*) by *sacramentum*, that is, upon the misinterpretation of the Greek word—that primarily *sacramentum* simply expresses what we have described above as a *sanctum*, and that marriage only came to be regarded as a sacrament, in the dogmatic sense of the word, quite late. The argument which is produced by KOHNSTAMM in his recent book (*Schepper en Schepping*, III, pp. 317–330) for the validity of the claim that marriage is a sacrament is wholly untenable. In the ecclesiastical sense of the word a "sacrament" does not denote a sacred symbol, but it means the communication of grace, by means of the Church. In Protestantism also the Sacrament belongs, of necessity, to the order of redemption, not to the order of creation, to the Church, and not to Nature as created by God. To make marriage into a sacrament means to connect it with the Church in the way in which Baptism and the Eucharist are connected with the Church, as a sign and a means of communicating the Divine grace of Redemption.

PAGE 349, NOTE 12.—The relation between man and woman outside the state of marriage—that is, outside the fellowship of love and companionship which is characterized by fidelity, and the recognition of the fact that these two individuals are bound to one another for life—is as a rule accompanied by a tinge of eroticism; pleasure in the individuality of another here becomes delight in the sex-aspect of individuality. This relationship does not itself, as it is, necessarily come under the condemnation of *Matthew v. 28*; but *actually* this will always be the case. Therefore, this question ought not to be treated only from the point of view of the order of creation but also from that of sin.

PAGE 349, NOTE 13.—A. V. OETTINGEN quotes with justifiable approval E. V. HARTMANN: "The non-periodic character of passion, and the sense of shame, are the earliest foundations upon which is based the fact that the sex relationships of human beings are in a higher sphere than those of the animals." See also the beautiful observations of VON OETTINGEN in his *Moralstatistik*, p. 76.

PAGE 351, NOTE 14.—To gain a real understanding of what this kind of ethical materialism means we need to let the gigantic work of the Jesuit SANCHEZ, *De Matrimonio*, or BUSENBAUM'S chapter on marriage in his *Medulla Theologiae Moralis* make its own impression upon our minds. Sexual faults are measured solely by the objective departure of the action from the natural sex function in "normal" marriage, so that, for instance, masturbation is considered worse than sex intercourse outside of marriage, refusal of the *debitum* after frequent *coitus* in one night is regarded as a sin, but the unreasonable attitude of the husband is not regarded as wrong.

PAGE 351, NOTE 15.—This spirit of legalism—in opposition to the spirit of Luther—comes out in an appalling way even in BULLINGER'S little book on marriage. It is no different, however, in the theology of Luther's followers.

PAGE 352, NOTE 16.—This is the point at which the modern conception of the erotic element, which is both Romantic and Naturalistic, shows that it is the offspring of the illusion of ROUSSEAU. An unsurpassed example of such erotic illusion is DIOTIMA: *School of Love*.

PAGE 352, NOTE 17.—This statement, a principle of the genuine ethic of marriage of the Reformation, is only valid on the similar Reformation presupposition that marriage is not made into a state of married life which conceals the life of a monk and a nun, which is the logical result of the Puritan and Pietist view of sex intercourse—most particularly since it has been found necessary, to some extent, to restrict the birth-rate.

NOTES ON CHAPTER XXXII

PAGE 356, NOTE 1.—The stages of the decline of the Reformation and Biblical idea of marriage can be determined at the following points: (1) Pietistic Puritanical legalism, making the idea of love (Eros) indifferent—rise of prudishness. (2) The exclusive basis of marriage upon love, with keen criticism of the objective view, in Romanticism. Here already the idea of "free love" over against marriage with its legal bonds, is theoretically and practically recognized. (3) Anthropology, determined by the biological idea of evolution, conceives love chiefly as the sex-instinct, and severs the satisfaction of the instinct from the spiritual and personal element, and then—of course—completely from the objective legal element in marriage. In this extreme form, as the well-known "glass of water" theory, it was introduced into the ideology of Bolshevism, but not without having a struggle with the genuine desire for love, and with the traditional Christian ideal of marriage. For a magnificent description of this controversy see KOLLONTHAIS: *Wege der Liebe*.

PAGE 357, NOTE 2.—A history of marriage within Pietism still needs to be written; it would be a work of merit. From this point of view the life of JOHN WESLEY is of very great interest.

PAGE 358, NOTE 3.—Naturally it was the Romantics who first began the process of ridiculing the public and legal aspect of marriage—the young SCHLEIERMACHER no less than his friend the author of the letters to *Lucinde*. We ought not to deny that to some extent this protest was necessary, and great confusion of thought has been caused by the fact that the contrast between free love and marriage has been conceived mainly as the difference between a marriage recognized by the State and one which has not been recognized by the State. It is not the recognition by the State which is the decisive sign of marriage as compared with free love, but the recognition of the obligation to *fidelity*. The real dissolution of the marriage relationship occurred when the obligation to mutual loyalty was abandoned, and when the following fatal argument gained increasing influence; that when love ceases it is immoral to carry on the marriage relationship any longer; it is this which annuls a marriage, not the refusal of legal and conventional legitimization to the marriage.

PAGE 359, NOTE 4.—At first it might seem as though this restriction has become absolutely unnecessary at the present time; but it seems to me that it is necessary, in view of the efforts which are again being made to regard marriage as a sacrament. We cannot be too earnest in our opposition to this tendency, in the interest of the genuinely "secular" character of marriage.

PAGE 361, NOTE 5.—We ought not to forget that owing to modern intellectual development the feeling for and sensitiveness to the compatibility or incompatibility of two individualities has been greatly intensified. It is not only a false kind of individualism which to-day makes it difficult to endure a marriage without love, but it is also a greater intellectual sensitiveness.

PAGE 362, NOTE 6.—It is my definite conviction, which I hold in common with many other scholars, that this phrase, "saving for the cause of fornication," was not uttered by Jesus Himself, but that it is an interpolation by the Early Church, which had already misunderstood the sayings of Jesus in a legalistic way, and therefore needed such a corrective. The theory of the reasons for divorce belongs to the saddest chapters in Christian ethics; nowhere is the mingling of law and ethics so crude as it is here, and accordingly there prevails an absolutely immoral materialism of thought, both in that which is recognized as a reason for divorce, as well in that which is not recognized as such.

PAGE 362, NOTE 7.—It is constantly asserted that this Catholic identification of the moral and the legal demand is of great educational value for the people as a whole, and that it is a stabilizing influence, and it is pointed out that since the introduction of civil marriage which can be dissolved, marriage relations have lost their previous stability. In making these statements people forget that it is not the modern legal situation but the movement of thought in the last few centuries, chiefly the sensitive self-consciousness of the individual, and individualism as a principle, which have produced this instability; that, on the other hand, the retention of the idea of marriage which, as far as possible, is indissoluble, has bred prostitution, the practice of keeping "mistresses," and so-called "free relationships." The fact that the increase in the number of divorces is not due to the greater ease in procuring divorce is shown by the fact that in countries where divorce is difficult to obtain the number of divorces is no less than in the opposite instance.

PAGE 363, NOTE 8.—The arguments used by H. MARCH, in his valuable work entitled *Der religiöse Sinn der sexuellen Krise* (1930) against JUDGE LINDSEY seem to me—like so many other protests against this American writer—to be lacking in fairness to Lindsey's real view, although his rejection of Lindsey's views is perfectly right. Lindsey's ideology is so superficial that it is enough to make one's hair stand on end! But behind it there is a real man, full of kindness of heart, and with an amazingly clear view of reality. It is very easy to demolish his arguments · but it is all the more difficult to deal with the problem to which he desires to draw our attention.

PAGE 364, NOTE 9.—Our ideas of the extent of this "surplus" are often rather fantastic. Even to-day it is not very great in the neutral countries. The figures for Switzerland for 1929 are the following: *Population* (as a whole): *Males*—1,871,123; *Females*—2,009,197; thus an excess of women of 138,074 or 3·6 per cent. The picture looks rather different certainly when we connect the figures with the years during which marriage is possible. So, for instance, the surpluses for the years 20–24 are 5·3 per cent; for 25–29, 6·4 per cent; for 30–34, 5·3 per cent; for 35–39, 2·9 per cent; for 40–44, 3·0 per cent. (These figures are taken from the statistics in the *Swiss Year Book of Statistics* for 1929.) Further, we must note that of course the neutral countries have also been affected by the loss of men in the countries at war, although naturally their losses have been much smaller. Whether, after this has been taken into account, the balance asserted by VON OETTINGEN would be the result, it is difficult to decide.

PAGE 366, NOTE 10.—DR. MARCH misrepresents the real situation in an absolutely monstrous manner when—in the work which we have just mentioned above—he says (p. 27): "Of the four hundred drones in a bee-hive only one for instance succeeds in mating. Accordingly it is purely a divine law of nature that one section of mankind should be destined for a life without sex-fulfilment." What is contrary to Nature cannot be expressed in a worse way than in explaining it as a Divine law of nature.

PAGE 366, NOTE 11.—Luther, as is well known, laid great emphasis on the right of marriage for every healthy person, from the point of view of the idea of Creation. ELLEN KEY's statement (in *Das Recht auf Mutterschaft*, p. 206): "One who steals in order to save his life ought not to be-punished," which refers to this act of self-defence on the part of women who are obliged to forgo marriage, would have been seriously considered by Luther, even if he could not have wholly endorsed it. The Church ought to be quite clear what she is asking when she *takes for granted*, as an obvious duty, the fact that so many millions of girls who are able, and willing, for marriage, have to renounce this most natural "right of woman." On this cf. LUTHER WA. VI, 558, and X, 2 Section, p. 278.

PAGE 367, NOTE 12.—We must not forget that in spite of the surplus number of women there is a large number of men—capable of marriage—who are still single (for Switzerland in 1929: in the years between 20–24, 92 per cent are single; 25–29, 59·7 per cent; 30–34, 34 per cent; 35–39, 22 per cent; 40–44, 16·7 per cent; 45–49, 14·8 per cent, etc.). It is evident that this large number of single men is closely connected with the readiness of so many girls for free relationships. On the other hand it must certainly be admitted that the gratifying decline in the number of prostitutes is due in whole or in part to the increase in the practice of free relationships among "decent people."

PAGE 367, NOTE 13.—At the present time this subject is often discussed in Church circles, but it is rarely discussed honestly and realistically. The "Copec" Conference, to its honour, was the first to dare to say something in opposition to the traditional view on this question; this it did in its Minority Report. On the German theological side the same has been done by H. WAGNER in his work: *Geburtenregelung als theologisches Problem*, 1930. His views agree to a very large extent with those which I have publicly expressed for several years, but which I here express for the first time in print.

PAGE 368, NOTE 14.—"He who neglects the sexual side of marriage will be called a sinner"; the Pharisee was only allowed to withdraw from his wife for short periods—for two weeks according to Shammai. PREISKER: *Christentum und Ehe*, pp. 73 and 83.

PAGE 368, NOTE 15.—The acceptance of this proposition alone would mean the final break with the Catholic ideal of marriage, and a very far-reaching upheaval. A great part of the present trouble, in the whole problem of marriage, is based upon the fact that it is not accepted. The proposition itself, however, is not free from danger. For, so it might be argued, why should not sexual intercourse take place between those who are not married, as an expression of erotic feelings, which in themselves are quite permissible? To this we would reply; definite erotic feelings outside marriage (and outside the relationship which should lead to marriage) are indeed, we human beings being what we are, always present in some way or other, but they are not simply "permitted"; they are always a sign of the incompleteness of married love which in its very essence is "monistic." Therefore perhaps an expression of such feelings under certain circumstances ought not to be absolutely condemned outright; but the more this expression of feeling approaches the actual sphere of sex the more dubious does it become.

PAGE 368, NOTE 16.—By this I do not mean that a marriage which is involuntarily childless is not a marriage, but it certainly is not a normal complete marriage; childlessness is a misfortune which has to be endured as such.

PAGE 368, NOTE 17.—At the present day we scarcely know what unrestricted fruitful marriage means, that is marriage apart from any kind of birth-control. In order to have some idea of this we need to study the figures for earlier periods in history, and especially the figures for countries which are wholly Catholic. J. WOLF, a scholar who has studied problems connected with population, gives some interesting figures (*Handwörterbuch der Soziologie*, pp. 52 ff) : in Scotland, in the years 1861–65 the average number of births was 7·8 per cent, in Norway, 10 per cent; and Catholic-French Canada had still higher figures. From this we can see that to-day, even in circles which do not approve of birth-control, actually—perhaps without knowing that this is what it is called—it is being practised.

PAGE 369, NOTE 18.—This is the view of the book (otherwise valuable) by HAUG : *Im Ringen um Reinheit und Kraft* (pp. 100 ff.). His *Hochehe* confuses the point of view of the order of creation with a law which is valid for actual practice.

PAGE 370, NOTE 19.—In his *Encyclica casti connubi* (authorized edition, Freiburg, p. 49) the Pope tries to meet the need of those married persons who are aware that they ought not to have any more children, and who yet do not wish to give up intercourse : the Pope tells them that he permits them to arrange it so that their intercourse shall take place on the days when there is the least likelihood of conception taking place. Obviously this means that the Catholic principle has broken down, sexual intercourse is permitted, even when its aim is not that of procreation, but indeed when the latter is to be avoided. The method alone distinguishes this kind of birth-control from that which is usually practised. The Catholic priesthood is, however, most relieved about this concession, and is now busily publishing *Konzeptkalender* (literally, conception-calendar) for popular use. Further, there is the complaint, which is heard on all hands, that even the Catholics no longer abide by the statutes of the Church, and priests who receive confessions are bidden not to probe into this question, save under special circumstances. The fact that Protestant moralists have joined in the enthusiastic admiration expressed for this Encyclical shows how deeply this legalism is also entrenched in "Protestant" thought.

PAGE 370, NOTE 20.—As a rule theologians do not remember sufficiently that during the last century Europe had an enormous increase in population, in spite of the fact that the birth-rate has, naturally, not increased, but has steadily decreased. About the year 1800 the population of Europe was reckoned to be about 160 millions, whereas to-day the total population of Europe has risen (according to the latest figures in *Brockhaus*) to *c.* 460 millions. Infant mortality used to be so great that, on the average, only a third of the children survived, so that a mother needed to bear six children in order to preserve the race; to-day three births per mother are considered adequate for this purpose (WOLF, op. cit.). Few people know that the average length of human life, which is now 56 for the man and 59 for the woman, even in 1870 was

35·6 and 38·5 respectively. At the time of Luther the average length of human life was reckoned at about 25.

PAGE 371, NOTE 21.—The figures for the births in Northern and Western Europe have gone down fairly steadily from 32·8 in the year 1876 to 19·2 in the year 1926, and the number of births from 4·4 millions to 3·6 millions. These certainly are very serious facts, and the causes which lie behind them are indeed often very serious. The way in which young married people of the present day will simply decide that they do not wish to have any children, in spite of the fact that there is no need to have these restrictions, is a sign of terrible irresponsibility and love of pleasure. But the arguments used by ecclesiastical and nationalistic bodies are so appallingly one-sided, since these same people will not see that the social conditions ought to be re-ordered in such a way that the proletariat could have larger families without a serious decline in the standard of living.

PAGE 372, NOTE 22.—The demand—in itself quite right—for the economic stability of the home comes into conflict with the far more elementary demand for the creation of satisfactory sex relationships ·and must give way to it. The Church ought to encourage people to marry young, but at the same time she must give up the traditional economic requirements of a "normal marriage."

NOTES ON CHAPTER XXXIII

PAGE 384, NOTE 1.—The word "civilization" is not used here in its original sense (*Civis*) but in a narrower sense, which has become current in modern German by being contrasted with the idea of culture (*Kultur*). Literally, however, "civilization" should mean— as it does in the French language—all that refers to historical life, and culture (*Kultur*), ought to refer to the mechanical aspect of "civilization" (cf. our word "agri-culture" (*Agri-kultur*).

PAGE 385, NOTE 2.—It is just as incorrect to speak of the work of animals as it is to speak of their play; both words presuppose freedom, whereas both the work and the play of an animal arise from an instinctive urge.

PAGE 386, NOTE 3.—"It is therefore not difficult to see that the young must be taught those useful arts that are indispensably necessary; but it is clear that . . . they must participate in such among the useful arts as will not render the person who participates in them vulgar ($\beta\acute{\alpha}\nu\alpha\nu\sigma o\nu$)[1]. . . . Hence we entitle vulgar ($\beta\alpha\nu\alpha\acute{\nu}\sigma o\nu\varsigma$) all such arts as deteriorate the condition of the body, and also the industries that earn wages; for they make the mind preoccupied and degraded" (*Aristotle, Politics*, 1337, b.) (H. RACK-

---

[1] The German rendering is *Handwerker* (manual worker).—TR.

HAM's Translation). The presupposition of this conception is slavery and helotry, which is taken for granted.

PAGE 386, NOTE 4.—On this cf. VON EICKEN: *Geschichte und System der mittelalterlichen Weltanschauung*, pp. 488 ff. One quotation gives the sense of many others: "Bernard of Clairvaux classified people according to three degrees of ascending perfection. On the lowest plane were the people in the 'world,' upon the middle plane stood the 'Active,' and upon the highest plane the 'Contemplative.'" "Of these three classes," he said, "some are within the mill, others are out in the fields, and the third class are reposing in the bedchamber. The mill is the secular life, the field is the soul of the person living in the world. The preachers of the word of God are in this field. But upon the bed rests the sacred love of the Spouse of Christ." By this classification Bernard described the lay folk, the secular clergy and the monastic orders. . . . "Happier and more perfect than the active life is the contemplative" (*de modo bene vivendi*) p. 490. Work is, however, always given a high place as a means of discipline. Work is therefore useful for the avoidance of vice, p. 492. On this point cf. THOMAS, *S.Th.* II, 2 *qu.* 182: *quanquam secundum conditionem praesentis necessitatis sit vita activa magis eligenda potior tamen est simpliciter vita contemplativa* (art. 1.), and: *Vita contemplativa ex suo genere majoris est meriti quam vita activa*; for *deum diligere secundum se es magis meritorium quam diligere proximum* (art 2). From this it is logical to conclude that the monastic life is the state of perfection, *qu.* 184–89.

PAGE 387, NOTE 5.—Cf. EGER, *Die Anschauungen Luthers vom Beruf.* STANGE: *Ethik der Arbeit, Ztschr. f. syst. Theologie*, 1927, Vol. 4. STANGE: *Luthers Theorie vom gesellschaftlichen Leben*, ibid 1930, Vol. 1.

PAGE 388, NOTE 6.—WÜNSCH says quite rightly, that the "distinctive element in Luther's view of work is that in principle he no longer measures the value of the activity according to the elevation of the value of the end which it serves, but according to the degree of its harmony with the Divine Command" (p. 546). Unfortunately, however, WÜNSCH has not noticed that with this absolutely correct statement his whole ethic, which is built upon the concept of Value, falls to the ground; that at this very point it becomes manifest that in principle it is impossible to combine his Platonist theory of value with the basic principle of the Reformation ethic. That kind of philosophy of Value can be combined, as in SCHELER, with a Catholic idea of God and of Salvation (*fruitio dei*, Highest Good, Vision of God, *vita contemplativa*), but not with the Reformation doctrine of obedience to God.

PAGE 390, NOTE 7.—That the idea of "the Mean" is really the central conception of the Aristotelian ethic, anyone can understand who has grasped the part played by the idea of the μεσότης within this system. In Thomism this Aristotelian idea gains a peculiar shade of meaning through the monastic ascetic ideal of life.

"Abstinence from the world" is the negative correlate to contemplation, as the highest ideal of life.

PAGE 393, NOTE 8.—It is not the rationalization of labour, with its vast system of distribution of labour, which is the real enemy of joy in work, but, on the one hand, it is the uncertainty of employment, and on the other, the fact that the workman is deprived of his rights (A. WEBER: *Das Berufsschicksal des Industriearbeiters*, in *Arch. f. Sozialwiss.* XXXIV, pp. 337 ff.). It is true of course that rationalization creates difficulties which must be overcome. The system of "scientific management" associated with the name of Taylor, if pushed to an extreme length, causes such a psychological over-stimulation by increasing the pace of work and the control to which it is subjected, that the human mind can only endure this artificial system at the cost of serious injury. But *this* type of rationalization is connected most closely with the economic desire for profit, and ought to be branded with the stigma of robbery of the greatest wealth of a people—its capacity for labour—as contrary to all economic common sense. On the other hand, rationalization in itself, even with the most widespread division of labour, is not an insuperable obstacle to delight in work; that is, if the social conditions under which the workman labours, and the economic reward for his work are satisfactory. Here there is a broad field—at present too little cultivated—for valuable efforts in the direction of the humanizing of labour which is quite compatible with modern developments in industry. On this point cf. ROSENSTOCK: *Lebensarbeit in der Industrie:* H. DE MAN: *Der Kampf um die Arbeitsfreude.*

PAGE 394, NOTE 9.—The problem of unemployment is undoubtedly one of the most difficult and complicated questions of all the many difficult and complicated questions of economic theory. Naturally the theological moralist is not in a position to see through its difficulties or even to suggest a solution. (On this point see E. SAITZEW: *Die Arbeitslosigkeit der Gegenwart*—a work which shows in a far-seeing way, and with a sense of urgency as well, both the complexity and the variety of the views which have to be taken into account in this question.) But this does not mean that it is impossible for a lay person to perceive the utter lack of sense in the fact that unemployment arises from over-production—an expression used by everybody. There can be two kinds of "over-production" · when more is produced than the market is able to use (which is obviously the case to-day), or, when more is produced than is required for *real* needs, which is obviously *not* the case to-day and would not be the case even if the power of production were greatly intensified. This is one point. But also the "purchasing power," which, as is evident from what has just been said, is such an important element in the question of "over-production," is in a different relation to production from that which is usually

657

accepted, that is, when we look at the economic sphere as a whole. If the collective economic sphere were a whole, then increased production would always mean increased purchasing power, since every (desirable, useful) product is also an object of exchange at our disposal, and thus represents purchasing power. In itself every increase of production ought to mean an increase in purchasing power, in national wealth, that is, if that which is necessary to sustain life is produced in sufficient measure (we have to-day so-called "over-production" in the necessities of life), and, further, if that is really produced which is wanted—so long as the production does not go beyond what is needed. Thus unemployment due to over-production can only call our attention to the utter irrationality of our present-day economic system in the distribution of goods; it shows us the insanity of being stifled by our riches, and of being destroyed by our want, at one and the same time. In America, masses of the necessities of life are destroyed because they cannot find a market, and yet at the same time, and in the same country, millions of human beings are starving because they cannot receive those goods which cannot find a market.

NOTES ON CHAPTER XXXIV

PAGE 395, NOTE 1.—The picture given in a standard work like the *Kompendium der Ethik*, by LUTHARDT, is typical of the Protestant ethics of last century as a whole. The whole economic problem is treated in one paragraph, which forms the tenth section of the chapter on "Christian Behaviour in the Family" (pp. 354–56), under the title: "Possessions and the Attitude of the Household towards Public Matters." The treatment is mainly confined to a threadbare argument in favour of private property. The Social Question, in the sense in which we use the words to-day, is likewise dealt with in one paragraph of the same chapter, under the heading: "Masters and Servants"; the only thing which is said on the subject is a sentence about the free contract of labour, which (apparently as opposed to slavery), is said to "lead to a similar result." "The dangers which spring out of this (!)" are to be "overcome by changing the merely legal relationship . . . into a relationship of personal sympathy" (p. 353). This is literally all. Again the only writer who constitutes an honourable exception is A. v. OETTINGEN. In his *Moralstatistik* he goes into a detailed examination of the relation between Labour, Capital, the division of labour, classification of callings, and Ethics, and arrives at a sharp criticism of Capitalism, even though his point of view is "socially conservative." In his *Sittenlehre* he tries to find a way out of the dilemma between "the extremes of modern industrialism" (the Manchester School, competition), and medieval quietism (the Guild System and the theory of stewardship) and sharply criticizes some of the typical phenomena of Capitalism. But his voice alone was raised in the desert of an individualistic Lutheranism. The first attempt on a large scale to outline a Protestant theory of the ethical aspect of economics is that of WÜNSCH. But his book, which in so many respects is most valuable and courageous, suffers from a disastrous confusion between the Idealistic ethic of Value and the thought of the Reformation; this emerges, in a most unfortunate manner, in all his explanations of concrete economic problems. His contempt for genuine theological statements of these problems which he shares with his friends of the Religious-Social Movement, revenges itself bitterly on his work, and prevents the considerable amount of good which his book contains from being worked out in a fruitful way. The members of the Religious-Social Movement have done a great service in drawing the attention of the Churches and of theological ethics to the economic system as a *problem*, and in calling attention to the problem of community as a "social question" which lies behind it; in this respect men like KUTTER and RAGAZ—whom WÜNSCH does not even mention—have opened up a new path by means of their disturbing questions, though we can learn less from their replies to the questions they have raised. The *evangelisch-soziale Kongress* was important in that it set the ball of discussion rolling between the two groups (cf. the Article "Evangelisch-sozial in RGG²); but the theological "modernism" which increasingly dominated its thinking did not provide a suitable basis for a fruitful statement of the problem in theological and ethical terms.

In England and America discussion between the Church and the economic sphere started much earlier, and with greater forces at its disposal; it has been in existence since the days of Carlyle, Ruskin, Robertson, and especially Kingsley; here too, however, and particularly in America, those who were critical of the existing régime more or less followed in the wake of Liberalism—and of that very Liberalism whose sociology (in the form of the Manchester School) they opposed, without perceiving that its theological bases and their own were the same (cf. VISSER T'HOOFT: *The Background of the Social Gospel in America*). The Anglican Church alone followed a strong line of her own; within this Church we find an ecclesiastical system which is loyal to the Church combined with the sharpest criticism of the Capitalist System, and with important constructive ideas; the Anglican Church has taken no small share in the movement for *Guild Socialism*, which is more widespread among leaders of the working classes in England than Marxism.

Catholic theology, to its honour, gave intensive thought to the ethical aspect of the economic problem all through the nineteenth century, and in the Papal *Encyclica rerum novarum* it has made a notable pronouncement, although of late there has been a certain tendency to rate this too highly. On the whole, however—that is, apart from a few free-lances who did not gain the approbation of the authorities—Catholic theology has remained within the confines of a view which defends Capitalism and suggests a few mild socio-political reforms. Still, when all is said and done, she was on the spot, and did express her mind, openly, plainly, and vigorously, whereas Protestant theology did not even know that these problems existed! (The book by LUTHARDT which I have mentioned bears the date 1898, and the new edition which I have before me now, is dated 1921.)

PAGE 395, NOTE 2.—Even the patristic period took the liveliest interest in economic questions. (On this point see TROELTSCH, *The Social Teaching of the Christian Churches*, and the literature mentioned by SCHILLING, op. cit. Further, see BRENTANO: *Die wirtschaftlichen Lehren des christlichen Altertums*, in *Sitzungsber. d. Münch. Akad.*, 1902, which also contains a wealth of illustrative material from other sources. Also UHLHORN: *Die Geschichte der Christlichen Liebestätigkeit*, 3 vols., a work which has never yet been surpassed, in spite of the patriarchal bias of its orthodox Lutheran author.)

PAGE 396, NOTE 3.—Christian Utopias have indeed arisen from time to time, mainly in connexion with Anabaptist ideals of the "communism of love," which have also occasionally been put into practice in small isolated economic communities. Religious Socialism has also constructed programmes of this kind; on the Protestant side we have *Ein soziales Programm*, issued by RAGAZ and his co-workers, and on the Catholic side there are the ideas of Professor UDE of Graz, who has now been silenced by the ecclesiastical authorities (*Soziologie: Leitfaden der natürlich vernünftigen Gesellschafts—und Wirtschaftslehre, Alpenland-Verlag, Schaan 1931*).

PAGE 396, NOTE 4.—A very informing criticism of previous definitions of this conception is provided by a book which has been both highly praised and hotly contested: *Fundament der Volkswirtschaftslehre* by OTHMAR SPANN, pp. 6–22; his own definition, however, like his sociology as a whole (see above, Note 12 on Chapter XXVII suffers from his romantic Idealism, especially from an *a priori* habit of mind which leads him to posit the Values as absolute: "economics is the sum-total of means for ends" (p. 25). It is, of course, true that economics is concerned with means; but that is also true of pedagogy, of politics, etc. And, on the other hand, economic ends—which he calls means (for instance the *end* of satisfying the actual needs of existence)—are just as much "self-ends" as the "aims" of art and science; or, rather, like all human ends, they have to be subordinated to the one sole self-end. But it is rather risky for a person who is not a specialist in these matters to meddle with them. (Cf. SOMBART: *Drei Nationalökonomien*, p. 7.)

PAGE 396, NOTE 5.—"Land Reform," whose first manifesto (in its own way very powerful) was the book entitled *Progress and Poverty*, by HENRY GEORGE (this is still a classical document, which strongly influenced TOLSTOY among others), which (through DAMASCHKE) became an influential conception, both from the scientific and the practical point of view, is certainly not a universal method of economic salvation; but, as a beginning, could there be any better starting-point? That is, with land which is not needed for agriculture, by socializing private property—here a definite beginning of this kind could have been made without any danger to society, and thus the terrible increase in land speculation and housing problems might have been checked. If only this had taken place some time ago, how much misery might have been avoided!

PAGE 398, NOTE 6.—The "universalist" or romantic school of political economy has rendered a great service by asserting the claims of this theory with great vigour, over against the abstract systems of SMITH and RICARDO (to which also Marxist Socialism belongs), which are more or less dominated by the idea of the *homo oeconomicus*. These ideas have been familiar to me from my student days through reading RUSKIN, where, although they are not very clearly defined, their ethical force is all the greater.

PAGE 399, NOTE 7.—Cf. SCHILLING (*Katholische Sozialethik*, p. 68) with LUTHER (WA. 16, 471).

PAGE 399, NOTE 8.—This idea of the corruption of the economic sphere by sin is a conception which we find in the writings of the Fathers, and to some extent also in Aquinas; but modern Catholics ignore it entirely. Their idea of "the Law of Nature" is so fully adapted to the actual state of things—think for instance of their doctrine of private property—that the contradiction either disappears entirely, or is concealed by the formula: "out of consideration for special circumstances."

PAGE 405, NOTE 9.—BRENTANO, in the work which has already been mentioned on the economic theories of Christian antiquity, has shown incontestably that "the Fathers of the Church in no wise regarded property as something which has been ordered by the Law of Nature; to them the natural thing was communism. To them property seems only an evil which has become necessary owing to the Fall" (p. 150), and indeed that is true, not only as TROELTSCH thought, of the later Church Fathers, but of TERTULLIAN, IRENAEUS, and CYPRIAN. The one who goes furthest in the assertion of communistic ideas is CHRYSOSTOM; in his exposition of the story of Ananias and Sapphira he outlines an absolutely communistic theory, which even extols communal consumption as the most natural method (loc. cit., p. 157). ST. THOMAS, on the other hand, not only asserts that private property is the best order for the world as it is at the present time, but he tries to modify the patristic communistic doctrine of the Primitive State; modern Catholicism alone, however, has "proved" that private property is an original order of creation, and from the time of Leo XIII this thesis has been sacrosanct, in spite of the reiterated opposition of some isolated individuals. (Cf. VORLÄNDER: *Katholizismus und Sozialismus*, in the *Archiv fur Sozialwissenschaft*, Vol. 51, pp. 765 ff.)

PAGE 405, NOTE 10.—The fundamental defect of the *Wirtschafts-ethik* of WÜNSCH is that it does not deal systematically with the decisive question of the nature of community—that is, the relation between the individual and society. That is why in its discussion of the question neither communism nor individualism is clearly presented; at one time the author asserts that communism is the consequence of the Christian ethic, and the next moment he says that private property is justified as the postulate of freedom, but immediately he goes off in another direction and inclines towards the communistic ideal of the cloister (p. 679 ff.).

PAGE 405, NOTE 11.—The theory of society, and the doctrine of political economy which has been erected upon it, of the Viennese sociologist SPANN (see also his excellent *Introduction* to the subject entitled *Haupttheorien der Volkswirtschaftslehre*) indubitably belongs to some of the most interesting phenomena of contemporary sociology. It is a pity that, as a rule, the Socialists save themselves the trouble of discussion with this very penetrating critic and creative thinker (*Der wahre Staat*) by calling him "a conservative reactionary." RUSKIN and CARLYLE were also "socially conservative," and SPANN follows the line laid down by them. The catchword "conservative" conceals an obscurity of thought: a system of political economy can be erected upon the basis of the romantic theory of the organism which is far more sharply opposed to the existing economic system than that of Marxist Socialism, which, by the very fact of its main conception—which is rationalistic and individualistic—is closely related to Capitalism.

In spite of this, however, I cannot accept this doctrine of society or of political economy (see above, Note 12 on Chapter 27) for the very reason that it uses the idea of the organism as its principle of construction, and therefore necessarily leads to an illusion. This renewal of the idea of the Platonic class-state indeed does all honour to the constructive imagination of the author, but to the sober thinker it sounds very fantastic. On the other hand, it is the duty of the Christian moralist in particular to seek what is living and formative for society beyond all catch-words and obstacles; English Socialism can show us that a Labour movement and radical criticism of Capitalism do not necessarily go with a sociology of the type of the Enlightenment (Marxism).

PAGE 405, NOTE 12.—The gigantic work by PESCH, a Jesuit writer, entitled *Lehrbuch der Nationalökonomie* (4 vols.) represents a theory of "solidarity" which at first sight looks very Christian and ethical, and whose postulates seem to agree with those in this book. But when we examine this work in greater detail we see that apart from moralizing demands, it deals with mild proposals for reform, which leave the essential basis of the Capitalist system untouched. This theory of solidarity moves loyally, without any originality whatsoever, along the lines laid down by Leo XIII for social reform; here certainly some isolated proposals for reform are made which are quite useful, but as a whole these proposals never touch the root of the trouble at all.

PAGE 406, NOTE 13.—The weakness of the Marxian conception of value—which cannot be denied—is that actually the only labour which counts is manual labour. This originally Marxian theory, which was long ago given up by modern Socialists, has become practical politics in Bolshevist Communism, in so far as the Communist Party, the ruling class which exercises the dictatorship, is deliberately drawn from the ranks of the manual workers. Those who live in secure economic conditions—and this means most of the Christians who belong to the Church—are far too easily satisfied with a simple denial of the ideas of Tolstoy; in any case the Apostle Paul—although he rejected the idea in principle—carried it out in practice, and worked hard with his own hands.

PAGE 406, NOTE 14.—Cf. SPANN: *Der wahre Staat*, who, in accordance with the Platonist classification of society, assigns the lowest stage in the social structure to the working classes.

PAGE 407, NOTE 15.—In his criticism of egalitarian sociology I agree with BRUNSTÄD (*Deutschland und der Sozialismus*), although, on the other hand, I very definitely reject his presentation of the Capitalist system, because he seeks to whitewash and justify it. SPANN has perceived the cancerous nature both of the Capitalist and of the Communist system more clearly than BRUNSTAD; only his organological principle leads him astray into seeking a solution in an hierarchical structure of society.

PAGE 409, NOTE 16.—The idea of the "economic spirit" is SOMBART's—we might well say "brilliant idea"—since he is the one who discovered it. The "Capitalist economic spirit" is something entirely different from the spirit of Mammon; it is, as SOMBART well says: the "objectification of the desire for gain." Mammon has always existed, but not the Capitalist spirit. See above on *Capitalism*.

PAGE 410, NOTE 17.—This conception of the daemonic element, as applied to the economic system, may have been introduced into literature by TILLICH, but it has been familiar to me for a long time from the lectures of my teacher RAGAZ, who is—quite unjustly—often treated as a *quantité négligeable* by those who speak on questions connected with Religious Socialism at the present day.

PAGE 411, NOTE 18.—The famous expressions *laissez-faire, laissez-aller* originated with the *Physiocrats* (Quesnay?). In the thought of the latter we can perceive most clearly the connexion between the ideas of classical political economy and the rationalistic and optimistic individualism of the Enlightenment.

PAGE 411, NOTE 19.—The following point must be kept in mind—

[although admitting the danger of sentimental exaggeration, and in contrast to the scepticism of BRENTANO (in the article by him which has already been mentioned, and in his book: *Die Anfänge des Kapitalismus*)]: unlike MAX WEBER and SOMBART this third leading political economist of the present day allowed himself to be too greatly influenced by economic materialism. Cf. also the article *Kirchliche Wirtschaftsgeschichte* by SOMMERLAD, in RGG².

PAGE 411, NOTE 20.—This idea is naturally not proof against misunderstanding; I am well aware what the political economists mean by a monopoly (cf. *Handwörterbuch der Staatswissenschaften*, "*Monopol*"). But I believe that my expansion of the conception will prove to be natural, and that it will help to illuminate the social problem in the sphere of economics. Even in the ordinary use of the term, in everyday language, a "monopoly" means something which I now possess and you do not, but which you need. The whole system of exchange is based upon *this* idea of monopoly; what is usually called a monopoly is a special instance, in which both the fact that only a certain person or class possesses something which another person or class needs, is specially emphasized by the absence of alternatives of equal value.

PAGE 412, NOTE 21.—Upon the theory that the monopoly of the possession of land—introduced by feudalism—is "the main key which opens all the locked doors of political economy as a science" (*Die soziale Frage und der Sozialismus*, p. 4), FRANZ OPPENHEIMER constructs his theory of "liberal Socialism," the chief idea of which is that the only solution of the social question can be found in "interior colonization." Probably DAMASCHKE's ideas on land reform are better known.

PAGE 413, NOTE 22.—The relative and indubitable right of the proletarian class consciousness and the proletarian assertion of the priority of manual labour is based upon this fact. On the other hand, it is this fact which is so frequently overlooked by the defenders of Capitalism, as well as by its organological critics.

PAGE 413, NOTE 23.—The idea of economic democracy has as many meanings as the idea of political democracy; its possibilities range from the "Labour Councils"—which also have their place in the bourgeois system of solidarity—to Soviet Communism. The Religious Socialists—I am thinking mainly of HEIMANN and TILLICH—ought to note the fact that the thought of our time is striving to leave rational democracy (the legacy of the French Revolution) behind, and to reach out after a more corporate form of democracy, which will not be based upon the arithmetical and untrue principle of the delegation of authority by means of election, which almost entirely excludes leadership and responsibility, but will also take inequality and mutuality into account. To apply the abstract parliamentarian principle to the economic sphere spells certain ruin; but this view does not by any means rule out democracy altogether. There is a kind of democracy which is not rationalistic. It seems as though all the vital thinkers of the present day, from all sides—breaking down the barriers erected by groups controlled by catchwords—were aiming in this direction; even Social Democracy itself cannot escape the influence of this idea; co-operative Socialism cannot, as BRUNSTÄD thinks, be brushed aside by using the term "Utopia" (p. 256).

NOTES ON CHAPTER XXXV

PAGE 416, NOTE 1.—BRUNSTÄD is of course right in saying that "in the name of Christianity we are not to take sides either for Capitalism or for Socialism, but simply to give ourselves with all earnestness and objectivity to wrestling with that which we discover through this earnest search as our service to the will of God" (p. 325). But what are we to do if by means of our "earnest objective search" we "discover" the radically immoral character of the Capitalist system? This does not mean, by any manner of means, that we must then become "Religious Socialists," but it certainly does mean that as Christians we feel obliged to oppose with all our might "the monster of Capitalism" (to use the language of SOMBART) as a Moloch which devours men's souls.

PAGE 417, NOTE 2.—Ever since I used to attend RAGAZ's lectures on the social question—that is, for more than twenty years—I have been trying to understand what Capitalism is; I have looked at this "monster" from very different angles, with the eyes of MARX, and SOMBART, as well as from the point of view of liberal political economy, with the eyes of RUSKIN, COLE (Guild Socialism), MAX WEBER, BRENTANO, and SPANN. But in spite of the keen criticism which BRENTANO (*Die Anfänge des Kapitalismus*) expends upon SOMBART, I keep returning to Sombart's analysis as the most satisfactory one; I venture therefore to make this the foundation of my presentation of the subject—and indeed in very close connexion with a brilliant summary of his views which SOMBART himself has given this year (*Handwörterbuch der Soziologie: Kapitalismus*)—I do not do so because I happen to have come across SOMBART accidentally, but because—with certain exceptions—I find him to be the thinker who has given the clearest and most illuminating analysis of the question. My own corrections are in the second part of my presentation of this question; here I owe much to BRENTANO.

I regard BRUNSTÄD's attempt to justify the Capitalist system as an enterprise which has been abandoned by all able thinkers; his fundamental defect is that he conceives the idea of Capitalism so narrowly that it becomes almost identical with a Capitalist economy; that, on the other hand, while he enumerates the advantages of Capitalism he forgets that these are due not so much to Capitalism as to technological science, and finally, that he rates the debit side too low, and forgets that times have changed (cf. the period of the development of the modern economic order with its various possibilities for pioneer experiment, with the "cut-and-dried economic world" of the present day). From the point of view of ethics the most important thing is that he does not understand the difference between the economic spirit of Capitalism and the spirit of "Mammon," which is fundamental to the thought of SOMBART (cf. pp. 252 and 307). The capitalistic economic spirit is the "spirit of Mammon" which is inherent in the system itself, the "objectification of the striving for gain." But in face of the present world-crisis any justification of the Capitalist system sounds absolutely grotesque.

PAGE 420, NOTE 3.—This fact is contested by those who defend Capitalism. From the point of view of statistics they may be, to some extent, right, but the whole question looks quite different from the dynamic point of view. For a large number of small businesses are often sociologically, and even legally, simply vassals of the large business enterprises. Their independence is a fiction.

PAGE 422, NOTE 4.—It is amazing how many defenders of Capitalism quite naïvely claim for Capitalism what can already be discerned as the result of the counter-movement. The fact that Capitalism, thanks to the Labour Movement and thanks to State interference, has not been able to stride over everything wholly unchecked is not to be reckoned as a virtue of Capitalism! Those phenomena which were established by the famous Report of ENGELS on the situation among the working classes in England in the Forties (of last century) were not just accidental accompaniments of Capitalism in its early stages, before it had reached maturity, but they represent the results of unchecked Capitalism everywhere, results which are inevitable if Capitalism is allowed to pursue its own sweet way without let or hindrance. The fact that to-day the situation is not *quite* so dark is the result of the struggle which has been waged against Capitalism by the State, the Churches, and above all by the organized Labour Movement. Capitalism will never be "moderated" from within; this will only take place through compulsory influence from outside. It would be more correct to speak of "taming" than of "moderating."

PAGE 423, NOTE 5.—This does not mean that I take back what I have said about the objective character of the economic spirit—as distinguished from the spirit of Mammon. Even if the capitalistic economic spirit is not within the *heart* of the Capitalist, it is present in his acts, in the "firm," in the "enterprise." That is the tragic element in the position of a genuinely Christian Capitalist. He is like a man in a huge crowd who is carried along by the pressure around him in a direction which is the very opposite of that in which he desires to go. A Christian Capitalist must be greedy for dividends, even if he himself is not anxious for large profits, for "the firm" wants dividends, and what can the individual do against this "objectified desire for profit" of the group of which he forms part?

PAGE 424, NOTE 6.—SOMBART takes too little account of these facts, as BRENTANO, with greater expert knowledge, has shown; where we are dealing with the demonstration of the *causal* genesis of the Capitalist system, then SOMBART's analysis must be judged inadequate. It is at this point that Marxist historical determinism is relatively—and to a very large extent—justified; and it is at this point that Utopian moralists fail completely because they do not recognize the element of destiny in history as a whole. On the other hand, however, it is just as dubious, with HEIMANN and TILLICH, to make this Destiny (in a pantheistically historical manner) into a god ("Idealistic dialectic," Heimann rightly calls it). Here it would be more to the point to speak of "the Prince of this world!"

PAGE 425, NOTE 7.—The most penetrating criticism of Capitalism from the purely economic point of view that I have been able to discover is in the book called *Business Enterprise*, by an American writer, VEBLEN.

PAGE 426, NOTE 8.—Here BRUNSTÄD also follows the traditional line of argument. I do not wish to maintain that during a certain period of economic expansion, by the immense increase of economic forces, and by the mobility of the economic system, supported by the free capitalist, Capitalism should not be reckoned one of the great productive factors of the last century. But that period is over. The representative type of the economic system of the present day is no longer the adventurous business man but the great financier. Capitalism has also severed the function of business administration from the possession of capital; to-day the business administrator is a paid official, or, if this is not legally the case, it is true sociologically, owing to his dependence on high finance.

PAGE 426, NOTE 9.—This lack of realism is justified by the fact that to-day a large section of the most important experts think in an anti-capitalistic way. This state of affairs is obscured by the antithesis of Capitalism versus Socialism, with all their slogans and catch-words. By no means every one who, from his knowledge of the subject, is an anti-capitalist, is on that account a Socialist, in the sense in which the usual party programmes use the term. We must accept the situation as it is: Capitalism stands condemned; but this does not mean that we already know exactly what ought to be put in its place. The right to criticize the existing order does not depend upon the fact that we already have a settled programme for the future up our sleeves. Indeed, I would go even further and say: just as surely as Capitalism is to be condemned, so also every tendency which believes that it can conquer Capitalism by means of a "programme" is on the wrong tack. In this, in spite of different opinions on other points, I agree with the "believing realism" of

667

TILLICH and his friends. (Cf. HEIMANN's Lecture at Heppenheim, which is now printed in *Kapitalismus und Sozialismus*, pp. 171–196.)

PAGE 427, NOTE 10.—KARL MARX too, so far as the goal which he visualizes of the economic revolution is concerned, is an anarchist, and that means a "Utopian." His dream of the future has no State, and, at bottom, it is wholly without community. SPANN (*Der wahre Staat*, p. 157) gives a quotation from a letter which is most instructive on the subject of this anarchist Utopianism: "In a higher stage of Communist society, after the enslaving subordination of individuals to the distribution of labour has disappeared, and with it the antithesis between manual and intellectual labour . . . after the productive energies of individuals have grown along with their all-round development, and all the springs of collective wealth flow with a fuller tide, only then will the narrow bourgeois legal horizon be wholly transcended and society be able to inscribe upon its banner: To each individual according to his capacities, to each according to his needs." This is a secular eschatology—it is that belief in progress characteristic of Rationalism of the Rousseau type which has been, and still is, such a decisive motive force, both for the original social Democratic Movement and for Communism, both inside and outside of Russia. It has indeed often been shown how Marx, in his programme of the future, completely evades the problem of the State and of legal administration. He believes in the goodness of man—who has become Socialist. The whole ideal is ultimately conceived from the point of view of the individual and of the welfare of the individual; on this point SPANN is entirely right. Marxist Socialism, both in its content of ideas and in its sentiment, is the child of the Rationalism of the Enlightenment. Here we are not concerned with the fact that in Russia an additional powerful motive lay in an Asiatic-primitive-Communistic impulse, coupled with the after-effects of the Orthodox idea of the Church.

PAGE 428, NOTE 11.—It is still truer of Socialism than of Capitalism to say that it is possible to mean all sorts of different things by the same word. If "Socialism is the urge for an intelligent moulding and transformation of life" (HEIMANN, loc. cit., p. 252) then everyone who is not satisfied with things as they are, but, whether as a Christian or as an Idealist, seeks for a more righteous social order, is a Socialist. This would be a fateful expansion of the meaning of the term. The following points should be kept distinct: (1) *The half-unconscious "urge" towards a new order*, which, welling up from hidden depths, has stirred "the masses" to demand a new social order in which not only shall the individual labourer have a fairer share in the economic goods, but, above all, in which his position within the economic community shall be different, more dignified and freer. This "urge" was greatly stimulated and made conscious by KARL MARX, and his intellectual followers; at the same time, however, it was guided in a definite direction, which is very closely connected with the Marxist Utopian visions of the future, with its historical materialism and its theory of value, and, finally, with the tactics and the programme of the Party. It is also true, as HEIMANN and TILLICH assert, that this "urge" manifests a kind of religion. But they forget that, at least to a very great extent, this is a pseudo-religion, it is secularized eschatology, Utopianism, a wish-fulfilment. Here there comes out very clearly, in a particularly unfortunate manner, the lack of clarity of a certain kind of Religious Socialism, which regards "religion" in itself as something positive, without enquiring what kind of religion it is. There is a kind of religion which is "daemonic" in character, and "Socialism" as such is full of this kind of religion. Everything that these representatives of the Religious-Social Movement say about the "religion of the proletariat" is far more true of Communism than of Socialism; why then do they not draw the logical inference? Communism is indubitably an elementary religious movement—even in its hatred of God and of Christ. Is it then our duty (as the "Religious Socialists" demand of Socialism) simply to "co-operate" with them? This religion which is inherent in the Labour Movement of the Extreme Left is itself a mixture of Christian elements, of vitalism, of the deification of Reason, and of the deification of Man; its dogma is the Party Programme, and its doctrines are of the economic, sociological, cultural type of Karl Marx, combined with his general philosophy of life. While we may not identify any religion with its dogma, we may at the same time also not ignore its dogma in our estimate of it. This, however, is precisely what those particular "Religious Socialists" do, since they no more accept this dogma than they accept the Christian dogma.

(2) *The Marxist Doctrine.*—Both in Communism and in the Social Democratic parties this doctrine is very powerful and influential, with which we have to reckon at least as much as with that "urge" towards a new order of which we have just spoken. Socialism—as a true child of the Enlightenment, and German Socialism in particular—is doctrinaire. At the present day it is less doctrinaire than it used to be—in contradistinction to Communism—but it is still full of this spirit, with the few exceptions of those who think for themselves. And this doctrine is not merely an economic doctrine, but it is a view of life as a whole, a theory which includes within its sweep a general philosophy of life and religion as well. A convinced Socialist must have a definite cultural programme, that is, the Marxist one; the opposition of certain independent thinkers who think clearly and deeply does not alter this fact. In essentials this general cultural programme, of which the economic programme only forms a part, is determined by the rationalism and the individualism of the Enlightenment; at this point critics of Socialism like BRUNSTÄD and SPANN are right. The labour leaders of Socialism

669

expect that anyone who calls himself a Socialist will also throw his weight into supporting this cultural programme just as much as the economic programme. It is cheering to note that quite recently this doctrinaire spirit has been making way for a more realistic and profound view of the situation; but at the moment, in the main, the view of the Enlightenment still holds the field, even in practical statements of the aims of Socialism.

(3) *There is also a non-Marxian Socialism*: it too is a force which assumes many forms, from the mild, semi-bourgeois reforming spirit of State Socialism or of the municipal Socialistic type to French anarchist Syndicalism and the American IWW (Industrial Workers of the World). Indeed, even German Fascism calls itself National-Socialism, and with a certain right, to this extent at least that even it has incorporated into its official programme strongly anti-capitalistic elements. Of practical importance are municipal Socialism on the one hand and Co-operative Socialism on the other. We are shutting our eyes to reality if we assert, like BRUNSTÄD, that these types of Socialism "are pointless and Utopian" (p. 256) Municipal Socialism, on the contrary—within the boundaries which are set to it by nature—has shown itself to be a practical possibility; only these boundaries are rather narrow (Cf. for both WILBRANDT: *Sozialismus*, pp. 165 ff.). Co-operative Socialism has at least in one form evinced great power of achievement: as a consumers' Co-operative, especially in England. The most promising element in it is the fact that it naturally regards the people as a whole, since *all* are consumers. But also the producers' co-operative Movement cannot be ruled out as a Utopia; we merely need to recall the development of agricultural co-operation (Denmark) in order to realize the practical possibilities which it contains. In this Co-operative Socialism this is the fruitful element, which separates it most widely from the ideology of the Enlightenment; but its best representatives easily fall a prey to an ethical delusion; since they expect that education in the habit of thought along co-operative lines will conquer selfishness, which sounds like emotional fanaticism to those who do not believe that education is so influential. (Cf. WILBRANDT: loc. cit., pp. 118, 188–90.)

(4) Most of the vital Socialistic thinkers of the present day—certainly a minority!—are more or less united in their rejection of State Socialism. This is a cheering phenomenon. But two urgent questions present themselves: firstly, does this opposition to State Socialism, which these individual intellectuals express, represent a real force within the Socialist Movement as a whole? Is not every victory of "Socialism" as such primarily a victory of State Socialism, and, more or less, of the general Marxist cultural programme? In any case this is a question which must be asked very seriously by anyone who reflects upon these things from the Christian point of view. Secondly, how will Co-operative Socialism of any kind

protect itself against the dangers of group-selfishness, and group competition, bureaucratism and demagogy? Of all the various tendencies within this group English Guild Socialism must be the one which takes this danger most seriously into its reckoning, and by means of its synthesis of corporative and political thought it is perhaps the group which is best fitted to withstand these dangers. (Cf. COLE: *A Social Theory,* and PENTY: *Auf dem Wege zu einer christlichen Soziologie* 1924.)

(5) However, as soon as we include the corporate idea within the sphere of Socialist thought—(we would indeed go so far as to assert that this type of thought is the most Socialistic of all)—and move away from the doctrinaire spirit of Marxist Socialism, the gulf between "bourgeois" and "Socialist" thought no longer seems impossible to bridge. A writer like SPANN, for instance, clearly feels an affinity with Guild Socialism·(*Der wahre Staat,* p. 285); that this "Guild Socialism" is more than an interesting theory will be familiar to anyone who knows anything about the English Labour Movement, and about the practical influence of the Fabian Society upon the public life of England. It is really no longer up to date to say, as WÜNSCH does, that there are only the two practical alternatives which are absolutely opposed to each other: Socialism and Capitalism, and that therefore we must decide for one or the other (loc. cit., p. 11). If we will only look steadily at the programme of Austrian Social Democracy, with its combination of municipal-Socialist, syndicalistic, and co-operative Socialistic elements (cf. WILBRANDT: *Sozialismus,* pp. 191 ff.), and, on the other side, at the influential ideas of Spann which envisage an economic community constructed on co-operative lines, upon the basis of the collective contract of labour, with its far-reaching restrictions on private property, then the alternatives proposed by WÜNSCH seem mere talk. The only thing which really does make a separation is this: Capitalism in the classic sense, or not. But *this* alternative has certainly become meaningless to-day. The fact is that the old slogans are no longer adequate, neither in economic theory nor in theology, if we are to come to terms with reality.

But the view which asserts that Socialism has attained its present high position through the influence of Reason, working within History (as certain Religious Socialists would have us believe), is equally untenable. For just as a doctrinaire emphasis on ethics, which tries to moralize the sphere of economics, contradicts the realism of the Christian Faith, so also does that "Idealistic dialectic . . . according to which the meaning which the spirit finds within itself, is at the same time also in things, because things are in the spirit, and only in the spirit" (HEIMANN, loc. cit., p. 174). For faith does not say, "Man does not live by bread alone . . . but by the totality of life"; faith does not set over against "bread alone" the "totality of life," but the Word of God, knowing very well that even the "totality of life," even historic life, is not God, and therefore that it does not contain its meaning within itself.

PAGE 430, NOTE 12.—When representatives of the bourgeoisie ascribe responsibility for the class war to the agitation engineered by Social Democracy, it is hypocrisy, pure and simple—it is the privileged classes themselves who are waging this class warfare, by asserting their inherited privileges, which they seldom modify by any consideration for the welfare of the people as a whole. It is perfectly natural that the aggressive section should be the proletariat, because it is fighting for its rights, which it does not possess. It must certainly be admitted that in this struggle Labour (dominated by the doctrinaire spirit of Marxism, and by a [psychologically intelligible, although wrong] spirit of retaliation, as well as by a kind of romantic glorification of the working class)—subordinates the welfare of the community to its own class interest, just as much as the "Bourgeoisie," which Labour rightly opposes, on account of its class selfishness. It cannot be denied that very often the Socialist proletariat has regarded the class bond as more important than the racial or national bond; but who can blame the proletarian, who does not own one rod of soil in his native land, for having no sense of "belonging" to the "fatherland," and no understanding for the community of his people as a whole?

PAGE 431, NOTE 13.—Purely from the point of view of economic requirements, it is wrong to demand that Christians ought to co-operate with Socialism—it is a curious fact that people are not so eager to make the same demand for Communism—because it cannot be taken for granted that that kind of Socialism which to-day is the standard kind would be able to substitute a better system for that of Capitalism; although we may absolutely agree with all that has to be said about Capitalism, under certain circumstances we might still be of the opinion that—purely from the economic point of view—it is still a lesser evil than official Socialism. To that too must be added the whole cultural programme of Socialism, its whole world-view, and its ethical doctrine, which a Socialism which had gained the reins of power would certainly strive with all its might to put into actual practice. But, apart from some important exceptions, this is naturalistic positivism. It is of course true that it is possible to understand Socialism in quite a different sense, indeed it can be understood in such a way that it absolutely agrees with the demands of the Gospel. Only this kind of Socialism is of no practical importance, but is the concern of individuals who like to paint a picture of "Socialism" which no one would ever recognize in the political world—where the word Socialism is used. Those who want to know what the "spirit" and the "Kultur" programme is like, which in spite of all opposition is still the standard in continental Social Democracy (which is fed on the most turbid sources of bourgeois ideology, and on naturalistic materialistic positivism), should read the work of the Socialist CUNOW: *Die Marxsche Geschichts-, Gesellschafts- und Staatstheorie,* 2 vols, 1920–23, or a book which is still "canonical": *Die Frau und der Sozialismus,* by BEBEL.

PAGE 432, NOTE 14.—By this I do not mean to say that under certain circumstances it may not be necessary that those who definitely wish to remain loyal to Jesus Christ and to the Church should join together in a special group, either in order to stir Christians everywhere to political action—as for instance the "Christliche Volksdienst" in Southern Germany has done—or in order to adopt a certain attitude towards questions of politics and political economy which affect the Church in a very intimate and special way. But the idea of "Christian Trades Unions" is and remains a Catholic idea, which is alien to the nature of the Protestant faith, and should remain so. For the object for which the Trades Union is struggling, and for which it should struggle, is indeed something for which a Christian also ought to fight, but it is not on that account by any means a "Christian" matter. The Name of Christ should only be used where we are certain that opposition to that which we represent is also opposition to the cause of Jesus Christ, that is, never in political groups, or in groups controlled by the principles of political economy. Anyone who is not happy in a Socialist Trades Union will find that there are other possibilities open to him of a more general character.

PAGE 434, NOTE 15.—It is very naïve to think that the Sermon on the Mount can be applied, as it stands, to the life of the economic sphere. "Give to him that asketh thee"—"Whoever takes thy coat let him take thy cloke also." History has shown plainly enough how serious are the results of the legal conception of the so-called prohibition of interest by Jesus (*Luke vi. 34, 35*). We might even say that the Jewish Question of the present day is one of these results. See the next note.

PAGE 434, NOTE 16.—The discussion of the ethical problem of interest can only be confused by a reference to the canonical prohibition of interest. Not only are the prohibitions of interest by the Second and Third Lateran Councils based on a complete misunderstanding of *Luke vi. 34, 35*—which already completely dominates Patristic thought on the question—(Jesus is not speaking about the renunciation of interest at all, but simply of returning what has been borrowed in general), but as a rule they deal only with the comparatively rare case of the loan for consumptive purposes. The practice which corresponds to interest on capital for productive capital at the present day, is not "usury," but the medieval practice of ground rent, of tithes. Very wisely the Medieval Church did not forbid tithes, because it knew that its own economic life was based upon them. The decisive factor in the economic life of the Middle Ages was not the inconsiderable practice of interest (usury) but the ground-rent, which corresponded to the economic system of that day which was based on barter. The ethical demand to abolish interest in the capitalist system of the present day would correspond to the abolition of ground-rent in the Middle Ages. It is well known that the peasants made this demand at the time of the Reformation; not only Luther, however, but Zwingli as well, saw how impossible it was; it would have meant the ruin of the economic system of that day. The same would be true of interest on capital at the present time. Further, it is also necessary to distinguish between interest, and reference to interest or enjoyment of interest (cf. HEIMANN, loc. cit., p.45). I suppose that even a Socialist economic system could not get on without calculation of interest (cf. HEIMANN: "Zins" in RGG[2]); but this is not an ethical question; it is a purely technical, economic question. The ethical problem is that of the *enjoyment of interest*. Whether (as the adherents of Silvio Gsell[1] maintain) it is possible to imagine an economic system apart from the practice of interest is a question of no importance to the moralist, quite apart from the different assumptions which are necessary to make the possibility of an economic system without interest seem plausible. The ethical danger-zone is not interest but profit, which would still be taken for granted in a system free from interest. The dangerous element in the Capitalist system is not that it is based upon capital which breeds interest, but that the only person who disposes of the interest is the employer of labour. See the following note.

PAGE 435, NOTE 17.—We understand the ethical meaning of interest best when we compare it with ground-rent. Just as the land-owner lives by the labour of his tenant, so does the capitalist live by the labour of those who do business with his capital. The fact that the capital bears interest is not a cause of offence, any more than the fruitfulness of the soil, in addition to the expenditure upon it, is objectionable. But what is objectionable is the fact that the one who does not work enjoys this fruit, that he alone has the power to dispose of it as he likes, although he has expended no labour upon it. Or in other words, the thing that is unsatisfactory from the point of view of ethics is this: that the capitalist can rake in large profits as the fruit of the present work of others, and for their work in the past—even when it is not his own work at all. The difficulty of the problem, however, consists in the fact that without this stimulus of gain, the "lease," the cession of capital as a whole, does not take place. Medieval theology, at a time when an economy based on money began to replace an economy based on barter (that is, when, alongside of ground-rent, productive capital began to have an equal position), tries very hard to discover some so-called

[1] A form of Social Credit. A movement widely spread in Switzerland under the name of "Freigeld."—TR.

"titles" which would make interest appear ethically innocent under certain conditions (cf. SCHILLING: *Sozialethik*, p. 104), as for instance premium on arrears or on risks, etc. At bottom all that they desired was to justify afterwards that which seemed psychologically inevitable. This justification was not altogether unfounded; indeed we may say that he who renounces the enjoyment of the fruits of his labour in order to make possible the fruit-bearing work of another person, subjectively (by renunciation) and objectively (by service) achieves something for which he has a fair claim to compensation. What Luther, for instance, finds objectionable in interest is the fact of the exploitation of the need of another person; he is thinking of interest on consumptive loans, not of productive interest. For this reason also Calvin, whose city of Geneva was economically orientated on the basis of productive interest, had a totally different view of the taking of interest from that of Luther. He regarded a moderate compensation for the loan of productive capital as just. But the ethical doubtfulness of the whole question comes out in the fact that it was impossible to justify the fixing of the rate of interest at 5 per cent.

This whole question of interest would vanish if private property in the means of production were abolished. But Socialism has never wrestled seriously with the question: What does private property actually mean, and what is the relation between property for consumption and productive business?—quite apart from the different forms which this socialization might take, and the difficulties to which they give rise. *Here* all we are concerned with is the question: How is the individual Christian to act towards the whole problem of interest within an economic system based on capitalism? It is not a responsible action to throw dust in his eyes by talking about the hope of an economic order in which money would be free, and there would be no interest, when his responsibility concerns his action here and now; theologians in particular ought not to do such things, pretending that they know the only possible economic solution where the most serious political economists are racking their brains over this problem and are only agreed at one particular point: that the theory of "free money" is based on obvious logical blunders.

The problem of interest ought not to be treated in isolation, but it should be treated in connexion with the whole ethical problem of wealth (or income), although every conscientious person will enjoy far more freely the income which he has himself earned than that which is based upon interest, and again he will make a distinction between the kinds of interest, those gained by earned and those gained by inherited income.

PAGE 436, NOTE 18.—Thus the Catholic writer UDE says: "No one ought to make any claim on the comforts of life until every one has first of all been provided with the necessaries of bare existence, to an adequate degree" (*Soziologie*, 1931, p. 168). However much we may admire the sense of serious responsibility which is expressed in this statement, the effect of this harsh Puritanism, were it put into practice, would be to make life terribly sterile. The same is true of his definition of luxury as "expenditure which goes beyond the measure of that which is necessary" (p. 286). UDE thinks it is possible to solve the question by having recourse to that which is "in accordance with nature." Thus from the long history of this conception, from the time of Diogenes and the Stoics down to Tolstoy and Gandhi, he has not learned that this conception can be understood in such a manner that it destroys all culture, and that it could only become a practical principle at all if another conception could fix clearly the exact distinction between that which is in accordance with nature and that which is not in accordance with nature, in such a way that at the same time the wealth and variety of historical life could be taken into account. Both Augustine and Calvin —not to mention Luther and modern Protestants and Catholics— had a different view of the permissibility of the comforts of life and of a satisfaction of need which goes beyond that of the satisfaction of bare necessity, than this Spartan Catholic, who, with the typical fanaticism of the reformer (see above, p. 202), declares that Total Abstinence both from alcoholic drinks and from tobacco, as well as vegetarianism, are absolute Christian duties, and who speaks of non-abstinence in the same breath with immoral pleasure (p. 287, etc.).

PAGE 437, NOTE 19.—At this point it is necessary also to emphasize clearly the profound contrast between Calvin and later Puritanism—especially that of the Anabaptist sects—after MAX WEBER and TROELTSCH have described the *Ethos* of Calvinism so very much from the point of view of asceticism. The Puritan ascetic view of life Calvin frequently describes as "*inhumana illa philosophia,*" *quae nullum nisi necessarium usum concedit ex creaturis* (*Institutio* III, 10; 3). God has not created the creatures only for our necessities but also for our comfort (cf. *Sermon 6: sur le Décal*). It is true, however, that he was more concerned with the prevention of licence; for this was the trouble he had to fight in Geneva.

NOTES ON CHAPTER XXXVI

PAGE 441, NOTE 1.—Finally it is simply a question of terminology whether, as some sociologists do (cf. HELLER: "Staat" in the *Handwörterbuch der Soziologie*), we speak of the "pre-State" beginnings of society or not. For even that kind of co-operative organization may be described as a kind of State, although it lacks some of the characteristics of the State as we know it at the present day, especially that of the relation of sovereignty. In any case modern ethnology has once for all made an end of Hobbes' idea of a "pre-State" existence in the sense of the *bellum omnium contra omnes*. I would describe as Utopian the idea of a possible abolition of the State altogether, which is the dream of Anarchism—of men like PROUDHON, BAKUNIN, or KROPOTKIN—haunting their imaginations as an ideal and an end, and in the form of a secular eschatology was taken over by MARX. Such a conception is only possible upon the basis of an unrealistic conception of man, on the basis of the optimistic rationalism of the Enlightenment; it is the favourite idea of the Stoics.

PAGE 442, NOTE 2.—This question splits political science at the present day into the two great currents of opinion: the idea of the State which is purely juridical, and the sociological conception of the State. The former conception, which is brilliantly represented by KELSEN, tries to interpret the State purely as an "order," as a "system of norms" (KELSEN: *Staatslehre*, p. 14). But when KELSEN further feels compelled to define this idea more exactly as "the system of positive legal norms," it then becomes evident that the "purity" so greatly desired in this method is more apparent than real. For "positive" norms do not in any way belong to the "world of norms," or to the "world of values," but—like a military regulation, or, to put it quite bluntly, like the recipes in a cookery book—in spite of their imperative character, are not genuine norms in the sense of *a priori* ideas, but are just *facts* which are present in experience. Everything positive is the subject of empirical knowledge, even if this positive element exists in the form of a command, or an instruction, of the way in which something ought to be done. The fact that a statement is made in the form of a command or an instruction is no proof that we are here dealing with a norm. At a decisive point (p. 17) KELSEN also confuses the purely psychological coercive effect of the legal norm with the validity of a genuine norm. It is only possible to talk about "positive norms" if one conceives the idea of a norm in a psychological way, and not in a transcendental way; positive norms belong to the world of the Actual, not to the world of the Ideal. This confusion has arisen in KELSEN's thought, and it dominates the whole of his doctrine of the State—because within the law there is always included a genuine norm, a genuine sense of obligation (on this point cf. also the criticisms of BINDER: *Philosophie des Rechtes*, pp. 183 ff). The second school of thought, represented during last century chiefly by GUMPLOWICZ, and at the present time (for instance) by OPPENHEIMER, in an extreme way, tries to interpret the State entirely from the point of view of "Sovereignty," that is, as an actual fact, due to actual causes. The more that sociology breaks away from its bondage to the causality of natural science, and the juridical philosophy of law from its formal insistence on *a priori* principles, and looks steadily at man as he really is, who is neither merely a fact of nature, nor an idea, but a being whose nature is influenced by ideas, the more the two conceptions will approximate to each other. There can be no "pure method" for the understanding of the real human being, the real State, and the real system of law, for such "purity" only exists in the abstract. The idea of pure law may be postulated thus—cf. what is said below about STAMMLER— but it is never an understanding of the positive law, on its positive side.

PAGE 442, NOTE 3.—The representatives of this positivist tendency—in the philosophical sense—are not only the "sociological" legal theorists, but also those described by BEROLZHEIMER (*System der Rechts- und Wirtschafts-philosophie*, II, Chapter 7) under the headings of Social Utilitarianism, ethnological jurisprudence, political and social philosophy on the basis of the theory of deterioration. According to GUMPLOWICZ (the most eminent and the "purest" representative of the naturalistic sociological school of thought), the State is "a social phenomenon, that is, it is a phenomenon which comes into being through the action of social elements according to natural law" (quoted from BEROLZHEIMER, p. 371). The idea of community which is determined by the naturalistic view of life, according to which the "social" element is conceived after the analogy of causal physical processes, is fully evident in this definition. See what was said above about the positivist theory of community, p. 298.

OPPENHEIMER in his book, *Der Staat*, holds similar views. It is of course obvious that in actual practice this naturalism is constantly interrupted by the observation of what is really human, which is no mere causal play of forces. The more that this inconsistency prevails, the more impossible does the task of classification become. It is naturally an "ideal picture."

PAGE 442, NOTE 4.—The above description is based on Hegel's philosophy of law. Here, too, Hegel shows himself to be the most logical and constructive thinker of objective Idealism. But the Catholic philosophy of law is to some extent in line with his thought, in that it deduced positive law from the *lex naturae*, and the corresponding philosophy of the State, that is, in so far as it undertsands the State only from the point of view of law, and not from that of irrational "might." In both respects modern Catholicism goes much further than the medieval scholastic thinkers, not to mention the Early Fathers. By means of the conception of the organism, so much used by Aquinas, the Catholic doctrine of the State already forms a bridge leading to the Romantic theory.

PAGE 443, NOTE 5.—The "organism theory" as the specific of the Romantic doctrine of society was first formulated by ADAM MÜLLER as a philosophy of the State (cf. STAHL: *Rechtsphilosophie*, I, pp. 568 ff). Its outstanding representative at the present day is O. SPANN: *Der wahre Staat*.

PAGE 443, NOTE 6.—The instructive work of my Zürich colleague, D. SCHINDLER (*Recht und Staat*, 1931), tries to do justice to this insoluble contradiction in the nature of the State. But his clear insight into the nature of this contradiction is somewhat obscured by his use of the idea of the "dialectical method." The dialectical method, in the sense of Hegel and of his modern disciples, aims at removing this contradiction by *logical* methods, whereas SCHINDLER sets forth this removal of the contradiction as a *practical* task which can only be approximately realized. SCHINDLER's aim is entirely different from the aim of the Hegelian dialectic; he demands, it explains. Another legal philosopher of Zürich, A. GYSIN, has also drawn attention to this contradiction in the nature of the State (*Rechtsphilosophie und Jurisprudenz*, 1927). Between the idea of law and positive law "there lies the abyss of an insoluble contradiction," p. 71. But to imagine that the fact of pointing out this contradiction also solves it, is a relic of Hegelian speculation, which cannot be combined with GYSIN's critical intention.

PAGE 443, NOTE 7.—It is a necessary consequence of the essential difference between Catholicism and Protestantism that there is a Catholic theory of law and of the State, but no Protestant theory. Wherever Protestantism has attempted to formulate such a theory it has always been already inwardly influenced by Catholicism.

The Catholic philosophy of the State—like the Catholic philosophy of law (see below, note 22)—is characterized by two features: (*a*) by the fact that it starts from the *lex naturae*, and here that means, from the idea of the divine purpose of the State; and (*b*) by the almost complete equation of the idea of the State and the conception of the State, in accordance with the fundamental attitude of the Aristotelian philosophy. Cf. the admirably clear outline of the doctrine of the State in CATHREIN, II, pp. 471–753. The decisive sentence, "The nature of the State can only be understood from the point of view of its end," p. 519. This "end" is, however, not to be understood, for instance, in the sense JHERING gives it, but in Aristotelian fashion, as an immanent idea. But in order to understand this idea, on its part, we must go back further to the idea of the Church. The Church is the actual State; the secular State is only its organ. It is true that all modern Catholic legal theorists maintain that even for the Catholic the State does exist independently alongside of the Church, in all secular matters. The Church ought merely to have "indirect authority over secular affairs" (p. 596). CATHREIN thinks GIERKE is not right when he says: "The Church, as the true State, in the authority given her by God, has received the fullness of all spiritual and secular conditions of power as integral parts of One authority." "Some theologians," he says, "have taught this, but not the Popes. When Gregory VII, Boniface VIII, and others, ascribe to the Church the highest power of judgment in secular matters this is true only of these things in so far

679

as they touch the spiritual sphere, or are touched by the so-called "indirect power" (p. 590). "In those instances in which the same matter comes under the jurisdiction of both authorities. from different points of view, and agreement by consent can be expected," the Church "can only be maintained by the fact that one of the two has the final decision. This latter power is the right of the Church" (p. 597). "The final decision, in the conflict between Church and State, can only belong to that society which both according to its end and its means is the higher" (ibid.). Since CATHREIN explicitly refers to the great Popes of the Middle Ages those who know their history will know in what sense we are to understand this "indirect authority." Some Papal sayings may give the authentic interpretation (quoted from the carefully documented selection of EICKEN, loc. cit., p. 370 ff). "Not merely a sacerdotal but also a royal sovereignty," says Innocent IV, "was founded by Christ, and He gave to St. Peter the reins of government both over the earthly and the heavenly kingdoms, which is sufficiently indicated by the number of the keys" (*Codex epist. Vatic. Nr. 4957, 49*). "We cannot do more for the freedom of the Church," wrote Innocent III, "than the Roman Church has done in asserting her full authority in secular as well as in spiritual matters" (*Ep. i, 27*) ; and the standard "doctor" of the Catholic Church, ST. THOMAS AQUINAS, expresses this clearly enough: "the uniform authority in the world as a whole is represented by the Pope alone" (*de regim. princip.* I, 14; III, 19). The brother of the Lord handed over to Peter "*non solum universam ecclesiam sed totum saeculum gubernandum*" (Innocent III, in SEEBERG: *Dogmengeschichte*, III, 286). And Boniface VIII : "*In hac eiusque potestate duos esse gladios. . . . Uterque ergo est in potestate ecclesiae, spiritualis gladius et materialis*" (ibid., p. 287). In order to avoid any possible misunderstanding, he emphasizes once more: "*opportet autem gladium esse sub gladio et temporalem auctoritatem spirituali subiici potestati*" (ibid., p. 288). This is exactly what GIERKE means; this is exactly what we mean when we say that the real Catholic idea of the State is the idea of the Church, to which the secular power is subordinate. The Church gives the latter a free hand in all matters which do not seem to her of sufficient importance to merit the special attention of the Church. "The military levy, and the conduct of war, right of coinage, collecting of rates and taxes, a limited power of jurisdiction, and the power of imposing police penalties constituted the whole content of the medieval State" (v. EICKEN, loc. cit., p. 370). Every question, however, which had any moral character at all came under the authority of the Church—even if it did not *actually* do so, this was at least the intention. And we know how this sphere was actually defined by the Popes. To this day this view, and this intention, is still that of the Catholic Church; only she knows that at the present day it is impossible to realize it.

The Reformers have no Christian philosophy of the State, any more than they recognize a divine *jus naturale*. They take seriously the statement that the State is a secular order *alongside* of the Church, and it is at this point that virtually the idea of a right of the State based on Christian ideas is abandoned. But the Reformers have a quite definite theory of the clear boundary between Church and State—a distinction which arises logically and inevitably out of their view of faith—of the independence of the State so far as the Church is concerned, and of the relation of the Christian to the State. Their emphasis on the secular nature of the order of the State does not mean, as Catholic theologians continually think it does, that the State has nothing to do with faith; but what they do mean is this: that God has given to the State a different function from that which He has given to the Church, and that the will of God which applies to the State cannot be perceived in the Scriptures, nor in a *Lex naturalis*, nor in faith itself, but that it must be sought, even by the Christian statesman, in view of the existing reality. When we look at this question as a whole we see that the differences between the Reformers with reference to the State are quite secondary. "The individual elements are almost wholly the same in both (LUTHER and CALVIN). The differences are mainly matters of emphasis and context" (HAUSSHERR: *Der Staat in Calvins Gedankenwelt*, 1923. See also HOLL: *Ges. Aufs.*, 1, 491). TROELTSCH has laid far too much stress on the differences between the Reformers in this respect—led astray by his erroneous conception of the Reformation doctrine of the Law of Nature—and in particular he has given a distorted picture of Luther's conception of the State; he has also under-estimated the agreement between Calvin and Luther, as much as he has over-estimated that between Calvin and the English sects. The Reformers' conception of the State is confined to the simple ideas which can be deduced from *Romans xiii*. The State is a divine order, instituted as a power of coercion on account of sin; its aim is the creation of order and the establishment of external justice; the Christian is therefore bound to yield obedience to it, even to a bad state and an unjust system of law, excepting when the State would try to force him to disobey God. Even at the point which is usually regarded as peculiar to the view of Calvin the two agree; the classes have a right to resist the monarch (although here the difference of emphasis becomes clear). Luther knows as well as Calvin that the question of the form of the State is a secondary question and one which is limited by history; Calvin is no more of a democrat than Luther; the fact that Calvin leans more to an oligarchy, and Luther more to the monarchy, does not affect their theory of the State, although historically this idea has been of great importance. Above all, however, neither of them regards the fact that "the powers that be are ordained of God" as meaning any kind of Divine Right in the sense of the Christian Romanticism of STAHL. Luther's "prince" and Calvin's "magis-

681

tratus" are bound to submit to the Command of God; in the one case the "sovereignty" of the ruler is limited by the command to serve the welfare of the people as a whole, and in the other instance by the Sovereignty of God Himself. And both Reformers make a clear distinction between the authority of the office and the one who holds the office. The patrimonial conception of Divine Right in STAHL's thought, that is, the conception according to which "the right of the State becomes the right of the Prince" (thus BLUNTSCHLI puts it in reference to STAHL: *Geschichte der Staatswissenschaft*, p. 703) is alien to the thought of Luther. Its source was not the Reformation, but the romanticism of the School of Historical Law, like the glorification of the State as "the moral world *par excellence*" (*Rechts- und Staatslehre auf der Grundlage christlicher Weltanschauung* 11, 2 Sect., p. 132). This "Christian" philosophy of the State has certainly influenced the thought of the Lutheran Church and of Lutheran theology more strongly than Luther himself. Modern Lutheranism is labelled with the name of the Reformation, but it actually contains the ideas of romantic Idealism. The same, however, is true of Dutch Reformed orthodoxy, whose "anti-revolutionary" philosophy of the State does not come from Calvin, but, through the intermediate stage of the writings of GROEN VAN PRINSTERER, from STAHL. This idealized picture of the State and this one-sided conservatism was not taught either by Calvin or by Luther. And, above all, the way in which German Lutheranism glorifies its own nation and its "soul" is pure Romanticism, and extremely non-Lutheran.

The fact that Calvin, as an ex-lawyer, in addition to his theological idea of the State, had also a theory of the State drawn from Aristotle and the Stoics, and that Luther, as a genuine lover of his own race, drew on the deep sources of the German popular consciousness of justice, does not form part of their theological doctrine, and therefore ought not to be confused with it, all the more since both Reformers were clearly conscious of this distinction, and always kept it in view.

PAGE 444, NOTE 8.—The philosopher may be within his rights in regarding the orders of creation (or the natural orders) as purely historical entities. But KNITTERMEYER also seems to wish to forbid the Christian to "regard these natural orders as divine orders" (in his otherwise excellent book, *Staat und Mensch*, p. 47). Can he really seriously think that the Christian is to regard marriage, for instance, as a purely historical natural order? Does he seriously believe that *Romans xiii* represents a point of view which is now out of date?

PAGE 444, NOTE 9.—We cannot blame ALTHAUS, BRUNSTÄD and HIRSCH for trying to argue that the individual nation is willed by God (ALTHAUS: *Staatsgedanke und Reich Gottes*; BRUNSTÄD: *Deutschland und der Sozialismus*; HIRSCH: *Deutschlands Schicksal*) but it is curious, to say the least, that they do not seem to have perceived that all nations which have hitherto existed have only existed for a comparatively short time, which shows that this idea is relative; it is strange, too, that they do not seem to reckon with the possibility that finally, even in the life of the State, God might have some more comprehensive unity in mind for mankind, in spite of the fact that the whole movement of history is actively and ardently aspiring after and striving for this larger unity. The dislike of modern Lutheran theologians for all that savours of the supra-national does not spring from their Lutheranism but from Romanticism. We shall see the romantic strain in the doctrine of the State outlined by ALTHAUS at another important point (see below, Note 26).

PAGE 445,. NOTE 10.—When ALTHAUS (loc. cit., p. 19) argues that the coercive character of the State itself arises from the order of creation, since the "conflict of aims" "does not always arise from evil," but from the natural variety of the created world, he inclines towards that remarkable theory of HIRSCH, according to which sin and creation are the same, looked at from two different angles (cf. above, Note 4 on Chapter XV). Where "conflict" exists which will only yield to force, there is *sin*, and not the divine creation; only certainly the idea of sin is vastly wider than that of the morally evil; a Lutheran theologian ought not to forget this. All the same, where what is necessary for the welfare of the whole has to be forced upon a reluctant people, there sin is involved, and I cannot agree with ALTHAUS when he says: "we see how insufficient it is to accept Luther's view that the necessity for the system of law and the coercion of the State is due exclusively to the power of evil over humanity." Here I decide for LUTHER against the historical romanticism of ALTHAUS.

PAGE 446, NOTE 11.—In these two words we may see the difference between Calvin's and Luther's idea of the State. In the thought of Calvin all the emphasis is upon *discipline* and to this extent upon the positively active estimate of the State; hence his observations on the subject of the State express a far more uniform opinion than that of Luther (cf. BARON: *Calvins Staatsauffassung*, p. 19). For in the thought of Luther about the State it is evident that the idea of *repentance* is uppermost, with its reminder of the fact of sin (cf. HOLL: *Luther*, p. 255). How closely, however, both approach each other, even in this respect—how, even in Calvin the remembrance of sin, and in Luther the thought of the divine rule through the State are vital elements in their thinking, cf. the fine remarks in DE QUERVAIN: *Die theologischen Voraussetzungen der Politik*, in the chapters entitled "Von der Fleischwerdung des Wortes," and "Vom Opfer des Christen," pp 60 ff. It is only Idealism, and the political romanticism strongly influenced by it, which is coloured by that glorification of the State which is characteristic of modern Lutheranism.

PAGE 446, NOTE 12.—"Power means every chance of enforcing

683

one's will, even against opposition, within a social relationship, regardless of the basis upon which this chance rests"—this is how MAX WEBER defines "power" (cf. the definition of *Machtverhältnisse* (conditions of power) by F. OPPENHEIMER, in the *Hdwb. der Soziologie*). This definition may be enough for certain purposes, but it is a definition *ab effectu*, it is not a definition of the essence of the matter. It leaves untouched also the deep connexions which are contained in the German word *Macht* (power, or might) especially the connexion with the idea of the *Schöpfermacht* (power of the Creator), *Allmacht* (omni*potence*), and that idea which defines the sphere of the Numinous, and is also the supporting basis of the power of the State.

PAGE 447, NOTE 13.—Modern thinkers on the question of the power of the State have rarely understood this aspect of power, since they are almost all under the influence of rationalism—neither MACHIAVELLI nor HOBBES, nor the modern Positivists, nor even the Idealists, for in place of the mysterious numinous "power" they place the glamour of the objective spirit. To a thinker like HEGEL, in the last resort, power is simply the World-reason, the Divine. A Protestant interpretation of *Macht* (power) ought to start from the idea of the Hidden God.

PAGE 447, NOTE 14.—It is absolutely wrong to ascribe to Primitive Christianity either indifference or hostility towards the State (cf. the article on *Christentum und Staat* in RGG[2], by ERICH FOERSTER). When Paul forbids the Christian to go to law in pagan courts this does not mean that he undervalues the State, but simply that he appeals to Christians to settle their difficulties voluntarily among themselves. The way in which, in the *Book of Acts*, Paul confronts the State—whether this is characteristic of Paul himself or of the later author of the *Acts*—shows no indifference towards the State, but a high sense of the value of the Roman civil administration. The assertion that the saying of Jesus: *Render to Caesar the things that are Caesar's* implies depreciation of the State, is unfounded. Certainly, as the One who was ushering in the New Age Jesus had nothing to do with the State, any more than He had to do with the other secular orders; but this does not mean that He regarded them with either indifference or contempt. The assertion that Christianity only gradually acquired a more positive attitude towards the State is pure imagination. What IRENAEUS says about the State (*adv. haer. V.* 24) is as much in accordance with the fundamental ideas of Paul, and of Primitive Christianity, as it is with those of the Reformation.

PAGE 447, NOTE 15.—For the fact that in Calvin's thought in particular the idea that those who wield the authority of the State are *Dei vicarii* (IV, 20, 6) *lieutenans de Dieu*, that the authorities are *velut delegata a Deo jurisdictio*, is contrary to the common idea of "Divine Right," see BEYERHAUS: *Studien zur Staatsanschauung*

Calvins, p. 90. "The intensification of this conception which allowed later theorists of the State to develop it into a metaphysical expression for the ruler's possession of sovereignty is moreover excluded by the exclusiveness of the Divine Sovereignty." The theory of Divine Right, in the form in which it was known in the later Prussian reigning dynasty, only appeared with FRIEDRICH WILHELM IV, that is, with the rise of Romanticism, and was theoretically justified in STAHL's semi-Lutheran and semi-Romantic and Idealistic *Rechtsphilosophie*.

PAGE 448, NOTE 16.—HEGEL: *Philosophie des Rechts*, § 258: "The State, as the reality of the substantial will . . . is that which in and for itself is rational. This substantial unity is an absolutely unmoved self-end, in which freedom attains its highest rights, just as this final end has its supreme right over against the individual, whose supreme duty it is to be a member of the State." "It is the course of God in the world which is the State: its foundation is the power of the Reason realizing itself as will . . . we must contemplate the Idea, this real God for itself" (*Wke VIII*, pp. 313–20).

The Hegelian absolutism of the State—somewhat modified by SCHLEIERMACHER—was introduced by STAHL into German Lutheranism, and by ROTHE into Liberal theology, and has stamped itself more or less upon the German theological thought of the nineteenth century. Its close connexion with "orthodox" Lutheranism in particular gave rise to the disastrous idea that LUTHER was the author of this absolutist doctrine of the State.

Outside theology this absolutism of the State prevails in the law schools which have been influenced by German Idealism. The doctrine of the omnipotence of the State (as we still find it for instance in the pages of JELLINEK, who says that: "The State has the formal right to determine the boundaries of its power according to its own judgment, in such a manner that in principle nothing which belongs to the common life of mankind is withdrawn from its power to regulate," *Allg. Staatslehre*, p. 327), is based on this Hegelian absolutism of the State. LASSON expresses it still more naïvely: "The State has the supreme right over all" (quoted by CATHREIN, loc. cit., p. 530), or BLUNTSCHLI, the task of the State is "to manifest its glory to the whole world" (quoted ibid.). In STAHL too we read that the State "is the realization of the moral kingdom" (quoted by BLUNTSCHLI, loc. cit., p. 702), it is "absolutely the moral world" (quoted by CATHREIN, loc. cit., p. 528). It should be one of the great tasks of the theology of the present day to put an end to this deification of the State, from a spirit of sacred regard for truth and sanity, the spirit of the great Reformers.

PAGE 448, NOTE 17.—The question whether the law of the State is the only law, is—as is well known—the subject of ardent controversy among scholars in jurisprudence at the present time. In the last resort, behind this controversy in the realm of the philosophy of law there are fundamental convictions, both religious and philosophical. Anyone who regards the Law of Nature as a real law will not admit the identification of law in general with the law of the State. For the Catholic the duty of refusing to identify the two is an absolute dogma; for to admit that there is no other law save the law of the State does away with ecclesiastical law, which is the basis of the Catholic Church.

The positivist philosophy of law has grown out of the philosophy of history, but it has thrown aside the doctrine of the latter concerning the consciousness of law which is diffused among the people, and the connexion which this implies between law and morality. Thus there is nothing left but to understand law as the accidental result, at any particular time, of the struggle for power. This is the view of GUMPLOWICZ, BERGBOHM, OPPENHEIMER, and—more important than all these (in spite of the fact that he was no legal philosopher)—KARL MARX. In its programme for the future and in its criticism of law Marxist Socialism unconsciously contains a good deal of the Stoic Law of Nature.

PAGE 448, NOTE 18.—The greatest modern representative of this conception of law is HEGEL. But Hegel's thought is too historical to be able to hold firmly to the fiction of the Law of Nature. To him it was precisely the law which had developed as the result of and in the course of history which was the development of the *idea* of law, and as such an element in the process of the objectification of Spirit. Even Roman Catholicism, since the contrast between the *lex naturae* and the positive law has been concealed as far as possible, approaches this Idealistic conception. Modern Catholicism does the same, as though positive law were on the whole an approximate realization of the *jus naturale*. See Note 4.

PAGE 449, NOTE 19.—Cf. STAMMLER: *Rechtsphilosophie*: "The statement that 'the powers that be are ordained by God' does not contradict what has been said. It offers to the believer the same thought, as well as the consideration that the self-imposed command of the law as such, that is, without any consideration of the goodness or the worthlessness of the content, is already absolutely necessary, and manifests itself as such" (p. 102).

PAGE 449, NOTE 20.—A particularly important attempt to define the idea of justice as absolute is contained in STAMMLER's philosophy of the law (*Die Lehre von dem richtigen Rechte* and *Lehrbuch der Rechtsphilosophie*). STAMMLER's ultimate intention has an affinity with our own, at least to this extent, that he regrets the idea of a timeless, universally valid Law of Nature, and in spite of this holds firmly to the idea of just law as the point of view for the positive formation of law and its treatment. His endeavour therefore is to conceive the idea of just law as formally as possible. But now, like his philosophical teacher KANT, he slips away from the purely critical way of thinking into a rationalistic way of thinking in positing an absolute rational *ideal* of law, which he deduces from a social ideal which is likewise rationally deduced. This social ideal, which he equates with the idea of pure community, he regards as the idea of "unconditioned harmony" (*Rechtsphilosophie*, § 80) which is further determined by the "unconditional absence of contradictions" in combined human effort (ibid., p. 214), or by the fact that "that which is desired personally must always be balanced in the other direction, in order that the increasing adjustment which thus takes place in the idea of an ideally imagined union of aims may receive its essentially definite sign" (ibid.). We have no desire to argue with the eminent legal philosopher as to whether this conception of the idea of justice is satisfying to juridical thought; but as moralists we have occasion to express the misgiving that such a conception would never lead to the idea of pure community. A community based on love is something quite different from a community of this kind based on the adjusted "efforts" of individuals. Behind this idea of adjustment there lies simply the *suum cuique*; Stammler's formula, like the Roman one, leaves it an open question concerning the nature of the principle according to which every one within the whole will receive his due. The purely formal conception of harmony, or of an existence without any contradictions, only conceals the concrete problem under a logically formal formula. Statements can be without contradiction; but what does it mean to speak of an adjustment of efforts without contradictions? What sort of adjustment is it that creates harmony? It is also interesting to see how STAMMLER deals with the problem of Love and Justice. Evidently under the influence of Kant, he conceives love quite subjectively as the *Dynamis* which effects that which is just (p. 208). Thus he does not see that love is a different way of meeting the claims of others, and he cannot see or admit this, because to him the final Good is something legal and therefore rational. Love, in the New Testament sense, precisely does *not* desire a fair adjustment, but sacrifice. It, too, absolutely creates a harmony—which is conceived in the idea of the Kingdom of God— but it is not a harmony which can be conceived in legal terms. STAMMLER's social ideal is, on the one hand, too indefinite to be an idea of law in the sense of constructive natural law, on the other hand it is too definite, too legalistic, to have a claim to the title of "pure community." But it is a happy formulation of the critical idea of law by the very fact of its formalism, apart from the idea of absence of contradiction, which suggests an unambiguous principle of construction which, when we look more closely, is not there; it is possible to imagine that which is most unjust as well as that which is most just. The principle of lack of contradiction here means absolutely nothing. But behind it there is the same logical perversion as we saw to be the case in the Kantian addition of the idea of the Law of Nature for the definition of the content of the Good.

687

PAGE 449, NOTE 21.—This is the right element in RITSCHL's contrast between the divine love and justice. He rightly calls attention to the fact that the word "justice," as it is used in the Old Testament, has a quite different meaning from that which it has when it has been influenced by the thought of Aristotle and of Roman jurisprudence. The "just man" in the Old Testament is not one who gives to every one his due, but one who submits himself wholly to the will of God. And again, the just (or righteous) will of God is not one which gives to every one according to his merits, but one which follows unfalteringly the aim of His Kingdom, and carries it out. Only at one point has RITSCHL gone astray, namely, in the fact that he wishes to eliminate the idea of reward, of Divine penalties, from the Biblical conception of God, and this leads him to a purely rational conception of love. The incomprehensible character of the divine love, as the New Testament speaks of it, is based upon the fact that while it is true that God rewards and punishes, His love transcends His justice. And, in the second place, RITSCHL does not understand that the holiness of God is never absorbed by His love. His holiness as it works itself out among men, however, is His justice in imposing penalties on man. The inviolability of His self-sovereign will—to use the language of STAMMLER—is His justice (or righteousness). But this is actually a wholly different conception of justice from that which is necessarily meant in the scientific language of jurisprudence. Justice, in the ordinary sense of the word, is rational; for in some way or other it presupposes equality between the parties concerned. But the Divine justice consists precisely in the absolutely incomparable character of God, in the fact—as *Romans ix* suggests—that God owes nothing to anyone. But a God who "as the Controller of the whole of human society must reward good actions and punish bad ones, in virtue of His distributive justice," as the Catholic moralists maintain (cf. CATHREIN, loc. cit., p. 511) is certainly just in a sense which is wholly alien to the thought of the Bible, but which is certainly possible in an ethic which makes the *lex naturae* the supreme principle.

PAGE 450, NOTE 22.—Here is one of the points at which the connexion between theology and thought about "secular matters" comes out very clearly. Roman Catholicism, as an integral part of its dogma, has a definite theory of law, which reveals the bases of Catholic theology. The fact that in so doing it appeals to its philosophy, and not to its theology, is all part of its fundamental theological conception, its doctrine of the *lex naturae*. This Catholic system of jurisprudence can in any case primarily point to the use of language in which the words "right" and "wrong"—"my just rights"—are used wholly in the sense of a supra-positive, "unwritten" eternal law. Indeed, apart from such a reference to the Moral, law cannot be understood at all. In this respect we must grant that the Catholic theory—which is not only held by Catholics but by others, for instance, by TRENDELENBURG, and which has been recently represented by many others—is right. Upon this basis the Catholic theory of jurisprudence is built up in the following manner.

The *jus naturale* is that part of the *lex naturae* which refers to that relation between human beings which is determined by the "Suum." The principle of the law of nature is the *suum cuique*—exactly in accordance with ULPIAN's definition of justice: *justitia est constans et perpetua voluntas jus suum cuique tribuendi* (cf. STAMMLER: *Rechtsphilosophie*, p. 201). From this proposition first of all the general propositions of the *jus gentium* and then all the propositions of just law are to be deduced "by an illuminating process of deduction" (CATHREIN, loc. cit., p. 558). That "suum" gains a definite content and meaning through reflection on that which "in a special way is connected with us and is destined for our use," as, for instance, the various parts of the body, freedom, that which has been gained by one's own efforts, and other things (loc. cit., p. 524). The total sum of all that is due to me "by means of the Law of nature" is taken for granted as equally due to every one else; this includes the idea of private property. But this theory of just law only now becomes significant from the point of view of the philosophy of law through the assumption that, as a whole, the positive law corresponds to this just law. It is at this point that the Catholic theory becomes on the one hand, hesitating, and on the other, dangerous. For the obligatory character of law, it is explicitly stated, is based *solely* upon this moral quality of law, so that, where the law does not correspond to this idea of the just law, this obligation of the law ceases. "A law which is obviously harmful to the common weal is not a true law" (p. 568). The judge may not judge according to the positive law if it is "obviously unjust" (p. 573). From the threat of inevitable and continual conflict between obedience to one's conscience and obedience to the law which this principle implies, one is only saved, to some extent, by the elastic protective determination of the "obviously" unjust which is practically extremely effective. Thus by means of a definition of a theory of knowledge the profound gulf which yawns between the positive and the just law is concealed, after, on the other hand, in the lapse of time the conception of just law itself (for instance, private property) has been adjusted to the actual law as part of it. The catastrophe of an actual clash between the just law and the positive law, when the Catholic would feel obliged to refuse to obey the positive law, can only be avoided by means of these two safety-valves. Only at this price also can the theoretical fiction be maintained that there is in existence a manifest Divine Law of Nature, from the point of view of which the positive law can be understood.

The historical and then the positivist school of thought has thrown over this fiction of an established Law of Nature, but in so doing it has overreached itself. It rightly calls attention to the fact of the immense variety and historically accidental character of the forms of law within the sphere of actual history, where the most contradictory demands have been made on the obedience of the individual, as the positive law of the State, and this is still going on. Further, it calls attention to the perversions by means of which the *suum cuique* has been filled with a quite definite content. But it goes astray when it regards the idea of just law as abolished. It then gives up the possibility of understanding international law, the legal practice of the judge, and many other elements of the reality of the law, where indubitably something like a *jus naturale* precedes the positive law, fills in its gaps, or gives it support. Hence the conflict between the defenders of the Law of Nature and the positivists of law will never cease, unless they find the critical conception of an idea of law which, as experience shows, and for good reasons, can only be understood by those jurists who are in connexion with the Reformation tradition of faith. (Cf. in addition to STAMMLER, for instance, W. BURCKHARDT, *L'état et le droit*, 1931.)

PAGE 450, NOTE 23.—The wealth of content which Catholicism —or to be more exact, modern Catholicism—gives to the *suum cuique*, originates in a Stoicism modified by the Christian belief in Creation. The dependence of Thomism on the Roman compilers of the Pandects of Justinian is as well known to us to-day as is its dependence on the popular philosophy of Stoicism. The "modifications" of egalitarian rationalism by means of the Scriptural belief in Creation are secretly introduced, as "illuminating" minor propositions, from the supposedly rational philosophy.

PAGE 451, NOTE 24.—Even the question whether force necessarily belongs to the sphere of law is a subject for controversy among jurists. If the question is denied, then it is difficult to distinguish between law and morality (unless one takes refuge in the Catholic definition of "relationship" (i.e. of the *jus naturale*—TR.) or in GIERKE's idea, that morality is only concerned with the inward disposition, which however is wrong); if we accept it, then it is difficult to explain certain provisions of positive law which evidently cannot be imposed by force—as for instance the most fundamental principles of common law—or even international law. This difficulty, however, lies in the very nature of the case, it is not due to the obstinacy of certain jurists. It points rather to the double origin of law. So much only can we say with certainty—with JHERING— that the law has the tendency to make it possible to impose it by force as far as possible, since only thus can it exercise its functions completely. We certainly would not agree with him in saying: "The law without force is an empty sound without any reality" (*Der Zweck im Recht*, p. 196), but we could very well endorse the following statement: "The social organization of force tallies with the State and with the Law" (p. 240) even when "within the administration of the law there are points at which force breaks down" (p. 256). STAMMLER's answer to this question, that only "the legal obligation according to its unchanging conception possesses the quality of permanent obligation" (*Rechtsphilosophie*, p. 236), is quite unsatisfying. In actual fact of course, looking at the question as a whole, the statement is correct, but it is only correct on account of the fact of evil, because human beings will not remain united without the compulsion of the law. The conception that the usefulness of the system of law is based precisely upon the power of compulsion by the forcible means it possesses, is the only conception which corresponds to the Christian knowledge of evil in men and in society, just as it is the only one of which Idealism and Rationalism would like to get rid because they do not see human nature as it really is. Hobbes' idea of the *bellum omnium contra omnes*, although it is not by any means the whole truth, still does express something which belongs to the real picture of humanity.

PAGE 452, NOTE 25.—Self-defence is one of these exceptions. The problem of self-defence absolutely belongs to *this* context, not to that of ethics in general, that is, it can only be understood from the standpoint of law. From the standpoint of the ethic of love, of the Sermon on the Mount, there is no right of self-defence, as indeed there are no "rights" at all. My own life, my own freedom is not a "right," it is the gracious gift of God. Therefore too I have no "right" to defend it where my direct relation to God and my neighbour is concerned. But in this sinful world God has set the "justice" of the State and of the law, in order to protect me from the attacks of violent men. Now where the established order, whose duty it is to ensure this protection, is lacking, then—from the point of view of this sphere of justice—the individual, acting vicariously for the regular authority, may protect himself. But this "right" is abrogated by the command of non-resistance, by the saying about "turning the other cheek." I may only act in self-defence, not as a Christian, but at the utmost as a citizen, and this means for the sake of justice within society. Where the latter is not the point at issue, the Christian must simply endure wrong. The father must somehow protect his children, he is not a free agent; his official duty modifies his purely personal duty. But how this is to take place, how we are to know which line to take, constitutes that *spatium* within which the decision of faith must be taken. The blunt common-sense attitude, "If I had not killed him he would have killed me," is in any case impossible for one who intends to live according to the obedience of faith.

PAGE 455, NOTE 26.—Modern Lutheranism has been greatly influenced by Romantic Idealism, both in its idea of the State and in its idea of the nation. This comes out, for instance, in what ALTHAUS says in his theory of the calling of a nation. Whereas

691

otherwise ALTHAUS knows perfectly well what the Lutheran idea of the Calling means, he formulates the idea of the national calling in a manner which could not be more clearly expressed by the purest representatives of romantic individualism: "the best, the most valuable internationalism is the obedient, serious, resolved development of one's own life. . . . Hence the people ought to regard its own calling alone. In great matters it should and may have nothing to do with any other nation for good or ill, but may only fulfil its own vocation" (*Staatsgedanke*, p. 45). This idea of vocation is not the fruit of Luther's thought but of the Romanticism of historical pantheism. For Luther the idea of the welfare of the Neighbour is inseparable from the idea of the Calling. We only act in accordance with our calling—and this applies also to a nation or a people—when we look not on our own things but on the things of others. The mixture of Hegelian deification of the State and sober obedience to a God-given command, is the dangerous element in this kind of Nationalism, glorified by religion.

PAGE 458, NOTE 27.—It is a relic of Idealistic State absolutism when KNITTERMEYER (*Staat und Mensch*, p. 10) says that "man is bound to the State by all his activities." "The individual human being must place himself, with all his activities, under the law of the State, under the claim of politics" (p. 35). The State must deteriorate if it claims to be the only court of appeal, in which the individual acknowledges and works out his responsibility towards the nation as a whole. In this respect Catholicism, with its opposition to the totalitarian authority of the State, carries on the genuine Christian tradition, which also corresponds to the thought of the Reformers, in a purer way than Protestantism, which has been so largely influenced by Idealism; the English dislike of the tendency of the State to unite all functions within itself must arise from a healthy instinct on the part of society to hold the power of the State in check.

PAGE 458, NOTE 28.—In saying this I do not retract what I said further back about the necessity for State intervention in the economic struggle. Temporarily the State may even have to become a subject of the economic sphere, but this would be a case of emergency, indicating an extraordinary disturbance of the equilibrium. The State, for the sake of its own health, must insist that it should delegate as much of its authority as possible to free corporations, for bureaucracy, which is the necessary result of the centralized State which desires to dominate and control everything, is the death of all free life. This is the same idea which lies behind federalistic Socialism, and indeed in all federal theories. When the one State, with its centralized apparatus of administration, is confronted by nothing but a mass of unorganized individuals, the effect is to kill all vitality. The wise State places between itself and the individual as many relatively autonomous groups as possible which are in close touch with life, and are endowed with strong legal powers.

NOTES ON CHAPTER XXXVII

PAGE 460, NOTE 1.—Luther's remarks in his *Schrift von weltlicher Obrigkeit* (on the Secular Authority) (WA. 11, pp. 246 ff) is most satisfactory in its frankness. The picture which he draws here of the behaviour of the Prince is certainly not far from the thought of MACHIAVELLI or HOBBES, but his *judgment* is the exact opposite. It has been reserved to German Idealism to declare this Unreason as Reason in accordance with the sentence of Hegel: "Philosophy glorifies the Real, which seems wrong, to the Rational" (*Philosophie der Weltgeschichte*, ed. LASSON, p. 55).

PAGE 460, NOTE 2.—It is therefore a Christian doctrine common to Christianity as a whole—both to Protestantism and to Catholicism—that in matters of conscience there is a right of passive resistance to the State. "Luther laid it down for the individual as a strict duty to defend his liberty of conscience, while at the same time, from the side of the State, he argues for a policy of yielding at this point, as that which is both reasonable and necessary" (HOLL, *Luther*, p. 484).

The same is true of Calvin. The right of resistance of the "classes" which has been so much discussed—thus not passive, but active resistance—is restricted in the teaching of Calvin nearly as much as it is in that of Luther (cf. HOLL, loc. cit., p. 491; BEYERHAUS, p. 96; HAUSSHERR, p. 58). In his teaching this is not based upon the idea of popular sovereignty—an idea which is not only alien to his way of thinking, but which flatly contradicts his view—but upon the recognition of a certain State federalism—not essentially different from the teaching of Luther. It was only later Calvinism which, upon a basis of natural law, renewed this theory of the right of resistance, which was already known in the Middle Ages, and thus laid the foundation of the doctrine of popular sovereignty (cf. GIERKE's *Althusius*).

PAGE 460, NOTE 3.—Cf. the valuable book by ARTHUR SALZ: *Imperialismus*, 1931. To-day, however, "imperialism" is also used in a narrower sense. It is "that stage in the period of Capitalism" in which Capitalistic Finance, by means of political coercion, takes possession of supra-national spheres, with the aim of holding a monopoly of the power to exploit . . . with the tendency of the autocratic world empire which includes all zones of influence and controls all raw materials." (SCHULZE-GÄVERNITZ, quoted in "Imperialismus," in the *Handwb. der Soziologie*.) Alongside of this is the definition of SULZBACH (ibid.): "Imperialism is the tendency of a State to enlarge its sphere of sovereignty." According to the views of certain modern Lutherans this imperialism is of the very essence of every healthy State, an idea which is opposed to that of the Reformation. For all the Reformers have severely condemned the forcible expansion of the State, all conquest. Luther "lays it down as the duty of the State not only to renounce the natural desire to expand, but also to suppress the sense of national honour which is of such importance for the national consciousness" (HOLL, loc. cit., p. 489).

PAGE 462, NOTE 4.—F. MEINECKE's book, *Die Idee der Staatsraison*, describes the tragedy of statecraft as well as its history. This profoundly serious, and in the broad sense, honest book can only be read with the deepest emotion. It deals indeed with the inescapable guilt, with the fact that one must inevitably incur guilt, of one who is called to guide the State in a responsible manner. How much more seriously this historian, who does not reckon himself a Christian, speaks of the evil which taints all the political exercise of power than the theologians who are still intoxicated by the Hegelian deification of the State! "The profound defect of German historical thought was the deceptive idealization of the policy of 'might' by the doctrine that it was in accordance with a higher morality. This gave rise, in spite of all the moral and idealistic exceptions which were made, to the development of a crudely naturalistic and biological ethic of force" (p. 533). "This is the most terrible and overwhelming fact of world history, that it cannot succeed in moralizing thoroughly precisely that human community which includes all other forms of community, as the force which protects and furthers their interests, which on that account ought to shed light on the path of all other forms of community which will follow, by the purity of its nature" (p. 15). How closely he comes to the Reformation doctrine of the Hidden God when he confesses at the end of the book: "In history we do not see God; we are simply aware of Him in the clouds which surround Him" (p. 542)! If MEINECKE had only understood the Christian Faith of the Reformers as well as Idealism he would perhaps have come to a rather different point of view from that which he expresses in the closing chapter of his book.

PAGE 463, NOTE 5.—The *Politische Ethik* of FRIEDRICH WILHELM FOERSTER is ethical pedantry. The "language of purely Christian idealism, which knows no compromise between Spirit and Nature" (MEINECKE, p. 532), is in reality the language of that fanatical sentimentalism which does not know what Original Sin means, of that legalism which believes that it is a sign of Christian earnestness to confront reality with *a priori* laws, whereas it is the sign of a superficial imagination. I do not wish to maintain that FOERSTER does not say several things which are worthy of consideration—for instance about a false *Real-politik*—or that he does not rightly call attention to certain imponderable elements which are frequently overlooked by politicians. Yet as a whole his work is the product of an idealism which is remote from reality, and therefore it is very far from genuine Christian thinking.

PAGE 464, NOTE 6.—The Reformers know nothing of the autonomy of the State, in the sense in which the statecraft of Machiavelli (and that of Hegel which comes very close to it) conceives it, which plays such a disastrous part in later theological discussions of the problem of the State. The acting State—for Calvin as for Luther this always means the authorities, the Prince, the *lieutenans de Dieu*—in the teaching of Calvin is always limited by the Sovereignty of God, and also by the welfare of the people, in the thought of Luther it is limited by the welfare of the people and also by the thought of the Sovereignty of God. (See BEYERHAUS, loc. cit., pp. 95 and 125.) Luther says the same. (WA. 11, 273.)

PAGE 465, NOTE 7.—Luther had very little occasion to enquire into the form of the State; there can be no question therefore of asserting that he held a theologically ethical argument for monarchy like that held by modern Lutheranism (see for instance the works of ALTHAUS, HIRSCH, and BRUNSTÄD). Calvin, in his *Institutes*, following ARISTOTLE, examines the various forms of the State, and for similar reasons to those which have been mentioned above, he came to the conclusion that he preferred a moderate aristocracy; but he makes it clear that this preference is founded on his own private opinion (*Institutio* 4, 20, 8). But he who certainly had good reason to know what authority means, feared the system of monarchy the longer he lived, on account of its daemonic dangers. (Cf. BEYERHAUS, loc. cit., pp. 109 ff.)

PAGE 468, NOTE 8.—The romantic vein in the ethic of the State of ALTHAUS comes out too in his exaggerated estimate of the "leader of genius." "Only those who combine the profound insight of genius with a strict conscience can really discover this knowledge (namely of the historical calling)." This religious estimate of the genius is a dominant feature in the thought of Romanticism. There can be no doubt that Bismarck is the model for all these ideas, as indeed for almost everything that German professors write about the vocation of the statesman; as though there were always such a "leader" at hand with his "genius" and his "rigid conscience"! And when ALTHAUS goes so far as to play off the idea of "the Leader" against that of democracy—as though on the one hand the ruler were the masses, and on the other hand the Leader of genius—it is rather extreme, in view of the fact that, for instance, the American democracy is quite inclined to assist the "able Leader" to gain power. That the "Crown," as it is venerated by ALTHAUS, HIRSCH and BRUNSTÄD, likewise is seldom successful has been shown more than sufficiently by history. But in any case this is the problem: we ought to seek for the constitution which will make most sure that really competent leaders are entrusted with the reins of government.

PAGE 469, NOTE 9.—At the present time, the word "pacifism," both by friend and foe, partly from malice and partly from thought-lessness, causes a great deal of mischievous nonsense to be talked. This is the place at which it is fitting to take stock of the various possibilities of pacifism.

Radical, fanatical pacifism is that type which condemns war because it is opposed to the command to love contained in the Sermon on the Mount. But once we appeal to the Sermon on the Mount we ought to go still further and reject all compulsion of every kind, even that which is represented by a police force, and all legal administration—even, for instance, all legislation for the protection of the workers—so far as it is a political method of compulsion. We need not concern ourselves any further with this fanatical type of pacifism. Throughout this work on ethics we have been engaged in a fierce struggle against it. But at the present time only a few people still take this position, although certainly the arguments from this side constantly reappear, even in those who take their stand upon the view of law—and this means, upon the view of the compulsory authority of the State.

There is, secondly, a newer kind of pacificism, represented for instance in Heering's valuable book, *Der Sündenfall des Christentums* (*The Fall of Christianity*: English translation). Here, apart from some digressions into the fanatical type of argument—law and its com-pulsory authority, that is, to put it briefly, the force exercised by the police, is recognized as an historical necessity. But, so the writer argues, there is a quantitative difference which becomes a quali-tative difference (loc. cit., pp. 200 ff). But war, says HEERING, is such a *quantum* of force that in no case can it be ethically justified. This argument is not devoid of value, indeed, in all "political ethics" it is of decisive importance. In the sphere of the Relative the "more or less" is the practically important element. We must also grant that war—quite apart from the war "of the present day"—by the very fact that it is a "more" of this kind, becomes a special ethical problem; without further argument we feel it to be a far more difficult problem than that of the force exercised by the police. But this type of argument is too doctrinaire to be true. If for instance "it should not please my wicked neighbour" to leave my nation in peace, must I renounce this sole method of defending the existence of my nation against the insatiable lust of conquest of my "wicked neighbour" simply because it would mean using the "more" of force, just because it is this "more"? Where anarchy prevails, that is, where Might is Right, the war of defence, as an emergency action, is the "just war." But pacifists like HEERING secretly use arguments which do not apply to this type of war in the old sense at all, but to war as it is now at the present time, and therefore, without noticing it, they slip into the third kind of pacifism which takes as its starting-point not war as a timeless problem, but the problem of war as it 'is to-day. This is the only serious way of stating the problem, and it alone is the one which is realistic and not fanatical or sentimental. But it is fatal to confuse this genuine type of pacifism with the sentimental kind, for it not only weakens discussion but it also weakens the influence of genuine pacifism, and constantly exposes it to the justified reproach of inconsistency and remoteness from the world. As Protestant and Biblical Christians we are under the obligation of affirming the necessity of the State, and with this the necessity for the compulsion exercised by the State. This deprives us of the right to appeal to the Sermon on the Mount in support of our pacifism and to estimate the wars of the past from an ethical point of view. Only so do we gain the right to oppose war at the present day with all the more energy.

There are also various types of anti-pacifism, from the justifiable rejection of sentimental pacifism to the most cold-blooded glorification of war. The statement of HIRSCH—"Without glorifying war in any way, it may be conceived as a necessary part of the divine order in creation . . ." (loc. cit., p. 95) comes perilously near to the latter extreme. This statement is not surprising from a theologian to whom sin and Creation are the same thing viewed from different angles! ALTHAUS discusses the problem of war in a very different spirit. See the next note.

PAGE 471, NOTE 10.—To a large extent I can agree with the observations of ALTHAUS on the subject of war (*Staatsgedanke und Reich Gottes*, pp. 58–108), and his article "Krieg" in RGG), and also with his rejection of absolute pacifism. We cannot rightly regard war as an abstract problem, but only as a problem of history and political action. The question is rightly stated: "Is war rightly part of the divine order of the State?" Absolute pacifism ignores the State altogether. We must also grant that ALTHAUS speaks of the necessity of war with bated breath, fully aware that here we are dealing with something which incurs serious guilt, and that he recognizes that it is the task of the Church to work for peace. But the charge I would bring against ALTHAUS is this: that his realism is defective. It is true that he sees that the problem of war at the present time is different from that of previous ages in history—this comes out especially plainly in the last section of the article mentioned above—but he does not see this clearly enough, and he does not draw from this fact the conclusions which it implies. He does not see that war at the present day is suicidal, that the meaning which it once had it has lost, that it has outlived its purpose; it is out of date. We agree with him when he says: the new situation does not mean in any way that we stand nearer to the Kingdom of God, or that humanity has become better; it merely means that humanity cannot tolerate any more wars. We require a political pacifism, a pacifism founded on statecraft, and indeed we require it as Christians. It is the duty of the Christian to think politically in matters which concern the State. This does not mean that the Christian has to forget his Christian faith, but that his faith must be connected with reality, and that it is under the obligation to do this through the Divine Command. For this very reason I regard the position of ALTHAUS as a kind of "half-way house," which is due to the fact that in his mind he oscillates between the thought of Romanticism and the thought of the Reformation.

He cannot shake himself free of the old idea of war, he has not yet heard the clock strike the new hour in world-history, he is still living in the past history of his nation, with its thirst for military glory. Only because this is so can we explain the fact that he can venture to make a statement like the following: "We have no more right to despise war than we have to glorify it." It is to-day the task of a Christian ethic to make war look despicable because it has become an insanity. And therefore the statement is no longer true, that "It is not the duty of the Church to educate the nations for war, but also not for peace, but for political seriousness and a sense of responsibility." Because the last part of the sentence is true, at the present time the central clause is untrue. At the present day every statesman ought to strive earnestly for the abolition of war, from a sense of political responsibility, just as a ship's captain would strain every nerve to extinguish a fire which had broken out upon his vessel. At the present day pacifism is the only rational political course of action—but it must be a realistic type of pacifism which is well aware of the necessities of the State.

NOTES ON CHAPTER XXXVIII

PAGE 483, NOTE 1.—There is a certain danger in speaking of a "Christian philosophy." *Vestigia terrent*. By this I do not mean—as FRANKEN (*Kritische Philosophie und dialektische Theologie*, p. 186) has understood me to mean—a universal philosophy, a system—for in that case it would cease to be a *critical* philosophy—but the philosophizing of a thinker who is a Christian, and who therefore, in spite of the fact that he thinks in a strictly philosophical manner, does not forget his faith, but indeed is preserved by it from rationalistic short circuits and speculative encroachments upon forbidden territory. Nor do I mean a merely formal philosophy, which could be called a critical philosophy in the narrower sense, but rather a treatment of the great concrete problems: Culture, the State, Law, Art, Morality, Religion. I see the promising beginnings of such a philosophy in the work of KNITTERMEYER and HEINRICH BARTH— although both still contain a relic of Platonist speculation, whose incompatibility with faith the theologian should point out to the philosopher, and thus give him occasion for renewed critical reflection. The work of GRISEBACH also stands in this context; but it is purely destructive; as such it is useful, but it is far from adequate. It is not the sole task of the critical philosopher to show where other philosophers have stepped out of their province! We need *positive* philosophical reflection upon culture, the State, education, etc. The philosophy of the present day, however, is still under the spell of the Idealistic or Positivistic world-view or metaphysic, and therefore it does not take into consideration the fact that the Christian Faith might be a regulative principle of thought; since it is satisfied with its substitute for faith in the form of Idealism or Positivism.

PAGE 483, NOTE 2.—The newer use of the word *Kultur* arose out of German Idealism, and other languages have no equivalent for it. It is therefore burdened with all the dangers of *Kultur*-absolutism which are peculiar to German Idealism.

PAGE 484, NOTE 3.—The idea of a "self-end" is not free from the danger of misconstruction. As we have said, from the point of view of faith there is no other self-end than the Kingdom, the Royal sovereignty of God. But the relative self-end, humanity, is incorporated into this absolute self-end. Science is not a self-end in the absolute sense of the word; in the last resort its aim is to serve man; but it can only do this if, once it is at work, it orders its activity according to its own laws. Here too a more detailed analysis—which we cannot attempt here—would lead us to the problem of the formal and the material. Science is a self-end by means of its form; it is connected with life by its content. Therefore the more formal science becomes—as, for instance, in the shape of logic and mathematics—the more autonomous it becomes, and the more material, and that means the more it approximates to human reality, the more it is connected with life, the more it is dependent upon the understanding of personality.

PAGE 485, NOTE 4.—HEINRICH BARTH has done real service in the fact that, undeterred by modern tendencies in philosophy, he has asserted this indispensable idea of PLATO and KANT (see above all his *Philosophie der praktischen Vernunft*) without which man cannot be understood in his being as man. Here FRANKEN—following in the steps of OVINK—is his follower, and for the first time delimits the boundaries between critical philosophy and genuine theology. Here a fruitful community of labour between philosophers and theologians may and should result. The philosopher must watch in order to see that the theologian never omits reflection on the nature of formal freedom, and the theologian must take care to see that the philosopher does not allow formal freedom to become material freedom and thus from the point of view of speculation go out of his province.

PAGE 487, NOTE 5.—Idealism with its fundamental idea of Reason which is identical with itself is not *ultimately* conscious of responsibility; responsibility only exists where a "Thou" is concerned which is not "I." Since for Idealism "at bottom" the *Thou* is the same as the "I", in it, "at bottom," the idea of responsibility disappears. Responsibility to oneself only means that the spiritual-self rules the sense-self; the spiritual self however has no master; it *is* master. Nor has it any "Thou" for it is the "I" in the "Thou." It has also no sense of guilt, for guilt can here only be understood as a distorted relationship between the spiritual and the sensual ego. It is solitary, like the Deity which as the All-Spirit, is the All.

PAGE 489, NOTE 6.—Cf. the discussion of the Dialectical Theology by E. SPRANGER in the book: *Der Kampf gegen den Idealismus, Sitz.-Ber. d. Preuss. Akad. d. Wiss.*, pp. 418–454. This is not the place to treat, once again, the subject of Idealism and Christianity in regard to the problem of truth, to which the article of SPRANGER is dedicated; a great deal would be gained if the champions of Idealism would once admit that the *aims* of Christianity and Idealism are totally different, that their views of God, Man, and the world are different, and are indeed mutually exclusive. Idealism with its emphasis on the Abstract—the Idea—is moreover just as "intolerant" and sure of itself as the Christian Faith with its insistence that all abstract values are subordinate to the Personal. But what ought never to happen again is the repetition of statements, which can clearly be refuted, and which have often been refuted. The Dialectical Theology—SPRANGER refers to me—has never given grounds for the assertion that it is "the theology of the radical denial of humanity, of culture, of religion" (p. 17); it would be difficult to prove that "it speaks of Reason as that which is absolutely non-divine, contrary to faith, and the pride of sin within man" (p. 23). We can willingly grant to SPRANGER, that "theology cannot shut itself out from those highly educated forms of intellectual life, represented by the Humanities, which through the medium of the historical school and Romanticism also go back to German Idealism" (p. 37). What we maintain is that Idealism, even in the form in which it is favourable to Christianity as in SPRANGER's thought, has always made this *form* of the spirit into the matter itself, that it has confused formal personality and freedom with material personality and freedom—that it has confused the formal fact that man is created "in the Image of God," of the *humanitas*, with the Divine itself, and for that very reason arrives at the equation of those abstractions—Idea, value, norm, law, culture —with the Divine itself, and contrasts this, as the final principle of interpretation, with that wholly different kind of knowledge of God (or at least sets it up as superior) which is perfected in personal revelation and in personal faith. For the Christian—not for the "theologian" but for everyone who believes in the sense of the New Testament, in the sense of the Reformers—"religious love" (to take only this one example) is never what it is for the Idealist SPRANGER: "Love which is applied to the developed divinity of the other (its revealed character) and love, turns to the divine in the other which is still wholly concealed" (*Lebensformen*, p. 61). The Christian can never understand true community in this way, yet the Idealist is always bound to understand it in this way. For, to the Idealist love always means "that a Super 'I' finds itself again in the 'Thou' " (ibid., p. 172), whereas for the Christian this can never be so. Between the Platonic *Eros*—SPRANGER's idea of love—and the Christian *Agape* there consists this primal contradiction: that in it the person is subordinated to the "higher" abstraction, to the Idea, while on the contrary in the Christian Faith that which is supposed to be higher, because it is abstract, is subordinated to the Personal.

In this subordination—not to theology but to faith—Christianity will at all times be obliged to admit the great relative truth of Idealism; but this subordination means at the same time renouncing the identification of those ideas which determine humanity in its indestructible form with God Himself. What I mean by this will be shown by the illustration of education in Chapter XLI.

NOTES ON CHAPTER XXXIX

PAGE 492, NOTE 1.—From many very different angles at the present time opposition to the rationalism of the Western idea of science has been aroused. NIETZSCHE already protested against it—and yet remained in its toils; after him came BERGSON, who with his doctrine of instinct and intuition established the idea of "intimate" knowledge. The stimulus received from both these sources was further developed by SCHELER, and in a different manner by SIMMEL. But psychology also, especially psycho-analysis, and research into the psychology of the primitive mind, prepared the way for the understanding of the fact that our scientific knowledge only offers one half of the experience of reality. Finally, possibly we may also regard the emphasis upon pre-rational knowledge as the real motive force in the philosophy of HEIDEGGER, and in the philosophy of GRISEBACH the contrast between *Gegenwarts-wirklichkeit* (present reality) and *"erinnertem" Idee-denken* (ideas thought in the memory). In this connexion, too, we should remember that even in the most "objective" science, in physics, in its final phase, the "objectivity" of the eighteenth and nineteenth century type was overcome by relativism; according to it the eye of the observer—the point which sees here and now—is an integral element in every scientific statement; thus here too the ideal of knowledge as *"pure* objectivity" has been abandoned.

PAGE 493, NOTE 2.—All the thinkers who are toiling to produce a new type of anthropology, and who have taken up the cudgels against intellectualism, belong to this category, from NIETZSCHE onwards, by way of BERGSON, SIMMEL, SCHELER down to HEIDEGGER

and GRISEBACH on the one side, and to EBNER, BUBER, and GOGAR-
TEN on the other. In a certain sense we ought also to place ADOLF
SCHLATTER in this series, in so far as he was one of the first to undertake to wage war on "the influence of Greek thought." But this
warfare cannot be waged solely by the methods of philosophy, but
—and GOGARTEN was the first to perceive this—only with the aid
of theology. The meaning of his previous work is the proof that
only in the Christian Faith is Man understood as really responsible,
and—it is the same thing—as one who is united with the "Thou."

PAGE 494, NOTE 3.—The fundamental question of ethics, the
problem of responsibility, will be understood in an abstract and
impersonal way (and this means it will *not* be understood at all) so
long as people think that the being of man and the moral imperative can be so divorced from one another that the understanding of
the real man is possible without knowledge of his "existence-in-
responsibility." Not only ethics, but the anthropology which precedes it, must grasp the idea of "existence-in-responsibility," in
order to know the real human being. But it is *this* which is impossible for an "objectifying" knowledge—whether it be that of natural
science or of the humanities. It is the Christian anthropology which
knows that man has his *being* in responsibility. The philosophy of
HEIDEGGER in particular shows that apart from the knowledge of
Christianity anthropology finally leads inevitably to the man who
has no connection with others. The *Eigentlich-Sein* of HEIDEGGER is,
in the last resort, as *ich-einsam* (solitary) as the Self in its action in
the teaching of FICHTE.

PAGE 495, NOTE 4.—It should be the task of a Christian anthropology—which is naturally part of theology—to develop this
conception of the "person." That which KANT calls by this
name remains abstract; he only arrives at the intelligible Self or
the rational Self, the Idea of Man, but not at the real man. In the
thought of Kant the real man remains somewhere between the
empirical, causally determined Self and the Intelligible Self; Kant
cannot grasp the idea of a real man who is both responsible and
guilty. But his conception also remains between the naturally
individual and the universally spiritual; he cannot grasp the individual in the sense in which KIERKEGAARD does. "Person" in the
literal sense of the word is a Christian conception, because it cannot be defined in any general sense, neither by that of Nature nor
by that of Reason. On this point cf. my article "Biblische Psychologie" in *Gott und Mensch*.

PAGE 495, NOTE 5.—No one has given a better description of this
despair which seizes the man for whom objective science has destroyed all understanding of the personal, by emptying life of all
meaning, than J. W. KRUTCH in his book: *The Modern Temper*.

PAGE 496, NOTE 6.—This is the theme of the new science of
"scientific sociology." KARL MARX, with his historical materialism,

made a magnificent even though one-sided beginning of this study. The second great figure in this series, who carries it further, is his exact opposite, NIETZSCHE. SIMMEL made an important contribution with his view of psychological sociology. The real founder of this science is, I suppose, MAX SCHELER. Since then this new branch of the science of the real man has made great progress. Cf. MANNHEIM: "Wissenschaftssoziologie" in the *Hdwb. d. Soziologie*.

PAGE 498, NOTE 7.—An absolutely classical example of this intellectualism, to which it is an *a priori* truth that nothing has any claim to truth save that which agrees with laws—whether they are causal or normative laws—is provided by KELSEN in his *Staatslehre*, § 16: *Staat und Gott*. The idea of a personal God is an anthropomorphic hypostasis of an abstract idea. Of course, this is not at all new, but from the time of the Neo-Platonists onwards this has been the struggle, constantly renewed, between the Abstract and the personalism of Christianity, of the βίος θεωρητικός against the demand for the decision of faith, of the solitary reason against the view of life which means community.

NOTES ON CHAPTER XL

PAGE 499, NOTE 1.—By this I do not mean to repeat the old misunderstanding that art is religious or irreligious, Christian or non-Christian according to its subject. The tendency and the dynamic of the Christian or non-Christian understanding of art must above all be sought in the form—understanding this word in the broadest sense. The slave figures of Michael Angelo could only be imagined within the sphere of Christianity, however little they may have to do with the Christian sphere so far as the subject is concerned, and the Deposition from the Cross of Rubens has nothing to do with Christian art, although its subject is connected with the central fact of Christianity. In spite of this, however, a purely formalistic view which disregards the subject altogether would certainly be bad aesthetics. For normally the selection of the subject of the painter, as well as of the poet, will certainly be important for what he has to "say." REMBRANDT could not "just as well" have renounced the use of Biblical subjects, any more than the fact that Dante turned to the "subject-matter" of Catholic eschatology was "accidental." The great artist does not only make the subject significant by means of his art, but he also is made great by his subject. This is true even of music: BACH is unthinkable apart from the hymnology of the Church, the Gospels, and the Lutheran liturgy.

PAGE 500, NOTE 2.—The recent attempt to understand the nature of art wholly from the point of view of religion breaks down on the fact that there is great and genuine art which has no other relation to the religious sphere than the element of form as such. On the other hand it is true that just as the profound thinker, in some way or another, is striving towards the religious question, so that the evidence of this aspiration is absolutely the measure of his depth, so is it also with great art. This is indeed intelligible if our conception of art is right; if art as such expresses the longing of man for redemption, then it is only natural that it should seek subjects in which the same question approaches it. The greatest art will therefore be always that in which ultimately the subject and the form both mean this ultimate thing.

PAGE 501, NOTE 3.—No one has given a more penetrating study of the problem of Aesthetics than KIERKEGAARD in his *Entweder-Oder* (Either-Or) and in the *Stadien*; he was particularly fitted for this, since he knew the whole problem from within, and he also possessed the equal capacity for artistic creation and the analysis of the thinker. Cf. also what was said at the beginning of this book (p. 24) about aestheticism.

PAGE 502, NOTE 4.—A distorted picture of the relation of Calvinistic Christianity to art is outlined by ELERT: *Morphologie des Luthertums*, p. 404. To him we would reply with the words of NEUMANN, who was an outstanding student of the works of REMBRANDT, on the relation of the latter to the Christian Faith—and this was its Calvinistic form—Neumann remarks: "In spite of the fact that from a thousand sources the influences of the art of the Renaissance flowed towards Rembrandt he remained aloof to an heroic degree from its pagan way of intensifying the (human) figure; he kept to the Biblical tradition of the "form of a Servant" and the preference for the weary and the heavy-laden. . . . Beauty and its love of admiration is scarcely expressed in his art. . . . He grew up in the atmosphere of earnest study of the Bible, and he lived in this atmosphere. He did not choose his subjects according to a theological plan; he is not determined in his choice of scenes by the Church Calendar of Festivals, but he has himself lived in the fundamental book, the Bible. Hence the difference in his selection of Bible stories, etc." (RGG[1], Vol. III, Col. 1862). The realism of Rembrandt in particular is most closely connected with his Calvinism: he is opposed to all deification of the creature, and thus provides one of the most convincing proofs that art can achieve great things even without those ingredients, which, according to ELERT, are the presupposition of Lutheran art. I cannot imagine what the "Divine Immanence" would have to do with BACH's art!

PAGE 502, NOTE 5.—It was not BACH—who is often appealed to as a witness—but BEETHOVEN who thought thus: "Music is a higher form of revelation than all wisdom and philosophy." BACH would have been horrified at any attempt to place his music on the same plane as the Bible. He had no desire to create a substitute for the Word of the Scripture and the proclamation of the Gospel, but he wanted to intensify the impression made by these, and to help to prepare the way for the Word to enter the soul. It was his aim to "create music for this end"—the greatness of his art is based upon this humility.

NOTES ON CHAPTER XLI

PAGE 504, NOTE 1.—Of course here too we are dealing with "ideal types" which do not exist in this pure form; on the contrary, within the sphere of the theory of education the type of experiment which prevails is synthetic. Here also Romanticism in particular is the path which is most often frequented in the endeavour to make the adjustment between nature and spirit; nearly all the outstanding examples of more recent pedagogy have been greatly influenced by it; on this point cf. the *Philosophy of Education*, by KRIECK (in BAEUMLER's and SCHRÖTER's *Handbuch der Philosophie*). The organic principle provides on the one hand a certain possibility of overcoming the abstract ideal of education of Idealism, but, on the other hand—as must be said of the organic theory in general—the individual tends to be absorbed by the collective body, in accordance with its idea that the "whole" precedes "the part" (this idea comes out very clearly also in KRIECK).

PAGE 505, NOTE 2.—There is absolutely no occasion to treat this naturalistic idea of education with contempt; in the hands of an educationalist as vital as DEWEY, one of the most influential of American educational reformers, owing to its healthy realism, it constitutes (certainly not without acceptance of motives which are really alien to its thought) an important corrective of German educational theory, which is almost exclusively under the influence of Idealism. The principle of "adaptation" is here, with cheerful inconsequence, made into a fruitful socio-pedagogical guiding principle. From personal observation I have been able to convince myself that in the schools influenced by Dewey's spirit there is a genuine revival of Pestalozzian ideas.

PAGE 505, NOTE 3.—To deal with this statement more fully by explanation and argument would lead us too far away from our subject. I would remind the reader of what has already been said in this connexion (Note 11 on Chapter IV). The fundamental idea of Greek Idealistic philosophy is that of the development of the inner potentiality. Its final point of reference is not the community—not even in PLATO, in spite of his views of the "State"—but the sage. The theory of Ideas is a theory of wisdom, and its aim is the spiritual life realized in contemplation of the Idea. German Idealism, mainly under Christian influence, has indeed modified this idea; but it still lives on in the idea of the truly educated person, of the "personality," which is the "Supreme Good of the children of men."

PAGE 506, NOTE 4.—The danger of all pedagogy is that owing to the fact that the problem of education comes so close to the "personal centre," that the educationalist cannot evade the question of the whole, it so easily goes beyond its province. Because, as a rule, it does not see that it is precisely this centre, this whole, which lies beyond its reach, it tries to define the whole as a harmony of the parts, and its ideal of education becomes that of the "harmonious personality." EDUARD SPRANGER has expressed this idea in a most attractive manner in his book *Lebensformen*, which is strongly influenced by HUMBOLDT's idea of Humanity. But in this influential book it becomes quite evident that Idealistic Humanism finally sticks in the mud of the Impersonal: the sum-total of the separate spheres of culture (*Lebensformen*) which are harmoniously adjusted within the personality of the cultivated human being, lacks the principle which could determine the adjustment and co-ordinate the whole. The Impersonal comes out most crudely where even personal fellowship is de-personalized by being defined as love present in the form of "values which point in the same direction." (Cf. Note 6 on Chapter XXXVIII.)

PAGE 507, NOTE 5.—Cf. E. STERN, article "Bildung" in RGG², Vol. I, Col. 1110: "Now this conception is confronted by another, which denies the possibility of such 'character building,' by stringing together separate and distinct tendencies; this view also rejects the idea that the consciousness can be 'built up' by placing certain separate elements side by side; in this view the *psyche* is regarded as a whole, is conceived as a unity, and this unity is its starting-point."

PAGE 507, NOTE 6.—This critical point of view is that of GRISE-BACH's pedagogy, *Gegenwart*. Only GRISEBACH forgets to say whence he has drawn his own critical principle, which lies behind his conception of the "Gegenwart" (present) or of "reality." It would clear the ground if he would openly confess that the background of his thinking, from the point of view of which he constructs his philosophy, is his Lutheran faith.

PAGE 507, NOTE 7.—This community in work appeared at the time of the Reformation in its connexion with Humanism. The Reformers, however, strictly observed the distinction between the formal *humanitas*, in which they made room for a formal autonomy within Humanism, and the material sphere of freedom and of human life, which is only realized in faith in God's Word as "the new man." The main theme of the Reformers' doctrine was how the "person," the "Werkmeister," could be "justified."

PAGE 508, NOTE 8.—Cf. KESSELER: *Pädagogische Charakterköpfe*, p. 183: "The task of education is the elevation of human beings into the spiritual world, the control of natural life by spiritual ideals, that is, freedom. The free human being, the humane human being, the human being who is rooted in the life of the spirit, and who is active for the life of the spirit, is the ideal and the aim of our educational activity." Or: E. Stern, loc. cit.: Education means "the development of the individual psychic structure to its maximum capacity in the experiencing and the shaping of values."

Page 508, Note 9.—Cf. Krieck: *Erziehungsphilosophie*: "Education is the adjustment of humanity to the aims incorporated in the possession of education." "By the process of education man takes a share in the culture-process and is actively related to it. Education therefore represents the subjective aspect of culture."

Page 508, Note 10.—The ideal of education is "the ideal of the supra-subjective unity, an ideal of community" (Häberlin, loc. cit., p. 32). "Perfected community would only be thinkable if there were no longer any members of the community" (!) (p. 62). For "harmony and the individual being are eternally at variance," therefore the only harmony which can be is relative (p. 61). So perfect harmony would be—identity!

Page 509, Note 11.—This partial right of Idealism ought not to be contested by the Christian Faith. This incorporation of Idealistic truth into Christian truth concerning Man is Kierkegaard's great merit, as compared with many of his followers of the present day, especially Grisebach, and perhaps also Gogarten.

Page 510, Note 12.—Cf. above, Note 6 on Chapter XXXVIII. The goods of civilization (*Kulturgüter*) do belong to the sphere of education, of course, but they only humanize if they are subordinated to something higher than themselves—and Idealism refuses to acknowledge this "higher element," since the Idea itself is visible in them alone. When Spranger defends Idealism against the reproach "that Idealism in its classical period deified culture quite regardless of its content, when it was rather the Idea, that is, the rays of the divine which it sought within culture" (*Der Kampf gegen den Idealismus*, loc. cit., p. 451), he actually confirms that which the Christian Faith charges against him: the deification of the Idea, as it is conceived as the content of culture. What ultimately lies behind this conception comes out clearly in another sentence of Spranger's: "He who discovers himself, also discovers God" (*Kultur und Erziehung*, p. 275).

Page 510, Note 13.—On this point, cf. the fundamental observations by Gogarten: *Wider die Ächtung der Autorität*. What E. Stern says in his valuable book: *Autorität und Erziehung*, does not weaken what Gogarten maintains; indeed, ultimately it only confirms it. For although Stern tries very hard to make a place for authority within education, in the end his thinking leads to this, that authority is only a method of attaining freedom (p. 53), and that its only justification lies in the superiority of the person who wields authority. On the other hand, in opposition to Gogarten, we must once more stress the point that even the authority which is based not on superiority but on the divine order can never be the decisive point of view of Christian ethics, and therefore it cannot be the decisive point of view of Christian pedagogy.

PAGE 510, NOTE 14.—Many leading educationalists of the present day have a positive relation to "religion" or even to Christianity. This ought to be recognized and taken into account. But the idea of education as a harmony of the separate spheres never permits any other conception to arise than that of SCHLEIERMACHER, namely, that "religion is a special province in the mind." Here there is no perception of the fact that *the* thing which makes a human being a *person* at all is the knowledge of and the recognition of God in faith, and that it is this alone which makes it possible to incorporate intelligently the whole of culture into life as a whole—and it is at this point that faith is compelled to become the enemy of Idealism. The point at issue is not the supremacy of the Church or of theology, but the sovereignty of God over all that is called "the realm of ideas."

PAGE 513, NOTE 15.—In saying this we do not overlook the fact that there are certain extreme instances, that is, that there are so many families in which there is no trace of this kind of community, which, therefore, as educational factors are only present in a negative sense, and where therefore radical severance from these associations is the only right course. We also do not overlook the fact of the terrible disturbance to family life due to economic conditions, which often goes so far as to produce the situation indicated in the preceding instance. But these extreme instances do not destroy the fundamental truth of our contention, but simply remind us that even that fundamental contention is a relative truth, that it is not absolute, and that even under the best conditions the blessing of the family is accompanied by a curse. But this does not take away the truth of the assertion that among the relative possibilities of culture as education the family occupies the first place.

NOTES ON CHAPTER XLII

PAGE 517, NOTE 1.—A wealth of shrewd ethical reflections on social life is provided by ROTHE's *Ethik*, 5, pp. 176–232; only here too—and here in particular—there appears the fundamental defect in ROTHE's ethic, namely, the monistic failure to distinguish between the cultural process and ethics.

PAGE 518, NOTE 2.—This is the reason why friendship is the favourite theme of Greek ethics and morality, and on the other hand, why it has not been treated with any special care in the Christian ethic. In the Aristotelian (Nicomachean) ethic the theory of friendship is the highest point of the victory over the purely individualistic ethos of education (Book 8). It forms the purest expression of the genuine Greek καλοκαγαθία, of aesthetic pleasure in the

Good: genuine friendship can only exist "between good people who resemble each other in virtue" (8, 4).

PAGE 519, NOTE 3.—Here for lack of space I have made no effort to define an actual theory of custom, although such a theory is urgently needed. Above all it would need to enquire into the criteria of "good customs" and their relation to faith; further, it would need to enquire into the relative rights of the modern criticism of all custom, and of emancipation from custom; it would be obliged to destroy the naïve equation of "good" with traditional customs, without at the same time abandoning the necessarily conservative character of custom. It would have to point out the inevitable tension between the conservative-collectivist tendency of custom, and the striving after individual sincerity and honesty in the shaping of life, and thence to the guilt of the Church in its one-sided support of the former to the disadvantage of the latter. But its most important task would be: to show that custom is merely relative in character, since it is a merely historical inheritance, which, as such, is not ethical in the real sense of the word.

PAGE 520, NOTE 4.—These natural group-formations, which are determined by intellectual reasons, are the favourite theme of discussion in contemporary sociology. The antithesis *Society v. Community*, to which the sociology of F. TÖNNIES first of all attracted the attention of scientific thinkers, can only be clearly perceived from the standpoint of the Christian Faith; only where the true meaning of "love" is known, "community" and forms of social life are clearly distinguished, and, on the other hand, the differences between (natural) personal community and (cultural or merely civilizing) societies (with such aims) are seen to be relative. But so long as the truly Personal, through the idea of "value," and true community, through the idea of spirit, is understood as an idea confusion must inevitably arise at this point, since the "personal" and the "communal" is sought just where it can least be found, and is not perceived where natural feeling finds it.

NOTES ON CHAPTER XLIII

PAGE 523, NOTE 1.—It would not be easy to find a clearer instance of the impotence of the would-be objective type of history to understand Christianity from the historical point of view, than in the fact that for so many years historical scholars were totally unable to understand the thought of the Reformation concerning the Church. In spite of the thorough equipment of knowledge in many points of detail in the school of Reformation research inaugurated by RITSCHL we must still say frankly: that the real understanding of the idea of the Church in the view of the Reformers, only begins with HOLL, and it has been powerfully supported by more recent developments in systematic theology. The only exception is someone who stands quite outside this movement—an "outsider"—but one who makes a congenial interpreter of Luther on account of his faith—I mean Sohm, the lawyer. Next to Holl and Kattenbusch, apart from my own particular theological friends—(especially Thurneysen)—I owe most to him.

Page 524, Note 2.—We may say, I suppose, that to-day—among theologians—to some extent we do know what is the fundamental Reformation Idea of the Church; the fine book by Althaus: *Communio sanctorum*, summarizes the result of this discovery in a selection of passages from the actual text of Luther's own writings. But what the relation is between this Church *proprie dicta*—the *una sancta* of the Creed—to the empirical Churches on the one hand, and to the secular orders on the other—on this question (so decisive from the practical point of view), most of the recent discussions leave us in the lurch. Holl's masterly work on Luther, and the system of church government of the Territorial Church, constitutes an important step forward in this direction: Kattenbusch's *Doppelschichtigkeit in Luthers Kirchenbegriff*, by means of a wholly new historical point of view (see Note 10 on this chapter) has further clarified the question, but a final, penetrating clarity in the question of this very central problem, which lies on the boundary line of the practical question of the formation of church order, can only be gained by systematic reflection which presses right through to the very heart of the problem. I must confess that through the question raised by Sohm I have felt compelled, and through the discovery of Kattenbusch, as I believe, I have been able to bring this question one step nearer to the goal.

Page 527, Note 3.—The account of the problem given above claims to represent the Reformation Idea of the Church, and this suggests that in what is essential we cannot and ought not to go beyond this knowledge of the Reformation. Opportunity will occur to show the points at which the idea of the Church of both Reformers (Luther and Calvin) needs correction; here too, however, upon the whole, we cannot do better than learn from them how to interpret the Bible. Anyone who tries to understand this subject by ignoring them, or who thinks that he understands it better than they do, will miss his way, so far as the main truth is concerned.

I say explicitly: the Idea of the Church of the *Reformation*, not Luther's idea of the Church, or Calvin's idea of the Church. The differences between the two are well known to me, but comparative study—from the time of Schneckenburger's rightly famous work—has exaggerated and coarsened them by misconstruction; and no one has done so in a more fatal manner—also most disastrous from the confessional point of view—than Ernst Troeltsch. This subject is so important that even in a work on ethics it ought not to be overlooked. Luther has been wrongly described in terms which would have been more suited to Melanchthon, and Calvin has also been misrepresented in the terms of later Calvinism. If we go to Luther and Calvin themselves for the decisive question and delve into the subject we find—not absolute identity, but an agreement which diverges far more widely from the usual picture than the doctrines between the Reformers themselves. So far as Luther's ideas are concerned, at least with reference to the bases of his idea of the Church, we are now clear—that is, since HOLL confuted the views attributed to Luther by TROELTSCH. Calvin's ideas are still, however, being presented from an incorrect point of view, based on unwarranted presuppositions, instead of being presented directly from the sources themselves.

1. It is not true that the idea of a twofold Predestination dominates Calvin's idea of the Church; rather in his thought the central point is the idea of belonging to Christ, of the *Insertio in Christum*, of the Body of Christ, of the Sovereignty of Christ, and indeed of the rule of Christ through His Word and through His Spirit. It is absolutely amazing how rarely in this connexion—inside or outside of the *Institutes*—the idea of a twofold Predestination appears. On the other hand, it is true—and this may be the reason for the misunderstanding—that in the thought of Calvin certainly here too the idea of Election is a guiding principle, but it is not represented in such a way as though through it the historic Word and membership in the *communio fidelium* were set aside. On the contrary, the striking thing about Calvin is with what energy he forces both these ideas to come together, which in Lutheranism—not in Luther's own thought—fall apart.

2. It is therefore also false to say that in Calvin's teaching the controlling idea is that of sanctification. There is no trace of this. But the idea that determines his thought is once more that of the Christ-community, of the Church as the depository of the good of salvation, of the share in the Kingdom of God, of the Word of Salvation, whereby certainly a stronger emphasis falls than in the thought of Luther on the *sovereignty* of Christ, and of the obedience of the true Christian. But we only need to read his discussion of Anabaptist perfectionism (*Inst.*, IV, 1, 13 ff.) to perceive how far Calvin was from the desire to establish a "gathered" or a "pure" Church.

3. It is likewise not correct to say that in the thought of Calvin the idea of the community based on the common enjoyment of the "means of grace" recedes behind the idea of the invisible Church of elect individuals. On the contrary, Calvin in particular —and perhaps still more clearly than Luther—perceived the connexion between the historic word and real community, and therefore he emphasized more strongly then Luther that the "Church is the mother of our faith." This is why he lays so much stress on the fact that the Church is a real community, on the *auctoritas*

of those who bear the office of preacher, and on the connexion between the individual Christian and the Christian community, on the impossibility of preserving the living faith outside the Christian community. But—this is certainly true: he never completely identifies the human word of preaching with the Divine Word, he leaves a *spatium* between the *ordinarius modus* and the freedom of God—but how cautiously and carefully limited!—he reckons with the possibility that a person might even belong to the invisible Church without belonging to the visible Church—but once more: how narrow is this opening, almost to the extent of closing it altogether, only just large enough to leave room for the divine freedom; man was only free to declare the message of salvation inside the visible Church.

The fact that it is a misunderstanding of Calvin to say that his attitude towards Church law, towards the institution of officials, his definition of the relation between Church and State is as a rule determined by his "legalism," will be shown in another place. In short: Luther has no important idea which is not also important to Calvin; at some particular points where Luther is represented as contrary to Calvin, we shall also show that the opposite is the case—as in the question of church law, of church discipline, of the *notae ecclesiae*, etc. Once again: Calvin and Luther cannot be equated with each other; but their difference here is a matter of emphasis, not of the subject itself.

PAGE 527, NOTE 4.—This is the meaning of the way in which Calvin puts together *fides* and *ordo* (*Inst.*, IV, I, 1), for *ordo* is above all the office of the preacher (ibid., I, 5); this also is the basis of the divine authority of the teaching office, which is due not to it, but to the Word alone (ibid. in countless passages, for instance, I, 1; I, 2: I, 5: 3, 1; and in particular 3, 3).

PAGE 527, NOTE 5.—CALVIN: *Inst.*, IV, I, 5.

PAGE 529, NOTE 6.—On this point there are innumerable illustrative passages in LUTHER's writings; I would merely call attention to the most familiar from the paper on the Councils and the Churches (WA. 50, 629). For CALVIN it is sufficient to indicate *Inst.*, IV, I, 9. But RIEKER is certainly right in saying (*Grundsätze reformierter Kirchenverfassung*, p. 61) that for Calvin the relation of the worshipping community to the Church of faith was closer and more necessary than it was to Luther. To this extent Calvin is more "churchly"; but this is drawing a very fine distinction, for how "churchly" Luther was also!

PAGE 529, NOTE 7.—SOHM has done great service by asserting this with great vigour; to him indeed it was no mere academic concern. He adduces several proofs to show how little this is understood by ecclesiastical lawyers; it would be just as easy to show that this idea is still alien to the thought of theology and of the Church, even without being obliged to point to OTTO DIBELIUS in particular.

PAGE 529, NOTE 8.—The Church, and indeed the Evangelical Church, was in existence where the Huguenot Bible colporteurs found the way to many hearts with their simple testimony to the message of the Scriptures, or it is now in existence where to-day the brothers Arnera do the same with their Bible lorry in the market-places of the country towns of France, and find faith among their hearers.

PAGE 530, NOTE 9.—Thus in particular CALVIN: loc. cit., 3, I. The gathering round the one preacher is a *vinculum caritatis* and *unitatis;* the communication of the Divine Word through men makes them into one Body (3, 2).

PAGE 531, NOTE 10.—This is the great contribution which KATTENBUSCH has rendered to the unravelling of the problem of the relation between the invisible and the visible Church. No one before him had seen it like this. Rather almost every one allowed themselves to be confused by the unfortunate contrast between the invisible Church and the visible Church. The decisive point is not that of the contrast between the invisible and the visible Church, but that between the Church of faith (KATTENBUSCH calls this the Church in its fundamental meaning) and the worshipping community. Only through this distinction does it become possible to clarify the relation of the Church of faith to the secular orders, and with this perception alone do we get rid of false ecclesiasticism, and free for a *weltliche Kirchlichkeit* (secular ecclesiasticism).

PAGE 532, NOTE 11.—In principle this is the same for Calvin as it is for Luther; all the elements which he regards as characteristic of the Church as a real unity, and as an "institution" over against a mere corporation, point to this. See the following note.

PAGE 533, NOTE 12.—I must agree with KATTENBUSCH against SOHM and RIEKER, in his opinion that in the Reformation (Lutheran) idea of the Church the "institutional" element and that of community are united (SOHM: *Kirchenrecht*, I, p. 35; KATTENBUSCH, loc. cit., pp. 54 and 105, RIEKER, loc. cit., p. 67). Certainly the Church in not an institution in the Catholic sense, any more than it is a corporation in the democratic sense. It is an "institution" in the sense that for each individual believer the Church is there before him, and stands over against him as the Bearer of the Word, and to this extent she has divine authority; she is a corporation to the extent in which, as an institution, she consists of nothing but believers, the "Christian people" (as Luther calls them). At this point there is no difference between Calvin and Luther; we might just as well assert that the institutional character of the Church predominates in Calvin as the opposite, when we look now at the authority of the Church and its office and then at the Church as the *communio sanctorum*.

PAGE 533, NOTE 13.—Even Calvin, who emphasizes the *rite vocatus* still more strongly than Luther, admits that there are some who have received an extraordinary vocation, who God *etiam interdum suscitat prout temporum necessitas postulat* (IV, 3, 4). May he not indeed have been thinking of himself!

PAGE 534, NOTE 14.—On this point Luther and Calvin teach exactly the same thing. (*For* LUTHER see WA. 50, 634, and for CALVIN, *Inst.*, IV, 8, 2.) Both conclude from this that there is no *character indelebilis*, that the minister who teaches errors may be deposed and become a layr̄ ̣n once more.

PAGE 535, NOTE 15.—This is a difference between Luther and Calvin which has been rightly noted by RIEKER (loc. cit., p. 68); although Calvin also holds the principle in common with Luther, he rightly emphasizes that the worshipping community itself ought to undertake works of mercy, because this is part of its life as a *communio*.

PAGE 535, NOTE 16.—That Calvin defends this idea is well known. But it is less well known that in so doing he is not thinking of any theocracy in the sense of the law of the State, for even his State stands upon its own feet. And the other, that we find the same idea in Luther too. Cf. what was said above about the State, p. 443, and note 2 on Chapter XXXVI.

PAGE 537, NOTE 17.—Calvin distinguishes explicitly between the ecclesiastical sentence of excommunication and the *anathema*, whose use *rarus aut nullus omnino est* (loc. cit., 12, 10), and he also ventures to say that exclusion from the Christian community does not mean being outside the Church.

PAGE 537, NOTE 18.—This is the meaning of the phrase the "invisible Church"; whoever maintains that believers know (with certainty) the true Church in its entirety do away with this idea altogether. This was taught not only by Calvin with his idea of Election, but also by Luther with his thought of the Hidden God. On this point cf. KATTENBUSCH, loc, cit., p. 61.

PAGE 537, NOTE 19.—What can become of a Bible whose content no longer lives on its oral proclamation but which is simply handed down from one generation to another in writing, was discovered by ANQUETIL DUPERRON when he sought in vain for Parsees who understood their Bible even only in its literal sense.

NOTES ON CHAPTER XLIV

PAGE 539, NOTE 1.—We have to thank Holl for the proof, at once convincing and important, that LUTHER, where the Church as the worshipping community was concerned (or as the Church which has to be organized), exactly like CALVIN, regarded the individual local congregation as primary (loc. cit., p. 350). Luther *wished* that each local congregation should choose its own pastors; he did not merely *wish*, but declared it to be absolutely necessary, that each congregation should have the right to give its consent to the pastor which was appointed to it. Likewise it should be autonomous in the ordering of public worship (ibid., pp. 352 ff.). Thus even at this important point the supposed contrast between Calvin and Luther is proved to be incorrect, all the more when we see how rigidly, even in Calvin's teaching, the idea of congregational autonomy is restricted.

PAGE 540, NOTE 2.—When RIEKER (loc. cit., pp. 81–82) sets CALVIN's "congregational" Church principle over against Luther's idea of the Church as an institution, he fails to distinguish between the Church in the fundamental sense of the word and the Church as a worshipping community. It is only this distinction, however, which makes it intelligible that in Calvin's thought the idea of congregational autonomy is strictly limited by that of Church unity. So far as Calvin is concerned there can be no idea of autonomy in the sense of formal democracy, or in the sense of natural law, as indeed RIEKER himself emphasizes very clearly over against modern Calvinism (pp. 144–170).

PAGE 542, NOTE 3.—Those who still want to make CALVIN responsible for the development of sects in the Western world, ought to take the trouble to read for themselves what Calvin says in Chapter I, 10–22, in the *Institutio*, IV. No one has ever grasped the idea of the sects in a more central manner and fought against it than he; his reasons for rejecting this view are the following: the false effort to achieve holiness; wrong impatience with the Church of sinners, with the erring, lax, secularized Church—and his whole polemic ends characteristically with the idea that the forgiveness of sins is bound up with the Church (I, 22).

PAGE 542, NOTE 4.—Once more it is not in harmony with the traditional views of CALVIN to realize that he deliberately defends the idea that in matters which concern practical holiness we ought to have greater *indulgentia* with the Church than where the preaching of right doctrine is concerned; at the same time he is quite convinced that no one preaches absolutely "pure" doctrine (*Institutio*, IV, 1, 13 and 1, 12).

PAGE 543, NOTE 5.—To how great an extent LUTHER recognized the possibility of this variety is shown to us by his "German Mass"; cf. also HOLL, loc. cit., pp. 351 ff. The same can be said of the Calvinists; cf. the Helvetic Confession: *unitas ecclesiae non est in externis ritibus*, for there is a *diversitas varia libera* (*Bekenntnisschriften*: E. F. K. MÜLLER, p. 199).

PAGE 544, NOTE 6.—I feel that it is not out of place to point out various things which are better in the Roman Catholic Church than they are with us—in view of the fact that the actual message of Protestantism has been so greatly weakened by Modernism, that patriotism of a certain kind is supposed to be identical with Protestant piety, that the Church reveals her lack of independence

715

when she is challenged by the demands of the State, and, finally, in view of the distracted, divided condition of Protestantism.

PAGE 545, NOTE 7.—SOHM rightly (*Kirchenrecht*, II, pp. 134 and 137) rejects TROELTSCH's view of Luther's attitude towards the authority of the Bible as too crude. For LUTHER, in particular, the Word of God in the Bible was not something which existed "ready-made," as it were, and the Bible was not a book of oracles to be consulted in a legalistic manner.

PAGE 545, NOTE 8.—This is the point at which the theology and the Church of the present day must move most definitely away from the view of the Reformers. Although CALVIN, to some extent, and LUTHER, to a greater extent, were aware that the Word of God was not identical with the letter of Scripture, still at this point they were more closely bound by the ecclesiastical tradition than we have any right to be. For the rest we may say: the rigorous Biblicism of the Calvinists is balanced by a stricter adhesion to the credal documents among the Lutherans.

PAGE 546, NOTE 9.—This important but relative difference between a charismatic and a legal Church order is the great truth in SOHM's *Kirchenrecht*; that he makes this relative truth into an absolute one is his error. (Cf. the following Note.)

PAGE 547, NOTE 10.—ERICH FOERSTER rightly raises the question "SOHM confutes? . . ." (*Ztschf. f. Kirchengesch*, 1929, pp. 307–343). How little even he is understood comes out in the new presentation of Protestant Church Law (*Die Grundlagen des evangelischen Kirchenrechts*) by GÜNTHER HOLSTEIN, who has been very little affected by the recent knowledge about Luther, and who still regards SCHLEIERMACHER as the great Church Father. SOHM himself, however, has rendered us great assistance, and he has raised questions which have not yet been answered; but his fundamental thesis, "Church law is opposed to the nature of the Church" (*Kirchenrecht*, I, p. 1), is wrong. It is based upon a failure to see the fundamental fact that even the invisible Church can never exist without something human and secular about it; it is based upon the incorrect opinion that a charismatic church order is purely spiritual, on the failure to perceive how fluctuating is the boundary between spontaneous church ordinances which necessarily arise out of the nature of the Church, and the more settled established church structure, as it is known, for instance, by the Church of Calvin; and finally, it is based upon the incorrect definition of the relation between the worshipping community and the Church of faith. Here the writer is influenced to some extent by a kind of "spiritual religion," as is the case in ERICH FOERSTER's defence, in many points so excellent. But, in truth, we have not yet done with SOHM, no, not for a long time to come.

PAGE 548, NOTE 11.—How carefully and surely Luther took into account these boundaries between Church and State just where they had to deal with each other, in the Church Visitation, has only been made clear to us since the publication of HOLL's article on "Luther and the Church Government of the Territorial Church"; how very different this picture is from that which is presented when the Lutheran conception of the emergency episcopate is taken as the starting-point (cf. RIEKER, loc. cit., p. 108; and SOHM: *Kirchenrecht*, I, pp. 542 ff.).

PAGE 549, NOTE 12.—That is doubtless the danger of the original Church structure elaborated by CALVIN; but it is only since the time of HOLL that we have come to know rightly that LUTHER had a dream which very closely resembled that which Calvin actually realized. Calvinism later fell a victim to ecclesiastical democracy just as Lutheranism fell a victim to the State Church system.

PAGE 550, NOTE 13.—On this point I cannot agree with HOLL's view that Luther really contributed to the confessional Church (*Bekenntniskirche*); Luther never wanted anything other than a people's Church (*Volkskirche*), even if an independent people's Church, or a Free Church. But how little a "Free Church" is identical with a confessional Church, many Reformed Free Churches will prove.

PAGE 551, NOTE 14.—That is why Luther did not want the confessional Church (*Bekenntniskirche*); this comes out clearly in HOLL's treatment of the question (loc. cit., p. 364). But this is also the very point which distinguishes Calvin's congregational principle from that of the Sect. The limitations of congregational autonomy by the collective Church are also far more important in Calvin than RIEKER admits (cf. on this point the quotations from French and Scottish church ordinances which are conceived absolutely in accordance with the meaning of Calvin (loc. cit., pp. 83 ff.).

PAGE 552, NOTE 15.—Even CALVIN would have accepted this statement. Where he speaks of the *notae ecclesiae*, he only mentions the Sermon and the Sacrament (loc. cit., I, 9); he is even able to declare that he would agree to an episcopal constitution of the Reformed Church in Poland, with its own Archbishop, if only the *Archiepiscopus non dominaretur in reliquos* (opp. 15, 332). See also the Helvetic Confession.

PAGE 553, NOTE 16.—This again is an important point, where against the prevailing opinion, the difference between LUTHER and CALVIN is only one of emphasis. Calvin never wishes to attack the independence of the State in the sense of the Catholic Theocratic view, and Luther never ceased to impress upon the State authorities that it was their duty to serve the Church of Christ.

PAGE 554, NOTE 17.—LUTHER, too, made this distinction extremely carefully. The State has direct authority within the Church only in reference to "the temporal sphere" and by this Luther means the authority of the secular system of law over the pastors. But where the Church is called in to make order within the Church it possesses no rights of compulsion. (Cf. HOLL, loc. cit., p. 33.) In this passage HOLL has finally dealt with the idea (set in motion by SOHM and RIEKER) that Luther had taken over the Catholic idea of the *Corpus Christianum*. The State is not, as RIEKER thinks it is, as such, a member of the invisible Church, but is only such in so far as the governing body consists of real Christians, just as Baptism does not, as such, make Christians, but only the Baptism which is affirmed in faith.

NOTES ON CHAPTER XLV

PAGE 555, NOTE 1.—Among the Reformers this idea of the "office" creates a disastrous obscurity; sometimes it is understood as a conception of faith, the necessity for the regular and permanent preaching of the Word which forms part of the very nature of the Church of faith, at other times it is taken to mean a conception of order: the administrative office, the official order as such.

PAGE 556, NOTE 2.—The usual idea of the relation between CALVIN and LUTHER is that Luther only took into account the Sermon and the Sacrament, but that Calvin added also Church discipline and service to the *notae verae ecclesiae*. Neither the one statement nor the other is correct. In the *Schrift von den Konzilien*, for instance, Luther enumerates *seven* necessary tokens of the true Church (Preaching, the two Sacraments, church discipline, the ecclesiastical office (ministerial), public worship, the bearing of the Cross), and where Calvin speaks of the *notae ecclesiae* as a standard, he only mentions the Word and the Sacrament (loc. cit., I, 9) and frequently). But it is true that Calvin endeavoured more vigorously than Luther to realize those other functions in practice, and to this end he founded and created an order which appeared to be too Biblicist and legalistic, whereas Luther let things take their course. The result was that Calvin realized something of that which Luther also desired, though in a very questionable form.

PAGE 556, NOTE 3.—On this point we do not need to waste any more words to-day to prove that Calvin's claim that his official Church order represents that of the Primitive Church is based upon an illusion. The presbyters of the New Testament are not a *collegium* with a President, nor is the bishop the minister, nor were there then any "ministers" in Calvin's sense of the word, and still less *eruditi*. This is undeniably the temporary element in Calvin's magnificent doctrine of the Church and system of Church Government.

PAGE 566, NOTE 4.—This ecclesiasticism has found its symbolically powerful expression in the book called *Das Jahrhundert der Kirche*, by OTTO DIBELIUS. There are far less attractive and far more solid expressions of this spirit. There is always reason in what DIBELIUS says, indeed in many points of detail we can agree with him. He is a practical churchman, who means well, and is able to make many suggestions which are well worth our consideration, based on his own wide experience and shrewd observation. But what gives its colour to the book is the fact that he is completely ignorant of the real nature of the Church, and still more the way in which he takes for granted that it is wholly unnecessary to enquire into this at all. FRICK (*Romantik und Realismus im Kirchenbegriff*) rightly describes him as a realist Romantic. He too is moved by a secret longing for the splendour of the Catholic Church; he is cheered by the sight of that renewed interest in the question of the Church, which he perceives everywhere, without enquiring into its causes. Rather, it is his plainly expressed conviction (p. 85) that "the sociological structure of the Church is not exclusively Christian." This is the reason why he could not understand the questions raised by BARTH (*Zwischen den Zeiten*, 1931, pp. 89-122). While the theologians, in their thought about the nature of the Church, often forget the problem of its relation to the empirical church, with him the process is reversed. He is not aware that it is precisely the empirical nature of the Church which must issue from its fundamental nature, that the Church in the Christian sense—even as an empirical fact—is something specifically Christian, in spite of all its connexions with other sociological factors. In this—in spite of his "realism"—he stands upon the same ground as TILLICH (*Kirche und Kultur*), who likewise believes it is possible to attack the problem of the Church as a general problem. But to Dibelius *this* Church is *the* Church. Hence he is able to say (p. 29): "Germany had no longer any Church" and *vice versa*: *habemus ecclesiam*—namely since 1919. It is true of course that now and again he happens to speak of the Church of faith; but that this does not interest him is shown by the fact that he does not enquire into the relation between the two. The fact that he is not aware of them comes out in the phrase "that the spirit of Jesus and His demands" are the standard set (p. 205). Thus this is churchmanship based upon a Modernist view of the Gospel. This, then, is why his churchmanship must be fed from other sources than those provided by faith; for this faith he knows will not bring forth any kind of churchmanship. Therefore he "surveys" the scene to try to discover all kinds of possible sociological factors, and expects from them, on the line of education, the new development of the religious life (cf. his remarks on the Bible, the Creed, custom, etc., in the last book). Truly, KARL BARTH has spoken the decisive word when he says: "Is it not time, and would it not in the end be more practical, and in the best sense of the word more realistic, if the Church were once more to begin really to 'seek first the Kingdom of God'?"

INDEX OF SUBJECTS

This index refers to the *text* of the book only, as all references to the "Notes and Appendices" will be found in the latter.

721

INDEX OF NAMES